W9-BFR-304

Jonathan Berk • Peter DeMarzo • Jarrad Harford

Fundamentals of Corporate Finance

FE 323
Questrom School of Business
Third Custom Edition for Boston University

Taken from:
Fundamentals of Corporate Finance, Fourth Edition
by Jonathan Berk, Peter DeMarzo, and Jarrad Harford.

The Pearson Series in Finance

Berk/DeMarzo
*Corporate Finance**
*Corporate Finance: The Core**

Berk/DeMarzo/Harford
*Fundamentals of Corporate Finance**

Brooks
*Financial Management: Core Concepts**

Copeland/Weston/Shastri
Financial Theory and Corporate Policy

Dorfman/Cather
Introduction to Risk Management and Insurance

Eakins/McNally
*Corporate Finance Online**

Eiteman/Stonehill/Moffett
*Multinational Business Finance**

Fabozzi
Bond Markets: Analysis and Strategies

Foerster
*Financial Management: Concepts and Applications**

Frasca
Personal Finance

Gitman/Zutter
*Principles of Managerial Finance**
*Principles of Managerial Finance—Brief Edition**

Haugen
The Inefficient Stock Market: What Pays Off and Why
Modern Investment Theory

Holden
Excel Modeling in Corporate Finance
Excel Modeling in Investments

Hughes/MacDonald
International Banking: Text and Cases

Hull
Fundamentals of Futures and Options Markets
Options, Futures, and Other Derivatives

Keown
*Personal Finance: Turning Money into Wealth**

Keown/Martin/Petty
*Foundations of Finance: The Logic and Practice of Financial Management**

Madura
*Personal Finance**

Marthinsen
Risk Takers: Uses and Abuses of Financial Derivatives

McDonald
Derivatives Markets
Fundamentals of Derivatives Markets

Mishkin/Eakins
Financial Markets and Institutions

Moffett/Stonehill/Eiteman
Fundamentals of Multinational Finance

Pennacchi
Theory of Asset Pricing

Rejda/McNamara
Principles of Risk Management and Insurance

Smart/Gitman/Joehnk
*Fundamentals of Investing**

Solnik/McLeavey
Global Investments

Titman/Keown/Martin
*Financial Management: Principles and Applications**

Titman/Martin
Valuation: The Art and Science of Corporate Investment Decisions

Weston/Mitchell/Mulherin
Takeovers, Restructuring, and Corporate Governance

*denotes titles with MyFinanceLab. Log onto **www.myfinancelab.com** to learn more.

To Rebecca, Natasha, and Hannah for the love and for being there. —J. B.

To Kaui, Pono, Koa, and Kai for all the love and laughter. —P. D.

To Katrina, Evan, and Cole for your love and support. —J. H.

Pearson Education, Inc., 330 Hudson Street, New York, New York 10013
A Pearson Education Company
www.pearsoned.com

Printed in the United States of America

4   17

000200010272108390

JK

ISBN 10: 1-323-78514-0
ISBN 13: 978-1-323-78514-0

Brief Contents

Detailed Contents

PART 8 Special Topics

CHAPTER 21 Option Applications and Corporate Finance 661

About the Authors

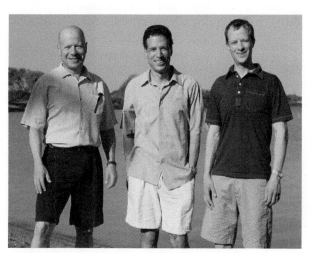

Jonathan Berk, Peter DeMarzo, and Jarrad Harford

Jonathan Berk is the A.P. Giannini Professor of Finance at the Graduate School of Business, Stanford University and is a Research Associate at the National Bureau of Economic Research. Before coming to Stanford, he was the Sylvan Coleman Professor of Finance at Haas School of Business at the University of California, Berkeley. Prior to earning his PhD, he worked as an Associate at Goldman Sachs (where his education in finance really began).

Professor Berk's research interests in finance include corporate valuation, capital structure, mutual funds, asset pricing, experimental economics, and labor economics. His work has won a number of research awards including the TIAA-CREF Paul A. Samuelson Award, the Smith Breeden Prize, Best Paper of the Year in *The Review of Financial Studies*, and the FAME Research Prize. His paper, "A Critique of Size-Related Anomalies," was selected as one of the two best papers ever published in *The Review of Financial Studies*. In recognition of his influence on the practice of finance he has received the Bernstein-Fabozzi/Jacobs Levy Award, the Graham and Dodd Award of Excellence, and the Roger F. Murray Prize. He served two terms as an Associate Editor of the *Journal of Finance*, and a term as a director of the American Finance Association, the Western Finance Association, and academic director of the Financial Management Association. He is a Fellow of the Financial Management Association and a member of the advisory board of the *Journal of Portfolio Management*.

Born in Johannesburg, South Africa, Professor Berk is married, with two daughters, and is an avid skier and biker.

Peter DeMarzo is the Mizuho Financial Group Professor of Finance at the Graduate School of Business, Stanford University. He is the current Vice President of the American Finance Association and a Research Associate at the National Bureau of Economic Research. He teaches MBA and PhD courses in Corporate Finance and Financial Modeling. In addition to his experience at the Stanford Graduate School of Business, Professor DeMarzo has taught at the Haas School of Business and the Kellogg Graduate School of Management, and he was a National Fellow at the Hoover Institution.

Professor DeMarzo received the Sloan Teaching Excellence Award at Stanford, and the Earl F. Cheit Outstanding Teaching Award at U.C. Berkeley. Professor DeMarzo has served as an Associate Editor for *The Review of Financial Studies*, *Financial Management*, and the *B.E. Journals in Economic Analysis and Policy*, as well as a Director of the American Finance Association. He has served as Vice President and President of the Western Finance Association. Professor DeMarzo's research is in the area of corporate investment and financing, asset securitization, and contracting, as well as market structure and regulation. His recent work has examined issues of the optimal design of contracts and securities, leverage dynamics and the role of bank capital regulation, and the influence of information asymmetries on stock prices and corporate investment. He has received numerous awards including the Western Finance Association Corporate Finance Award and the Barclays Global Investors/Michael Brennan best-paper award from *The Review of Financial Studies*.

Professor DeMarzo was born in Whitestone, New York, and is married with three boys. He and his family enjoy hiking, biking, and skiing.

Jarrad Harford is the Paul Pigott - PACCAR Professor of Finance at the University of Washington. Prior to Washington, Professor Harford taught at the Lundquist College of Business at the University of Oregon. He received his PhD in Finance with a minor in Organizations and Markets from the University of Rochester. Professor Harford has taught the core undergraduate finance course, Business Finance, for over nineteen years, as well as an elective in Mergers and Acquisitions, and "Finance for Non-financial Executives" in the executive education program. He has won numerous awards for his teaching, including the UW Finance Professor of the Year (2010, 2012, 2016), Panhellenic/Interfraternity Council Business Professor of the Year Award (2011, 2013), ISMBA Excellence in Teaching Award (2006), and the Wells Fargo Faculty Award for Undergraduate Teaching (2005). Professor Harford is currently a Managing Editor of the *Journal of Financial and Quantitative Analysis*, and serves as an Associate Editor for the *Journal of Financial Economics*, and *Journal of Corporate Finance*. His main research interests are understanding the dynamics of merger and acquisition activity as well as the interaction of corporate cash management policy with governance, payout and global tax considerations. Professor Harford was born in Pennsylvania, is married, and has two sons. He and his family enjoy traveling, hiking, and skiing.

Bridging Theory and Practice

EXAMPLE 7.1
Stock Prices
and Returns

MyFinanceLab

PROBLEM

Suppose you expect Longs Drug Stores to pay an annual dividend of $0.56 per share in the coming year and to trade for $45.50 per share at the end of the year. If investments with equivalent risk to Longs' stock have an expected return of 6.80%, what is the most you would pay today for Longs' stock? What dividend yield and capital gain rate would you expect at this price?

SOLUTION

PLAN

We can use Eq. 7.1 to solve for the beginning price we would pay now (P_0) given our expectations about dividends ($Div_1 = \$0.56$) and future price ($P_1 = \$45.50$) and the return we need to expect to earn to be willing to invest ($r_E = 0.068$). We can then use Eq. 7.2 to calculate the dividend yield and capital gain rate.

EXECUTE

Using Eq. 7.1, we have

$$P_0 = \frac{Div_1 + P_1}{1 + r_E} = \frac{\$0.56 + \$45.50}{1.0680} = \$43.13$$

Referring to Eq. 7.2, we see that at this price, Longs' dividend yield is $Div_1/P_0 = 0.56/43.13 = 1.30\%$. The expected capital gain is $\$45.50 - \$43.13 = \$2.37$ per share, for a capital gain rate of $2.37/43.13 = 5.50\%$.

EVALUATE

At a price of $43.13, Longs' expected total return is $1.30\% + 5.50\% = 6.80\%$, which is equal to its equity cost of capital (the return being paid by investments with equivalent risk to Longs'). This amount is the most we would be willing to pay for Longs' stock. If we paid more, our expected return would be less than 6.8% and we would rather invest elsewhere.

PROBLEM

Ellen is 35 years old and she has decided it is time to plan seriously for her retirement. At the end of each year until she is 65, she will save $10,000 in a retirement account. If the account earns 10% per year, how much will Ellen have in her account at age 65?

SOLUTION

PLAN

As always, we begin with a timeline. In this case, it is helpful to keep track of both the dates and Ellen's age:

35	36	37	65
0	1	2	30
	$10,000	$10,000	... $10,000

Ellen's savings plan looks like an annuity of $10,000 per year for 30 years. (*Hint:* It is easy to become confused when you just look at age, rather than at both dates and age. A common error is to think there are only $65 - 36 = 29$ payments. Writing down both dates and age avoids this problem.)

To determine the amount Ellen will have in her account at age 65, we'll need to compute the future value of this annuity.

EXECUTE

$$FV = \$10,000 \times \frac{1}{0.10}\left(1.10^{30} - 1\right)$$

$$= \$10,000 \times 164.49$$

$$= \$1.645 \text{ million at age 65}$$

Using a financial calculator or Excel:

	N	I/Y	PV	PMT	FV
Given:	30	10	0	−10,000	
Solve for:					1,644,940
Excel Formula:	=FV(RATE,NPER, PMT, PV)=FV(0.10,30,−10000,0)				

EVALUATE

By investing $10,000 per year for 30 years (a total of $300,000) and earning interest on those investments, the compounding will allow Ellen to retire with $1.645 million.

Study Aids with a Practical Focus

To be successful, students need to master the core concepts and learn to identify and solve problems that today's practitioners face.

- The **Valuation Principle** is presented as the foundation of all financial decision making: The central idea is that a firm should take projects or make investments that increase the *value* of the firm. The tools of finance determine the impact of a project or investment on the firm's value by comparing the costs and benefits in equivalent terms. The Valuation Principle is first introduced in Chapter 3, revisited in the part openers, and integrated throughout the text.

- **Guided Problem Solutions (GPS)** are Examples that accompany every important concept using a consistent problem-solving methodology that breaks the solution process into three steps: *Plan, Execute,* and *Evaluate.* This approach aids student comprehension, enhances their ability to model the solution process when tackling problems on their own, and demonstrates the importance of interpreting the mathematical solution.

- **Personal Finance GPS** Examples showcase the use of financial analysis in everyday life by setting problems in scenarios, such as purchasing a new car or house and saving for retirement.

- **Common Mistake** boxes alert students to frequently made mistakes stemming from misunderstanding of core concepts and calculations—in the classroom and in the field.

COMMON MISTAKE

Summing Cash Flows Across Time

Once you understand the time value of money, our first rule may seem straightforward. However, it is very common, especially for those who have not studied finance, to violate this rule, simply treating all cash flows as comparable regardless of when they are received. One example is in sports contracts. In 2011, Albert Pujols signed a contract with the Los Angeles Angels that was repeatedly referred to as a "$240 million" contract. The $240 million comes from simply adding up all the payments Pujols would receive over the 10 years of the contract—treating dollars received in 10 years the same as dollars received today. The same thing occurred when Lionel Messi signed a contract extension with FC Barcelona in 2013, giving him a "$150 million" contract through 2018, and in 2015 when Giancarlo Stanton signed a "$325 million" 13-year contract with the Florida Marlins.

Applications That Reflect Real Practice

Global Financial Crisis boxes reflect the reality of the recent financial crisis and sovereign debt crisis, noting lessons learned. Boxes interspersed through the book illustrate and analyze key details.

2008–2009: A Very Cold IPO Market

The drop in IPO issues during the 2008 financial crisis was both global and dramatic. The bar graph shows the total worldwide dollar volume of IPO proceeds in billions of dollars (blue bars) and number of deals (red line) by quarter, from the last quarter of 2006 to the first quarter of 2009. Comparing the fourth quarter of 2007 (a record quarter for IPO issues) to the fourth quarter of 2008, dollar volume dropped a stunning 97% from $102 billion to just $3 billion. Things got even worse in the first quarter of 2009 with just $1.4 billion raised. The market for IPOs essentially dried up altogether.

During the 2008 financial crisis, IPO markets were not the only equity issue markets that saw a collapse in volume. Markets for seasoned equity offerings and leveraged buyouts also collapsed. The extreme market uncertainty at the time created a "flight to quality." Investors, wary of taking risk, sought to move their capital into risk-free investments like U.S. Treasury securities. The result was a crash in existing equity prices and a greatly reduced supply of new capital to risky asset classes.

Source: Shifting Landscape—Are You Ready? Global IPO Trends report 2009, Ernst & Young.

Practitioner Interviews from notable professionals featured in many chapters highlight leaders in the field and address the effects of the financial crisis.

KEVIN M. WARSH

Kevin M. Warsh, a lecturer at Stanford's Graduate School of Business and a distinguished visiting fellow at the Hoover Institution, was a Federal Reserve governor from 2006 to 2011, serving as chief liaison to the financial markets.

QUESTION: *What are the main policy instruments used by central banks to control the economy?*

ANSWER: The Federal Reserve (Fed) deploys several policy tools to achieve its goals of price stability, maximum sustainable employment, and financial stability. Lowering the federal funds short-term interest rate, the primary policy instrument, stimulates the economy. Raising the federal funds rate generally slows the economy. Buying and selling short-term U.S. Treasury securities through *open market operations* is standard practice. Prior to the 2007–2009 financial crisis, the Fed's balance sheet ranged from $700–$900 billion. But when the Fed was unable to lower interest rates further because rates were so close to zero already, it resorted to large-scale, longer-term open market operations to increase liquidity in the financial system in the hopes of stimulating the economy further, thus growing its balance sheet significantly. With *open mouth operations*, the Fed's announcements of its intent to buy or sell assets indicates its desired degree of future policy accommodation, often prompting markets to react by adjusting interest rates immediately. The Fed's Lender-of-Last-Resort authority allows it to lend money against good collateral to troubled institutions under certain conditions.

QUESTION: *What factors limit the effectiveness of Fed policy?*

ANSWER: Monetary policy does not act in isolation. Fiscal (taxing and spending), trade, and regulatory policies have huge consequence on the state of economic and financial conditions. In the short term, monetary policy can help buy time for an economy to improve, but it cannot cure structural failings of an economy in isolation or compensate for the country's growing indebtedness.

QUESTION: *What tools did the Fed create to address the 2007–2009 financial crisis?*

ANSWER: During the darkest days of the crisis, markets did not operate effectively, prices for securities did not clear, and banks and other financial institutions lacked clarity and confidence in the financial wherewithal of each other. One effective, innovative tool, the *Term Auction Facility (TAF)*, stimulated the economy by providing cheap and readily available term funding to banks, large and small, on the front lines of the economy, thus encouraging them to extend credit to businesses and consumers. After reducing the policy rate to near zero to help revive the economy, the Fed instituted two *Quantitative Easing (QE)* programs—special purchases of government and agency securities—to increase money supply, promote lending, and according to some proponents, increase prices of riskier assets.

The Fed also addressed the global financial crisis by establishing temporary *central bank liquidity swap lines* with the European Central Bank and other major central banks. Using this facility, a foreign central bank is able to obtain dollar funding for its customers by swapping euros for dollars or another currency and agreeing to reverse the swap at a later date. The Fed does not take exchange rate risk, but it is subject to the credit risk of its central bank counterparty.

QUESTION: *What tools is the European Central Bank (ECB) using to address the sovereign debt crisis? How does its approach compare to the Fed's approach to the 2007–2009 financial crisis?*

ANSWER: As a novel economic federation, the ECB finds itself in a more difficult position than the Fed. The underlying economies and competitiveness are markedly different across the Eurozone—in Germany versus Greece, for example. From 2007 until mid-2010, many European financiers and policymakers believed that global financial crisis was largely American-made, with some strains exported to the continent. By mid-2010, however, they recognized that it was indeed a global crisis. The ECB is formally charged with a single mandate of ensuring price stability, rather than the broader mandate of the Fed. Still, its actions ultimately mirrored many of those undertaken by the Fed: lowering the effective policy rate to record lows, providing direct liquidity to the Eurozone's financial institutions to avoid a potential run on the banking system, and instituting the Security Market Purchase program (buying sovereign credit of some of its distressed countries).

General Interest boxes highlight timely material from current financial events that shed light on business problems and real company practices.

The Credit Crisis and Bond Yields

The financial crisis that engulfed the world's economies in 2008 originated as a credit crisis that first emerged in August 2007. At that time, problems in the mortgage market had led to the bankruptcy of several large mortgage lenders. The default of these firms, and the downgrading of many of the bonds backed by mortgages these firms had made, caused many investors to reassess the risk of other bonds in their portfolios. As perceptions of risk increased, and investors attempted to move into safer U.S. Treasury securities, the prices of corporate bonds fell and so their credit spreads rose relative to Treasuries, as shown in Figure 6.7. Panel (a) shows the yield spreads for long-term corporate bonds, where we can see that spreads of even the highest-rated Aaa bonds increased dramatically, from a typical level of 0.5% to over 2% by the fall of 2008. Panel (b) shows a similar pattern for the rate banks had to pay on short-term loans compared to the yields of short-term Treasury bills. This increase in borrowing costs made it more costly for firms to raise the capital needed for new investment, slowing economic growth. The decline in these spreads in early 2009 was viewed by many as an important first step in mitigating the ongoing impact of the financial crisis on the rest of the economy.

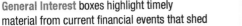

Teaching Every Student to Think Finance

Simplified Presentation of Mathematics

Because one of the hardest parts of learning finance for non-majors is mastering the jargon, math, and non-standardized notation, *Fundamentals of Corporate Finance* systematically uses:

- **Notation Boxes.** Each chapter begins with a Notation box that defines the variables and the acronyms used in the chapter and serves as a "legend" for students' reference.

- **Numbered and Labeled Equations.** The first time a full equation is given in notation form it is numbered. Key equations are titled and revisited in the summary and in end papers.

- **Timelines.** Introduced in Chapter 3, timelines are emphasized as the important first step in solving *every* problem that involves cash flows over time.

- **Financial Calculator** instructions, including a box in Chapter 4 on solving for future and present values, and appendices to Chapters 4, 6, and 15 with keystrokes for HP-10BII and TI BAII Plus Professional calculators, highlight this problem-solving tool.

- **Spreadsheet Tables.** Select tables are available on MyFinanceLab as Excel® files, enabling students to change inputs and manipulate the underlying calculations. Icons in the text show students where spreadsheets are available in the eText.

- **Using Excel** boxes describe Excel techniques and include screenshots to serve as a guide for students using this technology.

Using a Financial Calculator

Financial calculators are programmed to perform most present and future value calculations. However, we recommend that you develop an understanding of the formulas before using the shortcuts. We provide a more extensive discussion of financial calculators on page 95 and in the appendix to Chapter 4, but we'll cover the relevant functions for this chapter here. To use financial calculator functions, you always enter the known values first and then the calculator solves for the unknown.

To answer Example 3.4 with a financial calculator, do the following:

Concept	Number of Periods	Interest Rate per Period	Recurring Payments	Future Value
Calculator Key	**N**	**I/Y**	**PMT**	**FV**
Enter	10	6	0	15000

Because you are solving for the present value (PV), press the **FV** key last (on an HP calculator), or press **CPT** then the **PV** key on a TI calculator. The calculator will return −8375.92. Note that the calculator balances inflows with outflows, so because the FV is positive (an inflow), it returns the PV as a negative (an outflow).

If you were solving for the future value instead, you would enter:

N	**I/Y**	**PV**	**PMT**
10	6	−8375.92	0

And finally, on an HP, press the **FV** key or on a TI, press **CPT** and then the **FV** key.

TABLE 18.18

Pro Forma Statement of Cash Flows for KMS, 2016–2021

	Year	2016	2017	2018	2019	2020	2021
1	Statement of Cash Flows ($000s)						
2							
3	Net Income		7,600	8,807	11,141	13,739	16,827
4	Depreciation		7,443	7,498	7,549	7,594	7,634
5	Changes in Working Capital						
6	Accounts Receivable		−2,561	−2,827	−3,144	−3,491	−3,872
7	Inventory		−2,696	−2,976	−3,309	−3,675	−4,076
8	Accounts Payable		2,157	2,381	2,647	2,940	3,261
9	Cash from Operating Activities		11,942	12,884	14,884	17,107	19,574
10	Capital Expenditures		−25,000	−8,000	−8,000	−8,000	−8,000
11	Other Investment		—	—	—	—	—
12	Cash from Investing Activities		−25,000	−8,000	−8,000	−8,000	−8,000
13	Net Borrowing		20,000	—	—	—	—
14	Dividends		−4,786	−2,503	−4,237	−6,167	−8,313
15	Cash from Financing Activities		15,214	−2,503	−4,237	−6,167	−8,313
16							
17	Change in Cash (9 + 12 + 15)		2,157	2,381	2,647	2,940	3,261

USING EXCEL

Capital Budgeting Using a Spreadsheet Program

Capital budgeting forecasts and analysis are most easily performed in a spreadsheet program. Here, we highlight a few best practices when developing your own capital budgets.

Create a Project Dashboard

All capital budgeting analyses begin with a set of assumptions regarding future revenues and costs associated with the investment. Centralize these assumptions within your spreadsheet in a project dashboard so they are easy to locate, review, and potentially modify. Here, we show an example for the HomeNet project.

	A	B	C	D	E	F	G	H	I	J
1	HomeNet Capital Budget									
2	Key Assumptions									
3	Revenues & Costs		Year 0	Year 1	Year 2	Year 3	Year 4	Year 5		
4	HomeNet Units Sold			50	50	50	50			
5	HomeNet Avg. Price/Unit			$ 260.00	$ 260.00	$ 260.00	$ 260.00			
6	HomeNet Cost/Unit			$ 110.00	$ 110.00	$ 110.00	$ 110.00			
7	Operating Expenses									
8	Marketing, Support & Rent			(2,800)	(2,800)	(2,800)	(2,800)			
9	Capital Expenditures									
10	Purchase Equipment		(7,500)							
11	Other Assumptions									
12	Depreciation Schedule		0.0%	20.0%	20.0%	20.0%	20.0%	20.0%		
13	Corporate Tax Rate		40.0%	40.0%	40.0%	40.0%	40.0%	40.0%		
14	Receivables (% sales)		15.0%	15.0%	15.0%	15.0%	15.0%	15.0%		
15	Payables (% expenses)		15.0%	15.0%	15.0%	15.0%	15.0%	15.0%		
16										

Practice Finance
to Learn Finance

MyFinanceLab

Here is what you should know after reading this chapter. MyFinanceLab will help you identify what you know, and where to go when you need to practice.

KEY POINTS AND EQUATIONS	KEY TERMS	ONLINE PRACTICE
4.1 Valuing a Stream of Cash Flows • The present value of a cash flow stream is: $$PV = C_0 + \frac{C_1}{(1+r)} + \frac{C_2}{(1+r)^2} + \cdots + \frac{C_N}{(1+r)^N} \quad (4.3)$$	stream of cash flows, p. 94	MyFinanceLab Study Plan 4.1
4.2 Perpetuities • A perpetuity is a stream of equal cash flows C paid every period, forever. The present value of a perpetuity is: $$PV(C \text{ in Perpetuity}) = \frac{C}{r} \quad (4.4)$$	consol, p. 98 perpetuity, p. 98	MyFinanceLab Study Plan 4.2
4.3 Annuities • An annuity is a stream of equal cash flows C paid every period for N periods. The present value of an annuity is: $$C \times \frac{1}{r}\left(1 - \frac{1}{(1+r)^N}\right) \quad (4.5)$$ • The future value of an annuity at the end of the annuity is: $$C \times \frac{1}{r}\left((1+r)^N - 1\right) \quad (4.6)$$	annuity, p. 101	MyFinanceLab Study Plan 4.3 Interactive Annuity Calculator Financial Calculator Tutorials: Calculating the Present Value of an Annuity and Solving for the Future Value of an Annuity

Working problems is the proven way to cement and demonstrate an understanding of finance.

- **Concept Check questions** at the end of each section enable students to test their understanding and target areas in which they need further review.

- **End-of-chapter problems written personally by Jonathan Berk, Peter DeMarzo, and Jarrad Harford** offer instructors the opportunity to assign first-rate materials to students for homework and practice with the confidence that the problems are consistent with the chapter content. All end-of-chapter problems are available in MyFinanceLab, the fully integrated homework and tutorial system. Both the problems and solutions, which were also prepared by the authors, have been class-tested and accuracy checked to ensure quality. Excel icons indicate the availability of instructor solutions and student templates in the Textbook Resources tab of MyFinanceLab.

End-of-Chapter Materials Reinforce Learning

Testing understanding of central concepts is crucial to learning finance.

- **MyFinanceLab Chapter Summary** presents the key points and conclusions from each chapter, provides a list of key terms with page numbers, and indicates online practice opportunities.

- **Data Cases** present in-depth scenarios in a business setting with questions designed to guide students' analysis. Many questions involve the use of Internet resources.

- **Integrative Cases** occur at the end of most parts and present a capstone extended problem for each part with a scenario and data for students to analyze based on that subset of chapters.

DATA CASE

This is your second interview with a prestigious brokerage firm for a job as an equity analyst. You survived the morning interviews with the department manager and the vice president of equity. Everything has gone so well that they want to test your ability as an analyst. You are seated in a room with a computer and a list with the names of two companies—Ford (F) and Microsoft (MSFT). You have 90 minutes to complete the following tasks:

1. Download the annual income statements, balance sheets, and cash flow statements for the last four fiscal years from Morningstar (www.morningstar.com). Enter each company's stock symbol and then go to "financials." Copy and paste the financial statements into Excel.

2. Find historical stock prices for each firm from Yahoo! Finance (finance.yahoo.com). Enter the stock symbol, click "Historical Prices" in the left column, and enter the proper date range to cover the last day of the month corresponding to the date of each financial statement. Use the closing stock prices (not the adjusted close). To calculate the firm's market capitalization at each date, multiply the number of shares outstanding by the firm's historic stock price. You can find the number of shares by using "Basic" under "Weighted average shares outstanding" at the bottom of the Income Statement.

Preface

Finance professors are united by their commitment to shaping future generations of financial professionals as well as instilling financial awareness and skills in non-majors. Our goal with *Fundamentals of Corporate Finance* is to provide an accessible presentation for both finance and non-finance majors. We know from experience that countless undergraduate students have felt that corporate finance is challenging. It is tempting to make finance *seem* accessible by de-emphasizing the core principles and instead concentrating on the results. In our over 50 years of combined teaching experience, we have found that emphasizing the core concepts in finance—which are clear and intuitive at heart—is what makes the subject matter accessible. What makes the subject challenging is that it is often difficult for a novice to distinguish between these core ideas and other intuitively appealing approaches that, if used in financial decision making, will lead to incorrect decisions.

The 2007–2009 financial crisis was fueled in part by many practitioners' poor decision making when they did not understand—or chose to ignore—the core concepts that underlie finance and the pedagogy in this book. With this point in mind, we present finance as one unified whole based on two simple, powerful ideas: (1) valuation drives decision making—the firm should take projects for which the value of the benefits exceeds the value of the costs, and (2) in a competitive market, market prices (rather than individual preferences) determine values. We combine these two ideas with what we call the *Valuation Principle*, and from it we establish all of the key ideas in corporate finance.

New to This Edition

All text discussions and figures, tables, and facts have been updated to accurately reflect exciting developments in the field of finance in the last three years. Specific highlights include the following:

- **New Interviews** with Frank Hatheway, Chief Economist and Senior VP for NASDAQ; Ruth Porat, Senior VP and CFO of Alphabet and Google; Kevin Laws, COO of AngelList; and Douglas Kehring, Senior VP of Oracle.
- **Real-world examples** have been updated to reflect data through 2016.
- **New, Enhanced Media-Rich Pearson eText** includes Author Solution Videos that walk through the in-text examples using math, the financial calculator, and spreadsheets.
- **Using Excel boxes** have been updated and provide hands-on instruction of how to use Excel to solve financial problems and include screenshots to serve as a guide for students.
- **Added discussion of current issues** including negative interest rates, crowdfunding, new trading venues such as BATS and dark pools.

- **Added and revised end-of-chapter problems throughout the book,** once again personally writing and solving each one. In addition, every single problem is available in MyFinanceLab, the groundbreaking homework and tutorial system that accompanies the book.

- **We updated Data Cases and Integrative Cases** throughout the book, giving students a chance to apply the material with realistic data-analyzing exercises and problems that integrate material across chapters in each major part of the book.

Emphasis on Valuation

As painful as the financial crisis was, there is a silver lining: with the increasing focus on finance in the news, today's undergraduate students arrive in the classroom with an interest in finance. We strive to use that natural interest and motivation to overcome their fear of the subject and communicate time-tested core principles. Again, we take what has worked in the classroom and apply it to the text: By providing examples involving familiar companies such as Starbucks and Apple, making consistent use of real-world data, and demonstrating personal finance applications of core concepts, we strive to keep both non-finance and finance majors engaged.

By learning to apply the Valuation Principle, students develop the skills to make the types of comparisons—among loan options, investments, projects, and so on—that turn them into knowledgeable, confident financial consumers and managers. When students see how to apply finance to their personal lives and future careers, they grasp that finance is more than abstract, mathematically based concepts.

Table of Contents Overview

Fundamentals of Corporate Finance offers coverage of the major topical areas for introductory-level undergraduate courses. Our focus is on financial decision making related to the corporation's choice of which investments to make or how to raise the capital required to fund an investment. We designed the book with the need for flexibility and with consideration of time pressures throughout the semester in mind.

Part **1**	Introduction	
	Ch. 1: Corporate Finance and the Financial Manager	Introduces the corporation and its governance; updated to include comparison of traditional trading venues, new electronic exchanges, and how the market for trading stocks is changing
	Ch. 2: Introduction to Financial Statement Analysis	Introduces key financial statements; Coverage of financial ratios has been centralized to prepare students to analyze financial statements holistically
Part **2**	Interest Rates and Valuing Cash Flows	
	Ch. 3: Time Value of Money: An Introduction	Introduces the Valuation Principle and time value of money techniques for single-period investments
	Ch. 4: Time Value of Money: Valuing Cash Flow Streams	Introduces the mechanics of discounting; Includes examples with non-annual interest rates that provide time value of money applications in a personal loan context
	Ch. 5: Interest Rates	Presents how interest rates are quoted and compounding for all frequencies; Discusses key determinants of interest rates and their relation to the cost of capital; New discussion of negative interest rate

Ch. 22: Mergers and Acquisitions	Considers motives and methods for mergers and acquisitions, including leveraged buyouts
Ch. 23: International Corporate Finance	Analyzes the valuation of projects with foreign currency cash flows with integrated or segregated capital markets

Online Chapters
(on MyFinanceLab at www.myfinancelab.com)

Leasing	Opportunities for course customization with online-only chapter offerings
Insurance and Risk Management	
Corporate Governance	

A Complete Instructor and Student Support Package

MyFinanceLab

Not every student learns the same way or at the same rate. With the growing need for acceleration through many courses, it's more important than ever to meet students where they learn. Personalized learning in the MyFinanceLab gives you the flexibility to incorporate the approach that best suits your course and your students.

Study Plan

The **Study Plan** acts as a tutor, providing personalized recommendations for each of your students based on his or her ability to master the learning objectives in your course. This allows students to focus their study time by pinpointing the precise areas they need to review, and allowing them to use customized practice and learning aids—such as videos, eText, tutorials, and more—to get them back on track. Using the report available in the Gradebook, you can then tailor course lectures to prioritize the content where students need the most support—offering you better insight into classroom and individual performance.

Dynamic Study Modules

Dynamic Study Modules help students study effectively on their own by continuously assessing their activity and performance in real time. Here's how it works: students complete a set of questions with a unique answer format that also asks them to indicate their confidence level. Questions repeat until the student can answer them all correctly and confidently. Once completed, Dynamic Study Modules explain the concept using materials from the text. These are available as graded assignments prior to class, and accessible on smartphones, tablets, and computers. NEW! Instructors can now remove questions from Dynamic Study Modules to better fit their course.

Enhanced eText

The **Enhanced eText** keeps students engaged in learning on their own time, while helping them achieve greater conceptual understanding of course material. The worked examples bring learning to life, and algorithmic practice allows students to apply the very concepts they are reading about. Combining resources that illuminate content with accessible self-assessment, MyFinanceLab with Enhanced eText provides students with a complete digital learning experience—all in one place.

And with the **Pearson eText 2.0 mobile app** (available for select titles) students can now access the Enhanced eText and all of its functionality from their computer, tablet, or mobile phone. Because students' progress is synced across all of their devices, they can stop what they're doing on one device and pick up again later on another one—without breaking their stride.

Auto-Graded Excel Projects

Auto-graded Excel Projects allow instructors to seamlessly integrate Excel content into their course without having to manually grade spreadsheets. Students have the opportunity to practice important Finance skills in Microsoft Excel, helping them to master key concepts and gain proficiency with Excel.

Videos

Video clips available in MyFinanceLab profile well-known firms such as Boeing and Intel through interviews and analysis. The videos focus on core topical areas such as capital budgeting and risk and return. Author-created videos walk students through guided problem solutions for every in-text example.

Financial Calculator

The **Financial Calculator** is available as a smartphone application, as well as on a computer, and includes important functions such as cash flow, net present value, and internal rate of return. Fifteen helpful tutorial videos show the many ways to use the Financial Calculator in MyFinanceLab.

Interactive Figures

Select in-text graphs and figures have been digitally enhanced to allow students to interact with variables to affect outcomes and bring concepts to life.

Solutions Manual

The **Solutions Manual** provides students with detailed, accuracy-verified solutions to the problems in the book. The solutions, like the problems, were written by the authors themselves. Spreadsheet solutions in Excel, which allow the student to see the effect of changes in the input variables on the outcome, are also available to instructors for designated problems at the Instructor Resource Center (www.pearsonhighered.com/irc).

PowerPoint Presentations

The **PowerPoint Presentation**, authored by William Chittenden of Texas State University, is available in lecture form and includes art and tables from the book and additional examples. The PowerPoint presentation includes all tables and figures, examples, key terms, and spreadsheet tables from the textbook. All PowerPoint presentations are also available for download from the Instructor Resource Center at www.pearsonhighered.com/irc.

Test Bank

The **Test Bank** provides a wealth of accuracy-verified, algorithmic testing material. Each chapter offers a wide variety of true/false, short answer, and multiple-choice questions updated by Brian Nethercutt. Questions are verified by difficulty level and skill type, and correlated to the chapter topics. Numerical problems include step-by-step solutions and have been made algorithmic so they can be assigned for repeated practice.

TestGen

TestGen is a computerized test generation program, available exclusively from Pearson, that allows instructors to easily create and administer tests on paper, electronically, or online. Instructors can select test items from the publisher-supplied test bank, which is organized by chapter and based on the associated textbook material, or create their own questions from scratch. With both quick-and-simple test creation and flexible and robust editing tools, TestGen is a complete test generator system for today's educators.

Instructor's Manual

The **Instructor's Manual** was written by Mary R. Brown of the University of Illinois–Chicago, and contains annotated chapter outlines, lecture launchers, and questions for further class discussion. It also contains the solutions to the Data Cases and part-ending case problems, as well as answers to the end-of-chapter Critical Thinking questions in the book. As an additional resource to guide instructors with students who are planning to take the CFA exam, CFA learning outcomes met in each chapter are listed. A section also details how the end-of-chapter problems map to the accreditation standards set by the Association to Advance Collegiate Schools of Business (AACSB), so that instructors can track students' mastery of the AACSB standards. The Instructor's Manual is available for download as Microsoft Word files or as Adobe® PDF files from the Instructor Resource Center at www.pearsonhighered.com/irc.

Acknowledgments

Given the scope of this project, identifying the many people who made it happen is a tall order. This textbook was the product of the expertise and hard work of many talented colleagues. We are especially gratified with the work of those who developed the array of print supplements that accompany the book: William Chittenden for the PowerPoint presentations; Mary R. Brown, for the Instructor's Manual; James Linck, for serving as advisor for the videos; and our MyFinanceLab content development team, including Melissa Honig, Miguel Leonarte, Noel Lotz, and Sarah Peterson. We're also deeply appreciative of Susan White's contributions to the part-ending cases.

Creating a truly error-free text is a challenge we could not have lived up to without our team of expert error checkers. Jared Stanfield subjected the text and problem solutions to his exacting standards. We are also indebted to Jared for his adept research support throughout the writing process and Michael Wittry's assistance in providing updates.

At Pearson Education, we would like to single out Donna Battista, for her continued leadership and market insight; Kate Fernandes for her energy and fresh perspective as our new editor; Melissa Honig for her digital media expertise; and our production team, Meredith Gertz and especially Gillian Hall, for expertly managing the transformation of our files into a beautiful bound book. They were helped by Kalpana Arumugam at Spi Global, whose team provided the fantastic composition and artwork. We are truly thankful for the indispensable help provided by these and other professionals.

We are indebted to our colleagues for the time and expertise invested as manuscript reviewers, class testers, and focus group participants. We list all of these contributors on the following pages, but want to single out one group, our First Edition editorial board, for special notice: Tom Berry, *DePaul University*; Elizabeth Booth, *Michigan State University*; Julie Dahlquist, the *University of Texas–San Antonio*; Michaël Dewally, *Marquette University*; Robert M. Donchez, the *University of Colorado–Boulder*; Belinda Mucklow, the *University of Wisconsin–Madison*; Coleen Pantalone, *Northeastern University*; and Susan White, the *University of Maryland*. We strived to incorporate every contributor's input and are truly grateful for each comment and suggestion. The book has benefited enormously from this input.

Reviewers

Pankaj Agrrawal, *University of Maine*
Daniel Ahern, *California State University–Chico*
Paul Asabere, *Temple University*
Ajeyo Banerjee, *University of Colorado–Denver*
Tom Berry, *DePaul University*
Karan Bhanot, *University of Texas–San Antonio*
Rafiqul Bhuyan, *California State University–San Bernardino*
Eugene Bland, *Texas A&M University–Corpus Christi*
Matej Blasko, *University of Georgia*
Elizabeth Booth, *Michigan State University*
Mary Brown, *University of Illinois–Chicago*
Bill Brunsen, *Eastern New Mexico University*
David G. Cazier, *Brigham Young University–Provo*
Leo Chan, *Delaware State University*
Cindy Chen, *California State University–Long Beach*
Haiyu Chen, *Youngstown State University*
James F. Cotter, *Wake Forest University*
Vicentiu Covrig, *California State University–Northridge*
Julie Dahlquist, *University of Texas–San Antonio*
Pieter de Jong, *University of Texas–Arlington*
Andrea L. DeMaskey, *Villanova University*
Xiaohui Deng, *California State University–Fresno*
Michaël Dewally, *Marquette University*
Robert M. Donchez, *University of Colorado Boulder*
Gang Dong, *Rutgers University*
Dean Drenk, *Montana State University*
Robert Dubil, *University of Utah*
Hsing Fang, *California State University–Los Angeles*
David O. Fricke, *University of North Carolina–Pembroke*
Scott Fung, *California State University–East Bay*
Sharon Garrison, *University of Arizona*
Rakesh Gupta, *Central Queensland University*
Joseph D. Haley, *St. Cloud State University*
Thomas Hall, *Christopher Newport University*
Karen Hallows, *University of Maryland*
Karen L. Hamilton, *Georgia Southern University*
Robert Hanson, *Eastern Michigan University*
Mahfuzul Haque, *Indiana State University*
Edward C. Howell, *Northwood University*
Ping Hsiao, *San Francisco State University*
Xiaoqing Hu, *University of Illinois at Chicago*
Pankaj Jain, *University of Memphis*
Robert James, *Boston College*
Susan Ji, *Baruch College, City University of New York*
Domingo Joaquin, *Illinois State University*
Fred R. Kaen, *University of New Hampshire*
Terrill Keasler, *Appalachian State University*
Howard Keen, *Temple University*
Brett A. King, *University of North Alabama*
Daniel Klein, *Bowling Green State University*

Gregory Kuhlemeyer, *Carroll University*
Rose Neng Lai, *University of Macau*
Keith Lam, *University of Macau*
Reinhold P. Lamb, *University of North Florida*
Douglas Lamdin, *University of Maryland–Baltimore County*
Mark J. Laplante, *University of Georgia*
Sie Ting Lau, *Nanyang Technological University*
Richard LeCompte, *Wichita State University*
Adam Y.C. Lei, *Midwestern State University*
Qian Li, *Midwestern State University*
Chang Liu, *Washington State University*
Wei Liu, *Texas A&M University*
Hugh Marble III, *University of Vermont*
James Milanese, *University of North Carolina at Greensboro*
Sunil K. Mohanty, *University of St. Thomas*
Ted Moorman, *Northern Illinois University*
James Morris, *University of Colorado–Denver*
Belinda Mucklow, *University of Wisconsin–Madison*
Rick Nelson, *University of Minnesota*
Tom C. Nelson, *University of Colorado–Boulder*
Curtis Nicholls, *Bucknell University*
Anthony C. Ng, *Hong Kong Polytechnic University*
Coleen Pantalone, *Northeastern University*
Daniel Park, *Azusa Pacific University*
Janet Payne, *Texas State University*
Jay Peroni, *College of Charleston*
Lynn Pi, *Hong Kong University of Science and Technology*
J. Michael Pinegar, *Brigham Young University*
Annette Poulsen, *University of Georgia*
Eric Powers, *University of South Carolina*
Rose M. Prasad, *Central Michigan University*
Shoba Premkumar, *Iowa State University*
Mark K. Pyles, *College of Charleston*
A.A.B. Resing, *Hogeschool Van Amsterdam*
Greg Richey, *California State University, San Bernardino*
Scott Roark, *Boise State University*
David L. Robbins, *University of New Mexico*
Andrew Samwick, *Dartmouth College*
Salil K. Sarkar, *University of Texas–Arlington*
Oliver Schnusenberg, *University of North Florida*
Kenneth Scislaw, *University of Alabama–Huntsville*
Roger Severns, *Minnesota State University–Mankato*
Tatyana Sokolyk, *University of Wyoming*
Andrew C. Spieler, *Hofstra University*
Timothy G. Sullivan, *Bentley College*
Janikan Supanvanij, *St. Cloud State University*
Hugo Tang, *Purdue University*
Oranee Tawatnuntachai, *Pennsylvania State University–Harrisburg*
Robert Terpstra, *University of Macau*

Thomas Thomson, *University of Texas–San Antonio*
Olaf J. Thorp, *Babson College*
Ed Tiryakian, *Duke University*
Emery Trahan, *Northeastern University*
Joe Ueng, *University of St. Thomas*
Mo Vaziri, *California State University–San Bernardino*
Premal P. Vora, *Pennsylvania State University–Harrisburg*
Hefei Wang, *University of Illinois–Chicago*
Gwendolyn Webb, *Baruch College*
Paul M. Weinstock, *Ohio State University*
Susan White, *University of Maryland*
Annie Wong, *Western Connecticut State University*
Xiaoyan Xu, *San Jose State University*
Zhong-gou Zhou, *California State University–Northridge*
Kermit C. Zieg, Jr., *Florida Institute of Technology*

Focus Group Participants

Anne-Marie Anderson, *Lehigh University*
Sung Bae, *Bowling Green State University*
H. Kent Baker, *American University*
Steven Beach, *Radford University*
Rafiqul Bhuyan, *California State University–San Bernardino*
Deanne Butchey, *Florida International University*
Leo Chan, *Delaware State University*
George Chang, *Grand Valley State University*
Haiwei Chen, *California State University–San Bernardino*
Haiyu Chen, *Youngstown State University*
Massimiliano De Santis, *Dartmouth College*
Jocelyn Evans, *College of Charleston*
Kathleen Fuller, *University of Mississippi*
Xavier Garza Gomez, *University of Houston–Victoria*
William Gentry, *Williams College*
Axel Grossmann, *Radford University*
Pankaj Jain, *University of Memphis*
Zhenhu Jin, *Valparaiso University*
Steve Johnson, *University of Northern Iowa*
Steven Jones, *Samford University*
Yong-Cheol Kim, *University of Wisconsin–Milwaukee*
Robert Kiss, *Eastern Michigan University*
Ann Marie Klingenhagen, *DePaul University*
Thomas J. Krissek, *Northeastern Illinois University*
Olivier Maisondieu Laforge, *University of Nebraska–Omaha*
Douglas Lamdin, *University of Maryland–Baltimore County*
D. Scott Lee, *Texas A&M University*
Stanley A. Martin, *University of Colorado–Boulder*

Jamshid Mehran, *Indiana University, South Bend*
Sunil Mohanty, *University of St. Thomas*
Karyn L. Neuhauser, *State University of New York–Plattsburgh*
Thomas O'Brien, *University of Connecticut*
Hyuna Park, *Minnesota State University–Mankato*
G. Michael Phillips, *California State University–Northridge*
Wendy Pirie, *Valparaiso University*
Antonio Rodriguez, *Texas A&M International University*
Camelia S. Rotaru, *St. Edward's University*
Salil Sarkar, *University of Texas at Arlington*
Mark Sunderman, *University of Wyoming*
Chu-Sheng Tai, *Texas Southern University*
Oranee Tawatnuntachai, *Pennsylvania State University–Harrisburg*
Benedict Udemgba, *Alcorn State University*
Rahul Verma, *University of Houston–Downtown*
Angelo P. Vignola, *Loyola University–Chicago*
Premal Vora, *Pennsylvania State University–Harrisburg*
Eric Wehrly, *Seattle University*
Yan A. Xie, *University of Michigan–Dearborn*
Fang Zhao, *Siena College*
Sophie Zong, *California State University–Stanislaus*

Class Testers

Tom Berry, *DePaul University*
Eugene Bland, *Texas A&M University–Corpus Christi*
Charles Blaylock, *Murray State University*
Mary Brown, *University of Illinois–Chicago*
Bill Brunsen, *Eastern New Mexico University*
Sarah Bryant Bower, *Shippensburg University of Pennsylvania*
Alva Wright Butcher, *University of Puget Sound*
David G. Cazier, *Brigham Young University–Provo*
Asim G. Celik, *University of Nevada–Reno*
Michaël Dewally, *Marquette University*
Richard Gaddis, *Oklahoma Wesleyan University*
TeWhan Hahn, *Auburn University–Montgomery*
Matthew Hood, *University of Southern Mississippi*
Zhenhu Jin, *Valparaiso University*
Travis Jones, *Florida Gulf Coast University*
Francis E. Laatsch, *Bowling Green State University*
Diane Lander, *Saint Michael's College*
Vance Lesseig, *Texas State University*
Frances Maloy, *University of Washington*
Jamshid Mehran, *Indiana University–South Bend*
Belinda Mucklow, *University of Wisconsin–Madison*
Kuo-Chung Tseng, *California State University–Fresno*
Kermit C. Zieg, Jr., *Florida Institute of Technology*

2

Introduction to Financial Statement Analysis

LEARNING OBJECTIVES

- Know why the disclosure of financial information through financial statements is critical to investors

- Understand the function of the balance sheet

- Understand how the income statement is used

- Interpret a statement of cash flows

- Understand the management's discussion and analysis and the statement of stockholders' equity

- Analyze a firm through its financial statements, including using the DuPont Identity

- Understand the main purpose and aspects of the Sarbanes-Oxley reforms following Enron and other financial scandals

As we discussed in Chapter 1, anyone with money to invest is a potential investor who can own shares in a corporation. As a result, corporations are often widely held, with investors ranging from individuals who hold one share to large financial institutions that own millions of shares. For example, at the end of 2015, Microsoft Corporation had almost 8 billion shares outstanding held by hundreds of thousands of stockholders. Although the corporate organizational structure greatly facilitates the firm's access to investment capital, it also means that stock ownership is most investors' sole tie to the company. How, then, do investors learn enough about a company to know whether or not they should invest in it? One way firms evaluate their performance and communicate this information to investors is through their *financial statements*. Financial statements also enable financial managers to assess the success of their own firm and compare it to competitors.

Firms regularly issue financial statements to communicate financial information to the investment community. A detailed description of the preparation and analysis of these statements is sufficiently complicated that to do it justice would require an entire book. In this chapter, we briefly review the subject, emphasizing only the material that investors and corporate financial managers need in order to make the corporate finance decisions we discuss in the text.

We review the four main types of financial statements, present examples of these statements for a firm, and discuss where an investor or manager might find various types of information about the company. We also discuss some of the financial ratios used to assess a firm's performance and value. We close the chapter with a look at financial reporting abuses and the Sarbanes-Oxley regulatory response.

2.1 Firms' Disclosure of Financial Information

financial statements
Accounting reports issued by a firm quarterly and/or annually that present past performance information and a snapshot of the firm's assets and the financing of those assets.

Financial statements are accounting reports issued by a firm periodically (usually quarterly and annually) that present past performance information and a snapshot of the firm's assets and the financing of those assets. Public companies in the United States are required to file their financial statements with the U.S. Securities and Exchange Commission (SEC) on a quarterly basis on form *10-Q* and annually on form *10-K*.[1] They must also send an **annual report (10-K)** with their financial statements to their shareholders each year. Often, private companies also prepare financial statements, but they usually do not have to disclose these reports to the public. Financial statements are important tools with which investors, financial analysts, and other interested outside parties (such as creditors) obtain information about a corporation. They are also useful for managers within the firm as a source of information for the corporate financial decisions we discussed in Chapter 1. In this section, we examine the guidelines for preparing financial statements and introduce the different types of financial statements.

annual report (10-K) The yearly summary of business, accompanying or including financial statements, sent by U.S. public companies to their shareholders.

Preparation of Financial Statements

Generally Accepted Accounting Principles (GAAP) A common set of rules and a standard format for public companies to use when they prepare their financial reports.

Reports about a company's performance must be understandable and accurate. In the United States, the Financial Accounting Standards Board (FASB) establishes **Generally Accepted Accounting Principles (GAAP)** to provide a common set of rules and a standard format for public companies to use when they prepare their reports. This standardization also makes it easier to compare the financial results of different firms.

 International Financial Reporting Standards

Generally Accepted Accounting Principles (GAAP) differ among countries. As a result, companies face tremendous accounting complexities when they operate internationally. Investors also face difficulty interpreting financial statements of foreign companies, which discourages them from investing abroad. As companies and capital markets become more global, however, interest in harmonization of accounting standards across countries has increased.

The most important harmonization project began in 1973 when representatives of 10 countries (including the United States) established the International Accounting Standards Committee. This effort led to the creation of the International Accounting Standards Board (IASB) in 2001, with headquarters in London. Now the IASB has issued a set of International Financial Reporting Standards (IFRS).

The IFRS are taking root throughout the world. The European Union (EU) approved an accounting regulation in 2002 requiring all publicly traded EU companies to follow IFRS in their consolidated financial statements starting in 2005. As of 2016, more than 130 jurisdictions either require or permit the use of IFRS, including the EU, Australia, Brazil, Canada, Russia, Hong Kong, Taiwan, and Singapore. China, India, and Japan will soon follow suit. In fact,

currently all major stock exchanges around the world accept IFRS except the United States and Japan, which maintain their local GAAP.

The main difference between U.S. GAAP and IFRS is conceptual—U.S. GAAP are based primarily on accounting rules with specific guidance in applying them, whereas IFRS are based more on principles requiring professional judgment by accountants, and specific guidance in application is limited. Even so, some differences in rules also exist. For example, U.S. GAAP generally prohibit the upward revaluation of non-financial assets, whereas the IFRS allow the revaluation of some such assets to fair value. U.S. GAAP also rely more heavily on historical cost, as opposed to "fair value," to estimate the value of assets and liabilities.

Effort to achieve convergence between U.S. GAAP and IFRS was spurred by the Sarbanes-Oxley Act of 2002 in the United States. It included a provision that U.S. accounting standards move toward international convergence on high-quality accounting standards. Currently, SEC regulations still require public U.S. firms to report using U.S. GAAP. That said, modifications to both IFRS and U.S. GAAP have brought the two closer together, with the key remaining differences in the areas of revenue recognition, impairment charges, leasing, insurance, and the treatment of financial instruments. As of the early 2016, the SEC looks likely to allow U.S. companies to use IFRS to provide supplemental information, but will still require them to file their financials in accordance with U.S. GAAP.

---

[1]The Securities and Exchange Commission was established by Congress in 1934 to regulate securities (for example, stocks and bonds) issued to the public and the financial markets (exchanges) on which those securities trade.

INTERVIEW WITH RUTH PORAT

Ruth Porat is Senior Vice President and Chief Financial Officer of Alphabet and Google. Previously she spent 27 years at Morgan Stanley, where she last was Executive Vice President and Chief Financial Officer. As Morgan Stanley's Vice Chairman of Investment Banking and Global Head of the Financial Institutions Group, she advised the U.S. Treasury and the New York Federal Reserve Bank.

QUESTION: *What best practices do you recommend for financial managers?*

ANSWER:

1. *Maintain a tight financial control environment with respect to accounting controls and process.* Incorporate a strategic approach to IT architecture to ensure data integrity, consistency, and process controls while reducing reliance on human, manual processes—a source of risk and errors.

2. *Ensure a robust budgeting and capital allocation process built on a strong Financial Planning & Analysis team that is well integrated into the business.* Push data transparency to business leaders. They are best positioned to make difficult tradeoffs in the budgeting process, but often lack data granularity to make those choices (and to see the imperative).

3. *Culture matters.* A culture of honest, frank debate that challenges the status quo and avoids homogeneity of thought makes the job more fun and leads to better results. A broad range of experience, and even some "battle scars," ensures the organization recognizes patterns to foresee emerging risks. In that regard, a diverse team with respect to gender, race, and socioeconomic background brings differentiated perspectives, contributing to effective risk management.

4. *Make tough calls early and, ideally, once.* Lead.

QUESTION: *How has the crisis shaped the role of the CFO, or your view of it?*

ANSWER: In financial services, it redefined the perception of a CFO. Beyond focusing on accounting and external reporting functions, the CFO is now also the firm's most senior global manager for guardianship and risk management. Guardianship includes accounting (the controller function) and overseeing a comprehensive approach to IT systems. Risk management requires identifying sources of vulnerability, stress testing, and planning against them. The CFO has become a trusted adviser to the CEO, board and business leaders, which includes budgeting, capital allocation, and sensitivity analyses. Finally, in certain industries the CFO is the point person with regulators.

QUESTION: *What key lessons did you take from the financial crisis? What advice would you give future CFOs?*

ANSWER: I have three key takeaways from the financial crisis, relevant in both good and bad markets as well as across industries:

1. *Understand your greatest sources of vulnerability and defend against them.* For financial services, liquidity (access to cash) was a weak spot. In that period, we often said, "Liquidity is oxygen for a financial system: without it, you choke." Without sufficient liquidity, banks were forced into a negative cycle of selling assets to raise cash. As Morgan Stanley's CFO, I managed liquidity with the maxim that it was sacrosanct. We invested substantially in the amount and durability of the company's liquidity reserve. Similarly, regulators coming out of the crisis appropriately demanded higher capital, lower leverage, better liquidity, more durable funding, and rigorous stress testing, which imposed transparency on the banks and exposed their weaknesses.

2. *Build a robust control infrastructure ahead of needs, including financial and risk management controls, systems, and processes.* Just as one shouldn't drive a car at 100 mph with mud on the windshield, business leaders must have visibility about their business from accurate, insightful, and timely data consistent with strong financial controls. Rapid growth industries need to invest in infrastructure early because the business requirements continue to grow so rapidly.

3. *Recognize that time is your enemy.* Treasury Secretary Paulson told me during the financial crisis that you must have the will and the means to solve problems; too often, by the time you have the will, you no longer have the means. He was talking about policy, but that rule applies to any decision maker. The glaring examples, in retrospect, were the clear signs of crisis in August 2007 and the March 2008 collapse of Bear Stearns, but reactions were slow or nonexistent. Even in good times, business leaders must focus on resource optimization to maximize the potential for highest returns on investment.

auditor A neutral third party, which corporations are required to hire, that checks a firm's annual financial statements to ensure they are prepared according to GAAP, and provides evidence to support the reliability of the information.

Investors also need some assurance that the financial statements are prepared accurately. Publicly traded corporations are required to hire a neutral third party, known as an **auditor**, to check the annual financial statements, ensure they are prepared according to GAAP, and provide evidence to support the reliability of the information.

Types of Financial Statements

Every public company is required to produce four financial statements: the *balance sheet*, the *income statement*, the *statement of cash flows*, and the *statement of stockholders' equity*. These financial statements provide investors and creditors with an overview of the firm's financial performance. In the sections that follow, we take a close look at the content of these financial statements.

CONCEPT CHECK

1. What is the role of an auditor?
2. What are the four financial statements that all public companies must produce?

2.2 The Balance Sheet

balance sheet (or statement of financial position) A list of a firm's assets and liabilities that provides a snapshot of the firm's financial position at a given point in time.

assets The cash, inventory, property, plant, and equipment, and other investments a company has made.

liabilities A firm's obligations to its creditors.

shareholders' equity, stockholders' equity An accounting measure of a firm's net worth that represents the difference between the firm's assets and its liabilities.

common stock and paid-in surplus The amount that stockholders have directly invested in the firm through purchasing stock from the company.

retained earnings Profits made by the firm, but retained within the firm and reinvested in assets or held as cash.

The **balance sheet**, or **statement of financial position**,[2] lists the firm's *assets* and *liabilities*, providing a snapshot of the firm's financial position at a given point in time. Table 2.1 shows the balance sheet for a fictitious company, Global Corporation. Notice that the balance sheet is divided into two parts ("sides") with the assets on the left side and the liabilities on the right side.

1. The **assets** list the firm's cash, inventory, property, plant and equipment, and any other investments the company has made.
2. The **liabilities** show the firm's obligations to its creditors.
3. Also shown with liabilities on the right side of the balance sheet is the *stockholders' equity*. **Stockholders' equity** (also called **shareholders' equity**), the difference between the firm's assets and liabilities, is an accounting measure of the firm's net worth. For Global, the stockholders' equity has two parts: (1) **common stock and paid-in surplus**, the amount that stockholders have directly invested in the firm through purchasing stock from the company and (2) **retained earnings**, which are profits made by the firm, but retained within the firm and reinvested in assets or held as cash. We will take a more detailed look at retained earnings in our discussion of the statement of cash flows later in this chapter.

The assets on the left side show how the firm uses its capital (its investments), and the information on the right side summarizes the sources of capital, or how the firm raises the money it needs. Because of the way stockholders' equity is calculated, the left and right sides must balance:

The Balance Sheet Identity

$$\text{Assets} = \text{Liabilities} + \text{Stockholders' Equity} \tag{2.1}$$

In Table 2.1, total assets for 2016 ($170.1 million) are equal to total liabilities ($147.9 million) plus stockholders' equity ($22.2 million).

Let's examine Global's assets, liabilities, and stockholders' equity in more detail.

---

[2]In IFRS and recent U.S. GAAP pronouncements, the balance sheet is referred to as the *statement of financial position*.

TABLE 2.1

Global Corporation Balance Sheet for 2016 and 2015 ($ millions)

Assets	2016	2015	Liabilities and Stockholders' Equity	2016	2015
Current Assets			Current Liabilities		
Cash	23.2	20.5	Accounts payable	29.2	26.5
Accounts receivable	18.5	13.2	Notes payable/short-term debt	5.5	3.2
Inventories	15.3	14.3			
Total current assets	57.0	48.0	Total current liabilities	34.7	29.7
Long-Term Assets			Long-Term Liabilities		
Net property, plant, and equipment	113.1	80.9	Long-term debt	113.2	78.0
Total long-term assets	113.1	80.9	Total long-term liabilities	113.2	78.0
			Total Liabilities	147.9	107.7
			Stockholders' Equity		
			Common stock and paid-in surplus	8.0	8.0
			Retained earnings	14.2	13.2
			Total Stockholders' Equity	22.2	21.2
Total Assets	170.1	128.9	Total Liabilities and Stockholders' Equity	170.1	128.9

current assets Cash or assets that can be converted into cash within one year.

marketable securities Short-term, low-risk investments that can be easily sold and converted to cash.

accounts receivable Amounts owed to a firm by customers who have purchased goods or services on credit.

inventories A firm's raw materials as well as its work-in-progress and finished goods.

long-term assets Assets that produce tangible benefits for more than one year.

depreciation A yearly deduction a firm makes from the value of its fixed assets (other than land) over time, according to a depreciation schedule that depends on an asset's life span.

book value The acquisition cost of an asset less its accumulated depreciation.

Assets

In Table 2.1, Global's assets are divided into *current* and *long-term assets*. We discuss each in turn.

Current Assets. **Current assets** are either cash or assets that can be converted into cash within one year. This category includes:

1. Cash and other **marketable securities**, which are short-term, low-risk investments that can be easily sold and converted to cash (such as money market investments, like government debt, that mature within a year);

2. **Accounts receivable**, which are amounts owed to the firm by customers who have purchased goods or services on credit;

3. **Inventories**, which are composed of raw materials as well as work-in-progress and finished goods; and

4. Other current assets, which is a catch-all category that includes items such as prepaid expenses (such as rent or insurance).

Long-Term Assets. Assets such as real estate or machinery that produce tangible benefits for more than one year are called **long-term assets**. If Global spends $2 million on new equipment, this $2 million will be included with net property, plant, and equipment under long-term assets on the balance sheet. Because equipment tends to wear out or become obsolete over time, Global will reduce the value recorded for this equipment through a yearly deduction called **depreciation** according to a depreciation schedule that depends on an asset's life span. Depreciation is not an actual cash expense that the firm pays; it is a way of recognizing that buildings and equipment wear out and thus become less valuable the older they get. The **book value** of an asset, which is the value shown in the firm's financial statements, is equal to its acquisition cost less accumulated depreciation. The figures for net property, plant, and equipment show the total book value of these assets.

Other long-term assets can include such items as property not used in business operations, start-up costs in connection with a new business, trademarks and patents, and property held for sale. The sum of all the firms' assets is the total assets at the bottom of the left side of the balance sheet in Table 2.1.

Liabilities

We now examine the liabilities, shown on the right side of the balance sheet, which are divided into *current* and *long-term liabilities*.

Current Liabilities. Liabilities that will be satisfied within one year are known as **current liabilities**. They include:

current liabilities Liabilities that will be satisfied within one year.

1. **Accounts payable**, the amounts owed to suppliers for products or services purchased with credit.

accounts payable The amounts owed to creditors for products or services purchased with credit.

2. **Notes payable** and **short-term debt**, loans that must be repaid in the next year. Any repayment of long-term debt that will occur within the next year would also be listed here as current maturities of long-term debt.

notes payable, short-term debt Loans that must be repaid in the next year.

3. Accrual items, such as salary or taxes, that are owed but have not yet been paid, and deferred or unearned revenue, which is revenue that has been received for products or services that have not yet been delivered.

net working capital The difference between a firm's current assets and current liabilities that represents the capital available in the short term to run the business.

The difference between current assets and current liabilities is the firm's **net working capital**, the capital available in the short term to run the business. While notes payable and short-term debt are included in current liabilities, they are different from accounts payable and accrual items. Notes payable and short-term debt are related to financing decisions of the firm, while accounts payable and accruals arise from operating decisions of the firm. This distinction is important later when we see that financial managers generally try to keep these two decisions (operating and financing) separate.

$$\text{Net Working Capital} = \text{Current Assets} - \text{Current Liabilities} \tag{2.2}$$

For example, in 2016, Global's net working capital totaled $22.3 million ($57.0 million in current assets − $34.7 million in current liabilities). Firms with low (or negative) net working capital may face a shortage of funds. In such cases, the liabilities due in the short term exceed the company's cash and expected payments on receivables.

Long-Term Liabilities. Long-term liabilities are liabilities that extend beyond one year. When a firm needs to raise funds to purchase an asset or make an investment, it may borrow those funds through a long-term loan. That loan would appear on the balance sheet as **long-term debt**, which is any loan or debt obligation with a maturity of more than a year.

long-term debt Any loan or debt obligation with a maturity of more than a year.

Stockholders' Equity

book value of equity The difference between the book value of a firm's assets and its liabilities; also called *shareholders' equity* and *stockholders' equity*, it represents the net worth of a firm from an accounting perspective.

The sum of the current liabilities and long-term liabilities is total liabilities. The difference between the firm's assets and liabilities is the *stockholders' equity*; it is also called the **book value of equity** or *shareholders' equity*. As we stated earlier, it represents the net worth of the firm from an accounting perspective. The two main components are common stock and paid-in surplus and retained earnings. These two components form the book value of stockholders' ownership claims, stemming from their direct investment and reinvestment of profits.

Ideally, the balance sheet would provide us with an accurate assessment of the true value of the firm's equity. Unfortunately, this is unlikely to be the case. First, many of the assets listed on the balance sheet are valued based on their historical cost rather than their true value today. For example, an office building is listed on the balance sheet according to its historical cost less its accumulated depreciation. But the actual value of the office building today may be very different than this amount; in fact, if real estate prices went up it will be worth *more* than the amount the firm paid for it years ago. The same is true for other property, plant, and equipment: The true value today of an asset may be very different from, and even exceed, its book value. A second, and probably more important, problem is that *many of the firm's valuable assets are not captured on the balance sheet.* Consider, for example, the expertise of the firm's employees, the firm's reputation in the marketplace, the relationships with customers and suppliers, and the quality of the management team. All these assets add to the value of the firm but do not appear on the balance sheet. Although the book value of a firm's equity is not a good estimate of its true value as an ongoing firm, it is sometimes used as an estimate of the **liquidation value** of the firm, the value that would be left after its assets were sold and liabilities paid.

liquidation value The value of a firm after its assets are sold and liabilities paid.

Market Value Versus Book Value

For these reasons, the book value of equity is an inaccurate assessment of the actual value of the firm's equity. Thus, it is not surprising that it will often differ substantially from the amount investors are willing to pay for the equity. The total market value of a firm's equity equals the market price per share times the number of shares, referred to as the company's **market capitalization**. The market value of a stock does not depend on the historical cost of the firm's assets; instead, it depends on what investors expect those assets to produce in the future. To see the difference, think about what happens when a company like Boeing unveils a new plane. Investors' expectations about future cash flows from selling those planes increase the stock price immediately, elevating the market value of Boeing. However, the revenue from selling the planes will only be reflected in Boeing's financial statements when it actually sells them.

market capitalization The total market value of equity; equals the market price per share times the number of shares.

Finally, we note that the book value of equity can be negative (liabilities exceed assets), and that a negative book value of equity is not necessarily an indication of poor

---

EXAMPLE 2.1
Market Versus Book Value

MyFinanceLab

PROBLEM
If Global has 3.6 million shares outstanding, and these shares are trading for a price of $10.00 per share, what is Global's market capitalization? How does the market capitalization compare to Global's book value of equity?

SOLUTION

PLAN
Market capitalization is equal to price per share times shares outstanding. We can find Global's book value of equity at the bottom of the right side of its balance sheet.

EXECUTE
Global's market capitalization is ($10.00/share) $\times$ (3.6 million shares) = $36 million. This market capitalization is significantly higher than Global's book value of equity of $22.2 million.

EVALUATE
Global must have sources of value that do not appear on the balance sheet. These include potential opportunities for growth, the quality of the management team, relationships with suppliers and customers, etc.

performance. Successful firms are often able to borrow in excess of the book value of their assets because creditors recognize that the market value of the assets is far higher. For example, in June 2005 Amazon.com had total liabilities of $2.6 billion and a book value of equity of −$64 million. At the same time, the market value of its equity was over $15 billion. Clearly, investors recognized that Amazon's assets were worth far more than the book value reported on the balance sheet. By 2016, several years of strong growth had brought its book value of equity to over $13 billion and its market value of equity to around $300 billion!

Market-to-Book Ratio

market-to-book ratio (price-to-book [P/B] ratio) The ratio of a firm's market (equity) capitalization to the book value of its stockholders' equity.

In Example 2.1, we compared the market and book values of Global's equity. A common way to make this comparison is to compute the **market-to-book ratio** (also called the **price-to-book [P/B] ratio**), which is the ratio of a firm's market capitalization to the book value of stockholders' equity.

$$\text{Market-to-Book Ratio} = \frac{\text{Market Value of Equity}}{\text{Book Value of Equity}} \tag{2.3}$$

It is one of many financial ratios used to evaluate a firm. The market-to-book ratio for most successful firms substantially exceeds 1, indicating that the value of the firm's assets when put to use exceeds their historical cost (or liquidation value). The ratio will vary across firms due to differences in fundamental firm characteristics as well as the value added by management. Thus, this ratio is one way a company's stock price provides feedback to its managers on the market's assessment of their decisions.

In early-2016, AmeriServ Financial, Inc. (ASRV) had a market-to-book ratio of 0.57, a reflection of investors' assessment that many of AmeriServ's assets were unlikely to be profitable and were worth less than their book value. Citigroup's market-to-book ratio of 0.59 tells a similar story. Figure 2.1 shows that at the same time, the average market-to-book ratio for the financial services industry was about 1.9 and for large U.S. firms it was close to 3. In contrast, consider that Amazon.com, Inc. (AMZN) had a market-to-book ratio of over 20, and the average for technology firms was over 8. Analysts often classify firms with low market-to-book ratios as **value stocks**, and those with high market-to-book ratios as **growth stocks**.

value stocks Firms with low market-to-book ratios.

growth stocks Firms with high market-to-book ratios.

Enterprise Value

enterprise value The total market value of a firm's equity and debt, less the value of its cash and marketable securities. It measures the value of the firm's underlying business.

A firm's market capitalization measures the market value of the firm's equity, or the value that remains after the firm has paid its debts. So it includes any cash the firm holds. But what if you are interested in just the value of the business itself? The **enterprise value** of a firm assesses the value of the underlying business assets, unencumbered by debt and separate from any cash and marketable securities. We compute it as follows:

$$\text{Enterprise Value} = \text{Market Value of Equity} + \text{Debt} - \text{Cash} \tag{2.4}$$

For example, given its market capitalization from Example 2.1, Global's enterprise value in 2016 is $36 + 118.7 − 23.2 = \$131.5$ million. We can interpret the enterprise value as the cost to take over the business. That is, it would cost $36 + 118.7 = \$154.7$ million to buy all of Global's equity and pay off its debts. Because we would acquire Global's $23.2 million in cash (which can be used to pay off Global's debt), the net cost is only $154.7 − 23.2 = \$131.5$ million.

FIGURE 2.1

Market-to-Book
Ratios in 2016

This figure presents market-to-book ratios of different firms and groups of firms in 2016. Firms that might be classified as value stocks (low market-to-book ratios) are in red and those that might be classified as growth stocks (high market-to-book ratios) are in blue.

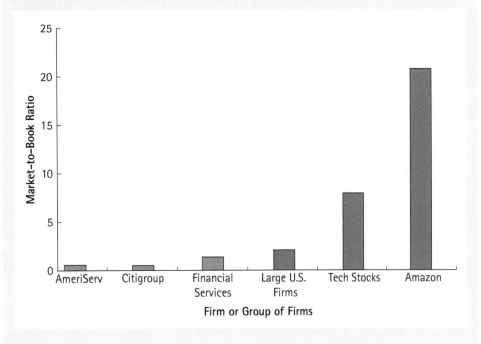

EXAMPLE 2.2

Computing
Enterprise Value

MyFinanceLab

PROBLEM

In June 2013, H.J. Heinz Co. (HNZ) had 320.7 million shares outstanding, a share price of $72.36, a book value of debt of $4.98 billion, and cash of $1.1 billion. What was Heinz's market capitalization (its market value of equity)? What was its enterprise value?

SOLUTION

PLAN

Share Price	$72.36
Shares Outstanding	320.7 million
Cash	$1.10 billion
Debt (book)	$4.98 billion

We will solve the problem using Eq. 2.4: Enterprise Value = Market Value of Equity + Debt − Cash. We can compute the market capitalization by multiplying the share price times the number of shares outstanding. We are given the amount of cash and the amount of debt.

EXECUTE

Heinz had a market capitalization of $72.36/share × 320.7 million shares = $23.21 billion. Thus, Heinz's enterprise value was 23.21 + 4.98 − 1.10 = $27.09 billion.

EVALUATE

The value of Heinz's underlying business, separate from any cash it holds, should be equal to the total value of the financial claims (equity and debt) on that business, which is its enterprise value of $27.09 billion.

CONCEPT
CHECK

3. What is depreciation designed to capture?

4. The book value of a company's assets usually does not equal the market value of those assets. What are some reasons for this difference?

2.3 The Income Statement

income statement A list of a firm's revenues and expenses over a period of time.

net income or earnings The last or "bottom" line of a firm's income statement that is a measure of the firm's income over a given period of time.

When you want someone to get to the point, you might ask them for the "bottom line." This expression comes from the *income statement.* The **income statement** lists the firm's revenues and expenses over a period of time. The last or "bottom" line of the income statement shows the firm's **net income**, which is a measure of its profitability during the period. The income statement is sometimes called a *profit and loss* or *P&L statement*, and the net income is also referred to as the firm's **earnings**. In this section, we examine the components of the income statement in detail and introduce ratios we can use to analyze this data.

Earnings Calculations

Whereas the balance sheet shows the firm's assets and liabilities at a given point in time, the income statement shows the flow of revenues and expenses generated by those assets and liabilities between two dates. Table 2.2 shows Global's income statement for 2016 and 2015. We examine each category on the statement.

gross profit The third line of an income statement that represents the difference between a firm's sales revenues and its costs.

Gross Profit. The first two lines of the income statement list the revenues from sales of products and the costs incurred to make and sell the products. Note that in accounting, the terms *revenues* and *net sales* are equivalent. Net sales is simply gross sales minus any returns, discounts, and allowances. We will simply use the term *sales* from here forward. The third line is **gross profit**, the difference between sales revenues and the cost of sales.

TABLE 2.2

Global Corporation's Income Statement Sheet for 2016 and 2015

GLOBAL CORPORATION Income Statement Year ended December 31 (in $ millions)		
	2016	**2015**
Net sales	186.7	176.1
Cost of sales	−153.4	−147.3
Gross Profit	33.3	28.8
Selling, general, and administrative expenses	−13.5	−13
Research and development	−8.2	−7.6
Depreciation and amortization	−1.2	−1.1
Operating Income	10.4	7.1
Other income	—	—
Earnings Before Interest and Taxes (EBIT)	10.4	7.1
Interest income (expense)	−7.7	−4.6
Pretax Income	2.7	2.5
Taxes	−0.7	−0.6
Net Income	2.0	1.9
Earnings per share:	$0.56	$0.53
Diluted earnings per share:	$0.53	$0.50

Operating Expenses. The next group of items is operating expenses. These are expenses from the ordinary course of running the business that are not directly related to producing the goods or services being sold. They include administrative expenses and overhead, salaries, marketing costs, and research and development expenses. The third type of operating expense, depreciation and amortization (a charge that captures the change in value of acquired assets), represents an estimate of the costs that arise from wear and tear or obsolescence of the firm's assets.[3] It is not an actual cash expense. The firm's gross profit less its operating expenses is called **operating income**.

operating income A firm's gross profit less its operating expenses.

Earnings Before Interest and Taxes. We next include other sources of income or expenses that arise from activities that are not the central part of a company's business. Cash flows from the firm's financial investments are one example of other income that would be listed here. After we have adjusted for other sources of income or expenses, we have the firm's earnings before interest and taxes, or **EBIT**.

EBIT A firm's earnings before interest and taxes are deducted.

Pretax and Net Income. From EBIT, we deduct the interest paid on outstanding debt to compute Global's pretax income, and then we deduct corporate taxes to determine the firm's net income.

Net income represents the total earnings of the firm's equity holders. It is often reported on a per-share basis as the firm's **earnings per share (EPS)**, which we compute by dividing net income by the total number of shares outstanding:

earnings per share (EPS) A firm's net income divided by the total number of shares outstanding.

$$EPS = \frac{\text{Net Income}}{\text{Shares Outstanding}} = \frac{\$2.0 \text{ million}}{3.6 \text{ million shares}} = \$0.56 \text{ per share} \qquad (2.5)$$

Although Global has only 3.6 million shares outstanding as of the end of 2016 (from Example 2.1), the number of shares outstanding may grow if Global has made commitments that would cause it to issue more shares. Consider these two examples:

stock options The right to buy a certain number of shares of stock by a specific date at a specific price.

1. Suppose Global compensates its employees or executives with **stock options** that give the holder the right to buy a certain number of shares by a specific date at a specific price. If employees "exercise" these options, the company issues new stock and the number of shares outstanding would grow.

2. The number of shares may also grow if the firm issues **convertible bonds**, a form of debt that can be converted into shares of common stock.

convertible bonds Corporate bonds with a provision that gives the bondholder an option to convert each bond owned into a fixed number of shares of common stock.

In the cases of stock options and convertible bonds, because there will be more total shares to divide the same earnings, this growth in the number of shares is referred to as **dilution**. Firms disclose the potential for dilution from options they have awarded by reporting **diluted EPS**, which shows the earnings per share the company would have if the stock options were exercised. For example, if Global has awarded options for 200,000 shares of stock to its key executives, its diluted EPS is $2.0 million/3.8 million shares = $0.53.

dilution An increase in the total number of shares that will divide a fixed amount of earnings.

diluted EPS The earnings per share a company would have based on the total number of shares including the effects of all stock options and convertible bonds.

EBITDA

As will become clear when we discuss the Statement of Cash Flows in the next section, neither EBIT nor net income are the same as the firm's cash flow. So, financial analysts often compute a firm's earnings before interest, taxes, depreciation, and amortization, or **EBITDA**. Because depreciation and amortization are not cash expenses for the firm,

---

[3]Only certain types of amortization are deductible as a pretax expense (e.g., amortization of the cost of an acquired patent). Amortization of goodwill is not a pretax expense and is generally included as an extraordinary item after taxes are deducted.

EBITDA A computation of a firm's earnings before interest, taxes, depreciation, and amortization are deducted.

EBITDA reflects the cash a firm has earned from its operations. If we add back Global's depreciation and amortization to its EBIT, we find that its EBITDA in 2016 was $10.4 + 1.2 = \$11.6$ million.

CONCEPT CHECK
5. What do a firm's earnings measure?
6. What is dilution?

2.4 The Statement of Cash Flows

The income statement provides a measure of the firm's profit over a given time period. However, it does not indicate the amount of *cash* the firm has earned. There are two reasons that net income does not correspond to cash earned. First, there are non-cash entries on the income statement, such as depreciation and amortization. Second, certain uses, such as the purchase of a building or expenditures on inventory, and sources of cash, such as the collection of accounts receivable, are not reported on the income statement. The firm's **statement of cash flows** utilizes the information from the income statement and balance sheet to determine how much cash the firm has generated, and how that cash has been allocated, during a set period. Cash is important: It is needed to pay bills and maintain operations and is the source of any return of investment for investors. Thus, from the perspective of an investor attempting to value the firm or a financial manager concerned about cash flows (vs. earnings), the statement of cash flows provides what may be the most important information of the four financial statements.

statement of cash flows An accounting statement that shows how a firm has used the cash it earned during a set period.

The statement of cash flows is divided into three sections: operating activities, investment activities, and financing activities. These sections roughly correspond to the three major jobs of the financial manager.

1. *Operating activities* starts with net income from the income statement. It then adjusts this number by adding back all non-cash entries related to the firm's operating activities.
2. *Investment activities* lists the cash used for investment.
3. *Financing activities* shows the flow of cash between the firm and its investors.

Global's statement of cash flows is shown in Table 2.3. In this section, we take a close look at each component of the statement of cash flows.

Operating Activity

The first section of Global's statement of cash flows adjusts net income by all non-cash items related to operating activity. For instance, depreciation is deducted when computing net income, but it is not an actual cash expense. Thus, we add it back to net income when determining the amount of cash the firm has generated. Similarly, we add back any other non-cash expenses (for example, deferred taxes).

Next, we adjust for changes to net working capital that arise from changes to accounts receivable, accounts payable, or inventory. When a firm sells a product, it records the revenue as income even though it may not receive the cash from that sale immediately. Instead, it may grant the customer credit and let the customer pay in the future. The customer's obligation adds to the firm's accounts receivable. We use the following guidelines to adjust for changes in working capital:

1. Accounts receivable: When a sale is recorded as part of net income, but the cash has not yet been received from the customer, we must adjust the cash flows by *deducting* the increases in accounts receivable. This increase represents additional lending by the firm to its customers and it reduces the cash available to the firm.

2. Accounts payable: We *add* increases in accounts payable. Accounts payable represents borrowing by the firm from its suppliers. This borrowing increases the cash available to the firm.

3. Inventory: Finally, we *deduct* increases in inventory. Increases in inventory are not recorded as an expense and do not contribute to net income (the cost of the goods are only included in net income when the goods are actually sold). However, the cost of increasing inventory is a cash expense for the firm and must be deducted.

Working capital adjustments address the difference between the time when sales and costs are recorded on the income statement and when the cash actually goes in and out of the firm. For example, Table 2.3 shows that in 2016 we *subtracted* the $5.3 million increase in accounts receivable from net income as part of the operating cash flow calculation. What happened? From Table 2.2, we see that Global had $10.6 million more in sales in 2016 than

TABLE 2.3

Global Corporation's Statement of Cash Flows for 2016 and 2015

GLOBAL CORPORATION Statement of Cash Flows Year ended December 31 (in $ millions)		
	2016	**2015**
Operating activities		
Net income	2.0	1.9
Depreciation and amortization	1.2	1.1
Cash effect of changes in		
Accounts receivable	−5.3	−0.3
Accounts payable	2.7	−0.5
Inventory	−1.0	−1.0
Cash from operating activities	−0.4	1.2
Investment activities		
Capital expenditures	−33.4	−4.0
Acquisitions and other investing activity	—	—
Cash from investing activities	−33.4	−4.0
Financing activities		
Dividends paid	−1.0	−1.0
Sale or purchase of stock	—	—
Increase in short-term borrowing	2.3	3.0
Increase in long-term borrowing	35.2	2.5
Cash from financing activities	36.5	4.5
Change in cash and cash equivalents	2.7	1.7

in 2015. However, from Table 2.1, we also see that Global's accounts receivable increased from $13.2 million in 2015 to $18.5 million in 2016. So, even though Global's sales were up considerably, it has not yet collected all the cash flow for those sales—instead, Global's customers owe it $5.3 million more at the end of 2016 than they did at the end of 2015. Because the statement of cash flows starts with net income, which includes sales for which Global has not yet been paid, we deduct the additional $5.3 million in sales Global is still owed when computing the actual cash flows it generated.

We must make a similar adjustment for inventory. Global does not record the cost of the inventory until it is sold, when it is included in the cost of goods sold. However, when it actually pays for the inventory, cash has flowed out of Global, decreasing operating cash flow. The opposite is true for accounts payable—Global has recorded additional expenses without actually paying for them yet. Those expenses reduce net income, but do not represent cash outflows.

Finally, we add depreciation to net income before calculating operating cash flow. Depreciation is an accounting adjustment to book value that is an expense, but not a cash outflow. That is, when Global's property, plant, and equipment depreciate by $1.2 million, it does not literally cost Global $1.2 million in cash flow. Because this is an expense that reduces net income, but not an actual cash outflow, we must add it back to calculate cash flow. We will talk more about depreciation when we do capital budgeting in Chapter 9. All these adjustments mean that cash flow can be very different from net income. Although Global showed positive net income on the income statement, it actually had a negative $0.4 million cash flow from operating activity, in large part because of the increase in accounts receivable.

EXAMPLE 2.3

The Impact of Depreciation on Cash Flow

MyFinanceLab

PROBLEM

Suppose Global had an additional $1 million depreciation expense in 2016. If Global's tax rate on pretax income is 26%, what would be the impact of this expense on Global's earnings? How would it impact Global's cash at the end of the year?

SOLUTION

PLAN

Depreciation is an operating expense, so Global's operating income, EBIT, and pretax income would be affected. With a tax rate of 26%, Global's tax bill will decrease by 26 cents for every dollar that pretax income is reduced. In order to determine how Global's cash would be impacted, we have to determine the effect of the additional depreciation on cash flows. Recall that depreciation is not an actual cash outflow, even though it is treated as an expense, so the only effect on cash flow is through the reduction in taxes.

EXECUTE

Global's operating income, EBIT, and pretax income would fall by $1 million because of the $1 million in additional operating expense due to depreciation.

This $1 million decrease in pretax income would reduce Global's tax bill by 26% $\times$ $1 million = $0.26 million. Therefore, net income would fall by $1 − $0.26 = $0.74 million.

On the statement of cash flows, net income would fall by $0.74 million, but we would add back the additional depreciation of $1 million because it is not a cash expense. Thus, cash from operating activities would rise by −$0.74 + 1 = $0.26 million. Therefore, Global's cash balance at the end of the year would increase by $0.26 million, the amount of the tax savings that resulted from the additional depreciation deduction.

EVALUATE

The increase in cash balance comes completely from the reduction in taxes. Because Global pays $0.26 million less in taxes even though its cash expenses have not increased, it has $0.26 million more in cash at the end of the year.

Investment Activity

capital expenditures
Purchases of new property, plant, and equipment.

The next section of the statement of cash flows shows the cash required for investment activities. Purchases of new property, plant, and equipment are **capital expenditures**. Recall that capital expenditures do not appear immediately as expenses on the income statement. Instead, the firm depreciates these assets and deducts depreciation expenses over time. To determine the firm's cash flow, we already added back depreciation because it is not an actual cash expense. Now, we subtract the actual capital expenditure that the firm made. Similarly, we also deduct other assets purchased or investments made by the firm, such as acquisitions. In Table 2.3, we see that in 2016, Global spent $33.4 million in cash on investing activities. This can be confirmed by adding the depreciation amount of $1.2 from Table 2.2 to the change in long-term assets of ($113.1 − $80.9) from Table 2.1.

Financing Activity

The last section of the statement of cash flows shows the cash flows from financing activities. Dividends paid to shareholders are a cash outflow. Global paid $1 million to its shareholders as dividends in 2016.

The difference between a firm's net income and the amount it spends on dividends is referred to as the firm's retained earnings for that year:

$$\text{Retained Earnings} = \text{Net Income} - \text{Dividends} \qquad (2.6)$$

payout ratio The ratio of a firm's dividends to its net income.

Global retained $2 million − $1 million = $1 million, or 50% of its earnings in 2016. This makes its *payout ratio* for 2016 equal to 50%. A firm's **payout ratio** is the ratio of its dividends to its net income:

$$\text{Payout Ratio} = \frac{\text{Dividends}}{\text{Net Income}} \qquad (2.7)$$

Also listed under financing activity is any cash the company received from the sale of its own stock, or cash spent buying (repurchasing) its own stock. Global did not issue or repurchase stock during this period.

The last items to include in this section result from changes to Global's short-term and long-term borrowing. Global raised money by issuing debt, so the increases in short-term and long-term borrowing represent cash inflows. The last line of the statement of cash flows combines the cash flows from these three activities to calculate the overall change in the firm's cash balance over the period of the statement. In this case, Global had cash inflows of $2.7 million in 2016, which matches the change in cash from 2015 to 2016 shown earlier in the balance sheet. By looking at the statement in Table 2.3 as a whole, we can determine that Global chose to borrow (mainly in the form of long-term debt) to cover the cost of its investment and operating activities. Although the firm's cash balance has increased, Global's negative operating cash flows and relatively high expenditures on investment activities might give investors some reasons for concern. If this pattern continues, Global will need to raise new external capital to remain in business.

CONCEPT CHECK
7. Why does a firm's net income not correspond to cash earned?
8. What are the components of the statement of cash flows?

2.5 Other Financial Statement Information

The most important elements of a firm's financial statements are the balance sheet, income statement, and the statement of cash flows, which we have already discussed. Several other pieces of information contained in the financial statements warrant brief mention: the *statement of stockholders' equity*, the *management discussion and analysis*, and *notes to the financial statements*.

Statement of Stockholders' Equity

statement of stockholders' equity An accounting statement that breaks down the stockholders' equity computed on the balance sheet into the amount that came from issuing new shares versus retained earnings.

The **statement of stockholders' equity** breaks down the stockholders' equity computed on the balance sheet into the amount that came from issuing shares (par value plus paid-in capital) versus retained earnings. Because the book value of stockholders' equity is not a useful assessment of value for financial purposes, financial managers use the statement of stockholders' equity infrequently (so we will skip the computational details here). We can, however, determine the change in stockholders' equity using information from the firm's other financial statements as follows:[4]

$$
\begin{aligned}
\text{Change in Stockholders' Equity} &= \text{Retained Earnings} + \text{Net Sales of Stock} \\
&= \text{Net Income} - \text{Dividends} + \text{Sales of Stock} \\
&\quad - \text{Repurchases of Stock} \quad\quad (2.8)
\end{aligned}
$$

For example, because Global had no stock sales or repurchases, its stockholders' equity increased by the amount of its retained earnings, or $1.0 million, in 2016. Note that this result matches the change in stockholders' equity shown earlier on Global's balance sheet.

Management Discussion and Analysis

management discussion and analysis (MD&A) A preface to the financial statements in which a company's management discusses the recent year (or quarter), providing a background on the company and any significant events that may have occurred.

The **management discussion and analysis (MD&A)** is a preface to the financial statements in which the company's management discusses the recent year (or quarter), providing a background on the company and any significant events that may have occurred. Management may also discuss the coming year, and outline goals and new projects.

Management must also discuss any important risks that the firm faces or issues that may affect the firm's liquidity or resources. Management is also required to disclose any **off-balance sheet transactions**, which are transactions or arrangements that can have a material impact on the firm's future performance yet do not appear on the balance sheet. For example, if a firm has made guarantees that it will compensate a buyer for losses related to an asset purchased from the firm, these guarantees represent a potential future liability for the firm that must be disclosed as part of the MD&A.

off-balance sheet transactions Transactions or arrangements that can have a material impact on a firm's future performance yet do not appear on the balance sheet.

Notes to the Financial Statements

In addition to the four financial statements, companies provide extensive notes with additional details on the information provided in the statements. For example, the notes document important accounting assumptions that were used in preparing the statements. They often provide information specific to a firm's subsidiaries or its separate product lines. They show the details of the firm's stock-based compensation plans for employees and the different types of debt the firm has outstanding. Details of acquisitions, spin-offs, leases, taxes, and risk management activities are also given. The information provided in the notes is often very important to a full interpretation of the firm's financial statements.

CONCEPT CHECK

9. Where do off-balance sheet transactions appear in a firm's financial statements?

10. What information do the notes to financial statements provide?

2.6   Financial Statement Analysis

Investors often use accounting statements to evaluate a firm in one of two ways:

1. Compare the firm with itself by analyzing how the firm has changed over time.

2. Compare the firm to other similar firms using a common set of financial ratios.

---

[4]Sales of stock would also include any stock-based compensation.

In this section, we will describe the most commonly used ratios—related to profitability, liquidity, asset efficiency, working capital, interest coverage, leverage, valuation, and operating returns—and explain how each one is used in practice.

Profitability Ratios

We introduce three profitability ratios: *gross margin, operating margin,* and *net profit margin.*

gross margin The ratio of gross profit to revenues (sales), it reflects the ability of the company to sell a product for more than the sum of the direct costs of making it.

Gross Margin. The **gross margin** of a firm is the ratio of gross profit to revenues (sales):

$$\text{Gross Margin} = \frac{\text{Gross Profit}}{\text{Sales}} \qquad (2.9)$$

The gross margin simply reflects the ability of the company to sell a product for more than the sum of the direct costs of making it. All of the firm's other expenses of doing business (those not directly related to producing the goods sold) must be covered by this margin. In 2016, Global's gross profit was $33.3 million and its sales were $186.7 million, for a gross margin of 33.3/186.7 = 17.84%.

operating margin The ratio of operating income to revenues, it reveals how much a company has earned from each dollar of sales before deducting interest and taxes.

Operating Margin. Because operating income reflects all of the expenses of doing business, another important profitability ratio is the **operating margin**, the ratio of operating income to revenues:

$$\text{Operating Margin} = \frac{\text{Operating Income}}{\text{Sales}} \qquad (2.10)$$

The operating margin reveals how much a company earns before interest and taxes from each dollar of sales. Global's operating margin in 2016 was 10.4/186.7 = 5.57%, an increase from its 2015 operating margin of 7.1/176.1 = 4.03%. By comparing operating margins across firms within an industry, we can assess the relative efficiency of firms' operations. For example, in 2015, United Continental Holdings (UAL) had an operating margin of 13.64% (i.e., they gained 13.64 cents for each dollar in revenues). However, competitor Alaska Air Group (ALK) had an operating margin of 23.19%.

Differences in operating margins can also result from differences in strategy. For example, in 2016, Walmart Stores had an operating margin of 5% while higher-end retailer Macy's had an operating margin of 9%. In this case, Walmart's lower operating margin is not a result of its inefficiency but is part of its strategy of offering lower prices to sell common products in high volume. Indeed, Walmart's sales were more than 17 times higher than those of Macy's.

net profit margin The ratio of net income to revenues, it shows the fraction of each dollar in revenues that is available to equity holders after the firm pays its expenses, plus interest and taxes.

Net Profit Margin. A firm's **net profit margin** is the ratio of net income to revenues:

$$\text{Net Profit Margin} = \frac{\text{Net Income}}{\text{Sales}} \qquad (2.11)$$

The net profit margin shows the fraction of each dollar in revenues that is available to equity holders after the firm pays its expenses, interest, and taxes. Global's net profit margin in 2016 was 2.0/186.7 = 1.07%. Differences in net profit margins can be due to differences in efficiency, but they can also result from differences in leverage (the firm's reliance on debt financing), which determines the amount of interest payments.

Liquidity Ratios

Creditors often compare a firm's current assets and current liabilities to assess whether the firm has sufficient working capital to meet its short-term needs. This comparison is sometimes summarized in the firm's **current ratio**, the ratio of current assets to current liabilities. A more stringent test of the firm's liquidity is the **quick ratio ("acid-test" ratio)**, which compares only cash and "near cash" assets, such as short-term investments and accounts receivable, to current liabilities.

$$\text{Current Ratio} = \frac{\text{Current Assets}}{\text{Current Liabilities}} \qquad (2.12)$$

$$\text{Quick Ratio} = \frac{\text{Current Assets} - \text{Inventory}}{\text{Current Liabilities}} \qquad (2.13)$$

In 2016, Global's quick ratio was $(57.0 - 15.3)/34.7 = 1.20$. A higher current or quick ratio implies less risk of the firm experiencing a cash shortfall in the near future. A reason to exclude inventory is that an increase in the current ratio that results from an unusual increase in inventory could be an indicator that the firm is having difficulty selling its products.

Ultimately, firms need cash to pay employees and meet other obligations. Running out of cash can be very costly for a firm, so firms often gauge their cash position by calculating the **cash ratio**, which is the most stringent liquidity ratio:

$$\text{Cash Ratio} = \frac{\text{Cash}}{\text{Current Liabilities}} \qquad (2.14)$$

Asset Efficiency

A financial manager can use the combined information in the firm's income statement and balance sheet to gauge how efficiently his or her firm is utilizing its assets. A first broad measure of efficiency is **asset turnover**, the ratio of sales to total assets:

$$\text{Asset Turnover} = \frac{\text{Sales}}{\text{Total Assets}} \qquad (2.15)$$

Low values of asset turnover indicate that the firm is not generating much revenue (sales) per dollar of assets. In 2016, Global's $170.1 million in assets generated $186.7 million in sales, for an asset turnover ratio of 1.1 (= $186.7/$170.1). Since total assets includes assets, such as cash, that are not directly involved in generating sales, Global's manager might also look at Global's fixed asset turnover, which is equal to sales divided by fixed assets:

$$\text{Fixed Asset Turnover} = \frac{\text{Sales}}{\text{Fixed Assets}} \qquad (2.16)$$

Global's fixed assets in 2016 were $113.1 million worth of property, plant, and equipment, yielding a fixed asset turnover of 1.7 (= $186.7/$113.1). Low asset turnover ratios indicate that the firm is generating relatively few sales given the amount of assets it employs.

Working Capital Ratios

Global's managers might be further interested in how efficiently they are managing their net working capital. We can express the firm's accounts receivable in terms of the number of days' worth of sales that it represents, called the **accounts receivable days**, **average collection period**, or **days sales outstanding:**[5]

$$\text{Accounts Receivable Days} = \frac{\text{Accounts Receivable}}{\text{Average Daily Sales}} \qquad (2.17)$$

accounts payable days An expression of a firm's accounts payable in terms of the number of days' worth of cost of goods sold that the accounts payable represents.

inventory days An expression of a firm's inventory in terms of the number of days' worth of cost of goods sold that the inventory represents.

inventory turnover ratio The cost of goods sold divided by either the latest cost of inventory or the average inventory over the year, it shows how efficiently companies turn their inventory into sales.

Given average daily sales of $186.7 million/365 = $0.51 million in 2016, Global's receivables of $18.5 million represent 18.5/0.51 = 36 days' worth of sales. In other words, Global takes a little over one month to collect payment from its customers, on average. In 2015, Global's accounts receivable represented only 27.5 days worth of sales. Although the number of receivable days can fluctuate seasonally, a significant unexplained increase could be a cause for concern (perhaps indicating the firm is doing a poor job collecting from its customers or is trying to boost sales by offering generous credit terms). Similar ratios exist for accounts payable and inventory. Those ratios are called **accounts payable days** (accounts payable divided by average daily cost of goods sold) and **inventory days** (inventory divided by average daily cost of goods sold).

We can also compute how efficiently firms use inventory. The **inventory turnover ratio** is equal to the cost of goods sold divided by either the latest cost of inventory or the average inventory over the year. We use the cost of goods sold because that is how inventory costs are reflected on the income statement. It is also common to use sales in the numerator to make the ratio more like the asset turnover ratios.

$$\text{Inventory Turnover} = \frac{\text{Cost of Goods Sold}}{\text{Inventory}} \qquad (2.18)$$

As with the other ratios in this section, a normal level for this ratio can vary substantially for different industries, although a higher level (more dollars of sales per dollar of inventory) is generally better.

EXAMPLE 2.4

Computing Working Capital Ratios

MyFinanceLab

PROBLEM

Compute Global's accounts payable days, inventory days, and inventory turnover for 2016.

SOLUTION

PLAN AND ORGANIZE

Working capital ratios require information from both the balance sheet and the income statement. For these ratios, we need inventory and accounts payable from the balance sheet and cost of goods sold from the income statement (often listed as cost of sales).

Inventory = 15.3, Accounts payable = 29.2, Cost of goods sold (cost of sales) = 153.4

EXECUTE

$$\text{Accounts payable days} = \frac{\text{Accounts Payable}}{\text{Average Daily Cost of Goods Sold}} = \frac{29.2}{(153.4/365)} = 69.48$$

$$\text{Inventory days} = \frac{\text{Inventory}}{\text{Average Daily Cost of Goods Sold}} = \frac{15.3}{(153.4/365)} = 36.40$$

$$\text{Inventory turnover} = \frac{\text{Cost of Goods Sold}}{\text{Inventory}} = \frac{153.4}{15.3} = 10.03$$

(*Continued*)

---

[5]Accounts receivable days can also be calculated based on the average accounts receivable at the end of the current and prior years.

Assuming that Global's accounts payable at year-end on its balance sheet is representative of the normal amount during the year, Global is able, on average, to take about 69.5 days to pay its suppliers. This compares well with the 27.5 days we calculated that it waits on average to be paid (its accounts receivable days). Global typically takes 36 days to sell its inventory. Note that inventory turnover and inventory days tell us the same thing in different ways—if it takes Global about 36 days to sell its inventory, then it turns over its inventory about 10 times per 365-day year. In Chapter 19 on working capital management, we'll see how a company's receivable, inventory, and payable days make up its operating cycle.

Interest Coverage Ratios

interest coverage ratio or times interest earned (TIE) ratio An assessment by lenders of a firm's leverage, it is equal to a measure of earnings divided by interest.

Lenders often assess a firm's leverage by computing an **interest coverage ratio**, also known as a **times interest earned (TIE) ratio**, which is equal to a measure of earnings divided by interest. Financial managers watch these ratios carefully because they assess how easily the firm will be able to cover its interest payments. There is no one accepted measure of earnings for these ratios; it is common to consider operating income, EBIT, or EBITDA as a multiple of the firm's interest expenses. When this ratio is high, it indicates that the firm is earning much more than is necessary to meet its required interest payments.

EXAMPLE 2.5

Computing Interest Coverage Ratios

MyFinanceLab

PROBLEM

Assess Global's ability to meet its interest obligations by calculating interest coverage ratios using both EBIT and EBITDA.

SOLUTION

PLAN AND ORGANIZE

Gather the EBIT, depreciation, and amortization and interest expense for each year from Global's income statement.

$$2015: \text{EBIT} = 7.1, \quad \text{EBITDA} = 7.1 + 1.1, \quad \text{Interest expense} = 4.6$$

$$2016: \text{EBIT} = 10.4, \quad \text{EBITDA} = 10.4 + 1.2, \quad \text{Interest expense} = 7.7$$

EXECUTE

In 2015 and 2016, Global had the following interest coverage ratios:

$$2015: \frac{\text{EBIT}}{\text{Interest}} = \frac{7.1}{4.6} = 1.54 \quad \text{and} \quad \frac{\text{EBITDA}}{\text{Interest}} = \frac{7.1 + 1.1}{4.6} = 1.78$$

$$2016: \frac{\text{EBIT}}{\text{Interest}} = \frac{10.4}{7.7} = 1.35 \quad \text{and} \quad \frac{\text{EBITDA}}{\text{Interest}} = \frac{10.4 + 1.2}{7.7} = 1.51$$

EVALUATE

The coverage ratios indicate that Global is generating enough cash to cover its interest obligations. However, Global's low—and declining—interest coverage could be a source of concern for its creditors.

Leverage Ratios

leverage A measure of the extent to which a firm relies on debt as a source of financing.

Another important piece of information that we can learn from a firm's balance sheet is the firm's **leverage**, or the extent to which it relies on debt as a source of financing. The **debt-equity ratio** is a common ratio used to assess a firm's leverage that we calculate by

debt-equity ratio The ratio of a firm's total amount of short- and long-term debt (including current maturities) to the value of its equity, which may be calculated based on market or book values.

dividing the total amount of short- and long-term debt (including current maturities) by the total stockholders' equity:

$$\text{Debt-Equity Ratio} = \frac{\text{Total Debt}}{\text{Total Equity}} \qquad (2.19)$$

We can calculate this ratio using either book or market values for equity and debt. From Table 2.1, Global's debt in 2016 includes notes payable ($5.5 million) and long-term debt ($113.2 million), for a total of $118.7 million. Therefore, using the book value of equity, its *book* debt-equity ratio is 118.7/22.2 = 5.3. Note the large increase from 2015, when the book debt-equity ratio was only (3.2 + 78)/21.2 = 3.8.

Because of the difficulty interpreting the book value of equity, the book debt-equity ratio is not especially useful. It is more informative to compare the firm's debt to the market value of its equity. Global's debt-equity ratio in 2016, using the market value of equity (from Example 2.1), is 118.7/36 = 3.3, which means Global's debt is a bit more than triple the market value of its equity.[6] As we will see later in the text, a firm's *market* debt-equity ratio has important consequences for the risk and return of its stock.

debt-to-capital ratio The ratio of total debt to total debt plus total equity.

We can also calculate the fraction of the firm financed by debt in terms of its **debt-to-capital ratio**:

$$\text{Debt-to-Capital Ratio} = \frac{\text{Total Debt}}{\text{Total Equity} + \text{Total Debt}} \qquad (2.20)$$

Again, this ratio can be computed using book or market values.

While leverage increases the risk to the firm's equity holders, firms may also hold cash reserves in order to reduce risk. Thus, another useful measure to consider is the firm's **net debt**, or debt in excess of its cash reserves:

net debt Debt in excess of a firm's cash reserves.

$$\text{Net Debt} = \text{Total Debt} - \text{Excess Cash \& Short-Term Investments} \qquad (2.21)$$

To understand why net debt may be a more relevant measure of leverage, consider a firm with more cash than debt outstanding: Because such a firm could pay off its debts immediately using its available cash, it has not increased its risk and has no effective leverage.

Analogous to the debt-to-capital ratio, we can use the concept of net debt to compute the firm's **debt-to-enterprise value ratio**:

debt-to-enterprise value ratio The ratio of a firm's net debt to its enterprise value.

$$\text{Debt-to-Enterprise Value Ratio} = \frac{\text{Net Debt}}{\text{Market Value of Equity} + \text{Net Debt}}$$

$$= \frac{\text{Net Debt}}{\text{Enterprise Value}} \qquad (2.22)$$

Given Global's 2016 cash balance of $23.2 million, and total long- and short-term debt of $118.7 million, its net debt is 118.7 − 23.2 = $95.5 million.[7] Given its market value of equity of $36.0 million, Global's enterprise value in 2016 is 36.0 + 95.5 = $131.5 million, and thus its debt-to-enterprise value ratio is 95.5/131.5 = 72.6%. That is, 72.6% of Global's underlying business activity is financed via debt.

---

[6]In this calculation, we have compared the market value of equity to the book value of debt. Strictly speaking, it would be best to use the market value of debt. But because the market value of debt is generally not very different from its book value, this distinction is often ignored in practice.

[7]While net debt should ideally be calculated by deducting cash in excess of the firm's operating needs, absent additional information, it is typical in practice to deduct all cash on the balance sheet.

equity multiplier A measure of leverage equal to total assets divided by total equity.

A final measure of leverage is a firm's **equity multiplier**, measured in book value terms as Total Assets/Book Value of Equity. As we will see shortly, this measure captures the amplification of the firm's accounting returns that results from leverage. The market value equity multiplier, which is generally measured as Enterprise Value/Market Value of Equity, indicates the amplification of shareholders' financial risk that results from leverage.

Valuation Ratios

Analysts and investors use a number of ratios to gauge the market value of a firm. The most important is the firm's **price-earnings ratio (P/E)**:

price-earnings ratio (P/E) The ratio of the market value of equity to the firm's earnings, or its share price to its earnings per share.

$$\text{P/E Ratio} = \frac{\text{Market Capitalization}}{\text{Net Income}} = \frac{\text{Share Price}}{\text{Earnings per Share}} \quad (2.23)$$

That is, the P/E ratio is the ratio of the value of equity to the firm's earnings, either on a total basis or on a per-share basis. Following Eq. 2.23, Global's P/E ratio in 2016 was $36/2.0 = 10/0.56 = 18$. The P/E ratio is a simple measure that is often used to assess whether a stock is over- or under-valued, based on the idea that the value of a stock should be proportional to the level of earnings it can generate for its shareholders. P/E ratios can vary widely across industries and tend to be higher for industries with high growth rates. For example, in 2016, the average large U.S. firm had a P/E ratio of about 25. But software firms, which tend to have above-average growth rates, had an average P/E ratio of 38. One way to capture the idea that a higher P/E ratio can be justified by a higher growth rate is to compare it to the company's expected earnings growth rate. For example, if Global's expected growth rate is 18%, then it would have a P/E to Growth, or **PEG ratio**, of 1. Some investors consider PEG ratios of 1 or below as indicating the stock is fairly priced, but would question whether the company is potentially overvalued if the PEG is higher than 1.

PEG ratio The ratio of a firm's P/E to its expected earnings growth rate.

The P/E ratio considers the value of the firm's equity and so depends on its leverage. Recall that the amount of assets controlled by the equity holders can be increased through the use of leverage. To assess the market value of the underlying business, it is common to consider valuation ratios based on the firm's enterprise value. Typical ratios include the ratio of enterprise value to revenue, or enterprise value to operating income, or EBITDA. These ratios compare the value of the business to its sales, operating profits, or cash flow. Similar to the P/E ratio, managers use these ratios to make intra-industry comparisons of how firms are priced in the market.

COMMON MISTAKE

Mismatched Ratios

When considering valuation (and other) ratios, be sure that the items you are comparing both represent amounts related to the entire firm or that both represent amounts related solely to equity holders. For example, a firm's share price and market capitalization are values associated with the firm's equity. Thus, it makes sense to compare them to the firm's earnings per share or net income, which are amounts to equity holders after interest has been paid to debt holders. We must be careful, however, if we compare a firm's market capitalization to its revenues, operating income, or EBITDA. These amounts are related to the whole firm, and both debt and equity holders have a claim to them. Therefore, it is better to compare revenues, operating income, or EBITDA to the enterprise value of the firm, which includes both debt and equity.

The P/E ratio is not useful when the firm's earnings are negative. In this case, it is common to look at the firm's enterprise value relative to sales. The risk in doing so, however, is that earnings might be negative because the firm's underlying business model is fundamentally flawed, as was the case for many Internet firms in the late 1990s.

EXAMPLE 2.6

Computing Profitability
and Valuation Ratios

MyFinanceLab

PROBLEM

Consider the following data for Walmart Stores and Target Corporation ($ billions):

	Walmart Stores (WMT)	**Target Corporation (TGT)**
Sales	469	73
Operating Income	28	5
Net Income	17	3
Market Capitalization	222	38
Cash	8	1
Debt	54	18

Compare Walmart's and Target's operating margin, net profit margin, P/E ratio, and the ratio of enterprise value to operating income and sales.

SOLUTION

PLAN

The table contains all of the raw data, but we need to compute the ratios using the inputs in the table.

Operating Margin = Operating Income/Sales
Net Profit Margin = Net Income/Sales
P/E Ratio = Price/Earnings = Market Capitalization/Net Income
Enterprise Value to Operating Income = Enterprise Value/Operating Income
Enterprise Value to Sales = Enterprise Value/Sales

EXECUTE

Walmart had an operating margin of 28/469 = 6.0%, a net profit margin of 17/469 = 3.6%, and a P/E ratio of 222/17 = 13.1. Its enterprise value was 222 + 54 − 8 = $268 billion. Its ratio to operating income is 268/28 = 9.6, and its ratio to sales is 268/469 = 0.57.

Target had an operating margin of 5/73 = 6.8%, a net profit margin of 3/73 = 4.1%, and a P/E ratio of 38/3 = 12.7. Its enterprise value was 38 + 18 − 1 = $55 billion. Its ratio to operating income is 55/5 = 11, and its ratio to sales is 55/73 = 0.75.

EVALUATE

Target has a slightly higher operating margin, net profit margin, and enterprise value ratio, but a slightly lower P/E ratio. This suggests that the market expects similar growth rates from Target and Walmart, despite large differences in size.

Operating Returns

Analysts and financial managers often evaluate the firm's return on investment by comparing its income to its investment using ratios such as the firm's **return on equity (ROE)**:[8]

return on equity (ROE) The ratio of a firm's net income to the book value of its equity.

$$\text{Return on Equity} = \frac{\text{Net Income}}{\text{Book Value of Equity}} \tag{2.24}$$

Global's ROE in 2016 was 2.0/22.2 = 9.0%. The ROE provides a measure of the return that the firm has earned on its past investments. A high ROE may indicate the firm is able to find investment opportunities that are very profitable. Of course, one weakness of this measure is the difficulty in interpreting the book value of equity.

---

[8]Because net income is measured over the year, the ROE can also be calculated based on the average book value of equity at the end of the current and prior years.

return on assets (ROA) The ratio of net income plus interest expense to the total book value of the firm's assets.

Another common measure is the **return on assets (ROA)**, which is net income plus interest expense divided by the total assets. The ROA calculation includes interest expense in the numerator because the assets in the denominator have been funded by both debt and equity investors. A firm must earn both a positive ROE and ROA to grow.

As a performance measure, ROA has the benefit that it is less sensitive to leverage than ROE. However, it is sensitive to working capital—for example, an equal increase in the firm's receivables and payables will increase total assets and thus lower ROA. To avoid this problem, we can consider the firm's **return on invested capital (ROIC)**:

return on invested capital (ROIC) The ratio of the after-tax profit before interest to the book value of invested capital not being held as cash (book equity plus net debt).

$$\text{Return on Invested Capital} = \frac{\text{EBIT} (1 - \text{Tax Rate})}{\text{Book Value of Equity} + \text{Net Debt}} \qquad (2.25)$$

The return on invested capital measures the after-tax profit generated by the business itself, excluding any interest expenses (or interest income), and compares it to the capital raised from equity and debt holders that has already been deployed (i.e., is not held as cash). Of the three measures of operating returns, ROIC is the most useful in assessing the performance of the underlying business.

EXAMPLE 2.7

Computing Operating Returns

MyFinanceLab

PROBLEM
Assess how Global's ability to use its assets effectively has changed in the last year by computing the change in its return on assets.

SOLUTION

PLAN AND ORGANIZE

In order to compute ROA, we need net income, interest expense, and total assets.

	2015	2016
Net Income	1.9	2.0
Interest Expense	4.6	7.7
Total Assets	128.9	170.1

EXECUTE

In 2016, Global's ROA was $(2.0 + 7.7)/170.1 = 5.7\%$, compared to an ROA in 2015 of $(1.9 + 4.6)/128.9 = 5.0\%$.

EVALUATE

The improvement in Global's ROA from 2015 to 2016 suggests that Global was able to use its assets more effectively and increase its return over this period.

The DuPont Identity

DuPont Identity Expresses return on equity as the product of profit margin, asset turnover, and a measure of leverage.

Global's financial manager will need to know that its ROE is 9%, but that financial manager would also need to understand the drivers of his or her firm's return on equity. High margins, efficient use of assets, or even simply high leverage could all lead to a higher return on equity. By delving deeper into the sources of return on equity, the financial manager can gain a clear sense of the firm's financial picture. One common tool for doing so is the **DuPont Identity**, named for the company that popularized it, which expresses return on equity as the product of profit margin, asset turnover, and a measure of leverage.

To understand the DuPont Identity, we start with ROE and decompose it in steps into the drivers identified in the identity. First, we simply multiply ROE by (sales/sales), which is just 1, and rearrange terms:

$$\text{ROE} = \left(\frac{\text{Net Income}}{\text{Total Equity}}\right)\left(\frac{\text{Sales}}{\text{Sales}}\right) = \left(\frac{\text{Net Income}}{\text{Sales}}\right)\left(\frac{\text{Sales}}{\text{Total Equity}}\right) \qquad (2.26)$$

This expression says that ROE can be thought of as net income per dollar of sales (profit margin) times the amount of sales per dollar of equity. For example, Global's ROE comes from its profit margin of 1.07% multiplied by its sales per dollar of equity (186.7/22.2 = 8.41): 1.07% × 8.41 = 9%. We can take the decomposition further by multiplying Eq. 2.26 by (total assets/total assets), which again is just 1, and rearranging the terms:

DuPont Identity

$$\text{ROE} = \left(\frac{\text{Net Income}}{\text{Sales}}\right)\left(\frac{\text{Sales}}{\text{Total Equity}}\right)\left(\frac{\text{Total Assets}}{\text{Total Assets}}\right)$$

$$= \left(\frac{\text{Net Income}}{\text{Sales}}\right)\left(\frac{\text{Sales}}{\text{Total Assets}}\right)\left(\frac{\text{Total Assets}}{\text{Total Equity}}\right) \qquad (2.27)$$

This final expression says that ROE is equal to net income per dollar of sales (profit margin) times sales per dollar of assets (asset turnover) times assets per dollar of equity (equity multiplier). Equation 2.27 is the DuPont Identity, expressing return on equity as the product of profit margin, asset turnover, and the equity multiplier. Turning to Global, its equity multiplier is 7.7(=170.1/22.2). A financial manager at Global looking for ways to increase ROE could assess the drivers behind its current ROE with the DuPont Identity. With a profit margin of 1.07%, asset turnover of 1.1, and an equity multiplier of 7.7, we have:

$$\text{ROE} = 9\% = (1.07\%)(1.1)(7.7)$$

This decomposition of ROE shows that leverage is already high (confirmed by the fact that the book debt-to-equity ratio shows that Global's debt is more than five times its equity). However, Global is operating with only 1% profit margins and relatively low asset turnover. Thus, Global's managers should focus on utilizing the firm's existing assets more efficiently and lowering costs to increase the profit margin.[9]

EXAMPLE 2.8
DuPont Analysis

MyFinanceLab

PROBLEM

The following table contains information about Walmart (WMT) and Nordstrom (JWN). Compute their respective ROEs and then determine how much Walmart would need to increase its profit margin in order to match Nordstrom's ROE.

	Profit Margin	Asset Turnover	Equity Multiplier
Walmart	3.6%	2.3	2.7
Nordstrom	6.1%	1.5	4.2

(*Continued*)

---

[9]Although the DuPont Identity makes it look like you can increase ROE just by increasing leverage, it is not quite that simple. An increase in leverage will increase your interest expense, decreasing your profit margin.

SOLUTION

PLAN AND ORGANIZE

The table contains all the relevant information to use the DuPont Identity to compute the ROE. We can compute the ROE of each company by multiplying together its profit margin, asset turnover, and equity multiplier. In order to determine how much Walmart would need to increase its profit margin to match Nordstrom's ROE, we can set Walmart's ROE equal to Nordstrom's, keep its turnover and equity multiplier fixed, and solve for the profit margin.

EXECUTE

Using the DuPont Identity, we have:

$$ROE_{WMT} = 3.6\% \times 2.3 \times 2.7 = 22.4\%$$
$$ROE_{JWN} = 6.1\% \times 1.5 \times 4.2 = 38.4\%$$

Now, using Nordstrom's ROE, but Walmart's asset turnover and equity multiplier, we can solve for the profit margin that Walmart needs to achieve Nordstrom's ROE:

$$38.4\% = \text{Margin} \times 2.3 \times 2.7$$
$$\text{Margin} = 38.4\%/6.21 = 6.2\%$$

EVALUATE

Walmart would have to increase its profit margin from 3.6% to 6.2% in order to match Nordstrom's ROE. It would be able to achieve Nordstrom's ROE with much lower leverage and around the same profit margin as Nordstrom (6.2% vs. 6.1%) because of its higher turnover.

Table 2.4 summarizes financial ratios and provides typical values of those ratios for the manufacturing, retail, and service sectors along with the 500 firms in the S&P 500 index. Because many companies with debt also held high levels of cash over the period, leverage ratios based on Net Debt are much lower than those based on Total Debt.

TABLE 2.4

A Summary of Key Financial Ratios

Ratio	Formula	Manufacturing	Retail	Service	S&P 500
Profitability Ratios					
Gross Margin	Gross Profit / Sales	33.8%	30.1%	51.4%	39.0%
Operating Margin	Operating Income / Sales	8.1%	7.3%	12.2%	16.2%
Net Profit Margin	Net Income / Sales	1.3%	2.6%	2.5%	4.5%
Liquidity Ratios					
Current Ratio	Current Assets / Current Liabilities	2.6	1.5	1.8	2.1
Quick Ratio	Current Assets − Inventory / Current Liabilities	1.9	0.8	1.7	1.6
Cash Ratio	Cash / Current Liabilities	0.9	0.3	0.9	0.7
Efficiency and Working Capital Ratios					
Accounts Receivable Days	Accounts Receivable / Average Daily Sales	57.6	7.8	63.0	60.2
Fixed Asset Turnover	Sales / Fixed Assets	5.4	6.6	10.6	4.8

Ratio	Formula	Manufacturing	Retail	Service	S&P 500
Total Asset Turnover	$\dfrac{\text{Sales}}{\text{Total Assets}}$	0.7	1.7	0.6	0.5
Inventory Turnover	$\dfrac{\text{Cost of Goods Sold}}{\text{Inventory}}$	4.2	6.9	26.9	5.7
Interest Coverage Ratios					
EBIT/Interest Coverage	$\dfrac{\text{EBIT}}{\text{Interest Expense}}$	3.2	5.5	2.3	3.9
EBITDA/Interest Coverage	$\dfrac{\text{EBITDA}}{\text{Interest Expense}}$	6.0	9.3	5.3	6.7
Leverage Ratios					
Book Debt-to-Equity Ratio	$\dfrac{\text{Total Debt}}{\text{Book Value of Total Equity}}$	27.1%	44.2%	21.5%	46.6%
Market Debt-to-Equity Ratio	$\dfrac{\text{Total Debt}}{\text{Market Value of Total Equity}}$	10.0%	17.2%	6.2%	21.8%
Debt-to-Capital Ratio	$\dfrac{\text{Total Debt}}{\text{Total Equity} + \text{Total Debt}}$	20.9%	30.6%	17.6%	32.0%
Debt-to-Enterprise Value	$\dfrac{\text{Net Debt}}{\text{Enterprise Value}}$	0.0%	4.7%	0.0%	2.0%
Equity Multiplier	$\dfrac{\text{Total Assets}}{\text{Total Equity}}$	1.8	2.4	1.98	2.4
Operating Returns					
Return on Equity	$\dfrac{\text{Net Income}}{\text{Book Value of Equity}}$	4.2%	10.4%	3.6%	7.1%
Return on Assets	$\dfrac{\text{Net Income} + \text{Interest Expense}}{\text{Total Assets}}$	3.6%	5.8%	3.3%	4.1%
Return on Invested Capital (ROIC)	$\dfrac{\text{EBIT}(1 - \text{Tax Rate})}{\text{Book Value of Equity} + \text{Net Debt}}$	18.0%	20.1%	18.3%	17.0%
Valuation Ratios					
Market-to-Book Ratio	$\dfrac{\text{Market Value of Equity}}{\text{Book Value of Equity}}$	2.7	2.7	3.5	2.1
Price-to-Earnings Ratio	$\dfrac{\text{Share Price}}{\text{Earnings per Share}}$	21.5	21.6	28.8	21.2
Enterprise Value Ratios (typical values shown are based on EV/EBITDA)	$\dfrac{\text{Enterprise Value}}{\text{EBIT or EBITDA or Sales}}$	8.3	11.7	10.5	12.1

Source: Standard and Poors' Compustat based on averages of fiscal years 2012 to 2015.

CONCEPT CHECK

11. What does a high debt-to-equity ratio tell you?
12. What is a firm's enterprise value?
13. How can a financial manager use the DuPont Identity to assess the firm's ROE?
14. How do you use the price-earnings (P/E) ratio to gauge the market value of a firm?

Financial Reporting in Practice

The various financial statements we have examined are of critical importance to investors and financial managers alike. Even with safeguards such as GAAP and auditors, financial reporting abuses unfortunately do take place. We now review one of the most infamous recent examples and offer some concluding thoughts to guide financial managers through the complexities of financial statements.

Enron

Enron is the most well-known of the accounting scandals of the early 2000s. Enron started as an operator of natural gas pipelines but evolved into a global trader dealing in a range of products including gas, oil, electricity, and even broadband Internet capacity. A series of events unfolded that led Enron to file what was at the time the largest bankruptcy filing in U.S. history in December 2001. By the end of 2001, the market value of Enron's shares had fallen by over $60 billion.

Interestingly, throughout the 1990s and up to late 2001, Enron was touted as one of the most successful and profitable companies in America. *Fortune* rated Enron "The Most Innovative Company in America" for six straight years, from 1995 to 2000. But while many aspects of Enron's business were successful, subsequent investigations suggest that Enron executives had been manipulating Enron's financial statements to mislead investors and artificially inflate the price of Enron's stock and to maintain its credit rating. In 2000, for example, 96% of Enron's reported earnings were the result of accounting manipulation.[10]

Although the accounting manipulation that Enron used was quite sophisticated, the essence of most of the deceptive transactions was surprisingly simple. Enron sold assets at inflated prices to other firms (or, in many cases, business entities that Enron's CFO Andrew Fastow had created), together with a promise to buy back those assets at an even higher future price. Thus, Enron was effectively borrowing money, receiving cash today in exchange for a promise to pay more cash in the future. But Enron recorded the incoming cash as revenue and then hid the promises to buy the assets back in a variety of ways.[11] In the end, much of their revenue growth and profits in the late 1990s were the result of this type of manipulation.

The Sarbanes-Oxley Act

Sarbanes-Oxley Act (SOX) Legislation passed by Congress in 2002, intended to improve the accuracy of financial information given to both boards and shareholders.

Accurate and up-to-date financial statements are essential to investors evaluating investment opportunities. In 2002, Congress passed the **Sarbanes-Oxley Act (SOX)**. While SOX contains many provisions, the overall intent of the legislation was to improve the accuracy of information given to both boards and shareholders. SOX attempted to achieve this goal in three ways: (1) by overhauling incentives and independence in the auditing process, (2) by stiffening penalties for providing false information, and (3) by forcing companies to validate their internal financial control processes.

Many of the problems at Enron and elsewhere were kept hidden from boards and shareholders until it was too late. In the wake of these scandals, many people felt that the

---

[10]John R. Kroger, "Enron, Fraud and Securities Reform: An Enron Prosecutor's Perspective," *University of Colorado Law Review*, December 2005, pp. 57–138.

[11]In some cases, these promises were called "price risk management liabilities" and hidden with other trading activities; in other cases they were off-balance sheet transactions that were not fully disclosed.

accounting statements of these companies, while often remaining true to the letter of GAAP, did not present an accurate picture of the financial health of the companies.

Auditing firms are supposed to ensure that a company's financial statements accurately reflect the financial state of the firm. In reality, most auditors have a long-standing relationship with their audit clients; this extended relationship and the auditors' desire to keep the lucrative auditing fees make auditors less willing to challenge management. More importantly, perhaps, most accounting firms have developed large and extremely profitable consulting divisions. Obviously, if an audit team refuses to accommodate a request by a client's management, that client will be less likely to choose the accounting firm's consulting division for its next consulting contract. SOX addressed this concern by putting strict limits on the amount of non-audit fees (consulting or otherwise) that an accounting firm can earn from the same firm that it audits. It also required that audit partners rotate every five years to limit the likelihood that auditing relationships become too cozy over time. Finally, SOX called on the SEC to force companies to have audit committees that are dominated by outside directors, and required that at least one outside director has a financial background.

SOX also stiffened the criminal penalties for providing false information to shareholders. It required both the CEO and the CFO to personally attest to the accuracy of the financial statements presented to shareholders and to sign a statement to that effect. Penalties for providing false or misleading financial statements were increased under SOX—fines of as much as $5 million and imprisonment of a maximum of 20 years are permitted. Further, CEOs and CFOs must return bonuses or profits from the sale of stock or the exercise of options during any period covered by statements that are later restated.

Finally, Section 404 of SOX requires senior management and the boards of public companies to attest to the effectiveness and validity of the process through which funds are allocated and controlled, and outcomes monitored throughout the firm. Section 404 has arguably garnered more attention than any other section in SOX because of the potentially enormous burden it places on every firm to validate its entire financial control system. When the SEC estimated the cost of implementing Section 404, its staff economists put the total cost at $1.24 billion. In 2005, surveys by Financial Executives International and the American Electronics Association predicted that the actual cost would be between $20 billion and $35 billion.[12] The burden of complying with this provision is greater, as a fraction of revenue, for smaller companies. The surveys cited earlier found that multibillion-dollar companies would pay less than 0.05% of their revenues to comply, whereas small companies with less than $20 million in revenues would pay more than 3% of their revenues to comply.

Dodd-Frank Act

To mitigate the compliance burden on small firms, the Dodd-Frank Wall Street Reform and Consumer Protection Act passed in 2010 exempts firms with less than $75 million in publicly held shares from the SOX Section 404 requirements. It also requires the SEC to study how it might reduce cost for medium-sized firms with a public float of less than $250 million, and to assess whether such measures would encourage more firms to list on U.S. exchanges.

Dodd-Frank also broadened the whistleblower provisions of SOX, so that an individual who provides "information related to a possible violation of the federal securities laws (including any rules or regulations thereunder)" that results in penalties or recoveries by the SEC or agencies is eligible to receive from 10 to 30% of that penalty or recovery.

---

[12]American Electronics Association, "Sarbanes-Oxley Section 404: The 'Section' of Unintended Consequences and Its Impact on Small Business" (2005).

Bernard Madoff's Ponzi Scheme

"It's only when the tide goes out that you learn who's been swimming naked."
—Warren Buffett

On December 11, 2008, federal agents arrested Bernie Madoff, one of the largest and most successful hedge fund managers. It turned out that the $65 billion[13] fund he ran was in fact a fraud. His spectacular performance of the last 17 years, generating consistent annual returns between 10% and 15%, was actually a complete fabrication. Madoff had been running the world's largest Ponzi scheme: That is, he used the capital contributed by new investors to pay off old investors. His strategy was so successful that for more than a decade investors ranging from Steven Spielberg to New York University, as well as a number of large banks and investment advisors, lined up to invest with him. Indeed, Madoff quite likely would have been able to hide the fraud until his deathbed had not the global financial crisis spurred many investors to seek to withdraw funds from their Madoff accounts in order to raise cash and cover losses elsewhere in their portfolios. In addition, the financial crisis meant there were fewer new investors with both the cash and the willingness to invest. As a result, Madoff did not have enough new capital to pay off the investors who wanted to withdraw their capital, and the scheme finally collapsed.

How was Madoff able to hide perhaps the largest fraud of all time for so long? Rather than simply manipulate his accounting statements, Madoff *made them up* with the assistance of a virtually unknown accounting firm with only one active accountant. Although many investors may have questioned why such a large fund, with $65 billion in assets, would choose an unknown and tiny audit firm, not enough of them recognized this choice as a potential red flag. In addition, because Madoff's firm was private, it was not subject to the strict regulatory requirements for public companies (such as the Sarbanes-Oxley Act) and so had weak reporting requirements. As this case makes clear, when making an investment decision, it is important not only to review the firm's financial statements, but also to consider the reliability and reputation of the auditors who prepared them.

The Financial Statements: A Useful Starting Point

In this chapter, we have highlighted the role of the financial statements in informing outside analysts, investors, and the financial managers themselves about the performance, position, and financial condition of the firm. However, especially from the financial manager's perspective, financial statements are only a starting point. For example, we have emphasized the importance of market values over book values. We have also shown that while much can be learned through ratio analysis, these ratios are only markers that point the financial manager toward areas where the firm is doing well or where he or she needs to focus an effort toward improvement. No single ratio tells the whole story. However, by studying all of the financial statements and considering ratios that assess profitability, leverage, and efficiency, you should be able to develop a clear sense of the health and performance of the firm. Finally, the usefulness of the financial statements to investors relies on the ethics of those constructing them. However, even in cases of deception, an informed reader of the financial statements could have spotted the warning signs by focusing on the statement of cash flows and carefully reading the notes to the financial statements.

CONCEPT CHECK

15. Describe the transactions Enron used to increase its reported earnings.

16. What is the Sarbanes-Oxley Act?

---

[13]$65 billion is the total amount Madoff had reported to his investors, including (fictitious) returns; investigators are still trying to determine the exact amount that investors had actually contributed to the fund, but it appears to be in excess of $17 billion (see www.madoff.com).

MyFinanceLab
Here is what you should know after reading this chapter. MyFinanceLab will help you identify what you know, and where to go when you need to practice.

KEY POINTS AND EQUATIONS	KEY TERMS	ONLINE PRACTICE
2.1 Firms' Disclosure of Financial Information • Financial statements are accounting reports that a firm issues periodically to describe its past performance. • Investors, financial analysts, managers, and other interested parties, such as creditors, rely on financial statements to obtain reliable information about a corporation. • The main types of financial statements are the balance sheet, the income statement, the statement of cash flows, and the statement of stockholders' equity. • While the U.S. maintains its own GAAP, most countries in the world are standardizing their accounting systems around International Financial Reporting Standards.	annual report (10-K), p. 28 auditor, p. 30 financial statements, p. 28 Generally Accepted Accounting Principles (GAAP), p. 28	MyFinanceLab Study Plan 2.1
2.2 The Balance Sheet • The balance sheet shows the current financial position (assets, liabilities, and stockholders' equity) of the firm at a single point in time. • The two sides of the balance sheet must balance: $$\text{Assets} = \text{Liabilities} + \text{Stockholders' Equity} \quad (2.1)$$ • Stockholders' equity is the book value of the firm's equity. It differs from the market value of the firm's equity, its market capitalization, because of the way assets and liabilities are recorded for accounting purposes. • A successful firm's market-to-book ratio typically exceeds 1. • The enterprise value of a firm is the total value of its underlying business operations: $$\text{Enterprise Value} = \text{Market Value of Equity} + \text{Debt} - \text{Cash} \quad (2.4)$$	accounts payable, p. 32 accounts receivable, p. 31 assets, p. 30 balance sheet, p. 30 book value, p. 31 book value of equity, p. 32 common stock and paid-in surplus, p. 30 current assets, p. 31 current liabilities, p. 32 depreciation, p. 31 enterprise value, p. 34 growth stocks, p. 34 inventories, p. 31 liabilities, p. 30 liquidation value, p. 33 long-term assets, p. 31 long-term debt, p. 32 market capitalization, p. 33 marketable securities, p. 31 market-to-book ratio (price-to-book [P/B] ratio), p. 34 net working capital, p. 32 notes payable, p. 32 retained earnings, p. 30 shareholders' equity, p. 30 short-term debt, p. 32 statement of financial position, p. 30 stockholders' equity, p. 30 value stocks, p. 34	MyFinanceLab Study Plan 2.2

2.3 The Income Statement • The income statement reports the firm's revenues and expenses, and it computes the firm's bottom line of net income, or earnings. • Net income is often reported on a per-share basis as the firm's earnings per share: Earnings per Share (EPS) = Net Income/ Shares Outstanding (2.5) • We compute diluted EPS by adding to the number of shares outstanding the possible increase in the number of shares from the exercise of stock options the firm has awarded.	convertible bonds, p. 37 diluted EPS, p. 37 dilution, p. 37 earnings per share (EPS), p. 37 EBIT, p. 37 EBITDA, p. 38 gross profit, p. 36 income statement, p. 36 net income or earnings, p. 36 operating income, p. 37 stock options, p. 37	MyFinanceLab Study Plan 2.3
2.4 The Statement of Cash Flows • The statement of cash flows reports the sources and uses of the firm's cash. It shows the adjustments to net income for non-cash expenses and changes to net working capital, as well as the cash used (or provided) from investing and financing activities.	capital expenditures, p. 41 payout ratio, p. 41 statement of cash flows, p. 38	MyFinanceLab Study Plan 2.4
2.5 Other Financial Statement Information • The management discussion and analysis section of the financial statement contains management's overview of the firm's performance, as well as disclosure of risks the firm faces, including those from off-balance sheet transactions. • The statement of stockholders' equity breaks down the stockholders' equity computed on the balance sheet into the amount that came from issuing new shares versus retained earnings. It is not particularly useful for financial valuation purposes. • The notes to a firm's financial statements generally contain important details regarding the numbers used in the main statements.	management discussion and analysis (MD&A), p. 42 off-balance sheet transactions, p. 42 statement of stockholders' equity, p. 42	MyFinanceLab Study Plan 2.5
2.6 Financial Statement Analysis • Profitability ratios show the firm's operating or net income as a fraction of sales, and they are an indication of a firm's efficiency and its pricing strategy. • Liquidity ratios help creditors assess whether the firm has enough cash to meet its short-term needs. • Asset efficiency ratios assess how efficiently the firm is using its assets by showing how many dollars of revenues the firm produces per dollar of assets. • Working capital ratios express the firm's working capital as a number of days of sales (for receivables) or cost of sales (for inventory or payables).	accounts payable days, p. 45 accounts receivable days, p. 44 asset turnover, p. 44 average collection period or days sales outstanding, p. 44 cash ratio, p. 44 current ratio, p. 44 debt-equity ratio, p. 47 debt-to-capital ratio, p. 47 debt-to-enterprise value ratio, p. 47 DuPont Identity, p. 50 equity multiplier, p. 48 gross margin, p. 43 interest coverage ratio, p. 46	MyFinanceLab Study Plan 2.6

- Interest coverage ratios indicate the ratio of the firm's income or cash flows to its interest expenses, and they are a measure of financial strength.
- A common ratio used to assess a firm's leverage is:

$$\text{Debt-Equity Ratio} = \frac{\text{Total Debt}}{\text{Total Equity}} \quad (2.19)$$

- This ratio is most informative when computed using the market value of equity. It indicates the degree of leverage of the firm.
- Valuation ratios compute market capitalization or enterprise value of the firm relative to its earnings or operating income.
- The P/E ratio computes the value of a share of stock relative to the firm's EPS. P/E ratios tend to be high for fast-growing firms.
- When comparing valuation ratios, it is important to be sure both the numerator and denominator match in terms of whether they include debt.
- ROE and ROA are typical operating return ratios. ROE expresses the firm's net income as a return on the book value of its equity. ROA expresses net income plus interest as a return on total assets.
- The DuPont Identity says that

$$\text{ROE} = \left(\frac{\text{Net Income}}{\text{Sales}}\right) \times \left(\frac{\text{Sales}}{\text{Total Assets}}\right)$$

$$\times \left(\frac{\text{Total Assets}}{\text{Total Equity}}\right) \quad (2.27)$$

inventory days, p. 45
inventory turnover ratio, p. 45
leverage, p. 46
net debt, p. 47
net profit margin, p. 43
operating margin, p. 43
PEG ratio, p. 48
price-earnings ratio (P/E), p. 48
quick ratio ("acid-test ratio"), p. 44
return on assets (ROA), p. 50
return on invested capital (ROIC), p. 50
return on equity (ROE), p. 49
times interest earned (TIE) ratio, p. 46

2.7 Financial Reporting in Practice
- Recent accounting scandals have drawn attention to the importance of financial statements. New legislation has increased the penalties for fraud, and tightened the procedures firms must use to ensure that statements are accurate.

Sarbanes-Oxley Act (SOX), p. 54

MyFinanceLab Study Plan 2.7

CRITICAL THINKING

1. Why do firms disclose financial information?
2. Who reads financial statements? List at least three different categories of people. For each category, provide an example of the type of information they might be interested in and discuss why?
3. What is the purpose of the balance sheet?
4. What is the purpose of the income statement?
5. How does the statement of cash flows differ from the income statement?
6. Can a firm with positive net income run out of cash? Explain.
7. How can you use the balance sheet to assess the health of a firm?

8. How are the balance sheet and the income statement related?

9. What is the DuPont Identity and how can a financial manager use it?

10. What can you learn from the management's discussion in the financial statements or the notes to the financial statements?

11. How did accounting fraud contribute to the collapse of Enron?

PROBLEMS

*All problems are available in MyFinanceLab. The [icon] icon indicates problems that are easier to solve using Excel and have data in an Excel format available in MyFinanceLab. An asterisk * indicates problems with a higher level of difficulty.*

Firms' Disclosure of Financial Information

1. What four financial statements can be found in a firm's 10-K filing? What checks are there on the accuracy of these statements?

2. What is GAAP and who oversees it?

3. Confirm that you can find the most recent financial statements for Starbucks Corporation (SBUX) using the following sources:
   a. From the company's Web page. (*Hint*: Search their Web site for "investor relations.")
   b. From the SEC Web site (www.sec.gov). (*Hint*: Search for company filings in the EDGAR database.)
   c. From the Yahoo! Finance Web site (finance.yahoo.com).
   d. From at least one other source. (*Hint*: Enter "SBUX 10K" at www.bing.com.)

The Balance Sheet

4. Consider the following potential events that might have occurred to Global on December 30, 2016. For each one, indicate which line items in Global's balance sheet would be affected and by how much. Also indicate the change to Global's book value of equity.
   a. Global used $20 million of its available cash to repay $20 million of its long-term debt.
   b. A warehouse fire destroyed $5 million worth of uninsured inventory.
   c. Global used $5 million in cash and $5 million in new long-term debt to purchase a $10 million building.
   d. A large customer owing $3 million for products it already received declared bankruptcy, leaving no possibility that Global would ever receive payment.
   e. Global's engineers discover a new manufacturing process that will cut the cost of its flagship product by more than 50%.
   f. A key competitor announces a radical new pricing policy that will drastically undercut Global's prices.

5. What was the change in Global's book value of equity from 2015 to 2016 according to Table 2.1? Does this imply that the market price of Global's shares increased in 2016? Explain.

6. Use EDGAR (www.sec.gov) to find Qualcomm's 10K filing for 2014. From the balance sheet, answer the following questions:
   a. How much did Qualcomm have in cash and short-term investments?
   b. What were Qualcomm's total accounts receivable?
   c. What were Qualcomm's total assets?
   d. What were Qualcomm's total liabilities? How much of this was long-term debt?
   e. What was the book value of Qualcomm's equity?

7. Find the annual 10-K report for Costco Wholesale Corporation (COST) for fiscal year 2015 (filed in October 2015). Answer the following questions from its balance sheet:
   a. How much cash did Costco have?
   b. What were Costco's total assets?
   c. What were Costco's total liabilities? How much debt did Costco have?
   d. What was the book value of Costco equity?

Income Statement

8. Find online the annual 10-K report for Costco Wholesale Corporation (COST) for fiscal year 2015 (filed in October 2015). Answer the following questions from the income statement:
   a. What were Costco revenues for 2015? By what percentage did revenues grow from the prior year?
   b. What were Costco operating and net profit margins in 2015? How do they compare with its margins in the prior year?
   c. What were Costco diluted earnings per share in 2015? What number of shares is this EPS based on?

TABLE 2.5

2012–2016 Financial Statement Data and Stock Price Data for Mydeco Corp.

Mydeco Corp. 2012–2016	(All data as of fiscal year end; $ in millions)				
Income Statement	**2012**	**2013**	**2014**	**2015**	**2016**
Revenue	404.3	363.8	424.6	510.7	604.1
Cost of Goods Sold	(188.3)	(173.8)	(206.2)	(246.8)	(293.4)
Gross Profit	215.9	190.0	218.3	263.9	310.7
Sales and Marketing	(66.7)	(66.4)	(82.8)	(102.1)	(120.8)
Administration	(60.6)	(59.1)	(59.4)	(66.4)	(78.5)
Depreciation & Amortization	(27.3)	(27.0)	(34.3)	(38.4)	(38.6)
EBIT	61.3	37.4	41.8	57.0	72.8
Interest Income (Expense)	(33.7)	(32.9)	(32.2)	(37.4)	(39.4)
Pretax Income	27.7	4.5	9.6	19.6	33.4
Income Tax	(9.7)	(1.6)	(3.4)	(6.9)	(11.7)
Net Income	18.0	2.9	6.2	12.7	21.7
Shares Outstanding (millions)	55.0	55.0	55.0	55.0	55.0
Earnings per Share	$0.33	$0.05	$0.11	$0.23	$0.39
Balance Sheet	**2012**	**2013**	**2014**	**2015**	**2016**
Assets					
Cash	48.8	68.8	86.2	77.4	84.9
Accounts Receivable	88.6	69.8	69.8	76.9	86.1
Inventory	33.7	30.9	28.4	31.7	35.3
Total Current Assets	171.1	169.4	184.4	186.1	206.3
Net Property, Plant, & Equipment	245.3	243.2	308.9	345.5	347.0
Goodwill & Intangibles	361.7	361.7	361.7	361.7	361.7
Total Assets	778.1	774.3	855.0	893.3	914.9

(Continued)

Mydeco Corp. 2012–2016		(All data as of fiscal year end; $ in millions)			
Balance Sheet (continued)	**2012**	**2013**	**2014**	**2015**	**2016**
Liabilities & Stockholders' Equity					
Accounts Payable	18.7	17.9	22.0	26.8	31.7
Accrued Compensation	6.7	6.4	7.0	8.1	9.7
Total Current Liabilities	25.5	24.2	29.0	34.9	41.4
Long-Term Debt	500.0	500.0	575.0	600.0	600.0
Total Liabilities	525.5	524.2	604.0	634.9	641.4
Stockholders' Equity	252.6	250.1	251.0	258.3	273.5
Total Liabilities & Stockholders' Equity	778.1	774.3	855.0	893.3	914.9
Statement of Cash Flows	**2012**	**2013**	**2014**	**2015**	**2016**
Net Income	18.0	2.9	6.2	12.7	21.7
Depreciation & Amortization	27.3	27.0	34.3	38.4	38.6
Change in Accounts Receivable	3.9	18.8	(0.0)	(7.2)	(9.1)
Change in Inventory	(2.9)	2.9	2.5	(3.3)	(3.6)
Change in Payables & Accrued Compensation	2.2	(1.3)	4.8	5.9	6.5
Cash from Operations	48.4	50.4	47.8	46.6	54.0
Capital Expenditures	(25.0)	(25.0)	(100.0)	(75.0)	(40.0)
Cash from Investing Activities	(25.0)	(25.0)	(100.0)	(75.0)	(40.0)
Dividends Paid	(5.4)	(5.4)	(5.4)	(5.4)	(6.5)
Sale (or Purchase) of Stock	—	—	—	—	—
Debt Issuance (Pay Down)	—	—	75.0	25.0	—
Cash from Financing Activities	(5.4)	(5.4)	69.6	19.6	(6.5)
Change in Cash	18.0	20.0	17.4	(8.8)	7.5
Mydeco Stock Price	$7.90	$3.29	$5.23	$8.70	$10.87

9. See Table 2.5 showing financial statement data and stock price data for Mydeco Corp.
a. By what percentage did Mydeco's revenues grow each year from 2013–2016?
b. By what percentage did net income grow each year?
c. Why might the growth rates of revenues and net income differ?

10. See Table 2.5 showing financial statement data and stock price data for Mydeco Corp. Suppose Mydeco repurchases 2 million shares each year from 2013–2016. What would its earnings per share be in 2016?

11. See Table 2.5 showing financial statement data and stock price data for Mydeco Corp. Suppose Mydeco had purchased additional equipment for $12 million at the end of 2013, and this equipment was depreciated by $4 million per year in 2014, 2015, and 2016. Given Mydeco's tax rate of 35%, what impact would this additional purchase have had on Mydeco's net income in years 2013–2016?

12. See Table 2.5 showing financial statement data and stock price data for Mydeco Corp. Suppose Mydeco's costs and expenses had been the same fraction of revenues in 2013–2016 as they were in 2012. What would Mydeco's EPS have been each year in this case?

13. Suppose a firm's tax rate is 35%.
    a. What effect would a $10 million operating expense have on this year's earnings? What effect would it have on next year's earnings?
    b. What effect would a $10 million capital expense have on this year's earnings if the capital is depreciated at a rate of $2 million per year for five years? What effect would it have on next year's earnings?

*14. Quisco Systems has 6.5 billion shares outstanding and a share price of $18. Quisco is considering developing a new networking product in house at a cost of $500 million. Alternatively, Quisco can acquire a firm that already has the technology for $900 million worth (at the current price) of Quisco stock. Suppose that absent the expense of the new technology, Quisco will have EPS of $0.80.
    a. Suppose Quisco develops the product in house. What impact would the development cost have on Quisco's EPS? Assume all costs are incurred this year and are treated as an R&D expense, Quisco's tax rate is 35%, and the number of shares outstanding is unchanged.
    b. Suppose Quisco does not develop the product in house but instead acquires the technology. What effect would the acquisition have on Quisco's EPS this year? (Note that acquisition expenses do not appear directly on the income statement. Assume the firm was acquired at the start of the year and has no revenues or expenses of its own, so that the only effect on EPS is due to the change in the number of shares outstanding.)
    c. Which method of acquiring the technology has a smaller impact on earnings? Is this method cheaper? Explain.

The Statement of Cash Flows

15. Find online the annual 10-K report for Costco Wholesale Corporation (COST) for fiscal year 2015 (filed in October 2015). Answer the following questions from its cash flow statement:
    a. How much cash did Costco generate from operating activities in 2015?
    b. What was Costco depreciation expense in 2015?
    c. How much cash was invested in new property and equipment (net of any sales) in 2015?
    d. How much did Costco raise from the sale of shares of its stock (net of any purchases) in 2015?

16. See the cash flow statement below (all values in thousands of dollars) (*see* MyFinanceLab *for the data in Excel format*):
    a. What were the company's cumulative earnings over these four quarters? What were its cumulative cash flows from operating activities?

Quarter	4	3	2	1
Net income	276,710	228,964	194,062	218,532
Operating Activities, Cash Flows Provided by or Used in				
Depreciation	69,997	75,733	74,570	73,173
Adjustments to net income	14,359	(13,142)	48,826	(47,993)
Changes in accounts receivable	(38,869)	(53,218)	100,732	(84,711)
Changes in liabilities	82,816	(111,577)	201,725	39,949
Changes in inventories	(195,186)	(114,121)	85,028	57,681
Changes in other operating activities	17,675	(26,574)	12,692	(2,097)

(*Continued*)

Quarter	4	3	2	1
Total Cash Flow from Operating Activities	227,502	(13,935)	717,635	254,534
Investing Activities, Cash Flows Provided by or Used in				
Capital expenditures	(82,584)	(41,634)	(100,109)	(69,170)
Investments	(5,465)	5,465	(93,153)	(48,330)
Other cash flows from investing activities	(108,903)	732	(58,069)	20,652
Total Cash Flows from Investing Activities	(196,952)	(35,437)	(251,331)	(96,848)
Financing Activities, Cash Flows Provided by or Used in				
Dividends paid	(131,483)	(131,333)	(119,452)	(121,404)
Sale purchase of stock	78,774	1,210	(76,807)	(79,288)
Net borrowings	515,709	114,766	(283,696)	64,885
Other cash flows from financing activities	(282)	2,000	(46,234)	39,763
Total Cash Flows from Financing Activities	462,718	(13,357)	(526,189)	(96,044)
Effect of exchange rate changes	(119,960)	(610)	32,807	6,890
Change in Cash and Cash Equivalents	$373,308	(63,339)	(27,078)	$68,532

    b. What fraction of the cash from operating activities was used for investment over the four quarters?

    c. What fraction of the cash from operating activities was used for financing activities over the four quarters?

17. Suppose your firm receives a $5 million order on the last day of the year. You fill the order with $2 million worth of inventory. The customer picks up the entire order the same day and pays $1 million up front in cash; you also issue a bill for the customer to pay the remaining balance of $4 million within 40 days. Suppose your firm's tax rate is 0% (i.e., ignore taxes). Determine the consequences of this transaction for each of the following:

    a. Revenues

    b. Earnings

    c. Receivables

    d. Inventory

    e. Cash

18. Nokela Industries purchases a $40 million cyclo-converter. The cyclo-converter will be depreciated by $10 million per year over four years, starting this year. Suppose Nokela's tax rate is 40%.

    a. What impact will the cost of the purchase have on earnings for each of the next four years?

    b. What impact will the cost of the purchase have on the firm's cash flow for the next four years?

Financial Statement Analysis

19. In December 2015, General Electric (GE) had a book value of equity of $98 billion, 9.4 billion shares outstanding, and a market price of $31 per share. GE also had cash of $102 billion, and total debt of $199 billion.
    a. What was GE's market capitalization? What was GE's market-to-book ratio?
    b. What was GE's book debt-equity ratio? What was GE's market debt-equity ratio?
    c. What was GE's enterprise value?

20. In December 2015, Apple had cash of $38.07 billion, current assets of $76.22 billion, and current liabilities of $76.09 billion. It also had inventories of $2.45 billion.
    a. What was Apple's current ratio?
    b. What was Apple's quick ratio?
    c. In January 2016, Hewlett-Packard had a quick ratio of 0.66 and a current ratio of 0.90. What can you say about the asset liquidity of Apple relative to Hewlett-Packard?

21. In early-2016, the following information was true about Abercrombie and Fitch (ANF) and The Gap (GPS), both clothing retailers. Values (except price per share) are in millions of dollars.

	Book Equity	Price per Share	Number of Shares (millions)
ANF	1,291	26.35	67.59
GPS	2,545	24.74	397.14

    a. What is the market-to-book ratio of each company?
    b. What conclusions do you draw from comparing the two ratios?

22. In fiscal year 2015, Walmart Stores. (WMT) had revenue of $485.65 billion, gross profit of $120.57 billion, and net income of $16.36 billion. Costco Wholesale Corporation (COST) had revenue of $116.20 billion, gross profit of $15.13 billion, and net income of $2.38 billion.
    a. Compare the gross margins for Walmart and Costco.
    b. Compare the net profit margins for Walmart and Costco.
    c. Which firm was more profitable in 2015?

23. Local Co. has sales of $10 million and cost of sales of $6 million. Its selling, general, and administrative expenses are $500,000 and its research and development is $1 million. It has annual depreciation charges of $1 million and a tax rate of 35%.
    a. What is Local's gross margin?
    b. What is Local's operating margin?
    c. What is Local's net profit margin?

24. If Local Co., the company in Problem 23, had an increase in selling expenses of $300,000, how would that affect each of its margins?

25. If Local Co., the company in Problem 23, had interest expense of $800,000, how would that affect each of its margins?

26. Chutes & Co. has interest expense of $1 million and an operating margin of 10% on total sales of $30 million. What is Chutes' interest coverage ratio?

27. Ladders, Inc. has a net profit margin of 5% on sales of $50 million. It has book value of equity of $40 million and total liabilities with a book value of $30 million. What is Ladders' ROE? ROA?

28. JPJ Corp has sales of $1 million, accounts receivable of $50,000, total assets of $5 million (of which $3 million are fixed assets), inventory of $150,000, and cost of goods sold of $600,000. What is JPJ's accounts receivable days? Fixed asset turnover? Total asset turnover? Inventory turnover?

 29. If JPJ Corp (the company in Problem 28) is able to increase sales by 10% but keep its total and fixed asset growth to only 5%, what will its new asset turnover ratios be?

 *30. Suppose that in 2016, Global launched an aggressive marketing campaign that boosted sales by 15%. However, their operating margin fell from 5.57% to 4.50%. Suppose that they had no other income, interest expenses were unchanged, and taxes were the same percentage of pretax income as in 2015.
   a. What was Global's EBIT in 2016?
   b. What was Global's income in 2016?
   c. If Global's P/E ratio and number of shares outstanding remained unchanged, what was Global's share price in 2016?

 31. You are analyzing the leverage of two firms and you note the following (all values in millions of dollars):

	Debt	Book Equity	Market Equity	Operating Income	Interest Expense
Firm A	500	300	400	100	50
Firm B	80	35	40	8	7

   a. What is the market debt-to-equity ratio of each firm?
   b. What is the book debt-to-equity ratio of each firm?
   c. What is the interest coverage ratio of each firm?
   d. Which firm will have more difficulty meeting its debt obligations?

 32. For 2015, Walmart and Target had the following information (all values are in millions of dollars):

	Sales (Income Statement)	Cost of Goods Sold (Income Statement)	Accounts Receivable (Balance Sheet)	Inventory (Balance Sheet)
Walmart	482,130	360,984	5,624	44,469
Target	73,785	51,997	779	8,601

   a. What is each company's accounts receivable days?
   b. What is each company's inventory turnover?
   c. Which company is managing its accounts receivable and inventory more efficiently?

 33. In January 2016, United Airlines (UAL) had a market capitalization of $20.6 billion, debt of $11.9 billion, and cash of $5.2 billion. United Airlines had revenues of $37.9 billion. Southwest Airlines (LUV) had a market capitalization of $27.5 billion, debt of $3.2 billion, cash of $3.0 billion, and revenues of $19.8 billion.
   a. Compare the market capitalization-to-revenue ratio (also called the price-to-sales ratio) for United Airlines and Southwest Airlines.
   b. Compare the enterprise value-to-revenue ratio for United Airlines and Southwest Airlines.
   c. Which of these comparisons is more meaningful? Explain.

34. Consider a retail firm with a net profit margin of 3.5%, a total asset turnover of 1.8, total assets of $44 million, and a book value of equity of $18 million.
    a. What is the firm's current ROE?
    b. If the firm increased its net profit margin to 4%, what would its ROE be?
    c. If, in addition, the firm increased its revenues by 20% (while maintaining this higher profit margin and without changing its assets or liabilities), what would its ROE be?

*35. Find online the annual 10-K report for Costco Wholesale Corporation (COST) for fiscal year 2015 (filed in October 2015).
    a. Compute Costco's net profit margin, total asset turnover, and equity multiplier.
    b. Verify the DuPont Identity for Costco ROE.
    c. If Costco managers wanted to increase its ROE by 1 percentage point, how much higher would their asset turnover need to be?

36. Repeat the analysis from parts a and b in Problem 35 using Walmart Stores (WMT) instead. Specifically, use Walmart's 2015 fiscal data, filed in October 2015. Based on the DuPont Identity, what explains the difference between the two firms' ROEs?

Other Financial Statement Information

37. Some balance sheet information is shown here (all values in millions of dollars) (*see* MyFinanceLab *for the data in Excel format*):

Balance Sheet: Assets	31-Mar-16	31-Dec-15	30-Sep-15	30-Jun-15
Assets				
Current Assets				
Cash and cash equivalents	293	300	255	232
Net receivables	401	362	385	460
Inventory	374	342	437	306
Other current assets	60	43	53	45
Total Current Assets	1,128	1,047	1,130	1,043
Long-term investments	128	97	—	200
Property, plant, and equipment	979	991	995	1,052
Goodwill	744	748	736	742
Other assets	777	827	911	797
Total Assets	3,756	3,710	3,772	3,834
Liabilities				
Current Liabilities				
Accounts payable	876	1,467	922	980
Short/current long-term debt	410	2	173	288
Other current liabilities	—	—	—	—
Total Current Liabilities	1,286	1,469	1,095	1,268
Long-term debt	2,381	2,124	474	475
Other liabilities	435	574	559	551
Total Liabilities	4,102	4,167	2,128	2,294
Total Stockholder Equity	−346	−457	1,644	1,540
Total Liabilities and Stockholder Equity	$3,756	$3,710	$3,772	$3,834

a. What change in the book value of the company's equity took place at the end of 2015?

b. Is the company's market-to-book ratio meaningful? Is its book debt-equity ratio meaningful? Explain.

c. Find the company's other financial statements from that time online. What was the cause of the change to its book value of equity at the end of 2015?

d. Does the company's book value of equity in 2016 imply that it is unprofitable? Explain.

Financial Reporting in Practice

38. Find online the annual 10-K report for Costco Wholesale Corporation (COST) for fiscal year 2015 (filed in October 2015).

a. Which auditing firm certified the financial statements?

b. Which officers of Costco certified the financial statements?

DATA CASE

This is your second interview with a prestigious brokerage firm for a job as an equity analyst. You survived the morning interviews with the department manager and the vice president of equity. Everything has gone so well that they want to test your ability as an analyst. You are seated in a room with a computer and a list with the names of two companies—Ford (F) and Microsoft (MSFT). You have 90 minutes to complete the following tasks:

1. Download the annual income statements, balance sheets, and cash flow statements for the last four fiscal years from Morningstar (www.morningstar.com). Enter each company's stock symbol and then go to "financials." Copy and paste the financial statements into Excel.

2. Find historical stock prices for each firm from Yahoo! Finance (finance.yahoo.com). Enter the stock symbol, click "Historical Prices" in the left column, and enter the proper date range to cover the last day of the month corresponding to the date of each financial statement. Use the closing stock prices (not the adjusted close). To calculate the firm's market capitalization at each date, multiply the number of shares outstanding by the firm's historic stock price. You can find the number of shares by using "Basic" under "Weighted average shares outstanding" at the bottom of the Income Statement.

3. For each of the four years of statements, compute the following ratios for each firm:

   Valuation Ratios
   Price-earnings ratio (for EPS use diluted EPS total)
   Market-to-book ratio
   Enterprise value-to-EBITDA
   (For debt, include long-term and short-term debt; for cash, include marketable securities.)

   Profitability Ratios
   Operating margin
   Net profit margin
   Return on equity

   Financial Strength Ratios
   Current ratio
   Book debt–equity ratio
   Market debt–equity ratio
   Interest coverage ratio (EBIT ÷ interest expense)

4. Obtain industry averages for each firm from Reuters (www.reuters.com/finance/stocks). Enter the stock symbol at the top of the page in the "Symbol lookup" and then click the "Financials" button, and then click "Search."

   a. Scroll down to "Valuation Ratios," and compare each firm's ratios to the available industry ratios for the most recent year. (Ignore the "Company" column as your calculations will be different.)

   b. Analyze the performance of each firm versus the industry and comment on any trends in each individual firm's performance. Identify any strengths or weaknesses you find in each firm.

5. Examine the market-to-book ratios you calculated for each firm. Which, if either, of the two firms can be considered "growth firms" and which, if either, can be considered "value firms"?

6. Compare the valuation ratios across the two firms. How do you interpret the difference between them?

7. Consider the enterprise value of both firms for each of the four years. How have the values of both firms changed over the time period?

8

Investment Decision Rules

LEARNING OBJECTIVES

- Calculate Net Present Value

- Use the NPV rule to make investment decisions

- Understand alternative decision rules and their drawbacks

- Choose between mutually exclusive alternatives

- Evaluate projects with different lives

- Rank projects when a company's resources are limited so that it cannot take all positive-NPV projects

notation

CF_n	cash flow that arrives at date n
g	growth rate
IRR	internal rate of return
$MIRR$	modified internal rate of return

NPV	net present value
PV	present value
r	discount rate

Managers are constantly faced with major investment decisions. In 2007, Apple decided to introduce its first mobile phone. In 2013, Microsoft tried to jumpstart its own phone business with a $7 billion acquisition of Nokia's phone unit. Amazon.com entered the mobile phone business in 2014 and exited it in 2015. That same year, Tesla started offering a mid-market sedan for pre-sale, priced at less than half of its popular premium S-series. Amazon.com decided to start flying its own cargo planes, leasing 20 Boeing 767 freighters in 2016. How did Apple, Microsoft, Amazon, and Tesla managers decide to commit substantial capital to these initiatives? In this chapter, we focus on the decision-making tools managers use to evaluate investment decisions. Examples of these decisions include new products, equipment purchases, and marketing campaigns.

We begin by introducing the *net present value (NPV) rule.* Although the NPV investment rule maximizes the value of the firm, some firms nevertheless use other techniques to evaluate investments and decide which projects to pursue. As a result, it is important to understand those techniques, so we will explain some commonly used alternative techniques—namely, the *payback rule* and the *internal rate of return (IRR) rule.* In each case, we define the decision rule and compare decisions based on this rule to decisions based on the NPV rule. We also illustrate the circumstances in which each of the alternative rules is likely to lead to bad investment decisions.

After establishing these rules in the context of a single, stand-alone project, we broaden our perspective to include evaluating multiple opportunities to select the best one. We conclude with a look at project selection when the firm faces limits on capital or managers' time.

8.1 The NPV Decision Rule

In the previous chapters, we learned how to convert between cash today and cash in the future using the discount rate. As long as we convert costs and benefits to the same point in time, we can use the Valuation Principle to make a decision. In practice, most corporations prefer to measure values in terms of their present value—that is, in terms of cash today. In this section, we apply the Valuation Principle to derive the concept of the *net present value* or *NPV*, which we can use to define the "golden rule" of financial decision making, the *NPV rule*.

Net Present Value

When the value of a cost or benefit is computed in terms of cash today, we refer to it as the present value (PV). Similarly, we define the **net present value (NPV)** of a project or investment as the difference between the present value of its benefits and the present value of its costs:

net present value (NPV)
The difference between the present value of a project's or investment's benefits and the present value of its costs.

Net Present Value

$$NPV = PV(\text{Benefits}) - PV(\text{Costs}) \tag{8.1}$$

Let's consider a simple example. Suppose your firm is offered the following investment opportunity: In exchange for $500 today, you will receive $550 in one year. If the interest rate is 8% per year, then:

$$PV(\text{Benefit}) = (\$550 \text{ in one year}) \div (\$1.08 \text{ in one year}/\$1 \text{ today})$$

$$= \$509.26 \text{ today}$$

This PV is the amount you would need to put in the bank today to generate $550 in one year ($509.26 × 1.08 = $550). In other words, *the present value is the amount you need to invest at the current interest rate to recreate the cash flow.* We can think of this as the cash cost today of generating the cash flow ourselves.

Once the costs and benefits are in present value terms, we can compare them by computing the investment's NPV:

$$NPV = \$509.26 - \$500 = \$9.26 \text{ today}$$

The NPV is positive, so the benefits outweigh the costs, which means the firm should undertake this investment opportunity.

But what if you don't have the $500 needed to cover the initial cost of the project? Does the project still have the same value? Because we computed the value using competitive market prices, it should not depend on your tastes or the amount of cash you have in the bank. If you don't have the $500, suppose you borrow $509.26 from the bank at the 8% interest rate and then take the project. What are your cash flows in this case?

Today: $509.26 (loan) − $500 (invested in the project) = $9.26

In one year: $550 (from project) − $509.26 × 1.08 (loan balance) = $0

This transaction leaves you with exactly $9.26 extra cash in your pocket today and no future net obligations. So taking the project is similar to having an extra $9.26 in cash upfront. Thus, the NPV expresses the value of an investment decision as an amount of cash received today. *As long as the NPV is positive, the decision increases the value of the firm and is a good decision regardless of your current cash needs or preferences regarding when to spend the money.*

EXAMPLE 8.1

The NPV Is Equivalent to Cash Today

MyFinanceLab

PROBLEM

After saving $1500 by waiting tables, you are about to buy a 50-inch TV. You notice that the store is offering a "one year same as cash" deal. You can take the TV home today and pay nothing until one year from now, when you will owe the store the $1500 purchase price. If your savings account earns 5% per year, what is the NPV of this offer? Show that its NPV represents cash in your pocket.

SOLUTION

PLAN

You are getting something worth $1500 today (the TV) and in exchange will need to pay $1500 in one year. Think of it as getting back the $1500 you thought you would have to spend today to get the TV. We treat it as a positive cash flow.
Cash flows:

Today	In one year
+$1500	−$1500

The discount rate for calculating the present value of the payment in one year is your interest rate of 5%. You need to compare the present value of the cost ($1500 in one year) to the benefit today (a $1500 TV).

EXECUTE

$$NPV = +1500 - \frac{1500}{(1.05)} = 1500 - 1428.57 = \$71.43$$

You could take $1428.57 of the $1500 you had saved for the TV and put it in your savings account. With interest, in one year it would grow to $1428.57 × (1.05) = $1500, enough to pay the store. The extra $71.43 is money in your pocket to spend as you like (or put toward the speaker system for your new media room).

EVALUATE

By taking the delayed payment offer, we have extra net cash flows of $71.43 today. If we put $1428.57 in the bank, it will be just enough to offset our $1500 obligation in the future. Therefore, this offer is equivalent to receiving $71.43 today, without any future net obligations.

The NPV Decision Rule

As shown in Example 8.1, the Valuation Principle implies that we should undertake projects with a positive NPV because undertaking those projects increases wealth. That is, good projects are those for which the present value of the benefits exceeds the present value of the costs. As a result, the value of the firm increases and investors are wealthier. Projects with negative NPVs have costs that exceed their benefits. Accepting them is equivalent to losing money today.

NPV decision rule When choosing among investment alternatives, take the alternative with the highest NPV. Choosing this alternative is equivalent to receiving its NPV in cash today.

We capture this logic in the **NPV Decision Rule**:

When making an investment decision, take the alternative with the highest NPV. Choosing this alternative is equivalent to receiving its NPV in cash today.

Because NPV is expressed in terms of cash today, using the NPV decision rule is a simple way to apply the Valuation Principle. Decisions that increase wealth are superior to those that decrease wealth. We don't need to know anything about the investor's preferences to reach this conclusion. As long as we have correctly captured all the cash flows of a project and applied the appropriate discount rate, we can determine whether the project makes us wealthier. Being wealthier increases our options and makes us better off, whatever our preferences are.

A common way companies apply the NPV rule in financial practices is when deciding whether to accept or reject a project. Because rejecting the project generally has $NPV = 0$ (there are no new costs or benefits from not doing the project), the NPV decision rule implies that we should

- Accept positive-NPV projects; accepting them is equivalent to receiving their NPV in cash today, and
- Reject negative-NPV projects; accepting them would reduce the value of the firm, whereas rejecting them has no cost $(\text{NPV} = 0)$.

If the NPV is exactly zero, then you will neither gain nor lose by accepting the project instead of rejecting it, which also has an NPV of zero. It is not a bad project because it does not reduce the firm's value, but it does not add value to the firm either.

CONCEPT CHECK
1. What is the NPV decision rule? How is it related to the Valuation Principle?
2. Why doesn't the NPV decision rule depend on the investor's preferences?

8.2 Using the NPV Rule

We continue our discussion of investment decision rules by considering a take-it-or-leave-it decision about a single, stand-alone project. By undertaking this project, the firm does not constrain its ability to take other projects. In the case of a stand-alone project, the alternatives we are considering are to accept or reject a project. The NPV rule then implies that we should compare the project's NPV to zero (the NPV of rejecting the project and doing nothing). Thus, we should accept the project if its NPV is positive.[1]

Organizing the Cash Flows and Computing the NPV

Researchers at Fredrick's Feed and Farm have made a breakthrough. They believe they can produce a new, environmentally friendly fertilizer at a substantial cost saving over the company's existing line of fertilizer. The fertilizer will require a new plant that can be built immediately at a cost of $81.6 million. Financial managers estimate that the benefits of the new fertilizer will be $28 million per year, starting at the end of the first year and lasting for four years, as shown by the following timeline:

Year:	0	1	2	3	4
Cash flow (in millions):	−$81.60	+$28	+$28	+$28	+$28

Thus, the cash flows are an immediate $81.6 million outflow followed by an annuity inflow of $28 million per year for four years. Therefore, given a discount rate r, the NPV of this project is:

---

[1]Some prefer to state the rule that the project should be accepted if its NPV is non-negative. Since the firm should be indifferent at an NPV of exactly zero (you will neither gain nor lose by accepting the project instead of rejecting it), we prefer to state it this way. A zero NPV project is not a bad project because it does not reduce the firm's value, but it does not add value to the firm either.

$$NPV = -81.6 + \frac{28}{1+r} + \frac{28}{(1+r)^2} + \frac{28}{(1+r)^3} + \frac{28}{(1+r)^4} \tag{8.2}$$

We can also use the annuity formula from Chapter 4 to write the NPV as:

$$NPV = -81.6 + \frac{28}{r}\left(1 - \frac{1}{(1+r)^4}\right) \tag{8.3}$$

To apply the NPV rule, we need to know the cost of capital. The financial managers responsible for this project estimate a cost of capital of 10% per year. If we replace r in Eq. 8.2 or 8.3 with the project's cost of capital of 10%, we get an NPV of $7.2 million, which is positive. Recall that a net present value tells us the present value of the benefits (positive cash flows) net of the costs (negative cash flows) of the project. By putting everything into present values, it puts all the costs and benefits on an equal footing for comparison. In this case, the benefits outweigh the costs by $7.2 million in present value. The NPV investment rule indicates that by making the investment, Fredrick's will increase the value of the firm today by $7.2 million, so Fredrick's should undertake this project.

The NPV Profile

NPV profile A graph of a project's NPV over a range of discount rates.

The NPV of the project depends on its appropriate cost of capital. Often, there may be some uncertainty regarding the project's cost of capital. In that case, it is helpful to compute an **NPV profile**, which graphs the project's NPV over a range of discount rates. It is easiest to prepare the NPV profile using a spreadsheet such as Excel. We simply repeat our calculation of the NPV above using a range of different discount rates instead of only 10%. Figure 8.1 presents the NPV profile for Fredrick's project by plotting the NPV as a function of the discount rate, r.[2]

FIGURE 8.1

NPV of Fredrick's New Project

The graph in Panel (b) shows the NPV as a function of the discount rate based on the data in Panel (a). The NPV is positive, represented by the green-shaded area, only for discount rates that are less than 14%, the *internal rate of return (IRR)*. Given the cost of capital of 10%, the project has a positive NPV of $7.2 million. The red-shaded area indicates discount rates above the 14% IRR with negative NPVs.

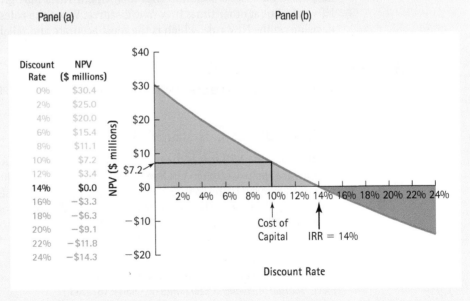

---

[2]In the online appendix to this chapter, we show you how to create an NPV profile in Excel. You can find this in the chapter resources section of MyFinanceLab.

internal rate of return (IRR) The interest rate that sets the net present value of the cash flows equal to zero.

Notice that the NPV is positive only for discount rates that are less than 14% (the green shaded area in Figure 8.1). Referring to the graph and the accompanying data table, we see that at 14% the NPV is zero. The discount rate that sets the net present value of the cash flows equal to zero is an investment's **internal rate of return (IRR)**. Thus, by constructing the NPV profile, we have determined that Fredrick's project has an IRR of 14%. We can also compute the IRR without graphing the NPV by using a financial calculator or a spreadsheet's IRR function (see the appendix to Chapter 4. The calculator instructions for solving for the rate of return can be used to solve for the IRR).

	N	I/Y	PV	PMT	FV
Given:	4		−81.6	28	0
Solve for:		14			
Excel Formula: =RATE(NPER,PMT,PV,FV)=RATE(4,28,−81.6,0)					

Measuring Sensitivity with IRR

In our Fredrick's example, the firm's managers provided the cost of capital. If you are unsure of your cost of capital estimate, it is important to determine how sensitive your analysis is to errors in this estimate. The IRR can provide this information. For Fredrick's, if the cost of capital estimate is more than the 14% IRR, the NPV will be negative (see the red shaded area in Figure 8.1). Therefore, as long as our estimate of the cost of capital of 10% is within 4% of the true cost of capital, our decision to accept the project is correct. In general, the difference between the cost of capital and the IRR tells us the amount of estimation error in the cost of capital estimate that can exist without altering the original decision.

Alternative Rules Versus the NPV Rule

The NPV rule indicates that Fredrick's should undertake the investment in fertilizer technology. As we evaluate alternative rules for project selection in the subsequent sections, keep in mind that sometimes other investment rules may give the same answer as the NPV rule, but at other times they may disagree. When the rules conflict, always base your decision on the NPV rule, which is the most accurate and reliable decision rule.

CONCEPT CHECK

3. Explain the NPV rule for stand-alone projects.

4. How can you interpret the difference between the cost of capital and the IRR?

8.3 Alternative Decision Rules

Even though the NPV rule is the most accurate and reliable rule, in practice a wide variety of rules are applied, often in tandem with the NPV rule. In a 2001 study, John Graham and Campbell Harvey[3] found that 75% of the firms they surveyed used the NPV rule for making investment decisions. This result is substantially different from that found in a similar study in 1977 by L. J. Gitman and J. R. Forrester,[4] who found that only 10% of firms used

---

[3]John Graham and Campbell Harvey, "The Theory and Practice of Corporate Finance: Evidence from the Field," *Journal of Financial Economics* 60 (2001): 187–243.

[4]L. J. Gitman and J. R. Forrester, Jr., "A Survey of Capital Budgeting Techniques Used by Major U.S. Firms," *Financial Management* 6 (1977): 66–71.

USING EXCEL

Computing NPV and IRR

Here we discuss how to use Microsoft Excel to solve for NPV and IRR. We also identify some pitfalls to avoid when using Excel.

NPV Function: Leaving Out Date 0

Excel's NPV function has the format *NPV (rate, value1, value2, . . .)*, where "rate" is the interest rate per period used to discount the cash flows, and "value1", "value2", etc., are the cash flows (or ranges of cash flows). The NPV function computes the present value of the cash flows *assuming the first cash flow occurs at date 1*. Therefore, if a project's first cash flow occurs at date 0, we cannot use the NPV function by itself to compute the NPV. We can use the NPV function to compute the present value of the cash flows from date 1 onward, and then we must add the date 0 cash flow to that result to calculate the NPV. The screenshot below shows the difference. The first NPV calculation (outlined in blue) is correct: we used the NPV function for all of the cash flows occurring at time 1 and later and then added on the first cash flow occurring at time 0 since it is already in present value. The second calculation (outlined in green) is incorrect: we used the NPV function for all of the cash flows, but the function assumed that the first cash flow occurs in period 1 instead of immediately.

NPV Function: Ignoring Blank Cells

Another pitfall with the NPV function is that cash flows that are left blank are treated differently from cash flows that are equal to zero. If the cash flow is left blank, *both the cash flow and the period are ignored*. For example, the second set of cash flows below is equivalent to the first—we have simply left the cash flow for date 2 blank instead of entering a "0." However, the NPV function ignores the blank cell at date 2 and assumes the cash flow is 10 at date 1 and 110 at date 2, which is clearly not what is intended and produces an incorrect answer (outlined in red).

Because of these idiosyncrasies, we avoid using Excel's NPV function. It is more reliable to compute the present value of each cash flow separately in Excel, and then sum them to determine the NPV.

IRR FUNCTION

Excel's IRR function has the format *IRR (values, guess)*, where "values" is the range containing the cash flows, and "guess" is an optional starting guess where Excel begins its search for an IRR. Two things to note about the IRR function:

1. The values given to the IRR function should include all of the cash flows of the project, including the one at date 0. In this sense, the IRR and NPV functions in Excel are inconsistent.

2. Like the NPV function, the IRR ignores the period associated with any blank cells.

FIGURE 8.2

The Most Popular
Decision Rules
Used by CFOs

The bar graph shows the most popular decision rules used by CFOs in Professors Graham and Harvey's 2001 survey. Many CFOs used more than one method, but no other methods were mentioned by more than half of CFOs.

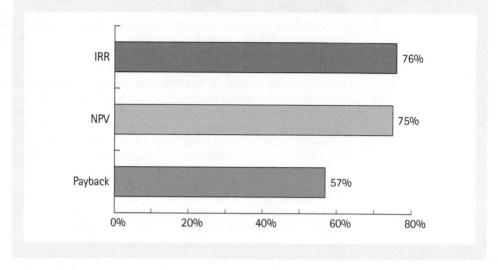

the NPV rule. Business students in recent years have been listening to their finance professors! Even so, Graham and Harvey's study indicates that one-fourth of U.S. corporations do not use the NPV rule. Exactly why other capital budgeting techniques are used in practice is not always clear. Figure 8.2 summarizes the top three decision rules given in the survey. Because you may encounter these techniques in the business world, you should know what they are, how they are used, and how they compare to NPV. In this section, we examine alternative decision rules for single, stand-alone projects within the firm. The focus here is on *the payback rule* and *the IRR rule*.

The Payback Rule

payback investment rule Only projects that pay back their initial investment within a prespecified period are undertaken.

The simplest investment rule is the **payback investment rule**, which states that you should only accept a project if its cash flows pay back its initial investment within a prespecified period. The rule is based on the notion that an opportunity that pays back its initial investment quickly is a good idea. To apply the payback rule,

payback period The amount of time until the cash flows from a project offset the initial investment. The time it takes to pay back the initial investment.

1. Calculate the amount of time it takes to pay back the initial investment, called the **payback period**.

2. Accept the project if the payback period is less than a prespecified length of time—usually a few years.

3. Reject the project if the payback period is greater than that prespecified length of time.

For example, a firm might adopt any project with a payback period of less than two years.

EXAMPLE 8.2

Using the
Payback Rule

MyFinanceLab

PROBLEM

Assume Fredrick's requires all projects to have a payback period of two years or less. Would the firm undertake the fertilizer project under this rule?

SOLUTION

PLAN

In order to implement the payback rule, we need to know whether the sum of the inflows from the project will exceed the initial investment before the end of two years. The project has inflows of $28 million per year and an initial investment of $81.6 million.

EXECUTE

The sum of the cash flows for years 1 and 2 is $28 $\times$ 2 = $56 million, which will not cover the initial investment of $81.6 million. In fact, it will not be until year 3 that the cash inflows exceed the initial investment ($28 $\times$ 3 = $84 million). Because the payback period for this project exceeds two years, Fredrick's will reject the project.

EVALUATE

While simple to compute, the payback rule requires us to use an arbitrary cutoff period in summing the cash flows. Furthermore, note that the payback rule does not discount future cash flows. Instead, it simply sums the cash flows and compares them to a cash outflow in the present. In this case, Fredrick's would have rejected a project that would have increased the value of the firm.

Relying on the payback rule analysis in Example 8.2, Fredrick's will reject the project. However, as we saw earlier, with a cost of capital of 10%, the NPV is $7.2 million. Following the payback rule would be a mistake because Fredrick's will pass up a project worth $7.2 million.

The payback rule is not as reliable as the NPV rule because it (1) ignores the time value of money, (2) ignores cash flows after the payback period, and (3) lacks a decision criterion grounded in economics (what is the right number of years to require for a payback period?). Some companies have addressed the first failing by computing the payback period using discounted cash flows, called the **discounted payback rule**. However, this does not solve the fundamental problem because the other two failings remain. Despite these failings, Graham and Harvey found that about 57% of the firms they surveyed reported using the payback rule as part of the decision-making process.

discounted payback rule Only accept projects where the sum of the discounted cash flows within the payback period is greater than or equal to the initial investment.

Why do some companies consider the payback rule? The answer probably relates to its simplicity. This rule is typically used for small investment decisions—for example, whether to purchase a new copy machine or to service the old one. In such cases, the cost of making an incorrect decision might not be large enough to justify the time required to calculate the NPV. The appeal of the payback rule is that it favors short-term projects. Some firms are unwilling to commit capital to long-term investments. Also, if the required payback period is short (one to two years), then most projects that satisfy the payback rule will have a positive NPV.

The Internal Rate of Return Rule

internal rate of return (IRR) investment rule A decision rule that accepts any investment opportunity where the IRR exceeds the opportunity cost of capital and otherwise rejects the opportunity.

Similar to NPV, the **internal rate of return (IRR) investment rule** is based on the concept that if the return on the investment opportunity you are considering is greater than the return on other alternatives in the market with equivalent risk and maturity (i.e., the project's cost of capital), you should undertake the investment opportunity. We state the rule formally as follows:

IRR investment rule: Take any investment opportunity whose IRR exceeds the opportunity cost of capital. Turn down any opportunity whose IRR is less than the opportunity cost of capital.

The IRR investment rule will give the correct answer (that is, the same answer as the NPV rule) in many—but not all—situations. For instance, it gives the correct answer for Fredrick's fertilizer opportunity. From Figure 8.1, whenever the cost of capital is in the green area below the IRR (14%), the project has a positive NPV and you should undertake the investment. Table 8.1 summarizes our analysis of Fredrick's new project. The NPV and IRR rules agree, but using the payback rule with a required payback period of two years or less would cause Fredrick's to reject the project.

TABLE 8.1

Summary of NPV, IRR, and Payback for Fredrick's New Project

NPV at 10%	$7.2 million	Accept ($7.2 million > 0)
Payback Period	3 years	Reject (3 years > 2 year required payback)
IRR	14%	Accept (14% > 10% cost of capital)

In general, the IRR rule works for a stand-alone project if all of the project's negative cash flows precede its positive cash flows. But in other cases, the IRR rule may disagree with the NPV rule and thus be incorrect. Let's examine several situations in which the IRR fails.

Delayed Investments. Star basketball player Evan Cole is graduating from college with a degree in finance and preparing for the NBA draft. Several companies have already approached him with endorsement contracts. Two competing sports drink companies are pursuing him. QuenchIt offers him a single up-front payment of $1 million to exclusively endorse their sports drink for three years. PowerUp offers $500,000 per year, payable at the end of each of the next three years, to endorse their product exclusively. Which offer is better? One direct way to compare the two contracts is to realize that signing with QuenchIt causes Evan to forgo the PowerUp contract, or $500,000 per year. Considering the risk of his alternative income sources and available investment opportunities, Evan estimates his opportunity cost of capital to be 10%. The timeline of Evan's investment opportunity is:

0	1	2	3
$1,000,000	−$500,000	−$500,000	−$500,000

The NPV of Evan's investment opportunity is:

$$NPV = 1,000,000 - \frac{500,000}{1+r} - \frac{500,000}{(1+r)^2} - \frac{500,000}{(1+r)^3}$$

By setting the NPV equal to zero and solving for r, we find the IRR. We can use either a financial calculator or a spreadsheet to find the IRR:

	N	I/Y	PV	PMT	FV
Given:	3		1,000,000	−500,000	0
Solve for:		23.38			
	Excel Formula: =RATE(NPER,PMT,PV,FV)=RATE(3,−500000,1000000,0)				

The 23.38% IRR is larger than the 10% opportunity cost of capital. According to the IRR rule, Evan should sign the deal. But what does the NPV rule say?

$$NPV = 1,000,000 - \frac{500,000}{1.1} - \frac{500,000}{1.1^2} - \frac{500,000}{1.1^3} = -\$243,426$$

At a 10% discount rate, the NPV is negative, so signing the deal would reduce Evan's wealth. He should not sign the endorsement deal with QuenchIt, and should sign with PowerUp instead.

To resolve this conflict, we can prepare an NPV profile for the QuenchIt contract. Figure 8.3 plots the NPV of the investment opportunity for a range of discount rates. It shows that, no matter what the cost of capital is, the IRR rule and the NPV rule will give exactly opposite recommendations. That is, the NPV is positive only when the opportunity cost of capital is *above* 23.38% (the IRR). Evan should accept the investment only when the opportunity cost of capital is greater than the IRR, the opposite of what the IRR rule recommends.

Figure 8.3 also illustrates the problem with using the IRR rule in this case. For most investment opportunities, expenses occur initially and cash is received later. In this case, Evan receives cash *upfront* from QuenchIt but the forgone cash flows from PowerUp occurred later. It is as if Evan borrowed money, and when you borrow money you prefer as *low* a rate as possible. Evan's optimal rule is to borrow money as long as the rate at which he borrows is *less* than the cost of capital.

Even though the IRR rule fails to give the correct answer in this case, the IRR itself still provides useful information *in conjunction* with the NPV rule. As mentioned earlier, the IRR provides information on how sensitive the investment decision is to uncertainty in the cost of capital estimate. In this case, the difference between the cost of capital and the IRR is large—10% versus 23.38%. Evan would have to have underestimated the cost of capital by 13.38% to make the NPV positive.

Multiple IRRs. Evan has informed QuenchIt that it needs to sweeten the deal before he will accept it. In response, the company has agreed to make an additional payment of $600,000 in 10 years as deferred compensation for the long-term increase in sales that

FIGURE 8.3

NPV of Evan Cole's $1 Million QuenchIt Deal

When all the benefits of an investment occur at time zero and before the costs, the NPV is an *increasing* function of the discount rate. The NPV is positive in the green-shaded areas and negative in the red-shaded areas. Notice that the NPV is positive when the cost of capital is above 23.38%, the IRR, so the NPV and IRR rules conflict.

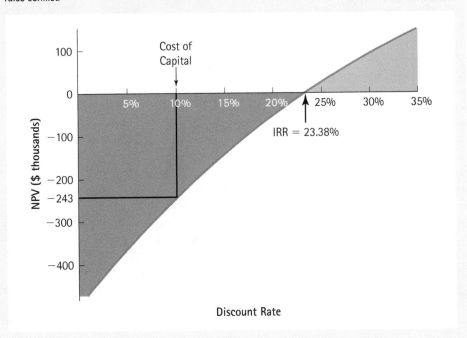

even a short-term endorsement by Evan would bring. Should he accept or reject the new offer?

We begin with the new timeline:

The NPV of Evan's new investment opportunity is:

$$NPV = 1,000,000 - \frac{500,000}{1+r} - \frac{500,000}{(1+r)^2} - \frac{500,000}{(1+r)^3} + \frac{600,000}{(1+r)^{10}}$$

We can find the IRR for this investment opportunity by creating an NPV profile and noting where it crosses zero. Figure 8.4 plots the NPV of the opportunity at different discount rates. In this case, there are *two* IRRs—that is, there are two values of r that set the NPV equal to zero. You can verify this fact by substituting IRRs of 5.79% and 13.80% for r into the equation. Because there is more than one IRR, we cannot apply the IRR rule. It is also worth noting that you should take special care when using a spreadsheet or financial calculator to determine the IRR. Both solve for the IRR through trial and error because you cannot calculate the IRR directly. In cases where there is more than one IRR, the spreadsheet or calculator will simply produce the first one that it finds, with no indication that there could be others! Some financial calculators will return an error message if there are multiple IRRs. Thus, it always pays to create the NPV profile.

For guidance, let's turn to the NPV rule. If the cost of capital were *either* below 5.79% or above 13.80%, Evan should undertake the opportunity. But given his cost of capital of 10%, he should still turn it down. Notice that even though the IRR rule fails in this case,

FIGURE 8.4

NPV of Evan's Sports Drink Deal with Additional Deferred Payments

The graph in Panel (b) shows the NPV of Evan's deal with additional deferred payment based on the data in Panel (a). In this case, there are two IRRs, invalidating the IRR rule. If the opportunity cost of capital is *either* below 5.79% or above 13.80%, Evan should accept the deal because the NPV is then positive, as indicated by the green-shaded areas. At any point between the two IRRs, the NPV is negative (see the red-shaded area).

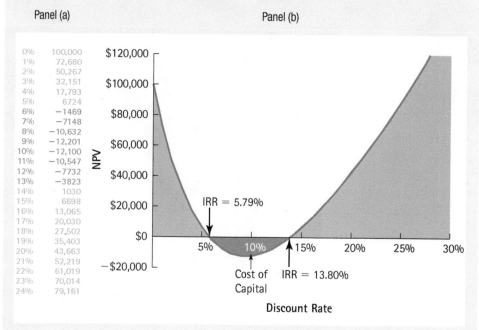

IRR Versus the IRR Rule

Throughout this subsection, we have distinguished between the IRR itself and the IRR rule. While we have pointed out the shortcomings of using the IRR rule to make investment decisions, *the IRR*

itself remains a very useful tool. The IRR measures the average return of the investment and indicates the sensitivity of the NPV to estimation error in the cost of capital. Thus, knowing the IRR can be very useful, but relying on it to make investment decisions can be hazardous.

the two IRRs are still useful as bounds on the cost of capital estimate. If the cost of capital estimate is wrong, and it is actually smaller than 5.79% or larger than 13.80%, the decision not to pursue the project will change because it will have a positive NPV.

There is no easy fix for the IRR rule when there are multiple IRRs. Although the NPV is negative between the IRRs in this example, the reverse is also possible (see Figure 8.5). In that case, the project would have a positive NPV for discount rates between the IRRs rather than for discount rates lower or higher than the IRRs. Furthermore, there are situations in which more than two IRRs exist.[5] In such situations, our only choice is to rely on the NPV rule.

modified internal rate of return (MIRR) The discount rate that sets the NPV of modified cash flows of a project equal to zero. Cash flows are modified so there is only one negative cash flow (and one sign change) to ensure that only one IRR exists.

Modified Internal Rate of Return

The fact that there can be multiple IRRs for the cash flows from a project is a clear disadvantage for the IRR. To overcome this, some have proposed various ways of modifying the cash flows before computing the IRR. All these modifications have the common feature that they group the cash flows so that there is only one negative cash flow, occurring at either the beginning or the end. In that case, there is only one sign change for the cash flows as a whole and hence only one IRR. This new IRR, computed as the discount rate that sets the NPV of the modified cash flows of the project equal to zero, is called the **modified internal rate of return (MIRR)**.

FIGURE 8.5

NPV Profile for a Project with Multiple IRRs

The graph shows the NPV profile for a multiple-IRR project with cash flows of −$1000, $2500, and −$1540 in years 0, 1, and 2, respectively. As the NPV profile shows, the project has two IRRs: 10% and 40%.

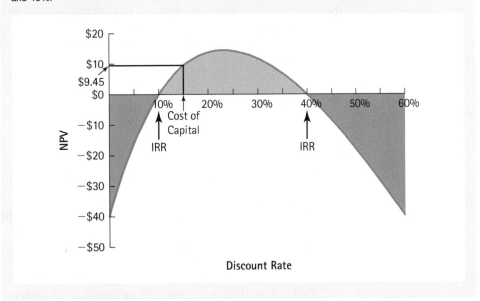

[5]In general, there can be as many IRRs as the number of times the project's cash flows change sign over time.

Why Do Rules Other Than the NPV Rule Persist?

Professors Graham and Harvey found that a sizable minority of firms (25%) in their study do not use the NPV rule at all. In addition, about 50% of firms surveyed used the payback rule. Furthermore, it appears that most firms use *both* the NPV rule and the IRR rule. Why do firms use rules other than NPV if they can lead to erroneous decisions?

One possible explanation for this phenomenon is that Graham and Harvey's survey results might be misleading. CFOs who were using the IRR as a sensitivity measure in conjunction with the NPV rule might have checked both the IRR box and the NPV box on the survey. The question they were asked was, "How frequently does your firm use the following techniques when deciding which projects or acquisitions to pursue?" By computing the IRR and using it in conjunction with the NPV rule to estimate the sensitivity of their results, they might have felt they were using *both* techniques.

Nevertheless, a significant minority of managers surveyed replied that they used only the IRR rule, so this explanation cannot be the whole story.

One common reason that managers give for using the IRR rule exclusively is that you do not need to know the opportunity cost of capital to calculate the IRR. On a superficial level, this is true: The IRR does not depend on the cost of capital. You may not need to know the cost of capital to *calculate* the IRR, but you certainly need to know the cost of capital when you *apply* the IRR rule. Consequently, the opportunity cost is as important to the IRR rule as it is to the NPV rule.

Nonetheless, part of the appeal of the IRR rule is that the IRR seems to sum up the attractiveness of an investment without requiring an assumption about the cost of capital. However, a more useful summary is the project's NPV profile, showing the NPV as a function of the discount rate. The NPV profile also does not require knowing the cost of capital, but it has the distinct advantage of being much more informative and reliable.

MIRR Technique. Let's clarify this with an example. You are considering a project that has the following three cash flows:

The NPV profile for this project, shown in Figure 8.5, identifies the two IRRs for this project as 10% and 40%.

Assume that your discount rate for this project is 15%. As Figure 8.5 shows, the NPV of the project at 15% is $9.45. We could modify the cash flows of the project to eliminate the multiple IRR problem. By discounting all of the negative cash flows to the present and compounding all of the positive cash flows to the end of the project, we have only two cash flows, yielding a single IRR. What discount rate and compounding rate should we use? One natural choice is our cost of capital for this project, which is 15%.

Figure 8.6 presents the NPV profile for our modified cash flows. As Figure 8.6 shows, there is now only a single IRR, at 15.25%. Because our cost of capital is 15%, we would properly accept the project using the IRR rule. Also note that the advantage of using 15% as our discount and compounding rates when modifying the cash flows is that the NPV of the modified cash flows at 15% is the same as the NPV of the true cash flows at 15%. Figure 8.6 also makes an important point: We are no longer evaluating the true cash flows of the project. Instead, we have modified them to force them to produce a single IRR. The NPV profile of the true cash flows of the project is given earlier in Figure 8.5 and is clearly different from the one produced by the modified cash flows in Figure 8.6.

FIGURE 8.6

NPV Profile of Modified
Cash Flows for the
Multiple-IRR Project
from Figure 8.5

The graph presents the NPV profile for the modified project cash flows of −2164.46 in year 0 and 2875 in year 2. The modified cash flows have only one IRR: 15.25%. Given the 15% cost of capital, the IRR rule confirms that we should accept the project.

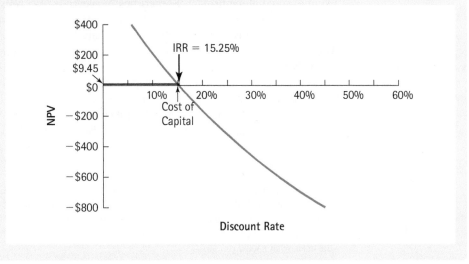

There is no set way to modify project cash flows to produce an MIRR. Two other approaches that each solve the multiple IRR problem are:

1. Discount all the negative cash flows to time 0 and leave the positive cash flows alone.

2. Leave the initial cash flow alone and compound all the remaining cash flows to the final period of the project. In this approach, you are implicitly reinvesting all the cash flows from the project at your compound rate until the project is complete.

Again, in either case, if you use the project's cost of capital as your discount and compounding rate, you will not alter the NPV of the project at that discount rate. Furthermore, a decision to accept or reject the project based on the modified IRR will be the same as the one based on the NPV decision rule.

MIRR: A Final Word. There is considerable debate about whether MIRR is actually better than IRR. Most of the argument centers on whether it is advisable to modify the cash flows of the project. The IRR is truly an internal rate of return based solely on the actual cash flows of the project. However, the IRR implicitly assumes that all cash flows generated by the project are reinvested at the project's IRR rather than at the firm's cost of capital until the project ends. For a project with a high IRR, this may be an unrealistic assumption. Furthermore, there may be more than one IRR, which complicates its use. The MIRR avoids these problems, but is based on a set of cash flows modified through the use of a chosen discount and compounding rate. Thus, it is not really an internal rate of return and is no longer based solely on the actual cash flows of the project. Finally, MIRR still does not solve some of the other problems associated with using IRR when choosing among projects.

CONCEPT CHECK

5. How do you apply the payback rule?

6. Under what conditions will the IRR rule lead to the same decision as the NPV rule?

8.4 Choosing Among Projects

Thus far, we have considered only decisions where the choice is either to accept or to reject a single, stand-alone project. Sometimes, however, a firm must choose just one project from among several possible projects. For example, a manager may be evaluating alternative package designs for a new product. The manager must choose only one of the designs. When choosing any one project excludes us from taking the other projects, we are facing **mutually exclusive projects**.

mutually exclusive projects Projects that compete with one another; by accepting one, you exclude the others.

When projects, such as the package designs, are mutually exclusive, it is not enough to determine which projects have positive NPVs. With mutually exclusive projects, the manager's goal is to rank the projects and choose the best one. In this situation, the NPV rule provides a straightforward answer: *Pick the project with the highest NPV.*

EXAMPLE 8.3
NPV and Mutually Exclusive Projects

MyFinanceLab

PROBLEM

You own a small piece of commercial land near a university. You are considering what to do with it. You have been approached with an offer to buy it for $220,000. You are also considering three alternative uses yourself: a bar, a coffee shop, and an apparel store. You assume that you would operate your choice indefinitely, eventually leaving the business to your children. You have collected the following information about the uses. What should you do?

	Initial Investment	Cash Flow in the First Year (CF_1)	Growth Rate (g)	Cost of Capital (r)
Bar	$400,000	$60,000	3.5%	12%
Coffee Shop	$200,000	$40,000	3%	10%
Apparel Store	$500,000	$75,000	3%	13%

SOLUTION

PLAN

Since you can develop only one project (you only have one piece of land), these are mutually exclusive projects. In order to decide which project is most valuable, you need to rank them by NPV. Each of these projects (except for selling the land) has cash flows that can be valued as a growing perpetuity, so from Chapter 4, the present value of the inflows is $CF_1/(r-g)$. The NPV of each investment will be:

$$\frac{CF_1}{r-g} - \text{Initial Investment}$$

EXECUTE

The NPVs are:

$$\text{Bar: } \frac{\$60,000}{0.12 - 0.035} - \$400,000 = \$305,882$$

$$\text{Coffee Shop: } \frac{\$40,000}{0.10 - 0.03} - \$200,000 = \$371,429$$

$$\text{Apparel Store: } \frac{\$75,000}{0.13 - 0.03} - \$500,000 = \$250,000$$

So, the ranking is

Alternative	NPV
Coffee Shop	$371,429
Bar	$305,882
Apparel Store	$250,000
Sell the Land	$220,000

You should choose the coffee shop.

EVALUATE

All the alternatives have positive NPVs, but you can take only one of them, so you should choose the one that creates the most value. Even though the coffee shop has the lowest cash flows, its lower start-up cost coupled with its lower cost of capital (it is less risky) make it the best choice.

Because the IRR is a measure of the expected return of investing in the project, you might be tempted to extend the IRR investment rule to the case of mutually exclusive projects by picking the project with the highest IRR. Unfortunately, picking one project over another simply because it has a larger IRR can lead to mistakes. Problems arise when the mutually exclusive investments have differences in scale (require different initial investments) and when they have different cash flow patterns. We discuss each of these situations in turn.

Differences in Scale

Would you prefer a 200% return on $1 or a 10% return on $1 million? The former return certainly sounds impressive and gives you great bragging rights, but at the end of the day you make only $2. The latter opportunity may sound much more mundane, but you make $100,000. This comparison illustrates an important shortcoming of IRR: Because it is a return, you cannot tell how much value has actually been created without knowing the basis for the return—a 10% IRR can have very different value implications for an initial investment of $1 million versus an initial investment of $100 million.

If a project has a positive NPV, then if we can double its size, its NPV will double: By the Valuation Principle, doubling the cash flows of an investment opportunity must make it worth twice as much. However, the IRR rule does not have this property—it is unaffected by the scale of the investment opportunity because the IRR measures the average return of the investment. Thus, the IRR rule cannot be used to compare projects of different scales. Let's illustrate this concept in the context of an example.

Identical Scale. We begin by considering two mutually exclusive projects with the same scale. Maria is evaluating two investment opportunities. If she goes into business with her boyfriend, she would need to invest $10,000 and the business would generate incremental cash flows of $6000 per year for three years. Alternatively, she could start a courier/delivery service using two high-end drones. The drone setup will cost $10,000 and will generate $5000 per year for three years. The opportunity cost of capital for both opportunities is 12% and both will require all her time, so Maria must choose between them. How valuable is each opportunity, and which one should she choose?

Let's consider both the NPV and IRR of each project. The timeline for the investment with Maria's boyfriend is:

0	1	2	3
−10,000	+6000	+6000	+6000

The NPV of the investment opportunity when $r = 0.12$ is:

$$NPV = -10{,}000 + \frac{6000}{1.12} + \frac{6000}{1.12^2} + \frac{6000}{1.12^3} = \$4411$$

We can determine the IRR of this investment by using a financial calculator or spreadsheet:

	N	I/Y	PV	PMT	FV
Given:	3		−10,000	6000	0
Solve for:		36.3			

Excel Formula: =RATE(NPER,PMT,PV,FV)=RATE(3,6000,−10000,0)

Thus, the IRR for Maria's investment in her boyfriend's business is 36.3%. The timeline for her investment in the drone delivery business is:

0	1	2	3
−10,000	+5000	+5000	+5000

The NPV of the investment opportunity when $r = 0.12$ is:

$$NPV = -10,000 + \frac{5000}{1.12} + \frac{5000}{1.12^2} + \frac{5000}{1.12^3} = \$2009$$

The $2009 NPV of the delivery business is lower than the $4411 NPV for her boyfriend's business, so Maria should join her boyfriend in business. Luckily, it appears that Maria does not need to choose between her money and her relationship!

We could also compare IRRs. For the delivery business, we would find that the IRR is 23.4%. The delivery business has a lower IRR than the investment in her boyfriend's business. As Figure 8.7 shows, in this case the project with the higher IRR has the higher NPV.

Change in Scale. What happens if we change the scale of one of the projects? Maria's finance professor points out that, given the potential for automation, she could manage

FIGURE 8.7

NPV of Maria's Investment Opportunities with the Two-Drone Delivery Service

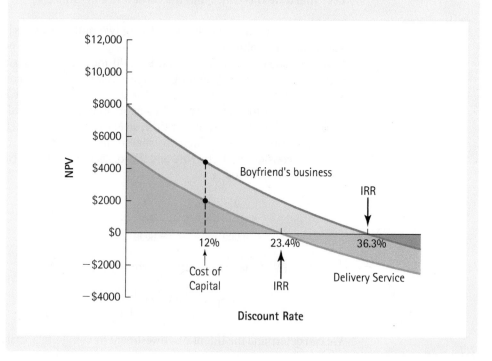

The NPV of her boyfriend's business is always larger than the NPV of the delivery service. The same is true for the IRR; the IRR of her boyfriend's business is 36.3%, while the IRR for the delivery service is 23.4%.

five times as many drones in her courier and delivery business. Her setup cost would now be $50,000 and her annual cash flows would be $25,000. What should Maria do now?

Note that the IRR is unaffected by the scale. Because we are scaling all the cash flows

	N	I/Y	PV	PMT	FV
Given:	3		−50,000	25,000	0
Solve for:		23.4			
Excel Formula: =RATE(NPER,PMT,PV,FV)=RATE(3,25000,−50000,0)					

up by a factor of 5, a 10-drone delivery service has exactly the same IRR as a 2-drone service, so her boyfriend's business still has a higher IRR than the delivery service:

However, the NPV of the delivery service does grow by the scale—it is five times larger:

$$NPV = -50,000 + \frac{25,000}{1.12} + \frac{25,000}{1.12^2} + \frac{25,000}{1.12^3} = \$10,046$$

Now Maria should invest in the 10-drone delivery service. As Figure 8.8 shows, the NPV of the 10-drone delivery service exceeds the NPV of going into business with her boyfriend whenever the cost of capital is less than 20%. In this case, even though the IRR of going into business with her boyfriend exceeds the IRR of the delivery service, picking the investment opportunity with the higher IRR does not result in taking the opportunity with the higher NPV.

Percentage Return Versus Dollar Impact on Value. This result might seem counterintuitive and you can imagine Maria having a difficult time explaining to her boyfriend why

FIGURE 8.8

NPV of Maria's Investment Opportunities with the Ten-Drone Delivery Service

As in Figure 8.7, the IRR of her boyfriend's business is 36.3%, while the IRR for the delivery service is 23.4%. But in this case, the NPV of her boyfriend's business is larger than the NPV of the 10-drone delivery service only for discount rates over 20%.

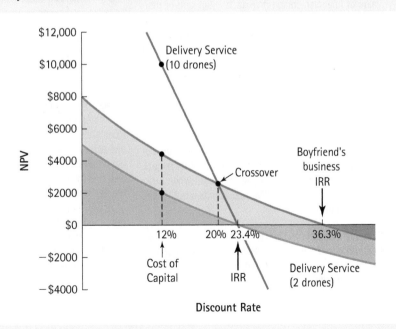

she is choosing a lower return over going into business with him. Why would anyone turn down an investment opportunity with a 36.3% return (IRR) in favor of one with only a 23.4% return? The answer is that the latter opportunity, the delivery service, makes more money. Recall the comparison at the beginning of this section: a 200% return on $1 versus a 10% return on $1 million. We agreed that ranking the returns was not the same as ranking the value created. The IRR is a measure of the average return, which can be valuable information. When you are comparing mutually exclusive projects of different scale, however, you need to know the dollar impact on value—the NPV.

INTERVIEW WITH DICK GRANNIS

Dick Grannis is Senior Vice President and Treasurer of QUALCOMM Incorporated, a world leader in digital wireless communications technology and semiconductors, headquartered in San Diego. He joined the company in 1991 and oversees the company's $10 billion cash investment portfolio. He works primarily on investment banking, capital structure, and international finance.

QUESTION: *QUALCOMM has a wide variety of products in different business lines. How does your capital budgeting process for new products work?*

ANSWER: QUALCOMM evaluates new projects (such as new products, equipment, technologies, research and development, acquisitions, and strategic investments) by using traditional financial measurements including DCF models, IRR levels, peak funding requirements, the time needed to reach cumulative positive cash flows, and the short-term impact of the investment on our reported net earnings. For strategic investments, we consider the possible value of financial, competitive, technology and/or market value enhancements to our core businesses—even if those benefits cannot be quantified. Overall, we make capital budgeting decisions based on a combination of objective analyses and our own business judgment.

We do not engage in capital budgeting and analysis if the project represents an immediate and necessary requirement for our business operations. One example is new software or production equipment to start a project that has already received approval.

We are also mindful of the opportunity costs of allocating our internal engineering resources on one project vs. another project. We view this as a constantly challenging but worthwhile exercise, because we have many attractive opportunities but limited resources to pursue them.

QUESTION: *How often does QUALCOMM evaluate its hurdle rates and what factors does it consider in setting them? How do you allocate capital across areas and regions and assess the risk of non-U.S. investments?*

ANSWER: QUALCOMM encourages its financial planners to utilize hurdle (or discount) rates that vary according to the risk of the particular project. We expect a rate of return commensurate with the project's risk. Our finance staff considers a wide range of discount rates and chooses one that fits the project's expected risk profile and time horizon. The range can be from 6.00% to 8.00% for relatively safe investments in the domestic market to 50% or more for equity investments in foreign markets that may be illiquid and difficult to predict. We re-evaluate our hurdle rates at least every year.

We analyze key factors including: (i) market adoption risk (whether or not customers will buy the new product or service at the price and volume we expect), (ii) technology development risk (whether or not we can develop and patent the new product or service as expected), (iii) execution risk (whether we can launch the new product or service cost effectively and on time), and (iv) dedicated asset risk (the amount of resources that must be consumed to complete the work).

QUESTION: *How are projects categorized and how are the hurdle rates for new projects determined? What would happen if QUALCOMM simply evaluated all new projects against the same hurdle rate?*

ANSWER: We primarily categorize projects by risk level, but we also categorize projects by the expected time horizon. We consider short-term and long-term projects to balance our needs and achieve our objectives. For example, immediate projects and opportunities may demand a great amount of attention, but we also stay focused on long-term projects because they often create greater long-term value for stockholders.

If we were to evaluate all new projects against the same hurdle rate, then our business planners would, by default, consistently choose to invest in the highest risk projects because those projects would appear to have the greatest expected returns in DCF models or IRR analyses. That approach would probably not work well for very long.

EXAMPLE 8.4

Computing the
Crossover Point

MyFinanceLab

PROBLEM

Solve for the crossover point for Maria from Figure 8.8.

SOLUTION

PLAN

The *crossover point* is the discount rate that makes the NPV of the two alternatives equal. We can find the discount rate by setting the equations for the NPV of each project equal to each other and solving for the discount rate. In general, we can always compute the effect of choosing the delivery service over her boyfriend's business as the difference of the NPVs. At the crossover point the difference is 0.

EXECUTE

Setting the difference equal to 0:

$$NPV = -50,000 + \frac{25,000}{1+r} + \frac{25,000}{(1+r)^2} + \frac{25,000}{(1+r)^3}$$

$$-\left(-10,000 + \frac{6000}{(1+r)} + \frac{6000}{(1+r)^2} + \frac{6000}{(1+r)^3}\right) = 0$$

combining terms, we have

$$-40,000 + \frac{19,000}{(1+r)} + \frac{19,000}{(1+r)^2} + \frac{19,000}{(1+r)^3} = 0$$

As you can see, solving for the crossover point is just like solving for the IRR, so we will need to use a financial calculator or spreadsheet:

	N	I/Y	PV	PMT	FV
Given:	3		−40,000	19,000	0
Solve for:		20.04			

Excel Formula: =RATE(NPER,PMT,PV,FV)=RATE(3,19000,−40000,0)

We find that the crossover occurs at a discount rate of 20.04%.

EVALUATE

Just as the NPV of a project tells us the value impact of taking the project, so the difference of the NPVs of two alternatives tells us the *incremental* impact of choosing one project over another. The crossover point is the discount rate at which we would be indifferent between the two projects because the incremental value of choosing one over the other would be zero.

Timing of the Cash Flows

Even when projects have the same scale, the IRR may lead you to rank them incorrectly due to differences in the timing of the cash flows. The reason for this is that the IRR is expressed as a return, but the dollar value of earning a given return—and therefore the NPV—depends on how long the return is earned. Consider a high-IRR project with cash flows paid back quickly. It may have a lower NPV than a project with a lower IRR whose cash flows are paid back over a longer period. This sensitivity to timing is another reason why you cannot use the IRR to choose between mutually exclusive investments. To see this in the context of an example, let's return to Maria's delivery business.

Maria believes that after starting the delivery business, she may be able to sell her stake in the business at the end of the first year for $40,000 (she will stay on and manage the business after she sells). Thus, counting her first-year profit of $25,000, she would earn a total of $65,000 after one year. In that case, the timeline is:

```
       0            1
       ├────────────┤
    −$50,000    +$65,000
```

FIGURE 8.9

NPV with and
without Selling

The IRR from selling after one year (30%) is larger than the IRR without selling (23.4%). However, the NPV from selling after one year exceeds the NPV without selling only for discount rates that are in excess of 16.3% (see the yellow-shaded area versus the blue-shaded area). Thus, given a cost of capital of 12%, it is better not to sell the delivery service after one year, despite the higher IRR.

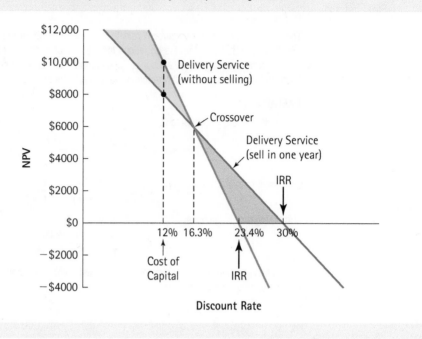

Figure 8.9 plots the NPV profile for the delivery service with and without selling it after one year. If Maria sells, the NPV profile crosses the *x*-axis at 30%, which is its IRR. The IRR for the delivery service if she does not sell is still 23.4%. Therefore, if Maria picks the alternative with the higher IRR, she will sell. However, since the height of each line indicates the NPV of that decision, we can see that his NPV given a 12% cost of capital is higher if she chooses not to sell. (In fact, the NPV is higher as long as the cost of capital is less than 16.3%.) The intuition is as follows: While the 30% IRR from selling is high, this return is only earned in the first year. While the 23.4% IRR from not selling is not as high, it is still attractive relative to the cost of capital, and it is earned over a longer period. Again, only by comparing the NPV can we determine which option is truly more valuable.

The Bottom Line on IRR. As these examples make clear, picking the investment opportunity with the largest IRR can lead to mistakes. In general, it is dangerous to use the IRR in cases where you are choosing between projects, or anytime when your decision to accept or reject one project would affect your decision on another project. In such a situation, always rely on NPV.

**CONCEPT
CHECK**

7. What is the most reliable way to choose between mutually exclusive projects?

8. For mutually exclusive projects, explain why picking one project over another because it has a larger IRR can lead to mistakes.

8.5 Evaluating Projects with Different Lives

Often, a company will need to choose between two solutions to the same problem. A complication arises when those solutions last for different periods of time. For example, a firm could be considering two vendors for its internal network servers. Each vendor offers the same level of service, but they use different equipment. Vendor A offers a more expensive server with lower per-year operating costs that it guarantees for three years. Vendor B offers a less expensive server with higher per-year operating costs that it guarantees for two years. The costs are shown in Table 8.2 along with the present value of the costs of each option, discounted at the 10% cost of capital for this project.

TABLE 8.2

Cash Flows ($ thousands) for Network Server Options

Year	PV at 10%	0	1	2	3
A	−12.49	−10	−1	−1	−1
B	−10.47	−7	−2	−2	

Note that all of the cash flows are negative, and so is the present value. This is a choice of an internal server, where the project must be taken and the benefits are diffuse (the company could not function effectively without an internal network). Thus, we are trying to minimize the cost of providing this service for the company. Table 8.2 shows that option A is more expensive on a present value basis (−$12,487 versus −$10,471). However, the comparison is not that simple: Option A lasts for three years while option B lasts for two. The decision comes down to whether it is worth paying $2000 more for option A to get the extra year. One method that is used to evaluate alternatives such as these that have different lives is to compute the **equivalent annual annuity (EAA)** for each project, which is the level annual cash flow with the same present value as the cash flows of the project. The intuition is that we can think of the cost of each solution as the constant annual cost that gives us the same present value of the lumpy cash flows of buying and operating the server. On a timeline, equivalent annual annuity cash flows would appear as follows:

equivalent annual annuity (EAA) The level annual cash flow that has the same present value as the cash flows of a project. Used to evaluate alternative projects with different lives.

When you have a level cash flow at a constant interval, you are dealing with an annuity and that is exactly how to approach this problem. We know the present value (−$12.49) the number of years (3), and the discount rate (10%). We need to solve for the cash flow, of an equivalent annuity. Recall from Chapter 4 that the formula (Eq. 4.9) for solving for the cash flow in an annuity is:

$$\text{Cash Flow} = \frac{\text{Present Value}}{\frac{1}{r}\left(1 - \frac{1}{(1+r)^N}\right)} = \frac{-12.49}{\frac{1}{0.10}\left(1 - \frac{1}{(1.10)^3}\right)} = -5.02$$

So, buying and operating server A is equivalent to spending $5020 per year to have a network server. We can repeat the calculation for server B, but for a two-year annuity because server B has only a two-year life (the change in exponent is highlighted):

$$\text{Cash Flow} = \frac{\text{Present Value}}{\frac{1}{r}\left(1 - \frac{1}{(1+r)^N}\right)} = \frac{-10.47}{\frac{1}{0.10}\left(1 - \frac{1}{(1.10)^2}\right)} = -6.03$$

Therefore, we can reinterpret the cost of each alternative as shown in Table 8.3:

Now we are ready to choose between the two servers. Server A is equivalent to spending $5020 per year and server B is equivalent to spending $6030 per year to have a network server. Seen in this light, server A appears to be the less expensive solution.

TABLE 8.3

Cash Flows ($ thousands) for
Network Server Options, Expressed
as Equivalent Annual Annuities

Year	PV at 10%	0	1	2	3
A	−12.49	0	−5.02	−5.02	−5.02
B	−10.47	0	−6.03	−6.03	

EXAMPLE 8.5

Computing
an Equivalent
Annual Annuity

MyFinanceLab

PROBLEM

You are about to sign the contract for server A from Table 8.2 when a third vendor approaches you with another option that lasts for four years. The cash flows for server C are given below. Should you choose the new option or stick with server A?

SOLUTION

PLAN

In order to compare this new option to server A, we need to put server C on an equal footing by computing its annual cost. We can do this by:

1. Computing its NPV at the 10% discount rate we used above.
2. Computing the equivalent four-year annuity with the same present value.

EXECUTE

$$PV = -14 - 1.2\left(\frac{1}{0.10}\right)\left[1 - \frac{1}{(1.10)^4}\right] = -17.80$$

$$\text{Cash Flow} = \frac{PV}{\frac{1}{r}\left[1 - \frac{1}{(1+r)^N}\right]} = \frac{-17.80}{\frac{1}{0.10}\left[1 - \frac{1}{(1.10)^4}\right]} = -5.62$$

Server C's annual cost of $5620 is greater than the annual cost of server A ($5020), so we should still choose server A.

EVALUATE

In this case, the additional cost associated with purchasing and maintaining server C is not worth the extra year we get from choosing it. By putting all of these costs into an equivalent annuity, the EAA tool allows us to see that.

Important Considerations When Using the Equivalent Annual Annuity

Although server A appears to be the lowest-cost alternative, there are several factors to consider before making our decision.

Required Life. We computed the equivalent annual cost of server A assuming we would use it for three years. But suppose it is likely that we will not need the server in the third year. Then we would be paying for something that we would not use. In that case, it may be cheaper to purchase server B, which provides coverage for the years we will need it at a lower total cost.[6]

---

[6]In this scenario, we should also consider any salvage value that server A might have if we sold it after two years.

Replacement Cost. When we compare servers A and B based on their equivalent annual cost, we are assuming that the cost of servers will not change over time. But suppose we believe a dramatic change in technology will reduce the cost of servers by the third year to an annual cost of $2000 per year. Then server B has the advantage that we can upgrade to the new technology sooner. The cost of three years of service from either server in this case can be represented as follows:

Year	PV at 10%	0	1	2	3
A	−12.49	0	−5.02	−5.02	−5.02
B	−11.97	0	−6.03	−6.03	−2.00

Therefore, when cost or performance is expected to change significantly over time, it may be cheaper to purchase server B despite its higher equivalent annual cost because it gives us the option to switch to the new technology sooner.

CONCEPT CHECK

9. Explain why choosing the option with the highest NPV is not always correct when the options have different lives.
10. What issues should you keep in mind when choosing among projects with different lives?

8.6 Choosing Among Projects When Resources Are Limited

In the previous sections, we compared projects that had *identical* resource needs. For example, in Maria's case, we assumed that both the delivery service and her boyfriend's business demanded all of her time. In this section, we develop an approach for situations where the choices have differing resource needs.

Evaluating Projects with Different Resource Requirements

In some situations, different investment opportunities demand different amounts of a particular resource. If there is a fixed supply of the resource so that you cannot undertake all possible opportunities, simply picking the highest NPV opportunity might not lead to the best decision.

We usually assume that you will be able to finance all positive NPV projects that you have. In reality, managers work within the constraint of a budget that restricts the amount of capital they may invest in a given period. Such a constraint would force a manager to choose among positive NPV projects to maximize the total NPV while staying within her budget. For example, assume you are considering the three projects in Table 8.4, and that you have a budget of $200 million. Table 8.4 shows the NPV of each project and the initial investment that each project requires. Project A has the highest NPV but it uses up the entire budget. Projects B and C can *both* be undertaken (together they use the entire budget), and their combined NPV exceeds the NPV of project A; thus, you should initiate them both. Together, their NPV is $145 million compared to $100 million for project A alone.

TABLE 8.4

Possible Projects for $200 Million Budget

Project	NPV ($ millions)	Initial Investment ($ millions)	NPV/Initial Investment
A	100	200	0.500
B	75	120	0.625
C	70	80	0.875

Profitability Index. Note that in the last column of Table 8.4 we included the ratio of the project's NPV to its initial investment. We can interpret this as telling us that for every dollar invested in project A, we will generate 50 cents in value (over and above the dollar investment).[7] Both projects B and C generate higher NPVs per dollar invested than project A, consistent with the fact that given our budget of $200 million, the two of them together created a higher NPV than project A alone.

In this simple example, identifying the optimal combination of projects to undertake is straightforward. In actual situations replete with many projects and resources, finding the optimal combination can be difficult. Practitioners often use the **profitability index (PI)** to help identify the optimal combination of projects to undertake in such situations:

profitability index (PI) Measures the NPV per unit of resource consumed.

Profitability Index

$$\text{Profitability Index} = \frac{\text{Value Created}}{\text{Resource Consumed}} = \frac{NPV}{\text{Resource Consumed}} \tag{8.4}$$

The profitability index measures the "bang for your buck"—that is, the value created in terms of NPV per unit of resource consumed. After computing the profitability index, we can rank projects based on it. Starting with the project with the highest index, we move down the ranking, taking all projects until the resource is consumed. In Table 8.4, the ratio in the last column is the profitability index. Note how the profitability index rule would correctly select projects B and C.

EXAMPLE 8.6

Profitability Index with a Human Resource Constraint

MyFinanceLab

PROBLEM

Your division at NetIt, a large networking company, has put together a project proposal to develop a new home networking router. The expected NPV of the project is $17.7 million, and the project will require 50 software engineers. NetIt has 190 engineers available, and is unable to hire additional qualified engineers in the short run. Therefore, the router project must compete with the following other projects for these engineers:

Project	NPV ($ millions)	Engineering Headcount (EHC)
Router	17.7	50
Project A	22.7	47
Project B	8.1	44
Project C	14.0	40
Project D	11.5	61
Project E	20.6	58
Project F	12.9	32
Total	107.5	332

How should NetIt prioritize these projects?

SOLUTION

PLAN

The goal is to maximize the total NPV that we can create with 190 engineers (at most). We can use Eq. 8.4 to determine the profitability index for each project. In this case, since engineers are our limited resource, we will use Engineering Headcount in the denominator. Once we have the profitability index for each project, we can sort them based on the index.

---

[7]Sometimes, practitioners add 1 to this ratio such that the interpretation would be that every dollar invested returned $1.50. Leaving off the additional 1 allows the ratio to be applied to resources other than budgets as we show in Example 8.6.

EXECUTE

Project	NPV ($ millions)	Engineering Headcount (EHC)	Profitability Index (NPV per EHC)	Cumulative EHC Required
Project A	22.7	47	0.483	47
Project F	12.9	32	0.403	$79\,(47+32)$
Project E	20.6	58	0.355	$137\,(79+58)$
Router	17.7	50	0.354	$187\,(137+50)$
Project C	14.0	40	0.350	
Project D	11.5	61	0.189	
Project B	8.1	44	0.184	

As shown in the table above, we assigned the resource to the projects in descending order according to the profitability index. The final column shows the cumulative use of the resource as each project is taken on until the resource is used up. To maximize NPV within the constraint of 190 engineers, NetIt should choose the first four projects on the list.

EVALUATE

By ranking projects in terms of their NPV per engineer, we find the most value we can create, given our 190 engineers. There is no other combination of projects that will create more value without using more engineers than we have. This ranking also shows us exactly what the engineering constraint costs us—this resource constraint forces NetIt to forgo three otherwise valuable projects (C, D, and B) with a total NPV of $33.6 million.

Shortcomings of the Profitability Index. Although the profitability index is simple to compute and use, in some situations it does not give an accurate answer. For example, suppose in Example 8.6 that NetIt has an additional small project with an NPV of only $100,000 that requires three engineers. The profitability index in this case is $0.1/3 = 0.03$, so this project would appear at the bottom of the ranking. However, notice that three of the 190 employees are not being used after the first four projects are selected. As a result, it would make sense to take on this project even though it would be ranked last because it would exactly use up our constraint.

In general, because the profitability index already includes the cost of capital (in computing the NPV), it would be better if the firm could raise additional funding to relieve the constraint. If the constraint is something else (such as engineers or physical capacity), there may be no way to relieve the constraint quickly enough to avoid having to choose among projects. Nonetheless, because all of the projects being ranked are value-increasing positive NPV projects, it is still better to focus on relieving the constraint.

A more serious problem occurs when multiple resource constraints apply. In this case, the profitability index can break down completely. The only surefire way to find the best combination of projects is to search through all of them. Although this process may sound exceedingly time-consuming, there are more advanced techniques that can tackle this specific kind of problem.[8] By using these techniques on a computer, the solution can usually be obtained almost instantaneously.

CONCEPT CHECK

11. Explain why picking the project with the highest NPV might not be optimal when you evaluate projects with different resource requirements.

12. What does the profitability index tell you?

---

[8]Specifically, there are techniques called *integer and linear programming* that can be used to find the combination with the highest NPV when there are multiple constraints that must be satisfied. These methods are available, for example, in many spreadsheet programs.

8.7 Putting It All Together

In Table 8.5, we summarize the decision rules outlined in this chapter. As a financial manager, you are likely to run into many different types of investment decision rules in your career. In fact, in the interview in this chapter, the Treasurer of QUALCOMM mentions five

TABLE 8.5

Summary of Decision Rules

NPV	
Definition	• The difference between the present value of an investment's benefits and the present value of its costs
Rule	• Take any investment opportunity where the NPV is positive; turn down any opportunity where it is negative
Advantages	• Corresponds directly to the impact of the project on the firm's value • Direct application of the Valuation Principle
Disadvantages	• Relies on an accurate estimate of the discount rate • Can be time-consuming to compute
IRR	
Definition	• The interest rate that sets the net present value of the cash flows equal to zero; the average return of the investment
Rule	• Take any investment opportunity where its IRR exceeds the opportunity cost of capital; turn down any opportunity where its IRR is less than the opportunity cost of capital
Advantages	• Related to the NPV rule and usually yields the same (correct) decision
Disadvantages	• Hard to compute • Multiple IRRs lead to ambiguity • Cannot be used to choose among projects • Can be misleading if inflows come before outflows
Payback Period	
Definition	• The amount of time it takes to pay back the initial investment
Rule	• Accept the project if the payback period is less than a prespecified length of time—usually a few years; otherwise, turn it down
Advantages	• Simple to compute • Favors liquidity
Disadvantages	• No guidance as to correct payback cutoff • Ignores cash flows after the cutoff completely • Not necessarily consistent with maximizing shareholder wealth
Profitability Index	
Definition	• NPV/Resource Consumed
Rule	• Rank projects according to their PI based on the constrained resource and move down the list accepting value-creating projects until the resource is exhausted
Advantages	• Uses the NPV to measure the benefit • Allows projects to be ranked on value created per unit of resource consumed
Disadvantages	• Breaks down when there is more than one constraint • Requires careful attention to make sure the constrained resource is completely utilized

different decision rules used by his company when evaluating investments. We have demonstrated that while alternative decision rules may sometimes (or even often) agree with the NPV decision rule, only the NPV decision rule is always correct. This is because the NPV provides you with a dollar-value measure of the impact of the project on shareholder wealth. Thus, it is the only rule that is directly tied to your goal of maximizing shareholder wealth. Computing the IRR can be a useful supplement to the NPV because knowing the IRR allows you to gauge how sensitive your decision is to errors in your discount rate. And some decision metrics are much simpler to calculate, such as the payback period. However, you should never rely on an alternative rule to make investment decisions.

If you are employed by a firm that uses the IRR rule (or another rule) exclusively, our advice is to always calculate the NPV. If the two rules agree, you can feel comfortable reporting the IRR rule recommendation. If they do not agree, you should investigate why the IRR rule failed by using the concepts in this chapter. Once you have identified the problem, you can alert your superiors to it and perhaps persuade them to adopt the NPV rule.

MyFinanceLab

Here is what you should know after reading this chapter. MyFinanceLab will help you identify what you know, and where to go when you need to practice.

KEY POINTS AND EQUATIONS	KEY TERMS	ONLINE PRACTICE
8.1 The NPV Decision Rule • The net present value (NPV) of a project is $$PV(\text{Benefits}) - PV(\text{Costs}) \qquad (8.1)$$ • A good project is one with a positive net present value. • The NPV decision rule states that when choosing from among a set of alternatives, choose the one with the highest NPV. The NPV of a project is equivalent to the cash value today of the project. • Regardless of our preferences for cash today versus cash in the future, we should always first maximize NPV. We can then borrow or lend to shift cash flows through time and find our most preferred pattern of cash flows.	net present value (NPV), p. 228 NPV decision rule, p. 229	MyFinanceLab Study Plan 8.1 Financial Calculator Tutorial: Calculating the Net Present Value of a Series of Uneven Cash Flows
8.2 Using the NPV Rule • If your objective is to maximize wealth, the NPV rule always gives the correct answer. • The difference between the cost of capital and the IRR is the maximum amount of estimation error that can exist in the cost of capital estimate without altering the original decision.	internal rate of return (IRR), p. 232 NPV profile, p. 231	MyFinanceLab Study Plan 8.2 Using Excel: Making an NPV Profile

8.3 Alternative Decision Rules	discounted payback	MyFinanceLab Study

8.3 Alternative Decision Rules
- Payback investment rule: Calculate the amount of time it takes to pay back the initial investment (the payback period). If the payback period is less than a prespecified length of time, accept the project. Otherwise, turn it down.
- IRR investment rule: Take any investment opportunity whose IRR exceeds the opportunity cost of capital. Turn down any opportunity whose IRR is less than the opportunity cost of capital.
- The IRR rule may give the wrong answer if the cash flows have an up-front payment (negative investment). When there are multiple IRRs or the IRR does not exist, the IRR rule cannot be used.
- Project cash flows can be modified to eliminate the multiple IRR problem. The modified IRR is calculated based on these modified cash flows.

discounted payback rule, p. 235
internal rate of return (IRR) investment rule, p. 235
modified internal rate of return (MIRR), p. 239
payback investment rule, p. 234
payback period, p. 234

MyFinanceLab Study Plan 8.3

Interactive IRR Analysis

Financial Calculator Tutorial: Solving for the Internal Rate of Return

8.4 Choosing Between Projects
- When choosing among mutually exclusive investment opportunities, pick the opportunity with the highest NPV. Do not use IRR to choose among mutually exclusive investment opportunities.

mutually exclusive projects, p. 242

MyFinanceLab Study Plan 8.4

8.5 Evaluating Projects with Different Lives
- When choosing among projects with different lives, you need a standard basis of comparison. First, compute an annuity with an equivalent present value to the NPV of each project. Then the projects can be compared on their cost or value created *per year*.

equivalent annual annuity (EAA), p. 249

MyFinanceLab Study Plan 8.5

8.6 Choosing Among Projects When Resources Are Limited
- When choosing among projects competing for the same resource, rank the projects by their profitability indices and pick the set of projects with the highest profitability indices that can still be undertaken given the limited resource.

profitability index (PI), p. 252

MyFinanceLab Study Plan 8.6

$$\text{Profitability Index} = \frac{\text{Value Created}}{\text{Resource Consumed}}$$
$$= \frac{NPV}{\text{Resource Consumed}} \quad (8.4)$$

CRITICAL THINKING

1. What is the NPV rule?

2. How is the NPV rule related to the goal of maximizing shareholder wealth?

3. What is the intuition behind the payback rule? What are some of its drawbacks?

4. What is the intuition behind the IRR rule? What are some of its drawbacks?

5. Under what conditions will the IRR rule and the NPV rule give the same accept/reject decision?

6. When is it possible to have multiple IRRs?

7. How does the MIRR solve the problem of multiple IRRs?

8. Why is it generally a bad idea to use IRR to choose between mutually exclusive projects?

9. When should you use the equivalent annual annuity?

10. What is the intuition behind the profitability index?

PROBLEMS

All problems are available in MyFinanceLab. *The* [icon] *icon indicates problems that are easier to solve using Excel and have data in an Excel format available in* MyFinanceLab. *An asterisk * indicates problems with a higher level of difficulty.*

The NPV Decision Rule

1. You have an opportunity to invest $50,000 now in return for $60,000 in one year. If your cost of capital is 8%, what is the NPV of this investment?

2. You have an opportunity to invest $100,000 now in return for $80,000 in one year and $30,000 in two years. If your cost of capital is 9%, what is the NPV of this investment?

3. Your storage firm has been offered $100,000 in one year to store some goods for one year. Assume your costs are $95,000, payable immediately, and the cost of capital is 8%. Should you take the contract?

4. You are preparing to produce some goods for sale. You will sell them in one year and you will incur costs of $80,000 immediately. If your cost of capital is 7%, what is the minimum dollar amount you need to expect to sell the goods for in order for this to be a non-negative NPV?

5. You run a construction firm. You have just won a contract to build a government office building. Building it will require an investment of $10 million today and $5 million in one year. The government will pay you $20 million in one year upon the building's completion. Assume the cost of capital is 10%.
   a. What is the NPV of this opportunity?
   b. How can your firm turn this NPV into cash today?

6. You have been offered a unique investment opportunity. If you invest $10,000 today, you will receive $500 one year from now, $1500 two years from now, and $10,000 ten years from now.
   a. What is the NPV of the opportunity if the cost of capital is 6% per year? Should you take the opportunity?
   b. What is the NPV of the opportunity if the cost of capital is 2% per year? Should you take it now?

7. Marian Plunket owns her own business and is considering an investment. If she undertakes the investment, it will pay $4000 at the end of each of the next three years. The opportunity requires an initial investment of $1000 plus an additional investment at the end of the second year of $5000. What is the NPV of this opportunity if the cost of capital is 2% per year? Should Marian take it?

Using the NPV Rule

8. Your factory has been offered a contract to produce a part for a new printer. The contract would be for three years and your cash flows from the contract would be $5 million per year. Your up-front setup costs to be ready to produce the part would

be $8 million. Your cost of capital for this contract is 8%.

a. What does the NPV rule say you should do?

b. If you take the contract, what will be the change in the value of your firm?

9. You are considering opening a new plant. The plant will cost $100 million up front and will take one year to build. After that, it is expected to produce profits of $30 million at the end of every year of production. The cash flows are expected to last forever. Calculate the NPV of this investment opportunity if your cost of capital is 8%. Should you make the investment? Calculate the IRR and use it to determine the maximum deviation allowable in the cost of capital estimate to leave the decision unchanged.

10. Bill Clinton reportedly was paid $10 million to write his book *My Life*. The book took three years to write. In the time he spent writing, Clinton could have been paid to make speeches. Given his popularity, assume that he could earn $8 million per year (paid at the end of the year) speaking instead of writing. Assume his cost of capital is 10% per year.

a. What is the NPV of agreeing to write the book (ignoring any royalty payments)?

b. Assume that, once the book was finished, it was expected to generate royalties of $5 million in the first year (paid at the end of the year) and these royalties were expected to decrease at a rate of 30% per year in perpetuity. What is the NPV of the book with the royalty payments?

*11. FastTrack Bikes, Inc., is thinking of developing a new composite road bike. Development will take six years and the cost is $200,000 per year. Once in production, the bike is expected to make $300,000 per year for 10 years. The cash inflows begin at the end of year 7.

Assuming the cost of capital is 10%:

a. Calculate the NPV of this investment opportunity. Should the company make the investment?

b. Calculate the IRR and use it to determine the maximum deviation allowable in the cost of capital estimate to leave the decision unchanged.

c. How long must development last to change the decision?

Assuming the cost of capital is 14%:

a. Calculate the NPV of this investment opportunity. Should the company make the investment?

b. How much must this cost of capital estimate deviate to change the decision?

c. How long must development last to change the decision?

12. OpenSeas, Inc., is evaluating the purchase of a new cruise ship. The ship will cost $500 million, and will operate for 20 years. OpenSeas expects annual cash flows from operating the ship to be $70 million and its cost of capital is 12%.

a. Prepare an NPV profile of the purchase.

b. Identify the IRR on the graph.

c. Should OpenSeas proceed with the purchase?

d. How far off could OpenSeas' cost of capital estimate be before your purchase decision would change?

13. You are CEO of Rivet Networks, maker of ultra-high performance network cards for gaming computers, and you are considering whether to launch a new product. The product, the Killer X3000, will cost $900,000 to develop upfront (year 0), and you expect revenues the first year of $800,000, growing to $1.5 million the second year, and then declining by 40% per year for the next 3 years before the product is fully obsolete. In years 1 through 5, you will have fixed costs associated with the product of $100,000 per year, and variable costs equal to 50% of revenues.

a. What are the cash flows for the project in years 0 through 5?
b. Plot the NPV profile for this investment using discount rates from 0% to 40% in 10% increments.
c. What is the project's NPV if the project's cost of capital is 10%?
d. Use the NPV profile to estimate the cost of capital at which the project would become unprofitable; that is, estimate the project's IRR.

Alternative Decision Rules

14. You are a real estate agent thinking of placing a sign advertising your services at a local bus stop. The sign will cost $5000 and will be posted for one year. You expect that it will generate additional free cash flow of $500 per month. What is the payback period?

15. Does the IRR rule agree with the NPV rule in Problem 8?

16. How many IRRs are there in part (a) of Problem 10? Does the IRR rule give the correct answer in this case?

17. How many IRRs are there in part (b) of Problem 10? Does the IRR rule work in this case?

18. Professor Wendy Smith has been offered the following deal: A law firm would like to retain her for an up-front payment of $50,000. In return, for the next year the firm would have access to eight hours of her time every month. Smith's rate is $550 per hour and her opportunity cost of capital is 15% per year. What does the IRR rule advise regarding this opportunity? What about the NPV rule?

19. Innovation Company is thinking about marketing a new software product. Up-front costs to market and develop the product are $5 million. The product is expected to generate profits of $1 million per year for 10 years. The company will have to provide product support expected to cost $100,000 per year in perpetuity. Assume all profits and expenses occur at the end of the year.
a. What is the NPV of this investment if the cost of capital is 6%? Should the firm undertake the project? Repeat the analysis for discount rates of 2% and 11%.
b. How many IRRs does this investment opportunity have?
c. What does the IRR rule indicate about this investment?

20. You have 3 projects with the following cash flows:

Year	0	1	2	3	4
Project 1	−150	20	40	60	80
Project 2	−825	0	0	7000	−6500
Project 3	20	40	60	80	−245

a. For which of these projects is the IRR rule reliable?
b. Estimate the IRR for each project (to the nearest 1%).
c. What is the NPV of each project if the cost of capital is 5%? 20%? 50%?

21. You own a coal mining company and are considering opening a new mine. The mine will cost $120 million to open. If this money is spent immediately, the mine will generate $20 million for the next 10 years. After that, the coal will run out and the site must be cleaned and maintained at environmental standards. The cleaning and maintenance are expected to cost $2 million per year in perpetuity. What does the IRR rule say about whether you should accept this opportunity? If the cost of capital is 8%, what does the NPV rule say?

22. Your firm is considering a project that will cost $4.55 million upfront, generate cash flows of $3.5 million per year for three years, and then have a cleanup and shutdown cost of $6 million in the fourth year.
    a. How many IRRs does this project have?
    b. Calculate a modified IRR for this project discounting the outflows and leaving the inflows unchanged. Assume a discount and compounding rate of 10%.
    c. Using the MIRR and a cost of capital of 10%, would you take the project?

23. You have just been offered a contract worth $1 million per year for five years. However, to take the contract, you will need to purchase some new equipment. Your discount rate for this project is 12%. You are still negotiating the purchase price of the equipment. What is the most you can pay for the equipment and not have a negative NPV?

*24. You are getting ready to start a new project that will incur some cleanup and shutdown costs when it is completed. The project costs $5.4 million up front and is expected to generate $1.1 million per year for 10 years and then have some shutdown costs in year 11. Use the MIRR approach to find the maximum shutdown costs you could incur and still meet your cost of capital of 15% on this project.

*25. You are considering investing in a new gold mine in South Africa. Gold in South Africa is buried very deep, so the mine will require an initial investment of $250 million. Once this investment is made, the mine is expected to produce revenues of $30 million per year for the next 20 years. It will cost $10 million per year to operate the mine. After 20 years, the gold will be depleted. The mine must then be stabilized on an ongoing basis, which will cost $5 million per year in perpetuity. Calculate the IRR of this investment. (*Hint*: Plot the NPV as a function of the discount rate.)

26. You are evaluating a project that will cost $500,000, but is expected to produce cash flows of $125,000 per year for 10 years, with the first cash flow in one year. Your cost of capital is 11% and your company's preferred payback period is three years or less.
    a. What is the payback period of this project?
    b. Should you take the project if you want to increase the value of the company?

27. You are considering making a movie. The movie is expected to cost $10 million upfront and take a year to produce. After that, it is expected to make $5 million in the year it is released and $2 million for the following four years. What is the payback period of this investment? If you require a payback period of two years, will you make the movie? Does the movie have positive NPV if the cost of capital is 10%?

Choosing Between Projects

28. You are choosing between two projects, but can only take one. The cash flows for the projects are given in the following table:

	0	1	2	3	4
A	−$50	25	20	20	15
B	−$100	20	40	50	60

    a. What are the IRRs of the two projects?
    b. If your discount rate is 5%, what are the NPVs of the two projects?
    c. Why do IRR and NPV rank the two projects differently?

29. You are deciding between two mutually exclusive investment opportunities. Both require the same initial investment of $10 million. Investment A will generate $2 million per year (starting at the end of the first year) in perpetuity. Investment B

will generate $1.5 million at the end of the first year and its revenues will grow at 2% per year for every year after that.

a. Which investment has the higher IRR?

b. Which investment has the higher NPV when the cost of capital is 7%?

c. In this case, when does picking the higher IRR give the correct answer as to which investment is the better opportunity?

30. You are considering the following projects and can take only one. Your cost of capital is 11%.

	0	1	2	3	4
A	−100	25	30	40	50
B	−100	50	40	30	20

a. What is the NPV of each project at your cost of capital?

b. What is the IRR of each project?

c. At what cost of capital are you indifferent between the two projects?

d. What should you do?

31. You need a particular piece of equipment for your production process. An equipment-leasing company has offered to lease you the equipment for $10,000 per year if you sign a guaranteed five-year lease. The company would also maintain the equipment for you as part of the lease. Alternatively, you could buy and maintain the equipment yourself. The cash flows (in thousands) from doing so are listed below (the equipment has an economic life of five years). If your discount rate is 7%, what should you do?

0	1	2	3	4	5
−40	−2	−2	−2	−2	−2

Evaluating Projects with Different Lives

32. You are trying to decide between two mobile phone carriers. Carrier A requires you to pay $200 for the phone and monthly charges of $60 for 24 months. Carrier B wants you to pay $100 for the phone and monthly charges of $70 for 12 months. Assume you will keep replacing the phone after your contract expires. Your cost of capital is 4%. Based on cost alone, which carrier should you choose?

33. Gateway Tours is choosing between two bus models. One is more expensive to purchase and maintain, but lasts much longer than the other. Its discount rate is 11%. It plans to continue with one of the two models for the foreseeable future; which should it choose? Based on the costs of each model shown below, which should it choose?

Model	0	1	2	3	4	5 ...	7
Old Reliable	−200	−4	−4	−4	−4	−4 ...	−4
Short and Sweet	−100	−2	−2	−2	−2		

34. Hassle-Free Web is bidding to provide Web hosting services for Hotel Lisbon. Hotel Lisbon pays its current provider $10,000 per year for hosting its Web page, handling transactions, etc. Hassle-Free figures that it will need to purchase equipment worth $15,000 upfront and then spend $2000 per year on monitoring, updates, and bandwidth to provide the service for three years. If Hassle-Free's cost of capital is 10%, can it bid less than $10,000 per year to provide the service and still increase its value by doing so?

35. You have to buy a new copier. The cost of the copier is $2000, plus $400 per year in maintenance costs. The copier will last for five years. Alternatively, a local company offers to lease the copier to you and do the maintenance as well. If your discount rate is 6%, what is the most you would be willing to pay per year to lease the copier (your first lease payment is due in one year)?

Choosing Among Projects When Resources Are Limited

36. Fabulous Fabricators needs to decide how to allocate space in its production facility this year. It is considering the following contracts:

	NPV	Use of Facility
A	$2 million	100%
B	$1 million	60%
C	$1.5 million	40%

    a. What are the profitability indexes of the projects?
    b. What should Fabulous Fabricators do?

37. Kartman Corporation is evaluating four real estate investments. Management plans to buy the properties today and sell them three years from today. The annual discount rate for these investments is 15%. The following table summarizes the initial cost and the sale price in three years for each property:

	Cost Today	Sale Price in Year 3
Parkside Acres	$650,000	$1,150,000
Real Property Estates	800,000	1,400,000
Lost Lake Properties	650,000	1,050,000
Overlook	150,000	350,000

    Kartman has a total capital budget of $800,000 to invest in properties. Which properties should it choose?

38. Orchid Biotech Company is evaluating several development projects for experimental drugs. Although the cash flows are difficult to forecast, the company has come up with the following estimates of the initial capital requirements and NPVs for the projects. Given a wide variety of staffing needs, the company has also estimated the number of research scientists required for each development project (all cost values are given in millions of dollars).

Project Number	Initial Capital	Number of Research Scientists	NPV
I	$10	2	$10.1
II	15	3	19.0
III	15	4	22.0
IV	20	3	25.0
V	30	12	60.2

    a. Suppose that Orchid has a total capital budget of $60 million. How should it prioritize these projects?
    b. Suppose that Orchid currently has 12 research scientists and does not anticipate being able to hire more in the near future. How should Orchid prioritize these projects?

DATA CASE

You have just purchased a house for $500,000 that is located very close to the university you attend. You plan to put $100,000 down and borrow $400,000. You need to decide which mortgage deal to take. To find out what your choices are, go to www.bankrate.com and select the appropriate buttons to get a quote for a 30-year fixed rate mortgage on a new purchase (not a refinancing). Assume your FICO score is very high and you are looking for a zero point mortgage. Find the best coupon rate on a mortgage that requires paying no upfront fees or points.[9] We will refer to this mortgage as the no-fee mortgage and assume that the rate on this mortgage is your cost of capital.

You are going to make the decision about which mortgage to consider by calculating the NPV of switching from the no-fee mortgage to each of the top six mortgages listed (sorted by their coupon). To calculate the NPV of this decision, calculate the difference in payments today, and over the life of the mortgage, by subtracting the alternative mortgage payments from the no-fee mortgage payments and calculating the NPV. For good measure, calculate the IRR as well.[10] Assume that you will be living in the house for the next 30 years for certain and you will never repay the mortgage early. Which mortgage should you undertake? Do the NPV and IRR rules agree?

Next, assume that the bank will allow you to borrow any fees and points, so the loan amount will increase by these charges. Repeat the above calculations.

Finally, repeat the calculations assuming that you will repay the outstanding balance on the mortgage after 5 years, using the same cost of capital. What can you say about which mortgage you should choose if you have a long horizon versus a shorter horizon?

Of course, the choice of cost of capital will vary by individual. Because your cost of capital might be different to the one used above, for both horizons, pick the option with the largest NPV and plot the NPV profile.

---

[9]The mortgage coupon is listed in the *rate* field (*not* the *APR*) and is quoted as a monthly APR. Both fees and "points" refer to money that must be paid upfront. Fees are specified in dollars, while points refer to a percentage of the amount borrowed. So, a $1000 fee together with a 1% point implies that you must pay $400,000 \times 1\% + 1000 = \$5000$ upfront. This means that although the loan amount will be $400,000 you will actually only borrow $395,000 (so you need to put down an extra $5000).

[10]Hint: If you are having trouble calculating the IRR, make sure it exists by first plotting the NPV profile.

9

Fundamentals of Capital Budgeting

LEARNING OBJECTIVES

- Identify the types of cash flows needed in the capital budgeting process

- Forecast incremental earnings in a pro forma earnings statement for a project

- Convert forecasted earnings to free cash flows and compute a project's NPV

- Recognize common pitfalls that arise in identifying a project's incremental free cash flows

- Assess the sensitivity of a project's NPV to changes in your assumptions

- Identify the most common options available to managers in projects and understand why these options can be valuable

notation

$CapEx$	capital expenditures
$EBIT$	earnings before interest and taxes
FCF_t	free cash flow in year t
IRR	internal rate of return

NPV	net present value
NWC_t	net working capital in year t
PV	present value
r	projected cost of capital

An important responsibility of corporate financial managers is determining which projects or investments a firm should undertake. *Capital budgeting*, the focus of this chapter, is the process of analyzing investment opportunities and deciding which ones to accept. In doing so, we are allocating the firm's funds to various projects—we are budgeting its capital. Chapter 8 covered the various methods for evaluating projects and proved that NPV will be the most reliable and accurate method for doing so. In retrospect, this may not be surprising as it is the only rule directly tied to the Valuation Principle. To implement the NPV rule, we must compute the NPV of our projects and accept only those projects for which the NPV is positive. In the last chapter, we spoke about Sony and Toshiba each using investment decision rules to pursue competing high-definition DVD standards (and eventually for Toshiba, to decide to abandon HD-DVD). In order to implement the investment decision rules, financial managers from Toshiba, for example, first had to forecast the incremental cash flows associated with the investments and later had to forecast the incremental cash flows associated with the decision to stop investing in HD-DVD. The process of forecasting those cash flows, crucial inputs in the investment decision process, is our focus in this chapter.

We begin by estimating the project's expected cash flows by forecasting the project's revenues and costs. Using these cash flows, we can compute the project's NPV—its contribution to shareholder value. Then, because the cash flow forecasts almost always contain uncertainty, we demonstrate how to compute the sensitivity of the NPV to the uncertainty in the forecasts. Finally, we examine the relationship between a project's flexibility and its NPV.

9.1 The Capital Budgeting Process

capital budget Lists the projects and investments that a company plans to undertake during the next period.

capital budgeting The process of analyzing projects and investment opportunities and deciding which ones to accept.

The first step in analyzing various investment opportunities is compiling a list of potential projects. A **capital budget** lists the projects and investments that a company plans to undertake during the next period. To create this list, firms analyze projects and investment opportunities and decide which ones to accept through a process called **capital budgeting**. This process begins with forecasts of each project's future consequences for the firm. Some of these consequences will affect the firm's revenues; others will affect its costs. Our ultimate goal is to determine the effect of the decision to accept or reject a project on the firm's cash flows, and evaluate the NPV of these cash flows to assess the consequences of the decision for the firm's value. Figure 9.1 depicts the types of cash flows found in a typical project. We will examine each of these as we proceed through our discussion of capital budgeting.

Of course, forecasting these cash flows is frequently challenging. We will often need to rely on different experts within the firm to obtain estimates for many of them. For example, the marketing department may provide sales forecasts, the operations manager may provide information about production costs, and the firm's engineers may estimate the up-front research and development expenses that are required to launch the project. Another important source of information comes from looking at past projects of the firm, or those of other firms in the same industry. In particular, practitioners often base their assessments of a project's revenues and costs using information on revenues and costs that can be learned from the historical financial statements of the firm or its competitors.

Once we have these estimates, how do we organize them? One common starting point is to consider the consequences of the project for the firm's earnings. Thus, we will *begin*

FIGURE 9.1

Cash Flows in a Typical Project

The diagram shows some typical cash flows in project analysis and their timing.

Initial Outlay	Ongoing Cash Flows	Terminal Cash Flows
Purchase Equipment	Incremental Revenues	Sale of Equipment (Net of any taxes)
Initial Development Costs	Incremental Costs	Shutdown Costs
	Taxes	
Increase in Net Working Capital (Increase inventories, raw materials, etc.)	Change in Net Working Capital (Change in inventories, raw materials, accounts receivable and payable)	Decrease in Net Working Capital (Decrease inventories, raw materials, etc.)

incremental earnings
The amount by which a firm's earnings are expected to change as a result of an investment decision.

our analysis in Section 9.2 by determining the **incremental earnings** of a project—that is, the amount by which a firm's earnings are expected to change as a result of an investment decision. The incremental earnings forecast tells us how the decision will affect the firm's reported profits from an accounting perspective. However, as we emphasized in Chapter 2, *earnings are not actual cash flows.* We need to estimate the project's cash flows to determine its NPV and decide whether it is a good project for the firm. Therefore, in Section 9.3, we demonstrate how to use the incremental earnings to forecast the actual cash flows of the project. Understanding how to compute the cash flow consequences of an investment based on its earning consequences is important for a number of reasons. First, as a practical matter, financial managers often begin by forecasting earnings. Second, if we are looking at historical data, accounting information is often the only information that is readily available.

CONCEPT CHECK

1. What is capital budgeting, and what is its goal?
2. Why is computing a project's effect on the firm's earnings insufficient for capital budgeting?

9.2 Forecasting Incremental Earnings

Let's begin our discussion of incremental earnings with a simple example that we will examine throughout this section. Suppose you are considering whether to upgrade your manufacturing plant to increase its capacity by purchasing a new piece of equipment. The equipment costs $1 million, plus an additional $20,000 to transport it and install it. You will also spend $50,000 on engineering costs to redesign the plant to accommodate the increased capacity. What are the initial earnings consequences of this decision?

Operating Expenses Versus Capital Expenditures

Most projects require some form of up-front investment—we may need to conduct a marketing survey, develop a prototype, or launch an ad campaign. These types of costs are accounted for as operating expenses in the year that they are incurred. However, many projects also include investments in plant, property, and/or equipment, called *capital expenditures*. Recall from Chapter 2 that while investments in plant, property, and equipment are cash expenses, they are not directly listed as expenses when calculating *earnings*. Instead, the firm deducts a fraction of the cost of these items each year as depreciation. Financial managers use several different methods to compute depreciation. The simplest method is

straight-line depreciation A method of depreciation in which an asset's cost is divided equally over its life.

straight-line depreciation, in which an asset's cost is divided equally over its depreciable life (we discuss another common method in Section 9.4).

In our example, the up-front costs associated with the decision to increase capacity have two distinct consequences for the firm's earnings. First, the $50,000 spent on redesigning the plant is an operating expense reported in year 0. For the $1,020,000 spent to buy, ship, and install the machine, accounting principles as well as tax rules require you to depreciate the $1,020,000 over the depreciable life of the equipment. Assuming that the equipment has a five-year depreciable life and that we use the straight-line method, we would expense $1,020,000/5 = $204,000 per year for five years. (The motivation for this accounting treatment is to match the cost of acquiring the machine to the timing of the revenues it will generate.)

	Year	0	1	2	3	4	5
2	Operating Expenses (Plant Redesign)	−$50,000					
3	Depreciation (New Equipment)		−$204,000	−$204,000	−$204,000	−$204,000	−$204,000

As the timeline shows, the up-front cash outflow of $1,020,000 to purchase and set up the machine is not recognized as an expense in year 0. Instead, it appears as depreciation expenses in years 1 through 5. Remember that these *depreciation expenses do not correspond to actual cash outflows.* This accounting and tax treatment of capital expenditures is one of the key reasons why earnings are not an accurate representation of cash flows. We will return to this issue in Section 9.3.[1]

Incremental Revenue and Cost Estimates

Our next step is to estimate the ongoing revenues and costs for the project. Forecasting future revenues and costs is challenging. The most successful practitioners collect as much information as possible before tackling this task—they will talk to members of marketing and sales teams as well as company economists to develop an estimate of sales, and they will talk to engineering and production teams to refine their estimate of costs.

There are several factors to consider when estimating a project's revenues and costs, including the following:

1. A new product typically has lower sales initially, as customers gradually become aware of the product. Sales will then accelerate, plateau, and ultimately decline as the product nears obsolescence or faces increased competition.

2. The average selling price of a product and its cost of production will generally change over time. Prices and costs tend to rise with the general level of inflation in the economy. The prices of technology products, however, often fall over time as newer, superior technologies emerge and production costs decline.

3. For most industries, competition tends to reduce profit margins over time.

Our focus here is on how to get from these forecasts to incremental earnings and then to cash flows. Chapter 18 discusses forecasting methods in more detail.

All our revenue and cost estimates should be *incremental,* meaning that we only account for additional sales and costs generated by the project. For example, if we are evaluating the purchase of a faster manufacturing machine, we are only concerned with how many additional units of the product we will be able to sell (and at what price) and any additional costs created by the new machine. We do not forecast total sales and costs because those include our production using the old machine. *Remember, we are evaluating how the project will change the cash flows of the firm. That is why we focus on incremental revenues and costs.*

Let's return to our plant upgrade example. Assume that after we have bought and installed the machine and redesigned the plant, our additional capacity will allow us to generate incremental revenues of $500,000 per year for five years. Those incremental revenues will be associated with $150,000 per year in incremental costs. In that case, our revenue, cost, and depreciation estimates for the project are as shown below (in thousands of dollars):

	Year	0	1	2	3	4	5
1							
2	Incremental Revenues		500	500	500	500	500
3	Incremental Costs	−50	−150	−150	−150	−150	−150
4	Depreciation		−204	−204	−204	−204	−204

Now that we have these estimates, we are ready to compute the consequences of our project for the firm's earnings. As we saw in Chapter 2, both depreciation expenses and

---

[1]Some students might note that for financial reporting, the asset should be depreciated to salvage value. For tax purposes, salvage value is always treated as zero, so this is the relevant method for capital budgeting.

the actual costs of producing (e.g., cost of goods sold) must be subtracted from revenues, so that:

$$\text{Incremental Earnings Before Interest and Taxes (EBIT)} = \text{Incremental Revenue}$$
$$- \text{Incremental Costs} - \text{Depreciation} \qquad (9.1)$$

Taxes

marginal corporate tax rate The tax rate a firm will pay on an incremental dollar of pretax income.

The final expense we must account for is corporate taxes. The correct tax rate to use is the firm's **marginal corporate tax rate**, which is the tax rate it will pay on an *incremental* dollar of pretax income. The incremental income tax expense is calculated as:

$$\text{Income Tax} = \text{EBIT} \times \text{The Firm's Marginal Corporate Tax Rate} \qquad (9.2)$$

Incremental Earnings Forecast

We're now ready to put the pieces together for an incremental earnings forecast. Assume our firm faces a marginal tax rate of 40% and that the firm as a whole has at least $50,000 in profits in year 0 for the incremental costs in that year to offset. Then the incremental earnings (or net income) are as follows (in thousands of dollars):[2]

	Year	0	1	2	3	4	5
1	Incremental Revenues		500	500	500	500	500
2	Incremental Costs	−50	−150	−150	−150	−150	−150
3	Depreciation		−204	−204	−204	−204	−204
4	**EBIT**	−50	146	146	146	146	146
5	Income Tax at 40%	20	−58.4	−58.4	−58.4	−58.4	−58.4
6	**Incremental Earnings**	−30	87.6	87.6	87.6	87.6	87.6

We can combine Eqs. 9.1 and 9.2 to compute incremental earnings directly. For example, in years 1 through 5 we have:

$$\text{Incremental Earnings} = (\text{Incremental Revenues} - \text{Incremental Cost}$$
$$- \text{Depreciation}) \times (1 - \text{Tax Rate}) \qquad (9.3)$$
$$\text{Incremental Earnings} = (500{,}000 - 150{,}000 - 204{,}000)$$
$$\times (1 - 0.4) = 87{,}600$$

EXAMPLE 9.1

Incremental Earnings

MyFinanceLab

PROBLEM

Suppose that the managers of the router division of Cisco Systems are considering the development of a wireless home networking appliance, called HomeNet, that will provide both the hardware and the software necessary to run an entire home from any Internet connection. In addition to connecting computers and smartphones, HomeNet will control Internet-capable televisions, streaming video services, heating and air-conditioning units, major appliances, security systems, office equipment, and so on. The major competitor for HomeNet is a product being developed by Brandt-Quigley Corporation.

Based on extensive marketing surveys, the sales forecast for HomeNet is 50,000 units per year. Given the pace of technological change, Cisco expects the product will have a four-year life and an expected

(Continued)

---

[2]While revenues and costs occur throughout the year, the standard convention, which we adopt here, is to list revenues and costs in the year in which they occur. Thus, cash flows that occur at the end of one year will be listed in a different column than those that occur at the start of the next year, even though they may occur only weeks apart. When additional precision is required, cash flows are often estimated on a quarterly or monthly basis.

wholesale price of $260 (the price Cisco will receive from stores). Actual production will be outsourced at a cost (including packaging) of $110 per unit.

To verify the compatibility of new consumer Internet-ready appliances, as they become available, with the HomeNet system, Cisco must also establish a new lab for testing purposes. It will rent the lab space, but will need to purchase $7.5 million of new equipment. The equipment will be depreciated using the straight-line method over a five-year life. Cisco's marginal tax rate is 40%.

The lab will be operational at the end of one year. At that time, HomeNet will be ready to ship. Cisco expects to spend $2.8 million per year on rental costs for the lab space, as well as marketing and support for this product. Forecast the incremental earnings from the HomeNet project.

SOLUTION

PLAN

We need four items to calculate incremental earnings: (1) incremental revenues, (2) incremental costs, (3) depreciation, and (4) the marginal tax rate:

Incremental revenues are:	Additional units sold × price = 50,000 × $260 = $13,000,000
Incremental costs are:	Additional units sold × production costs = 50,000 × $110 = $5,500,000 Selling, general, and administrative = $2,800,000 for rent, marketing, and support
Depreciation is:	Depreciable basis/Depreciable life = $7,500,000/5 = $1,500,000
Marginal tax rate is:	40%

Note that even though the project lasts for four years, the equipment has a five-year life, so we must account for the final depreciation charge in the fifth year.

EXECUTE (IN $000S)

1	Year	0	1	2	3	4	5
2	Revenues		13,000	13,000	13,000	13,000	—
3	Cost of Goods Sold		−5,500	−5,500	−5,500	−5,500	—
4	**Gross Profit**		7,500	7,500	7,500	7,500	—
5	Selling, General, and Administrative		−2,800	−2,800	−2,800	−2,800	—
6	Depreciation		−1,500	−1,500	−1,500	−1,500	−1,500
7	**EBIT**		3,200	3,200	3,200	3,200	−1,500
8	Income Tax at 40%		−1,280	−1,280	−1,280	−1,280	600
9	**Incremental Earnings**		1,920	1,920	1,920	1,920	−900

EVALUATE

These incremental earnings are an intermediate step on the way to calculating the incremental cash flows that would form the basis of any analysis of the HomeNet project. The cost of the equipment does not affect earnings in the year it is purchased, but does so through the depreciation expense in the following five years. Note that the depreciable life, which is based on accounting rules, does not have to be the same as the economic life of the asset—the period over which it will have value. Here, the firm will use the equipment for four years, but will depreciate it over five years.

pro forma Describes a statement that is not based on actual data but rather depicts a firm's financials under a given set of hypothetical assumptions.

Pro Forma Statement. The table calculating incremental earnings that we produced for our plant upgrade, and again in Example 9.1, is often referred to as a **pro forma** statement, because it is not based on actual data but rather depicts the firm's financials under a given set of hypothetical assumptions. In the HomeNet example, the firm's forecasts of revenues and costs were assumptions that allowed Cisco to forecast incremental earnings in a pro forma statement.

Taxes and Negative EBIT. Notice that in year 0 of our plant upgrade project, and in year 5 of the HomeNet example, EBIT is negative. Why are taxes relevant in this case? Consider the HomeNet example. HomeNet will reduce Cisco's taxable income in year 5 by $1.5

million. As long as Cisco earns taxable income elsewhere in year 5 against which it can offset HomeNet's losses, Cisco will owe $1.5 million $\times$ 40% = $600,000 *less* in taxes in year 5 than if it were not undertaking the project. Because the tax savings come from the depreciation expense on equipment for the HomeNet project, the firm should credit this tax savings to the HomeNet project.

EXAMPLE 9.2

Taxing Losses
for Projects
in Profitable
Companies

MyFinanceLab

PROBLEM

Suppose that Kellogg Company plans to launch a new line of high-fiber, gluten-free breakfast pastries. The heavy advertising expenses associated with the new product launch will generate operating losses of $15 million next year for the product. Kellogg expects to earn pretax income of $460 million from operations other than the new pastries next year. If Kellogg pays a 40% tax rate on its pretax income, what will it owe in taxes next year without the new pastry product? What will it owe with the new product?

SOLUTION

PLAN

We need Kellogg's pretax income with and without the new product losses and its tax rate of 40%. We can then compute the tax without the losses and compare it to the tax with the losses.

EXECUTE

Without the new product, Kellogg will owe $460 million $\times$ 40% = $184 million in corporate taxes next year. With the new product, Kellogg's pretax income next year will be only $460 million − $15 million = $445 million, and it will owe $445 million $\times$ 40% = $178 million in tax.

EVALUATE

Thus, launching the new product reduces Kellogg's taxes next year by $184 million − $178 million = $6 million. Because the losses on the new product reduce Kellogg's taxable income dollar for dollar, it is the same as if the new product had a tax bill of *negative* $6 million.

What About Interest Expenses? In Chapter 2, we saw that to compute a firm's net income, we must first deduct interest expenses from EBIT. When evaluating a capital budgeting decision, however, we generally *do not include interest expenses*. Any incremental interest expenses will be related to the firm's decision regarding how to finance the project, which is a separate decision. Here, we wish to evaluate the earnings contributions from the project on its own, separate from the financing decision. Ultimately, managers may also look at the additional earnings consequences associated with different methods of financing the project.

    Thus, we evaluate a project *as if* the company will not use any debt to finance it (whether or not that is actually the case), and we postpone the consideration of alternative financing choices until Parts 5 and 6 of the book. Because we calculate the net income assuming no debt (no leverage), we refer to the net income we compute using Eq. 9.3, as in the pro forma in Example 9.1, as the **unlevered net income** of the project, to indicate that it does not include any interest expenses associated with debt.

unlevered net income
Net income that does not include interest expenses associated with debt.

CONCEPT CHECK

3. How are operating expenses and capital expenditures treated differently when calculating incremental earnings?

4. Why do we focus only on incremental revenues and costs, rather than all revenues and costs of the firm?

9.3   Determining Incremental Free Cash Flow

As discussed in Chapter 2, earnings are an accounting measure of the firm's performance. They do not represent real profits: The firm cannot use its earnings to buy goods, pay employees, fund new investments, or pay dividends to shareholders. To do those things,

free cash flow The incremental effect of a project on a firm's available cash.

the firm needs cash. Thus, to evaluate a capital budgeting decision, we must determine its consequences for the firm's available cash. The incremental effect of a project on the firm's available cash is the project's incremental **free cash flow**.

Converting from Earnings to Free Cash Flow

As discussed in Chapter 2, there are important differences between earnings and cash flow. Earnings include non-cash charges, such as depreciation, but do not include expenditures on capital investment. To determine a project's free cash flow from its incremental earnings, we must adjust for these differences.

Capital Expenditures and Depreciation. As we have noted, depreciation is not a cash expense that is paid by the firm. Rather, it is a method used for accounting and tax purposes to allocate the original purchase cost of the asset over its life. Because depreciation is not a cash flow, we do not include it in the cash flow forecast. However, that does not mean we can ignore depreciation. The depreciation expense reduces our taxable earnings and in doing so reduces our taxes. Taxes are cash flows, so because depreciation affects our cash flows, it still matters. Our approach for handling depreciation is to add it back to the incremental earnings to recognize the fact that we still have the cash flow associated with it.

For example, a project has incremental gross profit (revenues minus costs) of $1 million and a $200,000 depreciation expense. If the firm's tax rate is 40%, then the incremental earnings will be $(\$1,000,000 - \$200,000) \times (1 - 0.40) = \$480,000$. However, the firm will still have $680,000 because the $200,000 depreciation expense is not an actual cash outflow. Table 9.1 shows the calculation to get the incremental free cash flow in this case. Blue boxes indicate all of the actual cash flows in the column labeled "Correct." A good way to check to make sure the incremental free cash flow is correct is to sum the actual cash flows. In this case, the firm generated $1,000,000 in gross profit (a positive cash flow), paid $320,000 in taxes (a negative cash flow), and was left with $1,000,000 - \$320,000 = \$680,000$, which is the amount shown as the incremental free cash flow. In the last column, labeled "Incorrect," we show what would happen if you just ignored depreciation altogether. Because EBIT would be too high, the taxes would be too high as well and consequently, the incremental free cash flow would be too low. (Note that the difference of $80,000 between the two cases is entirely due to the difference in tax payments.)

TABLE 9.1

Deducting and Then Adding Back Depreciation

	Correct	Incorrect
Incremental Gross Profit	$1,000,000	$1,000,000
Depreciation	−200,000	
EBIT	$800,000	$1,000,000
Tax at 40%	−$320,000	−$400,000
Incremental Earnings	$480,000	$600,000
Add Back Depreciation	$200,000	
Incremental Free Cash Flow	$680,000	$600,000

EXAMPLE 9.3

Incremental Free Cash Flows

MyFinanceLab

PROBLEM

Let's return to the HomeNet example. In Example 9.1, we computed the incremental earnings for HomeNet, but we need the incremental free cash flows to decide whether Cisco should proceed with the project.

SOLUTION

PLAN

The difference between the incremental earnings and incremental free cash flows in the HomeNet example will be driven by the equipment purchased for the lab. We need to recognize the $7.5 million cash outflow associated with the purchase in year 0 and add back the $1.5 million depreciation expenses from year 1 to 5 as they are not actually cash outflows.

EXECUTE (IN $000S)

We recognize the outflow for the equipment in row 11 and we add back the depreciation expenses in row 10.

	Year	0	1	2	3	4	5
1							
2	Revenues		13,000	13,000	13,000	13,000	–
3	Cost of Goods Sold		−5,500	−5,500	−5,500	−5,500	–
4	**Gross Profit**		7,500	7,500	7,500	7,500	–
5	Selling, General, and Administrative		−2,800	−2,800	−2,800	−2,800	–
6	Depreciation		−1,500	−1,500	−1,500	−1,500	−1,500
7	**EBIT**		3,200	3,200	3,200	3,200	−1,500
8	Income Tax at 40%		−1,280	−1,280	−1,280	−1,280	600
9	**Incremental Earnings**		1,920	1,920	1,920	1,920	−900
10	Add Back Depreciation		1,500	1,500	1,500	1,500	1,500
11	Purchase of Equipment	−7,500					
12	**Incremental Free Cash Flows**	−7,500	3,420	3,420	3,420	3,420	600

EVALUATE

By recognizing the outflow from purchasing the equipment in year 0, we account for the fact that $7.5 million left the firm at that time. By adding back the $1.5 million depreciation expenses in years 1 through 5, we adjust the incremental earnings to reflect the fact that the depreciation expense is not a cash outflow.

Net Working Capital (NWC). Another way that incremental earnings and free cash flows can differ is if there are changes in net working capital. We defined net working capital in Chapter 2 as the difference between current assets and current liabilities. The main components of net working capital are cash, inventory, receivables, and payables:

$$\text{Net Working Capital} = \text{Current Assets} - \text{Current Liabilities}$$
$$= \text{Cash} + \text{Inventory} + \text{Receivables} - \text{Payables} \qquad (9.4)$$

Note that as discussed in Chapter 2, we do not include short-term financing such as notes payable or short-term debt because those represent financing decisions that we keep separate from our investment decisions. Most projects will require the firm to invest in net working capital. Firms may need to maintain a minimum cash balance[3] to meet unexpected expenditures, and inventories of raw materials and finished product to accommodate production uncertainties and demand fluctuations. Also, customers may not pay for the goods they purchase immediately. While sales are immediately counted as part of earnings, the firm does not receive any cash until the customers actually pay. In the interim, the firm includes the amount that customers owe in its receivables. Thus, the firm's receivables measure the total credit that the firm has extended to its customers. In the same way, payables measure the credit the firm has received from its suppliers. The difference between receivables and payables is the net amount of the firm's capital that is consumed as a result of these credit transactions, known as **trade credit**.

trade credit The difference between receivables and payables (the net amount of a firm's capital consumed as a result of these credit transactions); the credit that a firm extends to its customers.

---

[3] The cash included in net working capital is cash that is *not* invested to earn a market rate of return. It includes cash held in the firm's checking account, in a company safe or cash box, in cash registers (for retail stores), and other sites.

We care about net working capital because it reflects a short-term investment that ties up cash flow that could be used elsewhere. For example, when a firm holds a lot of unsold inventory or has a lot of outstanding receivables, cash flow is tied up in the form of inventory or in the form of credit extended to customers. It is costly for the firm to tie up that cash flow because it delays the time until the cash flow is available for reinvestment or distribution to shareholders. Since we know that money has time value, we cannot ignore this delay in our forecasts for the project. Thus, whenever net working capital increases, reflecting additional investment in working capital, it represents a reduction in cash flow that year.

It is important to note that only changes in net working capital impact cash flows. For example, consider a three-year project that causes the firm to build up initial inventory by $20,000 and maintain that level of inventory in years 1 and 2, before drawing it down as the project ends and the last product is sold. It is often necessary for the initial increase in inventory to occur prior to the first sale so that the higher level of inventory would be achieved by the end of year 0. The level of the incremental net working capital in each year, the associated change in net working capital, and the cash flow implications, would be:

1	Year	0	1	2	3
2	Level of Incremental NWC	20,000	20,000	20,000	0
3	*Change* in Incremental NWC	+20,000	0	0	−20,000
4	**Cash Flow from Change in NWC**	**−20,000**	**0**	**0**	**+20,000**

Note that the cash flow effect from a change in net working capital is always equal and opposite in sign to the change in net working capital. For example, an increase in inventory represents an investment or cash outflow, while a reduction in that inventory frees up that investment of capital and represents a cash inflow. Thus, in capital budgeting we subtract changes in net working capital to arrive at the cash flows. Also notice that since the level of incremental net working capital did not change in years 1 and 2, there was no new cash flow effect. Intuitively, as the firm is using up inventory and replenishing it, the net new investment in inventory is zero, so no additional cash outflow is required. Finally, note that over the life of the project, the incremental net working capital returns to zero so that the changes (+20,000 in year 0 and −20,000 in year 3) sum to zero. Accounting principles ensure this by requiring the recapture of working capital over the life of the project.

More generally, we define the change in net working capital in year t as:

$$\text{Change in } NWC \text{ in Year } t = NWC_t - NWC_{t-1} \tag{9.5}$$

When a project causes a change in NWC, that change must be subtracted from incremental earnings to arrive at incremental free cash flows.

EXAMPLE 9.4

Incorporating Changes in Net Working Capital

MyFinanceLab

PROBLEM

Suppose that HomeNet will have no incremental cash or inventory requirements (products will be shipped directly from the contract manufacturer to customers). However, receivables related to HomeNet are expected to account for 15% of annual sales, and payables are expected to be 15% of the annual cost of goods sold (COGS). Fifteen percent of $13 million in sales is $1.95 million and 15% of $5.5 million in COGS is $825,000. HomeNet's net working capital requirements are shown in the following table:

1	Year	0	1	2	3	4	5
2	**Net Working Capital Forecast ($000s)**						
3	Cash Requirements	0	0	0	0	0	0
4	Inventory	0	0	0	0	0	0
5	Receivables (15% of Sales)	0	1,950	1,950	1,950	1,950	0
6	Payables (15% of COGS)	0	−825	−825	−825	−825	0
7	**Net Working Capital**	**0**	**1,125**	**1,125**	**1,125**	**1,125**	**0**

How does this requirement affect the project's free cash flow?

SOLUTION

PLAN

Any increases in net working capital represent an investment that reduces the cash available to the firm and so reduces free cash flow. We can use our forecast of HomeNet's net working capital requirements to complete our estimate of HomeNet's free cash flow. In year 1, net working capital increases by $1.125 million. This increase represents a cost to the firm. This reduction of free cash flow corresponds to the fact that in year 1, $1.950 million of the firm's sales and $0.825 million of its costs have not yet been paid.

In years 2–4, net working capital does not change, so no further contributions are needed. In year 5, when the project is shut down, net working capital falls by $1.125 million as the payments of the last customers are received and the final bills are paid. We add this $1.125 million to free cash flow in year 5.

EXECUTE (IN $000S)

1	Year	0	1	2	3	4	5
2	Net Working Capital	0	1,125	1,125	1,125	1,125	0
3	Change in NWC		+1,125	0	0	0	−1,125
4	Cash Flow Effect		−1,125	0	0	0	+1,125

The incremental free cash flows would then be:

1	Year	0	1	2	3	4	5
2	Revenues		13,000	13,000	13,000	13,000	0
3	Costs of Goods Sold		−5,500	−5,500	−5,500	−5,500	0
4	**Gross Profit**		7,500	7,500	7,500	7,500	0
5	Selling, General, and Administrative		−2,800	−2,800	−2,800	−2,800	0
6	Depreciation		−1,500	−1,500	−1,500	−1,500	−1,500
7	**EBIT**		3,200	3,200	3,200	3,200	−1,500
8	Income Tax at 40%		−1,280	−1,280	−1,280	−1,280	600
9	**Incremental Earnings**		1,920	1,920	1,920	1,920	−900
10	Add Back Depreciation		1,500	1,500	1,500	1,500	1,500
11	Purchase of Equipment	−7,500					
12	Subtract Changes in NWC		−1,125	0	0	0	1,125
13	**Incremental Free Cash Flows**	−7,500	2,295	3,420	3,420	3,420	1,725

EVALUATE

The free cash flows differ from unlevered net income by reflecting the cash flow effects of capital expenditures on equipment, depreciation, and changes in net working capital. Note that in the first year, free cash flow is lower than unlevered net income, reflecting the up-front investment in equipment. In later years, free cash flow exceeds unlevered net income because depreciation is not a cash expense. In the last year, the firm ultimately recovers the investment in net working capital, further boosting the free cash flow.

Calculating Free Cash Flow Directly

As we noted at the outset of this chapter, because practitioners usually begin the capital budgeting process by first forecasting earnings, we have chosen to do the same. However, we can calculate a project's free cash flow directly by using the following shorthand formula:

Free Cash Flow

$$\text{Free Cash Flow} = \overbrace{(\text{Revenues} - \text{Costs} - \text{Depreciation}) \times (1 - \text{Tax Rate})}^{\text{Unlevered Net Income}} \quad (9.6)$$
$$+ \text{Depreciation} - \text{CapEx} - \text{Change in } NWC$$

Note that we first deduct depreciation when computing the project's incremental earnings and then add it back (because it is a non-cash expense) when computing free cash flow.

Thus, the only effect of depreciation is to reduce the firm's taxable income. Indeed, we can rewrite Eq. 9.6 as:

$$\text{Free Cash Flow} = (\text{Revenues} - \text{Costs}) \times (1 - \text{Tax Rate}) - \text{CapEx} \\ - \text{Change in } NWC + \text{Tax Rate} \times \text{Depreciation} \qquad (9.7)$$

depreciation tax shield The tax savings that result from the ability to deduct depreciation.

The last term in Eq. 9.7, Tax Rate × Depreciation, is called the **depreciation tax shield**, which is the tax savings that result from the ability to deduct depreciation. As a consequence, depreciation expenses have a *positive* impact on free cash flow. Returning to our example in Table 9.1, if the firm ignored depreciation, its taxes were $400,000 instead of $320,000, leaving it with incremental free cash flow of $600,000 instead of $680,000. Notice that the $80,000 difference is exactly equal to the tax rate (40%) multiplied by the depreciation expense ($200,000). Every dollar of depreciation expense saves the firm 40 cents in taxes, so the $200,000 depreciation expense translates into an $80,000 tax savings.

Firms often report a different depreciation expense for accounting and for tax purposes. Because only the tax consequences of depreciation are relevant for free cash flow, we should use the depreciation expense that the firm will use for tax purposes in our forecast. For tax purposes, many firms use a system called *Modified Accelerated Cost Recovery System*, which we will discuss in the next section.

Calculating the NPV

The goal of forecasting the incremental free cash flows is to have the necessary inputs to calculate the project's NPV. To compute a project's NPV, we must discount its free cash flow at the appropriate cost of capital. As discussed in Chapter 5, the cost of capital for a project is the expected return that investors could earn on their best alternative investment with similar risk and maturity. We will develop the techniques needed to estimate the cost of capital in Part 4 of the text, when we discuss risk and return. For now, we take the cost of capital as given.

We compute the present value of each free cash flow in the future by discounting it at the project's cost of capital. As explained in Chapter 3, using r to represent the cost of capital, the present value of the free cash flow in year t (or FCF_t) is:

$$PV(FCF_t) = \frac{FCF_t}{(1+r)^t} = FCF_t \times \underbrace{\frac{1}{(1+r)^t}}_{t\text{-year discount factor}} \qquad (9.8)$$

EXAMPLE 9.5

Calculating the Project's NPV

MyFinanceLab

PROBLEM
Assume that Cisco's managers believe that the HomeNet project has risks similar to its existing projects, for which it has a cost of capital of 12%. Compute the NPV of the HomeNet project.

SOLUTION

PLAN

From Example 9.4, the incremental free cash flows for the HomeNet project are (in $000s):

	Year	0	1	2	3	4	5
1							
2	Incremental Free Cash Flows	−7,500	2,295	3,420	3,420	3,420	1,725

To compute the NPV, we sum the present values of all of the cash flows, noting that the year 0 cash outflow is already a present value.

EXECUTE

Using Eq. 9.8,

$$NPV = -7500 + \frac{2295}{(1.12)^1} + \frac{3420}{(1.12)^2} + \frac{3420}{(1.12)^3} + \frac{3420}{(1.12)^4} + \frac{1725}{(1.12)^5} = 2862$$

EVALUATE

Based on our estimates, HomeNet's NPV is $2.862 million. While HomeNet's up-front cost is $7.5 million, the present value of the additional free cash flow that Cisco will receive from the project is $10.362 million. Thus, taking the HomeNet project is equivalent to Cisco having an extra $2.862 million in the bank today.

USING EXCEL

Capital Budgeting Using a Spreadsheet Program

Capital budgeting forecasts and analysis are most easily performed in a spreadsheet program. Here, we highlight a few best practices when developing your own capital budgets.

Create a Project Dashboard

All capital budgeting analyses begin with a set of assumptions regarding future revenues and costs associated with the investment. Centralize these assumptions within your spreadsheet in a project dashboard so they are easy to locate, review, and potentially modify. Here, we show an example for the HomeNet project.

	A	B	C	D	E	F	G	H	I	J
1	**HomeNet Capital Budget**									
2	**Key Assumptions**									
3	*Revenues & Costs*			Year 0	Year 1	Year 2	Year 3	Year 4	Year 5	
4	HomeNet Units Sold				50	50	50	50		
5	HomeNet Ave. Price/Unit				$ 260.00	$ 260.00	$ 260.00	$ 260.00		
6	HomeNet Cost/Unit				$ 110.00	$ 110.00	$ 110.00	$ 110.00		
7	*Operating Expenses*									
8	Marketing, Support & Rent				(2,800)	(2,800)	(2,800)	(2,800)		
9	*Capital Expenditures*									
10	Purchase Equipment			(7,500)						
11	*Other Assumptions*									
12	Depreciation Schedule			0.0%	20.0%	20.0%	20.0%	20.0%	20.0%	
13	Corporate Tax Rate			40.0%	40.0%	40.0%	40.0%	40.0%	40.0%	
14	Receivables (% sales)			15.0%	15.0%	15.0%	15.0%	15.0%	15.0%	
15	Payables (% expenses)			15.0%	15.0%	15.0%	15.0%	15.0%	15.0%	
16										

Color Code for Clarity

In spreadsheet models, use a blue font to distinguish numerical assumptions from formulas. For example, HomeNet's revenue and cost estimates are set to a numerical value in year 1, whereas estimates in later years are set to equal the year 1 estimates. It is therefore clear which cells contain the main assumptions, should we wish to change them later.

Maintain Flexibility

In the HomeNet dashboard, note that we state all assumptions on an annual basis even if we expect them to remain constant. For example, we specify HomeNet's unit volume and average sale price for each year. We can then calculate HomeNet revenues each year based on the corresponding annual assumptions. Doing so provides flexibility if we later determine that HomeNet's adoption rate might vary over time or if we expect prices to follow a trend.

Never Hardcode

So that your assumptions are clear and easy to modify, reference any numerical values you need to develop your projections in the project dashboard. Never "hardcode," or enter numerical values directly into formulas. For example, in the computation of taxes in cell E24 below, we use the formula "=−E23*E13" rather than "=−E23*0.40". While the latter formula would compute the same answer, because the tax rate is hardcoded it would be difficult to update the model if the forecast for the tax rate were to change.

	A	B	C	D	E	F	G	H	I	J
22		*Incremental Earnings Forecast*			Year 0	Year 1	Year 2	Year 3	Year 4	Year 5
23		EBIT				$3,200	$3,200	$3,200	$3,200	($1,500)
24		Income Tax				=−E23*E13	($1,280)	($1,280)	($1,280)	$600
25		Net Income				$1,920	$1,920	$1,920	$1,920	($900)

CONCEPT
CHECK
5. If depreciation expense is not a cash flow, why do we have to subtract it and add it back? Why not just ignore it?

6. Why does an increase in net working capital represent a cash outflow?

9.4 Other Effects on Incremental Free Cash Flows

When computing the incremental free cash flows of an investment decision, we should include *all* changes between the firm's free cash flows with the project versus without the project. These include opportunities forgone due to the project and effects of the project on other parts of the firm. In this section, we discuss these other effects, some of the pitfalls and common mistakes to avoid, and the complications that can arise when forecasting incremental free cash flows.

Opportunity Costs

opportunity cost The value a resource could have provided in its best alternative use.

Many projects use a resource that the company already owns. Because the firm does not need to pay cash to acquire this resource for a new project, it is tempting to assume that the resource is available for free. However, in many cases, the resource could provide value for the firm in another opportunity or project. The **opportunity cost** of using a resource is the value it could have provided in its best alternative use.[4] Because this value is lost when the resource is used by another project, we should include the opportunity cost as an incremental cost of the project. For example, your company may be considering building a retail store on land that it owns. Even though it already owns the land, it is not free to the store project. If it does not put its store on the land, the company could sell the land, for example. This forgone market price for the land is an opportunity cost of the retail store project.

COMMON MISTAKE

The Opportunity Cost of an Idle Asset

A common mistake is to conclude that if an asset is currently idle, its opportunity cost is zero. For example, the firm might have a warehouse that is currently empty or a machine that is not being used. Often, the asset may have been idled in anticipation of taking on the new project, and would have otherwise been put to use by the firm. Even if the firm has no alternative use for the asset, the firm could choose to sell or rent the asset. The value obtained from the asset's alternative use, sale, or rental represents an opportunity cost that must be included as part of the incremental cash flows.

Project Externalities

project externalities Indirect effects of a project that may increase or decrease the profits of other business activities of a firm.

Project externalities are indirect effects of a project that may increase or decrease the profits of other business activities of the firm. For instance, some purchasers of Apple's larger iPad Pro would otherwise have bought Apple's iPad Air. When sales of a new product displace sales of an existing product, the situation is often referred

---

[4]In Chapter 5, we defined the opportunity cost of capital as the rate you could earn on an alternative investment with equivalent risk. We similarly define the opportunity cost of using an existing asset in a project as the cash flow generated by the next-best alternative use for the asset.

cannibalization When sales of a firm's new product displace sales of one of its existing products.

to as **cannibalization**. The lost sales of the existing product are an incremental cost to the company of going forward with the new product.

Sunk Costs

sunk cost Any unrecoverable cost for which a firm is already liable.

A **sunk cost** is any unrecoverable cost for which the firm is already liable. Sunk costs have been or will be paid regardless of the decision whether or not to proceed with the project. Therefore, they are not incremental with respect to the current decision and should not be included in its analysis. You may hire a market research firm to determine whether there is demand for a new product you are considering and the analysis may show that there is not enough demand, so you decide not to go forward with the project. Does that mean you do not have to pay the research firm's bill? Of course you still have to pay the bill, emphasizing that the cost is sunk and incurred whether you move forward with the project or not.

A good rule to remember is that *if your decision does not affect a cash flow, then the cash flow should not affect your decision.* If the cash flow is the same regardless of the decision, then it is not relevant to your decision. The following are some common examples of sunk costs you may encounter.

overhead expenses Expenses associated with activities that are not directly attributable to a single business activity but instead affect many different areas of a corporation.

Fixed Overhead Expenses. **Overhead expenses** are associated with activities that are not directly attributable to a single business activity but instead affect many different areas of a corporation. Examples include the cost of maintaining the company's headquarters and the salary of the CEO. These expenses are often allocated to the different business activities for accounting purposes. To the extent that these overhead costs are fixed and will be incurred in any case, they are not incremental to the project and should not be included. Only include as incremental expenses the *additional* overhead expenses that arise because of the decision to take on the project.

COMMON MISTAKE

The Sunk Cost Fallacy

Being influenced by sunk costs is such a widespread mistake that it has a special name: sunk cost fallacy. The most common problem is that people "throw good money after bad." That is, people sometimes continue to invest in a project that has a negative NPV because they have already invested a large amount in the project and feel that by not continuing it, the prior investment will be wasted. The sunk cost fallacy is also sometimes called the "Concorde effect," which refers to the British and French

governments' decision to continue funding the joint development of the Concorde aircraft even after it was clear that sales of the plane would fall far short of what was necessary to justify its continued development. The project was viewed by the British government as a commercial and financial disaster. However, the political implications of halting the project—and thereby publicly admitting that all past expenses on the project would result in nothing—ultimately prevented either government from abandoning the project.

Past Research and Development Expenditures. A pharmaceutical company may spend tens of millions of dollars developing a new drug, but if it fails to produce an effect in trials (or worse, has only negative effects), should it proceed? The company cannot get its development costs back and the amount of those costs should have no bearing on whether to continue developing a failed drug.

When a firm has already devoted significant resources to develop a new product, there may be a tendency to continue investing in the product even if market conditions have changed and the product is unlikely to be viable. The rationale that is sometimes given is that if the product is abandoned, the money that has already been invested will be "wasted." In other cases, a decision is made to abandon a project because it cannot possibly be successful enough to recoup the investment that has already been made. In fact, neither argument is correct: Any money that has already been spent is a sunk cost and therefore irrelevant. The decision to continue or abandon should be based only on the incremental costs and benefits of the product going forward.

Unavoidable Competitive Effects. When developing a new product, firms often worry about the cannibalization of their existing products. But if sales are likely to decline in any case as a result of new products introduced by competitors, then these lost sales are a sunk cost and we should not include them in our projections.

Adjusting Free Cash Flow

Here, we describe a number of complications that can arise when estimating a project's free cash flow.

Timing of Cash Flows. For simplicity, we have treated the cash flows in our examples as if they occur at annual intervals. In reality, cash flows are spread throughout the year. While it is common to forecast at the annual level, we can forecast free cash flow on a quarterly or monthly basis when greater accuracy is required. In practice, firms often choose shorter intervals for riskier projects so that they might forecast cash flows at the monthly level for projects that carry considerable risk. For example, cash flows for a new facility in Europe may be forecasted at the quarterly or annual level, but if that same facility were located in a politically unstable country, the forecasts would likely be at the monthly level.

Accelerated Depreciation. Because depreciation contributes positively to the firm's cash flow through the depreciation tax shield, it is in the firm's best interest to use the most accelerated method of depreciation that is allowable for tax purposes. By doing so, the firm will accelerate its tax savings and increase their present value. In the United States, the most accelerated depreciation method allowed by the IRS is *MACRS (Modified Accelerated Cost Recovery System) depreciation*. With **MACRS depreciation**, the firm first categorizes assets according to their recovery period. Based on the recovery period, MACRS depreciation tables assign a fraction of the purchase price that the firm can recover each year. We provide MACRS tables and recovery periods for common assets in the appendix to this chapter. As we explain in the appendix, MACRS allows for partial depreciation in the year when the asset is purchased and put into service.

> **MACRS depreciation** The most accelerated cost recovery system allowed by the IRS. Based on the recovery period, MACRS depreciation tables assign a fraction of the purchase price that the firm can depreciate each year.

EXAMPLE 9.6
Computing Accelerated Depreciation

MyFinanceLab

PROBLEM

What depreciation deduction would be allowed for HomeNet's $7.5 million lab equipment using the MACRS method, assuming the lab equipment is designated to have a five-year recovery period? For clarity, assume that the lab equipment is purchased and put into use in December of year 0, allowing the partial year depreciation in year 0. This means that year 0 is the first year of the MACRS schedule (year 1) in the appendix. (See the appendix to this chapter for information on MACRS depreciation schedules.)

SOLUTION

PLAN

Table 9.4 (in the appendix) provides the percentage of the cost that can be depreciated each year. Under MACRS, we take the percentage in the table for each year and multiply it by the original purchase price of the equipment to calculate the depreciation for that year.

EXECUTE

Based on the table, the allowable depreciation expense for the lab equipment is shown below (in thousands of dollars):

	Year	0	1	2	3	4	5
1							
2	**MACRS Depreciation**						
3	Lab Equipment Cost	−7,500					
4	MACRS Depreciation Rate	20.00%	32.00%	19.20%	11.52%	11.52%	5.76%
5	Depreciation Expense	−1,500	−2,400	−1,440	−864	−864	−432

EVALUATE

As long as the equipment is put into use by the end of year 0, the tax code allows us to take our first depreciation expense in the same year. Compared with straight-line depreciation, the MACRS method allows for larger depreciation deductions earlier in the asset's life, which increases the present value of the depreciation tax shield and so will raise the project's NPV. In the case of HomeNet, computing the NPV using MACRS depreciation leads to an NPV of $3.179 million.

Now compare what would happen if we put the machine into use at the very beginning of year 1 (the same year as we first recognize revenues in this example). Then, all of our depreciation expenses would shift by one year. Because we put the equipment *into use in year 1*, then the first time we can take a depreciation expense is in year 1. In that case, the table would be:

	Year	0	1	2	3	4	5	6
1								
2	MACRS Depreciation							
3	Lab Equipment Cost	−7,500						
4	MACRS Depreciation Rate		20.00%	32.00%	19.20%	11.52%	11.52%	5.76%
5	Depreciation Expense		−1,500	−2,400	−1,440	−864	−864	−432

In this case, the NPV would be $2.913 million because all of the depreciation tax shields are delayed by one year relative to the case where the equipment is put into use before year 1. Nonetheless, the NPV is still higher than in the case of straight-line depreciation because a larger percentage of the depreciation comes earlier.

Liquidation or Salvage Value. Assets that are no longer needed often have a resale value, or some salvage value if the parts are sold for scrap. Some assets may have a negative liquidation value. For example, it may cost money to remove and dispose of the used equipment.

In the calculation of free cash flow, we include the liquidation value of any assets that are no longer needed and may be disposed of. When an asset is liquidated, any capital gain is taxed as income. We calculate the capital gain as the difference between the sale price and the book value of the asset:

$$\text{Capital Gain} = \text{Sale Price} - \text{Book Value} \tag{9.9}$$

The book value is equal to the asset's original cost less the amount it has already been depreciated for tax purposes:

$$\text{Book Value} = \text{Purchase Price} - \text{Accumulated Depreciation} \tag{9.10}$$

We must adjust the project's free cash flow to account for the after-tax cash flow that would result from an asset sale:

$$\text{After-Tax Cash Flow from Asset Sale} = \text{Sale Price} - (\text{Tax Rate} \times \text{Capital Gain}) \tag{9.11}$$

EXAMPLE 9.7
Computing After-Tax Cash Flows from an Asset Sale

MyFinanceLab

PROBLEM

As production manager, you are overseeing the shutdown of a production line for a discontinued product. Some of the equipment can be sold for $50,000. The equipment was originally purchased and put into use five years ago for $500,000 and is being depreciated according to the five-year MACRS schedule (so that you are five years into the six years of the 5-year MACRS schedule). If your marginal tax rate is 35%, what is the after-tax cash flow you can expect from selling the equipment?

SOLUTION

PLAN

In order to compute the after-tax cash flow, you will need to compute the capital gain, which, as Eq. 9.9 shows, requires you to know the book value of the equipment. The book value is given in Eq. 9.10 as the original purchase price of the equipment less accumulated depreciation. Thus, you need to follow these steps:
1. Use the MACRS schedule to determine the accumulated depreciation.

(Continued)

2. Determine the book value as purchase price minus accumulated depreciation.
3. Determine the capital gain as the sale price less the book value.
4. Compute the tax owed on the capital gain and subtract it from the sale price, following Eq. 9.11, and then subtract the tax owed from the sale price.

EXECUTE

From the appendix, we see that the first five rates of the five-year MACRS schedule (including year 0) are:

Year	1	2	3	4	5
Depreciation Rate	20.00%	32.00%	19.20%	11.52%	11.52%
Depreciation Amount	100,000	160,000	96,000	57,600	57,600

Thus, the accumulated depreciation is $100,000 + 160,000 + 96,000 + 57,600 + 57,600 = 471,200$, such that the remaining book value is $500,000 - $471,200 = $28,800$. (Note we could have also calculated this by summing the rates for years remaining on the MACRS schedule: Year 6 is 5.76%, so $.0576 \times 500,000 = 28,800$).

The capital gain is then $50,000 - $28,800 = $21,200$ and the tax owed is

$$0.35 \times \$21,200 = \$7,420.$$

Your after-tax cash flow is then found as the sale price minus the tax owed:

$$\$50,000 - \$7,420 = \$42,580.$$

EVALUATE

Because you are only taxed on the capital gain portion of the sale price, figuring the after-tax cash flow is not as simple as subtracting the tax rate multiplied by the sale price. Instead, you have to determine the portion of the sale price that represents a gain and compute the tax from there. The same procedure holds for selling equipment at a loss relative to book value—the loss creates a deduction for taxable income elsewhere in the company.

Tax Loss Carryforwards and Carrybacks. A firm generally identifies its marginal tax rate by determining the tax bracket that it falls into based on its overall level of pretax income. Two features of the tax code, called **tax loss carryforwards** and **carrybacks**, allow corporations to take losses during a current year and offset them against gains in nearby years. Since 1997, companies can "carry back" losses for two years and "carry forward" losses for 20 years. This tax rule means that a firm can offset losses during one year against income for the last two years, or save the losses to be offset against income during the next 20 years. When a firm can carry back losses, it receives a refund for back taxes in the current year. Otherwise, the firm must carry forward the loss and use it to offset future taxable income. When a firm has tax loss carryforwards well in excess of its current pretax income, then additional income it earns today will simply increase the taxes it owes after it exhausts its carryforwards.

tax loss carryforwards and carrybacks Two features of the U.S. tax code that allow corporations to take losses during a current year and offset them against gains in nearby years. Since 1997, companies can "carry back" losses for two years and "carry forward" losses for 20 years.

Replacement Decisions

Often, the financial manager must decide whether to replace an existing piece of equipment. The new equipment may allow increased production, resulting in incremental revenue, or it may simply be more efficient, lowering costs. The typical incremental effects associated with such a decision are salvage value from the old machine, purchase of the new machine, cost savings and revenue increases, and depreciation effects.

EXAMPLE 9.8

Replacing an Existing Machine

MyFinanceLab

PROBLEM

You are trying to decide whether to replace a machine on your production line. The new machine will cost $1 million, but will be more efficient than the old machine, reducing costs by $500,000 per year. Your old machine is fully depreciated, but you could sell it for $50,000. You would depreciate the new machine over a five-year life using MACRS. The new machine will not change your working capital needs. Your tax rate is 35%, and your cost of capital is 9%. Should you replace the machine?

SOLUTION

PLAN

Incremental revenues: 0

Incremental costs: −500,000 (a reduction in costs will appear as a positive number in the costs line of our analysis)

Depreciation schedule (from the appendix):

	Year	1	2	3	4	5	6
2	Depreciation Rate	20.00%	32.00%	19.20%	11.52%	11.52%	5.76%
3	Depreciation Amount	200,000	320,000	192,000	115,200	115,200	57,600

Capital gain on salvage = $50,000 − $0 = $50,000
Cash flow from salvage value: +50,000 − (50,000)(.35) = 32,500

EXECUTE

(values in thousands)

	Year	0	1	2	3	4	5	6
1								
2	Incremental Revenues							
3	Incremental Costs of Goods Sold		500	500	500	500	500	
4	**Incremental Gross Profit**		500	500	500	500	500	
5	Depreciation		−200	−320	−192	−115.2	−115.2	−57.6
6	EBIT		300	180	308	384.8	384.8	−57.6
7	Income Tax at 35%		−105	−63	−107.8	−134.68	−134.68	20.16
8	**Incremental Earnings**		195	117	200.2	250.12	250.12	−37.44
9	Add Back Depreciation		200	320	192	115.2	115.2	57.6
10	Purchase of Equipment	−1000						
11	Salvage Cash Flow	32.5						
12	**Incremental Free Cash Flows**	−967.5	395	437	392.2	365.32	365.32	20.16

$$NPV = -967.5 + \frac{395}{1.09} + \frac{437}{1.09^2} + \frac{392.2}{1.09^3} + \frac{365.32}{1.09^4} + \frac{365.32}{1.09^5} + \frac{20.16}{1.09^6} = 573.81$$

EVALUATE

Even though the decision has no impact on revenues, it still matters for cash flows because it reduces costs. Furthermore, both selling the old machine and buying the new machine involve cash flows with tax implications. The NPV analysis shows that replacing the machine will increase the value of the firm by almost $574,000.

CONCEPT
CHECK

7. Should we include sunk costs in the cash flows of a project? Why or why not?

8. Explain why it is advantageous for a firm to use the most accelerated depreciation schedule possible for tax purposes.

9.5 Analyzing the Project

When evaluating a capital budgeting project, financial managers should make the decision that maximizes NPV. As we have discussed, to compute the NPV for a project you need to estimate the incremental free cash flows and choose a discount rate. Given these inputs, the NPV calculation is relatively straightforward. The most difficult part of capital budgeting is deciding how to estimate the cash flows and cost of capital. These estimates are often subject to significant uncertainty. In this section, we look at methods that assess the importance of this uncertainty and identify the drivers of value in the project.

sensitivity analysis An important capital budgeting tool that determines how the NPV varies as underlying assumptions change one at a time.

Sensitivity Analysis

An important capital budgeting tool for assessing the effect of uncertainty in forecasts is *sensitivity analysis*. **Sensitivity analysis** breaks the NPV calculation into its component assumptions and shows how the NPV varies as underlying assumptions change. In this way, sensitivity analysis allows us to explore the effects of errors in our NPV estimates for a project. By conducting a sensitivity analysis, we learn which assumptions are the most important; we can then invest further resources and effort to refine these assumptions. Such an analysis also reveals which aspects of a project are most critical when we are actually managing the project.

In fact, we have already performed a type of sensitivity analysis in Chapter 8 when we constructed an NPV profile. By graphing the NPV of a project as a function of the discount rate, we are assessing the sensitivity of our NPV calculation to uncertainty about the correct cost of capital to use as a discount rate. In practice, financial managers explore the sensitivity of their NPV calculation to many more factors than just the discount rate.

To illustrate, consider the assumptions underlying the calculation of HomeNet's NPV in Example 9.5. There is likely to be significant uncertainty surrounding each revenue and cost assumption. In addition to the base case assumptions about units sold, sale price, cost of goods sold, net working capital, and cost of capital, Cisco's managers would also identify best- and worst-case scenarios for each. For example, assume that they identified the best- and worst-case assumptions listed in Table 9.2. Note that these are best- and worst-case scenarios for each parameter rather than representing one worst-case scenario and one best-case scenario.

To determine the importance of this uncertainty, we recalculate the NPV of the HomeNet project under the best- and worst-case assumptions for each parameter. For example, if the number of units sold is only 35,000 per year, the NPV of the project falls to −$1.13 million. We repeat this calculation for each parameter. The result is shown in Figure 9.2, which reveals that the parameter assumptions with the largest effect on NPV are the number of units sold and the sale price per unit. As a result, these assumptions deserve the greatest scrutiny during the estimation process. In addition, as the most important drivers of the project's value, these factors deserve close attention when managing the project after it starts.

Break-Even Analysis

break-even The level of a parameter for which an investment has an NPV of zero.

A natural extension of the sensitivity analysis is to ask at what level of each parameter would the project have an NPV of zero. For each parameter, this level is its **break-even**. One example that we have already considered is the calculation of the internal rate of return (IRR). Recall from Chapter 8 that the difference between the IRR of a project and the cost of capital tells you how much error in the cost of capital it would take to change the investment decision. By either graphing the NPV profile or using the Excel IRR function, we would find that the incremental cash flows of HomeNet given in Example 9.5 imply an IRR of 26.6%. Thus, the true cost of capital can be as high as 26.6% and the project will still have a positive NPV.

break-even analysis A calculation of the value of each parameter for which the NPV of the project is zero.

We can determine the uncertainty of other parameters as well. In a **break-even analysis**, for each parameter we calculate the value at which the NPV of the project is zero. This would be tedious to do by hand, so in practice it is always done with a spreadsheet. As with the NPV profile for the discount rate, we can graph the NPV as a function of each of the critical assumptions. In each case, we keep all of the other parameters fixed at their initially assumed values and vary only the parameter in question. Figure 9.3 does this for HomeNet.

TABLE 9.2

Best- and Worst-Case Assumptions for Each Parameter in the HomeNet Project

Parameter	Initial Assumption	Worst Case	Best Case
Units Sold (thousands)	50	35	65
Sale Price ($/unit)	260	240	280
Cost of Goods ($/unit)	110	120	100
NWC ($ thousands)	1125	1525	725
Cost of Capital	12%	15%	10%

FIGURE 9.2

HomeNet's NPV Under Best- and Worst-Case Parameter Assumptions

Bars show the change in NPV going from the best-case assumption to the worst-case assumption for each parameter. For example, the NPV of the project ranges from −$1.13 million if only 35,000 units are sold to $6.85 million if 65,000 units are sold. Under the initial assumptions, HomeNet's NPV is $2.862 million.

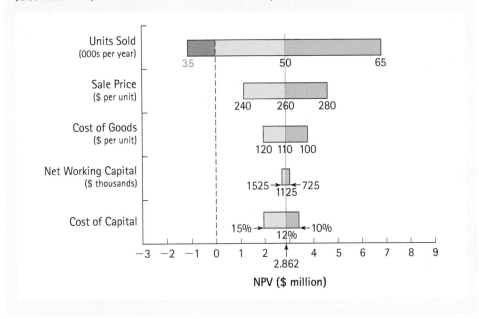

EBIT break-even The level of a particular parameter for which a project's EBIT is zero.	**Accounting Break-Even.** We have examined the break-even levels in terms of the project's NPV, which is the most useful perspective for decision making. Other accounting notions of break-even are sometimes considered, however. For example, we could compute the **EBIT break-even** for sales, which is the level of sales for which a project's EBIT is zero.	

FIGURE 9.3

Break-Even Analysis Graphs

The graphs in Panels (a) and (b) relate two of the key parameters to the project's NPV to identify the parameters' break-even points. For example, based on the initial assumptions, the HomeNet project will break even with a sales level of 39,242 units per year. Similarly, holding sales and the other parameters constant at their initial assumed values, the project will break even at a cost of goods sold of just over $142 per unit.

Panel (a) Break-Even Point Based on Units Sold

Panel (b) Break-Even Point Based on Costs of Goods Sold

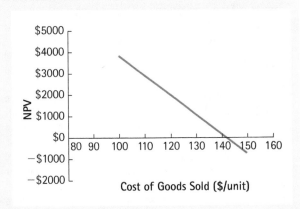

Recall from Eq. 9.1 that the project's EBIT is Revenues − Costs − Depreciation. Costs include cost of goods sold, and selling, general, and administrative expense (SG&A). Revenues equal Units Sold × Sale Price, and cost of goods sold equals Units Sold × Cost per Unit, so we have EBIT = (Units Sold × Sale Price) − (Units Sold × Cost per Unit) − SG&A − Depreciation. Setting this equal to zero and solving for units sold:

$$\text{Units Sold} \times (\text{Sale Price} - \text{Cost per Unit}) - \text{SG\&A} - \text{Depreciation} = 0$$

$$\text{Units Sold} = \frac{\text{SG\&A} + \text{Depreciation}}{\text{Sales Price} - \text{Cost per Unit}} = \frac{2,800,000 + 1,500,000}{260 - 110} = 28,667$$

INTERVIEW WITH DAVID HOLLAND

David Holland is currently Senior Vice President of Sports and Entertainment Solutions where he is responsible for accelerating development and adoption of Cisco solutions in that market. He was previously Senior Vice President and Treasurer of Cisco, and was responsible for managing all funding, risk, and capital market activities related to the firm's $50 billion balance sheet.

QUESTION: *What is the importance of considering free cash flow, as opposed to just the earnings implications of a financial decision?*

ANSWER: There is an adage saying, "Cash flow is a fact and earnings are an opinion." Earnings use an accounting framework and are governed by many rules, making it hard to know what earnings tell the investor. The economics of cash flow are clear: We can't dispute whether cash has come in or gone out. Cisco's investment decisions are based primarily on cash flow models because they take project risk into account and show the impact on value creation for owners of the business.

QUESTION: *What key financial metrics does Cisco use to make investment decisions?*

ANSWER: Cisco focuses primarily on net present value (NPV) for investment decisions. Robust NPV analysis goes beyond simply accepting projects with positive NPVs and rejecting those with negative NPVs. It identifies the key drivers that affect project success and demonstrates the interplay between factors that affect cash flow. For example, running a model using a lower margin approach shows us the impact on revenue growth and on operating cost structures. We can compare that to a higher margin (premium pricing) approach. The business unit manager learns how to control aspects of the business model to alleviate risk or accelerate the upside potential.

We prefer NPV to internal rate of return (IRR), which may return multiple answers or give false signals as to an investment's profitability, depending on the organization of cash flows. An attraction of IRR analysis is the ease of comparing percentage returns. However, this method hides the scope of a project. A project with a 25% return may generate $1 million in shareholder value, while another with a 13% IRR might produce $1 billion. NPV captures the size of the return in dollar terms and shows a project's impact on share price. NPV also creates an ownership framework for employees whose compensation package includes some form of stock ownership, directly tying the decision-making criteria to stock price.

QUESTION: *When developing a model to analyze a new investment, how do you deal with the uncertainty surrounding estimates, especially for new technologies?*

ANSWER: Cisco relies on strong financial modeling for the thousands of investment decisions we make every year. Our 2500 finance people worldwide work with the internal client—the business lead—to understand the assumptions in the model and to check the model's result against alternative assumptions. Evaluating the cash flows for technology projects, especially new technology, is difficult. When you buy an oil refinery, you can see the throughput and the cash flows. Identifying the relevant savings from a component technology for a larger router or switch product or a strategic move into a new area is more complex and intangible. Scenario and sensitivity analyses and game theory help us control risk by adjusting our strategy. We also look at the qualitative aspects, such as how the strategy fits into the customer sector and the directions customers are moving with their tech platforms.

QUESTION: *How does Cisco adjust for risk?*

ANSWER: To stay competitive in the technology space, we must be prepared to take some level of risk, even in down markets. We apply the same discount rate to all projects in a category, based on their market risk (i.e., sensitivity to market conditions). We do not adjust the discount rate to account for project-specific risks, because our required return has not changed and that would distort the true value of the company. To assess a project's unique risks, we model the upside or downside of cash flows with scenario and sensitivity analysis. We might analyze the sensitivity of a project's NPV to a 1% change in both revenue growth and operating costs. Then we run the model with other assumptions, developing base, optimistic, and bearish cases. We discuss these models with the business lead and rerun the models based on their input. This process improves our potential outcome and project profitability.

However, this EBIT break-even number is misleading. While HomeNet's EBIT break-even level of sales is only 28,667 units per year, given the large up-front investment required in HomeNet, its NPV is −$2.81 million at that sales level.

Scenario Analysis

scenario analysis
An important capital budgeting tool that determines how the NPV varies as multiple project parameters are changed simultaneously.

In the analysis thus far, we have considered the consequences of varying only one parameter at a time. In reality, certain factors may affect more than one parameter. **Scenario analysis** considers the effect on NPV of changing multiple project parameters simultaneously. For example, lowering HomeNet's price may increase the number of units sold. We can use scenario analysis to evaluate alternative pricing strategies for the HomeNet product in Table 9.3. In this case, the current strategy is optimal. Figure 9.4 shows the combinations of price and volume that lead to the same NPV of $2.862 million for HomeNet as the current strategy. Only strategies with price and volume combinations above the curve will lead to a higher NPV.

TABLE 9.3

Scenario Analysis of Alternative Pricing Strategies

Strategy	Sale Price ($/unit)	Expected Units Sold (thousands)	NPV ($ thousands)
Current Strategy	260	50	2862
Price Reduction	245	55	2729
Price Increase	275	45	2729

FIGURE 9.4

Price and Volume Combinations for HomeNet with Equivalent NPV

The graph shows alternative price per unit and annual volume combinations that lead to an NPV of $2.862 million. Pricing strategies with combinations above the curve will lead to a higher NPV and are superior. For example, if Cisco managers think they will be able to sell 48,000 units at a price of $275, this strategy would yield a higher NPV ($3,607 million).

USING EXCEL

Project Analysis
Using Excel

Here, we describe several useful Excel tools that assist with project analysis.

Goal Seek for Break-Even Analysis

Excel's goal seek function determines the break-even point for key assumptions in our model. For example, to determine the break-even level of units for annual sales, use the Goal Seek window (see the Data > What-If Analysis menu, or keyboard shortcut Alt-A-W-G). The set cell is the cell in which we calculated NPV (in this case, cell D31). To set its value to 0 (break-even), we change the average sale price (cell E5). Excel will then use trial and error to find the sale price at which the project's NPV is zero—in this case $227.73.

▲	A	B	C	D	E	F	G	H	I
1	**HomeNet Capital Budget**								
2	**Key Assumptions**			**Year 0**	**Year 1**	**Year 2**	**Year 3**	**Year 4**	**Year 5**
5		HomeNet Ave. Price/Unit			$ 260.00	$ 260.00	$ 260.00	$ 260.00	
30									
31		NPV		2,862					

Data Tables for Sensitivity Analysis

Data tables, which we introduced in the online appendix to Chapter 7 to construct the NPV profile, allow us to compute the sensitivity of NPV to any other input variable in our financial model. Excel can also compute a two-dimensional data table showing the sensitivity of NPV to two inputs simultaneously. For example, the data table below shows NPVs for different combinations of testing equipment cost and HomeNet's manufacturing costs.

▲	C	D	E	F	G	H
39	**NPV**			**HomeNet Cost/Unit**		
40		2,862	$110	$105	$100	$95
41		-7500	2,862	3,305	3,749	4,192
42		-7750	2,684	3,128	3,571	4,014
43		-8000	2,506	2,950	3,393	3,836
44		-8250	2,328	2,772	3,215	3,659
45		-8500	2,150	2,594	3,037	3,481
46		-8750	1,973	2,416	2,859	3,303
47		-9000	1,795	2,238	2,681	3,125
48		-9250	1,617	2,060	2,504	2,947
49		-9500	1,439	1,882	2,326	2,769
50		-9750	1,261	1,704	2,148	2,591
51		-10000	1,083	1,526	1,970	2,413

(Column C labeled "Equipment Cost" vertically)

To construct this data table, we put the values of each input along the sides of the table (shown in blue), and a formula for the value we want to compute in the upper-left corner (cell D36, which in this case is just a link to the cell in which we computed the NPV). We select the entire table (D36:H47), bring up the Data Table window (see the Data > What-If Analysis menu or keyboard shortcut Alt-D-T), and input the locations in our project dashboard (see page 277) of the cost assumption (row input cell E6) and equipment cost (column input cell D10). The data table shows, for example, that NPV increases if we lower our manufacturing cost to $100 per unit by spending an additional $1 million on equipment to test the design.

Scenarios in the Project Dashboard

The project dashboard on page 277 shows only our base-case assumptions. We can build multiple scenarios into our project dashboard by adding additional rows with alternative assumptions, and then using Excel's index function to select the scenario we would like to use in our analysis. For example, rows 5–7 on page 289 show alternative annual sales assumptions for HomeNet. We then select the scenario to analyze by entering the appropriate number (in this case 1, 2, or 3) in the highlighted cell (C4), and use the index function to pull the appropriate data into row 4.

	A	B	C	D	E	F	G	H	I	J
2	**Key Assumptions**			Year 0	Year 1	Year 2	Year 3	Year 4	Year 5	
3	*Revenues & Costs*									
4	HomeNet Units Sold		1		50	50	50	=INDEX(H5:H7,C4)		
5	*Base Case*		1		50	50	50	50		
6	*Fast Adoption*		2		65	80	100	80		
7	*Slow Adoption*		3		25	40	50	50		
8										
9	HomeNet Ave. Price/Unit			$	260.00 $	260.00 $	260.00 $	260.00		
10	HomeNet Cost/Unit			$	110.00 $	110.00 $	110.00 $	110.00		
11	*Operating Expenses*									
12	Marketing, Support & Rent				(2,800)	(2,800)	(2,800)	(2,800)		
13	*Capital Expenditures*									
14	Purchase Equipment			(7,500)						
15	*Other Assumptions*									
16	depreciation schedule			0.0%	20.0%	20.0%	20.0%	20.0%	20.0%	
17	corporate tax rate			40.0%	40.0%	40.0%	40.0%	40.0%	40.0%	
18	receivables (% sales)			15.0%	15.0%	15.0%	15.0%	15.0%	15.0%	
19	payables (% expenses)			15.0%	15.0%	15.0%	15.0%	15.0%	15.0%	
20										
21	**Incremental Earnings Forecast**			0	0	0	0	0		
22	Revenues				13000.0	13000.0	13000.0	13000.0		
23	Expenses				(5500.0)	(5500.0)	(5500.0)	(5500.0)		

We can then analyze the consequences for each scenario using the one-dimensional data table in C54:D57 below, with column input cell C4.

	A	B	C	D
53				**NPV**
54		**HomeNet Units Sold**		2,862
55		*Base Case*	1	2,862
56		*Fast Adoption*	2	11,029
57		*Slow Adoption*	3	319

CONCEPT CHECK

9. What is sensitivity analysis?

10. How does scenario analysis differ from sensitivity analysis?

9.6 Real Options in Capital Budgeting

real option The right to make a particular business decision, such as a capital investment.

Our approach to capital budgeting thus far has focused on the initial investment decision without explicitly considering future decisions that may need to be made over the life of a project. Rather, we assumed that our forecast of a project's expected future cash flows already incorporated the effect of future decisions that would be made. In truth, most projects contain *real options*. A **real option** is the right, but not the obligation, to make a particular business decision. Because you are not obligated to take the action, you will do so only if it increases the NPV of the project. In particular, because real options allow a decision maker to choose the most attractive alternative after new information has been learned, the presence of real options adds value to an investment opportunity. The tools to estimate the actual value created by real options are beyond the scope of this chapter and are contained later in the book. However, we introduce the concept here to give you a sense of the types of real options you may encounter and establish the intuition that flexibility (more options) is valuable. Let's look at some of the most common real options in the context of Cisco's HomeNet project.

Option to Delay

option to delay commitment The option to time a particular investment

The **option to delay commitment** (the option to time an investment) is almost always present. Cisco could wait to commit to the HomeNet project. Waiting could be valuable if Cisco expects prices of the components to decrease substantially, soon-to-be-released new technology that will make the existing components obsolete, or increased sales of Web-ready appliances (heightening the demand for HomeNet). In addition, Cisco may simply want more time to gather information about the potential market for HomeNet. As with any other capital budgeting decision, Cisco would only choose to delay if doing so would increase the NPV of the project.

Option to Expand

option to expand The option to start with limited production and expand only if the product is successful.

In the section on sensitivity analysis, we looked at changes in our assumptions about units sold. All of the analysis was performed, however, under the assumption that Cisco would fully commit to and roll out the HomeNet product worldwide. We did not consider the **option to expand**, which is the option to start with limited production and expand only if the product is successful. Cisco could, instead, test market the product in limited release before committing to it fully. Doing so would create an option to expand worldwide only if HomeNet were successful in limited release. It is possible that, by reducing its up-front commitment and choosing to expand only if the product is successful, Cisco will increase the NPV of the HomeNet product. However, in this particular case, there are large costs of development that would be paid whether Cisco sells one or one million units, so limiting the initial market does not reduce the financial commitment substantially. Thus, in the case of HomeNet, it is unlikely that Cisco would choose a limited release with an option to expand.

Option to Abandon

abandonment option The option for an investor to cease investing in a project. Abandonment options can add value to a project because a firm can drop a project if it turns out to be unsuccessful.

An **abandonment option** is the option to walk away. Abandonment options can add value to a project because a firm can drop a project if it turns out to be unsuccessful. Imagine that a competitor developed new technology that allowed it to introduce a successful competing product priced at $170. At that price, HomeNet would produce negative cash flows every year. But would Cisco continue to sell HomeNet if it had to do so at a loss? Probably not. Cisco has an option to abandon the project. It could stop producing HomeNet and sell the equipment. Depending on how much Cisco believes the equipment would sell for if it abandoned the project, the abandonment option could make HomeNet attractive even if there was a substantial risk of a competing product.

All these options point to the same conclusion: *If you can build greater flexibility into your project, you will increase its NPV.* In Chapter 21, we will discuss how to value options so that you can estimate just how much more valuable the project is with greater flexibility. Many industries regularly make use of real options. For example, most movie producers build in an option for a sequel if the first movie does well. Pharmaceutical developers like Merck develop new drugs in stages, allowing them to abandon development if tests do not go well.

CONCEPT CHECK

11. What are real options?

12. Why do real options increase the NPV of a project?

MyFinanceLab

Here is what you should know after reading this chapter. MyFinanceLab will help you identify what you know, and where to go when you need to practice.

KEY POINTS AND EQUATIONS	KEY TERMS	ONLINE PRACTICE
9.1 The Capital Budgeting Process • Capital budgeting is the process of analyzing investment opportunities and deciding which ones to accept. A capital budget is a list of all projects that a company plans to undertake during the next period. • We use the NPV rule to evaluate capital budgeting decisions, making decisions that maximize NPV. When deciding to accept or reject a project, we accept projects with a positive NPV.	capital budget, p. 266 capital budgeting, p. 266 incremental earnings, p. 267	MyFinanceLab Study Plan 9.1
9.2 Forecasting Incremental Earnings • The incremental earnings of a project comprise the amount by which the project is expected to change the firm's earnings. • Incremental earnings should include all incremental revenues and costs associated with the project. Incremental Earnings = (Incremental Revenues − Incremental Cost − Depreciation) × (1 − Tax Rate) (9.3) • Interest and other financing-related expenses are excluded to determine the project's unlevered net income.	marginal corporate tax rate, p. 269 pro forma, p. 270 straight-line depreciation, p. 267 unlevered net income, p. 271	MyFinanceLab Study Plan 9.2
9.3 Determining Incremental Free Cash Flow • We compute free cash flow from incremental earnings by eliminating all non-cash expenses and including all capital investment. • Depreciation is not a cash expense, so it is added back. • Actual capital expenditures are deducted. • Increases in net working capital are deducted and decreases are added. Net working capital is defined as: Cash + Inventory + Receivables − Payables (9.4) • The basic calculation for free cash flow is: Free Cash Flow = (Revenues − Costs − Depreciation) × (1 − Tax Rate) + Depreciation − CapEx − Change in NWC (9.6)	depreciation tax shield, p. 276 free cash flow, p. 272 trade credit, p. 273	MyFinanceLab Study Plan 9.3

9.4 Other Effects on Incremental Free Cash Flows

- An opportunity cost is the cost of using an existing asset.
- Project externalities are cash flows that occur when a project affects other areas of the company's business.
- A sunk cost is an unrecoverable cost that has already been incurred.
- Depreciation expenses affect free cash flow only through the depreciation tax shield. The firm should use the most accelerated depreciation schedule possible.
- The discount rate for a project is its cost of capital: the expected return of securities with comparable risk and horizon.
- When you sell an asset, the portion of the proceeds above its book value is taxed:

$$\text{After-Tax Cash Flow from Asset Sale} = \text{Sale Price} - (\text{Tax Rate} \times \text{Capital Gain}) \qquad (9.11)$$

cannibalization, p. 279
MACRS depreciation, p. 280
opportunity cost, p. 278
overhead expenses, p. 278
project externalities, p. 278
sunk cost, p. 279
tax loss carryforwards and carrybacks, p. 282

MyFinance Lab Study Plan 9.4

HomeNet Example Spreadsheet

9.5 Analyzing the Project

- Sensitivity analysis breaks the NPV calculation into its component assumptions, showing how the NPV varies as the values of the underlying assumptions change.
- Break-even analysis computes the level of a parameter that makes the project's NPV equal zero.
- Scenario analysis considers the effect of changing multiple parameters simultaneously.

break-even, p. 284
break-even analysis, p. 284
EBIT break-even, p. 285
scenario analysis, p. 287
sensitivity analysis, p. 283

MyFinanceLab Study Plan 9.5

Interactive Sensitivity Analysis, Using Excel: Performing Sensitivity Analysis

9.6 Real Options in Capital Budgeting

- Real options are options to make a business decision, often after gathering more information. The presence of real options in a project increases the project's NPV.

abandonment option, p. 290
option to delay commitment, p. 290
option to expand, p. 290
real option, p. 289

MyFinanceLab Study Plan 9.6

CRITICAL THINKING

1. What are pro forma incremental earnings?

2. What is the difference between pro forma incremental earnings and pro forma free cash flow?

3. Why do we convert from incremental earnings to free cash flow when performing capital budgeting?

4. What is the role of net working capital in projects?

5. How does net working capital affect the cash flows of a project?

6. Why is it important to adjust project sales and costs for externalities?

7. Does accelerated depreciation generally increase or decrease NPV relative to straight-line depreciation?

8. How is sensitivity analysis performed and what is its purpose?

PROBLEMS

All problems are available in MyFinanceLab. The *icon indicates problems that are easier to solve using Excel and have data in an Excel format available in MyFinanceLab. An asterisk * indicates problems with a higher level of difficulty.*

Forecasting Incremental Earnings

1. Daily Enterprises is purchasing a $10 million machine. It will cost $50,000 to transport and install the machine. The machine has a depreciable life of five years and will have no salvage value. If Daily uses straight-line depreciation, what are the depreciation expenses associated with this machine?

2. The machine in Problem 1 will generate incremental revenues of $4 million per year along with incremental costs of $1.2 million per year. If Daily's marginal tax rate is 35%, what are the incremental earnings associated with the new machine?

3. You are upgrading to better production equipment for your firm's only product. The new equipment will allow you to make more of your product in the same amount of time. Thus, you forecast that total sales will increase next year by 20% over the current amount of 100,000 units. If your sales price is $20 per unit, what are the incremental revenues next year from the upgrade?

4. Pisa Pizza, a seller of frozen pizza, is considering introducing a healthier version of its pizza that will be low in cholesterol and contain no trans fats. The firm expects that sales of the new pizza will be $20 million per year. While many of these sales will be to new customers, Pisa Pizza estimates that 40% will come from customers who switch to the new, healthier pizza instead of buying the original version.
   a. Assume customers will spend the same amount on either version. What level of incremental sales is associated with introducing the new pizza?
   b. Suppose that 50% of the customers who would switch from Pisa Pizza's original pizza to its healthier pizza will switch to another brand if Pisa Pizza does not introduce a healthier pizza. What level of incremental sales is associated with introducing the new pizza in this case?

5. Kokomochi is considering the launch of an advertising campaign for its latest dessert product, the Mini Mochi Munch. Kokomochi plans to spend $5 million on TV, radio, and print advertising this year for the campaign. The ads are expected to boost sales of the Mini Mochi Munch by $9 million this year and by $7 million next year. In addition, the company expects that new consumers who try the Mini Mochi Munch will be more likely to try Kokomochi's other products. As a result, sales of other products are expected to rise by $2 million each year.

   Kokomochi's gross profit margin for the Mini Mochi Munch is 35%, and its gross profit margin averages 25% for all other products. The company's marginal corporate tax rate is 35% both this year and next year. What are the incremental earnings associated with the advertising campaign?

6. Hyperion, Inc., currently sells its latest high-speed color printer, the Hyper 500, for $350. It plans to lower the price to $300 next year. Its cost of goods sold for the Hyper 500 is $200 per unit, and this year's sales are expected to be 20,000 units.
   a. Suppose that if Hyperion drops the price to $300 immediately, it can increase this year's sales by 25% to 25,000 units. What would be the incremental impact on this year's EBIT of such a price drop?
   b. Suppose that for each printer sold, Hyperion expects additional sales of $75 per year on ink cartridges for the next three years, and Hyperion has a gross profit margin of 70% on ink cartridges. What is the incremental impact on EBIT for the next three years of a price drop this year?

Determining Incremental Free Cash Flow

7. You have a depreciation expense of $500,000 and a tax rate of 35%. What is your depreciation tax shield?

8. You have forecast pro forma earnings of $1,000,000. This includes the effect of $200,000 in depreciation. You also forecast a decrease in working capital of $100,000 that year. What is your forecast of free cash flows for that year?

9. Your pro forma income statement shows sales of $1,000,000, cost of goods sold as $500,000, depreciation expense of $100,000, and taxes of $160,000 due to a tax rate of 40%. What are your pro forma earnings? What is your pro forma free cash flow?

10. You are evaluating a new product. In year 3 of your analysis, you are projecting pro forma sales of $5 million and cost of goods sold of $3 million. You will be depreciating a $1 million machine for 5 years using straight-line depreciation. Your tax rate is 35%. Finally, you expect working capital to increase from $200,000 in year 2 to $300,000 in year 3. What are your pro forma earnings for year 3? What are your pro forma free cash flows for year 3?

11. You are forecasting incremental free cash flows for Daily Enterprises. Based on the information in Problems 1 and 2, what are the incremental free cash flows associated with the new machine?

12. Castle View Games would like to invest in a division to develop software for a soon-to-be-released video game console. To evaluate this decision, the firm first attempts to project the working capital needs for this operation. Its chief financial officer has developed the following estimates (in millions of dollars) (*see* MyFinanceLab *for the data in Excel format*):

1	Year	1	2	3	4	5
2	Cash	6	12	15	15	15
3	Accounts Receivable	21	22	24	24	24
4	Inventory	5	7	10	12	13
5	Accounts Payable	18	22	24	25	30

Assuming that Castle View currently does not have any working capital invested in this division, calculate the cash flows associated with changes in working capital for the first five years of this investment.

13. In the HomeNet example from the chapter, its receivables are 15% of sales and its payables are 15% of COGS. Forecast the required investment in net working capital for HomeNet assuming that sales and cost of goods sold (COGS) will be as follows (*see* MyFinanceLab *for the data in Excel format*):

1	Year	0	1	2	3	4
2	Sales		23,500	26,438	23,794	8,566
3	COGS		9,500	10,688	9,619	3,483

14. Elmdale Enterprises is deciding whether to expand its production facilities. Although long-term cash flows are difficult to estimate, management has projected the following cash flows for the first two years (in millions of dollars) (*see* MyFinanceLab *for the data in Excel format*):
    a. What are the incremental earnings for this project for years 1 and 2?
    b. What are the free cash flows for this project for years 1 and 2?

Year	1	2
1		
Revenues	125	160
Operating Expenses (other than depreciation)	40	60
Depreciation	25	36
Increase in Net Working Capital	2	8
Capital Expenditures	30	40
Marginal Corporate Tax Rate	35%	35%

15. Cellular Access, Inc., a cellular telephone service provider, reported net income of $250 million for the most recent fiscal year. The firm had depreciation expenses of $100 million, capital expenditures of $200 million, and no interest expenses. Net working capital increased by $10 million. Calculate the free cash flow for Cellular Access for the most recent fiscal year.

16. Recall the HomeNet example from the chapter. Suppose HomeNet's lab will be housed in warehouse space that the company could have otherwise rented out for $200,000 per year during years 1 through 4. How does this opportunity cost affect HomeNet's incremental earnings?

*17. One year ago, your company purchased a machine used in manufacturing for $110,000. You have learned that a new machine is available that offers many advantages and you can purchase it for $150,000 today. It will be depreciated on a straight-line basis over 10 years and has no salvage value. You expect that the new machine will produce a gross margin (revenues minus operating expenses other than depreciation) of $40,000 per year for the next 10 years. The current machine is expected to produce a gross margin of $20,000 per year. The current machine is being depreciated on a straight-line basis over a useful life of 11 years, and has no salvage value, so depreciation expense for the current machine is $10,000 per year. The market value today of the current machine is $50,000. Your company's tax rate is 45%, and the opportunity cost of capital for this type of equipment is 10%. Should your company replace its year-old machine?

*18. Beryl's Iced Tea currently rents a bottling machine for $50,000 per year, including all maintenance expenses. It is considering purchasing a machine instead and is comparing two options:
   a. Purchase the machine it is currently renting for $150,000. This machine will require $20,000 per year in ongoing maintenance expenses.
   b. Purchase a new, more advanced machine for $250,000. This machine will require $15,000 per year in ongoing maintenance expenses and will lower bottling costs by $10,000 per year. Also, $35,000 will be spent upfront to train the new operators of the machine.

Suppose the appropriate discount rate is 8% per year and the machine is purchased today. Maintenance and bottling costs are paid at the end of each year, as is the rental cost of the machine. Assume also that the machines will be depreciated via the straight-line method over seven years and that they have a 10-year life with a negligible salvage value. The marginal corporate tax rate is 35%. Should Beryl's Iced Tea continue to rent, purchase its current machine, or purchase the advanced machine?

Other Effects on Incremental Free Cash Flows

19. You have just completed a $20,000 feasibility study for a new coffee shop in some retail space you own. You bought the space two years ago for $100,000, and if you sold it today, you would net $115,000 after taxes. Outfitting the space for a coffee shop would require

a capital expenditure of $30,000 plus an initial investment of $5,000 in inventory. What is the correct initial cash flow for your analysis of the coffee shop opportunity?

20. After spending a year and $50,000, you finally have the design of your new product ready. In order to start production, you will need $30,000 in raw materials and you will also need to use some existing equipment that you've fully depreciated, but which has a market value of $100,000. Your colleague notes that the new product could represent 10% of the company's overall sales and that 10% of overhead is $60,000. Your tax rate is 40%. As you start your analysis of the product, what should be your initial incremental free cash flow?

21. You purchased a machine for $1 million three years ago and have been applying straight-line depreciation to zero for a seven-year life. Your tax rate is 35%. If you sell the machine today (after three years of depreciation) for $700,000, what is your incremental cash flow from selling the machine?

22. The Jones Company has just completed the third year of a five-year MACRS recovery period for a piece of equipment it originally purchased for $300,000.
    a. What is the book value of the equipment?
    b. If Jones sells the equipment today for $180,000 and its tax rate is 35%, what is the after-tax cash flow from selling it?

23. Just before it is about to sell the equipment from Problem 22, Jones receives a new order. It can take the new order if it keeps the old equipment. Is there a cost to taking the order and if so, what is it? Explain.

24. Home Builder Supply, a retailer in the home improvement industry, currently operates seven retail outlets in Georgia and South Carolina. Management is contemplating building an eighth retail store across town from its most successful retail outlet. The company already owns the land for this store, which currently has an abandoned warehouse located on it. Last month, the marketing department spent $10,000 on market research to determine the extent of customer demand for the new store. Now Home Builder Supply must decide whether to build and open the new store.

    Which of the following should be included as part of the incremental earnings for the proposed new retail store?
    a. The original purchase price of the land where the store will be located.
    b. The cost of demolishing the abandoned warehouse and clearing the lot.
    c. The loss of sales in the existing retail outlet, if customers who previously drove across town to shop at the existing outlet become customers of the new store instead.
    d. The $10,000 in market research spent to evaluate customer demand.
    e. Construction costs for the new store.
    f. The value of the land if sold.
    g. Interest expense on the debt borrowed to pay the construction costs.

25. Nirvana Chip Designs has finished designing its next generation of chips, the XJ5000 series and is getting ready to start production. As the analyst on the project, you are required to prepare pro forma free cash flows. Which of the following are relevant to your analysis?
    a. Design costs for the chips.
    b. Potential lost sales of the XJ4000 chips.
    c. Proportional cost of the corporate jet lease.
    d. Start-up investment in raw materials.
    e. Upgrades to the chip fabrication facility required if the chip is produced.
    f. Market research done to guide the development of the new chip.
    g. Market value of land and buildings where new chip will be produced.

26. If Daily Enterprises uses MACRS instead of straight-line depreciation, which incremental free cash flows from Problem 11 would increase and which would decrease?

27. Markov Manufacturing recently spent $15 million to purchase some equipment used in the manufacture of disk drives. The firm expects that this equipment will have a useful life of five years, and its marginal corporate tax rate is 35%. The company plans to use straight-line depreciation.
    a. What is the annual depreciation expense associated with this equipment?
    b. What is the annual depreciation tax shield?
    c. Rather than straight-line depreciation, suppose Markov will use the MACRS depreciation method for the five-year life of the property. Calculate the depreciation tax shield each year for this equipment under this accelerated depreciation schedule.
    d. If Markov has a choice between straight-line and MACRS depreciation schedules, and its marginal corporate tax rate is expected to remain constant, which schedule should it choose? Why?
    e. How might your answer to part (d) change if Markov anticipates that its marginal corporate tax rate will increase substantially over the next five years?

28. Your company has been doing well, reaching $1 million in earnings, and is considering launching a new product. Designing the new product has already cost $500,000. The company estimates that it will sell 800,000 units per year for $3 per unit and variable non-labor costs will be $1 per unit. Production will end after year 3. New equipment costing $1 million will be required. The equipment will be depreciated to zero using the 7-year MACRS schedule. You plan to sell the equipment for book value at the end of year 3. Your current level of working capital is $300,000. The new product will require the working capital to increase to a level of $380,000 immediately, then to $400,000 in year 1, in year 2 the level will be $350,000, and finally in year 3 the level will return to $300,000. Your tax rate is 35%. The discount rate for this project is 10%. Do the capital budgeting analysis for this project and calculate its NPV.

29. You work for Apple. After toiling away on $10 million worth of prototypes, you have finally produced your answer to Google Glasses: iGlasses (the name alone is genius). iGlasses will instantly transport the wearer into the world as Apple wants you to experience it: iTunes with the wink of an eye and apps that can be activated just by looking at them. You think that these will sell for 5 years until the next big thing comes along (or until users are unable to interact with actual human beings). Revenues are projected to be $450 million per year along with expenses of $350 million. You will need to spend $60 million immediately on additional equipment that will be depreciated using the 5-year MACRS schedule. Additionally, you will use some fully depreciated existing equipment that has a market value of $10 million. As iGlasses are an outcome of the R&D center, Apple plans to charge $5 million of the annual costs of the center to the iGlasses product for 5 years. Finally, Apple's working capital levels will increase from their current level of $120 million to $140 million immediately. They will remain at the elevated level until year 5, when they will return to $120 million. Apple's discount rate for this project is 15% and its tax rate is 35%. Calculate the free cash flows and determine the NPV of this project.

30. After spending $10,000 on client development, you have just been offered a big production contract by a new client. The contract will add $200,000 to your revenues for each of the next 5 years and it will cost you $100,000 per year to make the additional product. You will have to use some existing equipment and buy new equipment as well. The existing equipment is fully depreciated, but could be sold for $50,000 now. If you use it in the project, it will be worthless at the end of the project. You will buy new equipment valued at $30,000 and use the 5-year MACRS schedule to depreciate it.

It will be worthless at the end of the project. Your current production manager earns $80,000 per year. Since she is busy with ongoing projects, you are planning to hire an assistant at $40,000 per year to help with the expansion. You will have to increase your inventory immediately from $20,000 to $30,000. It will return to $20,000 at the end of the project. Your company's tax rate is 35% and your discount rate is 15%. What is the NPV of the contract?

 31. You are a manager at Percolated Fiber, which is considering expanding its operations in synthetic fiber manufacturing. Your boss comes into your office, drops a consultant's report on your desk, and complains, "We owe these consultants $1 million for this report, and I am not sure their analysis makes sense. Before we spend the $25 million on new equipment needed for this project, look it over and give me your opinion." You open the report and find the following estimates (in thousands of dollars) (*see* MyFinanceLab *for the data in Excel format*):

1	Year	1	2	...	9	10
2	Sales Revenue	30,000	30,000		30,000	30,000
3	Costs of Goods Sold	18,000	18,000		18,000	18,000
4	**Gross Profit**	12,000	12,000		12,000	12,000
5	Selling, General, and Administrative Expenses	2,000	2,000		2,000	2,000
6	Depreciation	2,500	2,500		2,500	2,500
7	**EBIT**	7,500	7,500		7,500	7,500
8	Income Tax	2,625	2,625		2,625	2,625
9	**Net Income**	**4,875**	**4,875**		**4,875**	**4,875**

All of the estimates in the report seem correct. You note that the consultants used straight-line depreciation for the new equipment that will be purchased today (year 0), which is what the accounting department recommended. They also calculated the depreciation assuming no salvage value for the equipment, which is the company's assumption in this case. The report concludes that because the project will increase earnings by $4.875 million per year for 10 years, the project is worth $48.75 million. You think back to your glory days in finance class and realize there is more work to be done!

First, you note that the consultants have not included the fact that the project will require $10 million in working capital up front (year 0), which will be fully recovered in year 10. Next, you see they have attributed $2 million of selling, general, and administrative expenses to the project, but you know that $1 million of this amount is overhead that will be incurred even if the project is not accepted. Finally, you know that accounting earnings are not the right thing to focus on!

a. Given the available information, what are the free cash flows in years 0 through 10 that should be used to evaluate the proposed project?

b. If the cost of capital for this project is 14%, what is your estimate of the value of the new project?

Analyzing the Project

 32. Bauer Industries is an automobile manufacturer. Management is currently evaluating a proposal to build a plant that will manufacture lightweight trucks. Bauer plans to use a cost of capital of 12% to evaluate this project. Based on extensive research, it has prepared the incremental free cash flow projections shown on page 299 (in millions of dollars) (*see* MyFinanceLab *for the data in Excel format*).

a. For this base-case scenario, what is the NPV of the plant to manufacture lightweight trucks?

1	Year	0	1–9	10
2	Revenues		100.0	100.0
3	Manufacturing Expenses (other than depreciation)		−35.0	−35.0
4	Marketing Expenses		−10.0	−10.0
5	Depreciation		−15.0	−15.0
6	**EBIT**		40.0	40.0
7	Taxes at 35%		−14.0	−14.0
8	**Unlevered Net Income**		26.0	26.0
9	Depreciation		+15.0	+15.0
10	Additions to Net Working Capital		−5.0	−5.0
11	Capital Expenditures	−150.0		
12	Continuation Value			+12.0
13	**Free Cash Flow**	**−150.0**	**36.0**	**48.0**

b. Based on input from the marketing department, Bauer is uncertain about its revenue forecast. In particular, management would like to examine the sensitivity of the NPV to the revenue assumptions. What is the NPV of this project if revenues are 10% higher than forecast? What is the NPV if revenues are 10% lower than forecast?

c. Rather than assuming that cash flows for this project are constant, management would like to explore the sensitivity of its analysis to possible growth in revenues and operating expenses. Specifically, management would like to assume that revenues, manufacturing expenses, and marketing expenses are as given in the table for year 1 and grow by 2% per year every year starting in year 2. Management also plans to assume that the initial capital expenditures (and therefore depreciation), additions to working capital, and continuation value remain as initially specified in the table. What is the NPV of this project under these alternative assumptions? How does the NPV change if the revenues and operating expenses grow by 5% per year rather than by 2%?

d. To examine the sensitivity of this project to the discount rate, management would like to compute the NPV for different discount rates. Create a graph, with the discount rate on the x-axis and the NPV on the y-axis, for discount rates ranging from 5% to 30%. For what ranges of discount rates does the project have a positive NPV?

 *33. Billingham Packaging is considering expanding its production capacity by purchasing a new machine, the XC-750. The cost of the XC-750 is $2.75 million. Unfortunately, installing this machine will take several months and will partially disrupt production. The firm has just completed a $50,000 feasibility study to analyze the decision to buy the XC-750, resulting in the following estimates:

- *Marketing*: Once the XC-750 is operational next year, the extra capacity is expected to generate $10 million per year in additional sales, which will continue for the 10-year life of the machine.

- *Operations*: The disruption caused by the installation will decrease sales by $5 million this year. As with Billingham's existing products, the cost of goods for the products produced by the XC-750 is expected to be 70% of their sale price. The increased production will also require increased inventory on hand of $1 million during the life of the project, including year 0.

- *Human Resources*: The expansion will require additional sales and administrative personnel at a cost of $2 million per year.

- *Accounting*: The XC-750 will be depreciated via the straight-line method over the 10-year life of the machine. The firm expects receivables from the new sales to be 15% of revenues and payables to be 10% of the cost of goods sold. Billingham's marginal corporate tax rate is 35%.

a. Determine the incremental earnings from the purchase of the XC-750.

b. Determine the free cash flow from the purchase of the XC-750.

c. If the appropriate cost of capital for the expansion is 10%, compute the NPV of the purchase.

d. While the expected new sales will be $10 million per year from the expansion, estimates range from $8 million to $12 million. What is the NPV in the worst case? In the best case?

e. What is the break-even level of new sales from the expansion? What is the break-even level for the cost of goods sold?

f. Billingham could instead purchase the XC-900, which offers even greater capacity. The cost of the XC-900 is $4 million. The extra capacity would not be useful in the first two years of operation, but would allow for additional sales in years 3 through 10. What level of additional sales (above the $10 million expected for the XC-750) per year in those years would justify purchasing the larger machine?

Real Options in Captial Budgeting

34. Why must real options have positive value?

35. What kind of real option does the XC-900 machine provide to Billingham in Problem 33?

36. If Billingham knows that it can sell the XC-750 to another firm for $2 million in two years, what kind of real option would that provide?

DATA CASE

You have just been hired by Intel in its finance division. Your first assignment is to determine the net cash flows and NPV of a proposed new generation of mobile chips.

Capital expenditures to produce the new chips will initially require an investment of $1.2 billion. The R&D that will be required to finish the chips is $500 million this year. Any ongoing R&D for upgrades will be covered in the margin calculation in 2a below. The product family is expected to have a life of five years. First-year revenues for the new chip are expected to be $2,000,000,000 ($2,000 million). The chip family's revenues are expected to grow by 20% for the second year, and then decrease by 10% for the third, decrease by 20% for the 4th and finally decrease by 50% for the 5th (final) year of sales. Your job is to determine the rest of the cash flows associated with this project. Your boss has indicated that the operating costs and net working capital requirements are similar to the rest of the company's products. Since your boss hasn't been much help, here are some tips to guide your analysis:

1. Obtain Intel's financial statements. Download the annual income statements and balance sheets for the last four fiscal years from Google Finance (finance.google .com). Enter Intel's ticker symbol (INTC) and then go to "Financials." Click "Annual," to ensure you're getting annual, instead of quarterly, data. Next, copy and paste the income statements and balance sheets into Excel.

2. You are now ready to determine the free cash flow. Compute the free cash flow for each year using Eq. 9.6 from this chapter:

$$\overbrace{\text{Free Cash Flow} = (\text{Revenues} - \text{Costs} - \text{Depreciation}) \times (1 - \text{Tax Rate})}^{\text{Unlevered Net Income}}$$
$$+ \text{Depreciation} - \text{CapEx} - \text{Change in } NWC$$

Set up the timeline and computation of the free cash flow in separate, contiguous columns for each year of the project life. Be sure to make outflows negative and inflows positive.

a. Assume that the project's profitability will be similar to Intel's existing projects in 2015 and estimate costs each year by using the 2015 ratio of non-depreciation costs to revenue:

[(Cost of Revenue + SG&A + R&D)/ Total Revenue]

You should assume that this ratio will hold for this project as well. You do not need to break out the individual components of operating costs in your forecast. Simply forecast the total of Cost of Revenue + SG&A + R&D for each year.

b. Determine the annual depreciation by assuming Intel depreciates these assets by the straight-line method over a 5-year life.

c. Determine Intel's tax rate as [1 − (Income After Tax/Income Before Tax)] in 2015. Note that on Intel's income statement on Google Finance, there is a difference between operating income and income before tax. That difference is due to small adjustments. Ignore this issue and simply focus on the Income Before Tax line.

d. Calculate the net working capital required each year by assuming that the level of NWC will be a constant percentage of the project's sales. Use Intel's 2015 NWC/Sales to estimate the required percentage. (Use only accounts receivable, accounts payable, and inventory to measure working capital. Other components of current assets and liabilities are harder to interpret and are not necessarily reflective of the project's required NWC—e.g., Intel's cash holdings.)

e. To determine the free cash flow, calculate the *additional* capital investment and the *change* in net working capital each year.

3. Determine the IRR of the project and the NPV of the project at a cost of capital of 12% using the Excel functions. For the calculation of NPV, include cash flows 1 through 5 in the NPV function and then subtract the initial cost (i.e., $= NPV(\text{rate}, CF_1 : CF_5) + CF_0$). For IRR, include cash flows 0 through 5 in the cash flow range.

Chapter 9 APPENDIX

MACRS Depreciation

The U.S. tax code allows for accelerated depreciation of most assets. The depreciation method that you use for any particular asset is determined by the tax rules in effect at the time you place the asset into service. (Congress has changed the depreciation rules many times over the years, so many firms that have held property for a long time may have to use several depreciation methods simultaneously.)

For most business property placed in service after 1986, the IRS allows firms to depreciate the asset using the MACRS (Modified Accelerated Cost Recovery System) method. Under this method, you categorize each business asset into a recovery class that determines the time period over which you can write off the cost of the asset. The most commonly used items are classified as shown below:

- *3-year property*: Tractor units, race horses over 2 years old, and horses over 12 years old.

- *5-year property*: Automobiles, buses, trucks, computers and peripheral equipment, office machinery, and any property used in research and experimentation. Also includes breeding and dairy cattle.

- *7-year property*: Office furniture and fixtures, and any property that has not been designated as belonging to another class.
- *10-year property*: Water transportation equipment, single-purpose agricultural or horticultural structures, and trees or vines bearing fruit or nuts.
- *15-year property*: Depreciable improvements to land such as fences, roads, and bridges.
- *20-year property*: Farm buildings that are not agricultural or horticultural structures.
- *27.5-year property*: Residential rental property.
- *39-year property*: Nonresidential real estate, including home offices. (Note that the value of land may not be depreciated.)

Generally speaking, residential and nonresidential real estate is depreciated via the straight-line method, but other classes can be depreciated more rapidly in early years. Table 9.4 shows the standard depreciation rates for assets in the other recovery classes; refinements of this table can be applied depending on the month that the asset was placed into service (consult IRS guidelines). The table indicates the percentage of the asset's cost that may be depreciated each year, with year 1 indicating the year the asset was first put into use (typically year 0 in your spreadsheet as in Example 9.8).

The lower amount in year 1 reflects a "half-year convention" in which the asset is presumed to be in use (and thus depreciated) for half of the first year, no matter when it was actually put into use. After year 1, it is assumed that the asset depreciates more rapidly in earlier years.

TABLE 9.4

MACRS Depreciation Table Showing the Percentage of the Asset's Cost That May Be Depreciated Each Year Based on Its Recovery Period

			Depreciation Rate for Recovery Period			
Year	3 Years	5 Years	7 Years	10 Years	15 Years	20 Years
1	33.33	20.00	14.29	10.00	5.00	3.750
2	44.45	32.00	24.49	18.00	9.50	7.219
3	14.81	19.20	17.49	14.40	8.55	6.677
4	7.41	11.52	12.49	11.52	7.70	6.177
5		11.52	8.93	9.22	6.93	5.713
6		5.76	8.92	7.37	6.23	5.285
7			8.93	6.55	5.90	4.888
8			4.46	6.55	5.90	4.522
9				6.56	5.91	4.462
10				6.55	5.90	4.461
11				3.28	5.91	4.462
12					5.90	4.461
13					5.91	4.462
14					5.90	4.461
15					5.91	4.462
16					2.95	4.461
17						4.462
18						4.461
19						4.462
20						4.461
21						2.231

10

Stock Valuation:
A Second Look

LEARNING OBJECTIVES

- Value a stock as the present value of the company's free cash flows

- Value a stock by applying common multiples based on the values of comparable firms

- Understand how information is incorporated into stock prices through competition in efficient markets

- Describe some of the behavioral biases that influence the way individual investors trade

notation

Div_t	dividends paid in year t
$EBIT$	earnings before interest and taxes
$EBITDA$	earnings before interest, taxes, depreciation, and amortization
EPS_t	earnings per share on date t
FCF_t	free cash flow on date t
g	expected dividend growth rate
g_{FCF}	expected free cash flow growth rate
N	terminal date or forecast horizon
P_t	stock price at the end of year t
PV	present value
r_E	equity cost of capital
r_{wacc}	weighted average cost of capital
V_t	enterprise value on date t

In early-2016, the four most valuable U.S. companies were Alphabet (Google), Apple, Microsoft, and Facebook. Google and Facebook do not pay dividends, and until 2012, neither did Apple (yet in 2011 it was the most valuable company in the world). In Chapter 7, we discussed the basics of stocks and valued them using the dividend-discount model. As we pointed out at the end of that chapter, the dividend-discount model is not a practical approach for valuing the stock of the thousands of companies like Google and Facebook that do not pay dividends. We then modified the dividend-discount model to include other forms of payout such as repurchases.

Some companies, especially young ones, neither repurchase shares nor pay dividends. In this chapter, we develop a more broadly applicable method to value companies—it can even be used to value companies that currently make no cash payouts to investors. Termed the *Discounted Free Cash Flow* model, it is very closely linked to the concepts we just learned for capital budgeting. In fact, you will see that just as the discounted cash flows of a project determine the value of a project to the firm, the discounted cash flows of the firm as a whole determine its value to its investors.

The final valuation method we discuss in this chapter, the method of comparables, or "comps," is also broadly applicable to all types of companies. This method, in which we compare the firm to others in the same line of business, is based on the intuitive idea that similar companies should be valued similarly. We will learn how to use the market's valuation of one company to estimate a value of a similar company.

We close the chapter with a discussion of the role of competition in markets. We explain how information is reflected in stock prices through investor competition and discuss the implication for investors and corporate managers. Finally, we describe some common trading biases of individual investors.

10.1 The Discounted Free Cash Flow Model

In Chapter 7, we developed the dividend-discount model to value the stock of a dividend-paying firm. In this section, we outline an alternative approach to valuing the firm's shares that avoids some of the difficulties of the dividend-discount model. Specifically, we consider the *discounted free cash flow model*, which focuses on the cash flows to all of the firm's investors, both debt and equity holders. This model allows us to avoid the difficulties associated with estimating the impact of the firm's borrowing decisions on earnings. It also demonstrates the important connection between the capital budgeting analysis we did in Chapter 9 and its implications for the firm's stock price.

discounted free cash flow model A method for estimating a firm's enterprise value by discounting its future free cash flow.

The dividend-discount model values a single share of stock. In the total payout model, we first value the firm's equity, rather than just a single share. The **discounted free cash flow model** goes one step further and begins by determining the total value of the firm to all investors—both equity holders *and* debt holders. We begin by estimating the firm's enterprise value, which we defined in Chapter 2 as follows:[1]

$$\text{Enterprise Value} = \text{Market Value of Equity} + \text{Debt} - \text{Cash} \qquad (10.1)$$

Because the enterprise value is the value of the firm's underlying business, unencumbered by debt and separate from any cash or marketable securities, it is also the value of the underlying business to all investors. We can interpret the enterprise value as the net cost of acquiring the firm's equity, paying off all debt, and taking its cash; in essence, it is equivalent to owning the unlevered business. The advantage of the discounted free cash flow model is that it allows us to value a firm without explicitly forecasting its dividends, share repurchases, or use of debt.

Valuing the Enterprise

How can we estimate a firm's enterprise value? To estimate the value of the firm's equity, we compute the present value of the firm's total payouts to equity holders. Likewise, to estimate a firm's enterprise value, we compute the present value of the *free cash flow* (FCF) that the firm has available to pay all investors, both debt and equity holders. We saw how to compute the free cash flow for a project in Chapter 9; we now perform the same calculation for the entire firm:

$$\text{Free Cash Flow} = EBIT \times (1 - \text{Tax Rate}) + \text{Depreciation}$$
$$- \text{Capital Expenditures} - \text{Increases in Net Working Capital} \qquad (10.2)$$

Free cash flow measures the cash generated by the firm before any payments to debt or equity holders are considered.

---

[1]To be precise, when we say "cash," we are referring to the firm's cash in excess of its working capital needs, which is the amount of cash it has invested at a competitive market interest rate.

Thus, just as we determine the value of a project by calculating the NPV of the project's free cash flow, we estimate a firm's current enterprise value, V_0, by computing the present value of the firm's free cash flow:

Discounted Free Cash Flow Model

$$V_0 = PV(\text{Future Free Cash Flow of Firm}) \tag{10.3}$$

Given the enterprise value, we can estimate the share price by using Eq. 10.1 to solve for the value of equity and then divide by the total number of shares outstanding:

$$P_0 = \frac{V_0 + \text{Cash}_0 - \text{Debt}_0}{\text{Shares Outstanding}_0} \tag{10.4}$$

In the dividend-discount model, the firm's cash and debt are included indirectly through the effect of interest income and expenses on earnings. By contrast, in the discounted free cash flow model, we ignore interest income and expenses because free cash flow is based on EBIT (Earnings *Before* Interest and Taxes), but we then adjust for cash and debt directly (in Eq. 10.4).

Implementing the Model

A key difference between the discounted free cash flow model and the earlier models we have considered is the discount rate. In previous calculations, we used the firm's equity cost of capital, r_E, because we were discounting the cash flows to equity holders. Here, we are discounting the free cash flow that will be paid to both debt and equity holders. Thus, we should use the firm's **weighted average cost of capital (WACC)**, denoted by r_{wacc}. It is the cost of capital that reflects the risk of the overall business, which is the combined risk of the firm's equity *and* debt. We interpret r_{wacc} as the expected return the firm must pay to investors to compensate them for the risk of holding the firm's debt and equity together. If the firm has no debt, then $r_{wacc} = r_E$. We will develop methods to calculate the WACC explicitly in Part 4 of the text.

Given the firm's weighted average cost of capital, we implement the discounted free cash flow model in much the same way as we did the dividend-discount model. That is, we forecast the firm's free cash flow up to some horizon, together with a terminal (continuation) value of the enterprise:

> **weighted average cost of capital (WACC)** The cost of capital that reflects the risk of the overall business, which is the combined risk of the firm's equity and debt.

$$V_0 = \frac{FCF_1}{1 + r_{wacc}} + \frac{FCF_2}{(1 + r_{wacc})^2} + \cdots + \frac{FCF_N}{(1 + r_{wacc})^N} + \frac{V_N}{(1 + r_{wacc})^N} \tag{10.5}$$

Often, we estimate the terminal value by assuming a constant long-run growth rate g_{FCF} for free cash flows beyond year N, so that

$$V_N = \frac{FCF_{N+1}}{r_{wacc} - g_{FCF}} = \left(\frac{1 + g_{FCF}}{r_{wacc} - g_{FCF}} \right) \times FCF_N \tag{10.6}$$

The long-run growth rate g_{FCF} is typically based on the expected long-run growth rate of the firm's revenues.

EXAMPLE 10.1

Valuing Nike, Inc., Stock Using Free Cash Flow

MyFinanceLab

PROBLEM

Recall our example of Nike, Inc., from Chapter 7. Nike had sales of $25.3 billion in 2012. Suppose you expected its sales to grow at a rate of 10% in 2013, but then slow by 1% per year to the long-run growth rate that is characteristic of the apparel industry—5%—by 2018. Based on Nike's past profitability and investment needs, you expected EBIT to be 10% of sales, increases in net working capital requirements to be 10% of any increase in sales, and capital expenditures to equal depreciation expenses. If Nike had $3.3 billion in cash, $1.2 billion in debt, 893.6 million shares outstanding, a tax rate of 24%, and a weighted average cost of capital of 10%, what would have been your estimate of the value of Nike stock in early 2013?

(Continued)

SOLUTION

PLAN

We can estimate Nike's future free cash flow by constructing a pro forma statement as we did for HomeNet in Chapter 9. The only difference is that the pro forma statement is for the whole company, rather than just one project. Furthermore, we need to calculate a terminal (or continuation) value for Nike at the end of our explicit projections. Because we expected Nike's free cash flow to grow at a constant rate after 2018, we can use Eq.10.6 to compute a terminal enterprise value. The present value of the free cash flows during the years 2013–2018 and the terminal value will be the total enterprise value for Nike. From that value, we can subtract the debt, add the cash, and divide by the number of shares outstanding to compute the price per share (Eq. 10.4).

EXECUTE

The following spreadsheet presents a simplified pro forma for Nike based on the information we have:

	Year	2012	2013	2014	2015	2016	2017	2018
1								
2	**FCF Forecast ($ million)**							
3	Sales	25,300.0	27,830.0	30,334.7	32,761.5	35,054.8	37,158.1	39,016.0
4	*Growth Versus Prior Year*		*10.0%*	*9.0%*	*8.0%*	*7.0%*	*6.0%*	*5.0%*
5	**EBIT** (10% of sales)		2,783.0	3,033.5	3,276.1	3,505.5	3,715.8	3,901.6
6	Less: Income Tax (24%)		667.9	728.0	786.3	841.3	891.8	936.4
7	Plus: Depreciation		—	—	—	—	—	—
8	Less: Capital Expenditures		—	—	—	—	—	—
9	Less: Increase in NWC (10% ΔSales)		253.0	250.5	242.7	229.3	210.3	185.8
10	**Free Cash Flow**		1,862.1	2,055.0	2,247.2	2,434.8	2,613.7	2,779.4

Because capital expenditures are expected to equal depreciation, lines 7 and 8 in the spreadsheet cancel out. We can set them both to zero rather than explicitly forecast them.

Given our assumption of constant 5% growth in free cash flows after 2018 and a weighted average cost of capital of 10%, we can use Eq. 10.6 to compute a terminal enterprise value:

$$V_{2018} = \left(\frac{1 + g_{FCF}}{r_{wacc} - g_{FCF}} \right) \times FCF_{2018} = \left(\frac{1.05}{0.10 - 0.05} \right) \times 2,779.4 = \$58,367.9 \text{ million}$$

From Eq. 10.5, Nike's 2013 enterprise value is the present value of its free cash flows plus the present value of the firm's terminal value:

$$V_0 = \frac{1,862.1}{1.10} + \frac{2,055.0}{1.10^2} + \frac{2,247.2}{1.10^3} + \frac{2,434.8}{1.10^4} + \frac{2,613.7}{1.10^5} + \frac{2,779.4}{1.10^6} + \frac{58,367.9}{1.10^6} = \$42,881.5 \text{ million}$$

We can now estimate the value of a share of Nike stock using Eq. 10.4:

$$P_0 = \frac{\$42,881.5 + \$3,300 - \$1,200}{893.6} = \$50.34$$

EVALUATE

The total value of all of the claims, both debt and equity, on the firm must equal the total present value of all cash flows generated by the firm, in addition to any cash it currently has. The total present value of all cash flows to be generated by Nike is $42,881.5 million and it has $3,300 million in cash. Subtracting off the value of the debt claims ($1,200 million), leaves us with the total value of the equity claims and dividing by the number of shares produces the value per share.

Connection to Capital Budgeting

There is an important connection between the discounted free cash flow model and the NPV rule for capital budgeting we developed in Chapter 9. Because the firm's free cash flow is equal to the sum of the free cash flows from the firm's current and future investments, we can interpret the firm's enterprise value as the sum of the present value of its existing projects and the NPV of future ones. Hence, the NPV of any investment decision represents its contribution to the firm's enterprise value. To maximize the firm's share price, we should therefore accept those projects that have a positive NPV.

Recall also from Chapter 9 that many forecasts and estimates were necessary to estimate the free cash flows of a project. The same is true for the firm: We must forecast its future sales, operating expenses, taxes, capital requirements, and other factors to obtain its free cash flow. On the one hand, estimating free cash flow in this way gives us flexibility to incorporate many specific details about the future prospects of the firm. On the other hand, some uncertainty inevitably surrounds each assumption. Given this fact, it is important to conduct a sensitivity analysis, as described in Chapter 9, to translate this uncertainty into a range of potential values for the stock.

EXAMPLE 10.2

Sensitivity Analysis for Stock Valuation

MyFinanceLab

PROBLEM

In Example 10.1, Nike's EBIT was assumed to be 10% of sales. If Nike can reduce its operating expenses and raise its EBIT to 11% of sales, how would the estimate of the stock's value change?

SOLUTION

PLAN

In this scenario, EBIT will increase by 1% of sales compared to Example 10.1. From there, we can use the tax rate (24%) to compute the effect on the free cash flow for each year. Once we have the new free cash flows, we repeat the approach in Example 10.1 to arrive at a new stock price.

EXECUTE

In year 1, EBIT will be 1% × $27,830 million = $278.3 million higher. After taxes, this increase will raise the firm's free cash flow in year 1 by $(1 - 0.24) \times \$278.3 = \$211.5$ million, to $2,073.6 million. Doing the same calculation for each year, we get the following revised FCF estimates:

Year	2013	2014	2015	2016	2017	2018
FCF	2,073.6	2,285.5	2,496.2	2,701.2	2,896.1	3,075.9

We can now reestimate the stock price as in Example 10.1. The terminal value is $V_{2018} = [1.05/(0.10 - 0.05)] \times 3,075.9 = \$65,594.8$ million, so

$$V_0 = \frac{2,073.6}{1.10} + \frac{2,285.5}{1.10^2} + \frac{2,496.2}{1.10^3} + \frac{2,701.2}{1.10^4} + \frac{2,896.1}{1.10^5} + \frac{3,075.9}{1.10^6} + \frac{64,594.8}{1.10^6} = \$47,491 \text{ million}$$

The new estimate for the value of the stock is $P_0 = (47,491 + 3,300 - 1,200)/893.6 = \$55.50$ per share, a difference of about 10% compared to the result found in Example 10.1.

EVALUATE

Nike's stock price is fairly sensitive to changes in the assumptions about its profitability. A 1% permanent change in its margins affects the firm's stock price by 10%.

Figure 10.1 summarizes the different valuation methods we have discussed so far. We use the present value of a stock's future dividends to determine its value. We can estimate the total market capitalization of the firm's equity from the present value of the firm's total payouts, which includes dividends and share repurchases. Finally, the present value of the firm's free cash flow, which is the amount of cash the firm has available to make payments to equity or debt holders, determines the firm's enterprise value.

FIGURE 10.1

A Comparison of
Discounted Cash
Flow Models of Stock
Valuation

By computing the present value of the firm's dividends, total payouts, or free cash flows, we can estimate
the value of the stock, the total value of the firm's equity, or the firm's enterprise value. The final column
details what adjustment is necessary to obtain the stock price.

Present Value of...	Determines the...	To Get Stock Price Estimate...
Dividend Payments	Stock Price	No adjustment necessary
Total Payouts (all dividends and repurchases)	Equity Value	Divide by shares oustanding
Free Cash Flow (cash available to pay all security holders)	Enterprise Value	Subtract what does not belong to equity holders (debt and preferred stock), add cash and marketable securities, and divide by shares outstanding

CONCEPT
CHECK

1. What is the relation between capital budgeting and the discounted free cash flow model?

2. Why do we ignore interest payments on the firm's debt in the discounted free cash flow model?

10.2   Valuation Based on Comparable Firms

So far, we have valued a firm or its stock by considering the expected future cash flows it
will provide to its owner. The Valuation Principle then tells us that its value is the present
value of its future cash flows, because the present value is the amount we would need to
invest elsewhere in the market to replicate the cash flows with the same risk.

Another application of the Valuation Principle is the *method of comparables*. In the
method of comparables (or "comps"), rather than value the firm's cash flows directly, we
estimate the value of the firm based on the value of other, comparable firms or investments
that we expect will generate very similar cash flows in the future. For example, consider
the case of a new firm that is *identical* to an existing publicly traded company. Recall that
from competitive market prices, the Valuation Principle implies that two securities with
identical cash flows must have the same price. Thus, if these firms will generate identical
cash flows, we can use the market value of the existing company to determine the value
of the new firm.

Of course, identical companies do not really exist. Even two firms in the same industry selling the same types of products, while similar in many respects, are likely to be
of a different size or scale. For example, Intel Corporation and Advanced Micro Devices
(AMD) both develop and sell semiconductor chips. In 2015, Intel had sales of $55 billion,
whereas AMD had less than $4 billion. In this section, we consider ways to adjust for scale
differences to use comparables to value firms with similar businesses and then discuss the
strengths and weaknesses of this approach.

method of comparables
An estimate of the value of
a firm based on the value
of other, comparable firms
or other investments that
are expected to generate
very similar cash flows in
the future.

valuation multiple A ratio
of a firm's value to some
measure of the firm's
scale or cash flow.

Valuation Multiples

We can adjust for differences in scale between firms by expressing their value in terms
of a **valuation multiple**, which is a ratio of the value to some measure of the firm's scale.

As an analogy, consider valuing an office building. A natural measure to consider would be the price per square foot for other buildings recently sold in the area. Multiplying the size of the office building under consideration by the average price per square foot would typically provide a reasonable estimate of the building's value. We can apply this same idea to stocks, replacing square footage with some more appropriate measure of the firm's scale.

The Price-Earnings Ratio. The most common valuation multiple is the price-earnings ratio, which we introduced in Chapter 2. The P/E ratio is so common that it is almost always part of the basic statistics computed for a stock (as shown in Figure 10.2, the screenshot from Google Finance for Nike). A firm's P/E ratio is equal to the share price divided by its earnings per share. The intuition behind its use is that, when you buy a stock, you are in a sense buying the rights to the firm's future earnings. If differences in the scale of firms' earnings are likely to persist, you should be willing to pay proportionally more for a stock with higher current earnings. Using this idea, we can estimate the value of a share of stock of a firm by using the P/E ratios of other firms. For example, we can estimate the stock price of a private firm by multiplying its current earnings per share (EPS) by the average P/E ratio of comparable public firms.

FIGURE 10.2

Stock Price Quote for Nike (NKE)

This screenshot from Google Finance shows the basic stock price information and price history charting for the common stock of Nike. The historical price chart covers the period March through late June 2013. Notice that the price-earnings (P/E) ratio is listed as part of the basic information.

EXAMPLE 10.3

Valuation Using
the Price-Earnings
Ratio

MyFinanceLab

PROBLEM

Suppose furniture manufacturer Herman Miller, Inc., has earnings per share of $1.38. If the average P/E of comparable furniture stocks is 21.3, estimate a value for a share of Herman Miller stock using the P/E as a valuation multiple. What are the assumptions underlying this estimate?

SOLUTION

PLAN

We estimate a share price for Herman Miller by multiplying its EPS by the P/E of comparable firms:

EPS × P/E = Earnings per Share × (Price per Share ÷ Earnings per Share) = Price per Share

EXECUTE

$P_0 = \$1.38 \times 21.3 = \$29.39$. This estimate assumes that Herman Miller will have similar future risk, payout rates, and growth rates to comparable firms in the industry.

EVALUATE

Although valuation multiples are simple to use, they rely on some very strong assumptions about the similarity of the comparable firms to the firm you are valuing. It is important to consider whether these assumptions are likely to be reasonable—and thus to hold—in each case.

trailing earnings A firm's earnings over the prior 12 months.

forward earnings A firm's expected earnings over the coming 12 months.

trailing P/E A firm's price-earnings (P/E) ratio calculated using trailing (past) earnings.

forward P/E A firm's price-earnings (P/E) ratio calculated using forward (expected) earnings.

We can compute a firm's P/E ratio by using either **trailing earnings**—earnings over the prior 12 months—or **forward earnings**—expected earnings over the coming 12 months—with the resulting ratio being called the **trailing P/E** or the **forward P/E**, respectively. For valuation purposes, the forward P/E is generally preferred, as we are most concerned about future earnings.

To understand how P/E ratios relate to the other valuation techniques we have discussed, consider the dividend discount model introduced in Chapter 7.[2] For example, in the case of constant dividend growth (see Eq. 7.6), we had

$$P_0 = \frac{Div_1}{r_E - g}$$

Dividing through by EPS_1, we find that

$$\text{Forward P/E} = \frac{P_0}{EPS_1} = \frac{Div_1/EPS_1}{r_E - g} = \frac{\text{Dividend Payout Rate}}{r_E - g} \qquad (10.7)$$

In Chapter 7, we showed that Nike's current price is consistent with an equity cost of capital of 10% and an expected dividend growth rate of 8.5%. From the Nike quote, we can also see that Nike has earnings per share (EPS) of $2.52 and a dividend of $0.21 per quarter, or $0.84 per year which gives a dividend payout rate of 0.84/2.52 = 0.333. Assuming that earnings growth and payout rates remain at this level for the foreseeable future, then we could compute the forward P/E as:

$$\text{Forward P/E} = \frac{0.84/2.52}{.10 - 0.085} = 22.22, \text{ which is not far off its reported P/E of 24.00.}$$

Equation 10.7 suggests that firms and industries that have high growth rates, and that generate cash well in excess of their investment needs so that they can maintain high payout rates, should have high P/E multiples. Taking the example of Nike we showed that at

---

[2]We use the dividend discount model rather than discounted cash flows because price and earnings are variables associated exclusively with equity.

FIGURE 10.3

Relating the P/E Ratio
to Expected Future
Growth

The graph shows the expected growth in earnings under two growth scenarios for Nike: 8.5% and 5%. In 2013, earnings per share were $2.52. Higher growth increases the PV of the earnings stream, which means that the price increases. The result is that the higher price divided by current earnings yields a higher P/E ratio. We found that a growth rate of 8.5% implied a P/E ratio of 22.22 while a growth rate of 5% implied a P/E ratio of 6.67. The graph shows how higher expected growth translates into a higher P/E.

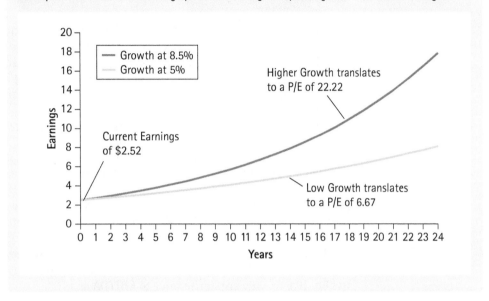

an expected growth rate of 8.5%, it would have a P/E ratio of 22.22. If our growth expectations were lower, its P/E would drop. Holding current earnings, dividends, and equity cost of capital constant, but decreasing the growth rate to 5%, we would have:

$$\text{Forward P/E} = \frac{0.84/2.52}{.10 - 0.05} = 6.67$$

This result is much lower than its current P/E of 24.00 making it clear that simply comparing P/E ratios without taking into account growth prospects can be highly misleading.

Figure 10.3 shows the relationship between expected earnings growth and P/E ratios.

EXAMPLE 10.4

Growth Prospects and
the Price-Earnings
Ratio

MyFinanceLab

PROBLEM

Amazon.com and Macy's are retailers. In 2016, Amazon had a price of $717.93 and forward earnings per share of $9.78. Macy's had a price of $31.21 and forward earnings per share of $3.77. Calculate their forward P/E ratios and explain the difference.

SOLUTION

PLAN

We can calculate their P/E ratios by dividing each company's price per share by its forward earnings per share. The difference we find is most likely due to different growth expectations.

EXECUTE

Forward P/E for Amazon = $717.93/$9.78 = 73.4. Forward P/E for Macy's = $31.21/$3.77 = 8.28. Amazon's P/E ratio is higher because investors expect its earnings to grow more than Macy's.

(Continued)

Enterprise Value Multiples. The P/E ratio has the same limitations as the dividend discount model—because it relates exclusively to equity, it ignores the effect of debt. Consequently, it is also common practice to use valuation multiples based on the firm's enterprise value. By representing the total value of the firm's underlying business rather than just the value of equity, the enterprise value allows us to compare firms with different amounts of leverage.

Because the enterprise value represents the entire value of the firm before the firm pays its debt, to form an appropriate multiple, we divide it by a measure of earnings or cash flows before interest payments are made. Common multiples to consider are enterprise value to EBIT, EBITDA (earnings before interest, taxes, depreciation, and amortization), and free cash flow. However, because capital expenditures can vary substantially from period to period (e.g., a firm may need to add capacity and build a new plant one year, but then may not need to expand further for many years), most practitioners rely on enterprise value to EBITDA (EV/EBITDA) multiples.

Enterprise value multiples value the entire firm, and so they are most closely related to the discount cash flow model. When expected free cash flow growth is constant, we can use Eq. 10.6 to write enterprise value to EBITDA as

$$\frac{V_0}{EBITDA_1} = \frac{\dfrac{FCF_1}{r_{wacc} - g_{FCF}}}{EBITDA_1} = \frac{FCF_1/EBITDA_1}{r_{wacc} - g_{FCF}} \tag{10.8}$$

As with the P/E multiple, this valuation multiple is higher for firms with high growth rates and low capital requirements (which means that free cash flow is high in proportion to EBITDA).

EXAMPLE 10.5

Valuation Using the Enterprise Value Multiple

MyFinanceLab

PROBLEM

Fairview, Inc., is an ocean transport company with EBITDA of $50 million, cash of $20 million, debt of $100 million, and 10 million shares outstanding. The ocean transport industry as a whole has an average EV/EBITDA ratio of 8.5. What is one estimate of Fairview's enterprise value? What is a corresponding estimate of its stock price?

SOLUTION

PLAN

To estimate Fairview's enterprise value, we multiply its EBITDA by the average EV/EBITDA ratio of its industry. From there, we can subtract Fairview's debt and add its cash to calculate its equity value. Finally, we can divide by the number of shares outstanding to arrive at its stock price.

EXECUTE

Fairview's enterprise value estimate is $50 million × 8.5 = $425 million.

Next, subtract the debt from its enterprise value and add in its cash:

$425 million − $100 million + $20 million = $345 million, which is an estimate of the equity value.

Its stock price estimate is equal to its equity value estimate divided by the number of shares outstanding:
$345 million ÷ 10 million = $34.50.

EVALUATE

If we assume that Fairview should be valued similarly to the rest of the industry, then $425 million is a reasonable estimate of its enterprise value and $34.50 is a reasonable estimate of its stock price. However, we are relying on the assumption that Fairview's expected free cash flow growth is similar to the industry average. If that assumption is wrong, so is our valuation.

Other Multiples. Many other valuation multiples are used. Looking at the enterprise value as a multiple of sales can be useful if it is reasonable to assume the firm will maintain a similar margin in the future. For firms with substantial tangible assets, the ratio of price-to-book value of equity per share is sometimes used as a valuation multiple. Some multiples are specific to an industry. In the cable TV industry, for example, analysts compare enterprise value per subscriber.

Limitations of Multiples

If comparable firms were identical to the firm being valued, the firms' multiples would match precisely. Of course, firms are not identical, so the usefulness of a valuation multiple will inevitably depend on the nature of the differences between firms and the sensitivity of the multiples to these differences.

Table 10.1 lists several valuation multiples, as of July 2013, for firms in the footwear industry that could be used as comparables for Nike. Also shown in the table is the average for each multiple, together with the range around the average (in percentage terms). The bottom rows showing the range make it clear that the footwear industry has a lot of dispersion for all the multiples (for example, Wolverine has a price-to-book (P/B) of 4.13,

TABLE 10.1

Stock Prices and Multiples for the Footwear Industry (excluding Nike), July 2013

Name	Market Capitalization ($ million)	Enterprise Value ($ million)	P/E	Price/Book	Enterprise Value/Sales	Enterprise Value/EBITDA
Nike, Inc.	55,970	54,023	23.29	5.07	2.03	15.71
Adidas AG	23,105	23,317	32.33	3.06	1.20	11.88
Puma AG	4,330	4,085	70.56	1.96	0.96	9.34
Wolverine World Wide	2,910	3,981	37.6	4.13	1.22	9.28
Steve Madden, Ltd.	2,320	2,140	18.4	3.68	1.74	10.70
Deckers Outdoor Corp.	1,990	1,923	16.74	2.67	1.36	8.73
Crocs, Inc.	1,470	1,240	11.46	2.4	1.10	6.74
Skechers U.S.A.	1,340	1,213	67.41	1.54	0.78	18.16
Weyco Group, Inc.	301	325	16.53	1.71	1.11	9.69
R. G. Barry Corp.	197	174	14.92	2.31	1.19	6.44
Rocky Brands, Inc.	113	132	12.46	0.89	0.58	6.61
		Average	29.84	2.44	1.12	9.76
		Maximum	+136%	+70%	+55%	+86%
		Minimum	−62%	−63%	−48%	−34%

while Rocky Brands, Inc. has a P/B of only 0.89). While the Enterprise Value/Sales multiple shows the smallest variation, even with it we cannot expect to obtain a precise estimate of a firm's value.

The differences in these multiples most likely reflect differences in expected future growth rates, risk (and therefore costs of capital), and, in the case of Puma and Adidas, differences in accounting conventions between the United States and Germany. Investors in the market understand that these differences exist, so the stocks are priced accordingly. When valuing a firm using multiples, however, there is no clear guidance about how to adjust for these differences other than by narrowing the set of comparables used.

Another limitation of comparables is that they provide only information regarding the value of the firm *relative to* the other firms in the comparison set. Using multiples will not help us determine whether an entire industry is overvalued, for example. This issue became especially important during the Internet boom of the late 1990s. Because many of these firms did not have positive cash flows or earnings, new multiples were created to value them (for instance, price to "page views"). While these multiples could justify the value of these firms in relationship to one another, it was much more difficult to justify the stock prices of many of these firms using a realistic estimate of cash flows and the discounted free cash flow approach.

Comparison with Discounted Cash Flow Methods

The use of a valuation multiple based on comparables is best viewed as a shortcut. Rather than separately estimate the firm's cost of capital and future earnings or free cash flows, we rely on the market's assessment of the value of other firms with similar future prospects. In addition to its simplicity, the multiples approach has the advantage of being based on actual stock prices of real firms, rather than on what may be unrealistic forecasts of future cash flows.

The most important shortcoming of the comparables approach is that it does not take into account materially important differences among firms. For example, the approach ignores the fact that some firms have exceptionally talented managers, others have developed more efficient manufacturing processes, and still others might hold a patent on a new technology. Discounted cash flow methods have an advantage because they allow us to incorporate specific information about the firm's cost of capital or future growth. Thus, because the true driver of value for any firm is its ability to generate cash flows for its investors, the discounted cash flow methods have the potential to be more accurate than the use of a valuation multiple.

CONCEPT 3. What are some common valuation multiples?
CHECK   4. What implicit assumptions do we make when valuing a firm using multiples based on comparable firms?

10.3 Stock Valuation Techniques: A Final Word

In the end, no single technique provides a final answer regarding a stock's true value. Indeed, all approaches inevitably require assumptions or forecasts that are too uncertain to provide a definitive assessment of the firm's value. Most real-world practitioners use a combination of these approaches and gain confidence in the outcome if the results are consistent across a variety of methods.

Figure 10.4 compares the ranges of values for Nike stock using the different valuation methods discussed in this chapter and in Chapter 7. The firm's stock price of $60.39 on June 25, 2013 was within the range of some methods, but higher than the range suggested by some of the multiples. Hence, based on this evidence alone, we would not conclude that the stock is obviously under- or over-priced. But if this were not the case—what if these valuation techniques produce valuations markedly different to what the stock is trading at in the market? In the next section, we tackle this question.

FIGURE 10.4

Range of Valuations
for Nike Stock Using
Various Valuation
Methods

Valuations from multiples are based on the low, high, and average values of the comparable firms from Table 10.1 (see Problems 17 and 18 at the end of this chapter). The constant dividend growth model is based on a 10% equity cost of capital and dividend growth rates of 6% to 9%, as discussed at the beginning of Section 7.5. The discounted free cash flow model is based on Example 10.1 with the range of parameters in Problem 9 at the end of this chapter. Midpoints are based on average multiples or base-case assumptions. Red and blue regions show the variation between the lowest-multiple/worst-case scenario and the highest-multiple/best-case scenario. Nike's actual share price of $60.39 is indicated by the gray line.

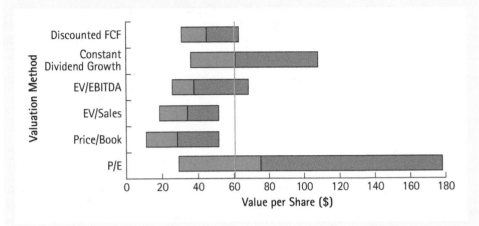

INTERVIEW WITH

DOUGLAS KEHRING

Since 2005, Douglas Kehring has been Senior Vice President of Oracle Corporation's Corporate Development and Strategic Planning group, providing planning, advisory, execution, and integration management services to Oracle on mergers and acquisitions and related transactions.

QUESTION: *How does Oracle target companies to acquire?*

ANSWER: Oracle uses an ongoing strategic planning process to identify potential acquisition targets. Top-down, the corporate development group works with the CEO's office looking for large, game-changing acquisitions. We also work bottom-up with engineering executives who sponsor potential acquisitions to fill customer needs and product gaps. Together we identify prospects, engage with targets, perform due diligence, develop business plans, and proceed with feasible transactions. Our group also provides the CEO's office with objective opinions of sponsor proposals, based on Oracle's overall needs and priorities. The CEO's office approves all transactions.

We see about 300 to 400 opportunities a year and show all to the appropriate product group executives, including those from venture capital firms and investment bankers. Typically, they express an interest in about 20 to 40, and we sign confidentiality agreements to proceed with a thorough analysis. About 12 of those reach the letter of intent stage, where we issue a term sheet and an exclusivity period to complete the transaction.

QUESTION: *Once you decide to try to acquire a company, how do you determine how much to pay for it?*

ANSWER: The pricing occurs after due diligence but before the letter of intent. From a practical standpoint, we negotiate the price point with the seller— that's where the art comes into play. Our DCF analysis is the most important part in justifying the value. We take into account what we believe we can do with the business from an income statement perspective, to determine the break-even valuation at the chosen hurdle rate. If we pay less, we'll earn a higher rate of return, and vice versa.

QUESTION: *Discuss the role of both discounted cash flow and comparables analysis in determining the price to pay.*

ANSWER: We use 5-year DCFs, because it takes that long to get to a steady state and predicting beyond that is difficult. The hardest part is determining the income statement inputs. The fifth-year numbers dominate value. Getting to that point depends on how fast you grow the business and how profitable it is. Assumptions are the key. We take a conservative approach, leveraging available information. Overly aggressive sponsor assumptions lead to extreme valuations, creating an acquirer's biggest problems.

(Continued)

The hurdle rate for a project varies. We might use cost of equity or the WACC. Then we ask, "What is right risk/return profile for this transaction?" and adjust the rate accordingly—for example, possibly requiring a higher return for a smaller, more volatile company.

Oracle's 80 completed transactions give us actual experience on which to base more realistic assumptions. We look at variables and attributes—was it a product line, a specific feature, a stand-alone acquisition?—and assess how well we did based on our models, to improve our cash flow analysis for future acquisitions. Then we benchmark using common valuation multiples based on comparable publicly traded companies and similar M&A transactions.

QUESTION: *How does your analysis differ for private versus public companies?*

ANSWER: The basic DCF analysis is no different: We perform the same due diligence for private and public companies and receive the same types of information. Typically, the larger the public company's revenues, the more stable it is and the more professional its orientation and systems. We feel more confident in our risk attributes and the information we receive. In acquiring a public company, we prepare a pro forma statement for the combined entity to determine whether it will increase or decrease our earnings per share.

Of greater concern to us is the target's size. A $2 billion company, whether public or private, has multiple product lines and larger installed bases, reducing its risk profile. A $100 million company may have only one product line and thus, higher risk and volatility. On the other hand, the small company may grow faster than a large one.

10.4 Information, Competition, and Stock Prices

As shown in Figure 10.5, the models described in this chapter and in Chapter 7 link the firm's expected future cash flows, its cost of capital (determined by its risk), and the value of its shares. But what conclusions should we draw if the actual market price of a stock does not appear to be consistent with our estimate of its value? Is it more likely that the stock is mispriced or that we are mistaken about its risk and future cash flows?

Information in Stock Prices

Suppose you are a new junior analyst assigned to research Nike stock and assess its value. You scrutinize the company's recent financial statements, look at the trends in the industry, and forecast the firm's future earnings, dividends, and free cash flows. After you carefully crunch the numbers, you estimate the stock's value to be $85 per share. On your way to present your analysis to your boss, you run into a slightly more experienced colleague in the elevator. It turns out that your colleague has been researching the same stock. But according to her analysis, the value of Nike stock is only $65 per share. What would you do?

Although you could just assume your colleague is wrong, most of us would reconsider our own analysis. The fact that someone else who has carefully studied the same stock has come to a very different conclusion is powerful evidence that you might be mistaken. In the face of this information from our colleague, you would probably adjust your assessment

FIGURE 10.5

The Valuation Triad

Valuation models determine the relationship among the firm's future cash flows, its cost of capital, and the value of its shares. We can use the stock's expected cash flows and cost of capital to assess its market price (share value). Conversely, we can use the market price to assess the firm's future cash flows or cost of capital.

of the stock's value downward. Of course, your colleague might also revise her opinion upward based on your assessment. After sharing the analyses, we would likely end up with a consensus estimate somewhere between $65 and $85 per share.

This type of encounter happens millions of times every day in the stock market. When a buyer seeks to buy a stock, the willingness of other parties to sell the same stock suggests that they value the stock differently. This information should lead both buyers and sellers to revise their valuations. Ultimately, investors trade until they reach a consensus regarding the value (market price) of the stock. In this way, stock markets aggregate the information and views of many different investors.

Thus, if your valuation model suggests a stock is worth $30 per share when it is trading for $20 per share in the market, the discrepancy is equivalent to knowing that thousands of investors—many of them professionals who have access to the best information about the stock available—disagree with your assessment. This knowledge should make you reconsider your original analysis. You would need a very compelling reason to trust your own estimate in the face of such contrary opinions.

What conclusion can we draw from this discussion? Recall Figure 10.5, in which a valuation model links the firm's future cash flows, its cost of capital, and its share price. In other words, given accurate information about any two of these variables, a valuation model allows us to make inferences about the third variable. Thus, the way we use a valuation model will depend on the quality of our information: The model will tell us the most about the variable for which our prior information is the least reliable.

For a publicly traded firm, its market price should already provide very accurate information, aggregated from a multitude of investors, regarding the true value of its shares. In these situations, the best use of a valuation model is to inform us about the things we cannot observe directly—the firm's future cash flows or cost of capital. Only in the relatively rare case in which we have some superior information that other investors lack regarding the firm's cash flows and cost of capital would it make sense to second-guess the stock price.

EXAMPLE 10.6

Using the Information in Market Prices

MyFinanceLab

PROBLEM

Suppose Tecnor Industries will have free cash flows next year of $40 million. Its weighted average cost of capital is 11%, and you expect its free cash flows to grow at a rate of approximately 4% per year, though you are somewhat unsure of the precise growth rate. Tecnor has 10 million shares outstanding, no debt, and $20 million in cash. If Tecnor stock is currently trading for $55.33 per share, how would you update your beliefs about its dividend growth rate?

SOLUTION

PLAN

If we apply the growing perpetuity formula for the growing FCF based on a 4% growth rate, we can estimate a stock price using Eqs.10.3 and 10.4. If the market price is higher than our estimate, it implies that the market expects higher growth in FCF than 4%. Conversely, if the market price is lower than our estimate, the market expects FCF growth to be less than 4%.

EXECUTE

Applying the growing perpetuity formula, we have $PV(FCF) = 40 \div (0.11 - 0.04) = \$571.43$ million. Applying Eq. 10.4, the price per share would be ($571.43 million − 0 + $20 million) $\div$ 10 million shares = $59.14 per share. The market price of $55.33, however, implies that most investors expect FCF to grow at a somewhat slower rate.

EVALUATE

Given the $55.33 market price for the stock, we should lower our expectations for the FCF growth rate from 4% unless we have very strong reasons to trust our own estimate.

efficient markets hypothesis The idea that competition among investors works to eliminate all positive-NPV trading opportunities. It implies that securities will be fairly priced, based on their future cash flows, given all information that is available to investors.

Competition and Efficient Markets

The notion that market prices reflect the information of many investors is a natural consequence of investor competition. If information were available that indicated buying a stock had a positive NPV, investors with that information would choose to buy the stock; their attempts to purchase it would then drive up the stock's price. By a similar logic, investors with information that selling a stock had a positive NPV would sell it, so the stock's price would fall.

The idea that competition among investors works to eliminate *all* positive-NPV trading opportunities is the **efficient markets hypothesis**. It implies that securities will be fairly priced, based on their future cash flows, given all information that is available to investors.

 ### Forms of Market Efficiency

The type of market efficiency we describe here, where all publicly available information is incorporated very quickly into stock prices, is often called *semistrong form market efficiency*. The term "semistrong" indicates that it is not as complete as *strong form market efficiency*, where prices immediately incorporate *all* information, including private information known, for example, only to managers. Finally, the term *weak form market efficiency* means that only the history of past prices is already reflected in the stock price. It helps to think of the different forms of market efficiency as meaning that prices incorporate a steadily increasing set of information, each of which encompasses all the lower forms. For example, since the history of past prices is public information, semistrong form efficiency encompasses weak form. The diagram illustrates the idea. In the diagram, the information sets of weak form, semistrong form, and strong form efficiency are represented by the blue, green, and yellow circles, respectively.

Not all market participants believe that the stock market is semistrong form efficient. Technical analysts, who look for patterns in stock prices, do not believe the market is even weak form efficient. Mutual fund managers and fundamental analysts, such as those who work for brokerages and make stock recommendations, believe that mispricing can be uncovered by careful analysis of company fundamentals. There is evidence that traders with inside information about upcoming merger or earnings announcements can make abnormal returns by trading (illegally) on that information, so the market is clearly not strong form efficient.

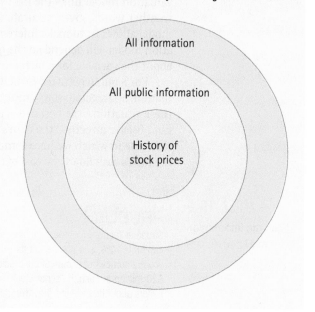

What happens when new information about a stock arrives? The answer depends on the degree of competition, that is, on the number of investors who have access to this new information. Consider two important cases.

Public, Easily Interpretable Information. Information that is available to all investors includes information in news reports, financial statements, corporate press releases, or other public data sources. If investors can readily ascertain the effects of this information on the firm's future cash flows, then all investors can determine how this information will change the firm's value.

In this situation, we expect competition among investors to be fierce and the stock price to react nearly instantaneously to such news. A few lucky investors might be able to trade a small quantity of shares before the price has fully adjusted. Most investors, however, would find that the stock price already reflected the new information before they were able to trade on it. In other words, the efficient markets hypothesis holds very well with respect to this type of information.

EXAMPLE 10.7

Stock Price Reactions
to Public Information

MyFinanceLab

PROBLEM

Myox Labs announces that it is pulling one of its leading drugs from the market, owing to the potential side effects associated with the drug. As a result, its future expected free cash flow will decline by $85 million per year for the next 10 years. Myox has 50 million shares outstanding, no debt, and an equity cost of capital of 8%. If this news came as a complete surprise to investors, what should happen to Myox's stock price upon the announcement?

SOLUTION

PLAN

In this case, we can use the discounted free cash flow method. With no debt, $r_{wacc} = r_E = 8\%$. The effect on the Myox's enterprise value will be the loss of a 10-year annuity of $85 million. We can compute the effect today as the present value of that annuity.

EXECUTE

Using the annuity formula, the decline in expected free cash flow will reduce Myox's enterprise value by

$$\$85 \text{ million} \times \frac{1}{0.08}\left(1 - \frac{1}{1.08^{10}}\right) = \$570.36 \text{ million}$$

Thus, the stock price should fall by 570.36 = $11.41 per share.

EVALUATE

Because this news is public and its effect on the firm's expected free cash flow is clear, we would expect the stock price to drop by $11.41 per share nearly instantaneously.

Private or Difficult-to-Interpret Information. Of course, some information is not publicly available. For example, an analyst might spend considerable time and effort gathering information from a firm's employees, competitors, suppliers, or customers that is relevant to the firm's future cash flows. This information is not available to other investors who have not devoted a similar effort to gathering it.

Even when information is publicly available, it may be difficult to interpret. Non-experts in the field may find it challenging to evaluate research reports on new technologies, for example. It may take a great deal of legal and accounting expertise and effort to understand the full consequences of a highly complicated business transaction. Certain consulting experts may have greater insight into consumer tastes and the likelihood of a product's acceptance. In these cases, while the fundamental information may be public, the *interpretation* of how that information will affect the firm's future cash flows is itself private information.

As an example, imagine that Phenyx Pharmaceuticals has announced the development of a new drug for which the company is seeking approval from the U.S. Food and Drug Administration (FDA). If the drug is approved and subsequently launched in the U.S. market, the future profits from the new drug will increase Phenyx's market value by $750 million, or $15 per share given its 50 million shares outstanding. Assume that the development of this drug comes as a surprise to investors, and that the average likelihood of FDA approval is 10%. In that case, because many investors probably know the chance of FDA approval is 10%, competition should lead to an immediate jump in Phenyx's stock price of 10% × $15 = $1.50 per share. Over time, however, analysts and experts in the field will likely make their own assessments of the probable efficacy of the drug. If they conclude that the drug looks more promising than average, they will begin to trade on their private information and buy the stock, and the firm's price will tend to drift higher over time. However, if the experts conclude that the drug looks less promising than average, they will tend to sell the stock, and the firm's price will drift lower over time. Of course, at the time of the announcement, uninformed investors do not know which way it will go. Examples of possible price paths are shown in Figure 10.6.

FIGURE 10.6

Possible Stock Price
Paths for Phenyx
Pharmaceuticals

Phenyx's stock price jumps on the announcement based on the average likelihood of FDA approval. The stock price then drifts up (green path) or down (orange path) as informed traders trade on their more accurate assessment of the drug's likelihood of approval and hence entry into the U.S. market. At the time of the announcement, uninformed investors do not know which way the stock will go.

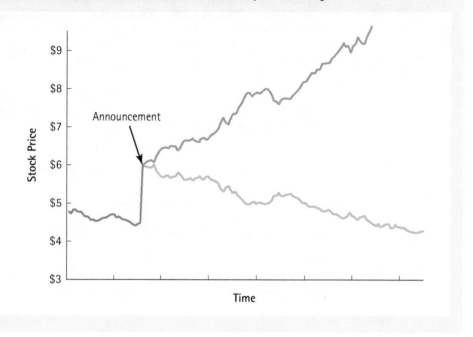

When private information is in the hands of a relatively small number of investors, these investors may be able to profit by trading on their information.[3] In this case, the efficient markets hypothesis will not hold in the strict sense. However, as these informed traders begin to trade, their actions will tend to move prices, so over time prices will begin to reflect their information as well.

If the profit opportunities from having this type of information are large, other individuals will attempt to gain the expertise and devote the resources needed to acquire it. As more individuals become better informed, competition to exploit this information will increase. Thus, in the long run, we should expect that the degree of "inefficiency" in the market will be limited by the costs of obtaining the information.

Lessons for Investors and Corporate Managers

The effect of competition based on information about stock prices has important consequences for both investors and corporate managers.

Consequences for Investors. As in other markets, investors should be able to identify positive-NPV trading opportunities in securities markets only if some barrier or restriction to free competition exists. An investor's competitive advantage may take several forms. For instance, the investor may have expertise or access to information known only to a few

---

[3]Even with private information, informed investors may find it difficult to profit from that information, because they must find others who are willing to trade with them; that is, the market for the stock must be sufficiently *liquid*. A liquid market requires that other investors in the market have alternative motives to trade (for example, selling shares of a stock to purchase a house) and so are willing to trade even when facing the risk that other traders may be better informed.

NOBEL PRIZE The 2013 Prize: An Enigma?

When the 2013 Nobel Prize in Economics was awarded to three financial economists, most people were surprised. The surprise was not that Eugene Fama, Robert Shiller, and Lars Peter Hansen had won the prize—most economists would agree they certainly deserved the prize for their contributions—rather it was that they won it *together*. After all, Fama is most well-known for what he termed the *efficient market hypothesis*, the assertion that markets are so competitive it is impossible to make money by trying to predict stock price movements. On the other hand, Robert Shiller argued the opposite, that the excess volatility in markets results from irrational behavior that can be exploited. Lars Peter Hansen is credited with developing statistical tools that can help distinguish these opposing views. Here is how the Nobel Prize committee justified its decision:

"Beginning in the 1960s, Eugene Fama and several collaborators demonstrated that stock prices are extremely difficult to predict in the short run, and that new information is very quickly incorporated into prices. . . . If prices are nearly impossible to predict over days or weeks, then shouldn't they be even harder to predict over several years? The answer is no, as Robert Shiller discovered in the early 1980s. He found that stock prices fluctuate much more than corporate dividends, and that the ratio of prices to dividends tends to fall when it is high, and to increase when it is low. This pattern holds not only for stocks, but also for bonds and other assets. Lars Peter Hansen developed a statistical method that is particularly well suited to testing rational theories of asset pricing. Using this method, Hansen and other researchers have found that modifications of these theories go a long way toward explaining asset prices."

Source: "The Prize in Economic Sciences 2013—Press Release." Nobelprize.org.

people. Alternatively, the investor may have lower trading costs than other market participants and so can exploit opportunities that others would find unprofitable. In all cases, the source of the positive-NPV trading opportunity must be something that is difficult to replicate; otherwise, any gains would be competed away in short order.

While the fact that positive-NPV trading opportunities are hard to come by may be disappointing, there is some good news as well. If stocks are fairly priced according to our valuation models, then investors who buy stocks can expect to receive future cash flows that fairly compensate them for the risk of their investment. In such cases, the average investor can invest with confidence, even if he or she is not fully informed.

Implications for Corporate Managers. If stocks are fairly valued according to the models we have described in this chapter and in Chapter 7, then the value of the firm is determined by the cash flows that it can pay to its investors. This result has several key implications for corporate managers:

- *Focus on NPV and free cash flow.* A manager seeking to boost the price of her firm's stock should make investments that increase the present value of the firm's free cash flow. Thus, the capital budgeting methods outlined in Chapter 9 are fully consistent with the objective of maximizing the firm's share price.

- *Avoid accounting illusions.* Many managers make the mistake of focusing on accounting earnings as opposed to free cash flows. According to the efficient markets hypothesis, the accounting consequences of a decision do not directly affect the value of the firm and should not drive decision making.

- *Use financial transactions to support investment.* With efficient markets, the firm can sell its shares at a fair price to new investors. As a consequence, the firm should not be constrained from raising capital to fund positive-NPV investment opportunities.

The Efficient Markets Hypothesis Versus No Arbitrage

There is an important distinction between the efficient markets hypothesis and the notion of no arbitrage that we introduced in Chapter 3. An arbitrage opportunity is a situation in which two securities (or portfolios) with *identical* cash flows have different prices. Because anyone can earn a sure profit in this situation by buying the low-priced security and selling the high-priced one, we expect investors to exploit and eliminate these opportunities immediately. Thus, arbitrage opportunities will not be found.

The efficient markets hypothesis states that the best estimate of the value of a share of stock is its market price. That is, investors' own estimates of value are not as accurate as the market price. But that does not mean that the market price always correctly estimates the value of a share of stock. There is a difference between the best estimate and being correct. Thus, there is no reason to expect the market price to always assess value accurately; rather, the price is best viewed as an approximation. However, because the price is the best estimate, the efficient market hypothesis implies that you cannot tell which prices overestimate and which underestimate the true value of the stock.

CONCEPT CHECK

5. State the efficient markets hypothesis.

6. What are the implications of the efficient markets hypothesis for corporate managers?

10.5 Individual Biases and Trading

Not all investors accept the notion that second guessing the stock prices requires specialized knowledge and unusual skills. Instead, they attempt to make money by trading and in most cases end up losing money. In this next section, we will briefly discuss some common psychological biases and consider how they affect individuals' trading behavior. In an efficient market, these biases can be costly, resulting in lower realized returns and reduced wealth.

Excessive Trading and Overconfidence

Trading is expensive; you must pay commissions on top of the difference between the bid and ask price, called the *spread*. Given how hard it should be to identify over- and undervalued stocks, you might then expect individual investors to take a conservative approach to trading. However, in an influential study of the trading behavior of individual investors that held accounts at a discount brokerage, researchers Brad Barber and Terrance Odean found that individual investors tend to trade very actively, with average turnover almost 50% above the average of all investors including institutions during the time period of their study.[4]

What might explain this trading behavior? Psychologists have known since the 1960s that uninformed individuals tend to overestimate the precision of their knowledge. For example, many sports fans sitting in the stands confidently second-guess the coaching decisions on the field, truly believing that they can do a better job. In finance we call investors' presumptuousness of their ability to beat the market by overtrading the **overconfidence hypothesis**. Barber and Odean hypothesized that this kind of behavior also characterizes individual investment decision making: Like sports fans, individual investors believe they can pick winners and losers when, in fact, they cannot; this overconfidence leads them to trade too much.

An implication of this overconfidence hypothesis is that, assuming they have no true ability, investors who trade more will not earn higher returns. Instead, their performance will be worse once we take into account the costs of trading (due to both commissions and bid-ask spreads). Figure 10.7 documents precisely this result, showing that much investor trading appears not to be based on rational assessments of performance.

overconfidence hypothesis The tendency of individual investors to trade too much based on the mistaken belief that they can pick winners and losers better than investment professionals.

disposition effect The tendency to hold on to stocks that have lost value and sell stocks that have risen in value since the time of purchase.

Hanging On to Losers and the Disposition Effect

Investors tend to hold on to stocks that have lost value and sell stocks that have risen in value since the time of purchase. We call this tendency to keep losers and sell winners the **disposition effect**. Researchers Hersh Shefrin and Meir Statman, building on the work of

---

[4]B. Barber and T. Odean, "Trading Is Hazardous to Your Wealth: The Common Stock Investment Performance of Individual Investors," *Journal of Finance*, 55 (2000) 773–806.

FIGURE 10.7

Individual Investor
Returns Versus
Portfolio Turnover

The plot shows the average annual return (net of commissions and trading costs) for individual investors at a large discount brokerage from 1991–1997. Investors are grouped into quintiles based on their average annual turnover. While the least-active investors had slightly (but not significantly) better performance than the S&P 500, performance declined with the rate of turnover.

Source: B. Barber and T. Odean, "Trading Is Hazardous to Your Wealth: The Common Stock Investment Performance of Individual Investors," *Journal of Finance*, 55 (2000): 773–806.

psychologists Daniel Kahneman and Amos Tversky, suggest that this effect arises due to investors' increased willingness to take on risk in the face of possible losses.[5] It may also reflect a reluctance to admit a mistake by taking the loss.

Researchers have verified the disposition effect in many studies. For example, in a study of all trades in the Taiwanese stock market from 1995–1999, investors in aggregate were twice as likely to realize gains as they were to realize losses. Also, nearly 85% of individual investors were subject to this bias.[6] On the other hand, mutual funds and foreign investors did not exhibit the same tendency, and other studies have shown that more sophisticated investors appear to be less susceptible to the disposition effect.[7]

This behavioral tendency to sell winners and hang on to losers is costly from a tax perspective. Because capital gains are taxed only when the asset is sold, it is optimal for tax purposes to postpone taxable gains by continuing to hold profitable investments; delaying the tax payment reduces its present value. On the other hand, investors should capture tax losses by selling their losing investments, especially near the year's end, in order to accelerate the tax write-off.

Of course, keeping losers and selling winners might make sense if investors forecast that the losing stocks would ultimately "bounce back" and outperform the winners going forward. While investors may in fact have this belief, it does not appear to be justified—if anything, the losing stocks that investors continue to hold tend to *underperform* the

---

[5]H. Shefrin and M. Statman, "The Disposition to Sell Winners Too Early and Ride Losers Too Long: Theory and Evidence," *Journal of Finance* 40 (1985): 777–790, and D. Kahneman and A. Tversky, "Prospect Theory: An Analysis of Decision under Risk," *Econometrica*, 47 (1979): 263–291.

[6]B. Barber, Y. T. Lee, Y. J. Liu, and T. Odean, "Is the Aggregate Investor Reluctant to Realize Losses? Evidence from Taiwan," *European Financial Management*, 13 (2007): 423–447.

[7]R. Dhar and N. Zhu, "Up Close and Personal: Investor Sophistication and the Disposition Effect," *Management Science*, 52 (2006): 726–740.

winners they sell. According to one study, losers underperformed winners by 3.4% over the year after the winners were sold.[8]

Investor Attention, Mood, and Experience

Individual investors generally are not full-time traders. As a result, they have limited time and attention to spend on their investment decisions and may be influenced by attention-grabbing news stories or other events. Studies show that individuals are more likely to buy stocks that have recently been in the news, engaged in advertising, experienced exceptionally high trading volume, or have had extreme (either positive or negative) returns.[9]

Investment behavior also seems to be affected by investors' moods. For example, sunshine generally has a positive effect on mood, and studies have found that stock returns tend to be higher when it is a sunny day at the location of the stock exchange. In New York City, the annualized market return on perfectly sunny days is approximately 24.8% per year versus 8.7% per year on perfectly cloudy days.[10] Further evidence of the link between investor mood and stock returns comes from the effect of major sports events on returns. One recent study estimates that a loss in the World Cup elimination stage lowers the next day's stock returns in the losing country by about 0.50%, presumably due to investors' poor moods.[11]

Finally, investors appear to put too much weight on their own experience rather than considering all the historical evidence. As a result, people who grow up and live during a time of high stock returns are more likely to invest in stocks than people who grow up and live during a time of low stock returns.[12]

Why would investors continue to make such mistakes? Even if they started with such misconceptions, wouldn't they be able to learn over time the cost of these errors? The challenge is that stock returns are extremely volatile, and this volatility masks the small differences in returns from different trading strategies. We will start Chapter 11 with a review of the historical evidence on average stock returns and their volatility. You will see how variable returns are and how there have been long stretches of good returns, as in the 1990s, and stretches in which the total return was negative, as in the 2000s.

CONCEPT CHECK

7. What are several systematic behavioral biases that individual investors fall prey to?

8. Why would excessive trading lead to lower realized returns?

---

[8]T. Odean, "Are Investors Reluctant to Realize Their Losses?" *Journal of Finance*, 53 (1998): 1775–1798.

[9]See G. Grullon, G. Kanatas, and J. Weston, "Advertising, Breadth of Ownership, and Liquidity," *Review of Financial Studies*, 17 (2004): 439–461; M. Seasholes and G. Wu, "Predictable Behavior, Profits, and Attention," *Journal of Empirical Finance*, 14 (2007): 590–610; B. Barber and T. Odean, "All That Glitters: The Effect of Attention and News on the Buying Behavior of Individual and Institutional Investors," *Review of Financial Studies*, 21 (2008): 785–818.

[10]Based on data from 1982–1997; see D. Hirshleifer and T. Shumway, "Good Day Sunshine: Stock Returns and the Weather," *Journal of Finance*, 58 (2003): 1009–1032.

[11]A. Edmans, D. Garcia, and O. Norli, "Sports Sentiment and Stock Returns," *Journal of Finance*, 62 (2007): 1967–1998.

[12]U. Malmendier and S. Nagel, "Depression Babies: Do Macroeconomic Experiences Affect Risk-Taking?" NBER working paper no. 14813.

MyFinanceLab

Here is what you should know after reading this chapter. MyFinanceLab will help you identify what you know, and where to go when you need to practice.

KEY POINTS AND EQUATIONS	KEY TERMS	ONLINE PRACTICE
10.1 The Discounted Free Cash Flow Model • When a firm has leverage, it is more reliable to use the discounted free cash flow model. In this model, the enterprise value of the firm equals the present value of the firm's future free cash flow: $$V_0 = PV(\text{Future Free Cash Flow of Firm})\quad(10.3)$$ • We discount cash flows using the weighted average cost of capital, which is the expected return the firm must pay to investors to compensate them for the risk of holding the firm's debt and equity together. • We can estimate a terminal enterprise value by assuming free cash flow grows at a constant rate (typically equal to the rate of long-run revenue growth). • We determine the stock price by subtracting debt and adding cash to the enterprise value, and then dividing by the initial number of shares outstanding of the firm: $$P_0 = \frac{V_0 + \text{Cash}_0 - \text{Debt}_0}{\text{Shares Outstanding}_0}\quad(10.4)$$	discounted free cash flow model, p. 304 weighted average cost of capital (WACC), p. 305	MyFinanceLab Study Plan 10.1 Interactive Discounted Cash Flow Valuation
10.2 Valuation Based on Comparable Firms • We can also value stocks by using valuation multiples based on comparable firms. Multiples commonly used for this purpose include the P/E ratio and the ratio of enterprise value (EV) to EBITDA. When we use multiples, we assume that comparable firms have the same risk and future growth as the firm being valued. • No valuation model provides a definitive value for the stock. It is best to use several methods to identify a reasonable range for the value.	forward earnings, p. 310 forward P/E, p. 310 method of comparables, p. 308 trailing earnings, p. 310 trailing P/E, p. 310 valuation multiple, p. 308	MyFinanceLab Study Plan 10.2
10.3 Stock Valuation Techniques: A Final Word • All valuation approaches require assumptions or forecasts that are too uncertain to provide a definitive assessment of the firm's value. • You can be more confident if the valuation is consistent across a variety of methods.		
10.4 Information, Competition, and Stock Prices • Stock prices aggregate the information of many investors. Therefore, if our valuation disagrees with the stock's market price, it is most likely an indication that our assumptions about the firm's cash flows are wrong.	efficient markets hypothesis, p. 318	MyFinanceLab Study Plan 10.3

- Competition between investors tends to eliminate positive-NPV trading opportunities. Competition will be strongest when information is public and easy to interpret. Privately informed traders may be able to profit from their information, which is reflected in prices only gradually.
- The efficient markets hypothesis states that competition eliminates all positive-NPV trades, which is equivalent to stating that securities with equivalent risk have the same expected returns.
- In an efficient market, investors will not find positive-NPV trading opportunities without some source of competitive advantage. By contrast, the average investor will earn a fair return on his or her investment.
- In an efficient market, to raise the stock price, corporate managers should focus on maximizing the present value of the free cash flow from the firm's investments, rather than accounting consequences or financial policy.

10.5 Individual Biases and Trading • Individual investors display many biases, including overconfidence, disposition effect, limited attention, and mood affects. • In an efficient market, these biases can lead to trading losses through excessive trading or biases in valuations.	disposition effect, p. 322 overconfidence hypothesis, p. 322	MyFinanceLab Study Plan 10.4

CRITICAL THINKING

1. What are the advantages of valuing a stock based on discounted free cash flows?

2. Explain the connection between the FCF valuation model and capital budgeting.

3. What is the intuition behind valuation by multiples and what are the major assumptions?

4. What are the limitations of valuation by multiples?

5. What is an efficient market?

6. How do interactions in a market lead to information being incorporated into stock prices?

7. Why does market efficiency lead a manager to focus on NPV and free cash flow?

8. Why don't investors always trade rationally?

9. What are some of the major behavioral trading biases?

PROBLEMS

All problems are available in MyFinanceLab. The ![icon] *icon indicates problems that are easier to solve using Excel and have data in an Excel format available in MyFinanceLab. An asterisk * indicates problems with a higher level of difficulty.*

The Discounted Free Cash Flow Model

1. This year, FCF, Inc., has earnings before interest and taxes of $10 million, depreciation expenses of $1 million, capital expenditures of $1.5 million, and has increased its net working capital by $500,000. If its tax rate is 35%, what is its free cash flow?

2. Victoria Enterprises expects earnings before interest and taxes (EBIT) next year of $1 million. Its depreciation and capital expenditures will both be $300,000, and it expects its capital expenditures to always equal its depreciation. Its working capital will increase by $50,000 over the next year. Its tax rate is 40%. If its WACC is 10% and its FCFs are expected to increase at 4% per year in perpetuity, what is its enterprise value?

3. The present value of JECK Co.'s expected free cash flows is $100 million. If JECK has $30 million in debt, $6 million in cash, and 2 million shares outstanding, what is its share price?

4. Portage Bay Enterprises has $1 million in excess cash, no debt, and is expected to have free cash flow of $10 million next year. Its FCF is then expected to grow at a rate of 3% per year forever. If Portage Bay's equity cost of capital is 11% and it has 5 million shares outstanding, what should be the price of Portage Bay stock?

5. River Enterprises has $500 million in debt and 20 million shares of equity outstanding. Its excess cash reserves are $15 million. They are expected to generate $200 million in free cash flows next year with a growth rate of 2% per year in perpetuity. River Enterprises' cost of equity capital is 12%. After analyzing the company, you believe that the growth rate should be 3% instead of 2%. How much higher (in dollars) would the price per share of stock be if you are right?

6. Heavy Metal Corporation is expected to generate the following free cash flows over the next five years:

Year	1	2	3	4	5
FCF ($ million)	53	68	78	75	82

After 5 years, the free cash flows are expected to grow at the industry average of 4% per year. Using the discounted free cash flow model and a weighted average cost of capital of 14%:
a. Estimate the enterprise value of Heavy Metal.
b. If Heavy Metal has no excess cash, debt of $300 million, and 40 million shares outstanding, estimate its share price.

*7. Covan, Inc., is expected to have the following free cash flows:

Year	1	2	3	4	...
FCF	10	12	13	14	Grow by 4% per year

a. Covan has 8 million shares outstanding, $3 million in excess cash, and it has no debt. If its cost of capital is 12%, what should its stock price be?
b. Covan reinvests all its FCF and has no plans to add debt or change its cash holdings. If you plan to sell Covan at the beginning of year 2, what should you expect its price to be?
c. Assume you bought Covan stock at the beginning of year 1. What is your expected return from holding Covan stock until year 2?

8. Sora Industries has 60 million outstanding shares, $120 million in debt, $40 million in cash, and the following projected free cash flow for the next four years (*see* MyFinanceLab *for the data in Excel format*):

1	Year	0	1	2	3	4
2	**Earnings and FCF Forecast ($ million)**					
3	Sales	433.0	468.0	516.0	547.0	574.3
4	*Growth Versus Prior Year*		8.1%	10.3%	6.0%	5.0%
5	Cost of Goods Sold		−313.6	−345.7	−366.5	−384.8
6	**Gross Profit**		154.4	170.3	180.5	189.5
7	Selling, General, and Administrative		−93.6	−103.2	−109.4	−114.9
8	Depreciation		−7.0	−7.5	−9.0	−9.5
9	**EBIT**		53.8	59.6	62.1	65.2
10	Less: Income Tax at 40%		−21.5	−23.8	−24.8	−26.1
11	Plus: Depreciation		7.0	7.5	9.0	9.5
12	Less: Capital Expenditures		−7.7	−10.0	−9.9	−10.4
13	Less: Increase in NWC		−6.3	−8.6	−5.6	−4.9
14	**Free Cash Flow**		25.3	24.6	30.8	33.3

a. Suppose Sora's revenues and free cash flow are expected to grow at a 5% rate beyond year 4. If Sora's weighted average cost of capital is 10%, what is the value of Sora stock based on this information?

b. Sora's cost of goods sold was assumed to be 67% of sales. If its cost of goods sold is actually 70% of sales, how would the estimate of the stock's value change?

c. Return to the assumptions of part (a) and suppose Sora can maintain its cost of goods sold at 67% of sales. However, the firm reduces its selling, general, and administrative expenses from 20% of sales to 16% of sales. What stock price would you estimate now? (Assume no other expenses, except taxes, are affected.)

*d. Sora's net working capital needs were estimated to be 18% of sales (their current level in year 0). If Sora can reduce this requirement to 12% of sales starting in year 1, but all other assumptions remain as in part (a), what stock price do you estimate for Sora? (*Hint*: This change will have the largest effect on Sora's free cash flow in year 1.)

9. Consider the valuation of Nike given in Example 10.1.

a. Suppose you believe Nike's initial revenue growth rate will be between 7% and 11% (with growth always slowing linearly to 5% by year 2018). What range of prices for Nike stock is consistent with these forecasts?

b. Suppose you believe Nike's initial revenue EBIT margin will be between 9% and 11% of sales. What range of prices for Nike stock is consistent with these forecasts?

c. Suppose you believe Nike's weighted average cost of capital is between 9.5% and 12%. What range of prices for Nike stock is consistent with these forecasts?

d. What range of stock prices is consistent if you vary the estimates as in parts (a), (b), and (c) simultaneously?

Valuation Based on Comparable Firms

10. You are evaluating the stock price of Kroger, a grocery store chain. It has forward earnings per share of $3. You notice that its competitor Safeway has a P/E ratio of 13. What is a good estimate of Kroger's stock price?

11. You notice that Coca-Cola has a stock price of $41.09 and EPS of $1.89. Its competitor PepsiCo has EPS of $3.90. But, Jones Soda, a small batch Seattle-based soda producer has a P/E ratio of 35. Based on this information, what is one estimate of the value of a share of PepsiCo stock?

12. CSH has EBITDA of $5 million. You feel that an appropriate EV/EBITDA ratio for CSH is 9. CSH has $10 million in debt, $2 million in cash, and 800,000 shares outstanding. What is your estimate of CSH's stock price?

13. Next year, BHH Co. is expected to pay a dividend of $3 per share from earnings of $5 per share. The equity cost of capital for BHH is 12%. What should BHH's forward P/E ratio be if its dividend growth rate is expected to be 4% for the foreseeable future?

14. GHL, Inc., has a dividend payout ratio of 50%. Its cost of equity is 11% and its dividend growth rate is 5%. If its forward EPS is $6, what is your estimate of its stock price?

15. SLYMN Enterprises has a P/E ratio of 12 and a dividend payout ratio of 40%. If its equity cost of capital is 13%, what growth rate is its P/E ratio consistent with?

16. After researching the competitors of EJH Enterprises, you determine that most comparable firms have the following valuation ratios (*see* MyFinanceLab *for the data in Excel format*):

	Comp 1	Comp 2	Comp 3	Comp 4
EV/EBITDA	12	11	12.5	10
P/E	19	18	20	17

EJH Enterprises has EPS of $2, EBITDA of $300 million, $30 million in cash, $40 million in debt, and 100 million shares outstanding. What range of prices is consistent with both sets of multiples?

17. Suppose that in July 2013, Nike had EPS of $2.52 and a book value of equity of $12.48 per share.
   a. Using the average P/E multiple in Table 10.1, estimate Nike's share price.
   b. What range of share prices do you estimate based on the highest and lowest P/E multiples in Table 10.1?
   c. Using the average price-to-book value multiple in Table 10.1, estimate Nike's share price.
   d. What range of share prices do you estimate based on the highest and lowest price-to-book value multiples in Table 10.1?

18. Suppose that in July 2013, Nike had sales of $25,313 million, EBITDA of $3,254 million, excess cash of $3,337 million, $1,390 million of debt, and 893.6 million shares outstanding.
   a. Using the average enterprise value to sales multiple in Table 10.1, estimate Nike's share price.
   b. What range of share prices do you estimate based on the highest and lowest enterprise value to sales multiples in Table 10.1?
   c. Using the average enterprise value to EBITDA multiple in Table 10.1, estimate Nike's share price.
   d. What range of share prices do you estimate based on the highest and lowest enterprise value to EBITDA multiples in Table 10.1?

*19. Suppose Rocky Brands has earnings per share of $2.30 and EBITDA of $30.7 million. The firm also has 5.4 million shares outstanding and debt of $125 million (net of cash). You believe Deckers Outdoor Corporation is comparable to Rocky Brands in terms of its underlying business, but Deckers has no debt. If Deckers has a P/E of 13.3 and an enterprise value to EBITDA multiple of 7.4, estimate the value of Rocky Brands stock using both multiples. Which estimate is likely to be more accurate?

20. Consider the following data for the airline industry for December 2015 (EV = enterprise value, Book = equity book value). Discuss the potential challenges of using multiples to value an airline.

Company Name	Market Capitalization	Enterprise Value (EV)	EV/Sales	EV/EBITDA	EV/EBIT	P/E	P/Book
Delta Air Lines (DAL)	40,857	45,846	1.1x	6.0x	7.6x	15.0x	4.0x
American Airlines (AAL)	27,249	38,937	0.9x	4.5x	5.5x	6.2x	7.5x
United Continental (UAL)	22,000	28,522	0.7x	4.2x	5.6x	3.4x	2.6x
Southwest Airlines (LUV)	28,499	28,125	1.5x	6.0x	7.4x	16.1x	4.1x
Alaska Air (ALK)	10,396	9,870	1.8x	6.3x	7.9x	13.4x	4.4x
JetBlue Airways (JBLU)	7,338	8,189	1.3x	6.1x	7.9x	13.8x	2.4x
SkyWest (SKYW)	1,039	2,590	0.8x	5.2x	11.1x	21.2x	0.7x
Hawaiian (HA)	1,974	2,281	1.0x	5.3x	6.9x	15.1x	5.3x

Source: Capital IQ and Yahoo! Finance.

21. Suppose Hawaiian Airlines (HA) has 53 million shares outstanding. Estimate Hawaiian's share value using each of the five valuation multiples in Problem 20, based on the median valuation multiple of the other seven airlines shown.

Information, Competition, and Stock Prices

22. Summit Systems has an equity cost of capital of 11%, will pay a dividend of $1.50 in one year and its dividends had been expected to grow by 6% per year. You read in the paper that Summit has revised its growth prospects and now expects its dividends to grow at a rate of 3% per year forever.
    a. What is the drop in the value of a share of Summit Systems stock based on this information?
    b. If you tried to sell your Summit Systems stock after reading this news, what price would you be likely to get? Why?

23. Assume that Cola Co. has a share price of $43. The firm will pay a dividend of $1.24 in one year, and you expect Cola Co. to raise this dividend by approximately 7% per year in perpetuity.
    a. If Cola Co.'s equity cost of capital is 8%, what share price would you expect based on your estimate of the dividend growth rate?
    b. Given Cola Co.'s share price, what would you conclude about your assessment of Cola Co.'s future dividend growth?

24. Roybus, Inc., a manufacturer of flash memory, just reported that its main production facility in Taiwan was destroyed in a fire. Although the plant was fully insured, the loss of production will decrease Roybus's free cash flow by $180 million at the end of this year and by $60 million at the end of next year.
    a. If Roybus has 35 million shares outstanding and a weighted average cost of capital of 13%, what change in Roybus's stock price would you expect upon this announcement? (Assume the value of Roybus's debt is not affected by the event.)
    b. Would you expect to be able to sell Roybus stock on hearing this announcement and make a profit? Explain.

*25. Apnex, Inc., is a biotechnology firm that is about to announce the results of its clinical trials of a potential new cancer drug. If the trials were successful, Apnex stock will be worth $70 per share. If the trials were unsuccessful, Apnex stock will be worth

$18 per share. Suppose that the morning before the announcement is scheduled, Apnex shares are trading for $55 per share.

a. Based on the current share price, what sort of expectations do investors seem to have about the success of the trials?

b. Suppose hedge fund manager Paul Kliner has hired several prominent research scientists to examine the public data on the drug and make their own assessment of the drug's promise. Would Kliner's fund be likely to profit by trading the stock in the hours prior to the announcement?

c. Which factors would limit the ability of Kliner's fund to profit on its information?

Individual Biases and Trading

26. You have a $100,000 portfolio made up of 15 stocks. You trade each stock five times this year and each time you trade, you pay about $30 in commissions and spread. You have no special knowledge, so you earn only the average market return of 12% on your investments. How much lower will your total return be because of your trades?

27. Assume the annual return for the lowest turnover portfolio is 18% and the annual return for the highest turnover portfolio is 12%. If you invest $100,000 and have the highest turnover, how much lower will the value of your portfolio be at the end of 10 years than if you had had the lowest turnover?

DATA CASE

As a new junior analyst for a large brokerage firm, you are excited to demonstrate the skills you learned in college and prove that you are worth your attractive salary. Your first assignment is to analyze Johnson & Johnson stock. Your boss recommends determining prices based on both the discounted free cash flow valuation method and the comparable P/E ratio method. You are a little concerned about your boss's recommendation because your finance professor explained that these two valuation methods can result in widely differing estimates when applied to real data. You are really hoping the two methods will reach similar prices. Good luck with that!

1. Go to Reuters (http://www.reuters.com) and enter the symbol for Johnson & Johnson (JNJ) in the "Search" box, then select Johnson and Johnson. From the main page for JNJ, gather the following information, and enter it into a spreadsheet:
   a. The current stock price (on the left side of the page)
   b. The EPS (TTM)
   c. The number of shares of stock outstanding
   d. The industry P/E (TTM) ratio

2. Click the "Analysts" tab. On the Analyst page, scroll down to find the LT (Long-Term) Growth Rate and enter the Mean value into your spreadsheet.

3. Go to Morningstar (http://www.morningstar.com) and enter "JNJ" into the "Quote" box.

4. Under "Financials," Click Income Statement. Copy and paste (or use the Export to Excel button to create a new file with the data) the most recent three years' worth of income statements into a new worksheet in your existing Excel file. Repeat this process for both the balance sheet and the cash flow statement for Johnson and Johnson. Keep all of the different statements in the same Excel worksheet. *Note*: Make sure you are collecting annual data, rather than quarterly or interim data.

5. To determine the stock value based on the discounted free cash flow method:

   a. Forecast the free cash flows. Start by using the historical data from the financial statements downloaded from Morningstar to compute the three-year average of the following ratios:

      i. EBIT/sales
      ii. Tax rate (income tax expense/income before tax)
      iii. Property plant and equipment/sales
      iv. Depreciation/property plant and equipment
      v. Net working capital/sales

   b. Create an empty timeline for the next five years.

   c. Forecast future sales based on the most recent year's total revenue growing at the LT growth rate from Reuters for the first five years.

   d. Use the average ratios computed in part (a) to forecast EBIT, property, plant and equipment, depreciation, and net working capital for the next five years.

   e. Forecast the free cash flow for the next five years using Eq. 10.2.

   f. Determine the horizon enterprise value for year 5 using Eq. 10.6 and a long-run growth rate of 4% and a cost of capital for JNJ of 11%.

   g. Determine the enterprise value of the firm as the present value of the free cash flows.

   h. Determine the stock price using Eq. 10.4. Note that your enterprise value is in $ thousands and the number of shares outstanding is in billions.

6. To calculate an estimate of JNJ price based on a comparable P/E ratio, multiply the industry average P/E ratio by JNJ EPS.

7. Compare the stock prices produced by the two methods to the actual stock price. What recommendations can you make as to whether clients should buy or sell JNJ stock based on your price estimates?

8. Explain to your boss why the estimates from the two valuation methods differ. Specifically address the assumptions implicit in the models themselves as well as the assumptions you made in preparing your analysis. Why do these estimates differ from the actual stock price of JNJ?

Integrative Case

This case draws on material from this and earlier chapters.

Nanovo, Inc., is a manufacturer of low-cost micro batteries for use in a wide variety of compact electronic devices such as children's toys, wireless transmitters, and sensors. The growth in the use of these devices has steadily increased, leading to an ever greater demand for Nanovo's products. Nanovo has responded to this increase in demand by expanding its production capacity, more than doubling the firm's size over the last decade. Despite this growth, however, Nanovo does not have sufficient capacity to meet the current demand for its ultra-long-life, low-voltage batteries. You have been asked to evaluate two proposals to expand one of Nanovo's existing plants, and make a recommendation.

Proposal 1

The current plant has a capacity of 25,000 cases per month. The first proposal is for a major expansion that would double the plant's current capacity to 50,000 cases per month. After talking with the firm's design engineers, sales managers, and plant operators, you have prepared the following estimates:

- Expanding the plant will require the purchase of $3.6 million in new equipment, and entail up-front design and engineering expenses of $3.9 million. These costs will be paid immediately when the expansion begins.
- Installing the new equipment and redesigning the plant to accommodate the higher capacity will require shutting down the plant for nine months. During that time, the plant's production will cease. After the expansion is finished, the plant will operate at double its original capacity.
- Marketing and selling the additional volume will lead to $1 million per year in additional sales, marketing, and administrative costs. These costs will begin in the first year (even while the plant is under construction and shut down).

Proposal 2

The engineers have put forth a second proposal for a minor expansion that will increase the firm's capacity by only 50%, to 37,500 cases per month. While the capacity is smaller, such an expansion would be cheaper and less disruptive:

- The smaller expansion will require only $2.4 million in new equipment, and $1.5 million in design and engineering expenses.
- The existing plant will need to be shut down for only four months.
- Sales, marketing, and administrative costs will only increase by $500,000.

Nanovo believes that with or without any expansion, the technology used at the plant will be obsolete after six years and will have no salvage value, and the plant itself will need to be completely overhauled at that time. You also have the following additional general information:

- With or without either proposed expansion, Nanovo will be able to sell all it can produce at an average wholesale price of $80 per case. This price is not expected to change during the next six years.
- Nanovo has a gross profit margin of 55% on these batteries.
- Nanovo's average net working capital at the end of each year will equal 15% of its annual revenue.
- Nanovo pays a 40% corporate tax rate.
- While all design and engineering costs are immediately deductible as operating expenses, all capital expenditures will be straight-line depreciated for tax purposes over the subsequent six years.

Management believes the risk of the expansion is similar to the risk of Nanovo's existing projects, and because Nanovo is all equity financed, the risk of the expansion is also similar to the risk of Nanovo stock. You have the following additional information about the stock:

- Nanovo has no debt and has 2 million shares outstanding. The firm's current share price is $75 per share.
- Analysts are expecting Nanovo to pay a $3 dividend at the end of this year, and to raise its dividend at an average rate of 8% per year in the future.

Based on this information, you have been tasked with preparing expansion recommendations for Nanovo (using Excel is optional but recommended).

Case Questions

1. Determine the annual incremental free cash flow associated with each expansion proposal relative to the status quo (no expansion).
2. Compute the IRR and payback period of each expansion proposal. Which plan has a higher IRR? Which has a shorter payback period?
3. Estimate Nanovo's equity cost of capital. Use it to determine the NPV associated with each expansion proposal. Which plan has a higher NPV?
4. Should Nanovo expand the plant? If so, which proposal should Nanovo adopt? Explain.
5. Suppose Nanovo decides to do the major expansion. If investors are not expecting this expansion, and if they agree with the forecasts above, how will the stock price change when the expansion is announced?
6. Suppose Nanovo announces the major expansion and the stock price reacts as in Question 5. Nanovo then issues new shares at this price to cover the up-front free cash flow required to launch the expansion, and thereafter pays out as dividends the total amount it expected to pay prior to the expansion, plus the additional free cash flow associated with the expansion. What dividend per share will Nanovo pay over the next eight years? What is the fair price today for Nanovo stock given these dividends?

11

Risk and Return in Capital Markets

LEARNING OBJECTIVES

- Identify which types of securities have historically had the highest returns and which have been the most volatile

- Compute the average return and volatility of returns from a set of historical asset prices

- Understand the tradeoff between risk and return for large portfolios versus individual stocks

- Describe the difference between common and independent risk

- Explain how diversified portfolios remove independent risk, leaving common risk as the only risk requiring a risk premium

notation

Div_t	dividend paid on date t
P_t	price on date t
R_t	realized or total return of a security from date $t-1$ to t

$\bar{R}$	average return
$SD(R)$	standard deviation of return R
$Var(R)$	variance of return R

Over the 10-year period of 2006 through 2015, investors in Consolidated Edison, Inc. (an electric utility) earned an average return of over 9% per year. Within this period there was considerable variation, with the annual return ranging from −16% in 2008 to nearly 31% in 2011. Over the same period, investors in Microsoft Corporation earned an average return of nearly 13%. However, the road was more rocky— these investors gained 60% in 2009, but lost 44% in 2008. At the same time, investors in three-month U.S. Treasury bills earned an average return of 1% during the period, with a high of nearly 5% in 2006 and a low of 0.02% in 2014. Thus, these three investments offered investors returns that were very different in terms of their average level and their variability. While Microsoft stock paid the highest return on average, its returns were also the most volatile.

In this chapter, our goal is to develop an understanding of how risk relates to return. In the last three chapters, we established that value in projects, and hence in the firm, is determined by the present value of free cash flows. Up until now, we have focused on how to forecast and discount those cash flows. In this chapter and the two that follow, we turn our attention to the discount rate. As we have emphasized, the discount rate should be our cost of capital, and our cost of capital is determined by the risk of the project. But how exactly do we measure risk and how does a particular level of risk imply a specific cost of capital?

We will see how holding many assets together affects our risk exposure. In Chapter 12, we will build on this foundation to develop a theory that explains how to determine the cost of capital for any investment opportunity. Then, in Chapter 13, we will apply what we've learned about the relation between risk and return to the cost of capital for a company as a whole.

We begin our investigation of the relationship between risk and return by looking at historical data for publicly traded securities. We will see, for example, that while stocks are riskier investments than bonds, they have also earned higher average annual returns. We interpret the higher average return on stocks versus bonds as compensation to investors for the greater risk they are taking. But we will also find that not all risk needs to be compensated. By holding a portfolio of many different investments, investors can eliminate risks that are specific to individual securities. Only risks that cannot be eliminated by holding a large portfolio determine the risk premium investors will require.

11.1 A First Look at Risk and Return

If your great-grandparents had invested only $100 in a portfolio of small companies in 1925, your family could be worth over $3 million today! As we will see, however, such a decision would have carried considerable risk and it is only with 20/20 hindsight that we know it would have been a profitable one.

We begin our look at risk and return by illustrating how the risk premium affects investor decisions and returns. Suppose your great-grandparents had indeed invested $100 on your behalf at the end of 1925. They instructed their broker to reinvest any dividends or interest earned in the account until the end of 2015. How would that $100 have grown if it were invested in one of the following?

1. Standard & Poor's 500 (S&P 500): A portfolio, constructed by Standard & Poor's, comprising 90 U.S. stocks up to 1957 and 500 U.S. stocks after that. The firms represented are leaders in their respective industries and are among the largest firms, in terms of market capitalization (share price times the number of shares in the hands of the shareholders), traded on U.S. markets.

2. Small stocks: A portfolio, updated quarterly, of U.S. stocks traded on the NYSE with market capitalizations in the bottom 20%.

3. World portfolio: A portfolio of international stocks from all of the world's major stock markets in North America, Europe, and Asia.

4. Corporate bonds: A portfolio of long-term, AAA-rated U.S. corporate bonds with maturities of approximately 20 years.[1]

5. Treasury bills: An investment in one-month U.S. Treasury bills (reinvested as the bills mature).

Figure 11.1 shows the result, through the end of 2015, of investing $100 at the end of 1925 for each of these five different investment portfolios. The results are striking—had your great-grandparents invested $100 in the small-stock portfolio, the investment would have been worth over $3.5 million at the end of 2015! On the other hand, if they had invested in Treasury bills, the investment would have been worth only $2043.

For comparison, consider how prices have changed during the same period based on the Consumer Price Index (CPI), the bottom line in Figure 11.1. From 1925–2015, small stocks

---

[1] Based on Moody's AAA Corporate Bond Index.

FIGURE 11.1

Value of $100 Invested at the End of 1925 in Small Stocks, U.S. Large Stocks (S&P 500), World Portfolio, Corporate Bonds, and Treasury Bills

Note that the investments that performed the best in the long run also had the greatest fluctuations from year to year. The change in the Consumer Price Index (CPI) is shown as a reference point. The vertical scale is such that a given vertical distance is always the same *percentage* change (going from 10 to 100 is 10 times, just like going from $10,000 to $100,000).

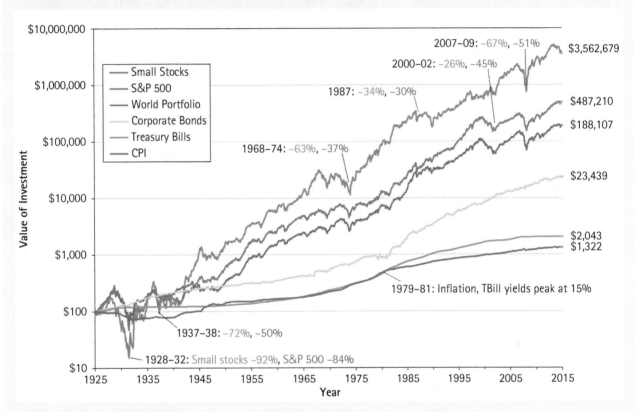

Source: Global Financial Data and CRSP.

in the United States experienced the highest long-term return, followed by the large stocks in the S&P 500, the international stocks in the world portfolio, corporate bonds, and finally Treasury bills. All of the investments grew faster than inflation (as measured by the CPI).

There is a second pattern evident in Figure 11.1. While the small-stock portfolio performed the best in the long run, its value also experienced the largest fluctuations. For example, investors in small stocks had the largest loss during the Depression era of the 1930s. To illustrate, suppose that in 1925 your great-grandparents put the $100 in a small-stock portfolio intended for their own retirement 15 years later in 1940. They would have had only $144 with which to retire, compared with $217 from an investment in corporate bonds. Moreover, during the 15-year period, they would have seen the value of their investment drop as low as $15. Yet if they had invested in Treasury bills, they would not have experienced any losses during the Depression period, but would have enjoyed steady—though modest—gains each year. Indeed, when ranking the investments by the size of their increases and decreases in value, we have the same ranking as before: small stocks had the most variable returns, followed by the S&P 500, the world portfolio, corporate bonds, and finally Treasury bills.

Investors are averse to fluctuations in the value of their investments, so they demand that riskier investments have higher expected returns. But even more importantly, when times are bad, investors do not like to have their problems exacerbated by experiencing losses on their investments. In fact, even if your great-grandparents had actually put the $100 into a small-stock portfolio in 1925, it is unlikely you would have received the proceeds. More likely, in the depths of the Great Depression your great-grandparents would have turned to their investments to supplement their income. Table 11.1 presents the first 10 years of returns that correspond to several of the investments in Figure 11.1. Negative returns (losses) are in red. Notice the string of large, negative returns from 1929–1931 for small stocks. Unfortunately, your great-grandparents' small-stock portfolio would have been of little help to them in the Great Depression—in June 1932 their original $100 investment would have been worth only $15. With the benefit of 85 years of hindsight, the small-stock portfolio looks like a great investment, but in 1932 it would have seemed like a huge mistake. Perhaps this is the reason your great-grandparents did not actually invest money for you in small stocks. The pleasure of knowing that their great-grandchild might one day be a millionaire does not really make up for the pain of the investment going bust at precisely the time that the money is needed for other things.

TABLE 11.1

Realized Returns, in Percent (%) for Small Stocks, the S&P 500, Corporate Bonds, and Treasury Bills, 1926–1935

Year	Small Stocks	S&P 500	Corp Bonds	Treasury Bills
1926	−7.20	11.14	6.29	3.19
1927	25.75	37.13	6.55	3.12
1928	46.87	43.31	3.38	3.82
1929	−50.47	−8.91	4.32	4.74
1930	−45.58	−25.26	6.34	2.35
1931	−50.22	−43.86	−2.38	1.02
1932	8.70	−8.86	12.20	0.81
1933	187.20	52.89	5.26	0.29
1934	25.21	−2.34	9.73	0.15
1935	64.74	47.21	6.86	0.17

Source: Global Financial Data.

We have established the general principle that investors do not like risk and therefore demand a risk premium to bear it. Our goal in this chapter is to further understand that because investors can eliminate some risk by holding large portfolios of stocks, not all risk is entitled to a risk premium. To show this, we must first develop tools that will allow us to measure risk and return.

CONCEPT CHECK

1. Historically, which types of investments have had the highest average returns and which have been the most volatile from year to year? Is there a relation?

2. Why do investors demand a higher return when investing in riskier securities?

11.2 Historical Risks and Returns of Stocks

In this section, we explain how to compute average returns and a measure of risk, or volatility, using historical stock market data. The distribution of past returns can be useful in estimating the possible future returns for investors. We start by explaining how to compute historical returns.

Computing Historical Returns

realized return The total return that occurs over a particular time period.

We begin with *realized returns* for an individual investment and a portfolio. The **realized return** is the total return that occurs over a particular time period.

Individual Investment Realized Return. Suppose you invested $10 in a stock a month ago. Today, it paid a dividend of $0.50 and you then sold it for $11. What was your return? Your return came from two sources: the dividend and the change in price. You earned $0.50 on your $10 investment through the dividend, for a return of $0.50/$10 = 5%, and you earned $1 from the increase in price, for a return of $1/$10 or 10%. Your total return was 15%:

$$\text{Return} = \frac{\$0.50}{\$10} + \frac{(\$11 - \$10)}{\$10} = 5\% + 10\% = 15\%$$

In general, assume you buy a stock on date t for price P_t. If the stock pays a dividend, Div_{t+1}, on date $t + 1$, and you sell the stock at that time for price P_{t+1}, then the timeline of your cash flows for the stock looks like this:

```
t                              t + 1
├──────────────┼────────────────┤
-P_t                          +Div_{t+1}
                               +P_{t+1}
```

The realized return from your investment in the stock from t to $t + 1$ is:

$$R_{t+1} = \frac{Div_{t+1} + P_{t+1} - P_t}{P_t} = \frac{Div_{t+1}}{P_t} + \frac{P_{t+1} - P_t}{P_t}$$

$$= \text{Dividend Yield} + \text{Capital Gain Yield} \qquad (11.1)$$

Your realized return for the period from t to $t + 1$ is the total of the dividend yield and the capital gain (as a percentage of the initial price); as discussed in Chapter 7, it is also called the *total return*. For each dollar invested at date t, you will have $1 + R_{t+1}$ at date $t + 1$. We can compute the total return for any security in the same way, by replacing the dividend payments with any cash flows paid by the security (for example, with a bond, coupon payments would replace dividends).

EXAMPLE 11.1
Realized Return

MyFinanceLab

PROBLEM

Microsoft paid a one-time special dividend of $3.08 on November 15, 2004. Suppose you bought Microsoft stock for $28.08 on November 1, 2004, and sold it immediately after the dividend was paid for $27.39. What was your realized return from holding the stock?

SOLUTION

PLAN

We can use Eq. 11.1 to calculate the realized return. We need the purchase price ($28.08), the selling price ($27.39), and the dividend ($3.08) and we are ready to proceed.

EXECUTE

Using Eq. 11.1, the return from Nov 1, 2004, until Nov 15, 2004, is equal to:

$$R_{t+1} = \frac{Div_{t+1} + P_{t+1} - P_t}{P_t} = \frac{3.08 + (27.39 - 28.08)}{28.08} = 0.0851, \text{ or } 8.51\%$$

(Continued)

This 8.51% can be broken down into the dividend yield and the capital gain yield:

$$\text{Dividend Yield} = \frac{Div_{t+1}}{P_t} = \frac{3.08}{28.08} = .1097, \text{ or } 10.97\%$$

$$\text{Capital Gain Yield} = \frac{P_{t+1} - P_t}{P_t} = \frac{27.39 - 28.08}{28.08} = -0.0246, \text{ or } -2.46\%$$

EVALUATE

These returns include both the capital gain (or in this case a capital loss) and the return generated from receiving dividends. Both dividends and capital gains contribute to the total realized return—ignoring either one would give a very misleading impression of Microsoft's performance.

If you hold the stock beyond the date of the first dividend, then to compute your return we must specify how you invest any dividends you receive in the interim. To focus on the returns of a single security, we assume that *all dividends are immediately reinvested and used to purchase additional shares of the same stock or security*. In this case, we can use Eq. 11.1 to compute a stock's return between dividend payments and then compound the returns from each dividend interval to compute the return over a longer horizon. If a stock pays dividends at the end of each quarter, with realized returns $R_1, \ldots, R_4$ each quarter, then we show the four quarterly returns for this stock as:

Its annual realized return, R_{annual}, is:

$$1 + R_{annual} = (1 + R_1)(1 + R_2)(1 + R_3)(1 + R_4) \tag{11.2}$$

EXAMPLE 11.2

Compounding
Realized Returns

MyFinanceLab

PROBLEM

Suppose you purchased Microsoft stock (MSFT) on Nov 1, 2004, and held it for one year, selling on Oct 31, 2005. What was your annual realized return?

SOLUTION

PLAN

We need to analyze the cash flows from holding MSFT stock for each quarter. In order to obtain the cash flows, we must look up MSFT's stock price data at the purchase date and selling date, as well as at any dividend dates (see Chapter 7 and the book's Web site for online sources of stock price and dividend data). From the data, we can construct the following table to fill out our cash flow timeline:

Date	Price	Dividend
Nov 01 04	28.08	
Nov 15 04	27.39	3.08
Feb 15 05	25.93	0.08
May 16 05	25.49	0.08
Aug 15 05	27.13	0.08
Oct 31 05	25.70	

Next, compute the realized return between each set of dates using Eq. 11.1. Then determine the annual realized return similarly to Eq. 11.2 by compounding the returns for all of the periods in the year.

EXECUTE

In Example 11.1, we already computed the realized return for November 1, 2004, to November 15, 2004, as 8.51%. We continue as in that example, using Eq. 11.1 for each period until we have a series of realized returns. For example, from November 15, 2004, to February 15, 2005, the realized return is:

$$R_{t+1} = \frac{Div_{t+1} + P_{t+1} - P_t}{P_t} = \frac{0.08 + (25.93 - 27.39)}{27.39} = -0.0504, \text{ or } -5.04\%$$

The following table includes the realized return in each period

Date	Price	Dividend	Return
Nov 01 04	28.08		
Nov 15 04	27.39	3.08	8.51%
Feb 15 05	25.93	0.08	−5.04%
May 16 05	25.49	0.08	−1.39%
Aug 15 05	27.13	0.08	6.75%
Oct 31 05	25.70		−5.27%

We then determine the one-year return by compounding.

Note that to use the method in Eq. 11.2, we must have an investment to compound, so just as in Chapter 3, when we compounded interest, we add 1 as if we are computing the outcome of investing $1. The first return is 8.51%, giving us $1 + .0851$ or 1.0851. The same is true when the return is negative: The second return is −5.04%, giving us $1 + (-.0504)$ or 0.9496. To compute the annual realized return, we simply subtract the initial $1, leaving only the return:

$$1 + R_{annual} = (1 + R_1)(1 + R_2)(1 + R_3)(1 + R_4)(1 + R_5)$$
$$1 + R_{annual} = (1.0851)(0.9496)(0.9861)(1.0675)(0.9473) = 1.0275$$
$$R_{annual} = 1.0275 - 1 = 0.0275 \text{ or } 2.75\%$$

EVALUATE

By repeating these steps, we have successfully computed the realized returns for an investor holding MSFT stock over this one-year period. From this exercise we can see that returns are risky. MSFT fluctuated up and down over the year and ended only slightly up (2.75%) at the end.

It is unlikely that anyone investing in Microsoft on November 1, 2004, expected to receive exactly the realized return we calculated in Example 11.2. In any given year we only observe one actual realized return from all of the possible returns that could have been realized. However, we can observe realized returns over many years. By counting the number of times the realized return falls in a particular range, we can start to graph the distribution of possible returns. Let's illustrate this process with the data in Table 11.1.

In Figure 11.2, we plot the annual returns for each U.S. investment in Table 11.1 in a histogram. In this histogram, the height of each bar represents the number of years that the annual returns were in each range indicated on the *x*-axis. Notice how much more variable stock returns are compared to Treasury bills.

Average Annual Returns

average annual return
The arithmetic average of an investment's realized returns for each year.

Out of the distribution of possible returns for each security depicted in Figure 11.2, we want to know the most likely return, represented by the average. The **average annual return** of an investment during some historical period is simply the average of the realized returns

FIGURE 11.2

The Distribution of Annual Returns for U.S. Large Company Stocks (S&P 500), Small Stocks, Corporate Bonds, and Treasury Bills, 1926–2015

The height of each bar represents the number of years that the annual returns were in each range. For example, the bar in the T-bills chart indicates that in more than 50% of the years, the annual return on one-month Treasury bills was between 0 and 5%. Note the greater variability of stock returns (especially small stocks) compared to the returns of corporate bonds or Treasury bills.

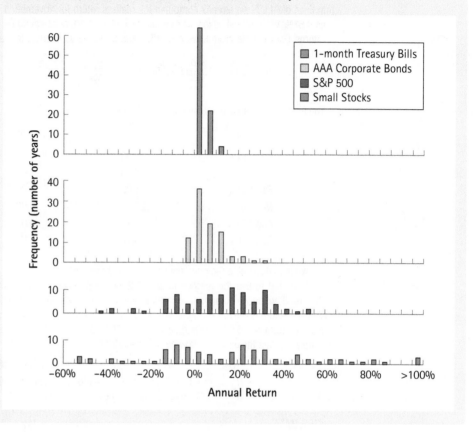

for each year. That is, if R_t is the realized return of a security in each year t, then the average annual return for years 1 through T is:

Average Annual Return of a Security

$$\overline{R} = \frac{1}{T}\left(R_1 + R_2 + \cdots + R_T\right) \tag{11.3}$$

If we assume that the distribution of possible returns is the same over time, the average return provides an estimate of the return we should expect in any given year—the expected return. This idea is not unique to returns. For example, a Starbucks manager cannot know exactly how many customers she will have today, but by looking at the average number of customers who have come in historically, she can form an expectation to use in staffing and stocking.

We can use Eq. 11.3 to calculate the average return for the S&P 500 for the years 2005–2009. The returns are:

2005	2006	2007	2008	2009
4.9%	15.8%	5.5%	−37.0%	26.5%

and the average return is:

$$\frac{1}{5}\left(4.9\% + 15.8\% + 5.5\% - 37.0\% + 26.5\%\right) = 3.1\%$$

The average Treasury bill return during the same period was 2.0%. Therefore, investors earned 1.1% (3.1% − 2.0%) more on average holding the S&P 500 than investing in Treasury bills during this period. This average is computed over just five years of data. Naturally, our estimate of the true average of the distribution is more precise the more data we use. We display the average returns for different U.S. investments from 1926–2012 in Figure 11.3.

 Arithmetic Average Returns Versus Compound Annual Returns

In Figure 11.1, we saw that $100 invested in the S&P 500 at the end of 1925 would have grown to $487,210 by the end of 2015. What if we wanted to know the average compound annual return for that investment? That's the same as asking what return, earned each year for 90 years, would have caused our $100 to grow into $487,210. We know that the formula for future value tells us that:

$$FV = PV(1 + R)^n$$

Thus:

$$\$487,210 = \$100(1 + R)^{90}$$

Solving for R, we get 9.894% (rounded).

But Figure 11.3 shows that the average annual return for the S&P 500 for this period was 11.84%. How can the two answers be different?

The difference is due to the fact that returns are volatile. To see the effect of volatility, suppose an investment has annual returns of +20% one year and −20% the next. The average annual return is:

$$\frac{20\% + (-20\%)}{2} = 0\%$$

But the value of $1 invested after two years is:

$$\$1 \times (1 + 0.20) \times (1 - 0.20) = \$0.96$$

This tells us that an investor would have lost money. Why? Because the 20% gain happens on a $1 investment for a total of 20 cents, whereas the 20% loss happens on a larger investment of $1.20. The loss is 20% of $1.20, or 24 cents.

```
                    $1.20
+20%($1) = +$0.20          -20%($1.20) = -$0.24
    $1.00
- - - - - - - - - - - - - - - - - - - - - - - -
                              $0.96
```

In this case, the compound annual return is

$$\$0.96 = \$1(1 + R)^2$$

so solving for R:

$$R = (0.96)^{1/2} - 1 = -2\%$$

We calculated the 11.84% average for the S&P 500 as a simple arithmetic average of the realized returns, while we calculated 9.9% as the average annual compound return that corresponds to the total gain on our $100 investment (called the *geometric average*).

Which is a better description of an investment's return? The compound annual return is a better description of the long-term *historical performance* of an investment. It describes the average annual compound return for that particular history of returns. The ranking of the long-term performance of different investments coincides with the ranking of their compound annual returns. Thus, the compound annual return is the return that is most often used for comparison purposes. For example, mutual funds generally report their compound annual returns over the last five or ten years.

On the other hand, the arithmetic average return should be used when trying to estimate an investment's *expected* return over a *future* horizon based on its past performance. If we view past annual returns as independent realizations of actual returns from the same set of possible returns, then we know from statistics that the arithmetic average provides the best estimate of the true mean. If the investment above is equally likely to have annual returns of +20% and −20% in the future, then the payoff from a $1 investment after two years will be:

25% of the time: $1 × (1.20) × (1.20) = $1.44
50% of the time: $1 × (1.20) × (0.80)
$$= (0.80) \times (1.20) = \$0.96$$
25% of the time: $1 × (0.80) × (0.80) = $0.64
The expected payoff is

$$25\% (1.44) + 50\% (0.96) + 25\% (0.64) = \$1$$

which is consistent with the arithmetic average return of 0%.

FIGURE 11.3

Average Annual
Returns of U.S. Small
Stocks, Large Stocks
(S&P 500), Corporate
Bonds, and Treasury
Bills, 1926–2015

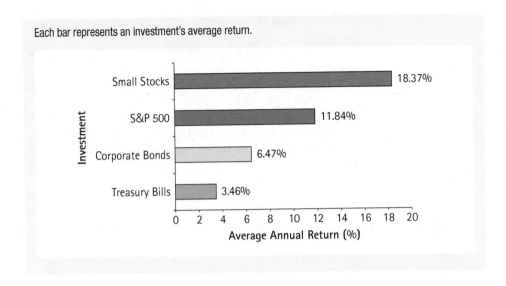

FIGURE 11.3

Average Annual
Returns of U.S. Small
Stocks, Large Stocks
(S&P 500), Corporate
Bonds, and Treasury
Bills, 1926–2015

The Variance and Volatility of Returns

Looking at Figure 11.2, we can see that the variability of the returns is very different for
each investment. The distribution of small stocks' returns is the most widely dispersed—if
you had invested in these stocks, you would have lost more than 50% in some years and
gained more than 100% in some years! The large company stocks in the S&P 500 have
returns that vary less than small company stocks, but much more than corporate bonds or
Treasury bills. While we can see these differences in variability in the chart, we need a way
to formally quantify them. To determine the variability of returns, we calculate the *standard deviation* of the distribution of realized returns. The **standard deviation** is the square
root of the *variance* of the distribution of realized returns. **Variance** measures the variability in returns by taking the differences of the returns from the average return and
squaring those differences. We have to square the difference of each return from the average because, by definition, the unsquared differences from an average must sum to zero.
Because we square the returns, the variance is in units of "$\%^2$" or percent-squared. That
is not very useful to us, so we take the square root, to get the standard deviation, in
units of %.

standard deviation A
common method used
to measure the risk of a
probability distribution; it
is the square root of the
variance.

variance A method to
measure the variability of
returns; it is the expected
squared deviation of
returns from the mean.

While that sounds a bit abstract, standard deviation simply indicates the tendency of
the historical returns to be different from their average and how far from the average they
tend to be. Standard deviation therefore captures our intuition of risk: How often will we
miss the mark and how far off will we be? Formally, we calculate the variance with the
following equation:[2]

Variance Estimate Using Realized Returns

$$Var(R) = \frac{1}{T-1}\left[(R_1 - \overline{R})^2 + (R_2 - \overline{R})^2 + \cdots + (R_T - \overline{R})^2 \right] \quad (11.4)$$

[2]You may wonder why we divide by $T-1$ rather than T here. The reason is that we are not computing
deviations from the true expected return; instead, we are computing deviations from the estimated average
return $\overline{R}$. Because the average return is derived from the same data, we lose a degree of freedom (in essence,
we have used up one of the data points), so that when computing the variance there are really only $T-1$
additional data points on which to base it.

The standard deviation, which we will call the *volatility*, is the square root of the variance:[3]

$$SD(R) = \sqrt{Var(R)} \tag{11.5}$$

EXAMPLE 11.3

Computing Historical Volatility

MyFinanceLab

PROBLEM

Using the following data, what is the standard deviation of the S&P 500's returns for the years 2005–2009?

2005	2006	2007	2008	2009
4.9%	15.8%	5.5%	−37.0%	26.5%

SOLUTION

PLAN

With the five returns, compute the average return using Eq. 11.3 because it is an input to the variance equation. Next, compute the variance using Eq. 11.4 and then take its square root to determine the standard deviation, as shown in Eq. 11.5.

EXECUTE

In the previous section we computed the average annual return of the S&P 500 during this period as 3.1%, so we have all of the necessary inputs for the variance calculation:
Applying Eq.11.4, we have:

$$Var(R) = \frac{1}{T-1}[(R_1 - \overline{R})^2 + (R_2 - \overline{R})^2 + \ldots + (R_T - \overline{R})^2]$$

$$= \frac{1}{5-1}[(.049 - .031)^2 + (.158 - .031)^2 + (.055 - .031)^2$$

$$+ (-.370 - .031)^2 + (.265 - .031)^2]$$

$$= .058$$

Alternatively, we can break out the calculation of this equation as follows:

	2005	2006	2007	2008	2009
Return	0.049	0.158	0.055	−0.370	0.265
Average	0.031	0.031	0.031	0.031	0.031
Difference	0.018	0.127	0.024	−0.401	0.234
Squared	0.000	0.016	0.001	0.161	0.055

Summing the squared differences in the last row, we get 0.233.

Finally, dividing by $(5 - 1 = 4)$ gives us 0.233/4 = 0.058. The standard deviation is therefore:

$$SD(R) = \sqrt{Var(R)} = \sqrt{.058} = 0.241, \text{ or } 24.1\%$$

EVALUATE

Our best estimate of the expected return for the S&P 500 is its average return, 3.1%, but it is risky, with a standard deviation of 24.1%.

---

[3]If the returns used in Eq. 11.4 are not annual returns, it is conventional to convert the variance to annual terms by multiplying the number of returns per year. Thus, when using monthly returns, we multiply the variance by 12, and equivalently, the standard deviation by $\sqrt{12}$.

COMMON MISTAKE

Mistakes When Computing Standard Deviation

Example 11.3 highlights two missteps often made in computing standard deviations.

1. Remember to divide by ONE LESS than the number of returns you have ($T - 1$, NOT T).

2. Don't forget to take the square root of the variance to obtain the standard deviation. You are not done when you calculate the variance—you have one more step to go.

We began our review of statistics with the goal of being able to quantify the difference in the variability of the distributions that we observed in Figure 11.2. We can now do so with the standard deviation of the returns on the U.S. investments as shown in Figure 11.4.

Comparing the standard deviations in Figure 11.4 we see that, as expected, small companies have had the most variable historical returns, followed by large companies. The returns of corporate bonds and Treasury bills are much less variable than stocks, with Treasury bills being the least volatile investment category.

USING EXCEL

Computing the Standard Deviation of Historical Returns

1. Enter or import the historical returns into Excel.
2. Next, highlight the cell where you want to produce the standard deviation and select **Function** from the **Insert** tab.
3. Select the "**STDEV**" function, highlight the returns for which you want to compute the average, and click **OK**.

4. *Make sure that you use the STDEV function and NOT the STDEVP function. STDEV calculates the sample standard deviation as in Eqs. 11.4 and 11.5, by dividing by $T - 1$. STDEVP assumes that you know with certainty the true mean and calculates the standard deviation by dividing by T. See footnote 2 for more discussion of this important distinction.*

FIGURE 11.4

Volatility (Standard
Deviation) of U.S. Small
Stocks, Large Stocks
(S&P 500), Corporate
Bonds, and Treasury
Bills, 1926–2015

Each bar represents the standard deviation of the investment's returns.

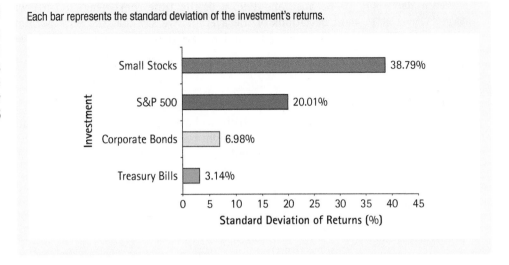

The Normal Distribution

normal distribution A
symmetric probability distribution that is completely
characterized by its average and standard deviation.
About 95% of all possible
outcomes fall within two
standard deviations above
and below the average.

The standard deviations that we have computed in Figure 11.4 are useful for more than
just ranking the investments from most to least risky. The standard deviation also plays an
important role in describing a **normal distribution**, shown in Figure 11.5, which is a symmetric probability distribution that is completely characterized by its average and standard
deviation. Importantly, about two-thirds of all possible outcomes fall within one standard
deviation above or below the average, and about 95% of all possible outcomes fall within
two standard deviations above and below the average. Figure 11.5 shows these outcomes
for small company stocks.

FIGURE 11.5

Normal Distribution

The height of the line reflects the likelihood of each return occurring. Using the data from Figures 11.3 and
11.4, if the returns of small companies are normally distributed, then about two-thirds of all possible outcomes
should lie within one standard deviation of the average return of 18.37% (given in Figure 11.3) and about 95%
should lie within two standard deviations. Figure 11.4 shows the standard deviation to be 38.79%, so that puts
95% of possible outcomes between −59.21% and +95.95% (the shaded area of the distribution).

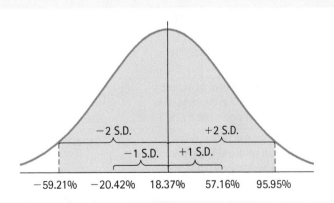

prediction interval A range of values that is likely to include a future observation. A 95% prediction interval should have a 95% chance of including the observed future observation.

Because about 95% of the time, next year's return will be within two standard deviations of the average, we say that the 95% **prediction interval** runs from [the average − 2 × standard deviation] to [the average + 2 × standard deviation]:

$$\text{Average} \pm (2 \times \text{standard deviation})$$
$$\bar{R} \pm (2 \times SD(R)) \tag{11.6}$$

Table 11.2 summarizes the central concepts and equations that we developed in this section. Calculating historical averages and volatilities indicates how investments performed in the past and might perform in the future. Of course, using the past to predict the future is fraught with uncertainty. In the next section, we will discuss that uncertainty.

EXAMPLE 11.4

Prediction Intervals

MyFinanceLab

PROBLEM

In Example 11.3, we found the average return for the S&P 500 from 2005 to 2009 to be 3.1% with a standard deviation of 24.1%. What is a 95% prediction interval for 2010's return?

SOLUTION

PLAN

We can use Eq. 11.6 to compute the prediction interval.

EXECUTE

Using Eq. 11.6, we have:

$$\text{Average} \pm (2 \times \text{standard deviation}) = 3.1\% - (2 \times 24.1\%) \text{ to } 3.1\% + (2 \times 24.1\%)$$
$$= -45.1\% \text{ to } 51.3\%.$$

EVALUATE

Even though the average return from 2005 to 2009 was 3.1%, the S&P 500 was volatile, so if we want to be 95% confident of 2010's return, the best we can say is that it will lie between −45.1% and +51.3%.

TABLE 11.2

Summary of Tools for Working with Historical Returns

Concept	Definition	Formula
Realized Returns	Total return earned over a particular period of time	$R_{t+1} = \dfrac{Div_{t+1} + P_{t+1} - P_t}{P_t}$
Average Annual Return	Average of realized returns for each year	$\bar{R} = \dfrac{1}{T}(R_1 + R_2 + \cdots + R_T)$
Variance of Returns	A measure of the variability of returns	$Var(R) = \dfrac{1}{T-1}[(R_1 - \bar{R})^2 + (R_2 - \bar{R})^2 + \cdots + (R_T - \bar{R})^2]$
Standard Deviation or Volatility of Returns	The square root of the variance (which puts it in the same units as the average—namely "%")	$SD(R) = \sqrt{Var(R)}$
95% Prediction Interval	The range of returns within which we are 95% confident that next period's return will lie	$\bar{R} \pm 2 \times SD(R)$

CONCEPT CHECK

3. For what purpose do we use the average and standard deviation of historical stock returns?

4. How does the standard deviation of historical returns affect our confidence in predicting the next period's return?

11.3 The Historical Tradeoff Between Risk and Return

Would you intentionally choose to accept additional risk without additional reward? In other words, are you willing to pursue riskier investments if they do not have the potential to generate higher returns? The answer to both of these questions is most likely "no." In this section, we will examine the historical tradeoff between risk (as measured by price volatility) and reward (as measured by returns) to see if historically investors behaved as you would.

The Returns of Large Portfolios

In Figures 11.3 and 11.4, we showed the historical average returns and volatilities for a number of different types of investments. In Figure 11.6, we plot the average return versus the volatility of each type of investment from those tables. We also include the world portfolio from Figure 11.1. Note that the investments with higher volatility, measured here with standard deviation, have rewarded investors with higher average returns. Figure 11.6 is consistent with our view that investors are risk averse. Riskier investments must offer investors higher average returns to compensate for the risk they are taking.

The Returns of Individual Stocks

Figure 11.6 suggests the following simple model of the risk premium: Investments with higher volatility should have a higher risk premium and therefore higher returns. Indeed, looking at the dotted line in Figure 11.6, it is tempting to conclude that all investments should lie on or near this line—that is, expected return should rise proportionately with volatility. This conclusion appears to be approximately true for the large portfolios we have looked at so far. Is it correct? Does it apply to individual stocks?

FIGURE 11.6

The Historical Tradeoff Between Risk and Return in Large Portfolios, 1926–2014

Note the general increasing relationship between historical volatility and average return for these large portfolios. In addition to the portfolios in Figure 11.1, also included is a mid-cap portfolio composed of the 10% of U.S. stocks whose size is just above the median of all U.S. stocks. (Data from 1926–2014.)

Source: CRSP, Morgan Stanley Capital International.

Actually, the answer to both questions is no. There is no clear relationship between volatility and returns for individual stocks. Figure 11.7 shows that, if we look at the volatility and return of individual stocks, we do not see any clear relationship between them. Each point represents the volatility and average return from investing in the *N*th largest stock traded in the United States (updated annually) for $N = 1$ to 500. Although it will take more work to establish the relation between risk and return for individual stocks, the following is true:

1. There is a relationship between size and risk—on average larger stocks have lower volatility than smaller stocks.
2. Even the largest stocks are typically more volatile than a portfolio of large stocks, such as the S&P 500.
3. All individual stocks have lower returns and/or higher risk than the portfolios in Figure 11.6.

Thus, while volatility (standard deviation) seems to be a reasonable measure of risk when evaluating a large portfolio, the volatility of an individual security doesn't explain the size of its average return. What are we to make of this? Why wouldn't investors demand a higher return from stocks with a higher volatility? And how is it that the S&P 500, a portfolio of 500 large stocks, is so much less risky than almost all of the 500 stocks individually? To answer these questions, we need to think more carefully about how to measure risk for an investor.

FIGURE 11.7

Historical Volatility and Return for 500 Individual Stocks, Ranked Annually by Size

Unlike the case for large portfolios, there is no precise relationship between volatility and average return for individual stocks. Individual stocks have higher volatility and lower average returns than the relationship shown for large portfolios. (Annual data from 1926–2014.)

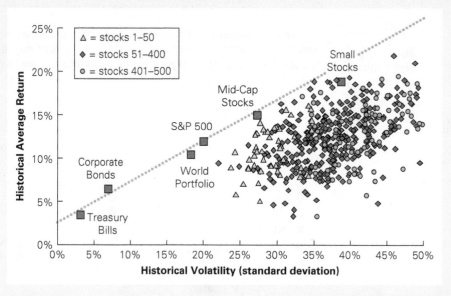

Source: CRSP.

11.4 Common Versus Independent Risk

In this section, we explain why the risk of an individual security differs from the risk of a portfolio composed of similar securities. We begin with an example from the insurance industry to understand how the portfolio of insurance products performs for the insurance company offering them.

Theft Versus Earthquake Insurance: An Example

Consider two types of home insurance an insurance company might offer: theft insurance and earthquake insurance. Let's assume, for the purpose of illustration, that the risk of each of these two hazards is similar for a given home in the San Francisco area—each year there is about a 1% chance the home will be robbed and also a 1% chance that the home will be damaged by an earthquake. In this case, the chance the insurance company will pay a claim for a single home is the same for the two types of insurance policies. Suppose an insurance company writes 100,000 policies of each type for homeowners in San Francisco. We know the risks of the individual policies are similar, but are the risks of the portfolios of 100,000 policies similar?

First consider theft insurance. Because the chance of a theft for any given home is 1%, we would expect about 1% of the 100,000 homes to experience a robbery. Thus, the number of theft claims will be about 1000 per year. The actual number of claims may be a bit higher or lower each year, but not by much. In this case, if the insurance company holds reserves sufficient to cover 1200 claims, it will almost certainly have enough to cover its obligations on its theft insurance policies.

Now consider earthquake insurance. There is a 99% chance that an earthquake will not occur. All the homes are in the same city, so if an earthquake does occur, all homes are likely to be affected and the insurance company can expect 100,000 claims. As a result, the insurance company can expect either 0 claims or 100,000 claims. Because it may have 100,000 claims, it will have to hold reserves of cash (or other investments) sufficient to cover claims on all 100,000 policies it wrote in order to meet its obligations if an earthquake occurs.

Thus, earthquake and theft insurance lead to portfolios with very different risk characteristics. For earthquake insurance, the percentage of claims is very risky—it will most likely be 0, but there is a 1% chance that the insurance company will have to pay claims on *all* the policies it wrote. So the risk of the portfolio of earthquake insurance policies is no different from the risk of any single policy. On the other hand, we've seen that for theft insurance the number of claims in a given year is quite predictable. Year in and year out, it will be very close to 1% of the total number of policies, or 1000 claims. The portfolio of theft insurance policies has almost no risk! That is, the insurance company's payouts are quite stable and predictable over time.

Types of Risk

common risk Risk that is linked across outcomes.

independent risk Risks that bear no relation to each other. If risks are independent, then knowing the outcome of one provides no information about the other.

diversification The averaging of independent risks in a large portfolio.

Why are the portfolios of insurance policies so different when the individual policies themselves are quite similar? Intuitively, the key difference between them is that an earthquake affects all houses simultaneously, and so the risk is linked across homes, meaning either all homes are damaged or all homes are not damaged. We call risk that is linked in this way **common risk**. In contrast, we have assumed that thefts in different houses are not related to each other—whether one house is burglarized has no effect on another house's chance of being burglarized. **Independent risk**, such as the risk of theft, is not linked across homes. When risks are independent, some individual homeowners are unlucky, others are lucky, but overall the number of claims is similar. The averaging out of risks in a large portfolio is called **diversification**.[4] Table 11.3 summarizes our discussion of common and independent risk.

---

[4]Harry Markowitz was the first to formalize the benefits from diversification. See H.M. Markowitz, "Portfolio Selection," *Journal of Finance*, 7(1) (1952): 77–91.

TABLE 11.3

Summary of Types of Risk

Type of Risk	Definition	Example	Risk Diversified in Large Portfolio?
Common Risk	Linked across outcomes	Risk of earthquake	No
Independent Risk	Risks that bear no relation to each other	Risk of theft	Yes

The principle of diversification is used routinely in the insurance industry. In addition to theft insurance, many other forms of insurance (life, health, auto) rely on the fact that the number of claims is relatively predictable in a large portfolio. Even in the case of earthquake insurance, insurers can achieve some diversification by selling policies in different geographical regions, or by combining different types of policies. Diversification is used to reduce risk in many other settings. For example, many systems are designed with redundancy to decrease the risk of a disruption. For example, firms often add redundancy to critical parts of the manufacturing process: NASA puts more than one antenna on its space probes, and automobiles contain spare tires.

In many settings, the risks lie somewhere between the common risks and independent risks. For example, you probably applied to more than one college. Your chances of being accepted (or rejected) at any one school are not perfectly linked across schools because schools have different admissions criteria and are looking for different types of students. However, your risk of rejection is not completely independent, either; all schools look at your high school grades and SAT/ACT scores, so their decisions will be related.

EXAMPLE 11.5

Diversification

MyFinanceLab

PROBLEM

You are playing a very simple gambling game with your friend: a $1 bet based on a coin flip. That is, you each bet $1 and flip a coin: heads you win your friend's $1, tails you lose and your friend takes your dollar. How is your risk different if you play this game 100 times versus just betting $100 (instead of $1) on a single coin flip?

SOLUTION

PLAN

The risk of losing one coin flip is independent of the risk of losing the next one: Each time you have a 50% chance of losing, and one coin flip does not affect any other coin flip. We can compute the expected outcome of any flip as a weighted average by weighting your possible winnings ($+\$1$) by 50% and your possible losses ($-\$1$) by 50%. We can then compute the probability of losing all $100 under either scenario.

EXECUTE

If you play the game 100 times, you should lose 50 times and win 50 times, so your expected outcome is $50 \times (+\$1) + 50 \times (-\$1) = \$0$. You should break even. But even if you don't win exactly half of the time, the probability that you would lose all 100 coin flips (and thus lose $100) is exceedingly small (in fact, it is 0.50^{100}, which is far less than even 0.0001%). If it happens, you should take a very careful look at the coin!

If instead you make a single $100 bet on the outcome of one coin flip, you have a 50% chance of winning $100 and a 50% chance of losing $100, so your expected outcome will be the same: break-even. However, there is a 50% chance you will lose $100, so your risk is far greater than it would be for 100 one-dollar bets.

EVALUATE

In each case, you put $100 at risk, but by spreading out that risk across 100 different bets, you have diversified much of your risk away, compared to placing a single $100 bet.

CONCEPT CHECK

7. What is the difference between common and independent risk?

8. How does diversification help with independent risk?

11.5 Diversification in Stock Portfolios

As the insurance example indicates, the risk of a portfolio depends upon whether the individual risks within it are common or independent. Independent risks are diversified in a large portfolio, whereas common risks are not. Our goal is to understand the relation between risk and return in the capital markets, so let's consider the implication of this distinction for the risk of stock portfolios.

Unsystematic Versus Systematic Risk

Over any given time period, the risk of holding a stock is that the dividends plus the final stock price will be higher or lower than expected, which makes the realized return risky. What causes dividends or stock prices, and therefore returns, to be higher or lower than we expect? Usually, stock prices and dividends fluctuate due to two types of news:

1. *Company or industry-specific news*: This is good or bad news about a company (or industry) itself. For example, a firm might announce that it has been successful in gaining market share within its industry. Or, the home-building industry may be damaged by a real estate slowdown.

2. *Market-wide news*: This is news that affects the economy as a whole and therefore affects all stocks. For instance, the Federal Reserve might announce that it will lower interest rates in an attempt to boost the economy.

Fluctuations of a stock's return that are due to company- or industry-specific news are independent risks. Similar to theft across homes, these are unrelated across stocks. This type of risk is also referred to as **unsystematic risk**.

unsystematic risk
Fluctuations of a stock's return that are due to company- or industry-specific news and are independent risks unrelated across stocks.

On the other hand, fluctuations of a stock's return that are due to market-wide news represent common risk. As with earthquakes, all stocks are affected simultaneously. This type of risk is also called **systematic risk**.

When we combine many stocks in a large portfolio, the unsystematic risks for each stock will average out and be eliminated by diversification. Good news will affect some stocks and bad news will affect others, but the amount of good or bad news overall will be relatively constant. The systematic risk, however, will affect all firms—and therefore the entire portfolio—and will not be eliminated by diversification.

systematic risk
Fluctuations of a stock's return that are due to market-wide news representing common risk.

Let's consider a hypothetical example. Suppose type S firms are *only* affected by the systematic risk of the strength of the economy, which has a 50-50 chance of being either strong or weak. If the economy is strong, type S stocks will earn a return of 40%, and if the economy is weak, their return will be −20%. Because the risk these firms face (the strength of the economy) is systematic risk, holding a large portfolio of type S stocks will not diversify the risk. When the economy is strong, the portfolio will have the same return of 40% as each type S firm. When the economy is weak, the portfolio will also have a return of −20%.

Now consider type U firms, which are only affected by unsystematic risks. Their returns are equally likely to be 35% or −25%, based on factors specific to each firm's local market. Because these risks are firm-specific, if we hold a portfolio of many type U stocks, the risk is diversified. About half of the firms will have returns of 35%, and half will have returns of −25%. The return of the portfolio will be the average return of 50% $(0.35) + 50\% (-0.25) = .05$ or 5%, no matter whether the economy is strong or weak.

Figure 11.8 illustrates how volatility, measured by standard deviation, declines with the size of the portfolio for type S and type U firms. Type S firms have only systematic risk. Similar to earthquake insurance, the volatility of the portfolio does not change as we increase the number of firms. Type U firms have only unsystematic risk. As with theft insurance, the risk is diversified as the number of firms increases, and volatility declines. As is evident from Figure 11.8, with a large number of firms, Type U firms' risk is, essentially, completely eliminated.

Of course, actual firms are not similar to type S or type U firms. Firms are affected by both systematic, market-wide risks, as well as unsystematic risks. Figure 11.8 also shows

FIGURE 11.8

Volatility of Portfolios of Type S and Type U Stocks

Because type S firms have only systematic risk, the volatility of the portfolio does not change. Type U firms have only unsystematic risk, which is diversified and eliminated as the number of firms in the portfolio grows. Typical stocks carry a mix of both types of risk, so that the risk of the portfolio declines as unsystematic risk is diversified, but systematic risk remains.

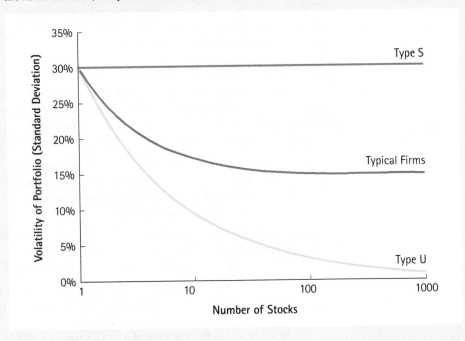

how the volatility changes with the number of stocks in a portfolio of typical firms. *When firms carry both types of risk, only the unsystematic risk will be eliminated by diversification when we combine many firms into a portfolio. The volatility will therefore decline until only the systematic risk, which affects all firms, remains.*

This example explains one of the puzzles from Section 11.3. There we saw that the S&P 500 had much lower volatility than any of the individual stocks. Now we can see why—the individual stocks each contain unsystematic risk, which is eliminated when we combine them into a large portfolio. Thus, the portfolio can have lower volatility than each of the stocks within it. Figure 11.9 illustrates this fact. The dotted lines show the extremes of the range of returns of a portfolio of Intel and Ford. The returns of each of the two stocks in the portfolio cross each of these extremes. Thus, the volatility of the portfolio is lower than the volatility of both of the stocks in the portfolio.

GLOBAL FINANCIAL CRISIS

Diversification Benefits During Market Crashes

The figure on page 357 illustrates the benefits of diversification over the last 40 years. The blue graph shows the historical volatility of the S&P 500 portfolio (annualized based on daily returns each quarter). The pink graph is the average volatility of the individual stocks in the portfolio (weighted according to the size of each stock). Thus, the pink shaded area is idiosyncratic risk—risk that has been diversified away by holding the portfolio. The blue area is market risk which cannot be diversified.

Market volatility clearly varies, increasing dramatically during times of crisis. But notice also that the fraction of risk that can be diversified away also varies, and seems to decline during times

of crisis. For example, since 1970, on average about 50% of the volatility of individual stocks is diversifiable (i.e., the pink area is about 50% of the total). But as the figure demonstrates, during the 1987 stock market crash, the 2008 financial crisis, and the recent Eurozone debt crisis, this fraction fell dramatically, so that only about 20% of the volatility of individual stocks could be diversified. The combined effect of increased volatility and reduced diversification during the 2008 financial crisis was so severe that the risk that investors care about—market risk—increased *seven*-fold, from 10% to 70%, between 2006 and the last quarter of 2008.

Although you are always better off diversifying, it is important to keep in mind that the benefits of diversification depend on economic conditions. In times of extreme crisis, the benefits may go down, making downturns in the market particularly painful for investors.

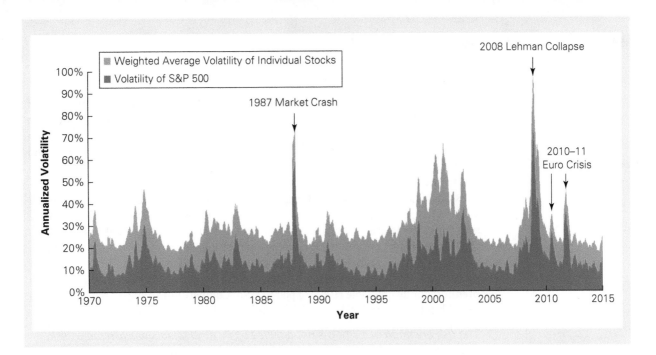

FIGURE 11.9

The Effect of
Diversification on
Portfolio Volatility

While Ford and Intel are each very volatile, some of their movements offset each other. If they are in a portfolio together, as represented by the green bars, the total movement of the portfolio is muted relative to the movement of either of the individual stocks. The dotted lines show the highest and lowest returns of the portfolio—note that the portfolio's worst return is better than the worst return of either stock on its own.

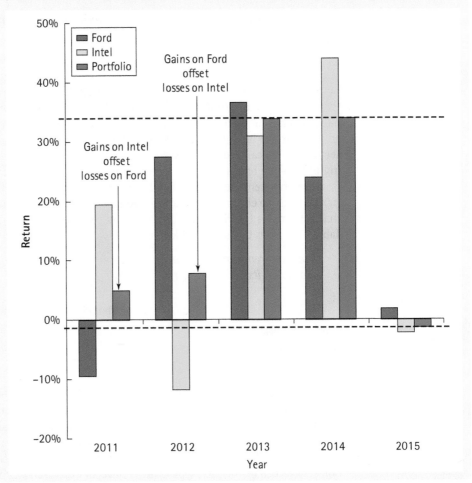

Diversifiable Risk and the Risk Premium

What if you hold only one or two stocks—wouldn't you be exposed to unsystematic risk and demand a premium for it? If the market compensated you with an additional risk premium for choosing to bear diversifiable risk, then other investors could buy the same stocks, earn the additional premium, while putting them in a portfolio so that they could diversify and eliminate the unsystematic risk. By doing so, investors could earn an additional premium without taking additional risk!

This opportunity to earn something for nothing is an arbitrage opportunity as we discussed in Chapter 3, and so it is something investors would find very attractive. As more and more investors take advantage of this situation and purchase shares that pay a risk premium for diversifiable, unsystematic risk, the current share price of those firms would rise, lowering their expected return—recall that the current share price P_t is the denominator when computing the stock's return as in Eq. 11.1. This trading would stop only when the risk premium for diversifiable risk dropped to zero. Competition among investors ensures that no additional return can be earned for diversifiable risk. The result is that

The risk premium of a stock is not affected by its diversifiable, unsystematic risk.

This argument is essentially an application of the Valuation Principle's Law of One Price. Imagine a large portfolio of type U firms, which have no systematic risk. As depicted in Figure 11.8, a large portfolio of type U firms eliminates all unsystematic risk, leaving no additional risk. Since that portfolio has no risk, it cannot earn a risk premium and instead must earn the risk-free interest rate. This line of reasoning suggests the following more general principle:

The risk premium for diversifiable risk is zero. Thus, investors are not compensated for holding unsystematic risk.

The Importance of Systematic Risk

Because investors can eliminate unsystematic risk "for free" by diversifying their portfolios, they will not require (nor deserve) a reward or risk premium for bearing it. On the other hand, diversification does not reduce systematic risk: Even when holding a large portfolio, an investor will be exposed to risks that affect the entire economy and therefore affect all securities. We can reduce the systematic risk of a portfolio by selling stocks and investing in risk-free bonds, but at the cost of giving up the higher expected return of stocks. Because unsystematic risk can be eliminated for free by diversifying, whereas systematic risk can only be eliminated by sacrificing expected returns, it is a security's systematic risk that determines the risk premium investors require to hold it. This fact, summarized in Table 11.4, leads to the second key principle:

The risk premium of a security is determined by its systematic risk and does not depend on its diversifiable risk.

TABLE 11.4

Systematic Risk Versus
Unsystematic Risk

	Diversifiable?	Requires a Risk Premium?
Systematic Risk	No	Yes
Unsystematic Risk	Yes	No

This principle implies that a stock's volatility, which is a measure of total risk (that is, systematic risk + unsystematic risk), is not useful in determining the risk premium that investors will earn. For example, consider again type S and type U firms. As shown in Figure 11.8, the volatility (standard deviation) of a single type S or type U firm is 30%. However, as Table 11.5 shows, although they have the same volatility, type S firms have an expected return of 10% and type U firms have an expected return of 5%.

TABLE 11.5

The Expected Return of Type S and Type U Firms, Assuming the Risk-Free Rate Is 5%

	S Firm	U Firm
Volatility (standard deviation)	30%	30%
Risk-Free Rate	5%	5%
Risk Premium	5%	0%
Expected Return	10%	5%

The difference in expected returns is due to the difference in the kind of risk each firm bears. Type U firms have only unsystematic risk, which does not require a risk premium, and so the expected return of 5% for type U firms equals the risk-free interest rate. Type S firms have only systematic risk. Because investors will require compensation for this risk, the expected return of 10% for type S firms provides investors with a 5% risk premium above the risk-free interest rate.

We now have an explanation for the second puzzle from Section 11.3. While volatility or standard deviation might be a reasonable measure of risk for a large portfolio, it is not appropriate for an individual security.

Thus, there is no relationship between volatility and average returns for individual securities.

Consequently, to estimate a security's expected return we need to find a measure of a security's systematic risk.

We began this chapter by showing in Figure 11.1 that your great-grandparents' investment in small stocks would have lost a lot of money in the Depression, potentially leaving them in dire straits. Thus, risk-averse investors will demand a premium to invest in securities that will do poorly in bad times. This idea coincides with the notion of systematic risk we have defined in this chapter. Economy-wide risk, the risk of recessions and booms, is systematic risk that cannot be diversified. Therefore, an asset that moves with the economy contains systematic risk and so requires a risk premium. In Chapter 12, we will discuss how to measure an investment's systematic risk and then use that measure to compute its expected return. We can then apply that return expected by investors as our cost of capital.

COMMON MISTAKE

A Fallacy of Long-Run Diversification

We have seen that investors can greatly reduce risk by dividing their investment dollars over many different investments, eliminating the diversifiable risk in their portfolios. It is sometimes argued that the same logic applies over time: By investing for many years, we can also diversify the risk we face during any particular year. Thus, young investors should choose risky portfolios because they have more time to make up their losses. Is this correct? In the long run, does risk still matter?

It is true that if returns each year are independent, the volatility of the average annual return does decline with the number of years that we invest. But, as long-term investors, we don't care about the volatility of our *average* return; instead we care about the volatility of our *cumulative* return over the period. This volatility grows with the investment horizon, as illustrated in the following example.

In 1925, large U.S. stocks increased in value by about 30%. So, a $77 investment at the start of 1925 would have grown to $77 × 1.30 = $100 by the end of the year. We see from Figure 11.1 that if that $100 were invested in the S&P 500 from 1926 onward, it would have grown to about $487,210 by the start of 2016. But suppose instead that mining and transportation strikes had caused stocks to drop by 35% in 1925. Then the initial $77 invested would only be worth $77 × (1 − 0.35) = $50 at the start of 1926. If returns from then on were unchanged, the investment would be worth half as much in 2016, or $243,605.

Thus, if future returns are not affected by today's return, then an increase or decline in the value of our portfolio today will translate into the same percentage increase or decrease in the value of our portfolio in the future, and so there is no diversification over time. The only way the length of the time horizon can reduce risk is if a below-average return this year implies that returns are

(Continued)

more likely to be above average in the future (and vice versa). If this were true, past low returns can be used to predict future high returns in the stock market.

For short horizons of a few years, there is no evidence of this predictability in the stock market. For longer horizons, there is some evidence of this historically, but it is not clear how reliable this evidence is (there are not enough decades of accurate stock market data available) or whether the pattern will continue. But even if there is long-run reversal in stock returns, a buy-and-hold diversification strategy is still not optimal: If past returns can be used to predict future returns, it is optimal to invest more in stocks when returns are predicted to be high, and less when they are predicted to be low. Note that this strategy is very different from the diversification we achieve by holding many stocks, where we cannot predict which stocks will have good or bad unsystematic shocks.

CONCEPT CHECK

9. Why is the risk of a portfolio usually less than the average risk of the stocks in the portfolio?

10. Does systematic or unsystematic risk require a risk premium? Why?

MyFinanceLab

Here is what you should know after reading this chapter. MyFinanceLab will help you identify what you know, and where to go when you need to practice.

KEY POINTS AND EQUATIONS	KEY TERMS	ONLINE PRACTICE
11.1 A First Look at Risk and Return • While in hindsight some investments have had very high returns, they have also had the most volatility over time.		MyFinanceLab Study Plan 11.1
11.2 Historical Risks and Returns of Stocks • The realized return from investing in a stock from time t to $t+1$ is: $$R_{t+1} = \frac{Div_{t+1} + P_{t+1} - P_t}{P_t} = \frac{Div_{t+1}}{P_t} + \frac{P_{t+1} - P_t}{P_t}$$ $$= \text{Dividend Yield} + \text{Capital Gain Yield} \quad (11.1)$$	average annual return, p. 343 normal distribution, p. 349 prediction interval, p. 350 realized return, p. 341 standard deviation, p. 346 variance, p. 346	MyFinanceLab Study Plan 11.2 Using Excel: Standard Deviation of Historical Returns

• We can calculate the average annual return and variance of realized returns:

$$\bar{R} = \frac{1}{T}(R_1 + R_2 + \cdots + R_T) \quad (11.3)$$

$$Var(R) = \frac{1}{T-1}[(R_1 - \bar{R})^2 + (R_2 - \bar{R})^2 + \cdots + (R_T - \bar{R})^2] \quad (11.4)$$

• The square root of the estimated variance is the standard deviation, an estimate of the volatility of returns.
• Based on historical data, small stocks have had higher volatility and higher average returns than large stocks, which have higher volatility and higher average returns than bonds.
• About 95% of possible outcomes lie within two standard deviations above or below the average outcome.

11.3 The Historical Tradeoff Between Risk and Return • There is no clear relationship between the volatility (standard deviation) and return of individual stocks. • Larger stocks tend to have lower overall volatility, but even the largest stocks are typically more risky than a portfolio of large stocks. • All stocks seem to have higher risk and lower returns than would be predicted based on extrapolation of data for large portfolios.		MyFinanceLab Study Plan 11.3
11.4 Common Versus Independent Risk • Common risk is risk that is perfectly linked across investments. • Independent risks are unrelated across investments. • Diversification is the averaging of risks in a large portfolio.	common risk, p. 353 diversification, p. 353 independent risk, p. 353	MyFinanceLab Study Plan 11.4
11.5 Diversification in Stock Portfolios • The total risk of a security represents both unsystematic risk and systematic risk. • Variation in a stock's return due to industry-specific or a firm's news is called unsystematic risk. • Systematic risk is risk due to market-wide news that affects all stocks simultaneously. • Diversification eliminates unsystematic risk but does not eliminate systematic risk. • Because investors can eliminate unsystematic risk, they do not require a risk premium for it. • Because investors cannot eliminate systematic risk, they must be compensated for it. So, the risk premium for a stock depends upon the amount of its systematic risk rather than its total risk.	systematic risk, p. 355 unsystematic risk, p. 355	MyFinanceLab Study Plan 11.5 Interactive Risk and Portfolio Diversification Analysis

CRITICAL THINKING

1. What does the historical relation between volatility and return tell us about investors' attitude toward risk?

2. What are the components of a stock's realized return?

3. What is the intuition behind using the average annual return as a measure of expected return?

4. How does standard deviation relate to the general concept of risk?

5. How does the relationship between the average return and the historical volatility of individual stocks differ from the relationship between the average return and the historical volatility of large, well-diversified, portfolios?

6. Consider two local banks. Bank A has 100 loans outstanding, each for $1 million, that it expects will be repaid today. Each loan has a 5% probability of default, in which case the bank is not repaid anything. The chance of default is independent across all the loans. Bank B has only one loan of $100 million outstanding that it also expects will be repaid today. It also has a 5% probability of not being repaid. Explain the difference between the type of risk each bank faces. Assuming you are averse to risk, which bank would you prefer to own?

7. What is meant by diversification and how does it relate to common versus independent risk?

8. Which of the following risks of a stock are likely to be unsystematic, diversifiable risks and which are likely to be systematic risks? Which risks will affect the risk premium that investors will demand?
   a. The risk that the founder and CEO retires
   b. The risk that oil prices rise, increasing production costs
   c. The risk that a product design is faulty and the product must be recalled
   d. The risk that the economy slows, reducing demand for the firm's products
   e. The risk that your best employees will be hired away
   f. The risk that the new product you expect your R&D division to produce will not materialize

9. What is the difference between systematic and unsystematic risk?

10. There are three companies working on a new approach to customer-tracking software. You work for a software company that thinks this could be a good addition to its software line. If you invest in one of them versus all three of them:
    a. Is your systematic risk likely to be very different?
    b. Is your unsystematic risk likely to be very different?

11. If you randomly select 10 stocks for a portfolio and 20 other stocks for a different portfolio, which portfolio is likely to have the lower standard deviation? Why?

12. Why doesn't the risk premium of a stock depend on its diversifiable risk?

13. Your spouse works for Southwest Airlines and you work for a grocery store. Is your company or your spouse's company likely to be more exposed to systematic risk?

PROBLEMS

All problems are available in MyFinanceLab. The ⊞ *icon indicates problems that are easier to solve using Excel and have data in an Excel format available in MyFinanceLab. An asterisk * indicates problems with a higher level of difficulty.*

Historical Risks and Returns of Stocks

1. You bought a stock one year ago for $50 per share and sold it today for $55 per share. It paid a $1 per share dividend today. What was your realized return?

2. How much of the return in Problem 1 came from dividend yield and how much came from capital gain?

3. Repeat Problems 1 and 2 assuming instead that the stock fell $5 to $45.
   a. Is your capital gain different? Why or why not?
   b. Is your dividend yield different? Why or why not?

4. Your portfolio consists of 100 shares of CSH and 50 shares of EJH, which you just bought at $20 and $30 per share, respectively.
   a. What fraction of your portfolio is invested in CSH? In EJH?
   b. If CSH increases to $23 and EJH decreases to $29, what is the return on your portfolio?

5. You have just purchased a share of stock for $20. The company is expected to pay a dividend of $0.50 per share in exactly one year. If you want to earn a 10% return on your investment, what price do you need if you expect to sell the share immediately after it pays the dividend?

6. You expect KStreet Co's trade at $100 per share right after paying a $2 dividend per share in one year. What is the most you would pay to buy the stock now if you want to earn at least a 15% return?

7. The following table contains prices and dividends for a stock. All prices are after the dividend has been paid. If you bought the stock on January 1 and sold it on December 31, what is your realized return?

	Price	Dividend
Jan 1	10.00	
Mar 31	11.00	0.20
Jun 30	10.50	0.20
Sep 30	11.10	0.20
Dec 31	11.00	0.20

 8. Using the data in the following table, calculate the return for investing in Boeing stock (BA) from January 2, 2008, to January 2, 2009, and also from January 3, 2011, to January 3, 2012, assuming all dividends are reinvested in the stock immediately.

Historical Stock and Dividend Data for Boeing

Date	Price	Dividend	Date	Price	Dividend
1/2/2008	86.62		1/3/2011	66.40	
2/6/2008	79.91	0.40	2/9/2011	72.63	0.42
5/7/2008	84.55	0.40	5/11/2011	79.08	0.42
8/6/2008	65.40	0.40	8/10/2011	57.41	0.42
11/5/2008	49.55	0.40	11/8/2011	66.65	0.42
1/2/2009	45.25		1/3/2012	74.22	

 9. The last four years of returns for a stock are as follows:

1	2	3	4
−4%	+28%	+12%	+4%

a. What is the average annual return?
b. What is the variance of the stock's returns?
c. What is the standard deviation of the stock's returns?

 10. Use the data in SBUX_GOOG.xlsx on MFL to answer the following questions:
a. What is the return for SBUX over the period without including its dividends? With the dividends?
b. What is the return for GOOG over the period?
c. If you have 30% of your portfolio in SBUX and 70% in GOOG, what was the return on your portfolio?

 11. Download the spreadsheet from the book's Web site containing the data for Figure 11.1.
a. Compute the average return for each of the assets from 1929 to 1940 (the Great Depression).
b. Compute the variance and standard deviation for each of the assets from 1929 to 1940.
c. Which asset was riskiest during the Great Depression? How does that fit with your intuition?

 12. Ten annual returns are listed in the following table.

−19.9%	16.6%	18.0%	−50.0%	43.3%	1.2%	−16.5%	45.6%	45.2%	−3.0%

a. What is the arithmetic average return over the 10-year period?

*b. What is the geometric average return over the 10-year period?

c. If you invested $100 at the beginning, how much would you have at the end?

13. Using the data in the following table, calculate the return for investing in this stock from January 1 to December 31. Prices are after the dividend has been paid (*see* MyFinanceLab *for the data in Excel format*).

Stock and Dividend Data

Date	Price	Dividend
Jan 1	33.88	
Feb 5	30.67	0.17
May 14	29.49	0.17
Aug 13	32.38	0.17
Nov 12	39.07	0.17
Dec 31	41.99	

14. What was your dividend yield from investing in the stock in Problem 12? What was your capital gain?

15. Using the data in the following table, calculate the return for investing in this stock from January 1 to December 31. Prices are after the dividend has been paid (*see* MyFinanceLab *for the data in Excel format*).

	Stock Price	Dividend
Jan 1	$50.00	
Mar 31	$51.00	$0.55
Jun 30	$49.47	$0.55
Sep 30	$51.94	$0.75
Dec 31	$52.46	$0.75

16. Consider the following five monthly returns:

a. Calculate the arithmetic average monthly return over this period.

*b. Calculate the geometric average monthly return over this period.

c. Calculate the monthly variance over this period.

d. Calculate the monthly standard deviation over this period.

0.05	−0.02	0.04	0.08	−0.01

17. Explain the difference between the arithmetic average return you calculated in Problem 16a and the geometric average return you calculated in Problem 16b. Are both numbers useful? If so, explain why.

18. The last four years of returns for a stock are as follows:

1	2	3	4
−4%	+28%	+12%	+4%

a. What is the average annual return?

b. What is the variance of the stock's returns?

c. What is the standard deviation of the stock's returns?

19. Calculate the 95% prediction intervals for the four different investments included in Figures 11.3 and 11.4.

20. You are choosing between the four investments from Problem 18 and you want to be 95% certain that you do not lose more than 8% on your investment. Which investments should you choose?

21. If returns of S&P 500 stocks are normally distributed, what range of returns would you expect to see 95% of the time? Base your answer on Figures 11.3 and 11.4.

22. You observe a portfolio for five years and determine that its average return is 12% and the standard deviation of its returns is 20%. Can you be 95% confident that this portfolio will not lose more than 30% of its value next year?

Common Versus Independent Risk

*23. Using the data in Critical Thinking Question 6, calculate the following:
   a. The expected overall payoff of each bank
   b. The standard deviation of the overall payoff of each bank

Diversification in Stock Portfolios

24. You are a risk-averse investor who is considering investing in one of two economies. The expected return and volatility of all stocks in both economies are the same. In the first economy, all stocks move together—in good times all prices rise together and in bad times they all fall together. In the second economy, stock returns are independent—one stock increasing in price has no effect on the prices of other stocks. Which economy would you choose to invest in? Explain.

25. Consider the following 6 months of returns for 2 stocks and a portfolio of those 2 stocks.

	Jan	Feb	Mar	Apr	May	Jun
Stock A	2%	5%	−6%	3%	−2%	4%
Stock B	0%	−3%	8%	−1%	4%	−2%
Portfolio	1%	1%	1%	1%	1%	1%

   a. What is the expected return and standard deviation of returns for each of the two stocks?
   b. What is the expected return and standard deviation of return for the portfolio?
   c. Is the portfolio more or less risky than the two stocks? Why?

DATA CASE

Today is April 30, 2016, and you have just started your new job with a financial planning firm. In addition to studying for all your license exams, you have been asked to review a portion of a client's stock portfolio to determine the risk/return profiles of 12 stocks in the portfolio. Unfortunately, your small firm cannot afford the expensive databases that would provide all this information with a few simple keystrokes, but that's why they hired you. Specifically, you have been asked to determine the monthly average returns and standard deviations for the 12 stocks for the past five years.

The stocks (with their symbols in parentheses) are:

Archer Daniels Midland (ADM)
Boeing (BA)
Caterpillar (CAT)
Deere & Co. (DE)

General Mills, Inc. (GIS)
eBay, Inc. (EBAY)
Hershey (HSY)
International Business Machines Corporation (IBM)
JPMorgan Chase & Co. (JPM)
Microsoft (MSFT)
Procter and Gamble (PG)
Walmart (WMT)

1. Collect price information for each stock from Yahoo! Finance (finance.yahoo.com) as follows:
   a. Enter the stock symbol. On the page for that stock, click "Historical Prices" on the left side of the page.
   b. Enter the "start date" as April 1, 2011, and the "end date" as April 30, 2016, to cover the five-year period. Make sure you click "monthly" next to the date.
   c. After hitting "Get Prices," scroll to the bottom of the first page and click "Download to Spreadsheet." If you are asked if you want to open or save the file, click open.
   d. Copy the entire spreadsheet, open Excel, and paste the Web data into a spreadsheet. Delete all the columns except the date and the adjusted close (the first and last columns).
   e. Keep the Excel file open and go back to the Yahoo! Finance Web page and hit the back button. If you are asked if you want to save the data, click no.
   f. When you return to the prices page, enter the next stock symbol and hit "Get Prices" again. Do not change the dates or frequency, but make sure you have the same dates for all the stocks you will download. Again, click "Download to Spreadsheet" and then open the file. Copy the last column, "Adj. Close," paste it into the Excel file and change "Adj. Close" to the stock symbol. Make sure that the first and last prices are in the same rows as the first stock.
   g. Repeat these steps for the remaining 10 stocks, pasting each closing price right next to the other stocks, again making sure that the correct prices on the correct dates all appear on the same rows.

2. Convert these prices to monthly returns as the percentage change in the monthly prices. (*Hint*: Create a separate worksheet within the Excel file.) Note that to compute a return for each month, you need a beginning and ending price, so you will not be able to compute the return for the first month.

3. Compute the mean monthly returns and standard deviations for the monthly returns of each of the stocks.[5] Convert the monthly statistics to annual statistics for easier interpretation (muliply the mean monthly return by 12, and multiply the monthly standard deviation by $\sqrt{12}$).

4. Add a column in your Excel worksheet with the average return across stocks for each month. This is the monthly return to an equally weighted portfolio of these 12 stocks. Compute the mean and standard deviation of monthly returns for the equally weighted portfolio. Double-check that the average return on this equally weighted portfolio is

---

[5]In Eq. 11.1, we showed how to compute returns with stock price and dividend data. The "adjusted close" series from Yahoo! Finance is already adjusted for dividends and splits, so we may compute returns based on the percentage change in monthly adjusted prices.

equal to the average return of all of the individual stocks. Convert these monthly statistics to annual statistics (as described in step 3) for interpretation.

5. Using the annual statistics, create an Excel plot with standard deviation (volatility) on the x-axis and average return on the y-axis as follows:

    a. Create three columns on your spreadsheet with the statistics you created in Questions 3 and 4 for each of the individual stocks and the equally weighted portfolio. The first column will have the ticker, the second will have annual standard deviation, and the third will have the annual mean return.

    b. Highlight the data in the last two columns (standard deviation and mean), choose > Insert > Chart > XY Scatter Plot. Complete the chart wizard to finish the plot.

6. What do you notice about the average of the volatilities of the individual stocks, compared to the volatility of the equally weighted portfolio?

12

Systematic Risk and the Equity Risk Premium

LEARNING OBJECTIVES

- Calculate the expected return and volatility (standard deviation) of a portfolio

- Understand the relation between systematic risk and the market portfolio

- Measure systematic risk

- Use the Capital Asset Pricing Model (CAPM) to compute the cost of equity capital for a stock

In Chapter 11, we started our exploration of the tradeoff between risk and return. We found that for large portfolios, while investors should expect to experience higher returns for higher risk, the same does not hold true for individual stocks. Stocks have both unsystematic, diversifiable risk and systematic, undiversifiable risk; only the systematic risk is rewarded with higher expected returns. With no reward for bearing unsystematic risk, rational investors should choose to diversify.

Put yourself in the role of a financial manager at a company such as Cisco. One part of your job would be to calculate Cisco's cost of equity capital so that its managers know what return its equity investors require. Recall that in Chapter 5 we defined the cost of capital as the best available expected return offered in the market on an investment of comparable risk and term. Since only systematic risk contributes to expected returns, we need to measure the systematic risk of Cisco and map it into an expected return for Cisco. To do so, we need to think about Apple's stock the way our investors would—as part of a portfolio. As a result, we begin where we left off in Chapter 11: with portfolios. After learning how to calculate the risk and expected return of a portfolio, we will focus on the biggest portfolio of them all: the portfolio of *all* risky securities. This portfolio has no diversifiable risk left and can be used as a baseline for measuring systematic risk. From there, we will develop a simple, powerful model that relates the systematic risk of an investment to its expected return. In other words, the model says that the return we should expect on any investment is equal to the risk-free rate of return plus a risk premium proportional to the amount of systematic risk in the investment.

12.1 The Expected Return of a Portfolio

In Chapter 11, we learned the important role that portfolios play in reducing unsystematic risk. As financial managers, we have to be mindful that investors hold our company's stock as part of a larger portfolio. Thus, it is important to understand how portfolios work and the implications for the return our investors expect on the stock of our company and the projects we undertake in that company.

Portfolio Weights

portfolio weights The fraction of the total investment in a portfolio held in each individual investment in the portfolio.

We begin by calculating the return and expected return of a portfolio. For example, consider a portfolio with 200 shares of Apple worth $200 per share ($40,000 total), and 1000 shares of Coca-Cola worth $60 per share ($60,000 total). The total value of the portfolio is $100,000, so Apple is 40% of the portfolio and Coca-Cola is 60% of the portfolio. More generally, we can describe a portfolio by its **portfolio weights**, which are the fractions of the total investment in a portfolio held in each individual investment in the portfolio:

$$w_i = \frac{\text{Value of Investment } i}{\text{Total Value of Portfolio}} \tag{12.1}$$

These portfolio weights add up to 100% (that is, $w_1 + w_2 + \ldots + w_N = 100\%$), so that they represent the way we have divided our money between the different individual investments in the portfolio. We can confirm the portfolio weights for our portfolio of Apple and Coca-Cola:

$$w_{Apple} = \frac{200 \times \$200}{\$100,000} = 40\% \text{ and } w_{Coca\text{-}Cola} = \frac{1000 \times \$60}{\$100,000} = 60\%$$

Portfolio Returns

Once you know the portfolio weights, you can calculate the return on the portfolio. For example, take the portfolio of Apple and Coca-Cola. If Apple earns a 10% return and Coca-Cola earns a 15% return, then 40% of the portfolio earns 10% and 60% of the portfolio earns 15%, so the portfolio as a whole earns: $(0.40)(10\%) + (0.60)(15\%) = 13\%$.

return of a portfolio The weighted average of the returns on the investments in a portfolio, where the weights correspond to the portfolio weights.

*The **return of a portfolio** is the weighted average of the returns on the investments in the portfolio, where the weights correspond to the portfolio weights.*

Formally, suppose $w_1, \ldots, w_n$ are the portfolio weights of the n investments in a portfolio and these investments have returns $R_1, \ldots, R_n$, then the formula for the return on the portfolio is:

$$R_p = w_1 R_1 + w_2 R_2 + \ldots + w_n R_n \tag{12.2}$$

EXAMPLE 12.1
Calculating Portfolio Returns

MyFinanceLab

PROBLEM

Suppose you invest $100,000 and buy 200 shares of Apple at $200 per share ($40,000) and 1000 shares of Coca-Cola at $60 per share ($60,000). If Apple's stock rises to $240 per share and Coca-Cola stock falls to $57 per share and neither paid dividends, what is the new value of the portfolio? What return did the portfolio earn? Show that Eq. 12.2 is true by calculating the individual returns of the stocks and multiplying them by their weights in the portfolio. If you don't buy or sell any shares after the price change, what are the new portfolio weights?

SOLUTION

PLAN

Your portfolio: 200 shares of Apple: $200 → $240 ($40 capital gain per share)
1000 shares of Coca-Cola: $60 → $57 ($3 capital loss per share)

A. To calculate the return on your portfolio, compute its value using the new prices and compare it to the original $100,000 investment.
B. To confirm that Eq. 12.2 is true, compute the return on each stock individually using Eq. 11.1 from Chapter 11, multiply those returns by their original weights in the portfolio, and compare your answer to the return you just calculated for the portfolio as a whole.

EXECUTE

The new value of your Apple stock is $200 \times \$240 = \$48,000$ and the new value of your Coca-Cola stock is $1000 \times \$57 = \$57,000$. So, the new value of your portfolio is $\$48,000 + 57,000 = \$105,000$, for a gain of $5000 or a 5% return on your initial $100,000 investment.

Since neither stock paid any dividends, we calculate their returns simply as the capital gain or loss divided by the purchase price. The return on Apple stock was $40/$200 = 20%, and the return on Coca-Cola stock was −$3/$60 = −5%.

The initial portfolio weights were $40,000/$100,000 = 40% for Apple and $60,000/$100,000 = 60% for Coca-Cola, so we can also compute the return of the portfolio from Eq. 12.2 as:

$$R_p = w_{Apple}\,R_{Apple} + w_{Coke}\,R_{Coke} = 0.40\,(20\%) + 0.60\,(-5\%) = 5\%$$

After the price change, the new portfolio weights are equal to the value of your investment in each stock divided by the new portfolio value:

$$w_{Apple} = \frac{200 \times \$240}{105,000} = 45.71\% \text{ and } w_{Coca\text{-}Cola} = \frac{1000 \times \$57}{105,000} = 54.29\%$$

As a check on your work, always make sure that your portfolio weights sum to 100%!

EVALUATE

The $3000 loss on your investment in Coca-Cola was offset by the $8000 gain in your investment in Apple, for a total gain of $5,000 or 5%. The same result comes from giving a 40% weight to the 20% return on Apple and a 60% weight to the −5% loss on Coca-Cola—you have a total net return of 5%.

After a year, the portfolio weight on Apple has increased and the weight on Coca-Cola has decreased. Note that without trading, the portfolio weights will increase for the stock(s) in the portfolio whose returns are above the overall portfolio return. The charts below show the initial and ending weights on Apple (shown in yellow) and Coca-Cola (shown in red).

Expected Portfolio Return

As we showed in Chapter 11, you can use the historical average return of a security as its expected return. With these expected returns, you can compute the **expected return of a portfolio**, which is simply the weighted average of the expected returns of the investments within it, using the portfolio weights:

$$E[R_P] = w_1 E[R_1] + w_2 E[R_2] + \ldots + w_n E[R_n] \tag{12.3}$$

We started by stating that you can describe a portfolio by its weights. These weights are used in computing both a portfolio's return and its expected return. Table 12.1 summarizes these concepts.

TABLE 12.1
Summary of Portfolio Concepts

Term	Concept	Equation
Portfolio weight	The relative investment in your portfolio	$w_i = \dfrac{\text{Value of Investment } i}{\text{Total Value of Portfolio}}$
Portfolio return	The total return earned on your portfolio, accounting for the returns of all of the securities in the portfolio and their weights	$R_P = w_1 R_1 + w_2 R_2 + \cdots + w_n R_n$
Portfolio expected return	The return you can expect to earn on your portfolio, given the expected returns of the securities in that portfolio and the relative amount you have invested in each	$E[R_P] = w_1 E[R_1] + w_2 E[R_2] + \cdots + w_n E[R_n]$

EXAMPLE 12.2
Portfolio Expected Return

MyFinanceLab

PROBLEM
Suppose you invest $10,000 in Boeing (BA) stock, and $30,000 in Merck (MRK) stock. You expect a return of 10% for Boeing and 16% for Merck. What is the expected return for your portfolio?

SOLUTION

PLAN
You have a total of $40,000 invested:

$10,000/$40,000 = 25% in Boeing and: $E[R_{BA}] = 10\%$

$30,000/$40,000 = 75% in Merck and: $E[R_{MRK}] = 16\%$

Using Eq. 12.3, compute the expected return on your whole portfolio by multiplying the expected returns of the stocks in your portfolio by their respective portfolio weights.

EXECUTE
The expected return on your portfolio is:

$$E[R_P] = w_{BA} E[R_{BA}] + w_{MRK} E[R_{MRK}]$$
$$E[R_P] = 0.25 \times 10\% + 0.75 \times 16\% = 14.5\%$$

EVALUATE
The importance of each stock for the expected return of the overall portfolio is determined by the relative amount of money you have invested in it. Most (75%) of your money is invested in Merck, so the overall expected return of the portfolio is much closer to Merck's expected return than it is to Boeing's.

CONCEPT CHECK

1. What do the weights in a portfolio tell us?

2. How is the expected return of a portfolio related to the expected returns of the stocks in the portfolio?

12.2 The Volatility of a Portfolio

Investors in a company such as Apple care not only about the return, but also about the risk of their portfolios. Understanding how Apple's investors think about risk requires us to understand how to calculate the risk of a portfolio. As we explained in Chapter 11, when we combine stocks in a portfolio, some of their risk is eliminated through diversification. The amount of risk that will remain depends upon the degree to which the stocks share common risk. The **volatility of a portfolio** is the total risk, measured as standard deviation, of the portfolio. In this section, we describe the tools to quantify the degree to which two stocks share risk and to determine the volatility of a portfolio.

volatility of a portfolio The total risk, measured as standard deviation, of a portfolio.

Diversifying Risks

Let's begin with a simple example of how risk changes when stocks are combined in a portfolio. Table 12.2 shows returns for three hypothetical stocks, along with their average returns and volatilities. Note that while the three stocks have the same volatility and average return, the pattern of returns differs. In years when the airline stocks performed well, the oil stock tended to do poorly (see 2011–2012), and when the airlines did poorly, the oil stock tended to do well (2014–2015).

Table 12.2 also shows the returns for two portfolios of the stocks. The first portfolio is an equal investment in the two airlines, North Air and West Air. The second portfolio is an equal investment in West Air and Texas Oil. The bottom two rows display the average return and volatility for each stock and portfolio of stocks. Note that the 10% average return of both portfolios is equal to the 10% average return of the stocks, consistent with Eq. 12.3. However, as Figure 12.1 illustrates, their volatilities (standard deviations)—12.1% for portfolio 1 and 5.1% for portfolio 2—are very different from the 13.4% volatility for the individual stocks *and* from each other.

This example demonstrates two important things that we learned in Chapter 11. *First, by combining stocks into a portfolio, we reduce risk through diversification.* Because the stocks do not move identically, some of the risk is averaged out in a portfolio. As a result, both portfolios have lower risk than the individual stocks.

Second, the amount of risk that is eliminated in a portfolio depends upon the degree to which the stocks face common risks and move together. Because the two airline stocks tend to perform well or poorly at the same time, the portfolio of airline stocks has a volatility that is only slightly lower than the volatility of the individual stocks. The airline and

TABLE 12.2

Returns for Three Stocks, and Portfolios of Pairs of Stocks

		Stock Returns		Portfolio Returns	
				(1) Half N.A. and Half W.A.	(2) Half W.A. and Half T.O.
Year	North Air	West Air	Texas Oil		
2011	21%	9%	−2%	15.0%	3.5%
2012	30%	21%	−5%	25.5%	8.0%
2013	7%	7%	9%	7.0%	8.0%
2014	−5%	−2%	21%	−3.5%	9.5%
2015	−2%	−5%	30%	−3.5%	12.5%
2016	9%	30%	7%	19.5%	18.5%
Avg. Return	10.0%	10.0%	10.0%	10.0%	10.0%
Volatility	13.4%	13.4%	13.4%	12.1%	5.1%

FIGURE 12.1

Volatility of Airline
and Oil Portfolios

The figures graph the portfolio returns from Table 12.2. In Panel (a), we see that the airline stocks move in synch, so that a portfolio made up of the two airline stocks does not achieve much diversification. In Panel (b), because the airline and oil stocks often move opposite each other, a portfolio of West Air and Texas Oil achieves greater diversification and lower portfolio volatility. Because both stocks have an average return of 10%, so does the portfolio, but it achieves that return with much less volatility than either of the individual stocks.

Panel (a): Portfolio split equally between West Air and North Air

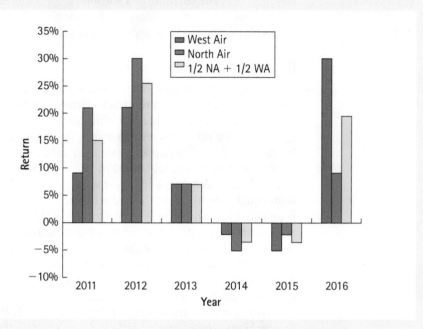

Panel (b): Portfolio split equally between West Air and Texas Oil

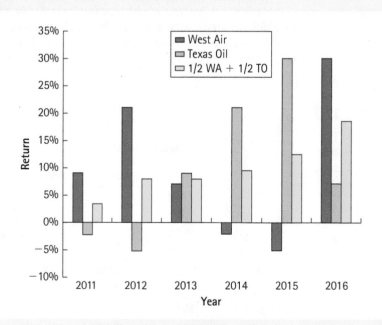

oil stocks, on the other hand, do not move together. Indeed, they tend to move in opposite directions. As a result, more risk is canceled out, making that portfolio much less risky.

Measuring Stocks' Co-Movement: Correlation

Figure 12.1 emphasizes the fact that to find the risk of a portfolio, we need to know more than just the risk of the component stocks: We need to know the degree to which the stocks' returns move together. The stocks' *correlation* is such a measure, ranging from −1 to +1.[1]

correlation A measure of the degree to which returns share common risk. It is calculated as the covariance of the returns divided by the product of the standard deviations of each return.

As Figure 12.2 shows, **correlation** is a barometer of the degree to which the returns share common risk. The closer the correlation is to +1, the more the returns tend to move together as a result of common risk. When the correlation equals 0, the returns are *uncorrelated*; that is, they have no tendency to move together or opposite of one another. Independent risks are uncorrelated. Finally, the closer the correlation is to −1, the more the returns tend to move in opposite directions.

When will stock returns be highly correlated with each other? Stock returns will tend to move together if they are affected similarly by economic events. Thus, stocks in the same industry tend to have more highly correlated returns than stocks in different industries. This tendency is illustrated in Table 12.3, which shows the volatility (standard deviation) of individual stock returns and the correlation between them for several common stocks. The blue-shaded boxes along the diagonal show the correlation of a stock with itself—which has to be 1 (a stock is perfectly correlated with itself). The table can be read across the rows or down the columns. Each correlation appears twice. For example, reading across the Coca-Cola row, the correlation between Coca-Cola and McDonald's (red box) is 0.59, which you could also find by reading across the McDonald's row for the correlation between McDonald's and Coca-Cola. McDonald's and Coca-Cola have the highest correlation in the table, 0.59, because both companies do

FIGURE 12.2

Correlation

The correlation measures how returns move in relation to each other. The correlation is between +1 (returns always move together) and −1 (returns always move oppositely). Independent risks have no tendency to move together and have zero correlation. The correlations of Microsoft with Boeing and Cisco are indicated on the continuum. Note that software company Microsoft is more correlated with a computer network infrastructure company than with an airplane manufacturer. See Table 12.3 for more examples of correlations.

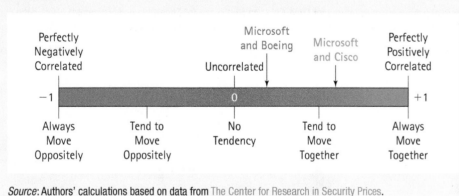

Source: Authors' calculations based on data from The Center for Research in Security Prices.

---

[1]Correlation is scaled covariance and is defined as:

$$Corr(R_i, R_j) = \frac{Covariance(R_i, R_j)}{SD(R_i)SD(R_j)}$$

TABLE 12.3

Estimated Annual Volatilities and Correlations for Selected Stocks
(Based on Monthly Returns, January 2006–December 2015)

Standard Deviation	Microsoft 25%	Starbucks 29%	Netflix 61%	Coca-Cola 16%	McDonald's 14%	Cisco 28%	Boeing 26%
Microsoft	1	0.35	0.18	0.40	0.43	0.52	0.28
Starbucks	0.35	1	0.19	0.23	0.17	0.52	0.48
Netflix	0.18	0.19	1	0.00	0.13	0.10	0.10
Coca-Cola	0.40	0.23	0.00	1	0.59	0.27	0.34
McDonald's	0.43	0.17	0.13	0.59	1	0.28	0.37
Cisco	0.52	0.52	0.10	0.27	0.28	1	0.46
Boeing	0.28	0.48	0.10	0.34	0.37	0.46	1

Source: Authors' calculations based on data from The Center for Research in Security Prices.

well when people buy more fast-food (and McDonald's serves only Coca-Cola products).
None of the correlations are negative, however, showing the general tendency of stocks
to move together. The lowest correlation is shown in the green boxes for Coca-Cola and
Netflix, which is <0.01 (it is actually 0.004), showing that there is little relation between
a soft drink company and an Internet television provider. Figure 12.3 shows scatter plots
of monthly returns for Coca-Cola and Netflix and for Coca-Cola and McDonald's. While
there is a clear positive relation between the returns of Coca-Cola and McDonald's, the
plot for Coca-Cola and Netflix looks like an unrelated cloud of returns.

FIGURE 12.3

Scatter Plots of Returns

Plots of pairs of monthly returns for Coca-Cola and Netflix and for Coca-Cola and McDonald's. Notice the clear positive relation between
Coca-Cola and McDonald's, which tend to move up and down together, versus the lack of a relation between Coca-Cola and Netflix.

Panel (a): Monthly Returns for Coca-Cola and Netflix   Panel (b): Monthly Returns for Coca-Cola and McDonald's

Source: Authors' calculations based on data from The Center for Research in Security Prices.

USING EXCEL

Calculating the
Correlation Between
Two Sets of Returns

The correlations presented in Table 12.3 were calculated by comparing the returns of two stocks. Here we describe how you can use Excel to calculate these correlations.

1. Enter or import the historical returns for the two stocks into Excel.
2. Next, from the Data Group, select **Data Analysis**, and then select **Correlation**.
3. For the "Input Range" field, highlight the two columns of returns, as shown in the screenshot.
4. Click **OK**.
5. The answer will appear in a new worksheet as the correlation between "column 1" and "column 2."

Note that if you don't have the Analysis Toolpak installed, you can use the CORREL function. In this case, you would type: =CORREL(B2:B145,C2:C145) into any empty cell. The function would return the correlation. The cell ranges B2:B145 and C2:C145 are the returns of Microsoft and Starbucks, respectively.

Computing a Portfolio's Variance and Standard Deviation

We now have the tools to formally compute portfolio variance. The formula for the variance of a two-stock portfolio is:

$$Var(R_p) = \overbrace{w_1^2 SD(R_1)^2}^{\substack{\text{Accounting} \\ \text{for the risk} \\ \text{of stock 1}}} + \overbrace{w_2^2 SD(R_2)^2}^{\substack{\text{Accounting} \\ \text{for the risk} \\ \text{of stock 2}}} + \overbrace{2w_1 w_2 Corr(R_1, R_2) SD(R_1) SD(R_2)}^{\substack{\text{Adjustment for} \\ \text{how much the two stocks move together}}} \quad (12.4)$$

Each part of Eq. 12.4 accounts for an important determinant of the overall variance of the portfolio: the risk of stock 1, the risk of stock 2, and an adjustment for how much the two stocks move together (their correlation, given as $Corr(R_1, R_2)$.[2] The equation demonstrates

---

[2]For three stocks, the formula is

$$Var(R_p) = w_1^2 SD(R_1)^2 + w_2^2 SD(R_2)^2 + w_3^2 SD(R_3)^2 + 2w_1 w_2 Corr(R_1, R_2) SD(R_1) SD(R_2)$$
$$+ 2w_2 w_3 Corr(R_2, R_3) SD(R_2) SD(R_3) + 2w_1 w_3 Corr(R_1, R_3) SD(R_1) SD(R_3)$$

and for n stocks, it is:

$$\sum_{i=1}^{n} \sum_{j=1}^{n} w_i w_j Corr(R_i, R_j) SD(R_i) SD(R_j)$$

that with a positive amount invested in each stock, the more the stocks move together and the higher their correlation, the more volatile the portfolio will be. The portfolio will have the greatest variance if the stocks have a perfect positive correlation of +1. In fact, when combining stocks into a portfolio, unless the stocks all have a perfect positive correlation of +1 with each other, the risk of the portfolio will be lower than the weighted average volatility of the individual stocks (as shown in Figure 12.1). Contrast this fact with a portfolio's expected return. The expected return of a portfolio is equal to the weighted average expected return of its stocks, but the volatility of a portfolio is less than the weighted average volatility. As a result, it is clear that we can eliminate some volatility by diversifying. Equation 12.4 formalized the concept of diversification introduced in Chapter 11. In the following example, we use it to compute the volatility of a portfolio.

EXAMPLE 12.3

Computing the Volatility of a Two-Stock Portfolio

MyFinanceLab

PROBLEM

Using the data from Table 12.3, what is the volatility (standard deviation) of a portfolio with equal amounts invested in Microsoft and Cisco stock? What is the standard deviation of a portfolio with equal amounts invested in Microsoft and Starbucks stock?

SOLUTION

PLAN

	Weight	Volatility	Correlation with Microsoft
Microsoft	0.50	0.25	1
Cisco	0.50	0.28	0.52
Microsoft	0.50	0.25	1
Starbucks	0.50	0.29	0.35

A. With the portfolio weights, volatility, and correlations of the stocks in the two portfolios, we have all the information we need to use Eq. 12.4 to compute the variance of each portfolio.
B. After computing the portfolio's variance, we can take the square root to get the portfolio's standard deviation.

EXECUTE

For Microsoft and Cisco, from Eq. 12.4 the portfolio's variance is:

$$Var(R_P) = w_{MSFT}^2 SD(R_{MSFT})^2 + w_{CSCO}^2 SD(R_{CSCO})^2$$
$$+ 2w_{MSFT}w_{CSCO}Corr(R_{MSFT}, R_{CSCO}) SD(R_{MSFT}) SD(R_{CSCO})$$
$$= (.50)^2(.25)^2 + (.50)^2(.28)^2 + 2(.50)(.50)(.52)(.25)(.28)$$
$$= 0.05343$$

The standard deviation is therefore:

$$SD(R_P) = \sqrt{Var(R_P)} = \sqrt{0.05343} = 0.231, \text{ or } 23.1\%$$

For the portfolio of Microsoft and Starbucks:

$$Var(R_P) = w_{MSFT}^2 SD(R_{MSFT})^2 + w_{SBUX}^2 SD(R_{SBUX})^2$$
$$+ 2w_{MSFT}w_{SBUX}Corr(R_{MSFT}, R_{SBUX}) SD(R_{MSFT}) SD(R_{SBUX})$$
$$= (.50)^2(.25)^2 + (.50)^2(.29)^2 + 2(.50)(.50)(.35)(.25)(.29)$$
$$= 0.04934$$

The standard deviation in this case is:

$$SD(R_P) = \sqrt{Var(R_P)} = \sqrt{0.04934} = 0.222, \text{ or } 22.2\%.$$

EVALUATE

The weights, standard deviations, and correlation of the two stocks are needed to compute the variance and then the standard deviation of the portfolio. Here, we computed the standard deviation of the portfolio of Microsoft and Cisco to be 23.1% and of Microsoft and Starbucks to be 22.2%. Note that both portfolios are less volatile than any of the individual stocks in the portfolios. The portfolio of Microsoft and Starbucks is actually less volatile than the portfolio of Microsoft and Cisco. Even though Starbucks is more volatile than Cisco, its lower correlation with Microsoft leads to greater diversification benefits in the portfolio, which offsets Starbuck's higher volatility.

In the next example, we show how portfolios can be used to reduce risk without giving up too much expected return.

EXAMPLE 12.4
Reducing Risk Without Sacrificing Return

MyFinanceLab

PROBLEM

Based on historical data, your expected annual return for Boeing is 13% and for Coca-Cola is 12%. What is the expected return and risk (standard deviation) of your portfolio if you hold only Boeing? If you split your money evenly between Boeing and Coca-Cola, what is the expected return and risk of your portfolio?

SOLUTION

PLAN

A. From Table 12.3 we can get the standard deviations of Boeing (BA) and Coca-Cola (KO) stock along with their correlation:

$$SD(R_{BA}) = 0.26, \quad SD(R_{KO}) = .16 \quad Corr(R_{BA}, R_{KO}) = 0.34$$

B. With this information and the information from the problem, we can compute the expected return of the portfolio using Eq. 12.3 and its variance using Eq. 12.4.

EXECUTE

For the all-Boeing portfolio, we have 100% of our money in Boeing stock, so the expected return and standard deviation of our portfolio is simply the expected return and standard deviation of that stock:

$$E[R_{BA}] = .13, \quad SD(R_{BA}) = 0.26$$

However, when we invest our money 50% in Coca-Cola and 50% in Boeing, the expected return is:

$$E[R_P] = w_{KO}E[R_{KO}] + w_{BA}E[R_{BA}] = 0.5(.12) + 0.5(.13) = 0.125$$

and the variance is:

$$Var(R_P) = w_{KO}^2 SD(R_{KO})^2 + w_{BA}^2 SD(R_{BA})^2$$
$$+ 2w_{KO}w_{BA} Corr(R_{KO}, R_{BA}) SD(R_{KO}) SD(R_{BA})$$
$$= (.50)^2(.16)^2 + (.50)^2(.26)^2 + 2(.50)(.50)(.34)(.16)(.26)$$
$$= 0.0304$$

The standard deviation is therefore:

$$SD(R_P) = \sqrt{Var(R_P)} = \sqrt{0.0304} = 0.174$$

EVALUATE

For a very small reduction in expected return, we gain a large reduction in risk. This is the advantage of portfolios: By selecting stocks with low correlation but similar expected returns, we achieve our desired expected return at the lowest possible risk.

The Volatility of a Large Portfolio

We can gain additional benefits of diversification by holding more than two stocks in our portfolio. As we add more stocks to our portfolio, the diversifiable firm-specific risk for each stock matters less and less. Only risk that is common to all of the stocks in the portfolio continues to matter.

In Figure 12.4, we graph the volatility for an *equally weighted portfolio* with different numbers of stocks. In an **equally weighted portfolio**, the same amount of money is invested in each stock. Note that the volatility declines as the number of stocks in the portfolio grows. In fact, nearly half the volatility of the individual stocks is eliminated in a large portfolio by diversification. The benefit of diversification is most dramatic initially—the decrease in volatility going from one to two stocks is much larger than the decrease going from 100 to 101 stocks. Even for a very large portfolio, however, we cannot eliminate all of the risk—the systematic risk remains.

equally weighted portfolio A portfolio in which the same amount of money is invested in each stock.

FIGURE 12.4

Volatility of an Equally Weighted Portfolio Versus the Number of Stocks

The graph in Panel (b) is based on the data in Panel (a). Note that the volatility declines as we increase the number of stocks in the portfolio. Yet even in a very large portfolio, systematic (market) risk remains. Also note that the volatility declines at a decreasing rate (the effect of going from one to two stocks—an 8-percentage point decrease in volatility—is bigger than the effect of going from four to five stocks, which is a 1.1-percentage point decrease). The graph is formed based on the assumption that each stock has a volatility of 40% and a correlation with other stocks of 0.28. Both are average for large stocks in the United States.

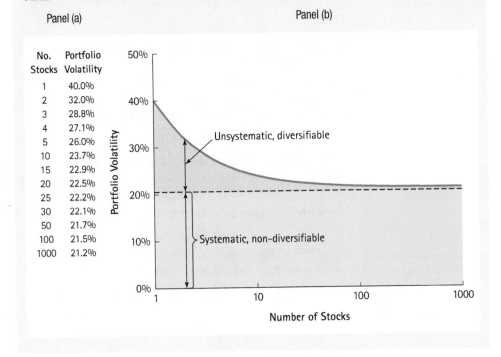

No. Stocks	Portfolio Volatility
1	40.0%
2	32.0%
3	28.8%
4	27.1%
5	26.0%
10	23.7%
15	22.9%
20	22.5%
25	22.2%
30	22.1%
50	21.7%
100	21.5%
1000	21.2%

Harry Markowitz

The techniques that allow an investor to find the portfolio with the highest expected return for any level of standard deviation (or volatility), were developed in an article, "Portfolio Selection," published in the *Journal of Finance* in 1952 by Harry Markowitz. Markowitz's approach has become one of the main methods of portfolio optimization used on Wall Street. In recognition for his contribution, Markowitz was awarded the Nobel Prize in Economics in 1990.

CONCEPT CHECK
3. What determines how much risk will be eliminated by combining stocks in a portfolio?
4. When do stocks have more or less correlation?

Measuring Systematic Risk

Our goal is to understand the impact of risk on the firm's investors. By understanding how they view risk, we can quantify the relation between risk and required return to produce a discount rate for our present value calculations. In Chapter 11, we established that the only risk that is related to return is systematic risk, but standard deviation measures *total* risk, including the unsystematic part. We need a way to measure just the systematic risk of an investment opportunity. The previous section contains two important insights that we will now build on to determine the sensitivity of individual stocks to risk. To recap:

1. *The amount of a stock's risk that is removed by diversification depends on its correlation with other stocks in the portfolio.* For example, in Example 12.3 we showed that much less of Microsoft's risk is diversified away in a portfolio with Cisco than in a portfolio with Starbucks.

2. *If you build a large enough portfolio, you can remove all unsystematic risk by diversification, but you will still be left with systematic risk.* Figure 12.4 shows that as the number of stocks in your portfolio grows, the unsystematic positive and negative events affecting only a few stocks will cancel out, leaving systematic events as the only source of risk for the portfolio.

Role of the Market Portfolio

As we explained in Chapter 11, investors should diversify their portfolios in order to reduce their risk. If investors choose their portfolios optimally, they will do so until no further diversifiable risk is present, and only systematic risk remains. Let's assume that all investors behave in this way; that is

Suppose all investors hold portfolios that contain only systematic risk.

If that is the case, then consider the portfolio we obtain by combining the portfolios of every investor. Because each investor's portfolio contains only systematic risk, the same is true for this "aggregate" portfolio. So, the aggregate portfolio held by all investors is a fully diversified, optimal portfolio. Moreover, we can identify this portfolio: Because all securities are held by someone, the aggregate portfolio contains all shares outstanding of every risky security. We call this portfolio the **market portfolio**.

market portfolio The portfolio of all risky investments, held in proportion to their value.

To illustrate, imagine that there are only two companies in the world, each with 1000 shares outstanding:

	Number of Shares Outstanding	Price per Share	Market Capitalization
Company A	1000	$40	$40,000
Company B	1000	$10	$10,000

market capitalization The total market value of a firm's equity; equals the market price per share times the number of shares.

In this simple setting, the market portfolio consists of 1000 shares of each stock and has a total value of $50,000. Stock A's portfolio weight is therefore 80% ($40,000/$50,000) and B's is 20% ($10,000/$50,000). Because all of the shares of A and all of the shares of B must be held by someone, the sum of all investors' portfolios must equal this market portfolio. Note from this example that the portfolio weight of each stock is proportional to the total market value of its outstanding shares, which is called its **market capitalization**:

$$\text{Market Capitalization} = (\text{Number of Shares Outstanding}) \times (\text{Price per Share}) \quad (12.5)$$

Generally, the market portfolio will consist of all risky securities in the market, with portfolio weights proportional to their market capitalization. Thus, for example, if Microsoft's market capitalization were equal to 3% of the total market value of all securities, then it would have a 3% weight in the market portfolio. Because stocks are held in proportion to their market capitalization (value), we say that the market portfolio is **value weighted**.

value-weighted portfolio A portfolio in which each security is held in proportion to its market capitalization.

Because the market portfolio only contains systematic risk, we can use it to measure the amount of systematic risk of other securities in the market. In particular, any risk that is correlated with the market portfolio must be systematic risk. Therefore, by looking at the sensitivity of a stock's return to the overall market, we can calculate the amount of systematic risk the stock has.

Stock Market Indexes as the Market Portfolio

While the market portfolio is easy to identify, actually constructing it is a different matter. Because it should contain all risky securities, we need to include all stocks, bonds, real estate, commodities, etc., both in the United States and around the world. Clearly, it would be impractical, if not impossible, to collect and update returns on all risky assets everywhere. In practice, we use a **market proxy**—a portfolio whose return should track the underlying, unobservable market portfolio. The most common proxy portfolios are *market indexes*, which are broadly used to represent the performance of the stock market. A **market index** reports the value of a particular portfolio of securities. We list the most popular indexes below, but you can also read the box on page 16 in Section 1.5 of Chapter 1 that compares the different market indexes.

market proxy A portfolio whose return should closely track the true market portfolio.

market index The market value of a broad-based portfolio of securities.

Dow Jones Industrial Average. The most familiar stock index in the United States is the Dow Jones Industrial Average, or DJIA. This index consists of a portfolio of 30 large stocks. While these stocks are chosen to be representative of different sectors of the economy, they clearly do not represent the entire market. Despite being non-representative of the entire market, the DJIA remains widely cited because it is one of the oldest stock market indexes (it was first published in 1884).

S&P 500. A better representation of the entire U.S. stock market is the S&P 500, a value-weighted portfolio of 500 of the largest U.S. stocks.[3] The S&P 500 was the first widely publicized value-weighted index (S&P began publishing its index in 1923), and it is a standard benchmark for professional investors. This index is the most commonly cited index when evaluating the overall performance of the U.S. stock market. It is also the standard portfolio used to represent "the market" in practice. As we show in Figure 12.5, even though the S&P 500 includes only 500 of more than 7000 individual U.S. stocks, because the S&P 500 includes the largest stocks, it represents more than 70% of the U.S. stock market in terms of market capitalization.

Market Risk and Beta

Now that we have established that the market portfolio is a good basis for measuring systematic risk, we can use the relation between an individual stock's returns and the market portfolio's returns to measure the amount of systematic risk present in that stock. The intuition is that if a stock's returns are highly sensitive to the market portfolio's returns,

---

[3]There is no precise formula for determining which stocks will be included in the S&P 500. Standard & Poor's periodically replaces stocks in the index (on average about seven or eight stocks per year). While size is one criterion, Standard & Poor's also tries to maintain appropriate representation of different segments of the economy and chooses firms that are leaders in their industries.

FIGURE 12.5

The S&P 500

The Panel (a) pie chart shows the 500 firms in the S&P 500 as a fraction of the approximately 3600 U.S. public operating firms. Panel (b) shows the S&P 500 firms' importance in terms of market capitalization— these 500 firms represent approximately 80% of the total capitalization of the 3600 public firms.

Index Funds

One easy way investors can buy (an approximation of) the market portfolio is to invest in an *index fund*, which invests in stocks and other securities with the goal of matching the performance of a particular market index. The Vanguard Group was the largest mutual fund company in 2013 and it specializes in index funds. Vanguard was founded in 1974 by John Bogle, who advocates the benefits of index funds for individual investors. Comparing index funds to the strategy of trying to pick hot stocks, Bogle reportedly said, "What's the point of looking for the needle in the haystack? Why not own the haystack?"

In August of 1976, Vanguard created its well-known S&P 500 Index Fund, which tries to match the performance of the S&P 500 index as closely as possible. As of April 2016, this fund had nearly $230 billion in assets. Vanguard's Total Stock Market Index Fund is designed to track the performance of the MSCI US Broad Market index, an index that measures the performance of all U.S. stocks with available price data.

then that stock is highly sensitive to systematic risk. That is, events that are systematic and affect the whole market are also strongly reflected in that stock's returns. If a stock's returns do not depend on the market's returns, then it has little systematic risk—when systematic events happen, they are not strongly reflected in its returns. So stocks whose returns are volatile *and* are highly correlated with the market's returns are the riskiest in the sense that they have the most systematic risk.

Specifically, we can measure a stock's systematic risk by estimating the stock's sensitivity to the market portfolio, which we refer to as its **beta** (β):

beta (β) The expected percentage change in the excess return of a security for a 1% change in the excess return of the market (or other benchmark) portfolio.

A stock's beta (β) is the percentage change in its return that we expect for each 1% change in the market's return.

There are many data sources that provide estimates of beta based on historical data. Typically, these data sources estimate betas using two-to-five years of weekly or monthly returns and use the S&P 500 as the market portfolio. Table 12.4 shows estimates of betas for a number of large stocks and their industries. You can find the betas of other companies

TABLE 12.4

Average Betas for Stocks by Industry and the Betas of a Selected Company in Each Industry

Industry	Average Beta	Ticker	Company	Beta
Electric Utilities	0.8	EIX	Edison International	0.2
Personal & Household Prods.	0.5	PG	The Procter & Gamble Company	0.5
Food Processing	0.9	CPB	Campbell Soup Co.	0.4
Restaurants	0.5	SBUX	Starbucks Corporation	0.8
Beverages (Nonalcoholic)	0.2	KO	The Coca-Cola Company	0.5
Retail (Grocery)	0.6	KR	Kroger Co	0.8
Major Drugs	0.7	PFE	Pfizer Inc.	0.9
Beverages (Alcoholic)	0.6	SAM	Boston Beer Company Inc.	0.7
Apparel/Accessories	1.2	ANF	Abercrombie & Fitch	1.2
Retail (Home Improvement)	0.7	HD	Home Depot Inc.	0.9
Software & Programming	0.9	MSFT	Microsoft Corporation	1.0
Consumer (Discretionary)	0.5	TRIP	TripAdvisor Inc.	2.3
Auto & Truck Manufacturers	1.2	F	Ford Motor Company	1.4
Communications Equipment	1.1	CSCO	Cisco Systems Inc.	1.3
Forestry & Wood Products	0.6	WY	Weyerhaeuser Company	1.4
Computer Services	1.0	GOOGL	Alphabet Inc. (Google)	0.9
Computer Hardware	0.8	HPQ	Hewlett Packard	1.7
Semiconductors	1.3	INTC	Intel Corporation	1.0

Source: Reuters, May 2016.

by going to http://finance.google.com or http://finance.yahoo.com. Note that because different Web sites use different time frames for estimating betas, they can display different betas from each other and from your own calculation for a stock's beta.

As we explain below, the beta of the overall market portfolio is 1, so you can think of a beta of 1 as representing average exposure to systematic risk. However, as the table demonstrates, many industries and companies have betas much higher or lower than 1. The differences in betas by industry are related to the sensitivity of each industry's profits to the general health of the economy. For example, Hewlett Packard, Abercrombie & Fitch, and TripAdvisor all have high betas (near or above 1.2) because demand for their products usually varies with the business cycle (cyclical stocks): People tend to indulge in new computers, new clothes, and travel when times are good, but cut back on these purchases when the economy slows. Thus, systematic events have a greater-than-average impact on these firms and their exposure to systematic risk is greater than average. On the other hand, the demand for personal and household products such as shampoo has very little relation to the state of the economy (stocks of companies providing these types of products are often called *defensive stocks*). Firms producing these types of goods, such as Procter & Gamble, tend to have low betas (near 0.5). Note also that even within an industry, each company's specific strategy and focus can lead to different exposures to systematic events, so that there is variation in beta even within industries (see, for example, how different Weyerhaeuser's beta is than the average beta in the forestry and wood products industry).

COMMON MISTAKE

Mixing Standard Deviation and Beta

Volatility (standard deviation) and beta are measured in different units (standard deviation is measured in % and beta is unitless). So even though total risk (volatility) is equal to the sum of systematic risk (measured by beta) and firm-specific risk, our measure of volatility does not have to be a bigger number than our measure for beta. To illustrate, consider Microsoft. It has total risk (volatility), measured as standard deviation, of 25% or 0.25 (see Table 12.3),

but Table 12.4 shows that it has systematic risk, measured as a beta, of 1.0, which is greater than 0.25. Volatility (standard deviation) is measured in percentage terms, but beta is not, so 0.25 does not have to be greater than 1.0. For the same reason, it is possible for Boston Beer Company to have a higher standard deviation than Microsoft (35%), but a lower beta (0.7). Figure 12.6 illustrates one possible breakdown of total risk for Microsoft and Boston Beer Company that would be consistent with these data.

FIGURE 12.6

Systematic Versus Firm-Specific Risk in Boston Beer and Microsoft

Beta, measuring systematic risk, and standard deviation, measuring total risk, are in different units. Even though Microsoft's total risk (standard deviation) is 0.25 (25%), its beta, measuring only systematic risk, is 1.0. In this case, the beta of 1.0 corresponds to a breakdown in total risk as depicted in the figure. Formally, the portion of Microsoft's total risk that is in common with the market is calculated by multiplying the correlation between Microsoft and the market by the standard deviation (total risk) of Microsoft. We can do a similar breakdown of Boston Beer's risk. Note that Boston Beer has more total, but less systematic, risk than Microsoft.

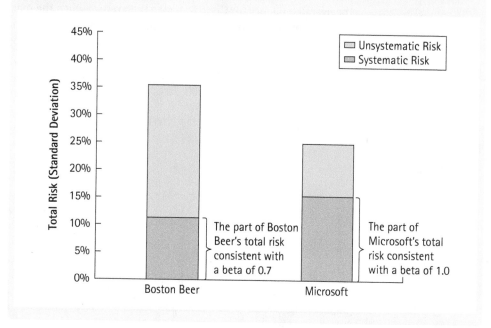

EXAMPLE 12.5

Total Risk Versus Systematic Risk

MyFinanceLab

PROBLEM

Suppose that in the coming year, you expect SysCo's stock to have a standard deviation of 30% and a beta of 1.2, and UniCo's stock to have a standard deviation of 41% and a beta of 0.6. Which stock carries more total risk? Which has more systematic risk?

SOLUTION

PLAN

	Standard Deviation (Total Risk)	Beta (β) (Systematic Risk)
SysCo	30%	1.2
UniCo	41%	0.6

(Continued)

Estimating Beta from Historical Returns

A security's beta is the expected percentage change in the return of the security for a 1% change in the return of the market portfolio. That is, beta represents the amount by which risks that affect the overall market are amplified or dampened in a given stock or investment. As demonstrated in Table 12.4, securities whose returns tend to move one for one with the market on average have a beta of one. Securities that tend to move more than the market have higher betas, while those that move less than the market have lower betas.

For example, let's look at Cisco's stock. Figure 12.7 shows the monthly returns for Cisco and the monthly returns for the S&P 500 from January 2011 through December 2015. Note the overall tendency for Cisco to have a high return when the market is up and a low return when the market is down. Indeed, Cisco tends to move in the same direction as the market, but its movements are larger. The pattern suggests that Cisco's beta is greater than one.

FIGURE 12.7

Monthly Excess Returns for Cisco Stock and for the S&P 500, January 2011 through December 2015

Note that Cisco's returns tend to move in the same direction but farther than those of the S&P 500.

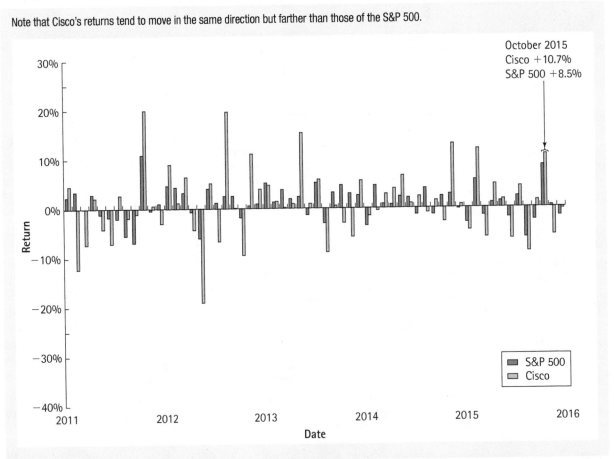

We can see Cisco's sensitivity to the market even more clearly by plotting Cisco's return as a function of the S&P 500 return, as shown in Figure 12.8. Each point in this figure represents the returns of Cisco and the S&P 500 for one of the months in Figure 12.7. For example, in October 2015, Cisco's return was 10.7% and the S&P 500's was 8.5%.

As the scatter plot makes clear, Cisco's returns have a positive correlation with the market: Cisco tends to be up when the market is up, and vice versa. In practice, we use linear regression to estimate the relation between Cisco's returns and the market's return. The output of the linear regression analysis is the best-fitting line that represents the historical relation between the stock and the market. The slope of this line is our estimate of its beta. That slope tells us how much, on average, the stock's return changes for a 1% change in the market's return.[4]

For example, in Figure 12.8, the best-fitting line shows that a 1% change in the market's return corresponds to about a 1.3% change in Cisco's return. That is, Cisco's return moves about 1.3 times the overall market's movement, and so Cisco's beta is about 1.3.

To fully understand this result, recall that beta measures the systematic, market risk of a security. The best-fitting line in Figure 12.8 captures the components of a security's returns that can be explained by market-risk factors. In any individual month, the security's returns will be higher or lower than the best-fitting line. Such deviations from the best-fitting line result from risk that is not related to the market as a whole. This risk is diversifiable risk that averages out in a large portfolio.

But what is the beta of the market portfolio? Imagine plotting the returns of the S&P 500 against themselves. You would have a line with a slope of one and no deviations from that line. Thus, the beta of the market portfolio is 1. What about a risk-free investment?

FIGURE 12.8

Scatter Plot of Monthly Returns for Cisco Versus the S&P 500, January 2011 through December 2015

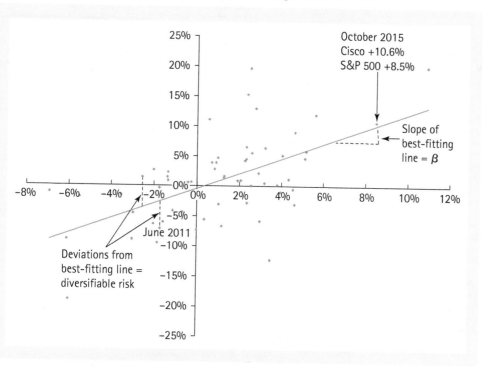

Beta corresponds to the slope of the best-fitting line. Beta measures the expected change in Cisco's return per 1% change in the market's return. Deviations from the best-fitting line, such as in June 2011, correspond to diversifiable, unsystematic risk.

---

[4]Formally, the beta of an investment is defined as:

$$\beta_i = \frac{\overbrace{SD(R_i) \times Corr(R_i, R_{Mkt})}^{\text{Volatility of } i \text{ that is common with the market}}}{SD(R_{Mkt})} = \frac{Covariance(R_i, R_{Mkt})}{Var(R_{Mkt})}$$

Because the risk-free return is the return earned on a Treasury bond and is therefore known in advance, it has no volatility and hence no correlation with the market. Therefore, the beta of the risk-free investment is 0.

USING EXCEL

Calculating a
Stock's Beta

1. Enter or import the historical returns for the stock and the S&P 500 into Excel.
2. Next, from the Data Tab, select **Data Analysis**, and then select **Regression**.
3. For the "Input Y Range" box, highlight the stock's returns.
4. For the "Input X Range" box, highlight the S&P 500's returns, as shown in the screenshot.
5. Click **OK**.

6. The output will appear in a separate sheet. The stock's beta is the coefficient on "X Variable 1." In this case, the beta is 1.247, circled in the screenshot.

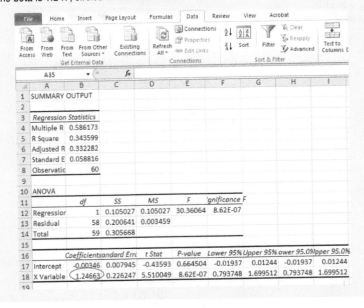

CONCEPT 5. What is the market portfolio?
CHECK 6. What does beta (β) tell us?

12.4 Putting It All Together: The Capital Asset Pricing Model

One of our goals in this chapter is to compute the cost of equity capital for Apple, which is the best available expected return offered in the market on an investment of comparable risk and term. Thus, in order to compute the cost of capital, we need to know the relation between Apple's risk and its expected return. In the last three sections, we have laid the foundation for a practical way of measuring this relation. In this section, we put all the pieces together to build a model for determining the expected return of any investment.

The CAPM Equation Relating Risk to Expected Return

As we have learned, only common, systematic risk determines expected returns—firm-specific risk is diversifiable and does not warrant extra return. In the introduction to this chapter, we stated that, intuitively, the expected return on any investment should come from two components:

1. A baseline risk-free rate of return that we would demand to compensate for inflation and the time value of money, even if there were no risk of losing our money.
2. A risk premium that varies with the amount of systematic risk in the investment.

Expected Return = Risk-Free Rate + Risk Premium for Systematic Risk

We devoted the last section to measuring systematic risk. Beta is our measure of the amount of systematic risk in an investment:

Expected Return for Investment i =
Risk-Free Rate + $\beta_i \times$ Risk Premium per Unit of Systematic Risk (per unit of β).

But what is the risk premium per unit of systematic risk? Well, we know that the market portfolio, by definition, has exactly one unit of systematic risk (it has a beta of 1). So, a natural estimate of the risk premium per unit of systematic risk is the historical average excess return on the market portfolio, also known as the **market** or **equity risk premium**. Historically, the average excess return of the S&P 500 over the return on U.S. Treasury bonds (the risk-free rate) has been 5% to 7%, depending on the period of measurement (we'll discuss issues in determining the risk premium and risk-free rate in Chapter 13). With this last piece of the puzzle, we can write the equation for the expected return of an investment:

market risk premium (equity risk premium) The historical average excess returns on the market portfolio.

Capital Asset Pricing Model

$$E[R_i] = r_f + \underbrace{\beta_i(E[R_{Mkt}] - r_f)}_{\text{Risk premium for security } i}$$

(12.6)

Capital Asset Pricing Model (CAPM) An equilibrium model of the relationship between risk and return that characterizes a security's expected return based on its beta with the market portfolio.

This equation for the expected return of any investment is the **Capital Asset Pricing Model (CAPM)**. In words, the CAPM simply says that the return we should expect on any investment is equal to the risk-free rate of return plus a risk premium proportional to the amount of systematic risk in the investment. Specifically, the risk premium of an investment is equal to the market risk premium $(E[R_{Mkt}] - r_f)$ multiplied by the amount of systematic (market) risk present in the investment, measured by its beta with the market (β_i).

Why Not Estimate Expected Returns Directly?

If we have to use historical data to estimate beta and determine a security's expected return (or an investment's cost of capital), why not just use the security's historical average return as an estimate for its expected return instead? This method would certainly be simpler and more direct.

The answer is that it is extremely difficult to infer the average return of individual stocks from historical data. Because stock returns are so volatile, even with 100 years of data we would have little confidence in our estimate of the true average. (Imagine drawing 100 numbers from a swimming pool full of widely ranging

numbers and being asked to guess the average of all of the numbers in the pool.) Worse, few stocks have existed for 100 years, and those that have probably bear little resemblance today to what they were like 100 years ago. If we use less than ten years of data, we would have very little confidence in our estimate at all. In fact, if the volatility of the stock's return is 20%, it turns out that we would need 1600 years of data to be 95% confident that our estimate of its true average return was within $+/-1\%$ of being correct!

On the other hand, the linear regression technique allows us to infer beta from historical data reasonably accurately with just a few years of data. Thus, in theory at least, using beta and the CAPM can provide much more accurate estimates of expected returns for stocks than we could obtain from their historical average return.

required return The expected return of an investment that is necessary to compensate for the risk of undertaking the investment.

Because investors will not invest in this security unless they can expect at least the return given in Eq. 12.6, we also call this return the investment's **required return**.

The CAPM is the main method used by most major corporations to determine the equity cost of capital. In a survey of CFOs, Graham and Harvey found that more than 70% rely on the CAPM, and Bruner, Eades, Harris, and Higgins reported that 85% of a sample of large firms rely on it.[5] It has become the most important model of the relationship between risk and return, and for his contributions to the theory, William Sharpe was awarded the Nobel Prize in Economics in 1990.

EXAMPLE 12.6

Computing the Expected Return of a Stock

MyFinanceLab

PROBLEM

Suppose the risk-free return is 3% and you measure the market risk premium to be 6%. Cisco has a beta of 1.3. According to the CAPM, what is its expected return?

SOLUTION

PLAN

We can use Eq. 12.6 to compute the expected return according to the CAPM. For that equation, we will need the market risk premium, the risk-free return, and the stock's beta. We have all of these inputs, so we are ready to go.

EXECUTE

Using Eq. 12.6:

$$E[R_{CSCO}] = r_f + \beta_{CSCO}(E[R_{Mkt}] - r_f) = 3\% + 1.3(6\%)$$

$$= 10.8\%$$

EVALUATE

Because of Cisco's beta of 1.3, investors will require a risk premium of 7.8% over the risk-free rate for investments in its stock to compensate for the systematic risk of Apple stock. This leads to a total expected return of 10.8%.

---

[5]J. Graham and C. Harvey, "The Theory and Practice of Corporate Finance: Evidence from the Field," *Journal of Financial Economics*, 60 (2001): 187–243; and R. Bruner, K. Eades, R. Harris, and R. Higgins, "Best Practices in Estimating the Cost of Capital: Survey and Synthesis," *Financial Practice and Education*, 8 (1998): 13–28.

William Sharpe

The CAPM was proposed as a model of risk and return by William Sharpe in a 1964 paper, and in related papers by Jack Treynor (1961), John Lintner (1965), and Jan Mossin (1966).*

Below is an excerpt from a 1998 interview with William Sharpe:

Portfolio Theory focused on the actions of a single investor with an optimal portfolio. I said what if everyone was optimizing? They've all got their copies of Markowitz and they're doing what he says. Then some people decide they want to hold more IBM, but there aren't enough shares to satisfy demand. So they put price pressure on IBM and up it goes, at which point they have to change their estimates of risk and return, because now they're paying more for the stock. That process of upward and downward pressure on prices continues until prices reach an equilibrium and everyone collectively wants to hold what's available. At that point, what can you say about the relationship between risk and return? The answer is that expected return is proportional to beta relative to the market portfolio.

The CAPM was and is a theory of equilibrium. Why should anyone expect to earn more by investing in one security as opposed to another? You need to be compensated for doing badly when times are bad. The security that is going to do badly just when you need money when

times are bad is a security you have to hate, and there had better be some redeeming virtue or else who will hold it? That redeeming virtue has to be that in normal times you expect to do better. The key insight of the Capital Asset Pricing Model is that higher expected returns go with the greater risk of doing badly in bad times. Beta is a measure of that. Securities or asset classes with high betas tend to do worse in bad times than those with low betas.

Source: Jonathan Burton, "Revisiting the Capital Asset Pricing Model." *Dow Jones Asset Manager* (May/June 1998): 20–28.

---

*W. F. Sharpe: "Capital Asset Prices: A Theory of Market Equilibrium Under Conditions of Risk." *Journal of Finance*, 19 (September 1964): 425–442.

Jack Treynor, "Toward a Theory of the Market Value of Risky Assets." Unpublished manuscript (1961).

J. Lintner: "The Valuation of Risk Assets and the Selection of Risky Investments in Stock Portfolios and Capital Budgets." *Review of Economics and Statistics*, 47 (February 1965): 13–37.

J. Mossin "Equilibrium in a Capital Asset Market." *Econometrica*, 34 (4) (1966): 768–783.

The Security Market Line

Figure 12.9 graphs the relations between expected return and both total risk and systematic risk (beta) for the stocks in Table 12.4. Recall from Chapter 11 that there is no clear relation between a stock's standard deviation (total risk) and its expected return, as shown in Panel (a). However, the CAPM equation (Eq. 12.6) implies that there is a linear relation between a stock's beta and its expected return. This line is graphed in Panel (b) as the line through the risk-free investment (with a beta of zero) and the market (with a beta of one); it is called the **security market line (SML)**. We see that the relation between risk and return for individual securities is only evident when we measure market risk as in Panel (b), rather than total risk as in Panel (a).

The security market line in Figure 12.9 raises the subject of negative beta stocks. While the vast majority of stocks have a positive beta, it is possible to have returns that co-vary negatively with the market. Firms that provide goods or services that are in greater demand in economic contractions than in booms fit this description.

security market line (SML) The pricing implication of the CAPM; it specifies a linear relation between the risk premium of a security and its beta with the market portfolio.

FIGURE 12.9

Expected Return, Volatility, and Beta

Panel (a) Expected Return and Total Risk (Standard Deviation)
The graph compares the standard deviation and expected returns of the stocks in Table 12.4. There is no relation between total risk and expected return. Some of the stocks are identified. It is clear that we could not predict Boston Beer's expected return using its total risk (volatility).

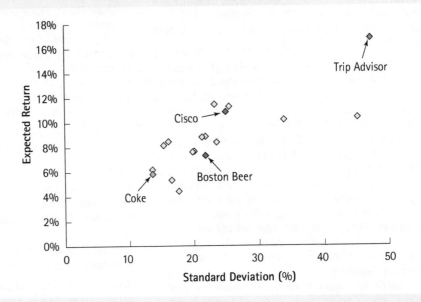

Panel (b) Expected Return and Beta
The security market line shows the expected return for each security in Table 12.4 as a function of its beta with the market. According to the CAPM, all stocks and portfolios (including the market portfolio) should lie on the security market line. Thus, Boston Beer's expected return can be determined by its beta, which measures its systematic risk.

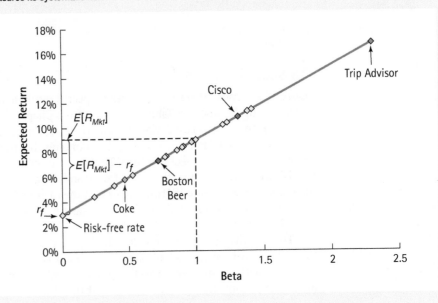

EXAMPLE 12.7

A Negative Beta Stock

MyFinanceLab

PROBLEM

Suppose the stock of Bankruptcy Auction Services Inc. (BAS) has a negative beta of -0.30. How does its expected return compare to the risk-free rate, according to the CAPM? Does your result make sense?

SOLUTION

PLAN

We can use the CAPM equation, Eq. 12.6, to compute the expected return of this negative beta stock just as we would with a positive beta stock. We don't have the risk-free rate or the market risk premium, but the problem doesn't ask us for the exact expected return, just whether or not it will be more or less than the risk-free rate. Using Eq. 12.6, we can answer that question.

EXECUTE

Because the expected return of the market is higher than the risk-free rate, Eq. 12.6 implies that the expected return of Bankruptcy Auction Services (BAS) will be *below* the risk-free rate. As long as the market risk premium is positive (as long as people demand a higher return for investing in the market than for a risk-free investment), then the second term in Eq. 12.6 will have to be negative if the beta is negative. For example, if the risk-free rate is 4% and the market risk premium is 6%:

$$E[R_{BAS}] = 4\% - 0.30\ (6\%) = 2.2\%.$$

(See Figure 12.9—the security market line drops below r_f for $\beta < 0$.)

EVALUATE

This result seems odd—why would investors be willing to accept a 2.2% expected return on this stock when they can invest in a safe investment and earn 4%? The answer is that a savvy investor will not hold BAS alone; instead, the investor will hold it in combination with other securities as part of a well-diversified portfolio. These other securities will tend to rise and fall with the market. But because BAS has a negative beta, its correlation with the market is negative, which means that BAS tends to perform well when the rest of the market is doing poorly. Therefore, by holding BAS, an investor can reduce the overall market risk of the portfolio. In a sense, BAS is "recession insurance" for a portfolio, and investors will pay for this insurance by accepting a lower expected return.

The CAPM and Portfolios

Because the security market line applies to all securities, we can apply it to portfolios as well. For example, the market portfolio is on the SML, and according to the CAPM, other portfolios (such as mutual funds) are also on the SML. Therefore, the expected return of a portfolio should correspond to the portfolio's beta. We calculate the beta of a portfolio made up of securities each with weight w_i as follows:

$$\beta_P = w_1\beta_1 + w_2\beta_2 + \cdots + w_n\beta_n \tag{12.7}$$

That is, the *beta of a portfolio is the market value weighted average beta of the securities in the portfolio.*

EXAMPLE 12.8

The Expected Return of a Portfolio

MyFinanceLab

PROBLEM

Suppose drug-maker Pfizer (PFE) has a beta of 0.9, whereas the beta of Abercrombie & Fitch (ANF) is 1.2. If the risk-free interest rate is 3% and the market risk premium is 6%, what is the expected return of an equally weighted portfolio of Pfizer and Abercrombie & Fitch, according to the CAPM?

SOLUTION

PLAN

We have the following information:

$$r_f = 3\%, \qquad E[R_{Mkt}] - r_f = 6\%$$

PFE: $\quad \beta_{PFE} = 0.9, \quad w_{PFE} = 0.50$

ANF: $\quad \beta_{ANF} = 1.2, \quad w_{ANF} = 0.50$

(Continued)

We can compute the expected return of the portfolio two ways. First, we can use the CAPM (Eq. 12.6) to compute the expected return of each stock and then compute the expected return of the portfolio using Eq. 12.3.

Or, we can compute the beta of the portfolio using Eq. 12.7 and then use the CAPM (Eq. 12.6) to find the portfolio's expected return.

EXECUTE

Using the first approach, we compute the expected return for PFE and GOOG:

$$E[R_{PFE}] = r_f + \beta_{PFE}(E[R_{Mkt}] - r_f) \qquad E[R_{ANF}] = r_f + \beta_{GOOG}(E[R_{Mkt}] - r_f)$$

$$E[R_{PFE}] = 3\% + 0.9(6\%) = 8.4\% \qquad E[R_{ANF}] = 3\% + 1.2(6\%) = 10.2\%$$

Then the expected return of the equally weighted portfolio P is:

$$E[R_P] = 0.5(8.4\%) + 0.5(10.2\%) = 9.3\%$$

Alternatively, we can compute the beta of the portfolio using Eq.12.7:

$$\beta_P = w_{PFE}\beta_{PFE} + w_{ANF}\beta_{ANF}$$
$$\beta_P = (0.5)(0.9) + (0.5)(1.2) = 1.05$$

We can then find the portfolio's expected return from the CAPM:

$$E[R_P] = r_f + \beta_P(E[R_{Mkt}] - r_f)$$
$$E[R_P] = 3\% + 1.05(6\%) = 9.3\%$$

EVALUATE

The CAPM is an effective tool for analyzing securities and portfolios of those securities. You can compute the expected return of each security using its beta and then compute the weighted average of those expected returns to determine the portfolio's expected return. Or, you can compute the weighted average of the securities' betas to get the portfolio's beta and then compute the expected return of the portfolio using the CAPM. Either way, you will get the same answer.

Summary of the Capital Asset Pricing Model

The CAPM is a powerful tool that is widely used to estimate the expected return on stocks and investments within companies. To summarize the model and its use:

- Investors require a risk premium proportional to the amount of *systematic* risk they are bearing.
- We can measure the systematic risk of an investment by its β, which is the sensitivity of the investment's return to the market's return. For each 1% change in the market portfolio's return, the investment's return is expected to change by β percent due to risks that it has in common with the market.
- The most common way to estimate a stock's beta is to regress its historical returns on the market's historical returns. The stock's beta is the slope of the line that best explains the relation between the market's return and the stock's return.
- The CAPM says that we can compute the expected, or required, return for any investment using the following equation:

$$E[R_i] = r_f + \beta_i(E[R_{Mkt}] - r_f)$$

which when graphed is called the *security market line*.

The Big Picture

The CAPM marks the culmination of our examination of how investors in capital markets trade off risk and return. It provides a powerful and widely used tool to quantify the return that should accompany a particular amount of systematic risk. We have already reached our goal (in Example 12.6) of estimating the cost of equity capital for Cisco. While our finding that equity investors in Cisco should reasonably expect (and therefore require) a return of 10.8% on their investments is an important piece of information to Cisco's managers, it is not the whole picture. While some firms have only equity investors, most have debt investors as well. In Chapters 13, we will apply what we have learned here and in Chapters 6, 7, and 10 on bonds and stocks to develop the overall cost of capital for a company. The Valuation Principle tells us to use this cost of capital to discount the future expected cash flows of a firm to arrive at the value of the firm. Thus, the cost of capital is an essential input to the financial manager's job of analyzing investment opportunities, and so knowing this overall cost of capital is critical to the company's success at creating value for its investors.

CONCEPT CHECK

7. What does the CAPM say about the required return of a security?

8. What is the security market line?

MyFinanceLab

Here is what you should know after reading this chapter. MyFinanceLab will help you identify what you know, and where to go when you need to practice.

KEY POINTS AND EQUATIONS	KEY TERMS	ONLINE PRACTICE
12.1 The Expected Return of a Portfolio • The portfolio weight is the initial fraction w_i of an investor's money invested in each asset. Portfolio weights add up to one: $$w_i = \frac{\text{Value of Investment } i}{\text{Total Value of Portfolio}} \quad (12.1)$$ • The expected return of a portfolio is the weighted average of the expected returns of the investments within it, using the portfolio weights: $$E[R_P] = w_1 E[R_1] + w_2 E[R_2] + \cdots + w_n E[R_n] \quad (12.3)$$	expected return of a portfolio, p. 372 portfolio weights, p. 370 return of a portfolio, p. 370	MyFinanceLab Study Plan 12.1
12.2 The Volatility of a Portfolio • To find the risk of a portfolio, we need to know the degree to which stock returns move together. Correlation measures the co-movement of returns. The correlation is always between -1 and $+1$. It represents the fraction of the volatility due to risk that is common to the securities. • The variance of a portfolio depends on the correlation of the stocks. For a portfolio with two stocks, the portfolio variance is: $$Var(R_p)$$ $$= w_1^2 SD(R_1)^2 + w_2^2 SD(R_2)^2$$ $$+ 2w_1 w_2 Corr(R_1, R_2) SD(R_1) SD(R_2) \quad (12.4)$$ • As we lower the correlation between the two stocks in a portfolio, we lower the portfolio variance. • Diversification eliminates independent, firm-specific risks, and the volatility of a large portfolio results from the common systematic risk between the stocks in the portfolio.	correlation, p. 375 equally weighted portfolio, p. 380 volatility of a portfolio, p. 373	MyFinanceLab Study Plan 12.2 Using Excel: Correlation Between Two Sets of Returns

12.3 Measuring Systematic Risk

- The market portfolio in theory is a value-weighted index of all risky investments. In practice, we often use a stock market index such as the S&P 500 to represent the market.
- A stock's beta is the percentage change in its return that we expect for each 1% change in the market's return.
- To estimate beta, we often use historical returns. Most data sources use five years of monthly returns to estimate beta.
- Beta also corresponds to the slope of the best-fitting line in the plot of a security's excess returns versus the market's excess returns. We use linear regression to find the best-fitting line.
- The beta of a portfolio is the weighted-average beta of the securities in the portfolio.

beta (β), p. 383
market capitaliza-
tion, p. 381
market index,
p. 382
market portfolio,
p. 381
market proxy,
p. 382
value-weighted
portfolio, p. 382

MyFinanceLab
Study Plan 12.3

Interactive Beta
Calculation, Using
Excel: Calculating
a Stock's Beta

12.4 Putting It All Together: The Capital Asset Pricing Model

- According to the CAPM, the risk premium of any security is equal to the market risk premium multiplied by the beta of the security. This relationship is called the security market line (SML), and it determines the expected or required return for an investment:

$$E[R_i] = r_f + \underbrace{\beta_i(E[R_{Mkt}] - r_f)}_{\text{Risk premium for security } i} \qquad (12.6)$$

Capital Asset
Pricing Model
(CAPM), p. 389
market or equity risk
premium, p. 389
required return,
p. 390
security market line
(SML), p. 391

MyFinanceLab
Study Plan 12.4

CRITICAL THINKING

1. What information do you need to compute the expected return of a portfolio?

2. What does correlation tell us?

3. Why isn't the total risk of a portfolio simply equal to the weighted average of the risks of the securities in the portfolio?

4. What does beta measure? How do we use beta?

5. What, intuitively, does the CAPM say drives expected return?

6. What relation is described by the security market line?

PROBLEMS

All problems are available in MyFinanceLab. The 🗔 *icon indicates problems that are easier to solve using Excel and have data in an Excel format available in MyFinanceLab. An asterisk * indicates problems with a higher level of difficulty.*

The Expected Return of a Portfolio

1. You buy 100 shares of Tidepool Co. for $40 each and 200 shares of Madfish, Inc., for $15 each. What are the weights in your portfolio?

2. Fremont Enterprises has an expected return of 15% and Laurelhurst News has an expected return of 20%. If you put 70% of your portfolio in Laurelhurst and 30% in Fremont, what is the expected return of your portfolio?

3. HNL has an expected return of 18% and KOA has an expected return of 22%. If you create a portfolio that is 60% HNL and 40% KOA, what is the expected return of the portfolio?

4. You are considering how to invest part of your retirement savings. You have decided to put $200,000 into three stocks: 50% of the money in GoldFinger (currently

$25/share), 25% of the money in Moosehead (currently $80/share), and the remainder in Venture Associates (currently $2/share). If GoldFinger stock goes up to $30/share, Moosehead stock drops to $60/share, and Venture Associates stock rises to $3 per share,

a. What is the new value of the portfolio?

b. What return did the portfolio earn?

c. If you don't buy or sell shares after the price change, what are your new portfolio weights?

5. You have $70,000. You put 20% of your money in a stock with an expected return of 12%, $30,000 in a stock with an expected return of 15%, and the rest in a stock with an expected return of 20%. What is the expected return of your portfolio?

6. There are two ways to calculate the expected return of a portfolio: Either calculate the expected return using the value and dividend stream of the portfolio as a whole, or calculate the weighted average of the expected returns of the individual stocks that make up the portfolio. Which return is higher?

The Volatility of a Portfolio

7. If the returns of two stocks have a correlation of 1, what does this imply about the relative movements in the stock prices?

8. Stocks A and B have the following returns (*see* MyFinanceLab *for the data in Excel format*):

	Stock A	Stock B
1	0.10	0.06
2	0.07	0.02
3	0.15	0.05
4	−0.05	0.01
5	0.08	−0.02

a. What are the expected returns of the two stocks?

b. What are the standard deviations of the returns of the two stocks?

c. If their correlation is 0.46, what is the expected return and standard deviation of a portfolio of 70% stock A and 30% stock B?

9. Using the data in the following table, estimate the average return and volatility for each stock (*see* MyFinanceLab *for the data in Excel format*).

	Realized Returns	
Year	Stock A	Stock B
2008	−10%	21%
2009	20%	30%
2010	5%	7%
2011	−5%	−3%
2012	2%	−8%
2013	9%	25%

10. Using your estimates from Problem 9 and the fact that the correlation of A and B is 0.48, calculate the volatility (standard deviation) of a portfolio that is 70% invested in stock A and 30% invested in stock B.

11. The following spreadsheet contains monthly returns for Cola Co. and Gas Co. for 2013. Using these data, estimate the average monthly return and volatility for each stock (*see* MyFinanceLab *for the data in Excel format*).

Date	Cola Co.	Gas Co.
Jan	−10.84%	−6.00%
Feb	2.36%	1.28%
Mar	6.60%	−1.86%
Apr	2.01%	−1.90%
May	18.36%	7.40%
June	−1.22%	−0.26%
July	2.25%	8.36%
Aug	−6.89%	−2.46%
Sep	−6.04%	−2.00%
Oct	13.61%	0.00%
Nov	3.51%	4.68%
Dec	0.54%	2.22%

12. Using the spreadsheet from Problem 11 and the fact that Cola Co. and Gas Co. have a correlation of 0.6083, calculate the volatility (standard deviation) of a portfolio that is 55% invested in Cola Co. stock and 45% invested in Gas Co. stock. Calculate the volatility by
a. Using Eq. 12.4.
b. Calculating the monthly returns of the portfolio and computing its volatility directly.
c. How do your results compare?

13. Using the data in Table 12.2,
a. Compute the annual returns for a portfolio with 25% invested in North Air, 25% invested in West Air, and 50% invested in Texas Oil.
b. What is the lowest annual return for your portfolio in part a? How does it compare with the lowest annual return of the individual stocks or portfolios in Table 12.2?

14. Using the data from Table 12.3, what is the volatility of an equally weighted portfolio of Microsoft and Coca-Cola stock?

15. Suppose Johnson & Johnson and the Walgreen Company have the expected returns and volatilities shown below, with a correlation of 22%.

	E[R]	SD[R]
Johnson & Johnson	7%	16%
Walgreen Company	10%	20%

For a portfolio that is equally invested in Johnson & Johnson's and Walgreen's stock, calculate
a. The expected return.
b. The volatility (standard deviation).

16. Arbor Systems and Gencore stocks both have a volatility of 40%. Compute the volatility of a portfolio with 50% invested in each stock if the correlation between the stocks is (a) +1, (b) 0.50, (c) 0, (d) −0.50, and (e) −1.0. In which cases is the volatility lower than that of the original stocks?

17. Suppose Wesley Publishing stock has a volatility of 60%, while Addison Printing stock has a volatility of 30%. If the correlation between these stocks is 25%, what is the volatility of the following portfolios of Addison and Wesley: (a) 100% Addison, (b) 75% Addison and 25% Wesley, and (c) 50% Addison and 50% Wesley?

18. You have a portfolio with a standard deviation of 30% and an expected return of 18%. You are considering adding one of the two stocks in the following table. If after adding the stock you will have 20% of your money in the new stock and 80% of your money in your existing portfolio, which one should you add?

	Expected Return	Standard Deviation	Correlation with Your Portfolio's Returns
Stock A	15%	25%	0.2
Stock B	15%	20%	0.6

19. Your client has $100,000 invested in stock A. She would like to build a two-stock portfolio by investing another $100,000 in either stock B or C. She wants a portfolio with an expected return of at least 14% and as low a risk as possible, but the standard deviation must be no more than 40%. What do you advise her to do, and what will be the portfolio's expected return and standard deviation?

	Expected Return	Standard Deviation	Correlation with A
A	15%	50%	1
B	13%	40%	0.2
C	13%	40%	0.3

Measuring Systematic Risk

20. Suppose all possible investment opportunities in the world are limited to the five stocks listed in the following table. What are the market portfolio weights (*see* MyFinanceLab *for the data in Excel format*)?

Stock	Price/Share ($)	Number of Shares Outstanding (millions)
A	10	10
B	20	12
C	8	3
D	50	1
E	45	20

21. Given the information below, construct a value-weighted portfolio of the four stocks if you have $500,000 to invest. That is, how much of your $500,000 would you invest in each stock?

Stock	Market Cap
OGG	$50 million
HNL	$75 million
KOA	$20 million
LIH	$10 million

22. Given $100,000 to invest, construct a value-weighted portfolio of the four stocks listed below (*see* MyFinanceLab *for the data in Excel format*).

Stock	Price/Share ($)	Number of Shares Outstanding (millions)
Golden Seas	13	1.00
Jacobs and Jacobs	22	1.25
MAG	43	30
PDJB	5	10

23. If one stock in a value-weighted portfolio goes up in price and all other stock prices remain the same, what trades are necessary to keep the portfolio value weighted?

24. You hear on the news that the S&P 500 was down 2% today relative to the risk-free rate (the market's excess return was −2%). You are thinking about your portfolio and your investments in Zynga and Procter & Gamble.
    a. If Zynga's beta is 1.4, what is your best guess as to Zynga's excess return today?
    b. If Procter & Gamble's beta is 0.5, what is your best guess as to P&G's excess return today?

25. The risk-free rate is 3% and you believe that the S&P 500's excess return will be 10% over the next year. If you invest in a stock with a beta of 1.2 (and a standard deviation of 30%), what is your best guess as to its expected return over the next year?

26. Go to Chapter Resources on MyFinanceLab and use the data in the spreadsheet provided to estimate the beta of Nike stock using linear regression.

27. The Chapter Resources section of MyFinanceLab has data on Microsoft and the S&P 500 from 1986 to 2006.
    a. Estimate Microsoft's beta using linear regression over the periods 1987–1991, 1992–1996, 1997–2001, and 2002–2006.
    b. Compare the four estimated betas. What do you conclude about how Microsoft's exposure to systematic risk changed over that 20-year period? What do you think explains the change?

Putting It All Together: The Capital Asset Pricing Model

28. Suppose the risk-free return is 4% and the market portfolio has an expected return of 10% and a standard deviation of 16%. Johnson & Johnson Corporation stock has a beta of 0.32. What is its expected return?

29. What is the sign of the risk premium of a negative-beta stock? Explain. (Assume the risk premium of the market portfolio is positive.)

30. EJH has a beta of 1.2, CSH has a beta of 0.6, and KMS has a beta of 1.0. If you put 25% of your money in EJH, 25% in CSH, and 50% in KMS, what is the beta of your portfolio?

31. Suppose Autodesk stock has a beta of 2.16, whereas Costco stock has a beta of 0.69. If the risk-free interest rate is 4% and the expected return of the market portfolio is 10%, what is the expected return of a portfolio that consists of 60% Autodesk stock and 40% Costco stock, according to the CAPM?

32. Suppose Intel stock has a beta of 1.6, whereas Boeing stock has a beta of 1. If the risk-free interest rate is 4% and the expected return of the market portfolio is 10%, according to the CAPM,
    a. What is the expected return of Intel stock?
    b. What is the expected return of Boeing stock?

    c. What is the beta of a portfolio that consists of 60% Intel stock and 40% Boeing stock?

    d. What is the expected return of a portfolio that consists of 60% Intel stock and 40% Boeing stock? (Show both ways to solve this.)

*33. You are thinking of buying a stock priced at $100 per share. Assume that the risk-free rate is about 4.5% and the market risk premium is 6%. If you think the stock will rise to $117 per share by the end of the year, at which time it will pay a $1 dividend, what beta would it need to have for this expectation to be consistent with the CAPM?

*34. You are analyzing a stock that has a beta of 1.2. The risk-free rate is 5% and you estimate the market risk premium to be 6%. If you expect the stock to have a return of 11% over the next year, should you buy it? Why or why not?

35. You have risen through the ranks of a coffee company, from the lowly green-apron barista to the coveted black apron, and all the way to CFO. A quick Internet check shows that your company's beta is 0.6. The risk-free rate is 5% and you believe the market risk premium to be 5.5%. What is your best estimate of investors' expected return on your company's stock (its cost of equity capital)?

36. At the beginning of 2007 (the year the iPhone was introduced), Apple's beta was 1.4 and the risk-free rate was about 4.5%. Apple's price was $84.84. Apple's price at the end of 2007 was 198.08. If you estimate the market risk premium to have been 6%, did Apple's managers exceed their investors' required return as given by the CAPM?

*37. You want to invest $50,000 in a portfolio with a beta of no more than 1.4 and an expected return of 12.4%. Bay Corp. has a beta of 1.2 and an expected return of 11.2%, and City Inc. has a beta of 1.8 and an expected return of 14.8%. The risk-free rate is 4%. You can invest in Bay Corp. and City Inc. How much will you invest in each?

Chapter 12 APPENDIX

Alternative Models of Systematic Risk

While the CAPM is the most widely used model for estimating the cost of capital in practice, recently some practitioners have tried to improve on the CAPM.

Problems with the CAPM in Practice

Researchers have found that using only the S&P 500, or some other simple proxy for the true market portfolio, has led to consistent pricing errors from the CAPM. That is, some stocks and portfolios of stocks earn consistently higher or lower returns than the CAPM would predict. For example, researchers have found that small stocks, stocks with high ratios of book-to-market value of equity, and stocks that have recently performed very well have consistently earned higher returns than the CAPM would predict using a simple stock market proxy for the market portfolio.

Multi-Factor Models

These findings have led researchers to add new portfolios to the CAPM pricing equation in an attempt to construct a better proxy for the true market portfolio. The goal is a proxy that captures the components of systematic risk that just using the S&P 500 alone misses.

risk factors Different components of systematic risk (used in a multi-factor model).

multi-factor model A model that uses more than one portfolio to capture systematic risk. Each portfolio can be thought of as either the risk factor itself or a portfolio of stocks correlated with an unobservable risk factor.

Arbitrage Pricing Theory (APT) One of the earliest multi-factor models, relying on the absence of arbitrage to price securities.

Although we might not be able to identify a perfect proxy for the true market portfolio, the market portfolio can be constructed from other portfolios. This observation implies that as long as the market portfolio can be constructed from a collection of portfolios, the collection itself can be used to measure risk. *Thus, it is not actually necessary to identify the market portfolio itself.* All that is required is to identify a collection of portfolios from which it can be constructed.

Thus, we can use a collection of portfolios to capture the components of systematic risk, referred to as **risk factors**. A model with more than one portfolio to capture risk is known as a **multi-factor model**. Each portfolio can be thought of as either the risk factor itself or a portfolio of stocks correlated with an unobservable risk factor. This particular form of the multi-factor model was originally developed by Professor Stephen Ross, but Professor Robert Merton developed an alternative multi-factor model earlier.[6] The model is also referred to as the **Arbitrage Pricing Theory (APT)**.

Fama-French-Carhart Factor Specification

Practitioners have added portfolios specifically to address the CAPM pricing errors. One such portfolio is constructed by buying small firms and selling large firms. This portfolio is widely known as the *small-minus-big (SMB) portfolio*. A second portfolio buys high book-to-market firms and sells low book-to-market firms, and we call it the *high-minus-low (HML) portfolio*. A third portfolio buys stocks that have recently done extremely well and sells those that have done extremely poorly. Since this portfolio addresses the problem that this extremely good and bad performance continues in the short run, it is called the *prior 1-year (PR1YR) momentum portfolio*.

The collection of these four portfolios—the stock market (Mkt), SMB, HML, and PR1YR—is the most popular collection of portfolios used as an alternative model to the CAPM and is one example of a multi-factor model. Using this collection, the expected return of security i is given by:

$$E[R_i] = r_f + \beta_i^{Mkt}(E[R_{Mkt}] - r_f) + \beta_i^{SMB}E[R_{SMB}] + \beta_i^{HML}E[R_{HML}]$$
$$+ \beta_i^{PR1YR}E[R_{PR1YR}] \qquad (12.8)$$

Fama-French-Carhart (FFC) factor specification A multi-factor model of risk and return in which the factor portfolios are the market, small-minus-big, high-minus-low, and prior 1-year momentum portfolios identified by Fama, French, and Carhart.

where β_i^{Mkt}, β_i^{SMB}, β_i^{HML}, and β_i^{PR1YR} are the factor betas of stock i and measure the sensitivity of the stock to each portfolio. Because the collection of portfolios in Eq. 12.8 (Mkt, SMB, HML, and PR1YR) were identified by Professors Eugene Fama, Kenneth French, and Mark Carhart, we refer to this collection of portfolios as the **Fama-French-Carhart (FFC) factor specification**.

The average monthly returns for each of the four portfolios in the FFC factor specification are given in Table 12.5.

TABLE 12.5

FFC Portfolio Average Monthly Returns (1926–2008)

	Average Monthly Return (%)
Mkt–r_f	0.61
SMB	0.25
HML	0.38
PR1YR	0.70

Source: Kenneth French: http://mba.tuck.dartmouth.edu/pages/faculty/ken.french/data_library.html.

---

[6]See Stephen A. Ross, "The Arbitrage Theory of Capital Asset Pricing," *Journal of Economic Theory*, 3 (December 1976): 343–362, and Robert C. Merton "An Intertemporal Capital Asset Pricing Model," *Econometrica*, 41(1973): 867–887.

EXAMPLE 12.9

Using the FFC Factor Specification to Calculate the Cost of Capital

MyFinanceLab

PROBLEM

You are currently considering making an investment in the fast food industry. You determine the project has the same level of non-diversifiable risk as investing in McDonald's stock. You use data over the past nine years to estimate the factor betas of McDonald's stock (ticker symbol: MCD). Specifically, you regress the monthly excess return (the realized return in each month minus the risk-free rate) of McDonald's stock on the return of each of the four-factor portfolios. You determine that the factor betas for MCD are:

$$\beta_{MCD}^{Mkt} = 0.687$$

$$\beta_{MCD}^{SMB} = -0.299$$

$$\beta_{MCD}^{HML} = -0.156$$

$$\beta_{MCD}^{PR1YR} = 0.123$$

The current risk-free monthly rate is 1.5%/12 = 0.125%. Determine the cost of capital by using the FFC factor specification.

SOLUTION

PLAN

First, gather the information you have. Combining the information in the problem with the data in Table 12.5, you have:

	Average Monthly Return (%)	MCD's β with Factor
Mkt$-r_f$	0.61	0.687
SMB	0.25	-0.299
HML	0.38	-0.156
PR1YR	0.70	0.123

Using the information you have collected along with the monthly risk-free rate of 0.125%, you can use Eq. 12.8 to calculate the monthly expected return for investing in McDonald's. From there, you can multiply by 12 to get the annual expected return, represented as an APR.

EXECUTE

Using Eq. 12.8, the monthly expected return of investing in McDonald's is:

$$E[R_{MCD}] = r_f + \beta_{MCD}^{Mkt}(E[R_{Mkt}] - r_f) + \beta_{MCD}^{SMB}E[R_{SMB}] + \beta_{MCD}^{HML}E[R_{HML}] + \beta_{MCD}^{PR1YR}E[R_{PR1YR}]$$

$$= 0.125\% + 0.687 \times 0.61\% - 0.299 \times 0.25\% - 0.156 \times 0.38\% + 0.123 \times 0.70\%$$

$$= 0.496\%$$

Expressed as an APR, the expected return is 0.496% × 12 = 5.95%

EVALUATE

By gathering all of the inputs and applying the FFC factor specification in the same way we would apply the CAPM, we can calculate this alternative estimate of the cost of capital for McDonald's stock. According to this approach, we would conclude that the annual cost of capital of the investment opportunity is about 5.95%.

As a comparison, a standard CAPM regression over the same time period leads to an estimated market beta of 0.54 for McDonald's—the market beta differs from the estimate of 0.687 above because we are using only a single factor in the CAPM regression. Using the historical excess return on the market implies an expected return of 0.125% + 0.54 × 0.61% = 0.454% per month, or about 5.5% per year.

13

The Cost of Capital

LEARNING OBJECTIVES

- Understand the drivers of the firm's overall cost of capital

- Measure the costs of debt, preferred stock, and common stock

- Compute a firm's overall, or weighted average, cost of capital

- Apply the weighted average cost of capital to value projects

- Adjust the cost of capital for the risk associated with the project

- Account for the direct costs of raising external capital

notation

$D\%$	fraction of the firm financed with debt		P_E	price of common stock equity
Div_1	dividend due in one year		P_{pfd}	price of preferred stock
Div_{pfd}	dividend on preferred stock		r_D	required return (cost of capital) for debt
$E\%$	fraction of the firm financed with equity		r_E	required return (cost of capital) of levered equity
FCF_t	incremental free cash flow in year t		r_{pfd}	required return (cost of capital) for preferred stock
g	expected growth rate for dividends		r_{wacc}	weighted average cost of capital
$P\%$	fraction of the firm financed with preferred stock		T_C	marginal corporate tax rate
			V_0^L	initial levered value

In Chapter 12, we learned how to determine a firm's equity cost of capital. In reality, most firms are financed with a combination of equity, debt, and other securities such as preferred stock. As a result, financial managers must determine their firm's overall cost of capital based on all sources of financing. This overall cost of capital is a critical input into the capital budgeting process. The Valuation Principle tells us that the value of a project is the present value of its benefits net of the present value of its costs. In capital budgeting, we implement this important concept with net present value (NPV). To calculate a project's NPV, we need a cost of capital to use as a discount rate.

In this chapter, we will learn how to calculate and use the firm's overall cost of capital, which is typically referred to as its *weighted average cost of capital (WACC)*. We will see that the WACC is a weighted average of the costs of capital from each of the firm's different financing sources. After we have learned how to estimate the WACC, we will apply it in capital budgeting. As part of that discussion, we will learn the conditions under which we can use the firm's overall cost of capital as a discount rate and identify those situations in which we will instead need to determine a cost of capital specific to a project or division of the firm.

13.1 A First Look at the Weighted Average Cost of Capital

Most firms draw on some combination of equity, debt, and other securities to raise the funds they need for investment. In this section, we examine the role of financing sources in determining the firm's overall cost of capital. We begin by stepping back to assess these financing sources in the context of the firm's balance sheet.

The Firm's Capital Structure

capital A firm's sources of financing—debt, equity, and other securities that it has outstanding.

A firm's sources of financing, which usually consist of debt and equity, represent its **capital**. The typical firm raises funds to invest by selling shares to stockholders (its equity) and borrowing from lenders (its debt). Recall the most basic form of the balance sheet, as represented in Figure 13.1. The left side of the balance sheet lists the firm's assets, and the right side describes the firm's capital.

capital structure The relative proportions of debt, equity, and other securities that a firm has outstanding.

The relative proportions of debt, equity, and other securities that a firm has outstanding constitute its **capital structure**. When corporations raise funds from outside investors, they must choose which type of security to issue. The most common choices are financing through equity alone and financing through a combination of debt and equity. Figure 13.2 shows the capital structures of Facebook, Apple, and UnitedContinental Holdings. Capital structures vary widely across firms. In Chapter 16, we will discuss how a firm sets its capital structure.

Opportunity Cost and the Overall Cost of Capital

Financial managers take into account each component of the firm's capital structure when determining the firm's overall cost of capital. Throughout the discussion that follows, keep in mind the intuition behind the term "cost of capital." When investors buy the stock

FIGURE 13.1

A Basic Balance Sheet

This figure provides a very basic balance sheet for reference. As discussed in Chapter 2, the two sides of the balance sheet must equal each other: Assets = Liabilities + Equity. The right side represents the way the assets are financed. In this chapter, we will focus on the required returns for the different forms of financing found on the right side of the balance sheet.

Assets	Liabilities and Equity
Current Assets	Debt
Long-Term Assets	Preferred Stock
	Equity

FIGURE 13.2

Two Capital Structures

This figure shows the capital structures of three real firms. Facebook is financed almost 100% with equity (shown in blue), Apple is financed 89% with equity, while United Continental Holdings is financed 56% with equity and 44% with debt, shaded in beige.

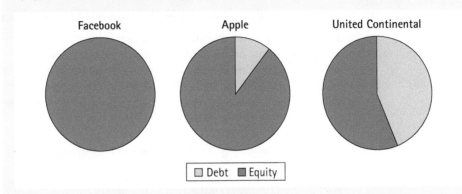

Source: Authors' calculations based on publicly available data in 2016. Percentages are based on market value of equity.

or bonds of a company, they forgo the opportunity to invest that money elsewhere. The expected return from those alternative investments constitutes an opportunity cost to them. Thus, to attract their investments as capital to the firm, the firm must offer potential investors an expected return equal to what they could expect to earn elsewhere for assuming the same level of risk. Providing this return is the cost a company bears in exchange for obtaining capital from investors.

Weighted Averages and the Overall Cost of Capital

Intuitively, the firm's overall cost of capital should be a blend of the costs of the different sources of capital. In fact, we calculate the firm's overall cost of capital as a weighted average of its equity and debt costs of capital, known as the firm's **weighted average cost of capital (WACC)**.

weighted average cost of capital (WACC) The average of a firm's equity and debt costs of capital, weighted by the fractions of the firm's value that correspond to equity and debt, respectively.

But what should the weights be? Imagine you owned all of the stock and all of the debt of the firm. If that was all you had in your portfolio, the return on your portfolio would be the total return of the firm. As we showed in Chapter 12, a portfolio return is the weighted average of the returns of the securities in the portfolio. In this case, the return on your portfolio—the total return of the firm—is a weighted average of the return you earn holding all the stock of the firm and the return you earn holding all of the debt. Since you hold all of each, your portfolio weights are just the relative amount of debt and equity issued by the firm. Thus, the weights we use in the WACC are the proportions of debt and equity used in the firm's capital structure. For example, if the firm is financed 30% by debt and 70% by equity, then the weights used in its WACC would be 30% on the debt cost of capital and 70% on the equity cost of capital.

This example suggests that you can determine the weights by looking at the right side of the firm's balance sheet. That assumption is correct, with one important modification: You must use the *market values* of the debt and equity to determine the proportions, not the accounting-based *book values* listed on the balance sheet. Recall from Chapter 2 that book values reflect historical costs, but market values are forward-looking, based on what the assets are expected to produce in the future. Holders of the firm's financial claims—equity and, if the firm has it, debt—assess the firm based on the market value of its assets, not the book value.

market-value balance sheet Similar to an accounting balance sheet, but all values are current market values rather than historical costs.

In fact, it is useful to think about the **market-value balance sheet**, where the assets, debt, and equity are all listed in terms of their market values, instead of their book values. Of course, the market-value balance sheet must still balance:

$$\text{Market Value of Equity} + \text{Market Value of Debt} = \text{Market Value of Assets} \qquad (13.1)$$

Equation 13.1 states that the total market value of all the claims (equity and debt) issued by the firm must be equal to the total market value of all its assets. This equality drives home the point that the equity and debt issued by the firm derive their value from the underlying assets they claim. The risk, and hence the required return, of the debt and equity of the firm are determined by the risk of the firm's assets. This point will be useful as we derive the firm's WACC.

Weighted Average Cost of Capital Calculations

In this section, we will develop the intuition behind the use of market-value weights as well as the link between the risk of the assets and the risk of the debt and equity claims on those assets.

unlevered A firm that does not have debt outstanding.

levered A firm that has debt outstanding.

leverage The relative amount of debt on a firm's balance sheet.

We begin with the straightforward case of the firm that does not issue debt—the **unlevered** firm that pays out all of the free cash flows generated by its assets to its equity holders. When some of a firm's financing comes from debt, we say the firm is **levered**. Just as a lever allows you to lift a heavy object by exerting relatively little force, so borrowing money through debt allows equity holders to control highly valued assets with relatively little investment of their own money. We refer to the relative amount of debt on the balance sheet as the firm's **leverage**.

The Weighted Average Cost of Capital: Unlevered Firm. If a firm is unlevered, so that it has no debt, all of the free cash flows generated by its assets are ultimately paid out to its equity holders. Because the free cash flows to the equity holders are the same as the free cash flows from the assets, the Valuation Principle tells us that the market value, risk, and cost of capital for the firm's equity are equal to the corresponding amounts for its assets. Given this relationship, we can estimate the firm's equity cost of capital using the Capital Asset Pricing Model (CAPM). The resulting estimate is the cost of capital for the firm as a whole. For example, Zynga does do not issue debt, so the cost of capital for Zynga's assets is the same as Zynga's cost of equity.

The Weighted Average Cost of Capital: Levered Firm. But what if the firm has debt? How should we incorporate the cost of this debt to determine the cost of capital for the firm's assets as a whole? The market-value balance sheet provides the answer. We can interpret the equality in Eq. 13.1 in terms of a portfolio: By holding a portfolio of the firm's equity and debt, we can get the same cash flows as if we held the assets directly. Because the return of a portfolio is equal to the weighted average of the returns of the securities in it, this equality implies the following relationship between the required returns (costs) of equity, debt, and assets:

Weighted Average Cost of Capital (Pretax)

$$r_{wacc} = \left(\begin{array}{c}\text{Fraction of Firm Value}\\\text{Financed by Equity}\end{array}\right)\left(\begin{array}{c}\text{Equity}\\\text{Cost of Capital}\end{array}\right)$$

$$+ \left(\begin{array}{c}\text{Fraction of Firm Value}\\\text{Financed by Debt}\end{array}\right)\left(\begin{array}{c}\text{Debt}\\\text{Cost of Capital}\end{array}\right)$$

$$= \left(\begin{array}{c}\text{Asset}\\\text{Cost of Capital}\end{array}\right) \qquad (13.2)$$

We now have the justification for our intuition that the overall cost of capital for a firm should be a weighted average of its equity and debt costs of capital. Eq. 13.2 shows that we can calculate the cost of capital of the firm's assets by computing the weighted average of the firm's equity and debt cost of capital. In the next section, we explore how to estimate the firm's costs of equity and debt capital.

EXAMPLE 13.1

Calculating the Weights in the WACC

MyFinanceLab

PROBLEM

Suppose Kenai Corp. has debt with a book (face) value of $10 million, trading at 95% of face value. It also has book equity of $10 million, and 1 million shares of common stock trading at $30 per share. What weights should Kenai use in calculating its WACC?

SOLUTION

PLAN

Equation 13.2 tells us that the weights are the fractions of Kenai financed with debt and financed with equity. Furthermore, these weights should be based on market values because the cost of capital is based on investors' current assessment of the value of the firm, not on accounting-based book values. As a consequence, we can ignore the book values of debt and equity.

EXECUTE

$10 million in debt trading at 95% of face value is $9.5 million in market value. One million shares of stock at $30 per share is $30 million in market value. So, the total market value of the firm is $39.5 million.
    The weights are

$$9.5 \div 39.5 = 24.1\% \text{ for debt and } 30 \div 39.5 = 75.9\% \text{ for equity.}$$

EVALUATE

When calculating its overall cost of capital, Kenai will use a weighted average of the cost of its debt capital and the cost of its equity capital, giving a weight of 24.1% to its cost of debt and a weight of 75.9% to its cost of equity.

CONCEPT CHECK

1. Why does a firm's capital have a cost?

2. Why do we use market-value weights in the weighted average cost of capital?

13.2   The Firm's Costs of Debt and Equity Capital

Section 13.1 made it clear that to measure the firm's overall cost of capital, we need to start by determining the cost of each type of capital a firm might use. We now turn to how a company measures the costs of its debt, preferred stock, and common stock. We will use General Electric (GE) as an example.

Cost of Debt Capital

We will start at the top of the right side of the balance sheet with the cost of the firm's debt. A firm's cost of debt is the interest rate it would have to pay to refinance its existing debt, such as through new bond issues. This rate differs from the coupon rate on the firm's existing debt, which reflects the interest rate the firm had to offer at the time the debt was issued.

Yield to Maturity and the Cost of Debt. Existing debt trades in the marketplace, so its price fluctuates to reflect both changes in the overall credit environment and changes in the risk specifically associated with the firm. As we learned in Chapter 6, the market price of the firm's existing debt implies a yield to maturity, which is the return that current purchasers of the debt would earn if they held the debt to maturity and received all of the payments as promised. So, we can use the yield to maturity to estimate the firm's current cost of debt: It is the yield that investors demand to hold the firm's debt (new or existing).[1]

Suppose General Electric has debt due in 2021 with a coupon rate of 5.3% priced at $1147.93 per $1000 face value. Because the market price of the debt is above its face value, investors in debt earn a yield that is lower than the 5.3% coupon rate. In fact, based on the timing of the remaining payments, this price implies a yield to maturity of 1.98%, which is an estimate of General Electric's current cost of debt. You would not need to actually compute the yield to maturity yourself because prices and their implied yields to maturity are always quoted together in the bond market.[2]

COMMON MISTAKE

Using the Coupon Rate as the Cost of Debt

A common mistake in estimating a company's overall cost of capital is to use the coupon rate on its existing debt as its debt cost of capital. The company's cost of capital is forward-looking and based on current conditions. By contrast, the coupon rate on existing debt is historical and set under potentially very different conditions. A better estimate of the firm's debt cost of capital is the yield to maturity of its existing debt, which is the promised return its lenders currently demand. As we mention in the text, it would be even better to adjust the promised yield to maturity for expected losses to get an estimate of investors' actual expected return.

Consider KB Homes as an example. KB had bonds due in 2014 that were originally issued in 2004; these bonds had a coupon rate of 5.75%. With the collapse of the U.S. real estate market in 2008, KB Homes' performance suffered and the risk that it might not be able to meet all of its debt obligations increased. By mid-2010, those 5.75% coupon bonds were rated BB (below investment grade) and trading at a yield to maturity of about 8.6%. Thus, to be willing to take a creditor position in KB, investors demanded a yield to maturity of 8.6%. Taking into account the probability of default and the expected loss in default, BB-rated bonds had an average expected loss of 1.3%. Thus, the true expected return was closer to 7.3% (8.6% promised minus 1.3% expected loss).

So, which is a better estimate of the cost of debt capital for KB in 2010: the 5.75% coupon or something based on the 8.6% yield to maturity? It would be a mistake for KB to use 5.75% as its cost of debt capital. The 5.75% rate, which was set under different circumstances, is not a relevant measure of KB's debt holders' required return in 2010, so it should not enter into the WACC calculation. Because of the default risk, the 7.3% we calculated would be a much better estimate of KB's cost of debt capital.

Taxes and the Cost of Debt. In the case of debt, the return paid to the debt holders is not the same as the cost to the firm. How could this be? The difference arises because interest paid on debt is a tax-deductible expense. When a firm uses debt financing, the cost of the interest it must pay is offset to some extent by the tax savings from the tax deduction.

For example, suppose a firm with a 35% tax rate borrows $100,000 at 10% interest per year. Then its net cost at the end of the year is calculated as follows:

		Year-End
Interest expense	$r_D \times \$100,000 =$	$10,000
Tax savings	$- \text{Tax Rate} \times r_D \times \$100,000 =$	−$3500
Effective after-tax interest expense	$r_D \times (1 - \text{Tax Rate}) \times \$100,000 =$	$6500

effective cost of the debt A firm's net cost of interest on its debt after accounting for the interest tax deduction.

The **effective cost of the debt**—the firm's net cost of interest on its debt after taxes—is only $6500/$100,000 = 6.50% of the loan amount, rather than the full 10% interest. Thus, the tax deductibility of interest lowers the effective cost of debt financing for the firm.

---

[1]In fact, the yield to maturity is the *most* the firm will pay because there is some risk the firm may not repay its debt. The expected return on the bond can be significantly less than the *promised* yield to maturity during times when the firm might be close to financial distress. However, outside of these times, the yield on an A-rated bond such as General Electric's provides a reasonable estimate of its expected return.

[2]Chapter 6 demonstrated how to find current prices and yields to maturity for corporate bonds online using the Web site http://www.finra.org/marketdata.

More generally, with tax-deductible interest and denoting the corporate tax rate as T_C, the effective after-tax borrowing rate is

$$r_D(1 - T_C) \tag{13.3}$$

EXAMPLE 13.2

Effective Cost of Debt

MyFinanceLab

PROBLEM

By using the yield to maturity on General Electric's debt, we found that its pretax cost of debt is 1.98%. If General Electric's tax rate is 35%, what is its effective cost of debt?

SOLUTION

PLAN

We can use Eq. 13.3 to calculate General Electric's effective cost of debt:

$$r_D = 0.0198 \, (\text{pretax cost of debt})$$
$$T_C = 0.35 \, (\text{corporate tax rate})$$

EXECUTE

General Electric's effective cost of debt is $0.0198\,(1 - 0.35) = 0.01287 = 1.287\%$.

EVALUATE

For every new $1000 it borrows, General Electric would pay its bondholders $0.0198\,(\$1000) = \$19.80$ in interest every year. Because it can deduct that $19.80 in interest from its income, every dollar in interest saves General Electric 35 cents in taxes, so the interest tax deduction reduces the firm's tax payment to the government by $0.35\,(\$19.80) = \$6.93$. Thus, General Electric's net cost of $1000 of debt is the $19.80 it pays minus the $6.93 in reduced tax payments, which is $12.87 per $1000 or 1.287%.

We have used corporate bonds as an example for estimating the cost of debt. Many smaller companies do not have access to the bond market and use bank debt instead. In their case, they typically have a good sense of their cost of debt from discussions with their banker about interest rates on new loans.

Cost of Preferred Stock Capital

Firms may also raise capital by issuing preferred stock. Typically, holders of the preferred stock are promised a fixed dividend, which must be paid "in preference to" (i.e., before) any dividends can be paid to common stockholders.

If the preferred dividend is known and fixed, we can estimate the preferred stock's cost of capital using Eq. 7.7 of Chapter 7,

$$r_E = \frac{Div_1}{P_0} + g$$

where the growth rate $g = 0$. Thus,

$$\text{Cost of Preferred Stock Capital} = \frac{\text{Preferred Dividend}}{\text{Preferred Stock Price}} = \frac{Div_{pfd}}{P_{pfd}} \tag{13.4}$$

For example, assume General Electric's series D preferred stock has a price of $85.83 and an annual dividend of $3.50. Its cost of preferred stock, therefore, is $3.50 \div 85.83 = 4.08\%$.[3]

---

[3]General Electric previously had three sets of outstanding preferred shares, but exchanged them for Series D in early 2016.

Cost of Common Stock Capital

As we learned in Chapter 12, a company cannot directly observe its cost of common stock (equity), but must instead estimate it. We now present and compare the two major methods for doing so.

Capital Asset Pricing Model. The most common approach is to use the CAPM as presented in Chapter 12. To summarize that approach:

1. Estimate the firm's beta of equity, typically by regressing 60 months of the company's returns against 60 months of returns for a market proxy such as the S&P 500.
2. Determine the risk-free rate, typically by using the yield on Treasury bills or bonds.
3. Estimate the market risk premium, typically by comparing historical returns on a market proxy to historical risk-free rates.
4. Apply the CAPM:

$$\text{Cost of Equity} = \text{Risk-Free Rate} + \text{Equity Beta} \times \text{Market Risk Premium}$$

For example, suppose the equity beta of General Electric is 1.30, the yield on 10-year Treasury notes is 3%, and you estimate the market risk premium to be 6%. General Electric's cost of equity is $3\% + 1.30 \times 6\% = 10.8\%$.

Constant Dividend Growth Model. Another way to estimate a company's cost of equity comes from the constant dividend growth model (CDGM) introduced in Chapter 7. Equation 7.7 from Chapter 7 shows that

$$\text{Cost of Equity} = \frac{\text{Dividend (in one year)}}{\text{Current Price}} + \text{Dividend Growth Rate} = \frac{Div_1}{P_E} + g \quad (13.5)$$

Thus, to estimate the cost of equity, we need the current price of the stock, the expected dividend in one year, and an estimate of the dividend growth rate. The current price of the stock is easy to obtain online. We may even have a reasonable estimate of next year's dividend. However, as we discussed in Chapter 7, estimating the future dividend growth rate can be very difficult. For example, General Electric's recent annual dividend history is $0.58 (2011), $0.68 (2012), $0.76 (2013), $0.88 (2014), and $0.92 (2015). Perhaps it is reasonable to assume that 2016's dividend will also be $0.92 per year, but what about the dividend's long-term growth rate? The historical growth has been uneven.

Rather than looking backward at historical growth, one common approach is to use estimates produced by stock analysts, as these estimates are forward-looking. As discussed in Chapter 7, if General Electric keeps its dividend payout rate constant, then the long-run growth in dividends will equal the long-run growth in earnings. In early-2016, the average forecast for GE's long-run earnings growth rate was 12.7%. Thus, with an expected dividend in one year of $0.92, a price of $30.05, and long-run dividend growth of 12.7%, the CDGM estimates GE's cost of equity as follows (using Eq. 13.5):

$$\text{Cost of Equity} = \frac{Div_1}{P_E} + g = \frac{\$0.92}{\$30.05} + 0.127 = 0.158, \text{ or } 15.8\%$$

We should not be surprised that the two estimates of General Electric's cost of equity (10.8% and 15.8%) do not match, because each was based on different assumptions. Furthermore, even given an estimate of future growth of dividends, Eq. 13.5 makes an assumption that future dividend growth will continue at a constant rate. This assumption is unlikely to be valid for most firms. For example, even though General Electric's dividend has grown steadily over 5 years, it was forced to reduce its dividend substantially in 2009 during the financial crisis. Also note that many young, growing firms do not pay a dividend and have no plans to do so in the near future.

	Capital Asset Pricing Model	**Constant Dividend Growth Model**
TABLE 13.1		
Estimating the Cost of Equity		
Inputs	Equity beta	Current stock price
	Risk-free rate	Expected dividend next year
	Market risk premium	Future dividend growth rate
Major Assumptions	Estimated beta is correct	Dividend estimate is correct
	Market risk premium is accurate	Growth rate matches market expectations
	CAPM is the correct model	Future dividend growth is constant

We could use any model relating a firm's stock price to its future cash flows to estimate its cost of equity—the CDGM is just one of the possible models. For example, we could use the discounted free cash flow model from Chapter 10 to solve for the firm's cost of equity.

CAPM and CDGM Comparison. Because of the difficulties with the CDGM, the CAPM is the most popular approach for estimating the cost of equity. Table 13.1 compares the two approaches.

EXAMPLE 13.3

Estimating the Cost of Equity

MyFinanceLab

PROBLEM

Assume the equity beta for Johnson & Johnson (ticker: JNJ) is 0.55. The yield on 10-year treasuries is 3%, and you estimate the market risk premium to be 6%. Furthermore, Johnson & Johnson issues dividends at an annual rate of $2.81. Its current stock price is $92.00, and you expect dividends to increase at a constant rate of 4% per year. Estimate J&J's cost of equity in two ways.

SOLUTION

PLAN

The two ways to estimate J&J's cost of equity are to use the CAPM and the CDGM.
1. The CAPM requires the risk-free rate, an estimate of the equity's beta, and an estimate of the market risk premium. We can use the yield on 10-year Treasury notes as the risk-free rate.
2. The CDGM requires the current stock price, the expected dividend next year, and an estimate of the constant future growth rate for the dividend.

Risk-free rate: 3%	Current price: $92.00
Equity beta: 0.55	Expected dividend: $2.81
Market risk premium: 6%	Estimated future dividend growth rate: 4%

We can use the CAPM from Chapter 12 to estimate the cost of equity using the CAPM approach and Eq. 13.5 to estimate it using the CDGM approach.

EXECUTE

1. The CAPM says that

$$\text{Cost of Equity} = \text{Risk-Free Rate} + \text{Equity Beta} \times \text{Market Risk Premium}$$

For J&J, this implies that its cost of equity is 3% + 0.55 × 6% = 6.3%.

2. The CDGM says

$$\text{Cost of Equity} = \frac{\text{Dividend (in one year)}}{\text{Current Price}} + \text{Dividend Growth Rate} = \frac{\$2.81}{\$92.00} + 4\% = 7.1\%$$

EVALUATE

According to the CAPM, the cost of equity capital is 6.3%; the CDGM produces a result of 7.1%. Because of the different assumptions we make when using each method, the two methods do not have to produce the same answer—in fact, it would be highly unlikely that they would. When the two approaches produce

(Continued)

different answers, we must examine the assumptions we made for each approach and decide which set of assumptions is more realistic. We can also see what assumption about future dividend growth would be necessary to make the answers converge. By rearranging the CDGM and using the cost of equity we estimated from the CAPM, we have

$$\text{Dividend Growth Rate} = \text{Cost of Equity} - \frac{\text{Dividend (in one year)}}{\text{Current Price}} = 6.3\% - 3.1\% = 3.2\%$$

Thus, if we believe that J&J's dividends will grow at a rate of 3.2% per year, the two approaches would produce the same cost of equity estimate.

CONCEPT CHECK

3. How can you measure a firm's cost of debt?
4. What are the major tradeoffs in using the CAPM versus the CDGM to estimate the cost of equity?

13.3 A Second Look at the Weighted Average Cost of Capital

Now that we have estimated the costs of General Electric's different sources of capital, we are ready to calculate the firm's overall WACC. The weights are the percentage of the firm's value financed by equity, preferred stock, and debt. We can represent these as $E\%$, $P\%$, and $D\%$, respectively, and note that they must sum to 100% (i.e., we must account for all the sources of financing).

WACC Equation

Formally, denoting the cost of equity, preferred and debt capital as r_E, r_{pfd}, and r_D, and the corporate tax rate as T_C, the WACC is

Weighted Average Cost of Capital

$$r_{wacc} = r_E E\% + r_{pfd} P\% + r_D (1 - T_C) D\% \tag{13.6}$$

For a company that does not have preferred stock, the WACC condenses to

$$r_{wacc} = r_E E\% + r_D (1 - T_C) D\% \tag{13.7}$$

For example, in 2016, the market values of General Electric's common stock, preferred stock, and debt were $276,880 million, $6,000 million, and $198,270 million, respectively. Its total value was, therefore, $276,880 million + $6,000 million + $198,270 million = $481,150 million. Given the costs of common stock (CAPM estimate), preferred stock, and debt we have already computed, General Electric's WACC in 2016 was

$$r_{wacc} = r_E E\% + r_{pfd} P\% + r_D (1 - T_C) D\%$$

$$r_{wacc} = 10.8\%\left(\frac{276,880}{481,150}\right) + 4.08\%\left(\frac{6,000}{481,150}\right) + 1.98\% (1 - 0.35)\left(\frac{198,270}{481,150}\right)$$

$$r_{wacc} = 6.8\%$$

EXAMPLE 13.4
Computing the WACC

MyFinanceLab

PROBLEM

Assume the expected return on Target's equity is 11.5%, and the firm has a yield to maturity on its debt of 6%. Debt accounts for 18% and equity for 82% of Target's total market value. If its tax rate is 35%, what is an estimate of this firm's WACC?

SOLUTION

PLAN

We can compute the WACC using Eq. 13.7. To do so, we need to know the costs of equity and debt, their proportions in Target's capital structure, and the firm's tax rate. We have all that information, so we are ready to proceed.

EXECUTE

$$r_{wacc} = r_E E\% + r_D (1 - T_C) D\% = (0.115)(0.82) + (0.06)(1 - 0.35)(0.18)$$
$$= 0.101, \text{ or } 10.1\%$$

EVALUATE

Even though we cannot observe the expected return of Target's investments directly, we can use the expected return on its equity and debt and the WACC formula to estimate it, adjusting for the tax advantage of debt. Target needs to earn at least a 10.1% return on its investment in current and new stores to satisfy both its debt and equity holders.

Weighted Average Cost of Capital in Practice

The WACC is driven by the risk of a company's line of business and, because of the tax effect of interest, its leverage. As a result, WACCs vary widely across industries and companies. Figure 13.3 presents the WACC for several real companies to provide a sense of the degree to which the cost of capital can vary. Some lines of business are clearly riskier than others.

FIGURE 13.3

WACCs for Real Companies

The cost of equity is computed using the company's equity beta, a risk-free rate of 3%, and a market risk premium of 6%. The cost of debt is based on market yield to maturities of the debt. The percent equity and percent debt are determined from the company's market capitalization and balance sheet. The WACC is computed using Eq. 13.7 with a 35% tax rate and is shown in the accompanying bar graph. "N/A" means that the cost of debt is not applicable and refers to companies that have no debt.

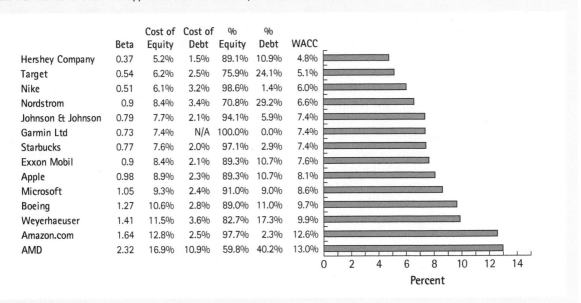

	Beta	Cost of Equity	Cost of Debt	% Equity	% Debt	WACC
Hershey Company	0.37	5.2%	1.5%	89.1%	10.9%	4.8%
Target	0.54	6.2%	2.5%	75.9%	24.1%	5.1%
Nike	0.51	6.1%	3.2%	98.6%	1.4%	6.0%
Nordstrom	0.9	8.4%	3.4%	70.8%	29.2%	6.6%
Johnson & Johnson	0.79	7.7%	2.1%	94.1%	5.9%	7.4%
Garmin Ltd	0.73	7.4%	N/A	100.0%	0.0%	7.4%
Starbucks	0.77	7.6%	2.0%	97.1%	2.9%	7.4%
Exxon Mobil	0.9	8.4%	2.1%	89.3%	10.7%	7.6%
Apple	0.98	8.9%	2.3%	89.3%	10.7%	8.1%
Microsoft	1.05	9.3%	2.4%	91.0%	9.0%	8.6%
Boeing	1.27	10.6%	2.8%	89.0%	11.0%	9.7%
Weyerhaeuser	1.41	11.5%	3.6%	82.7%	17.3%	9.9%
Amazon.com	1.64	12.8%	2.5%	97.7%	2.3%	12.6%
AMD	2.32	16.9%	10.9%	59.8%	40.2%	13.0%

Source: Authors' calculations based on publicly available information in 2016.

For example, selling chocolate, as Hershey does, is a fairly low-risk proposition, but being an online retailer (Amazon) or semiconductor company (AMD) is much riskier.

Methods in Practice

We now turn to some issues that arise for financial managers when they are estimating the WACC in practice.

Net Debt. When calculating the weights for the WACC, it is increasingly common practice to make an adjustment to the debt. Many practitioners now use **net debt**, the total debt outstanding minus any cash balances:

net debt Total debt outstanding minus any cash balances.

$$\text{Net Debt} = \text{Debt} - \text{Cash and Risk-Free Securities} \tag{13.8}$$

Why subtract a company's cash from its debt? The assets on a firm's balance sheet include any holdings of cash or risk-free securities. If a firm holds $1 in cash and has $1 of risk-free debt, then the interest earned on the cash will equal the interest paid on the debt. The cash flows from each source cancel each other, just as if the firm held no cash and no debt. In fact, we can view cash as being equivalent to negative debt. Significant excess cash on a firm's balance sheet can complicate the assessment of the risk (and hence the cost of capital) of the assets the firm actually uses in the course of business. Thus, when trying to evaluate a firm's business assets separate from any cash holdings, practitioners often measure the leverage of the firm in terms of its net debt and measure the market value of a firm's business assets using its enterprise value. Recall Chapter 2's definition of the enterprise value as the market value of its equity plus its net debt.

Using this approach, the weights in the WACC would then be

$$\left(\frac{\text{Market Value of Equity}}{\text{Enterprise Value}} \right) \text{ and } \left(\frac{\text{Net Debt}}{\text{Enterprise Value}} \right)$$

For firms with substantial excess cash reserves, this adjustment could be important. For firms with relatively low levels of cash, it will not have a large effect on the overall WACC estimate.

The Risk-Free Interest Rate. Estimating the equity cost of capital using the CAPM requires the risk-free interest rate. The risk-free interest rate is generally determined using the yields of U.S. Treasury securities, which are free from default risk. But which horizon should we choose? The CAPM states that we should use the risk-free interest corresponding to the investment horizon of the firm's investors. When surveyed, the vast majority of large firms and financial analysts report using the yields of long-term (10- to 30-year) bonds to determine the risk-free rate.[4]

The Market Risk Premium. Using the CAPM also requires an estimate of the market risk premium. As mentioned in Chapter 11, one way to estimate the market risk premium is to look at historical data. Because we are interested in the *future* market risk premium, we face a tradeoff in terms of the amount of data we use. As noted in Chapter 11, it takes many years of data to produce even moderately accurate estimates of expected returns—yet data that are very old may have little relevance for investors' expectations of the market risk premium today.

Table 13.2 reports excess returns of the S&P 500 versus one-year and 10-year Treasury rates. Since 1926, the S&P 500 has produced an average return of 7.7% above the rate

[4]See Robert Bruner, et al., "Best Practices in Estimating the Cost of Capital: Survey and Synthesis," *Financial Practice and Education* 8 (1998): 13–28.

TABLE 13.2

Historical Excess
Returns of the S&P 500
Compared to One-Year
Treasury Bills
and 10-Year U.S.
Treasury Securities

| S&P 500 Excess | Period | |
Return Versus	1926–2015	1965-2015
One-year Treasury	7.7%	5.0%
10-year Treasury*	5.9%	3.9%

*Based on a comparison of compounded returns over a 10-year holding period.

for one-year Treasury securities. However, some evidence indicates that the market risk premium has declined over time. Since 1965, the S&P 500 has shown an excess return of only 5.0% over the rate for one-year Treasury securities. Compared with 10-year Treasury securities, the S&P 500 had an average excess return of only 3.9% (due primarily to the fact that 10-year Treasury bond rates tend to be higher than one-year rates).

How can we explain this decline? One explanation may be that as more investors have begun to participate in the stock market and the costs of constructing a diversified portfolio have declined, investors have tended to hold less risky portfolios. As a result, the return they require as compensation for taking on that risk has diminished. In addition, the overall volatility of the market has declined over time. Some researchers believe that the future expected returns for the market are likely to be even lower than these historical numbers, in a range of 3% to 5% over Treasury bills.[5] Consequently, many financial managers currently use market risk premiums closer to 5%, rather than 7%.

CONCEPT
CHECK

5. Why do different companies have different WACCs?

6. What are the tradeoffs in estimating the market risk premium?

13.4 Using the WACC to Value a Project

A project's cost of capital depends on its risk. When the market risk of the project is similar to the average market risk of the firm's investments, then its cost of capital is equivalent to the cost of capital for a portfolio of all the firm's securities. In other words, the project's cost of capital is equal to the firm's WACC. As shown in Eq. 13.6, the WACC incorporates the benefit of the interest tax deduction by using the firm's *after-tax* cost of capital for debt.

Because the WACC incorporates the tax savings from debt, we can compute the value of an investment including the benefit of the interest tax deduction given the firm's leverage policy, sometimes called the investment's **levered value**. To do so, we discount the firm's future incremental free cash flow using the WACC, a process we refer to as the **WACC method**. Specifically, if FCF_t is the expected incremental free cash flow of an investment at the end of year t, then the Valuation Principle tells us that the investment's levered value, V_0^L, is

levered value The value of an investment, including the benefit of the interest tax deduction, given the firm's leverage policy.

WACC method Discounting future incremental free cash flows using the firm's WACC. This method produces the levered value of a project.

$$V_0^L = FCF_0 + \frac{FCF_1}{1 + r_{wacc}} + \frac{FCF_2}{(1 + r_{wacc})^2} + \frac{FCF_3}{(1 + r_{wacc})^3} + \cdots \qquad (13.9)$$

The intuition for the WACC method is that the firm's WACC represents the average return the firm must pay to its investors (both debt and equity holders) on an after-tax basis. Thus, to have a positive NPV, a project with the same risk as the average risk for the firm's projects should generate an expected return of at least the firm's WACC.

___

[5]See I. Welch, "Views of Financial Economists on the Equity Premium and Other Issues," *Journal of Business* 73 (2000): 501–537 (with 2009 update), and J. Graham and C. Harvey, "The Equity Risk Premium in 2008: Evidence from the Global CFO Outlook Survey," SSRN 2008, "The Equity Risk Premium in 2008: Evidence from the Global CFO Outlook Survey," SSRN 2008, and Ivo Welch and Amit Goyal, "A Comprehensive Look at The Empirical Performance of Equity Premium Prediction," Review of Financial Studies 21 (2008): 1455–1508.

EXAMPLE 13.5

The WACC Method

MyFinanceLab

PROBLEM

Suppose Anheuser-Busch InBev is considering introducing a new ultra-light beer with zero calories to be called BudZero. The firm believes that the beer's flavor and appeal to calorie-conscious drinkers will make it a success. The cost of bringing the beer to market is $200 million, but Anheuser-Busch InBev expects first-year incremental free cash flows from BudZero to be $100 million and to grow at 3% per year thereafter. If Anheuser-Busch InBev's WACC is 5.7%, should it go ahead with the project?

SOLUTION

PLAN

We can use the WACC method shown in Eq. 13.9 to value BudZero and then subtract the up-front cost of $200 million. We will need Anheuser-Busch InBev's WACC, which is 5.7%.

EXECUTE

The cash flows for BudZero are a growing perpetuity. Applying the growing perpetuity formula with the WACC method, we have

$$V_0^l = FCF_0 + \frac{FCF_1}{r_{wacc} - g} = -\$200 \text{ million} + \frac{\$100 \text{ million}}{0.057 - 0.03} = \$3,503.7 \text{ million } (\$3.5 \text{ billion})$$

EVALUATE

The BudZero project has a positive NPV because it is expected to generate a return on the $200 million far in excess of Anheuser-Busch InBev's WACC of 5.7%. As discussed in Chapter 8, taking positive-NPV projects adds value to the firm. Here, we can see that the value is created by exceeding the required return of the firm's investors.

Key Assumptions

While it is common practice to use the WACC as the discount rate in capital budgeting, it is important to be aware of the underlying assumptions. We examine the critical assumptions here and then explore these assumptions further in the context of an application.

Assumption 1: Average Risk. We assume initially that the market risk of the project is equivalent to the average market risk of the firm's investments. In that case, we assess the project's cost of capital based on the risk of the firm.

debt-equity ratio A ratio of the market value of debt to the market value of equity.

Assumption 2: Constant Debt-Equity Ratio. We assume that the firm adjusts its leverage continuously to maintain a constant ratio of the market value of debt to the market value of equity—a relationship referred to as the **debt-equity ratio**. This policy determines the amount of debt the firm will take on when it accepts a new project. It also implies that the risk of the firm's equity and debt, and therefore its WACC, will not fluctuate owing to leverage changes.

Assumption 3: Limited Leverage Effects. We assume initially that the main effect of leverage on valuation follows from the interest tax deduction. We assume that any other factors (such as possible financial distress) are not significant at the level of debt chosen. We discuss these other factors in detail in Chapter 16.

Assumptions in Practice. These assumptions are reasonable for many projects and firms. The first assumption is likely to fit typical projects of firms with investments concentrated in a single industry. In that case, the market risk of both the project and the firm will primarily depend on the sensitivity of the industry to the overall economy. The second assumption, while unlikely to hold exactly, reflects the fact that firms tend to increase their levels of debt as they grow larger; some may even have an explicit target for their debt-equity ratio.[6] Finally, for firms without very high levels of debt, the interest tax deduction is likely to be the most important factor affecting the capital budgeting decision. Hence, the third assumption is a reasonable starting point to begin our analysis.

Of course, while these three assumptions may be a reasonable approximation in many situations, there are certainly projects and firms for which they do not apply. In the following section, we apply the WACC method under all three assumptions. Next, we relax the first assumption, which states that the project has average risk. (We will relax the other two assumptions in later chapters.)

WACC Method Application: Extending the Life of a GE Facility

Let's apply the WACC method to value a project. Suppose GE is considering an investment that would extend the life of one of its facilities for four years. The project would require up-front costs of $6.67 million plus a $24 million investment in equipment. The equipment will be obsolete in four years and will be depreciated via the straight-line method over that period. During the next four years, however, GE expects annual sales of $60 million per year from this facility. Material costs and operating expenses are expected to total $25 million and $9 million, respectively, per year. Finally, GE expects no net working capital requirements for the project, and it pays a corporate tax rate of 35%.

Using this information, the spreadsheet in Table 13.3 forecasts the project's expected free cash flow. Assume that the market risk of the project of extending the life of the facility is the same as that for GE's overall business. As a consequence, we can use GE's WACC to compute the NPV of the project.

We can determine the value of the project, including the present value of the interest tax deduction from the debt, by calculating the present value of its future free cash flows, V_0^L, using the WACC method and GE's WACC of 6.8%, which we computed in Section 13.3:

$$V_0^L = \frac{19}{1.068} + \frac{19}{1.068^2} + \frac{19}{1.068^3} + \frac{19}{1.068^4} = \$64.65 \text{ million}$$

TABLE 13.3

Expected Free Cash Flow from GE's Facility Project

	Year	0	1	2	3	4
1						
2	**Incremental Earnings Forecast ($million)**					
3	Sales	—	60.00	60.00	60.00	60.00
4	Cost of Goods Sold	—	−25.00	−25.00	−25.00	−25.00
5	**Gross Profit**	—	35.00	35.00	35.00	35.00
6	Operating Expenses	−6.67	−9.00	−9.00	−9.00	−9.00
7	Depreciation	—	−6.00	−6.00	−6.00	−6.00
8	**EBIT**	−6.67	20.00	20.00	20.00	20.00
9	Income Tax at 35%	2.33	−7.00	−7.00	−7.00	−7.00
10	**Unlevered Net Income**	−4.34	13.00	13.00	13.00	13.00
11	**Incremental Free Cash Flow ($ million)**					
12	Plus: Depreciation	—	6.00	6.00	6.00	6.00
13	Less: Capital Expenditures	−24.00	—	—	—	—
14	Less: Increases in NWC	—	—	—	—	—
15	**Incremental Free Cash Flow**	−28.34	19.00	19.00	19.00	19.00

---

[6]We discuss the tradeoff between debt and equity and the concept of a target debt-equity ratio in Chapter 16.

Because the up-front after-tax cost of extending the facility's life is only $28.34 million, this project is a good idea. Taking the project results in an NPV of $64.65 million − $28.34 million = $36.31 million for the firm.

Summary of the WACC Method

To summarize, the key steps in the WACC valuation method are as follows:

1. Determine the incremental free cash flow of the investment.
2. Compute the weighted average cost of capital using Eq. 13.6.
3. Compute the value of the investment, including the tax benefit of leverage, by discounting the incremental free cash flow of the investment using the WACC.

In many firms, the corporate treasurer performs the second step, calculating the firm's WACC. This rate can then be used throughout the firm as the companywide cost of capital for new investments *that are of comparable risk to the rest of the firm and that will not alter the firm's debt-equity ratio*. Employing the WACC method in this way is very simple and straightforward. As a result, this method is the most commonly used in practice for capital budgeting purposes.

CONCEPT CHECK

7. What are the main assumptions you make when you use the WACC method?
8. What inputs do you need to be ready to apply the WACC method?

13.5 Project-Based Costs of Capital

Up to this point we have assumed that both the risk and the leverage of the project under consideration matched those characteristics for the firm as a whole. This assumption allowed us, in turn, to assume that the cost of capital for a project matched the firm's cost of capital.

In reality, specific projects often differ from the average investment made by the firm. Consider again General Electric Company (GE), a large firm with many divisions that operate in completely different lines of business. Projects in GE's health-care division are likely to have different market risk than projects in its air transportation equipment division or in its appliance division. Projects may also vary in terms of the amount of leverage they will support—for example, acquisitions of real estate or capital equipment are often highly levered, while investments in intellectual property are not. We will study the effect of leverage on the cost of capital when we cover the leverage decision in Chapter 16. In this section, we show how to calculate the cost of capital for the project's cash flows when a project's risk differs from the firm's overall risk.

COMMON MISTAKE

Using a Single Cost of Capital in Multi-Divisional Firms

Many firms combine business units with widely different market risk. Yet some of them use a single cost of capital to evaluate projects throughout the organization. Using the same cost of capital for projects that have different riskiness, is, of course, a mistake, and will result in the firm taking on too many risky projects and too few safer projects. That is, when the same cost of capital is used for all investment opportunities, regardless of their riskiness, riskier projects will be discounted at too low a cost of capital, making negative NPV investments appear to be positive NPV and be accepted. Similarly, less risky projects will be discounted at too high a cost of capital, and so may be erroneously rejected.

Because survey evidence suggests that this mistake is quite common, Professors Philipp Krüger, Augustin Landier, and David Thesmar* looked at the behavior of conglomerates and found evidence that they were making this mistake. For each conglomerate, they identified the most important division, what they termed the *core-division*. They then demonstrated that, on average, conglomerates invest relatively less in divisions that are less risky than the core-division, and relatively more in divisions that are more risky than the core-division.

*"The WACC Fallacy: The Real Effects of Using a Unique Discount Rate," *Journal of Finance*, 70 (2015): 1253–1285.

Cost of Capital for a New Acquisition

We begin by explaining how to calculate the cost of capital of a project with market risk that is different from the risk for the rest of the firm. Suppose GE wants to enter the athletic shoe business. To do so, it is considering acquiring Nike, a company that is focused on that business. Nike faces different market risks than GE does in GE's broad range of businesses. What cost of capital should GE use to value a possible acquisition of Nike?

Because the risks are different, GE's WACC would be inappropriate for valuing Nike. Instead, GE should calculate and use Nike's WACC when assessing the acquisition. In Figure 13.3, we find the following information for Nike, where the WACC is based on a tax rate of 35%:

	Beta	Cost of Equity	Cost of Debt	% Equity	% Debt	WACC
Nike	0.51	6.1%	3.2%	99%	1%	6.0%

Assuming that GE will find it appropriate to continue to finance Nike with the same mix of debt and equity after it buys Nike,[7] we can use Nike's WACC as the cost of capital for acquiring it. Thus, GE would use a cost of capital of 6.0% to value Nike for purchase.

Divisional Costs of Capital

Now assume GE makes a different decision: It decides to create an athletic shoes division internally, rather than buying Nike. What should the cost of capital for the new division be? If GE plans to finance the division with the same proportion of debt as is used by Nike, then GE would use Nike's WACC as the WACC for its new division. Because Nike's WACC is the right cost of capital given the risks of athletic shoes and 1% debt financing, it has to be the right cost of capital for an internally created athletic shoes division that is financed 1% with debt.

In most cases, firms with more than one division should not use a single companywide WACC to evaluate projects. More typically, they perform analyses similar to GE's analysis of Nike. Multidivisional firms benchmark their own divisions off of companies that compete with their division and are focused in that single line of business. By performing the same analysis as we did in Figure 13.3, the multidivisional firm can estimate the WACCs of its divisions' competitors—adjusting for different financing if necessary—to estimate the cost of capital for each division.

EXAMPLE 13.6

A Project in a New Line of Business

MyFinanceLab

PROBLEM

You are working for Microsoft evaluating the possibility of selling digital video recorders (DVRs). Microsoft's WACC is 8.6%. DVRs would be a new line of business for Microsoft, however, so the systematic risk of this business would likely differ from the systematic risk of Microsoft's current business. As a result, the assets of this new business should have a different cost of capital. You need to find the cost of capital for the DVR business. Assuming that the risk-free rate is 3% and the market risk premium is 6%, how would you estimate the cost of capital for this type of investment?

SOLUTION

PLAN

The first step is to identify a company operating in Microsoft's targeted line of business. TiVo, Inc., is a well-known marketer of DVRs. In fact, that is its sole business. Thus, the cost of capital for TiVo would be a good estimate of the cost of capital for Microsoft's proposed DVR business. Many Web sites are available that provide betas for traded stocks, including http://finance.yahoo.com. Suppose you visit that site and find that the beta of TiVo stock is 1.45. With this beta, the risk-free rate, and the market risk premium, you can use the CAPM to estimate the cost of equity for TiVo. Fortunately for us, TiVo has no debt, so its cost of equity is the same as its cost of capital for its assets.

(Continued)

---

[7]We consider what to do if GE wants to change Nike's financing mix in Chapter 16.

EXECUTE

Using the CAPM, we have

$$\text{TiVo's Cost of Equity} = \text{Risk-Free Rate} + \text{TiVo's Equity Beta} \times \text{Market Risk Premium}$$
$$= 3\% + 1.45 \times 6\% = 11.7\%$$

Because TiVo has no debt, its WACC is equivalent to its cost of equity.

EVALUATE

The correct cost of capital for evaluating a DVR investment opportunity is 11.7%. If we had used the 8.6% cost of capital that is associated with Microsoft's *existing* business, we would have mistakenly used too low of a cost of capital. That could lead us to go ahead with the investment, even if it truly had a negative NPV.

INTERVIEW WITH SHELAGH GLASER

Shelagh M. Glaser is vice president of Finance and Group Controller of the Client Computing Group at Intel Corporation. Her responsibilities include profit and loss forecasting, reporting and controls.

QUESTION: *Does Intel set the discount rate at the corporate or project level?*

ANSWER: We typically set the discount rate at the corporate level. As a company, Intel makes a broad set of products that sell into similar markets, so one hurdle rate makes sense for our core business. To justify an investment, every project has to earn or exceed that level of return for our shareholders.

We may use a different discount rate for mergers and acquisitions. For example, recently we've done more software acquisitions. That industry is very different from semiconductors and has different risk factors, so we take those considerations into account to set the hurdle rate.

QUESTION: *How does Intel compute the cost of capital for new investment opportunities?*

ANSWER: We reexamine our weighted average cost of capital (WACC) each year to see that we have the right inputs and if any have changed: What is the current market risk premium? Are we using the right risk-free rate? How should we weight historical data? We use the CAPM to determine beta but consider whether to continue using the five-year weekly beta or to change to a daily or monthly beta in the calculation. We also look at the latest studies from academia on what the inputs should be.

Once we have estimated the WACC, we think about the appropriate hurdle rate for our circumstances. We have not changed the hurdle rate in recent years—even though the WACC may have changed—and continue to use a hurdle rate that is above the WACC. This higher hurdle rate reflects our ability to time our investments and helps us choose projects that maximize our expected returns. Intel has more projects with returns above our hurdle than we can invest in, so assessing opportunity cost is a significant aspect of decision making. We may invest in some projects with NPVs below the hurdle rate if they are of strategic importance.

QUESTION: *How do project-specific considerations affect Intel's cost of capital calculation?*

ANSWER: When deciding whether to invest billions in wafer fabrication plants, Intel considers both the physical plant and the product line. We calculate the margin we would need from the product and develop a comprehensive set of metrics to justify the large capital investment. Typically we use our standard hurdle rate and also look at risk factors and the timing of the product launch. Intel's business is driven by the economics of Moore's Law, allowing us to double transistors every two years. Each generation of new technology creates cost reductions that enable new fabrication plants to clear the hurdle rate. These plants produce our leading-edge product, which earn our highest margins. To get a premium price, our customers require a product that takes advantage of the performance and power efficiency of the latest technology.

QUESTION: *Did the 2008 financial crisis affect how you evaluate investment opportunities?*

ANSWER: In 2008, the market was very depressed. We continued making R&D investments and reduced spending in other areas, such as marketing and short-term promotion. Cutting R&D would have left us with a gap in our product line in several years, because product development cycles typically run four years. In this industry, not keeping the R&D machine flowing, to boost short-term earnings, will harm the company's long-term viability. R&D is critical to our fundamental business model, which may require long-term decisions that negatively impact short-term results.

Intel has a long history of investing to maintain performance leadership during downturns. Intel carries almost no debt. Our capital policy is to maintain sufficient cash for fabrication plants and multiple years of R&D expenses, to avoid depending on capital markets to finance ongoing operations. A painful experience in the 1980s, when Intel's access to capital markets was curtailed, highlighted how this conservative capital policy pays off. Going into this crisis with no debt and an extremely strong cash position has served us well.

9. When evaluating a project in a new line of business, which assumptions for the WACC method are most likely to be violated?

10. How can you estimate the WACC to be used in a new line of business?

13.6 When Raising External Capital Is Costly

So far, we have assumed that there are no important factors to consider in seeking capital other than taxes. Among other things, this implies that we can raise external capital without any extra costs associated with the capital-raising transaction. As a consequence, we have no reason to treat a project financed with new external funds any differently than a project financed with internal funds (retained earnings).

In reality, issuing new equity or bonds carries a number of costs. These costs include the costs of filing and registering with the Securities and Exchange Commission and the fees charged by investment bankers to place the securities. We will discuss the process for issuing equity and bonds in detail in Chapters 14 and 15. Here, we mention it briefly in the context of the cost of capital.

Because of these issuing costs, a project that can be financed from internal funds will be less costly overall than the same project if it were financed with external funds. One approach would be to adjust the costs of equity and debt capital in the WACC to incorporate the issuing costs. A better and far more direct route is to simply treat the issuing costs as what they are—cash outflows that are necessary to the project. We can then incorporate this additional cost as a negative cash flow in the NPV analysis.

EXAMPLE 13.7

Evaluating an
Acquisition with Costly
External Financing

MyFinanceLab

PROBLEM

You are analyzing GE's potential acquisition of Nike. GE plans to offer $100 billion as the purchase price for Nike, and it will need to issue additional debt and equity to finance such a large acquisition. You estimate that the issuance costs will be $800 million and will be paid as soon as the transaction closes. You estimate the incremental free cash flows from the acquisition will be $3.3 billion in the first year and will grow at 3% per year thereafter. What is the NPV of the proposed acquisition?

SOLUTION

PLAN

We know from Section 13.5 that the correct cost of capital for this acquisition is Nike's WACC. We can value the incremental free cash flows as a growing perpetuity:

$$PV = \frac{FCF_1}{r - g}$$

where

$$FCF_1 = \$3.3 \text{ billion}$$

$$r = \text{Nike's WACC} = 0.06 \text{ (from Figure 13.3)}$$

$$g = 0.03$$

The NPV of the transaction, including the costly external financing, is the present value of this growing perpetuity net of both the purchase cost and the transaction costs of using external financing.

EXECUTE

Noting that $800 million is $0.8 billion,

$$NPV = -\$100 - \$0.8 + \frac{\$3.3}{0.06 - 0.03} = \$9.2 \text{ billion}$$

EVALUATE

It is not necessary to try to adjust Nike's WACC for the issuance costs of debt and equity. Instead, we can subtract the issuance costs from the NPV of the acquisition to confirm that the acquisition remains a positive-NPV project even if it must be financed externally.

In this chapter, we learned what a firm's cost of capital is, where it comes from, and how it is used in capital budgeting. The role of capital budgeting is to identify positive-NPV projects that allow a firm to cover the costs of its various types of capital. Now, we turn to another aspect of capital financing—where the firm gets that capital. In Chapters 14 through 16, we explore how a firm raises equity and debt capital and how it decides the proportion of each to have in its capital structure.

CONCEPT CHECK

11. What types of additional costs does a firm incur when accessing external capital?

12. What is the best way to incorporate these additional costs into capital budgeting?

MyFinanceLab

Here is what you should know after reading this chapter. MyFinanceLab will help you identify what you know, and where to go when you need to practice.

KEY POINTS AND EQUATIONS	KEY TERMS	ONLINE PRACTICE
13.1 A First Look at the Weighted Average Cost of Capital • A firm's debt and equity represent its capital. The relative proportions of debt, equity, and other securities that a firm has outstanding constitute its capital structure. • Investors of each type of capital have a required return. Providing this return is the cost a company bears to obtain capital from investors. • We calculate the firm's overall cost of capital as a weighted average of its equity and debt costs of capital, referred to as the firm's weighted average cost of capital. • The weights in the WACC must be based on the market values of both the firm's debt and equity, not the book values.	capital, p. 406 capital structure, p. 406 leverage, p. 408 levered, p. 408 market-value balance sheet, p. 408 unlevered, p. 408 weighted average cost of capital (WACC), p. 407	MyFinanceLab Study Plan 13.1
13.2 The Firm's Costs of Debt and Equity Capital • To estimate the cost of capital for a company as a whole, we usually start by estimating the cost of each of the company's sources of capital. • The cost of debt is the interest a firm would need to pay on *new* debt. Generally, it will differ from the coupon rate on existing debt, but can be estimated from the yield to maturity on existing debt. • The cost of preferred stock is straightforward to estimate because of its constant and known dividend: $$\text{Cost of Preferred Stock Capital} = \frac{Div_{pfd}}{P_{pfd}} \quad (13.4)$$	effective cost of the debt, p. 410	MyFinanceLab Study Plan 13.2

- The Capital Asset Pricing Model (CAPM) is the most common approach for estimating the cost of equity capital. To apply the CAPM, we need an estimate of the firm's equity beta, the market risk premium, and the risk-free rate:

$$\text{Cost of Equity} = \text{Risk-Free Rate} + \text{Equity Beta} \times \text{Market Risk Premium}$$

- Another approach to estimating the cost of equity is to use the constant dividend growth model (CDGM). To apply this model, we need the current stock price, the expected future dividend, and an estimate of the dividend's constant growth rate:

$$\text{Cost of Equity} = \frac{Div_1}{P_E} + g \qquad (13.5)$$

13.3 A Second Look at the Weighted Average Cost of Capital

- The WACC equation is

$$r_{wacc} = r_E E\% + r_{pfd} P\% + r_D(1 - T_C)D\% \quad (13.6)$$

- For a company that does not have preferred stock, the WACC equation condenses to

$$r_{wacc} = r_E E\% + r_D(1 - T_C)D\% \qquad (13.7)$$

- The WACC is driven by the risk of a company's line of business and, because of the tax effect of interest, its leverage. As a result, WACCs vary widely across industries and companies.

net debt, p. 416

MyFinanceLab
Study Plan 13.3

13.4 Using the WACC to Value a Project

- Assuming a project has average risk for the firm, that the firm will maintain its current leverage ratio, and that a firm's leverage affects its value only through taxes, the WACC can be used to value the cash flows from a new project.

debt-equity ratio, p. 418
levered value, p. 417
WACC method, p. 417

MyFinanceLab
Study Plan 13.4

Spreadsheet
Table 13.3

13.5 Project-Based Costs of Capital

- If the project's risk differs from the average risk for the firm, the WACC will not be the appropriate discount rate for the project. Instead, you must estimate the WACC from the WACC of other firms operating in the same line of business as the new project.

MyFinanceLab
Study Plan 13.5

13.6 When Raising External Capital Is Costly

- The WACC is calculated without accounting for the direct costs of raising external financing. Rather than adjusting the WACC, the correct way to account for these costs is to subtract their present value from the NPV of the project.

MyFinanceLab
Study Plan 13.6

1. What does the WACC measure?

2. Why are market-based weights important?

3. Why is the coupon rate of existing debt irrelevant for finding the cost of debt capital?

4. Why is it easier to determine the costs of preferred stock and of debt than it is to determine the cost of common equity?

5. Describe the steps involved in the CAPM approach to estimating the cost of equity.

6. Why would the CDGM and CAPM produce different estimates of the cost of equity capital?

7. Under what assumptions can the WACC be used to value a project?

8. What possible problems might be associated with the assumptions used in applying the WACC method?

9. How should you value a project in a line of business with risk that is different than the average risk of your firm's projects?

10. What is the right way to adjust for the costs of raising external financing?

PROBLEMS

All problems are available in MyFinanceLab.

A First Look at the Weighted Average Cost of Capital

1. MV Corporation has debt with market value of $100 million, common equity with a book value of $100 million, and preferred stock worth $20 million outstanding. Its common equity trades at $50 per share, and the firm has 6 million shares outstanding. What weights should MV Corporation use in its WACC?

2. Andyco, Inc., has the following balance sheet and an equity market-to-book ratio of 1.5. Assuming the market value of debt equals its book value, what weights should it use for its WACC calculation?

Assets	Liabilities and Equity	
1000	Debt	400
	Equity	600

3. Book Co. has 1 million shares of common equity with a par (book) value of $1, retained earnings of $30 million, and its shares have a market value of $50 per share. It also has debt with a par value of $20 million that is trading at 101% of par.
   a. What is the market value of its equity?
   b. What is the market value of its debt?
   c. What weights should it use in computing its WACC?

4. Consider a simple firm that has the following market-value balance sheet:

Assets	Liabilities and Equity	
1000	Debt	400
	Equity	600

Next year, there are two possible values for its assets, each equally likely: $1200 and $960. Its debt will be due with 5% interest. Because all of the cash flows from the assets must go either to the debt or the equity, if you hold a portfolio of the debt and equity in the same proportions as the firm's capital structure, your portfolio should earn exactly the expected return on the firm's assets. Show that a portfolio invested 40% in the firm's debt and 60% in its equity will have the same expected return as the assets of the firm. That is, show that the firm's pretax WACC is the same as the expected return on its assets.

The Firm's Costs of Debt and Equity Capital

5. Aluminum maker Alcoa has a beta of about 2.0, whereas Hormel Foods has a beta of 0.45. If the expected excess return of the marker portfolio is 5%, which of these firms has a higher equity cost of capital, and how much higher is it?

6. Avicorp has a $10 million debt issue outstanding, with a 6% coupon rate. The debt has semiannual coupons, the next coupon is due in six months, and the debt matures in five years. It is currently priced at 95% of par value.
    a. What is Avicorp's pretax cost of debt?
    b. If Avicorp faces a 40% tax rate, what is its after-tax cost of debt?

7. Laurel, Inc., has debt outstanding with a coupon rate of 6% and a yield to maturity of 7%. Its tax rate is 35%. What is Laurel's effective (after-tax) cost of debt?

8. Dewyco has preferred stock trading at $50 per share. The next preferred dividend of $4 is due in one year. What is Dewyco's cost of capital for preferred stock?

9. Steady Company's stock has a beta of 0.20. If the risk-free rate is 6% and the market risk premium is 7%, what is an estimate of Steady Company's cost of equity?

10. Wild Swings Inc.'s stock has a beta of 2.5. If the risk-free rate is 6% and the market risk premium is 7%, what is an estimate of Wild Swings' cost of equity?

11. HighGrowth Company has a stock price of $20. The firm will pay a dividend next year of $1, and its dividend is expected to grow at a rate of 4% per year thereafter. What is your estimate of HighGrowth's cost of equity capital?

12. Slow 'n Steady, Inc., has a stock price of $30, will pay a dividend next year of $3, and has expected dividend growth of 1% per year. What is your estimate of Slow 'n Steady's cost of equity capital?

13. Mackenzie Company has a price of $36 and will issue a dividend of $2 next year. It has a beta of 1.2, the risk-free rate is 5.5%, and it estimates the market risk premium to be 5%.
    a. Estimate the equity cost of capital for Mackenzie.
    b. Under the CGDM, at what rate do you need to expect Mackenzie's dividends to grow to get the same equity cost of capital as in part (a)?

A Second Look at the Weighted Average Cost of Capital

14. CoffeeCarts has a cost of equity of 15%, has an effective cost of debt of 4%, and is financed 70% with equity and 30% with debt. What is this firm's WACC?

15. AllCity, Inc., is financed 40% with debt, 10% with preferred stock, and 50% with common stock. Its pretax cost of debt is 6%, its preferred stock pays an annual dividend of $2.50 and is priced at $30. It has an equity beta of 1.1. Assume the risk-free rate is 2%, the market risk premium is 7% and AllCity's tax rate is 35%. What is its after-tax WACC?

16. Pfd Company has debt with a yield to maturity of 7%, a cost of equity of 13%, and a cost of preferred stock of 9%. The market values of its debt, preferred stock, and equity are $10 million, $3 million, and $15 million, respectively, and its tax rate is 40%. What is this firm's after-tax WACC?

17. Growth Company's current share price is $20 and it is expected to pay a $1 dividend per share next year. After that, the firm's dividends are expected to grow at a rate of 4% per year.
    a. What is an estimate of Growth Company's cost of equity?
    b. Growth Company also has preferred stock outstanding that pays a $2 per share fixed dividend. If this stock is currently priced at $28, what is Growth Company's cost of preferred stock?
    c. Growth Company has existing debt issued three years ago with a coupon rate of 6%. The firm just issued new debt at par with a coupon rate of 6.5%. What is Growth Company's pretax cost of debt?
    d. Growth Company has 5 million common shares outstanding and 1 million preferred shares outstanding, and its equity has a total book value of $50 million. Its liabilities have a market value of $20 million. If Growth Company's common and preferred shares are priced as in parts (a) and (b), what is the market value of Growth Company's assets?
    e. Growth Company faces a 35% tax rate. Given the information in parts (a) through (d), and your answers to those problems, what is Growth Company's WACC?

Using the WACC to Value a Project

18. A retail coffee company is planning to open 100 new coffee outlets that are expected to generate $15 million in free cash flows per year, with a growth rate of 3% in perpetuity. If the coffee company's WACC is 10%, what is the NPV of this expansion?

19. RiverRocks, Inc., is considering a project with the following projected free cash flows:

0	1	2	3	4
−50	10	20	20	15

The firm believes that, given the risk of this project, the WACC method is the appropriate approach to valuing the project. RiverRocks' WACC is 12%. Should it take on this project? Why or why not?

Project-Based Costs of Capital

20. RiverRocks (whose WACC is 12%) is considering an acquisition of Raft Adventures (whose WACC is 15%). What is the appropriate discount rate for RiverRocks to use to evaluate the acquisition? Why?

21. RiverRocks' purchase of Raft Adventures (from Problem 20) will cost $100 million, and will generate cash flows that start at $15 million in one year and then grow at 4% per year forever. What is the NPV of the acquisition?

22. Your firm is planning to invest in an automated packaging plant. Harburtin Industries is an all-equity firm that specializes in this business. Suppose Harburtin's equity beta is 0.85, the risk-free rate is 4%, and the market risk premium is 5%. If your firm's project is all equity financed, estimate its cost of capital.

23. CoffeeStop primarily sells coffee. It recently introduced a premium coffee-flavored liquor. Suppose the firm faces a tax rate of 35% and collects the following information. If it plans to finance 11% of the new liquor-focused division with debt and the rest with equity, what WACC should it use for its liquor division? Assume a cost of debt of 4.8%, a risk-free rate of 3%, and a risk premium of 6%.

	Beta	% Equity	% Debt
CoffeeStop	0.61	96%	4%
BF Liquors	0.26	89%	11%

24. Your company has two divisions: One division sells software and the other division sells computers through a direct sales channel, primarily taking orders over the Internet. You have decided that Dell Computer is very similar to your computer division, in terms of both risk and financing. You go online and find the following information: Hewlett Packard's beta is 1.21, the risk-free rate is 4.5%, its market value of equity is $67 billion, and it has $700 million worth of debt with a yield to maturity of 6%. Your tax rate is 35% and you use a market risk premium of 5% in your WACC estimates.
    a. What is an estimate of the WACC for your computer sales division?
    b. If your overall company WACC is 12% and the computer sales division represents 40% of the value of your firm, what is an estimate of the WACC for your software division?

When Raising External Capital Is Costly

25. RiverRocks realizes that it will have to raise the financing for the acquisition of Raft Adventures (described in Problem 21) by issuing new debt and equity. The firm estimates that the direct issuing costs will come to $7 million. How should it account for these costs in evaluating the project? Should RiverRocks go ahead with the project?

26. You are planning to issue debt to finance a new project. The project will require $20 million in financing and you estimate its NPV to be $15 million. The issue costs for the debt will be 3% of face value. Taking into account the costs of external financing, what is the NPV of the project?

DATA CASE

You work in Walt Disney Company's corporate finance and treasury department and have been assigned to the team estimating Disney's WACC. You must estimate this WACC in preparation for a team meeting later today. You quickly realize that the information you need is readily available online.

1. Go to http://finance.yahoo.com. Under "Market Data" you will find the yield to maturity for 10-year Treasury bonds listed as "10 Yr Bond(%)." Collect this number as your risk-free rate.

2. In the box next to the "Look Up" button, type Walt Disney's ticker symbol (DIS), and click "Search." Once you see the basic information for Disney, find and click "Key Statistics" on the left side of the screen. From the key statistics, collect Disney's market capitalization (its market value of equity), enterprise value (market value equity + net debt), cash, and beta.

3. To get Disney's cost of debt and the market value of its long-term debt, you will need the price and yield to maturity on the firm's existing long-term bonds. Go to http://finra-markets.morningstar.com/BondCenter/Default.jsp?, click "Search," click "Corporate," type Disney's ticker symbol (DIS), and click "Show Results." A list of Disney's outstanding bond issues will appear. Assume that Disney's policy is to use the yield to maturity on non-callable 10-year obligations as its cost of debt. Find the non-callable bond issue that is as close to 10 years from maturity as possible. (*Hint*: You will see a column titled "Callable"; make sure the issue you choose has "No" in this column.) You may have to choose a bond issued by one of its subsidiaries, like ABC. Find the yield to maturity for your chosen bond issue (it is in the column titled "Yield") and enter that yield as your pretax cost of debt into your spreadsheet. Next, copy and paste the data in the entire table into Excel.

4. You now have the price for each bond issue, but you need to know the size of the issue. Returning to the Web page, go to the row of the bond you chose and click the Issuer Name in the first column (this will either be Walt Disney Company or ABC or another subsidiary). This brings up a Web page with all of the information

about the bond issue. Scroll down until you find "Amount Outstanding" on the right side. Noting that this amount is quoted in thousands of dollars (e.g., $60,000 means $60 million = $60,000,000), record the issue amount in the appropriate row of your spreadsheet. Repeat this step for all of the bond issues.

5. The price for each bond issue in your spreadsheet is reported as a percentage of the bond's par value. For example, 104.50 means that the bond issue is trading at 104.5% of its par value. You can calculate the market value of each bond issue by multiplying the amount outstanding by (Price ÷ 100). Do so for each issue and then calculate the total of all the bond issues. This is the market value of Disney's debt.

6. Compute the weights for Disney's equity and debt based on the market value of equity and Disney's market value of debt, computed in step 5.

7. Calculate Disney's cost of equity capital using the CAPM, the risk-free rate you collected in step 1, and a market risk premium of 5%.

8. Assuming that Disney has a tax rate of 35%, calculate its effective cost of debt capital.

9. Calculate Disney's WACC.

10. Calculate Disney's net debt by subtracting its cash (collected in step 2) from its debt. Recalculate the weights for the WACC using the market value of equity, net debt, and enterprise value. Recalculate Disney's WACC using the weights based on the net debt. How much does it change?

11. How confident are you of your estimate? Which implicit assumptions did you make during your data collection efforts?

PART 4

Integrative Case

This case draws on material from Chapters 11–13.

You work for HydroTech, a large manufacturer of high-pressure industrial water pumps. The firm specializes in natural disaster services, ranging from pumps that draw water from lakes, ponds, and streams in drought-stricken areas to pumps that remove high water volumes in flooded areas. You report directly to the CFO. Your boss has asked you to calculate HydroTech's WACC in preparation for an executive retreat. Too bad you're not invited, as water pumps and skiing are on the agenda in Sun Valley, Idaho. At least you have an analyst on hand to gather the following required information:

1. The risk-free rate of interest, in this case, the yield of the 10-year government bond, which is 3%
2. HydroTech's:
   a. Market capitalization (its market value of equity), $100 million
   b. CAPM beta, 1.2
   c. Total book value of debt outstanding, $50 million
   d. Cash, $10 million
3. The cost of debt (using the quoted yields on HydroTech's outstanding bond issues), which is 5%

With this information in hand, you are now prepared to undertake the analysis.

Case Questions

1. Calculate HydroTech's net debt.
2. Compute HydroTech's equity and (net) debt weights based on the market value of equity and the book value of net debt.
3. Calculate the cost of equity capital using the CAPM, assuming a market risk premium of 5%.
4. Using a tax rate of 35%, calculate HydroTech's effective cost of debt capital.
5. Calculate HydroTech's WACC.
6. When is it appropriate to use this WACC to evaluate a new project?

16

Capital Structure

LEARNING OBJECTIVES

- Examine how capital structures vary across industries and companies

- Understand why investment decisions, rather than financing decisions, fundamentally determine the value and cost of capital of a firm

- Describe how leverage increases the risk of a firm's equity

- Demonstrate how debt can affect a firm's value through taxes and bankruptcy costs

- Show how the optimal mix of debt and equity trades off the costs (including financial distress costs) and benefits (including the tax advantage) of debt

- Analyze how debt can alter the incentives of managers to choose different projects and can be used as a signal to investors

- Weigh the many costs and benefits to debt that a manager must balance when deciding how to finance the firm's investments

notation

D	market value of debt
E	market value of levered equity
EPS	earnings per share
NPV	net present value
PV	present value
r_D	expected return (cost of capital) of debt
r_E	expected return (cost of capital) of levered equity

r_U	expected return (cost of capital) of unlevered equity
r_{wacc}	weighted average cost of capital
T_c	marginal corporate tax rate
V^L	value of the firm with leverage
V^U	value of the unlevered firm

When a firm needs to raise new funds to undertake its investments, it must decide which type of financing security it will issue to investors. What considerations should guide this decision and how does this decision affect the value of the firm?

Consider the case of Facebook from Chapter 14 issuing new equity in a seasoned equity offering to fund its expansion, or Hertz from Chapter 15 substantially increasing its leverage through its leveraged buyout. In the summer of 2007, Home Depot dramatically changed its capital structure by reducing its equity by $22 billion and increasing its debt by $12 billion. What led managers at Facebook to rely on equity for its expansion and Hertz and Home Depot to choose to increase their debt instead? How might such capital structure decisions impact the value of these firms?

In this chapter, first we explore these questions in a setting of *perfect capital markets*, in which all securities are fairly priced, there are no taxes or transaction costs, and the total cash flows of the firm's projects are not affected by how the firm finances them. Although in reality capital markets are not perfect, this setting provides an important benchmark.

We devote the remainder of the chapter to exploring how violations of our perfect capital markets assumptions affect our conclusions. We further explore how the tax advantage of debt that we briefly discussed in Chapter 13 makes debt a potentially attractive financing source. Then we discuss the costs of financial distress and bankruptcy faced by firms with debt. This discussion leads us to the insight that managers choose debt by balancing the tax advantages against the distress costs of debt. After discussing other influences on capital structure, including agency problems and differences in information between managers and investors, we conclude with some recommendations for a financial manager making capital structure decisions.

16.1 Capital Structure Choices

Recall that the relative proportions of debt, equity, and other securities that a firm has outstanding constitute its *capital structure*. When corporations raise funds from outside investors, they must choose which type of security to issue and what type of capital structure to have. The most common choices are financing through equity alone and financing through a combination of debt and equity. How do firms arrive at their capital structures and what factors should a financial manager consider when choosing among financing alternatives?

First and foremost, various financing choices will promise different future amounts to each security holder in exchange for the cash that is raised today. But beyond that, the firm may also need to consider whether the securities it issues will receive a fair price in the market, have tax consequences, entail transactions costs, or even change its future investment opportunities. A firm's capital structure is also affected by decisions on whether to accumulate cash, pay off debt or pay dividends, or conduct share repurchases. Before exploring the theory underpinning this analysis, we place these financing decisions in the context of actual firm practices.

Capital Structure Choices Across Industries

Figure 16.1 shows the median debt-to-value ratios across industries for U.S. stocks. A firm's **debt-to-value ratio**—$D/(E + D)$—is the fraction of the firm's total value that corresponds to debt. Notice that the debt levels financial managers choose differ across industries. For example, software companies such as Microsoft are far less levered (have less debt relative to their equity) than are construction equipment manufacturers such as Caterpillar Company.

debt-to-value ratio The fraction of a firm's total value that corresponds to debt.

Capital Structure Choices Within Industries

The differences in capital structures across industries are striking. However, even within industries, two competing firms may make different choices about their debt-to-value ratios. For example, Intel and ARM Holdings, PLC, both members of the semiconductor

FIGURE 16.1

Debt-to-Value Ratio [$D/(E + D)$] for Select Industries

The bars represent debt-to-value ratios across a wide variety of industries. Debt levels are determined by book values, and equity by market values. The average debt financing for all U.S. stocks was about 22%, but note the large differences by industry.

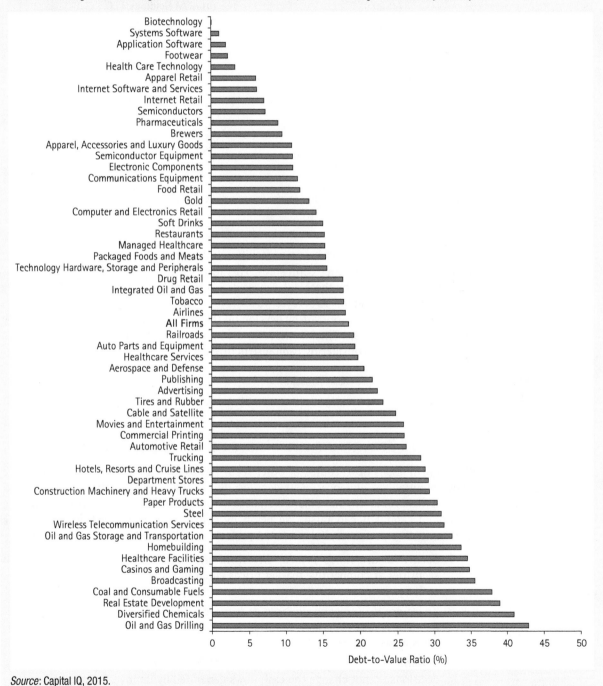

Source: Capital IQ, 2015.

industry, have different capital structures, as depicted in Panels (a) and (b) of Figure 16.2. Intel has 15% debt and 85% equity, as shown in Panel (a), and ARM has no debt, as shown in Panel (b)! Even though the companies are direct competitors, they have very different assets and histories. ARM, which has enjoyed strong growth recently due to the use of its

FIGURE 16.2

Capital Structures of
Intel and ARM Holdings

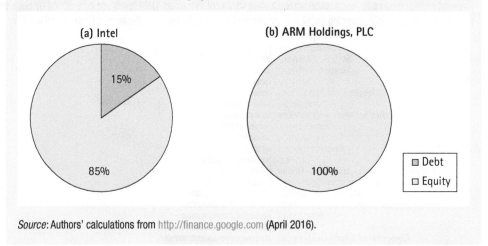

The pie charts in panels (a) and (b) show the split between debt and equity in two competing firms, Intel and ARM Holdings, PLC. Both are part of the semiconductor industry. Even within an industry, two companies can choose a different mix of debt and equity.

(a) Intel

(b) ARM Holdings, PLC

15%

85%

100%

□ Debt
□ Equity

Source: Authors' calculations from http://finance.google.com (April 2016).

chips in tablets, has no chip fabrication facilities. Unlike Intel, ARM licenses its chip designs to be manufactured by other companies. This leaves it with few physical assets. In this chapter, we will learn why these differences in assets and business plans would naturally lead to the different capital structures we observe today.

In the next section, we start by developing the critical theoretical foundation of any capital structure analysis. Then we move on to important real-world factors that managers must trade off when considering capital structure decisions.

1. What constitutes a firm's capital structure?

2. What are some factors a manager must consider when making a financing decision?

16.2   Capital Structure in Perfect Capital Markets

When a firm issues debt, equity, or other securities to fund a new investment, there are many potential consequences of its decision. By far the most important question for a financial manager is whether different choices will affect the value of the firm and thus the amount of capital it can raise. We begin by considering this question in a simple environment—a perfect capital market. A **perfect capital market** is a market in which:

perfect capital markets A set of conditions in which investors and firms can trade the same set of securities at competitive market prices; there are no frictions and the firm's financing decisions do not change the cash flows generated by its investments.

1. *Securities are fairly priced.* Investors and firms can trade the same set of securities at competitive market prices equal to the present value of their future cash flows.

2. *There are no tax consequences or transactions costs.* There are no tax consequences, transactions costs, or other issuance costs associated with financing decisions or security trading.

3. *Investment cash flows are independent of financing choices.* A firm's financing decisions do not change the cash flows generated by its investments, nor do they reveal new information about those cash flows.

The assumption of perfect capital markets may seem narrow and unrealistic. We will see, however, that by starting with them we will gain important insight into the true benefits and costs of leverage.

Application: Financing a New Business

Let's begin with an example of a possible financing decision in a perfect capital market. Imagine you have one year left in college and you want to earn some extra money before graduation. You have been offered the opportunity to run the coffee shop in the lobby of a nearby office building. The owner of the building is willing to grant you this right on a one-year basis prior to a major remodeling of the building.

Your research indicates that you will need to make an up-front investment of $24,000 to start the business. After covering your operating costs, including paying yourself a nice wage, you expect to generate a cash flow of $34,500 at the end of the year. The current risk-free interest rate is 5%. You believe, however, that your profits will be somewhat risky and sensitive to the overall market (which will affect the level of activity in the building and demand for your business), so that a 10% risk premium is appropriate, for a total discount rate of 15% (5% + 10%). Therefore, you calculate the NPV of this investment in the coffee shop as:

$$NPV = -\$24,000 + \frac{\$34,500}{1.15} = -\$24,000 + \$30,000 = \$6000$$

Thus, the investment has a positive NPV.

Even though the investment looks attractive, you still need to raise the money for the up-front investment. How should you raise the funds, and what is the amount you will be able to raise?

Equity Financing. First, you consider raising money solely by selling equity in the business to your friends and family. Given the cash flow estimates, how much would they be willing to pay for those shares? Recall that the value of a security equals the present value of its future cash flows. In this case, equity holders in your firm will expect to receive the payoff of $34,500 at the end of the year, with the same risk as the cash flows generated by the coffee shop. Therefore, your firm's equity cost of capital will be 15% and the value of its equity today will be:

$$PV \text{ (Equity Cash Flows)} = \frac{\$34,500}{1.15} = \$30,000$$

unlevered equity Equity in a firm with no debt.

Recall that the absence of debt means the absence of financial leverage. Equity in a firm with no debt is therefore called **unlevered equity**. Because the present value of the equity cash flows is $30,000, you can raise $30,000 by selling all the unlevered equity in your firm. Doing so allows you to keep the NPV of $6000 as profit after paying the investment cost of $24,000. In other words, the project's NPV represents the value to the initial owner of the firm (in this case, you, the entrepreneur) created by the project.

levered equity Equity in a firm with outstanding debt.

Levered Financing. As an alternative, you also consider borrowing some of the money you will need to invest. Suppose the business's cash flow is certain to be at least $16,000. Then you can borrow $15,000 at the current risk-free interest rate of 5%. You will be able to pay the debt of $15,000 × 1.05 = $15,750 at the end of the year without any risk of defaulting.

How much can you raise selling equity in your business now? Equity in a firm that also has outstanding debt is called **levered equity**. After the debt is repaid, equity holders can expect to receive $34,500 − $15,750 = $18,750. What discount rate should we use to value levered equity? What expected return will investors demand?

It is tempting to use the same 15% equity cost of capital as before. In that case, by selling levered equity, you could raise $18,750/1.15 = $16,304. If this result were correct, then using leverage would allow you to raise a total amount, including the debt, of $15,000 + $16,304 = $31,304, or $1304 more than in the case without leverage.

Thus, it would seem that simply financing a project with leverage can make it more valuable. *But if this sounds too good to be true, it is*. Our analysis assumed that your firm's equity cost of capital remained unchanged at 15% after adding leverage. But as we will see shortly, that will not be the case—leverage will increase the risk of the firm's equity and raise its equity cost of capital. To see why, and to understand what will actually happen, we turn to the hallmark work of researchers Franco Modigliani and Merton Miller.

Leverage and Firm Value

In an important paper, researchers Modigliani and Miller (or simply MM) considered whether leverage would increase the total value of the firm. Their answer to this question surprised researchers and practitioners at the time.[1] They argued that with perfect capital markets, the total value of a firm should *not* depend on its capital structure. Their reasoning: Your firm's total cash flows—those paid to both debt and equity holders—still equal the cash flows of the coffee shop, with the same expected value of $34,500 and the same total risk as before, as shown in Figure 16.3. Because the total cash flows of the debt and equity equal the cash flows of the unlevered firm, the Valuation Principle tells us that their market values must be the same. Specifically, we calculated earlier that the value of the unlevered firm, V^U, is:

$$V^U = \$34{,}500/1.15 = \$30{,}000$$

FIGURE 16.3

Unlevered Versus Levered Cash Flows with Perfect Capital Markets

When the firm has no debt, as shown in Panel (a), the cash flows paid to equity holders correspond to the free cash flows generated by the firm's assets. When the firm has the debt, shown in Panel (b), these cash flows are divided between debt and equity holders. However, with perfect capital markets, the total amount paid to all investors still corresponds to the free cash flows generated by the firm's assets. Therefore, the value of the unlevered firm, V^U, must equal the total value of the levered firm, V^L, which is the combined value of its debt D and levered equity E.

Panel (a), Unlevered Cash Flows

Panel (b), Levered Cash Flows

[1]F. Modigliani and M. Miller, "The Cost of Capital, Corporation Finance and the Theory of Investment," *American Economic Review*, 48 (3) (1958): 261–297.

Thus, the total value of the levered firm, V^L, which is the combined value of its debt, D, and levered equity, E, must be the same:

$$V^L = D + E = \$30,000$$

Therefore, if the initial market value of the debt is $D = \$15,000$ (the amount borrowed), the initial market value of the levered equity must be $E = \$30,000 - \$15,000 = \$15,000$.

Thus, Modigliani and Miller argued that leverage merely changes the allocation of cash flows between debt and equity without altering the total cash flows of the firm in a perfect capital market. As a result, they concluded that:

MM Proposition I: *In a perfect capital market, the total value of a firm is equal to the market value of the free cash flows generated by its assets and is not affected by its choice of capital structure.*

We can write this result in an equation as follows:

$$V^L = E + D = V^U \tag{16.1}$$

This equation states that the total value of the firm is the same with or without leverage.

Note in our example that because the cash flows of levered equity are smaller than those of unlevered equity, levered equity will sell for a lower price than unlevered equity ($15,000 versus $30,000). However, the fact that the equity is less valuable with leverage does not mean that you are worse off. You will still raise a total of $30,000 by issuing both debt and levered equity, just as you did with unlevered equity alone, and still keep the $6000 difference between the $30,000 you raise and your $24,000 cost as profit. As a consequence, you will be indifferent between these two choices for the firm's capital structure.

The Effect of Leverage on Risk and Return

Modigliani and Miller's conclusion went against the common view that even with perfect capital markets, leverage would affect a firm's value. In particular, it was thought that the value of the levered equity should exceed $15,000, because the present value of its expected cash flow at a 15% discount rate is $18,750/1.15 = $16,304, as we calculated earlier. The reason this is *not* correct is that leverage increases the risk of the equity of a firm. Therefore, it is inappropriate to discount the cash flows of levered equity at the same discount rate of 15% that we used for unlevered equity.

Let's take a closer look at the effect of leverage on the firm's equity cost of capital. If equity holders are only willing to pay $15,000 for the levered equity, then given its expected payoff of $18,750, their expected return is:

Expected Return of Levered Equity = $18,750/\$15,000 - 1 = 25\%$

Although this return may seem like a good deal for investors, remember that the coffee shop cash flows are uncertain. Table 16.1 considers the different levels of demand and free

TABLE 16.1

Returns to Equity in Different Scenarios with and Without Leverage

	Coffee Shop	Security Cash Flows			Security Returns		
Demand	Free Cash Flows	Unlevered Equity	Debt	Levered Equity	Unlevered Equity	Debt	Levered Equity
Weak	$27,000	$27,000	$15,750	$11,250	−10%	5%	−25%
Expected	$34,500	$34,500	$15,750	$18,750	15%	5%	25%
Strong	$42,000	$42,000	$15,750	$26,250	40%	5%	75%

cash flows that the coffee shop may generate, and compares the security payoffs and returns with unlevered equity to the case in which you borrow $15,000 and raise an additional $15,000 using levered equity. Note that the returns are very different with and without leverage. With no debt, the returns of unlevered equity range from −10% to 40%, with an expected return of 15%. With leverage, the debt holders receive a risk-free return of 5%, whereas the returns of levered equity are much more volatile, with a range of −25% to 75%. To compensate for this higher risk, levered equity holders receive a higher expected return of 25%.

We further illustrate the effect of leverage on returns in Figure 16.4. By adding leverage, the returns of the unlevered firm are effectively "split" between low-risk debt and much higher-risk levered equity. Note that the returns of levered equity fall twice as fast as those of unlevered equity if the coffee shops cash flows decline. This doubling of the risk justifies a doubling of the risk premium, which is 15% − 5% = 10% for unlevered equity and 25% − 5% = 20% for levered equity. As this example shows, *leverage increases the risk of equity even when there is no risk that the firm will default.*

FIGURE 16.4

Unlevered Versus Levered Returns with Perfect Capital Markets

Leverage splits the firm's return between low-risk debt and high-risk levered equity compared to the equity of an unlevered firm. In this example, the returns of levered equity are twice as sensitive to the firm's cash flows as the returns of unlevered equity. This doubling of risk implies a doubling of the risk premium from 10% to 20%.

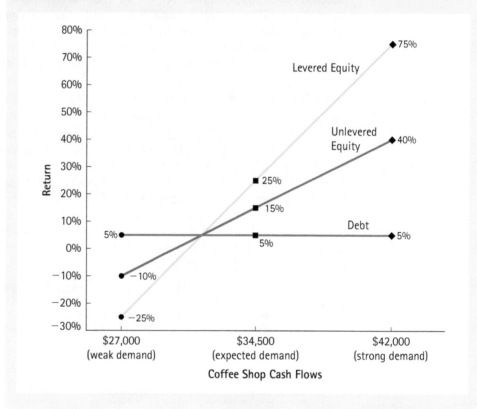

EXAMPLE 16.1

The Risk and Return of Levered Equity

MyFinanceLab

PROBLEM

Suppose you borrow only $6000 when financing your coffee shop. According to Modigliani and Miller, what should the value of the equity be? What is the expected return?

SOLUTION

PLAN

The value of the firm's total cash flows does not change: It is still $30,000. Thus, if you borrow $6000, your firm's equity will be worth $24,000. To determine the equity's expected return, we will compute the cash flows to equity under the two scenarios. The cash flows to equity are the cash flows of the firm net of the cash flows to debt (repayment of principal plus interest).

EXECUTE

The firm will owe debt holders $6000 × 1.05 = $6300 in one year. Thus, the expected payoff to equity holders is $34,500 − $6300 = $28,200, for a return of $28,200/$24,000 − 1 = 17.5%.

EVALUATE

While the total value of the firm is unchanged, the firm's equity in this case is more risky than it would be without debt, but less risky than if the firm borrowed $15,000. To illustrate, note that if demand is weak, the equity holders will receive $27,000 − $6300 = $20,700, for a return of $20,700/$24,000 − 1 = −13.75%. Compare this return to −10% without leverage and −25% if the firm borrowed $15,000. As a result, the expected return of the levered equity is higher in this case than for unlevered equity (17.5% versus 15%), but not as high as in the previous example (17.5% versus 25%).

Homemade Leverage

MM showed that the firm's value is not affected by its choice of capital structure. But suppose investors would prefer an alternative capital structure to the one the firm has chosen. MM demonstrated that in this case, investors can borrow or lend on their own and achieve the same result. For example, an investor who would like more leverage than the firm has chosen can borrow and thus add leverage to his or her own portfolio. Adding leverage in this way will lower the out-of-pocket cost of the security, but increase the risk of the portfolio. When investors use leverage in their own portfolios to adjust the leverage choice made by the firm, we say that they are using **homemade leverage**. As long as investors can borrow or lend at the same interest rate as the firm, which is true in perfect capital markets, homemade leverage is a perfect substitute for the use of leverage by the firm. Thus, because different choices of capital structure offer no benefit to investors in perfect capital markets, those choices do not affect the value of the firm.

homemade leverage When investors use leverage in their own portfolios to adjust the leverage choice made by a firm.

Leverage and the Cost of Capital

We can use the insight of Modigliani and Miller to understand the effect of leverage on the firm's cost of capital. Recall from Figure 16.3 and Eq. 16.1 that if we look at a portfolio of the equity and debt of a levered firm together, that portfolio has the same value and cash flows as the unlevered firm. Therefore, the expected return of the portfolio should equal the expected return of the unlevered firm. Recall from Chapter 12 that the expected return of the portfolio equity and debt is simply the weighted average of the expected returns of each security. Thus, with r_E representing the expected return of levered equity, r_D the expected return of debt, and r_U the expected return of the unlevered equity, we have:

Weighted Average Cost of Capital (Pretax)

$$\underbrace{r_E \frac{E}{E + D} + r_D \frac{D}{E + D}}_{\text{Pretax WACC}} = r_U \tag{16.2}$$

The amounts $\frac{E}{E+D}$ and $\frac{D}{E+D}$ represent the fraction of the firm's value financed by equity and debt, respectively. Thus, the left side of Eq. 16.2 is the weighted average cost of capital

(WACC) of the firm, which we defined in Chapter 13. Note that the cost of debt is not adjusted for taxes, because we are assuming "perfect capital markets" and thus are ignoring taxes. When we compute the weighted average cost of capital without taxes, we refer to it as the firm's **pretax WACC**. Equation 16.2 states that for any choice of capital structure, the firm's pretax WACC is unchanged and remains equal to the firm's unlevered cost of capital.

pretax WACC The weighted average cost of capital computed using the pretax cost of debt.

Let's check this result for our coffee shop example. With leverage, the firm's debt cost of capital was $r_D = 5\%$, and its equity cost of capital rose to $r_E = 25\%$. What about the portfolio weights? In this case, the firm borrowed $D = 15,000$, and issued equity worth $E = 15,000$, for a total value $V^L = E + D = 30,000$. Therefore, its pretax WACC is:

$$r_E \frac{E}{E+D} + r_D \frac{D}{E+D} = 25\% \left(\frac{15,000}{30,000} \right) + 5\% \left(\frac{15,000}{30,000} \right) = 15\%$$

Thus, the pretax WACC does indeed equal the firm's unlevered cost of capital, $r_U = 15\%$.

How is it that the firm's weighted average cost of capital stays the same even after adding leverage? There are two offsetting effects of leverage: We finance a larger fraction of the firm with debt, which has a lower cost of capital, but at the same time adding leverage raises the firm's equity cost of capital. Because the firm's total risk has not changed (it has just been split between these two securities), these two effects should exactly cancel out

---

COMMON MISTAKE

Capital Structure Fallacies

Here, we take a critical look at two incorrect arguments that are sometimes cited in favor of leverage.

Leverage and Earnings per Share

Fallacy 1: Leverage can increase a firm's expected earnings per share; by doing so, leverage should also increase the firm's stock price.

Consider the coffee shop example. In the all-equity case, if you issued 1000 shares, they would each be worth $30 and the expected earnings per share (EPS) would be $34,500/1000 = $34.50. EPS would vary from $27 per share to $42 per share in the case of weak or strong demand. In the case with debt, as shown in Table 16.1, you only need to raise $15,000 in equity and so could issue only 500 shares, each worth $30. In this case, your expected EPS will be $18,750/500 = $37.50, with a range from $22.50 to $52.50. Thus, although the expected EPS

is greater with leverage, the variation in EPS is also much greater, as shown in the blue and yellow bars. With leverage, EPS falls to $22.50 when cash flows are low, which is much further than EPS would have dropped without leverage ($27). Although EPS increases on average, this increase is necessary to compensate shareholders for the additional risk they are taking. As a result, the entrepreneur's share price does not increase as a result of issuing debt.

Equity Issuances and Dilution

Fallacy 2: Issuing equity will *dilute* existing shareholders' ownership, so debt financing should be used instead.
Dilution means that if the firm issues new shares, the cash flows generated by the firm must be divided among a larger number of shares, thereby reducing the value of each individual share.

This line of reasoning ignores the fact that the cash raised by issuing new shares will increase the firm's assets. Consider Google's September 2005 seasoned equity offering of 14,159,265 Class A shares at $295 apiece. Google priced the shares to match the market price of Class A shares on NASDAQ at the time of the offer. The amount raised was then $4,176,983,175, so the total value of Google increased to $60,560,157,355, which when divided by the new total number of shares (205,288,669), still results in a price of $295 per share.

In general, as long as the firm sells the new shares of equity *at a fair price*, there will be no gain or loss to shareholders associated with the equity issue itself. The money taken in by the firm as a result of the share issue exactly offsets the dilution of the shares. *Any gain or loss associated with the transaction will result from the NPV of the investments the firm makes with the funds raised.*

and leave the firm's WACC unchanged. In fact, we can use Eq. 16.2 to determine the precise impact of leverage on the firm's equity cost of capital. Solving the equation for r_E, we have:

MM Proposition II: The Cost of Capital of Levered Equity

$$r_E = r_U + \frac{D}{E}(r_U - r_D) \tag{16.3}$$

Or, in words:

MM Proposition II: *The cost of capital of levered equity is equal to the cost of capital of unlevered equity plus a premium that is proportional to the debt-equity ratio (measured using market values).*

Let's check MM Proposition II for the coffee shop example. In this case:

$$r_E = r_U + \frac{D}{E}(r_U - r_D) = 15\% + \frac{15{,}000}{15{,}000}(15\% - 5\%) = 25\%$$

This result matches the expected return for levered equity we calculated in Table 16.1.

Figure 16.5 illustrates the effect of increasing the amount of leverage in a firm's capital structure on its equity cost of capital, its debt cost of capital, and its WACC. In the

FIGURE 16.5   WACC and Leverage with Perfect Capital Markets

Panel (a) represents the data in Panel (b) for the coffee shop example. As the fraction of the firm financed with debt increases, both the equity and the debt become riskier and their cost of capital rises. Yet because more weight is put on the lower-cost debt, the weighted average cost of capital, r_{wacc}, remains constant.

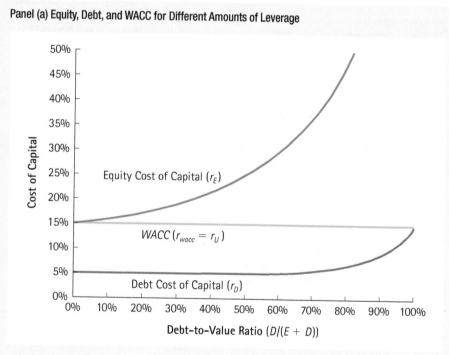

Panel (a) Equity, Debt, and WACC for Different Amounts of Leverage

Panel (b) WACC Data for Alternative Capital Structures

E	D	r_E	r_D	$r_E \dfrac{E}{E+D} + r_D \dfrac{D}{E+D}$	$= r_{wacc}$
30,000	0	15.0%	5.0%	15.0% × 1.0 + 5.0% × 0.0	= 15%
24,000	6,000	17.5%	5.0%	17.5% × 0.8 + 5.0% × 0.2	= 15%
15,000	15,000	25.0%	5.0%	25.0% × 0.5 + 5.0% × 0.5	= 15%
3,000	27,000	75.0%	8.3%	75.0% × 0.1 + 8.3% × 0.9	= 15%

figure, we measure the firm's leverage in terms of its debt-to-value ratio, $D/(E + D)$. With no debt, the WACC is equal to the unlevered equity cost of capital. As the firm borrows at the low cost of capital for debt, its equity cost of capital rises, according to Eq. 16.3. The net effect is that the firm's WACC is unchanged. Of course, as the amount of debt increases, the debt becomes riskier because there is a chance the firm will default; as a result, the debt cost of capital also rises. With close to 100% debt, the debt would be almost as risky as the assets themselves (similar to unlevered equity). But even though the debt and equity costs of capital both rise when leverage is high, because more of the firm is financed with debt (which has lower cost), the WACC remains constant.

GLOBAL FINANCIAL CRISIS

Bank Capital Regulation and the ROE Fallacy

In banking jargon, a "capital requirement" obligates a bank to finance itself with a certain minimum amount of equity to ensure that its debt-to-equity ratio will stay below a set level. The permitted level of leverage is very high—international standards allow common equity to represent as little as 2% of a bank's total funding.[2] To put this number in perspective, the equity of a typical non-financial firm exceeds 50% of firm value. Such extreme leverage makes bank equity very risky.

These extreme levels of bank leverage were an important contributing factor to the financial meltdown in 2008 and the subsequent recession: With such a small equity cushion, even a minor drop in asset values can lead to insolvency. Post-crisis, banks have come under increased pressure to reduce leverage with new international rules more than doubling the required proportion of equity financing. Many policymakers believe capital requirements should be increased much more to reduce the risk of the financial sector and the consequent spillovers to the broader economy.

Bankers counter that decreased leverage will lower their return on equity, limiting their ability to compete effectively.

According to Josef Ackermann, then CEO of Deutsche Bank, new capital requirements would "depress ROE to levels that make investment into the banking sector unattractive relative to other business sectors."[3] The return on equity is indeed a function of the firm's leverage. As with EPS, lower leverage will tend to decrease the firm's ROE on average, though it will raise the ROE in bad times. But this decrease in average ROE is compensated for by a reduction in the riskiness of equity and therefore the required risk premium. Thus, from an investor's perspective, the reduction in ROE that results solely from a decrease in leverage does not make investing in the firm any less attractive. Franco Modigliani and Merton Miller were awarded the Nobel Prize for pointing out that in a perfect market the bank's capital structure cannot affect its competitiveness.

The only way a change in leverage can affect the "attractiveness" of equity (and the competitiveness of banks) is if there is a market imperfection. The most important imperfections come from deposit insurance, too-big-to-fail policies, and the tax deductibility of interest, giving banks a strong incentive to maximize their leverage. These imperfections derive from government subsidies, so the banks' gains from leverage come largely at taxpayer expense.

EXAMPLE 16.2
Computing the Equity Cost of Capital

MyFinanceLab

PROBLEM
Suppose you borrow only $6000 when financing your coffee shop. According to MM Proposition II, what will your firm's equity cost of capital be?

SOLUTION

PLAN

Because your firm's assets have a market value of $30,000, according to MM Proposition I the equity will have a market value of $24,000 = $30,000 − $6000. We can use Eq. 16.3 to compute the cost of equity. We know the unlevered cost of equity is $r_u = 15\%$. We also know that r_D is 5%.

---

[2]Two percent is the Tier 1 Common Equity Requirement of the Basel II Accord, the global regulatory standard for bank capital. Starting in 2013, the new Basel III Accord will raise this requirement gradually to 4.5% by 2015.

[3]J. Ackermann, "The new architecture of financial regulation: Will it prevent another crisis?" Special Paper 194, FMG Deutsche Bank Conference, London School of Economics, October 2010.

EXECUTE

$$r_E = 15\% + \frac{6000}{24{,}000}\,(15\% - 5\%) = 17.5\%$$

EVALUATE

This result matches the expected return calculated in Example 16.1 where we also assumed debt of $6000. The equity cost of capital should be the expected return of the equity holders.

MM and the Real World

Our conclusions so far may seem striking at first: In perfect capital markets, leverage does not affect either the cost of capital or a firm's value, and so the firm's choice of capital structure would be irrelevant! However, capital markets are not perfect in the real world. What then are we to make of Modigliani and Miller's results?

NOBEL PRIZE Franco Modigliani and Merton Miller

Franco Modigliani and Merton Miller, authors of the Modigliani-Miller Propositions, each won the Nobel Prize in Economics for their work in financial economics, including their capital structure propositions. Modigliani won the Nobel Prize in 1985 for his work on personal savings and for his capital structure theorems with Miller. Miller earned his prize in 1990 for his analysis of portfolio theory and capital structure.

Miller once described the MM propositions in an interview this way:

People often ask, "Can you summarize your theory quickly?" Well, I say, you understand the MM theorem if you know why this is a joke: The pizza delivery man comes to Yogi Berra after the game and says, "Yogi, how do you want this pizza cut, into quarters or eighths?" And Yogi says, "Cut it in eight pieces. I'm feeling hungry tonight."

Everyone recognizes that's a joke because obviously the number and shape of the pieces don't affect the size of the pizza. And similarly, the stocks, bonds, warrants, etc., issued don't affect the aggregate value of the firm. They just slice up the underlying earnings in different ways.*

Modigliani and Miller each won the Nobel Prize in large part for their observation that the value of a firm should be unaffected by its capital structure in perfect capital markets. Whereas the intuition underlying the MM propositions may be as simple as slicing pizza, their implications for corporate finance are far-reaching. The propositions imply that the true role of a firm's financial policy is to deal with (and potentially exploit) financial market imperfections such as taxes and transaction costs. Modigliani and Miller's work began a long line of research into these market imperfections, which we will look at in the rest of the chapter.

*Peter J. Tanous, Investment Gurus (New York: Institute of Finance, 1997).

As an analogy, consider Galileo's law of falling bodies. Galileo overturned the conventional wisdom by showing that without friction, free-falling bodies will fall at the same rate, independent of their mass. If you test this law, you will likely find it does not hold exactly. The reason, of course, is that unless we are in a vacuum, air friction tends to slow some objects more than others.

MM's results are similar. In practice, we will find that capital structure can have an effect on a firm's value. Galileo's law of falling bodies reveals that we must look to air friction, rather than any underlying property of gravity, to explain differences in the speeds of falling objects. MM's propositions reveal that any effects of capital structure must similarly be due to frictions that exist in capital markets. We explore the important sources of these frictions, and their consequences, in the remainder of this chapter.

CONCEPT CHECK

3. How does leverage affect the risk and cost of equity for the firm?

4. In a perfect capital market, can you alter the firm's value or WACC by relying more on debt capital?

16.3   Debt and Taxes

So far, we have used the perfect capital markets setting to focus on the fundamental point that the firm's choice of projects and investments is the primary determinant of its value and risk, and hence its overall cost of capital. But in the real world, markets are imperfect and these imperfections can create a role for the firm's capital structure. In this section, we focus on one important market friction—corporate taxes—and show how the firm's choice of capital structure can affect the taxes that it must pay and therefore its value to investors.

The Interest Tax Deduction and Firm Value

As we discussed in Chapter 13, corporations can deduct interest expenses from their taxable income. The deduction reduces the taxes they pay and thereby increases the amount available to pay investors. In doing so, the interest tax deduction increases the value of the corporation.

To illustrate, let's consider the impact of interest expenses on the taxes paid by The Kroger Co., a grocery store chain. In 2015, Kroger had earnings before interest and taxes of $3.58 billion, and interest expenses of $480 million. Given a corporate tax rate of 35%, we can compare Kroger's actual net income with what it would have been without debt, as shown in Table 16.2.

TABLE 16.2

Kroger's Income with and Without Leverage, 2012 ($ million)

	With Leverage	Without Leverage
EBIT	$3580	$3580
Interest expense	−480	0
Income before tax	3100	3580
Taxes (35%)	−1085	−1253
Net income	$2015	$2327

As we can see from Table 16.2, Kroger's net income in 2015 was lower with leverage than it would have been without leverage. Thus, Kroger's debt obligations reduced the value of its equity. But more importantly, the *total* amount available to *all* investors was higher with leverage:

	With Leverage	Without Leverage
Interest paid to debt holders	480	0
Income available to equity holders	2015	2327
Total available to all investors	**$2495**	**$2327**

With leverage, Kroger was able to pay out $2495 million in total to its investors, versus only $2327 million without leverage, representing an increase of $168 million.

It might seem odd that a firm can be better off with leverage even though its earnings are lower. But recall from Section 16.1 that the value of a firm is the total amount it can raise from all investors, not just equity holders who receive the earnings. Thus, if the firm can pay out more in total with leverage, it will be able to raise more total capital initially.

Where does the additional $168 million come from? Looking at Table 16.2, we can see that this gain is equal to the reduction in taxes with leverage: $1253 million − $1085 million = $168 million. Because Kroger does not owe taxes on the $480 million of pretax earnings that were used to make interest payments, this $480 million is *shielded* from the corporate tax, providing the tax savings of $0.35 \times \$480$ million = $168 million.

In general, the gain to investors from the tax deductibility of interest payments is referred to as the **interest tax shield**. The interest tax shield is the additional amount a firm can pay to investors by saving the taxes it would have paid if it did not have leverage. We can calculate the amount of the interest tax shield each year as follows:

interest tax shield The reduction in taxes paid due to the tax deductibility of interest payments.

$$\text{Interest Tax Shield} = \text{Corporate Tax Rate} \times \text{Interest Payments} \quad (16.4)$$

EXAMPLE 16.3

Computing the Interest Tax Shield

MyFinanceLab

PROBLEM

Shown below is the income statement for E. C. Builders (ECB). Given its marginal corporate tax rate of 35%, what is the amount of the interest tax shield for ECB in years 2010 through 2013?

	ECB Income Statement ($ million)	2010	2011	2012	2013
1					
2	Total sales	$3369	$3706	$4077	$4432
3	Cost of sales	−2359	−2584	−2867	−3116
4	Selling, general, and administrative expense	−226	−248	−276	−299
5	Depreciation	−22	−25	−27	−29
6	**Operating income**	762	849	907	988
7	Other income	7	8	10	12
8	**EBIT**	769	857	917	1000
9	Interest expense	−50	−80	−100	−100
10	**Income before tax**	719	777	817	900
11	Taxes (35%)	−252	−272	−286	−315
12	**Net income**	$467	$505	$531	$585

SOLUTION

PLAN

From Eq. 16.4, the interest tax shield is the tax rate of 35% multiplied by the interest payments in each year.

EXECUTE

	($ million)	2010	2011	2012	2013
1					
2	Interest expense	50	80	100	100
3	**Interest tax shield (35% × interest expense)**	17.5	28	35	35

EVALUATE

By using debt, ECB is able to reduce its taxable income and therefore decrease its total tax payments by $115.5 million over the four-year period. Thus, the total amount of cash flows available to all investors (debt holders and equity holders) is $115.5 million higher over the four-year period.

Value of the Interest Tax Shield

When a firm uses debt, the interest tax shield provides a corporate tax benefit each year. To determine the benefit of leverage for the value of the firm, we must compute the present value of the stream of future interest tax shields the firm will receive.

As we saw with Kroger and in Example 16.3, each year a firm makes interest payments, the cash flows it pays to investors will be higher than they would be without leverage by the amount of the interest tax shield:

$$\begin{pmatrix} \text{Cash Flows to Investors} \\ \text{with Leverage} \end{pmatrix} = \begin{pmatrix} \text{Cash Flows to Investors} \\ \text{Without Leverage} \end{pmatrix} + (\text{Interest Tax Shield})$$

Figure 16.6 illustrates this relationship. Notice how each dollar of pretax cash flows is divided. The firm uses some fraction to pay taxes, and it pays the rest to investors. By increasing the amount paid to debt holders through interest payments, the amount of the pretax cash flows that must be paid as taxes decreases. The gain in total cash flows to investors is the interest tax shield.[4]

Because the cash flows of the levered firm are equal to the sum of the cash flows from the unlevered firm plus the interest tax shield, according to the Valuation Principle the same must be true for the present values of these cash flows. Thus, letting V^L and V^U represent the value of the firm with and without leverage, respectively, we have the following change to MM Proposition I in the presence of taxes:

The total value of the levered firm exceeds the value of the firm without leverage due to the present value of the tax savings from debt:

$$V^L = V^U + PV \text{ (Interest Tax Shield)} \tag{16.5}$$

Clearly, there is an important tax advantage to the use of debt financing. But how large is this tax benefit? To compute the increase in the firm's total value associated with the interest tax shield, we need to forecast how a firm's debt—and therefore its interest payments—will vary over time. Given a forecast of future interest payments, we can determine the interest tax shield and compute its present value by discounting it at a rate that corresponds to its risk.

FIGURE 16.6

The Cash Flows of the Unlevered and Levered Firm

By increasing the cash flows paid to debt holders through interest payments, a firm reduces the amount paid in taxes. The increase in total cash flows paid to investors is the interest tax shield. (The figure assumes a 40% marginal corporate tax rate.)

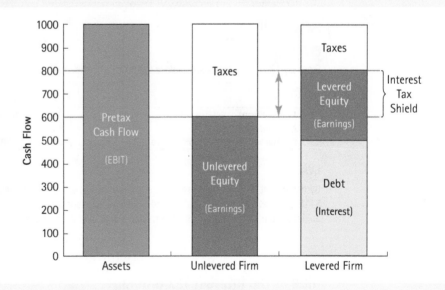

EXAMPLE 16.4

Valuing the Interest Tax Shield

MyFinanceLab

PROBLEM

Suppose ECB from Example 16.3 borrows $2 billion by issuing 10-year bonds. ECB's cost of debt is 6%, so it will need to pay $120 million in interest each year for the next 10 years, and then repay the principal of $2 billion in year 10. ECB's marginal tax rate will remain 35% throughout this period. By how much does the interest tax shield increase the value of ECB?

---

[4]If investors are taxed on interest income at a higher rate than they are on capital gains, this personal tax *disadvantage* of debt will partly offset the corporate tax advantage of debt.

SOLUTION

PLAN

In this case, the interest tax shield lasts for 10 years, so we can value it as a 10-year annuity. Because the tax savings are as risky as the debt that creates them, we can discount them at ECB's cost of debt: 6%.

EXECUTE

The interest tax shield each year is 35% × $120 million = $42 million. Valued as a 10-year annuity with a discount rate of 0.06, we have:

$$PV\,(\text{Interest Tax Shield}) = \$42 \text{ million} \times \frac{1}{0.06}\left(1 - \frac{1}{1.06^{10}}\right)$$

$$= \$309 \text{ million}$$

Because only interest is tax deductible, the final repayment of principal in year 10 is not deductible, so it does not contribute to the tax shield.

EVALUATE

We know that in perfect capital markets, financing transactions have an NPV of zero—the interest and principal repayment have a present value of exactly the amount of the bonds: $2 billion. However, the interest tax deductibility makes this a positive-NPV transaction for the firm. Because the government effectively subsidizes the payment of interest, issuing these bonds has an NPV of $309 million.

The Interest Tax Shield with Permanent Debt

Many factors can affect the future tax savings from interest. Typically, the level of future interest payments varies due to:

Changes the firm makes in the amount of debt outstanding,
Changes in the interest rate on that debt,
Changes in the firm's marginal tax rate, and
The risk that the firm may default and fail to make an interest payment.

Rather than attempting to account for all possibilities here, we will consider the special case in which the firm issues debt and plans to keep the dollar amount of debt constant forever.

For example, the firm might issue a perpetual consol bond, making only interest payments but never repaying the principal. More realistically, suppose the firm issues short-term debt such as a five-year coupon bond. When the principal is due, the firm raises the money needed to pay it by issuing new debt. In this way, the firm never pays off the principal but simply refinances it whenever it comes due. In this situation, the debt is effectively permanent.

Many large firms have a policy of maintaining a certain amount of debt on their balance sheets. As old bonds and loans mature, they start new loans and issue new bonds. Note that we are considering the value of the interest tax shield with a *fixed* dollar amount of outstanding debt, rather than an amount that changes with the size of the firm.

As we learned in Chapter 6, if the debt is fairly priced, the Valuation Principle implies that the market value of the debt today must equal the present value of the future interest payments:[5]

$$\text{Market Value of Debt} = D = PV\,(\text{Future Interest Payments}) \qquad (16.6)$$

---

[5]Equation 16.6 is valid even if interest rates fluctuate and the debt is risky, as long as any new debt is fairly priced. It requires only that the firm never repay the principal on the debt (it either refinances or defaults on the principal).

If the firm's marginal tax rate (T_c) is constant, then we have the following general formula:

Value of the Interest Tax Shield of Permanent Debt

$$PV \text{ (Interest Tax Shield)} = PV(T_c \times \text{Future Interest Payments})$$
$$= T_c \times PV \text{ (Future Interest Payments)}$$
$$= T_c \times D \tag{16.7}$$

This formula shows the magnitude of the interest tax shield. Given a 35% corporate tax rate, it implies that for every $1 in new permanent debt that the firm issues, the value of the firm increases by $0.35.

Leverage and the WACC with Taxes

There is another way we can incorporate the benefit of the firm's future interest tax shield. Recall from Chapter 13 that for companies without preferred stock (which is most companies), we defined the WACC with taxes as:

Weighted Average Cost of Capital with Taxes

$$r_{wacc} = r_E \frac{E}{E+D} + r_D(1 - T_C)\frac{D}{E+D} \tag{16.8}$$

In Eq. 16.8, we incorporate the benefit of the interest tax shield by adjusting the cost of debt to the firm. If the firm pays interest rate r_D on its debt, then because it receives a tax shield of $T_C \times r_D$, the effective after-tax cost of debt is reduced to $r_D(1 - T_C)$. Comparing Eq. 16.8 with Eq. 16.2 for the pretax WACC, we can see that corporate taxes lower the effective cost of debt financing, which translates into a reduction in the weighted average cost of capital. In fact, Eq. 16.8 implies:

$$r_{wacc} = \underbrace{r_E \frac{E}{E+D} + r_D \frac{D}{E+D}}_{\text{Pretax WACC}} - \underbrace{r_D T_C \frac{D}{E+D}}_{\substack{\text{Reduction Due} \\ \text{to Interest Tax Shield}}} \tag{16.9}$$

Thus, the reduction in the WACC increases with the amount of debt financing. The higher the firm's leverage, the more the firm exploits the tax advantage of debt and the lower its WACC. Figure 16.7 illustrates this decline in the WACC with leverage. The figure also shows the pretax WACC as shown in Figure 16.5.

Debt and Taxes: The Bottom Line

In this section, we have seen that the deductibility of interest expenses for corporate taxes creates an advantage for debt financing. We can calculate the value of this benefit to the firm in two ways. First, we can forecast the firm's future interest tax shields and determine their present value. This approach is especially simple when the amount of debt is fixed permanently, in which case the value of the tax shield is equal to $T_C \times D$.

A second way to calculate the benefit of the interest tax shield is to incorporate it in the firm's cost of capital by using the WACC. Unlike the pretax WACC, the WACC with taxes declines with leverage because of the interest tax shield. If we use this lower discount rate to compute the present value of the firm's or an investment's free cash flow, the present value will be higher by an amount that reflects the benefit of the future interest tax shields. This approach is simplest to apply when the firm adjusts its debt to keep the fraction of debt financing (its debt-to-value ratio) constant over time.

FIGURE 16.7

The WACC with and Without Corporate Taxes

We compute the WACC as a function of leverage using Eq. 16.9. Whereas the pretax WACC remains constant, with taxes the WACC declines as the firm increases its reliance on debt financing and the benefit of the interest tax deduction grows. The figure assumes a marginal corporate income tax rate of 35%.

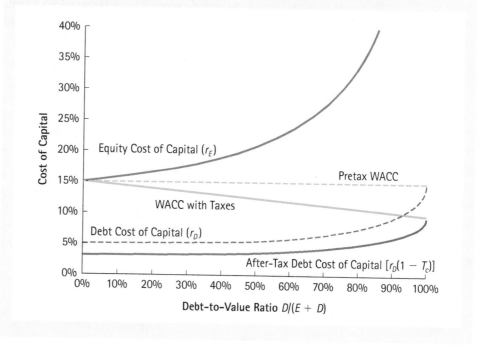

To summarize, we can include the interest tax shield when assessing the value of a firm or an investment by *either* of these methods:

1. Discounting its free cash flow using the pretax WACC, and adding the present value of expected future interest tax shields, or

2. Discounting its free cash flow using the WACC (with taxes).

Using either of these methods, we will find the value of the firm will increase with leverage. Thus, unlike the setting with perfect capital markets, capital structure matters. But now we face a new puzzle: Given the tax benefit, why don't firms use debt financing almost exclusively?

CONCEPT CHECK

5. How does the interest tax deduction affect firm value?

6. How does the firm's WACC change with leverage?

16.4 The Costs of Bankruptcy and Financial Distress

The last section presents us with an interesting question: If increasing debt increases the value of the firm, why not shift to nearly 100% debt? One part of the answer comes from bankruptcy costs. With more debt, there is a greater chance that the firm will be unable to make its required interest payments and will default on its debt obligations. A firm that has trouble meeting its debt obligations is in **financial distress**. Bankruptcy is a long and complicated process that imposes both direct and indirect costs on the firm and its investors that the assumption of perfect capital markets ignores.

financial distress When a firm has difficulty meeting its debt obligations.

Direct Costs of Bankruptcy

Each country has a bankruptcy code that details the process for dealing with a firm in default of its debt obligations (see the appendix to this chapter). The bankruptcy code is designed to provide an orderly process for settling a firm's debts. However, the process is still complex, time-consuming, and costly. When a corporation becomes financially distressed, outside professionals, such as legal and accounting experts, consultants, appraisers, auctioneers, and others with experience selling distressed assets, are generally hired. Investment bankers may also assist with a potential financial restructuring.

In addition to the money spent by the firm, the creditors may incur costs during the bankruptcy process. In the case of reorganization, creditors must often wait several years for a reorganization plan to be approved and to receive payment. To ensure that their rights and interests are respected, and to assist in valuing their claims in a proposed reorganization, creditors may seek separate legal representation and professional advice.

Studies typically report that the average direct costs of bankruptcy are approximately 3% to 4% of the pre-bankruptcy market value of total assets. The costs are likely to be higher for firms with more complicated business operations and for firms with larger numbers of creditors, because it may be more difficult to reach agreement among many creditors regarding the final disposition of the firm's assets. Because many aspects of the bankruptcy process are independent of the size of the firm, the costs are typically higher, in percentage terms, for smaller firms.

 Bankruptcy Can Be Expensive

Outside experts that specialize in aiding distressed firms are costly. At the time Enron entered bankruptcy, it reportedly spent a record $30 million per month on legal and accounting fees, and the total cost ultimately exceeded $750 million. WorldCom paid its advisors $657 million as part of its reorganization to become MCI. Between 2003 and 2005, United Airlines paid a team of more than 30 advisory firms an average of $8.6 million per month for legal and professional services related to its bankruptcy reorganization. Whether paid by the firm or its creditors, these direct costs of bankruptcy reduce the value of the assets that the firm's investors will ultimately receive. In the case of Enron, reorganization costs were expected to approach 10% of the value of the assets.

Source: Julie Johnsson, "UAL a Ch. 11 Fee Machine," *Crain's Chicago Business*, June 27, 2005.

Indirect Costs of Financial Distress

Aside from the direct legal and administrative costs of bankruptcy, many other *indirect* costs are associated with financial distress (whether or not the firm has formally filed for bankruptcy). Whereas these costs are difficult to measure accurately, they are often much larger than the direct costs of bankruptcy.

Indirect bankruptcy costs often occur because the firm may renege on both implicit and explicit commitments and contracts when in financial distress. For example, a bankrupt software manufacturer need not fulfill an obligation to support one of its products. Knowing this, customers who rely on such support might choose to buy software from companies that have a low chance of bankruptcy; that is, companies with lower leverage. Importantly, many of these indirect costs may be incurred even if the firm is not yet in financial distress, but simply faces a significant possibility of bankruptcy in the future. Consider the following examples:

Loss of Customers. Because bankruptcy may enable firms to walk away from future commitments to their customers, those customers may be unwilling to purchase products whose value depends on future support or service from the firm.

Loss of Suppliers. Suppliers may be unwilling to provide a firm with inventory if they fear they will not be paid. For example, Swiss Air was forced to shut down in 2001 because financial concerns caused its suppliers to refuse to fuel its planes.

Cost to Employees. One important cost that often receives a great deal of press coverage is the cost of financial distress to employees. Most firms offer their employees explicit long-term employment contracts, or an implicit promise regarding job security. However, during bankruptcy these contracts and commitments are often ignored and significant numbers of employees may be laid off. In anticipation of this, employees will be less willing to work for firms with significant bankruptcy risk and so will demand a higher compensation to do so. Thus, hiring and retaining key employees may be costly for a firm with high leverage: Pacific Gas and Electric Corporation implemented a retention program costing over $80 million to retain 17 key employees while it was in bankruptcy in 2003.

Fire Sales of Assets. A company in distress may be forced to sell assets quickly to raise cash, possibly accepting a lower price than the assets are actually worth to the firm. This cost is likely to be large when creditors are more pessimistic than management regarding the value of the assets, and so creditors will try to force liquidation even at low prices.

In total, the indirect costs of financial distress may be substantial. A study of highly levered firms by Gregor Andrade and Steven Kaplan estimated a potential loss due to financial distress of 10% to 20% of firm value.[6] Importantly, many of these indirect costs may be incurred even if the firm is not yet in financial distress, but simply faces a significant possibility that it may occur in the future.

CONCEPT CHECK

7. What are the direct costs of bankruptcy?

8. Why are the indirect costs of financial distress likely to be more important than the direct costs of bankruptcy?

16.5 Optimal Capital Structure: The Tradeoff Theory

We can now combine our knowledge of the benefits of leverage from the interest tax shield with the costs of financial distress to determine the amount of debt that a firm should issue to maximize its value. The analysis presented in this section is called the *tradeoff theory* because it weighs the benefits of debt that result from shielding cash flows from taxes against the costs of financial distress associated with leverage. This theory is also sometimes referred to as the *static tradeoff theory*.

tradeoff theory The total value of a levered firm equals the value of the firm without leverage plus the present value of the tax savings from debt, less the present value of financial distress costs.

According to the **tradeoff theory**, the total value of a levered firm equals the value of the firm without leverage plus the present value of the tax savings from debt, less the present value of financial distress costs:

$$V^L = V^U + PV(\text{Interest Tax Shield}) - PV(\text{Financial Distress Costs}) \quad (16.10)$$

Equation 16.10 shows that leverage has costs as well as benefits. Firms have an incentive to increase leverage to exploit the tax benefits of debt. But with too much debt, they are more likely to risk default and incur financial distress costs.

Differences Across Firms

Whereas we have seen in Section 16.3 how to calculate the benefits of the interest tax shield, calculating the precise present value of financial distress costs is very difficult if not impossible. Two key qualitative factors determine the present value of financial distress costs: (1) the probability of financial distress and (2) the magnitude of the direct and indirect costs related to financial distress that the firm will incur.

---

[6]G. Andrade, and S. Kaplan, 1998, "How Costly Is Financial (Not Economic) Distress? Evidence from Highly Leveraged Transactions that Became Distressed," *Journal of Finance* 53: 1443–1493.

What determines each of these factors? The magnitude of the financial distress costs will depend on the relative importance of the sources of these costs and is likely to vary by industry. For example, technology firms are likely to incur high costs associated with financial distress, due to the potential for loss of customers and key personnel, as well as a lack of tangible assets that can be easily liquidated. In contrast, forest products companies are likely to have low costs of financial distress, as much of their value derives from tangible assets (timber land and mills) that can be sold if necessary. Not surprisingly, by reviewing Figure 16.1 we can see that these two industries have very different leverage policies: Technology companies have very low debt, whereas forest products companies tend to be highly levered. Similarly, in Figure 16.2 we saw that Intel has debt whereas ARM Holdings has none. Intel has patents and large chip fabrication facilities that can be sold to meet the claims of lenders. ARM has design facilities and also has patents, but little else that could be sold to meet the demands of creditors.

The probability of financial distress depends on the likelihood that a firm will be unable to meet its debt commitments and therefore default. This probability increases with the amount of a firm's liabilities (relative to its assets). It also increases with the volatility of a firm's cash flows and asset values. Thus, firms with steady, reliable cash flows such as utility companies are able to use high levels of debt and still have a very low probability of default. Firms whose value and cash flows are very volatile (for example, semiconductor firms) must have much lower levels of debt to avoid a significant risk of default.

Optimal Leverage

Figure 16.8 shows how the value of a levered firm, V^L, varies with the level of permanent debt, D, according to Eq. 16.10. With no debt, the value of the firm is V^U. For low levels of debt, the risk of default remains low and the main effect of an increase in leverage is an

FIGURE 16.8

Optimal Leverage with Taxes and Financial Distress Costs

As the level of debt increases, the tax benefits of debt increase until the interest expense exceeds the firm's EBIT. However, the probability of default, and hence the present value of financial distress costs, also increases. The optimal level of debt, D^*, occurs when these effects balance out and the value of the levered firm is maximized. D^* will be lower for firms with higher costs of financial distress.

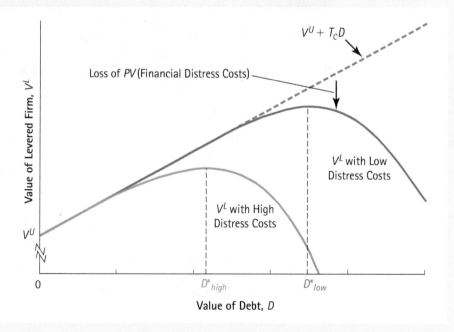

increase in the interest tax shield, which has present value $T_C D$ as shown in Eq. 16.7. If there were no costs of financial distress, the value would continue to increase at this rate until the interest on the debt exceeds the firm's earnings before interest and taxes, and the tax shield is exhausted.

The costs of financial distress reduce the value of the levered firm, V^L. The amount of the reduction increases with the probability of default, which in turn increases with the level of the debt D. The tradeoff theory states that firms should increase their leverage until it reaches the level D^* for which V^L is maximized. At this point, the tax savings that result from increasing leverage are just offset by the increased probability of incurring the costs of financial distress.

Figure 16.8 also illustrates the optimal debt choices for two types of firms. The optimal debt choice for a firm with low costs of financial distress is indicated by D^*_{low}, and the optimal debt choice for a firm with high costs of financial distress is indicated by D^*_{high}. Not surprisingly, with higher costs of financial distress, it is optimal for the firm to choose lower leverage.

The tradeoff theory helps to resolve two important facts about leverage:

1. The presence of financial distress costs can explain why firms choose debt levels that are too low to fully exploit the interest tax shield.

2. Differences in the magnitude of financial distress costs and the volatility of cash flows can explain the differences in the use of leverage across industries.

CONCEPT CHECK

9. According to the tradeoff theory, how should a financial manager determine the right capital structure for a firm?

10. Why would managers in one industry choose different capital structures from those in another industry?

16.6 Additional Consequences of Leverage: Agency Costs and Information

Taxes and financial distress costs are not the only capital market imperfections that arise in practice. In this section, we continue to relax the assumption of perfect capital markets to see other ways in which capital structure can affect a firm's value. We begin by discussing how leverage alters managers' incentives and changes their investment decisions. We then address the complexities of stakeholders in the firm having different information.

Agency Costs

agency costs The costs that arise when there are conflicts of interest among stakeholders.

Agency costs are costs that arise when there are conflicts of interest among stakeholders. In Chapter 1, we briefly mentioned the agency problem that arises when managers put their own interests ahead of shareholders' interest. Here, we discuss how debt can mitigate this problem. However, it may also distort equity holders' preferences for the types of projects pursued by the firm.

management entrenchment A situation arising as a result of the separation of ownership and control, in which managers may make decisions that benefit themselves at investors' expense.

Managerial Entrenchment. Although managers often do own shares of the firm, in most large corporations they own only a very small fraction of the outstanding shares. Shareholders, through the board of directors, have the power to fire managers. In practice, they rarely do so unless the firm's performance is exceptionally poor.

This separation of ownership and control creates the possibility of **management entrenchment**; facing little threat of being fired and replaced, managers are free to run the firm in their own best interests. As a result, managers may make decisions that benefit themselves at investors' expense. Managers may reduce their effort, spend excessively on perks such as corporate jets, or undertake wasteful projects that increase the size of the firm (and their paychecks) at the expense of shareholder value, often called "empire building." If these decisions have a negative NPV for the firm, they are a form of agency cost.

These agency costs are most likely to arise when equity ownership is highly diluted (so that no individual shareholder has an incentive to monitor management closely) and when the firm has a great deal of cash available for managers to spend on wasteful projects. Debt can therefore help in two ways. First, by borrowing rather than raising funds by issuing shares, ownership of the firm may remain more concentrated, improving the monitoring of management. Second, by forcing the firm to pay out cash to meet interest and principal payments, debt reduces the funds available at management's discretion. For managers to engage in wasteful investment, they must have the cash to invest. Only when cash is tight will managers be motivated to run the firm as efficiently as possible. Thus, leverage can provide incentives for managers to run the firm efficiently and effectively. These benefits provide an additional incentive to use debt rather than equity financing.

 ### Airlines Use Financial Distress to Their Advantage

The need to generate cash flows sufficient to make interest payments may also tie managers' hands and commit them to pursue sound business strategies with greater vigor than they would without the threat of financial distress. For example, when American Airlines was in labor negotiations with its unions in April 2003, the firm was able to win wage concessions by explaining that higher costs would push it into bankruptcy. (A similar situation enabled Delta Airlines to persuade its pilots to accept a 33% wage cut in November 2004.) Without the threat of

financial distress, American's managers might not have reached agreement with the union as quickly or achieved the same wage concessions.

A firm with greater leverage may also become a fiercer competitor and act more aggressively in protecting its markets because it cannot risk the possibility of bankruptcy. This commitment to aggressive behavior can scare off potential rivals. (However, this argument can also work in reverse, as a firm weakened by too much leverage might become so financially fragile that it crumbles in the face of competition, allowing other firms to erode its markets.)

Equity-Debt Holder Conflicts. When a firm has leverage, a conflict of interest exists if investment decisions have different consequences for the value of equity and the value of debt. Such a conflict is most likely to occur when the risk of financial distress is high. In some circumstances, managers may take actions that benefit shareholders but harm the firm's creditors and lower the total value of the firm.

To illustrate, put yourself in the place of the shareholders of a company in distress that is likely to default on its debt. You could continue as normal, in which case you will very likely lose the value of your shares and control of the firm to the bondholders. Alternatively, you could:

1. Roll the dice and take on a risky project that could save the firm, even though its expected outcome is so poor that you normally would not take it on.

2. Conserve funds rather than invest in new, promising projects.

3. Cash out by distributing as much of the firm's capital as possible to the shareholders before the bondholders take over.

excessive risk-taking
A situation that occurs when a company is near distress and shareholders have an incentive to invest in risky negative-NPV projects that will destroy value for debt holders and the firm overall.

Why would you roll the dice? Even if the project fails, you are no worse off because you were headed to default anyway. If it succeeds, then you avoid default and retain ownership of the firm. This incentive leads to **excessive risk-taking**, a situation that occurs when a company is near distress and shareholders have an incentive to invest in risky negative-NPV projects that will destroy value for debt holders and the firm overall. Anticipating this behavior, security holders will pay less for the firm initially. This cost is likely to be highest for firms that can easily increase the risk of their investments.

Moral Hazard and Government Bailouts

The term **moral hazard** refers to the idea that individuals will change their behavior if they are not fully exposed to its consequences. Discussion of moral hazard's role in the 2008 financial crisis has centered on mortgage brokers, investment bankers, and corporate managers who earned large bonuses when their businesses did well, but did not need to repay those bonuses later when things turned sour. The agency costs described in this chapter represent another form of moral hazard, as equity holders may take excessive risk or pay excessive dividends if the negative consequences will be borne by bondholders.

How are such abuses by equity holders normally held in check? Bondholders will either charge equity holders for the risk of this abuse by increasing the cost of debt, or, more likely, equity holders will credibly commit not to take on excessive risk by, for example, agreeing to very strong bond covenants and other monitoring.

Ironically, despite the potential immediate benefits of the federal bailouts in response to the 2008 financial crisis, by protecting the bondholders of many large corporations, the government may have simultaneously weakened this disciplining mechanism and thereby increased the likelihood of future crises. With this precedent in place, all lenders to corporations deemed "too big to fail" may presume they have an implicit government guarantee, thus lowering their incentives to insist on strong covenants and to monitor whether those covenants are being satisfied.[7] Without this monitoring, the likelihood of future abuses by equity holders and managers has probably been increased, as has the government's liability.

On the other hand, when default is very likely, a firm may pass up a good project before default because some or most of the benefit will go to bondholders (by reducing the risk or extent of default). For example, if a firm can invest $100 in a project that will increase the value of its debt by $30 and the value of its equity by $90, then the project has a positive NPV of $30 + $90 − $100 = $20. Equity holders will not want to fund it as their gain ($90) is less than the project's cost of $100. In this case, there is an **under-investment problem**: Shareholders choose not to invest in a positive-NPV project because the firm is in financial distress and the value of undertaking the investment opportunity will accrue to bondholders rather than themselves. This failure to invest is costly for debt holders and for the overall value of the firm, because it is giving up the NPV of the missed opportunities. The cost is highest for firms that are likely to have profitable future growth opportunities requiring large investments.

The ultimate form of under-investment is cashing out. Knowing that they are likely to lose the firm to the bondholders, shareholders have an incentive to withdraw as much capital from the firm as possible before it enters bankruptcy and transfers to the debt holders. An extreme example of this would be to sell all the assets of the firm and distribute the proceeds to shareholders as a special dividend. The firm would then enter bankruptcy as a worthless shell. As we discussed in Chapter 15, bondholders can anticipate this problem and often require restrictions on the size of dividends and source of funds for those dividends.

Our discussion suggests that we can create a more complete tradeoff model of capital structure by incorporating the possible agency costs and benefits of debt in addition to tax benefits and financial distress costs. This tradeoff model representing optimal leverage is illustrated in Figure 16.9. When debt is too low, adding leverage increases the value of the firm by providing tax benefits and motivating managers to run the firm more efficiently (and avoid wasteful investment). But if debt is too high, the firm will incur financial distress costs and suffer from excessive risk taking and under-investment. The optimal level of debt D^* is the point that maximizes firm value by balancing these positive and negative consequences of leverage.

under-investment problem A situation in which shareholders choose not to invest in a positive-NPV project because the firm is in financial distress and the value of undertaking the investment opportunity will accrue to bondholders rather than to shareholders.

---

[7]As an example, a number of large banks continued to pay dividends during the crisis even after receiving bailout funds. Had the funds been raised from outside investors without any government guarantee, it is very likely the new investors would have restricted such payouts.

FIGURE 16.9

Optimal Leverage
with Taxes, Financial
Distress, and
Agency Costs

As the level of debt increases, the value of the firm increases from the interest tax shield ($T_C D$) as well as improvements in managerial incentives. If leverage is too high, however, the present value of financial distress costs, as well as the agency costs from debt holder–equity holder conflicts, dominates and reduces firm value. The optimal level of debt, D^*, balances these benefits and costs of leverage.

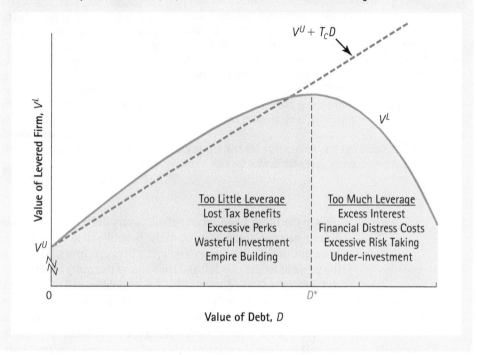

Financial Distress and Rolling the Dice, Literally

Shortly after launching FedEx, founder Frederick Smith was running out of cash and on the verge of shuttering the company's operations. The problem was massive fixed costs (airplanes, sorting facilities, delivery personnel, etc.) and low initial volume.

"By 1973, Smith was so desperate for cash that he flew to Las Vegas to play the blackjack tables. He wired the $27,000 he won back to FedEx."* The company used the winnings to pay its fuel bills, and the rest is history.

*"Frederick W. Smith: No Overnight Success," *Business Week*, September 20, 2004.

Debt and Information

Our final market imperfection is related to the role of information. Throughout this chapter, we have assumed that managers, stockholders, and creditors have the same information. We have also assumed that securities are fairly priced: The firm's shares and debt are priced according to their true underlying value. These assumptions may not always be accurate in practice. Due to **asymmetric information**, managers' information about the firm and its future cash flows is likely to be superior to that of outside investors. This asymmetric information may motivate managers to alter a firm's capital structure.

asymmetric information
A situation in which parties have different information. It can arise when, for example, managers have superior information to that of outside investors regarding the firm's future cash flows.

Leverage as a Credible Signal. To convince the stock market that it has great projects, a firm may commit to large future debt payments. If the projects are great, then the firm will have no trouble making the debt payments. But if the firm is making false claims and then does not grow, it will have trouble paying its creditors and will experience financial distress. This distress will be costly for the firm and also for its managers, who will likely lose their jobs. Thus, the managers can use leverage as a way to convince investors that they do have information that the firm will grow, even if they cannot provide verifiable details about the sources of growth. Investors will interpret the additional leverage as a credible signal of the managers' confidence. The use of leverage as a way to signal good information to investors is known as the **signaling theory of debt**.

signaling theory of debt The use of leverage as a way to signal good information to investors.

market timing When managers sell new shares because they believe the stock is overvalued, and rely on debt and retained earnings (and possibly repurchasing shares) if they believe the stock is undervalued.

Market Timing. When managers have better information than outside investors regarding the value of the firm, they may attempt to engage in **market timing** by selling new shares when they believe the stock is overvalued, and relying on debt and retained earnings (and possibly repurchasing shares) if they believe the stock is undervalued. Managers who successfully time the market in this way benefit long-term shareholders by trading the firm's shares whenever they are mispriced. The firm's capital structure would change as the managers issued new equity (decreasing the leverage) or new debt (increasing the leverage) while attempting to time the market. As a result, the firm's capital structure may deviate above or below the optimal level described by the tradeoff theory, depending on management's view of the share price relative to its true value.

Adverse Selection and the Pecking Order Hypothesis. Suppose managers do try to issue equity when it is overpriced relative to its true value. Knowing this, how would investors react? Recall from Chapter 14 the adverse selection or lemons effect in seasoned equity offerings. Fearful that they are being sold a "lemon," investors will discount the price they are willing to pay for the stock.

The adverse selection problem has implications for capital structure. Managers do not want to sell equity if they have to discount it to find buyers. Therefore, they may seek alternative forms of financing. Debt issues may also suffer from adverse selection. Because the value of low-risk debt is not very sensitive to managers' private information about the firm (but is instead determined mainly by interest rates), the discount needed to attract buyers will be smaller for debt than for equity. Of course, a firm can avoid underpricing altogether by financing investment using its cash (retained earnings) when possible. The **pecking order hypothesis** therefore states that to avoid this "lemons cost":

pecking order hypothesis The idea that managers will have a preference to fund investment using retained earnings, followed by debt, and will only choose to issue equity as a last resort.

Managers will have a preference to fund investment using retained earnings, followed by debt, and will only choose to issue equity as a last resort.

This hypothesis has implications for firms' capital structure. When firms are profitable and generate sufficient cash to fund their investments, they will not issue debt or equity, but just rely on retained earnings. Thus, highly profitable firms will have little debt in their capital structure. Only firms that need to raise external capital will have significant debt financing. According to the pecking order hypothesis, firms should almost never issue equity. In reality, it is likely that multiple forces will shape the firm's capital structure, and firms will issue equity when the agency costs or financial distress costs of debt are too great.

EXAMPLE 16.5
The Pecking Order of Financing Alternatives

MyFinanceLab

PROBLEM

Axon Industries needs to raise $9.5 million for a new investment project. If the firm issues one-year debt, it may have to pay an interest rate of 8%, although Axon's managers believe that 6% would be a fair rate given the level of risk. However, if the firm issues equity, the managers believe the equity may be underpriced by 5%. What is the cost to current shareholders of financing the project out of retained earnings, debt, and equity?

SOLUTION

PLAN

We can evaluate the financing alternatives by comparing what the firm would have to pay to get the financing versus what its managers believe it should pay if the market had the same information they do.

(Continued)

EXECUTE

If the firm spends $9.5 million out of retained earnings, rather than paying that money out to shareholders as a dividend, the cost of financing the project is $9.5 million.

Using one-year debt costs the firm $9.5 \times (1.08) = $10.26 million in one year, which has a present value based on management's view of the firm's risk of $10.26 \div (1.06) = $9.68 million.

If equity is underpriced by 5%, then to raise $9.5 million the firm will need to issue shares that are actually worth $10 million. (For example, if the firm's shares are each worth $50, but it sells them for $0.95 \times $50 = $47.50 per share, it will need to sell $9.5 million $\div$ $47.50/share = 200,000 shares. These shares have a true value of 200,000 shares $\times$ $50/share = $10 million.) Thus, the cost of financing the project with equity will be $10 million.

EVALUATE

Comparing the three options, retained earnings are the cheapest source of funds, followed by debt, and finally by equity. The ranking reflects the effect of differences in information between managers and investors that result in a lemons problem when they issue new securities, and particularly when they issue new equity.

CONCEPT CHECK

11. How can too much debt lead to excessive risk-taking?

12. What is the "pecking order" hypothesis?

16.7 Capital Structure: Putting It All Together

In this chapter, we have examined a number of factors that might influence a firm's choice of capital structure. What is the bottom line for a financial manager devising the optimal capital structure for a firm? The optimal capital structure depends on market imperfections such as taxes, financial distress costs, agency costs, and asymmetric information, as follows:

1. *Make use of the interest tax shield if your firm has consistent taxable income.* The interest tax shield allows firms to repay investors and avoid the corporate tax.

2. *Balance the tax benefits of debt against the costs of financial distress when determining how much of the firm's income to shield from taxes with leverage.* Whereas the risk of default is not itself a problem, financial distress may lead to other consequences that reduce the value of the firm.

3. *Consider short-term debt for external financing when agency costs are significant.* Too much debt can motivate managers and equity holders to take excessive risks or under-invest in a firm. When free cash flows are high, too little leverage may encourage wasteful spending.

4. *Increase leverage to signal managers' confidence in the firm's ability to meet its debt obligations.* Investors understand that bankruptcy is costly for managers.

5. *Be mindful that investors are aware that you have an incentive to issue securities that you know are overpriced.* Thus, when an issue is announced, investors will lower their valuation of that security. This effect is most pronounced for equity issues because the value of equity is most sensitive to the manager's private information.

6. *Rely first on retained earnings, then debt, and finally equity.* This pecking order of financing alternatives will be most important when managers are likely to have a great deal of private information regarding the value of the firm.

7. *Do not change the firm's capital structure unless it departs significantly from the optimal level.* Actively changing a firm's capital structure (for example, by selling or repurchasing shares or bonds) entails transactions costs. Most changes to a firm's debt-equity ratio are likely to occur passively, as the market value of the firm's equity fluctuates with changes in the firm's stock price.

MyFinanceLab

Here is what you should know after reading this chapter. MyFinanceLab will help you identify what you know, and where to go when you need to practice.

KEY POINTS AND EQUATIONS	KEY TERMS	ONLINE PRACTICE
16.1 Capital Structure Choices • The collection of securities that a firm issues to raise capital from investors is called the firm's capital structure. Equity and debt are the securities most commonly used by firms. • Various financing choices will promise different future amounts to each security holder in exchange for the cash that is raised today. • Managers also need to consider whether the securities that the firm issues will receive a fair price in the market, have tax consequences, entail transactions costs, or even change its future investment opportunities.	debt-to-value ratio, p. 498	MyFinanceLab Study Plan 16.1
16.2 Capital Structure in Perfect Capital Markets • When equity is used without debt, the firm is said to be unlevered. Otherwise, the amount of debt determines the firm's leverage. • The owner of a firm should choose the capital structure that maximizes the total value of the securities issued. • According to MM Proposition II, the cost of capital for levered equity is: $$r_E = r_U + \frac{D}{E}(r_U - r_D) \qquad (16.3)$$ • Debt is less risky than equity, so it has a lower cost of capital. Leverage increases the risk of equity, however, raising the equity cost of capital. The benefit of debt's lower cost of capital is offset by the higher equity cost of capital, leaving a firm's weighted average cost of capital (WACC) unchanged with perfect capital markets. • According to MM Proposition I, with perfect capital markets, the value of a firm is independent of its capital structure. With perfect capital markets, homemade leverage is a perfect substitute for firm leverage.	homemade leverage, p. 505 levered equity, p. 501 perfect capital markets, p. 500 pretax WACC, p. 506 unlevered equity, p. 501	MyFinanceLab Study Plan 16.2 Interactive Leverage Effect Analysis
16.3 Debt and Taxes • Because interest expense is tax deductible, leverage increases the total amount of income available to all investors. The gain to investors from the tax deductibility of interest payments is called the interest tax shield. Interest Tax Shield = Corporate Tax Rate $\times$ Interest Payments $\qquad (16.4)$ • When we consider corporate taxes, the total value of a levered firm equals the value of an unlevered firm plus the present value of the interest tax shield. $$V^L = V^U + PV(\text{Interest Tax Shield}) \qquad (16.5)$$	interest tax shield, p. 511	MyFinanceLab Study Plan 16.3

- When securities are fairly priced, the original shareholders of a firm capture the full benefit of the interest tax shield from an increase in leverage.
- When we introduce corporate taxes, the weighted average cost of capital is:

$$r_{wacc} = r_E \frac{E}{E+D} + r_D(1-T_C)\frac{D}{E+D} \quad (16.8)$$

- Absent other market imperfections, the WACC declines with a firm's leverage because interest expense is tax deductible.
- To capture the effect of the interest tax deduction on firm value, you can either compute the PV of the future tax shields or use the WACC with taxes to discount the firm's free cash flows, but not both!

16.4 The Costs of Bankruptcy and Financial Distress • Bankruptcy is a costly process that imposes both direct and indirect costs on a firm and its investors. • Some direct costs are fees paid to lawyers and bankruptcy experts. • Some indirect costs are loss of customers, suppliers, and employees or being forced to sell assets at a deep discount to raise money.	financial distress, p. 515	MyFinanceLab Study Plan 16.4
16.5 Optimal Capital Structure: The Tradeoff Theory • According to the tradeoff theory, the total value of a levered firm equals the value of the firm without leverage plus the present value of the tax savings from debt minus the present value of financial distress costs: $$V^L = V^U + PV(\text{Interest Tax Shield}) - PV(\text{Financial Distress Costs}) \quad (16.10)$$ • The optimal leverage is the level of debt that maximizes V^L.	tradeoff theory, p. 517	MyFinanceLab Study Plan 16.5
16.6 Additional Consequences of Leverage: Agency Costs and Information • Leverage has agency benefits and can improve incentives for managers to run a firm more efficiently and effectively. However, when a firm enters financial distress, leverage can create incentives to forgo good projects or to take excessive risks. • When managers have better information than investors, the result is asymmetric information. Given asymmetric information, managers may use leverage as a credible signal to investors of the firm's ability to generate future free cash flow. • Managers who perceive that the firm's equity is underpriced will have a preference to fund investment using retained earnings, or debt, rather than equity. This result is called the pecking order hypothesis.	agency costs, p. 519 asymmetric information, p. 522 excessive risk-taking, p. 520 management entrenchment, p. 519 market timing, p. 523 pecking order hypothesis, p. 523 signaling theory of debt, p. 523 under-investment problem, p. 521	MyFinanceLab Study Plan 16.6

CRITICAL THINKING

1. Absent tax effects, why can't we change the cost of capital of the firm by using more debt financing and less equity financing?

2. Explain what is wrong with the following argument: "If a firm issues debt that is risk-free because there is no possibility of default, the risk of the firm's equity does not change. Therefore, risk-free debt allows the firm to get the benefit of a low cost of capital of debt without raising its cost of capital of equity."

3. What are the channels through which financing choices can affect firm value?

4. How do taxes affect the choice of debt versus equity?

5. What is meant by "indirect costs of financial distress"?

6. Which type of firm is more likely to experience a loss of customers in the event of financial distress:
   a. Campbell Soup Company or Intuit, Inc. (a maker of accounting software)?
   b. Allstate Corporation (an insurance company) or Reebok International (a footwear and clothing firm)?

7. According to the tradeoff theory, how is capital structure determined?

8. For each pair below, which type of asset is more likely to be liquidated for close to its full market value in the event of financial distress:
   a. An office building or a brand name?
   b. Product inventory or raw materials?
   c. Patent rights or engineering "know-how"?

9. Which of the following industries have low optimal debt levels according to the tradeoff theory? Which have high optimal levels of debt?
   a. Tobacco firms
   b. Accounting firms
   c. Established restaurant chains
   d. Lumber companies
   e. Cell phone manufacturers

10. How can leverage alter the incentives of managers?

PROBLEMS

All problems are available in MyFinanceLab. The ⊞ *icon indicates problems that are easier to solve using Excel and have data in an Excel format available in MyFinanceLab. An asterisk * indicates problems with a higher level of difficulty.*

Capital Structure in Perfect Capital Markets

For problems in this section assume no taxes or distress costs.

1. Consider a project with free cash flows in one year of $130,000 or $180,000, with each outcome being equally likely. The initial investment required for the project is $100,000, and the project's cost of capital is 20%. The risk-free interest rate is 10%.
   a. What is the NPV of this project?
   b. Suppose that to raise the funds for the initial investment, the project is sold to investors as an all-equity firm. The equity holders will receive the cash flows of the project in one year. How much money can be raised in this way—that is, what is the initial market value of the unlevered equity?
   c. Suppose the initial $100,000 is instead raised by borrowing at the risk-free interest rate. What are the cash flows of the levered equity, and what is its initial value according to MM?

2. You are an entrepreneur starting a biotechnology firm. If your research is successful, the technology can be sold for $30 million. If your research is unsuccessful, it will be worth nothing. To fund your research, you need to raise $2 million. Investors are willing to provide you with $2 million in initial capital in exchange for 50% of the unlevered equity in the firm.
   a. What is the total market value of the firm without leverage?
   b. Suppose you borrow $1 million. According to MM, what fraction of the firm's equity must you sell to raise the additional $1 million you need?
   c. What is the value of your share of the firm's equity in cases (a) and (b)?

3. Acort Industries owns assets that will have an 80% probability of having a market value of $50 million in one year. There is a 20% chance that the assets will be worth only $20 million. The current risk-free rate is 5%, and Acort's assets have a cost of capital of 10%.
   a. If Acort is unlevered, what is the current market value of its equity?
   b. Suppose instead that Acort has debt with a face value of $20 million due in one year. According to MM, what is the value of Acort's equity in this case?
   c. What is the expected return of Acort's equity without leverage? What is the expected return of Acort's equity with leverage?
   d. What is the lowest possible realized return of Acort's equity with and without leverage?

*4. Suppose there are no taxes. Firm ABC has no debt, and firm XYZ has debt of $5000 on which it pays interest of 10% each year. Both companies have identical projects that generate free cash flows of $800 or $1000 each year. After paying any interest on debt, both companies use all remaining free cash flows to pay dividends each year.

	ABC		XYZ	
FCF	Debt Payments	Equity Dividends	Debt Payments	Equity Dividends
$ 800				
$1000				

   a. Fill in the table above showing the debt payments and equity dividends each firm will receive given each of the two possible levels of free cash flows.
   b. Suppose you hold 10% of the equity of ABC. What is another portfolio you could hold that would provide the same cash flows?
   c. Suppose you hold 10% of the equity of XYZ. If you can borrow at 10%, what is an alternative strategy that would provide the same cash flows?

5. Hardmon Enterprises is currently an all-equity firm with an expected return of 12%. It is considering borrowing money to buy back some of its existing shares, thus increasing its leverage.
   a. Suppose Hardmon borrows to the point that its debt-equity ratio is 0.50. With this amount of debt, the debt cost of capital is 6%. What will be the expected return of equity after this transaction?
   b. Suppose instead Hardmon borrows to the point that its debt-equity ratio is 1.50. With this amount of debt, Hardmon's debt will be much riskier. As a result, the debt cost of capital will be 8%. What will be the expected return of equity in this case?
   c. A senior manager argues that it is in the best interest of the shareholders to choose the capital structure that leads to the highest expected return for the stock. How would you respond to this argument?

6. Suppose Microsoft has no debt and a WACC of 9.2%. The average debt-to-value ratio for the software industry is 5%. What would be its cost of equity if it took on the average amount of debt for its industry at a cost of debt of 6%?

7. Your firm is financed 100% with equity and has a cost of equity capital of 12%. You are considering your first debt issue, which would change your capital structure to 30% debt and 70% equity. If your cost of debt is 7%, what will be your new cost of equity?

8. One of your new employees notes that your debt has a lower cost of capital (5%) than your equity (15%). So, he suggests that the firm swap its capital structure from 30% debt and 70% equity to 70% debt and 30% equity instead. He estimates that after the swap, your cost of equity would be 20%.
   a. What would be your new cost of debt?
   b. Have you lowered your overall cost of capital?

Debt and Taxes

9. Pelamed Pharmaceuticals had EBIT of $325 million in 2013. In addition, Pelamed had interest expenses of $125 million and a corporate tax rate of 40%.
   a. What was Pelamed's 2013 net income?
   b. What was the total of Pelamed's 2013 net income and interest payments?
   c. If Pelamed had no interest expenses, what would its 2013 net income have been? How does it compare to your answer in part (b)?
   d. What was the amount of Pelamed's interest tax shield in 2013?

10. Grommit Engineering expects to have net income next year of $20.75 million and free cash flow of $22.15 million. Grommit's marginal corporate tax rate is 35%.
    a. If Grommit increases leverage so that its interest expense rises by $1 million, how will its net income change?
    b. For the same increase in interest expense, how will its free cash flow change?

11. Braxton Enterprises currently has debt outstanding of $35 million and an interest rate of 8%. Braxton plans to reduce its debt by repaying $7 million in principal at the end of each year for the next five years. If Braxton's marginal corporate tax rate is 40%, what is the interest tax shield from Braxton's debt in each of the next five years?

12. Assume that Microsoft has a total market value of $300 billion and a marginal tax rate of 35%. If it permanently changes its leverage from no debt by taking on new debt in the amount of 13% of its current market value, what is the present value of the tax shield it will create?

13. Suppose the corporate tax rate is 40%. Consider a firm that earns $1000 before interest and taxes each year with no risk. The firm's capital expenditures equal its depreciation expenses each year, and it will have no changes to its net working capital. The risk-free interest rate is 5%.
    a. Suppose the firm has no debt and pays out its net income as a dividend each year. What is the value of the firm's equity?
    b. Suppose instead the firm makes interest payments of $500 per year. What is the value of its equity? What is the value of its debt?
    c. What is the difference between the total value of the firm with leverage and without leverage?
    d. To what percentage of the value of the debt is the difference in part (c) equal?

14. Your firm currently has $100 million in debt outstanding with a 10% interest rate. The terms of the loan require the firm to repay $25 million of the balance each year. Suppose that the marginal corporate tax rate is 40%, and that the interest tax shields have the same risk as the loan. What is the present value of the interest tax shields from this debt?

15. Arnell Industries has $10 million in permanent debt outstanding. The firm will pay interest only on this debt. Arnell's marginal tax rate is expected to be 35% for the foreseeable future.
    a. Suppose Arnell pays interest of 6% per year on its debt. What is its annual interest tax shield?
    b. What is the present value of the interest tax shield, assuming its risk is the same as the loan?
    c. Suppose instead that the interest rate on the debt is 5%. What is the present value of the interest tax shield in this case?

16. Rogot Instruments makes fine violins, violas, and cellos. It has $1 million in debt outstanding, equity valued at $2 million, and pays corporate income tax at a rate of 35%. Its cost of equity is 12% and its cost of debt is 7%.
    a. What is Rogot's pretax WACC?
    b. What is Rogot's (effective after-tax) WACC?

17. Rumolt Motors has 30 million shares outstanding with a price of $15 per share. In addition, Rumolt has issued bonds with a total current market value of $150 million. Suppose Rumolt's equity cost of capital is 10%, and its debt cost of capital is 5%.
    a. What is Rumolt's pretax WACC?
    b. If Rumolt's corporate tax rate is 35%, what is its after-tax WACC?

18. Summit Builders has a market debt-equity ratio of 0.65 and a corporate tax rate of 40%, and it pays 7% interest on its debt. By what amount does the interest tax shield from its debt lower Summit's WACC?

19. Milton Industries expects free cash flows of $5 million each year. Milton's corporate tax rate is 35%, and its unlevered cost of capital is 15%. The firm also has outstanding debt of $19.05 million, and it expects to maintain this level of debt permanently.
    a. What is the value of Milton Industries without leverage?
    b. What is the value of Milton Industries with leverage?

20. NatNah, a builder of acoustic accessories, has no debt and an equity cost of capital of 15%. NatNah decides to increase its leverage to maintain a market debt-to-value ratio of 0.5. Suppose its debt cost of capital is 9% and its corporate tax rate is 35%. If NatNah's pretax WACC remains constant, what will be its (effective after-tax) WACC with the increase in leverage?

*21. Kurz Manufacturing is currently an all-equity firm with 20 million shares outstanding and a stock price of $7.50 per share. Although investors currently expect Kurz to remain an all-equity firm, Kurz plans to announce that it will borrow $50 million and use the funds to repurchase shares. Kurz will pay interest only on this debt, and it has no further plans to increase or decrease the amount of debt. Kurz is subject to a 40% corporate tax rate.
    a. What is the market value of Kurz's existing assets before the announcement?
    b. What is the market value of Kurz's assets (including any tax shields) just after the debt is issued, but before the shares are repurchased?
    c. What is Kurz's share price just before the share repurchase? How many shares will Kurz repurchase?
    d. What are Kurz's market value balance sheet and share price after the share repurchase?

22. Kohwe Corporation plans to issue equity to raise $50 million to finance a new investment. After making the investment, Kohwe expects to earn free cash flows of $10 million each year. Kohwe currently has 5 million shares outstanding, and it has no other assets or opportunities. Suppose the appropriate discount rate for Kohwe's future free cash flows is 8%, and the only capital market imperfections are corporate taxes and financial distress costs.
    a. What is the NPV of Kohwe's investment?
    b. What is Kohwe's share price today?

23. Suppose Kohwe borrows the $50 million instead. The firm will pay interest only on this loan each year, and it will maintain an outstanding balance of $50 million on the loan. Suppose that Kohwe's corporate tax rate is 40%, and expected free cash flows are still $10 million each year. What is Kohwe's share price today if the investment is financed with debt?

24. Now suppose that with leverage, Kohwe's expected free cash flows will decline to $9 million per year due to reduced sales and other financial distress costs. Assume that the appropriate discount rate for Kohwe's future free cash flows is still 8%. What is Kohwe's share price today given the financial distress costs of leverage?

*25. Rally, Inc., is an all-equity firm with assets worth $25 billion and 10 billion shares outstanding. Rally plans to borrow $10 billion and use these funds to repurchase shares. The firm's corporate tax rate is 35%, and Rally plans to keep its outstanding debt equal to $10 billion permanently.
    a. Without the increase in leverage, what would Rally's share price be?
    b. Suppose Rally offers $2.75 per share to repurchase its shares. Would shareholders sell for this price?
    c. Suppose Rally offers $3.00 per share, and shareholders tender their shares at this price. What will Rally's share price be after the repurchase?
    d. What is the lowest price Rally can offer and have shareholders tender their shares? What will be its stock price after the share repurchase in that case?

Optimal Capital Structure: The Tradeoff Theory

26. With its current leverage, Impi Corporation will have net income next year of $4.5 million. If Impi's corporate tax rate is 35% and it pays 8% interest on its debt, how much additional debt can Impi issue this year and still receive the benefit of the interest tax shield next year?

27. Now that your firm has matured, you are considering adding debt to your capital structure for the first time. Your all-equity firm has a market value of $20 million and you are considering issuing $2 million in debt with an interest rate of 7% and using it to repurchase shares. You pay a corporate tax rate of 40%. Assume taxes are the only imperfection and the debt is expected to be permanent.
    a. What will be the total value of the firm after the change in capital structure?
    b. What will be the value of the remaining equity after the change in capital structure?

28. Hawar International is a shipping firm with a current share price of $5.50 and 10 million shares outstanding. Suppose that Hawar announces plans to lower its corporate taxes by borrowing $20 million and repurchasing shares, that Hawar pays a corporate tax rate of 30%, and that shareholders expect the change in debt to be permanent.
    a. If the only imperfection is corporate taxes, what will the share price be after this announcement?

b. Suppose the only imperfections are corporate taxes and financial distress costs. If the share price rises to $5.75 after this announcement, what is the PV of financial distress costs Hawar will incur as the result of this new debt?

29. Marpor Industries has no debt and expects to generate free cash flows of $16 million each year. Marpor believes that if it permanently increases its level of debt to $40 million, the risk of financial distress may cause it to lose some customers and receive less favorable terms from its suppliers. As a result, Marpor's expected free cash flows with debt will be only $15 million per year. Suppose Marpor's tax rate is 35%, the risk-free rate is 5%, the expected return of the market is 15%, and the beta of Marpor's free cash flows is 1.10 (with or without leverage).
   a. Estimate Marpor's value without leverage.
   b. Estimate Marpor's value with the new leverage.

*30. Colt Systems will have EBIT this coming year of $15 million. It will also spend $6 million on total capital expenditures and increases in net working capital, and have $3 million in depreciation expenses. Colt is currently an all-equity firm with a corporate tax rate of 35% and a cost of capital of 10%.
   a. If Colt's free cash flows are expected to grow by 8.5% per year, what is the market value of its equity today?
   b. If the interest rate on its debt is 8%, how much can Colt borrow now and still have non-negative net income this coming year?
   c. Is there a tax incentive today for Colt to choose a debt-to-value ratio that exceeds 50%? Explain.

Additional Consequences of Leverage: Agency Costs and Information

31. Dynron Corporation's primary business is natural gas transportation using its vast gas pipeline network. Dynron's assets currently have a market value of $150 million. The firm is exploring the possibility of raising $50 million by selling part of its pipeline network and investing the $50 million in a fiber-optic network to generate revenues by selling high-speed network bandwidth. Whereas this new investment is expected to increase profits, it will also substantially increase Dynron's risk. If Dynron is levered, would this investment be more or less attractive to equity holders than if Dynron had no debt?

32. Consider a firm whose only asset is a plot of vacant land, and whose only liability is debt of $15 million due in one year. If left vacant, the land will be worth $10 million in one year. Alternatively, the firm can develop the land at an up-front cost of $20 million. The developed land will be worth $35 million in one year. Suppose the risk-free interest rate is 10%, assume all cash flows are risk-free, and assume there are no taxes.
   a. If the firm chooses not to develop the land, what is the value of the firm's equity today? What is the value of the debt today?
   b. What is the NPV of developing the land?
   c. Suppose the firm raises $20 million from equity holders to develop the land. If the firm develops the land, what is the value of the firm's equity today? What is the value of the firm's debt today?
   d. Given your answer to part (c), would equity holders be willing to provide the $20 million needed to develop the land?

*33. Zymase is a biotechnology start-up firm. Researchers at Zymase must choose one of three different research strategies. The payoffs (after taxes) and their likelihood for each strategy are shown below. The risk of each project is diversifiable.

Strategy	Probability	Payoff ($ million)
A	100%	75
B	50%	140
	50%	0
C	10%	300
	90%	40

a. Which project has the highest expected payoff?

b. Suppose Zymase has debt of $40 million due at the time of the project's payoff. Which strategy has the highest expected payoff for equity holders?

c. Suppose Zymase has debt of $110 million due at the time of the strategy's payoff. Which strategy has the highest expected payoff for equity holders?

d. If management chooses the strategy that maximizes the payoff to equity holders, what is the expected agency cost to the firm from having $40 million in debt due? What is the expected agency cost to the firm from having $110 million in debt due?

*34. You own a firm, and you want to raise $30 million to fund an expansion. Currently, you own 100% of the firm's equity, and the firm has no debt. To raise the $30 million solely through equity, you will need to sell two-thirds of the firm. However, you would prefer to maintain at least a 50% equity stake in the firm to retain control.

a. If you borrow $20 million, what fraction of the equity will you need to sell to raise the remaining $10 million? (Assume perfect capital markets.)

b. What is the smallest amount you can borrow to raise the $30 million without giving up control? (Assume perfect capital markets.)

*35. Empire Industries forecasts net income this coming year as shown below (in thousands of dollars):

EBIT	$1000
Interest expense	0
Income before tax	1000
Taxes	−350
Net income	$650

Approximately $200,000 of Empire's earnings will be needed to make new, positive-NPV investments. Unfortunately, Empire's managers are expected to waste 10% of its net income on needless perks, pet projects, and other expenditures that do not contribute to the firm. All remaining income will be distributed to shareholders.

a. What are the two benefits of debt financing for Empire?

b. By how much would each $1 of interest expense reduce Empire's distributions to shareholders?

c. What is the increase in the *total* funds Empire will pay to investors for each $1 of interest expense?

*36. Info Systems Technology (IST) manufactures microprocessor chips for use in appliances and other applications. IST has no debt and 100 million shares outstanding. The correct price for these shares is either $14.50 or $12.50 per share. Investors view both possibilities as equally likely, so the shares currently trade for $13.50.

IST must raise $500 million to build a new production facility. Because the firm would suffer a large loss of both customers and engineering talent in the event of financial distress, managers believe that if IST borrows the $500 million, the present value of financial distress costs will exceed any tax benefits by $20 million. At the same time, because investors believe that managers know the correct share price, IST faces a lemons problem if it attempts to raise the $500 million by issuing equity.

a. Suppose that if IST issues equity, the share price will remain at $13.50. To maximize the long-term share price of the firm once its true value is known, would managers choose to issue equity or borrow the $500 million if:

   i. They know the correct value of the shares is $12.50?
   ii. They know the correct value of the shares is $14.50?

b. Given your answer to part (a), what should investors conclude if IST issues equity? What will happen to the share price?

c. Given your answer to part (a), what should investors conclude if IST issues debt? What will happen to the share price in that case?

d. How would your answers change if there were no distress costs, but only the tax benefits of leverage?

Chapter 16 Appendix	# The Bankruptcy Code

When a firm fails to make a required payment to debt holders, it is in default. Debt holders can then take legal action against the firm to collect payment by seizing the firm's assets. Because most firms have multiple creditors, coordination is required to guarantee that each creditor will be treated fairly. Moreover, because the assets of the firm might be more valuable if kept together, creditors seizing assets in a piecemeal fashion might destroy much of the remaining value of the firm.

The U.S. bankruptcy code was created to organize this process so that creditors are treated fairly and the value of the assets is not needlessly destroyed. According to the provisions of the 1978 Bankruptcy Reform Act, U.S. firms can file for two forms of bankruptcy protection: Chapter 7 or Chapter 11.

In Chapter 7 liquidation, a trustee is appointed to oversee the liquidation of the firm's assets through an auction. The proceeds from the liquidation are used to pay the firm's creditors, and the firm ceases to exist.

In the more common form of bankruptcy for large corporations, Chapter 11 reorganization, all pending collection attempts are automatically suspended, and the firm's existing management is given the opportunity to propose a reorganization plan. While developing the plan, management continues to operate the business. The reorganization plan specifies the treatment of each creditor of the firm. In addition to cash payment, creditors may receive new debt or equity securities of the firm. The value of cash and securities is generally less than the amount each creditor is owed, but more than the creditors would receive if the firm were shut down immediately and liquidated. The creditors must vote to accept the plan, and it must be approved by the bankruptcy court.[8] If an acceptable plan is not put forth, the court may ultimately force a Chapter 7 liquidation of the firm.

---

[8]Specifically, management holds the exclusive right to propose a reorganization plan for the first 120 days, and this period may be extended indefinitely by the bankruptcy court. Thereafter, any interested party may propose a plan. Creditors who will receive full payment or have their claims fully reinstated under the plan are deemed unimpaired, and do not vote on the reorganization plan. All impaired creditors are grouped according to the nature of their claims. If the plan is approved by creditors holding two-thirds of the claim amount in each group and a majority in the number of the claims in each group, the court will confirm the plan. Even if all groups do not approve the plan, the court may still impose the plan (in a process commonly known as a "cram down") if it deems the plan fair and equitable with respect to each group that objected.

18

Financial Modeling and Pro Forma Analysis

LEARNING OBJECTIVES

- Understand the goals of long-term financial planning

- Create pro forma income statements and balance sheets using the *percent of sales method*

- Develop financial models of the firm by directly forecasting capital expenditures, working capital needs, and financing events

- Distinguish between the concepts of sustainable growth and value-increasing growth

- Use pro forma analysis to model the value of the firm under different scenarios, such as expansion

notation

FCF	free cash flow		*ROE*	return on equity
PV	present value		*SGR*	sustainable growth rate
ROA	return on assets			

Most decisions a financial manager makes have long-term consequences. For example, in the late 1990s, Airbus managers decided to bet the future of the company on the market for megajets, giving the green light to development of the 555-seat A380. Shortly thereafter, Boeing managers bet that airlines would favor improvements in fuel efficiency and gave the go-ahead to the all-composite, technologically advanced 787. The outcomes of these decisions are still playing out today. In this chapter, we will learn how to build a financial model to analyze the consequences of our financial decisions well into the future. In particular, we will use these models to forecast when the firm will need to secure additional external funding and to determine how the decision will affect the value of the firm.

We will start by explaining the goals of forecasting through financial modeling and pro forma analysis, and how this analysis relates to the overall goal of maximizing firm value. Then, we will move to a basic forecasting technique based on projections of the firm's future sales. Next, we will develop an improved approach to forecasting that produces a more realistic financial model of the firm. We will end with a discussion of value-increasing versus value-decreasing growth. Putting the elements of the chapter together, we will see the connection between the role of forecasting, NPV analysis, and the Valuation Principle that underlies all of finance.

18.1 Goals of Long-Term Financial Planning

The goal of the financial manager is to maximize the value of the stockholders' stake in the firm. One tool to help with this goal is long-term financial planning and modeling. In the following sections, we will develop specific methods to forecast the financial statements and cash flows for the firm as a whole. For context, in this section we discuss the objectives of long-term planning.

Identify Important Linkages

As you will see in Sections 18.2 and 18.3, when you build a model of the future course of the firm, by necessity you will uncover important linkages between, for example, sales, costs, capital investment, and financing. A well-designed spreadsheet model will allow you to examine how a change in your cost structure will impact your future free cash flows, financing needs, and other items in the firm's budget. Some links may be obvious, but others are much more difficult to determine without building a forecast of the entire firm's financial statements years into the future. For example, technological improvements leading to reduced costs could allow the firm to reduce prices and sell more product. However, increased production will require more equipment and facilities, and the associated capital expenditures will require financing and create additional depreciation tax shields. None of these links would be easy to see without a careful forecasting model. This is an important outcome of long-term planning because it allows the financial manager to understand the business and, through that understanding, to increase its value.

Analyze the Impact of Potential Business Plans

Perhaps your firm is planning a big expansion or considering changes in how it manages its inventory. By building a long-term model of your firm's financials, you can examine exactly how such business plans will impact the firm's free cash flows and hence value. In Chapter 9, we developed the tools of capital budgeting with the goal of deciding whether to invest in a new project. To consider a fundamental change in the firm's business plan, the financial manager models the firm as a whole, rather than just a single project. In Section 18.3, we will analyze the impact of a firm-wide expansion plan, including necessary capital investment and debt financing. In Section 18.5, we will determine whether the expansion is a good idea by forecasting changes in free cash flows and calculating the change in firm value.

Plan for Future Funding Needs

Building a model for long-term forecasting reveals points in the future where the firm will need additional external financing—for example, where its retained earnings will not be enough to fund planned capital investment. Identifying the firm's funding needs in advance gives financial managers enough time to plan for them and line up the source of financing that is most advantageous for the firm. In a perfect capital market, this would be unnecessary—you would be able to secure financing instantaneously for any positive-NPV project and the source of financing would have no effect on the firm's value. However, in reality, market frictions mean that you need time to issue debt or new equity and, as we learned in Chapter 16, that financing decisions impact firm value. Thus, identifying and planning for these financing decisions far in advance is a valuable exercise.

1. How does long-term financial planning support the goal of the financial manager?
2. What are the three main things that the financial manager can accomplish by building a long-term financial model of the firm?

18.2 Forecasting Financial Statements: The Percent of Sales Method

We will illustrate our discussion of forecasting financial statements via an application: the fictional company KMS Designs. Assume KMS Designs is a boutique women's fashion house, specializing in affordable fashion-forward separates, with its own production facility. KMS Designs is a growing firm and its financial managers predict that it will need external financing to fuel its growth. In order to predict when KMS will need this financing and the amount the managers will need to secure, we need to prepare a financial model in Excel for KMS that will allow us to produce pro forma income statements and balance sheets. After developing a technique for forecasting, we will turn to the steps involved in preparing the pro forma income statement and balance sheet.

Percent of Sales Method

percent of sales method A forecasting method that assumes that as sales grow, many income statement and balance sheet items will grow, remaining the same percent of sales.

A common starting point for forecasting is the *percent of sales method*. The **percent of sales method** assumes that as sales grow, many income statement and balance sheet items will grow, remaining the same percent of sales. For example, Table 18.1 shows that KMS's costs excluding depreciation were 78% of sales in 2016. There were sales of $74,889 (in thousands). If KMS forecasts that sales will grow by 18% in 2017, then:

- Sales will grow to $74,889 \times 1.18 = \$88,369$.
- Costs excluding depreciation will remain 78% of sales, so that costs will be $88,369 \times 0.78 = \$68,928$ in 2017.[1]

We are essentially assuming that KMS will maintain its profit margins as its sales revenues grow. We proceed by making similar assumptions about working capital items on the balance sheet such as cash, accounts receivable, inventory, and accounts payable. The far-right column of Table 18.1 shows what percent of sales each of these items was in 2016. We can use those percentages to forecast part of the balance sheet in 2017. For example, if sales grow to $88,369 as we predict, then our inventory will need to grow to $88,369 \times 0.20 = \$17,674$ to support those sales.

Some of the items in the percent of sales column are marked "NM" for "Not Meaningful." For example, our assets and accounts payables might reasonably be expected to grow in line with sales, but our long-term debt and equity will not naturally grow in line with sales. Instead, the change in equity and debt will reflect choices we make about dividends and net new financing.

---

[1] For ease of exposition, we will base our forecast on a single year, 2016. Companies often take into account averages and trends over several years in forecasting for the future.

1	Year	2016	% of Sales
2	**Income Statement ($000s)**		
3	**Sales**	74,889	100%
4	Costs Except Depreciation	−58,413	78%
5	**EBITDA**	16,476	22%
6	Depreciation	−5,492	7.333%
7	**EBIT**	10,984	15%
8	Interest Expense (net)	−306	NM*
9	**Pretax Income**	10,678	14%
10	Income Tax (35%)	−3,737	NM
11	**Net Income**	6,941	9%

*NM indicates representing the item as a percent of sales is not meaningful.

1	Year	2016	% of Sales
2	**Balance Sheet ($000s)**		
3	**Assets**		
4	Cash and Equivalents	11,982	16%
5	Accounts Receivable	14,229	19%
6	Inventories	14,978	20%
7	**Total Current Assets**	41,189	55%
8	Property, Plant, and Equipment	49,427	66%
9	**Total Assets**	90,616	121%
10	**Liabilities and Stockholders' Equity**		
11	Accounts Payable	11,982	16%
12	Debt	4,500	NM
13	**Total Liabilities**	16,482	NM
14	**Stockholders' Equity**	74,134	NM
15	**Total Liabilities and Equity**	90,616	121%

Pro Forma Income Statement

Table 18.2 shows KMS's pro forma income statement for 2017 along with how each line was determined. KMS is forecasting 18% growth in sales from 2016 to 2017. In addition to the sales forecast, we require three other details to prepare the pro forma income statement: costs excluding depreciation in 2016 as a percent of sales, depreciation as a percent of sales, and the tax rate. KMS's info from Table 18.1 is as follows:

- Costs excluding depreciation were 78% of sales.
- Depreciation was 7.333% of sales in 2016.
- KMS pays a 35% tax rate.

1	Year	2016	2017	Calculation
2	**Income Statement ($000s)**			
3	**Sales**	74,889	88,369	74,889 × 1.18
4	Costs Except Depreciation	−58,413	−68,928	78% of Sales
5	**EBITDA**	16,476	19,441	Lines 3 + 4
6	Depreciation	−5,492	−6,480	7.333% of Sales
7	**EBIT**	10,984	12,961	Lines 5 + 6
8	Interest Expense (net)	−306	−306	Remains the same
9	**Pretax Income**	10,678	12,655	Lines 7 + 8
10	Income Tax (35%)	−3,737	−4,429	35% of Line 9
11	**Net Income**	**6,941**	**8,226**	Lines 9 + 10

The one final assumption we need to make is about our interest expense.[2] We assume for now that it will remain the same as in 2016 because we will determine if our debt needs will change as part of the forecasting process.

Based on our pro forma balance sheet, we are forecasting an increase in net income of $8226 − $6941 = $1285, which represents an 18.5% increase over 2016 net income.[3] We now turn to forecasting the balance sheet to determine whether we will need any new financing in 2017 to pay for our growth. The net income we forecast in Table 18.2 will be one of the inputs to the pro forma balance sheet. The part of that net income not distributed as dividends will add to stockholders' equity on the balance sheet.

EXAMPLE 18.1

Percent of Sales

MyFinanceLab

PROBLEM

KMS has just revised its sales forecast downward. If KMS expects sales to grow by only 10% next year, what are its costs, except for depreciation, projected to be?

SOLUTION

PLAN

Forecasted 2017 sales will now be: $74,889 \times (1.10) = $82,378. With this figure in hand and the information from Table 18.1, we can use the percent of sales method to calculate KMS's forecasted costs.

EXECUTE

From Table 18.1, we see that costs are 78% of sales. With forecasted sales of $82,378, that leads to forecasted costs except depreciation of $82,378 \times (0.78) = $64,255.

EVALUATE

If costs remain a constant 78% of sales, then our best estimate is that they will be $64,255.

Pro Forma Balance Sheet

Forecasting the balance sheet using the percent of sales method requires a few iterating steps. In any balance sheet analysis, we know that assets and liabilities/equity must be equal. The assets and liabilities/equity sides of the pro forma balance sheet will not balance, however, until we make assumptions about how our equity and debt will grow with sales. We see this point in Table 18.3, where we have taken a first stab at the pro forma balance sheet (we will explain the details of the calculation below). Our assets are projected to be $8396 more than our liabilities and equity. The imbalance indicates that we will need $8396 in *net new financing* to fund our growth. **Net new financing** is the amount of additional external financing we will need to secure to pay for the planned increase in assets. It can be computed as:

net new financing The amount of additional external financing a firm needs to secure to pay for the planned increase in assets.

$$\text{Net New Financing} = \text{Projected Assets} - \text{Projected Liabilities and Equity}$$

Let's take a closer look at how we arrived at the $8396 figure. Because we are using the percent of sales method, we assume that assets increase in line with sales. Thus, total assets have increased by 18%, the same as sales. The liabilities side of the balance sheet is more complicated. The amount of dividends a company pays will affect the retained earnings it has to finance growth. Furthermore, any increases in debt or equity reflect capital

---

[2]The interest expense should be interest paid on debt, net of interest earned on any invested cash—just as interest paid is tax deductible, interest earned is taxable—so KMS's tax shield comes from its net interest expense. In order to focus on forecasting, we will assume that all cash held by KMS is a necessary part of its working capital needed for transactions. Thus, we assume that KMS holds all of its cash in a non-interest-bearing account. In Chapter 19, we will discuss alternative ways to invest cash.

[3]This is higher than the sales growth of 18% because we assumed that interest expenses would not increase.

TABLE 18.3

First-Pass Pro Forma
Balance Sheet for 2017

	Year	2016	2017	Calculation
1				
2	**Balance Sheet ($000s)**			
3	**Assets**			
4	Cash and Cash Equivalents	11,982	14,139	16% of Sales
5	Accounts Receivable	14,229	16,790	19% of Sales
6	Inventories	14,978	17,674	20% of Sales
7	**Total Current Assets**	41,189	48,603	Lines 4 + 5 + 6
8	Property, Plant, and Equipment	49,427	58,324	66% of Sales
9	**Total Assets**	90,616	106,927	Lines 7 + 8
10	**Liabilities**			
11	Accounts Payable	11,982	14,139	16% of Sales
12	Debt	4,500	4,500	Remains the same
13	**Total Liabilities**	16,482	18,639	Lines 11 + 12
14	**Stockholders' Equity**	74,134	79,892	74,134 + 70% of 8,226
15	**Total Liabilities and Equity**	90,616	98,531	Lines 13 + 14
16	**Net New Financing**		8,396	Line 9 − Line 15

structure decisions and require managers to actively raise capital, as discussed in Chapters 14 and 15. The bottom line is that we cannot simply assume debt and equity increase in line with sales.

In KMS's case, it has a policy of paying out 30% of its net income as dividends. Thus, $2468 of its forecasted $8226 net income will be distributed to stockholders as dividends:

2017 Net Income:	$8,226
−2017 Dividends (30% of NI)	−$2,468
=2017 Retained Earnings	= $5,758

The $5758 in retained earnings (the remaining 70% of net income after dividends are paid) adds to stockholders' equity on the balance sheet. As a result, stockholders' equity is forecast to increase from $74,134 to $79,892 in Table 18.3.

2016 Stockholders' Equity:	$74,134
+2017 Retained Earnings	+$5,758
=2017 Stockholders' Equity	= $79,892

We also assume that accounts payable will grow along with sales, remaining at 16% of sales as they were in 2016, so they are forecast to grow to $14,139. However, our initial assumption is that debt will remain the same, so our forecasted growth in liabilities and equity falls short of our forecasted growth in assets by $8396.

COMMON MISTAKE

Confusing Stockholders' Equity with Retained Earnings

It is easy to confuse new retained earnings, total retained earnings, and stockholders' equity. As in the example above, new retained earnings are the amount of net income left over after paying dividends. These new retained earnings are then added to the *total* accumulated retained earnings from the life of the firm. Total retained earnings makes up one part of stockholders' equity, which also includes the par value of the stock and any paid-in capital.

Making the Balance Sheet Balance: Net New Financing

How do we address this $8396 difference between assets and liabilities? The projected difference between KMS's assets and liabilities in the pro forma balance sheet indicates that KMS will need to obtain new financing from its investors. The net new financing of $8396 in this case is the amount we have to add to the liabilities and equity side of the pro forma balance sheet to make it balance.

While KMS definitely has to secure $8396 in new financing, it could come from new debt or new equity. We discussed the issues involved in the equity versus debt decision in Chapter 16. It is a complex decision weighing many factors. Rather than complicating our analysis here, we assume that KMS's financial managers have evaluated these factors and decided that the best way to finance the growth is through additional debt. Table 18.4 shows our second-pass pro forma balance sheet including the $8396 in additional debt financing that brings the sheet into balance.

TABLE 18.4

Second-Pass Pro Forma Balance Sheet for KMS

	Year	2016	2017	Calculation
1	**Year**	**2016**	**2017**	**Calculation**
2	**Balance Sheet ($000s)**			
3	**Assets**			
4	Cash and Cash Equivalents	11,982	14,139	16% of Sales
5	Accounts Receivable	14,229	16,790	19% of Sales
6	Inventories	14,978	17,674	20% of Sales
7	**Total Current Assets**	41,189	48,603	Lines 4 + 5 + 6
8	Property, Plant, and Equipment	49,427	58,324	66% of Sales
9	**Total Assets**	90,616	106,927	Lines 7 + 8
10	**Liabilities**			
11	Accounts Payable	11,982	14,139	16% of Sales
12	Debt	4,500	**12,896**	4,500 + 8,396
13	**Total Liabilities**	16,482	27,035	Lines 11 + 12
14	**Stockholders' Equity**	74,134	79,892	74,134 + 70% of 8,226
15	**Total Liabilities and Equity**	90,616	106,927	Lines 13 + 14

We should note that the decision to take on additional debt in 2017 makes our initial assumption that our interest expense would remain constant in 2017 potentially incorrect. If KMS takes on the debt before the end of the year, then there will be a partial-year interest expense from the debt. We would need to adjust the pro forma income statement and iterate with the pro forma balance sheet to get the exact amount of new debt needed. However, we have achieved our primary objective: to identify a future funding need and determine approximately how much we will need and how we will fund it. This will give KMS's managers enough time to begin the debt-issuance process with its bankers. We also note that debt has more than doubled, which justifies our original decision not to assume that it will increase in proportion to sales.

EXAMPLE 18.2

Net New Financing

MyFinanceLab

PROBLEM

If instead of paying out 30% of earnings as dividends, KMS decides not to pay any dividend and instead retains all its 2016 earnings, how would its net new financing change?

SOLUTION

PLAN

KMS currently pays out 30% of its net income as dividends, so rather than retaining only $5758, it will retain the entire $8226. This will increase stockholders' equity, reducing the net new financing.

EXECUTE

The additional retained earnings are $8226 − $5758 = $2468. Compared to Table 18.3, stockholders' equity will be $79,892 + $2468 = $82,360 and total liabilities and equity will also be $2468 higher, rising to $100,999. Net new financing, the imbalance between KMS's assets and liabilities and equity, will decrease to $8396 − $2468 = $5928.

(Continued)

1	Year	2016	2017
2	**Balance Sheet ($000s)**		
3	**Liabilities**		
4	Accounts Payable	11,982	14,139
5	Debt	4,500	4,500
6	**Total Liabilities**	16,482	18,639
7	**Stockholders' Equity**	74,134	82,360
8	**Total Liabilities and Equity**	90,616	100,999
9	**Net New Financing**		5,928

EVALUATE

When a company is growing faster than it can finance internally, any distributions to shareholders will cause it to seek greater additional financing. It is important not to confuse the need for external financing with poor performance. Most growing firms need additional financing to fuel that growth as their expenditures for growth naturally precede their income from that growth. We will revisit the issue of growth and firm value in Section 18.4.

Choosing a Forecast Target

Forecasting by assuming fixed ratios of sales is very common. Another approach is to forecast by targeting specific ratios that the company either wants or needs to maintain. For example, debt covenants (such as those discussed in Chapter 15) often require a company to maintain certain levels of liquidity or minimum interest coverage. The lender does this by specifying, for example, a minimum current ratio (current assets/current liabilities) of 1.5, or a minimum cash flow to interest ratio of 1.2. The company would then incorporate these target ratios into its forecasts to ensure it will be in compliance with its loan covenants.

The need to consider other target ratios is an example of a larger issue in forecasting—that the firm's investment, payout, and financing decisions are linked together and cannot be treated separately. As we saw in Table 18.4, the balance sheet must balance. So a financial manager must understand that the firm can set an investment budget and a financing plan, and those will then determine what is available to pay out. Alternatively, a firm could decide on an investment budget and payout policy, and those will then determine the firm's financing position—perhaps in unintended ways. The bottom line is that a financial manager must balance all these linked decisions, and a careful forecast allows him or her to see the consequences of decisions.

CONCEPT CHECK

3. What is the basic idea behind the percent of sales method for forecasting?

4. How does the pro forma balance sheet help the financial manager forecast net new financing?

18.3 Forecasting a Planned Expansion

The percent of sales method is a useful starting point and may even be sufficient for mature companies with relatively stable but slow growth. Its shortcoming is handling the realities of fast growth requiring "lumpy" investments in new capacity. The typical firm cannot smoothly add capacity in line with expected sales. Instead, it must occasionally make a large investment in new capacity that it expects to be sufficient for several years. This kind of capacity expansion also implies that new funding will happen in large, infrequent financing rounds, rather than small increments each year as sales grow. However, we can address these realities in our long-term forecasting by modeling our capacity needs and capital expenditures directly. In this section, we consider a planned expansion by KMS and generate pro forma statements that allow us to decide whether the expansion will increase the value of KMS. First, we identify capacity needs and how to finance that capacity. Next, we construct pro forma income statements and forecast future free cash flows. Finally, we use those forecasted free cash flows to assess the impact of the expansion on firm value.

KMS's managers have constructed a detailed sales forecast by first forecasting the size of the market and what market share KMS can expect to capture. While the size of the market is generally based on demographics and the overall economy, KMS's market share will depend on the appeal of its product and its price, which KMS has forecast as well. KMS currently has the capacity to produce a maximum of 1.1 million units (i.e., 1100 thousand units). However, as detailed in Table 18.5, KMS expects both the total market size and its share of the market to grow to the point where the company will quickly exceed that capacity. Thus, KMS is considering an expansion that will increase its capacity to 2 million units—enough to handle its projected requirements through 2021.

TABLE 18.5

KMS's Forecasted Production Capacity Requirements

1	Year	2016	2017	2018	2019	2020	2021
2	**Production Volume (000s units)**						
3	Market Size	10,000	10,500	11,025	11,576	12,155	12,763
4	Market Share	10.0%	11.0%	12.0%	13.0%	14.0%	15.0%
5	Production Volume (Line 3 × Line 4)	1,000	1,155	1,323	1,505	1,702	1,914
6	**Additional Market Information**						
7	Average Sales Price	$ 74.89	$ 76.51	$ 78.04	$ 79.60	$ 81.19	$ 82.82

KMS Designs' Expansion: Financing Needs

The first step in our analysis is estimating KMS's financing needs based on the capital expenditures required for the expansion.

Capital Expenditures for the Expansion. The new equipment to increase KMS's capacity will cost $20 million and will need to be purchased in 2017 to meet the company's production needs. Table 18.6 details KMS's forecasted capital expenditures and depreciation over the next five years. Based on the estimates for capital expenditures and depreciation, this spreadsheet tracks the book value of KMS's plant, property, and equipment starting from the book value level at the beginning of 2016.[4] The depreciation entries in Table 18.6 are based on the appropriate depreciation schedule for each type of property. Those calculations are quite specific to the nature of the property; they are not detailed here but follow the conventions discussed in the appendix to Chapter 9. The depreciation shown will be

TABLE 18.6

KMS's Forecasted Capital Expenditures

1	Year	2016	2017	2018	2019	2020	2021
2	**Fixed Assets and Capital Investment ($000s)**						
3	Opening Book Value	49,919	49,427	66,984	67,486	67,937	68,344
4	Capital Investment	5,000	25,000	8,000	8,000	8,000	8,000
5	Depreciation	−5,492	−7,443	−7,498	−7,549	−7,594	−7,634
6	Closing Book Value	49,427	66,984	67,486	67,937	68,344	68,709

[4]In this table and elsewhere in the chapter, we display rounded numbers. Calculations such as Closing Book Value are based on the actual numbers in the spreadsheet with all significant digits. As a result, there will occasionally be a small discrepancy between the Excel-calculated value shown and the hand-calculated value using the rounded numbers displayed.

used for tax purposes.[5] KMS has ongoing capital investment requirements to cover the replacement of existing equipment—these were expected to be $5 million per year without the new equipment. The additional $20 million is reflected in 2017, bringing the total to $25 million for 2017 and increasing expected recurring investment to $8 million per year in years 2018–2021.

Financing the Expansion. While KMS believes it can fund recurring investment from its operating cash flows, as shown in Table 18.7, it will have to seek external financing for the $20 million in new equipment. KMS plans to finance the new equipment by issuing 10-year coupon bonds with a coupon rate of 6.8%. Thus, KMS will pay only interest on the bonds until the repayment of principal in 10 years. The principal on its outstanding debt of $4500 is also not due before 2021.

TABLE 18.7

KMS's Planned Debt and Interest Payments

1	Year		2016	2017	2018	2019	2020	2021
2	Debt and Interest Table ($000s)							
3	Outstanding Debt		4,500	24,500	24,500	24,500	24,500	24,500
4	Net New Borrowing		—	20,000	—	—	—	—
5	Interest on Debt	6.80%	306	306	1,666	1,666	1,666	1,666

Given KMS's outstanding debt, its interest expense each year is computed as:[6]

$$\text{Interest in Year } t = \text{Interest Rate} \times \text{Ending Balance in Year } (t - 1) \quad (18.1)$$

As we saw in Chapter 16, the interest on the debt will provide a valuable tax shield to offset KMS's taxable income.

KMS Designs' Expansion: Pro Forma Income Statement

The value of any investment opportunity arises from the future cash flows it will generate. To estimate the cash flows resulting from the expansion, we begin by projecting KMS's future earnings. We then consider KMS's working capital and investment needs and estimate its free cash flows. With its free cash flows and projected interest tax shields, we can compute the value of KMS with and without the expansion to decide whether the benefit of the new equipment is worth the cost.

Forecasting Earnings. To build the pro forma income statement, we begin with KMS's sales. We calculate sales for each year from the estimates in Table 18.5 as follows:

$$\text{Sales} = \text{Market Size} \times \text{Market Share} \times \text{Average Sales Price} \quad (18.2)$$

For example, in 2017, KMS has projected sales (in thousands) of 10,500 units × 11% market share × $76.51 average sales price = $88,369. We will assume that costs except depreciation will continue to be 78% of sales, so that our projected costs, except depreciation in 2017, will be 78% × $88,369 = $68,928. To arrive at forecasted earnings, we take the following steps:

- Deducting these operating expenses from KMS's sales, we can project EBITDA over the next five years, as shown in Table 18.8.

---

[5]Firms often maintain separate books for accounting and tax purposes, and they may use different depreciation assumptions for each. Because depreciation affects cash flows through its tax consequences, tax depreciation is more relevant for valuation.

[6]Equation 18.1 assumes that changes in debt occur at the end of the year. If debt changes during the year, it is more accurate to compute interest expenses based on the average level of debt during the year.

1	Year	2016	2017	2018	2019	2020	2021
2	**Income Statement ($000s)**						
3	**Sales**	74,889	88,369	103,247	119,793	138,167	158,546
4	Costs Except Depreciation	−58,413	−68,928	−80,533	−93,438	−107,770	−123,666
5	**EBITDA**	16,476	19,441	22,714	26,354	30,397	34,880
6	Depreciation	−5,492	−7,443	−7,498	−7,549	−7,594	−7,634
7	**EBIT**	10,984	11,998	15,216	18,806	22,803	27,246
8	Interest Expense (net)	−306	−306	−1,666	−1,666	−1,666	−1,666
9	**Pretax Income**	10,678	11,692	13,550	17,140	21,137	25,580
10	Income Tax	−3,737	−4,092	−4,742	−5,999	−7,398	−8,953
11	**Net Income**	6,941	7,600	8,807	11,141	13,739	16,627

- Subtracting the depreciation expenses we estimated in Table 18.6, we arrive at KMS's earnings before interest and taxes.
- Next, we deduct interest expenses according to the schedule given in Table 18.7.
- The final expense is the corporate income tax. KMS pays a 35% tax rate, and the income tax is computed as:

$$\text{Income Tax} = \text{Pretax Income} \times \text{Tax Rate} \qquad (18.3)$$

After subtracting the income tax from the pretax income, we arrive at the forecasted net income as the bottom line in Table 18.8.

Working Capital Requirements. We have one more step before we are ready to forecast the free cash flows for KMS. Recall that increases in working capital reduce free cash flows. Thus, we still need to forecast KMS's working capital needs. The spreadsheet in Table 18.9 lists KMS's current working capital requirements and forecasts the firm's future working capital needs. (See Chapter 19 for a further discussion of working capital requirements and their determinants.) We have forecast that the minimum required cash will be 16% of sales, accounts receivable will be 19% of sales, inventory will be 20% of sales, and accounts payable will be 16% of sales, all as they were in 2016.

The minimum required cash represents the minimum level of cash needed to keep the business running smoothly, allowing for the daily variations in the timing of income and expenses. Firms generally earn little or no interest on these balances, which are held in cash or in a checking or short-term savings account. As a consequence, we account for this opportunity cost by including the cash balance as part of the firm's working capital. We will make the assumption that KMS distributes all cash in excess of the minimum required cash as dividends. If our forecast shows that KMS's cash flows will be insufficient to

1	Year	2016	2017	2018	2019	2020	2021
2	**Working Capital ($000s)**						
3	**Assets**						
4	Cash	11,982	14,139	16,520	19,167	22,107	25,367
5	Accounts Receivable	14,229	16,790	19,617	22,761	26,252	30,124
6	Inventory	14,978	17,674	20,649	23,959	27,633	31,709
7	**Total Current Assets**	41,189	48,603	56,786	65,886	75,992	87,201
8	**Liabilities**						
9	Accounts Payable	11,982	14,139	16,520	19,167	22,107	25,367
10	**Total Current Liabilities**	11,982	14,139	16,520	19,167	22,107	25,367
11	**Net Working Capital**						
12	Net Working Capital (7 − 10)	29,207	34,464	40,266	46,719	53,885	61,833
13	Increase in Net Working Capital		5,257	5,802	6,453	7,166	7,948

fund the minimum required cash, then we know that we need to plan to finance those cash needs. Again, identifying these future funding needs is one of the advantages of forecasting.

If KMS instead retained some cash above the amount needed for transactions, the company would likely invest it in some short-term securities that earn interest. Most companies choose to do this to provide funds for future investment so that they do not need to raise as much capital externally. In this case, the excess amount of cash would not be included in working capital. We will discuss cash management in Chapter 19.

COMMON MISTAKE

Treating Forecasts as Fact

Forecasts, like much of finance, give the illusion of precision—we can produce an answer down to dollars and cents. As a result, it is easy to lose sight of the fact that the answer depends on a number of big assumptions that could easily turn out to be wrong. Although it is the financial manager's job to build the forecast and analyze it,

he or she is highly dependent on all the other functional areas for input. Good financial managers will talk to operations, marketing, and sales people to develop reliable estimates of future production costs and potential revenues for each product. However, even the best forecasts can be wrong. That's why it is so important to perform sensitivity and scenario analysis as we did in Chapter 9.

Forecasting the Balance Sheet

We have enough data now to forecast the balance sheet for our planned expansion. Recall from Section 18.2 with the percent of sales method that forecasting the balance sheet helps us identify any future funding needs because the balance sheet must balance. Here, we have explicitly planned for the funding of the expansion in 2017. Nonetheless, we can check to make sure that our debt issue will be enough and then forecast past the expansion to see if we will need any future financing. Table 18.10 shows the balance sheet for 2016 and 2017 filled in with the information we have so far. The only piece of information we are missing is the dividend amount, so we assume for now that we will not pay any dividends in 2017.

As we can see from the column for 2017 in the pro forma balance sheet, KMS's balance sheet does not initially balance: the liabilities and equity are greater than the assets. In Section 18.2, KMS faced the opposite situation—its assets were greater than its liabilities

TABLE 18.10

Pro Forma Balance Sheet for KMS, 2017

	Year	2016	2017	Source for 2017 Data	2017 (Revised)
1	Year	2016	2017	Source for 2017 Data	(Revised)
2	**Balance Sheet ($000s)**				
3	**Assets**				
4	Cash and Cash Equivalents	11,982	14,139	Table 18.9	14,139
5	Accounts Receivable	14,229	16,790	Table 18.9	16,790
6	Inventories	14,978	17,674	Table 18.9	17,674
7	**Total Current Assets**	41,189	48,603	Lines 4 + 5 + 6	48,603
8	Property, Plant, and Equipment	49,427	66,984	Table 18.6	66,984
9	**Total Assets**	90,616	115,587	Lines 7 + 8	115,587
10	**Liabilities**				
11	Accounts Payable	11,982	14,139	Table 18.9	14,139
12	Debt	4,500	24,500	Table 18.7	24,500
13	**Total Liabilities**	16,482	38,639	Lines 11 + 12	38,639
14	**Stockholders' Equity**				
15	Starting Stockholders' Equity	69,275	74,134	2016 Line 18	74,134
16	Net Income	6,941	7,600	Table 18.8	7,600
17	Dividends	−2,082	0	**Assumed**	**−4,786**
18	**Stockholders' Equity**	74,134	81,734	Lines 15 + 16 + 17	76,948
19	**Total Liabilities and Equity**	90,616	120,373	Lines 13 + 18	115,587

and equity—and this told KMS's managers that they needed external financing. When liabilities and equity are greater than the assets, we have generated more cash than we had planned to consume and we need to decide what to do with it. KMS's options are:

- Build-up extra cash reserves (which would increase the cash account to bring assets in line with liabilities and equity).
- Pay down (retire) some of its debt.
- Distribute the excess as dividends.
- Repurchase shares.

Let's assume KMS's managers choose to distribute the excess as dividends. The excess is the amount by which liabilities and equity exceeds assets: $120,373 - $115,587 = $4786. The final column of Table 18.10, labeled "2017 (Revised)," shows the new pro forma balance sheet, including KMS's planned dividend. The balance sheet now balances! We can do this for the full forecast horizon (2017–2021). The completed pro forma balance sheet is shown in the appendix to this chapter.

The general lesson from the example in Section 18.2, as well as from this section, is summarized in Table 18.11.

TABLE 18.11

Pro Forma Balance Sheets and Financing

Liabilities and equity are . . .	less than assets	greater than assets
	New financing is needed—the firm must reduce dividends, borrow, or issue new equity to fund the shortfall.	Excess cash is available—the firm can retain it as extra cash reserves (thus increasing assets), pay dividends, or reduce external financing by retiring debt or repurchasing shares.

CONCEPT CHECK

5. What is the advantage of forecasting capital expenditures, working capital, and financing events directly?
6. What role does minimum required cash play in working capital?

18.4 Growth and Firm Value

We just analyzed an expansion for KMS that involved an expensive capital investment. For KMS, this forecast would be a starting point for the capital budgeting analysis necessary to decide whether the expansion is a positive-NPV project. It is important to remember that not all growth is worth the price. It is possible to pay so much to enable growth that the firm, on net, is worth less. Even if the cost of the growth is not an issue, other aspects of growth can leave the firm less valuable. For example, expansion may strain managers' capacity to monitor and handle the firm's operations. It may surpass the firm's distribution capabilities or quality control or even change customers' perceptions of the firm and its brand.

For example, in Starbucks' 2005 annual report, Chairman Howard Schultz and CEO Jim Donald wrote to shareholders that Starbucks planned to continue opening new stores—1800 in 2006 alone—and planned revenue growth of approximately 20% for the next five years. Around the time Starbucks' shareholders were reading this (early 2006), the price of the company's stock was about $36. By the end of 2007, Starbucks' stock price had fallen to $21, Jim Donald had been fired as CEO, and chairman and founder Howard Schultz had written a memo to employees that Starbucks' recent expansion had caused it to "lose its soul," meaning that the Starbucks experience—the key to its success and the loyalty of its customers—had been watered down. To distinguish between growth that adds to or detracts from the value of the firm, we will discuss two growth rates that factor in financing needs and revisit our top decision rule: NPV analysis.

Sustainable Growth Rate and External Financing

The Starbucks example makes the point that not all growth is valuable growth. The distinction between value-enhancing and value-destroying growth can be made only through careful NPV analysis such as we perform in the next section. However, this distinction is often confused with the concept of a firm's **internal growth rate**—the maximum growth rate a firm can achieve without resorting to external financing. Intuitively, this is the growth the firm can support by reinvesting its earnings. A closely related and more commonly used measure is the firm's **sustainable growth rate**—the maximum growth rate the firm can sustain without issuing new equity or increasing its debt-to-equity ratio. Let's discuss each of these in turn.

internal growth rate The maximum growth rate a firm can achieve without resorting to external financing.

sustainable growth rate The maximum growth rate a firm can achieve without issuing new equity or increasing its debt-to-equity ratio.

Internal Growth Rate Formula. Both these benchmark growth rates are aimed at identifying how much growth a firm can support based on its existing net income. For a firm that does not pay any dividends, its internal growth rate is its return on assets, because that tells us how fast it could grow its assets using only its net income. If the firm pays some of its net income out as a dividend, then its internal growth rate is reduced to only the growth supported by its retained earnings. This reasoning suggests a more general formula for the internal growth rate:

$$\text{Internal Growth Rate} = \left(\frac{\text{Net Income}}{\text{Beginning Assets}} \right) \times (1 - \text{Payout Ratio})$$

$$= \text{ROA} \times \text{Retention Rate} \tag{18.4}$$

Recall from Chapter 7 that the fraction of net income retained for reinvestment in the firm is called the retention rate. In the context of internal and sustainable growth rates, the retention rate is often called the **plowback ratio**. The internal growth rate is simply the ROA multiplied by the retention rate (plowback ratio).[7]

plowback ratio One minus the payout ratio of the firm, also called the *retention rate*.

Sustainable Growth Rate Formula. The sustainable growth rate allows for some external financing. It assumes that no new equity will be issued and that the firm's managers want to maintain the same debt-to-equity ratio. Thus, it tells us how fast the firm can grow by reinvesting its retained earnings and issuing only as much new debt as can be supported by those retained earnings. The formula for the sustainable growth rate is:[8]

$$\text{Sustainable Growth Rate} = \left(\frac{\text{Net Income}}{\text{Beginning Equity}} \right) \times (1 - \text{Payout Ratio})$$

$$= \text{ROE} \times \text{Retention Rate} \tag{18.5}$$

Sustainable Growth Rate Versus Internal Growth Rate. Because your ROE will be larger than your ROA any time you have debt, the sustainable growth rate will be greater than the internal growth rate. While the internal growth rate assumes no external financing, the sustainable growth rate assumes you will make use of some outside financing equal to the amount of new debt that will keep your debt-to-equity ratio constant as your equity grows through reinvested net income.

---

[7]It is common to define ROA as Net Income / End-of-Period Assets. If that is the case, the formula is more complicated but still has the same intuition: (ROA × Retention Rate)/(1 − ROA × Retention Rate).

[8]Just as with the internal growth rate, if you define ROE using end-of-period equity, the formula changes but maintains its intuition: (ROE × Retention Rate)/(1 − ROE × Retention Rate).

EXAMPLE 18.3

Internal and
Sustainable Growth
Rates and Payout
Policy

MyFinanceLab

PROBLEM

Your firm has $70 million in equity and $30 million in debt and forecasts $14 million in net income for the year. It currently pays dividends equal to 20% of its net income. You are analyzing a potential change in payout policy—an increase in dividends to 30% of net income. How would this change affect your internal and sustainable growth rates?

SOLUTION

PLAN

We can use Eqs. 18.4 and 18.5 to compute your firm's internal and sustainable growth rates under the old and new policy. To do so, we'll need to compute its ROA, ROE, and retention rate (plowback ratio). The company has $100 million (= $70 million in equity + $30 million in debt) in total assets.

$$ROA = \frac{\text{Net Income}}{\text{Beginning Assets}} = \frac{14}{100} = 14\% \quad ROE = \frac{\text{Net Income}}{\text{Beginning Equity}} = \frac{14}{70} = 20\%$$

$$\text{Old Retention Rate} = (1 - \text{Payout Ratio}) = (1 - 0.20) = 0.80$$

$$\text{New Retention Rate} = (1 - 0.30) = 0.70$$

EXECUTE

Using Eq. 18.4 to compute the internal growth rate before and after the change, we have:

$$\text{Old Internal Growth Rate} = ROA \times \text{Retention Rate} = 14\% \times 0.80 = 11.2\%$$

$$\text{New Internal Growth Rate} = 14\% \times 0.70 = 9.8\%$$

Similarly, we can use Eq. 18.5 to compute the sustainable growth rate before and after:

$$\text{Old Sustainable Growth Rate} = ROE \times \text{Retention Rate} = 20\% \times 0.80 = 16\%$$

$$\text{New Sustainable Growth Rate} = 20\% \times 0.70 = 14\%$$

EVALUATE

By reducing the amount of retained earnings available to fund growth, an increase in the payout ratio necessarily reduces your firm's internal and sustainable growth rates.

Whenever you forecast growth greater than the internal growth rate, you will have to reduce your payout ratio (increase your plowback ratio), plan to raise additional external financing, or both. If your forecasted growth is greater than your sustainable growth rate, you will have to increase your plowback ratio, raise additional equity financing, or increase your leverage (increase your debt faster than keeping your debt-to-equity ratio constant would allow). Table 18.12 compares internal and sustainable growth rates.

While the internal and sustainable growth rates are useful in alerting you to the need to plan for external financing, they cannot tell you whether your planned growth increases or decreases the firm's value. The growth rates do not evaluate the future costs and benefits of the growth, and the Valuation Principle tells us that the value implications of the growth can be assessed only by doing so.

TABLE 18.12

Summary of Internal
Growth Rate Versus
Sustainable Growth
Rate

	Internal Growth Rate	Sustainable Growth Rate
Formula:	ROA × Retention Rate	ROE × Retention Rate
Maximum growth financed only by:	Retained earnings	Retained earnings and new debt that keeps D/E ratio constant
To grow faster, a firm must:	Reduce payout or raise external capital	Reduce payout, raise new equity, or increase leverage

There is nothing inherently bad or unsustainable about growth greater than your sustainable growth rate as long as that growth is value-increasing. Your firm will simply need to raise additional capital to finance the growth.

For example, in the 1990s, Starbucks' average growth was above 60% even though its average ROE was 20%. Until 2010, Starbucks never paid dividends, so its retention rate was 1, making its sustainable growth rate (SGR) at the time also 20%.

$$\text{SGR} = \text{ROE} \times \text{Retention Rate} = 20\% \times 1 = 20\%$$

Despite expanding at three times its sustainable growth rate, Starbucks' value increased almost 10 times (1000%) during that period.

Conversely, Starbucks' recent experience illustrates that sustainable growth need not be value-increasing growth, as seen in Figure 18.1. We noted at the beginning of this section that starting in 2006, Starbucks was aiming for annual growth of 20%. How does this compare to its sustainable growth rate at the time? When Schultz and Donald wrote their letter to shareholders, Starbucks' ROE was 20% (based on its 2005 annual report). Again, until 2013, Starbucks never paid dividends, so its retention rate was 1, making its sustainable growth rate also 20%. Thus, 20% growth was sustainable—it just wasn't value-increasing.[9]

FIGURE 18.1

Starbucks' Stock Price During Periods of Growth At, Above, and Below Its SGR

The figure graphs Starbucks' stock price since 2000. During most of its early years, Starbucks grew at well above its sustainable growth rate (SGR) and its value increased substantially. In 2006, it planned growth at its SGR but suffered a share decrease in value. Following a change in strategy to slow growth, it grew below its SGR and saw a turnaround in its stock price performance. The figure demonstrates that there is no necessary relationship between a firm's growth relative to its SGR and whether that growth is valuable.

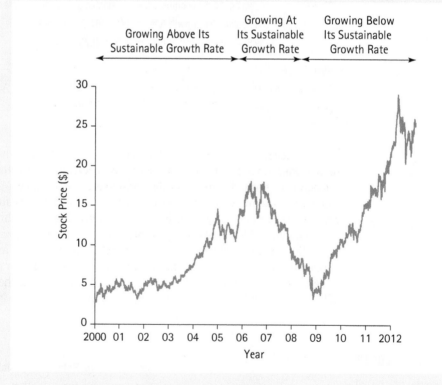

Source: http://finance.yahoo.com, Compustat, and authors' calculations.

---

[9]The book's Web site (www.myfinancelab.com) contains a spreadsheet with a proposed expansion of KMS Designs that allows you to explore the differences between sustainable growth, internal growth rate, and value-increasing growth.

As we discussed in Chapters 14 and 15, there are costs to seeking external financing—the flotation and issuance costs associated with issuing new equity or new bonds. Thus, the internal growth rate indicates the fastest growth possible without incurring any of these costs. The sustainable growth rate still assumes some new debt will be sought, so the company reduces, but does not eliminate entirely, its costs of external financing when growing at the sustainable growth rate. Thus, managers, especially those at small firms, concerned with these costs might track these growth rates. However, for most value-enhancing investment decisions, one would expect these costs to be small relative to the NPV of the decision.

While these costs are usually small relative to the NPV of expanding the business, it would be wrong to ignore them completely. The proper way to incorporate them is to calculate the cash outflow associated with these costs and subtract it from the NPV of the expansion. The point remains that growth above a firm's internal or sustainable growth rates is not necessarily bad but will require external financing and the costs associated with that financing.

CONCEPT CHECK

7. What is the difference between internal growth rate and sustainable growth rate?
8. If a firm grows faster than its sustainable growth rate, is that growth value decreasing?

18.5 Valuing the Expansion

As the last section made clear, growth can increase or decrease the value of the firm. Planning for and forecasting the impact of growth is just the first step in the analysis of whether the growth will make sense for the shareholders. Our forecasting exercise in Section 18.3 gave us estimates of the implications of the planned expansion for the debt, net income, and working capital of KMS. Now we are ready to determine whether the expansion is a good idea. The Valuation Principle guides us here—we need to forecast the cash flows and compute their present value.

Forecasting Free Cash Flows

We now have the data needed to forecast KMS's free cash flows over the next five years. KMS's earnings are available from the income statement (Table 18.8), as are its depreciation and interest expenses. Capital expenditures are available from Table 18.6, and changes in net working capital can be found in Table 18.9. We combine these items to estimate the free cash flows in the spreadsheet shown in Table 18.13.

To compute KMS's free cash flows, which exclude cash flows associated with leverage, we first adjust net income by adding back the after-tax interest payments associated with the net debt in its capital structure. Our net interest expense is interest paid on debt minus

TABLE 18.13

KMS Forecasted Free Cash Flows

	Year	2017	2018	2019	2020	2021
1						
2	**Free Cash Flow ($000s)**					
3	**Net Income**	7,600	8,807	11,141	13,739	16,627
4	Plus: After-Tax Interest Expense	199	1,083	1,083	1,083	1,083
5	**Unlevered Net Income**	7,799	9,890	12,224	14,822	17,710
6	Plus: Depreciation	7,443	7,498	7,549	7,594	7,634
7	Less: Increases in NWC	−5,257	−5,802	−6,453	−7,166	−7,948
8	Less: Capital Expenditures	−25,000	−8,000	−8,000	−8,000	−8,000
9	**Free Cash Flow of Firm**	−15,015	3,586	5,320	7,250	9,396

interest earned on excess cash balances. Recall that interest *paid* is tax deductible, and interest *earned* is taxable, so we adjust each by $(1 - \text{Tax Rate})$:[10]

$$\text{After-Tax Interest Expense} = (1 - \text{Tax Rate}) \times (\text{Interest on Debt})$$
$$- (1 - \text{Tax Rate}) \times (\text{Interest on Excess Cash}) \quad (18.6)$$

Because KMS has no excess cash, its after-tax interest expense in 2017 is $(1 - 35\%) \times \$306 = \$199$ (thousand), providing unlevered net income of $\$7600 + 199 = \$7799$. We could also compute the unlevered net income in Table 18.13 by starting with EBIT and deducting taxes. For example, in 2017 EBIT is forecasted as $11.998 million (Table 18.8), which amounts to:

$$\$11.998 \times (1 - 35\%) = \$7.799 \text{ million after taxes}$$

To compute KMS's free cash flows from its unlevered net income, we add back depreciation (which is not a cash expense), and deduct KMS's increases in net working capital and capital expenditures. The free cash flows on line 9 of Table 18.13 show the cash the firm will generate for its investors, both debt and equity holders.[11] While KMS will generate substantial free cash flows over the next five years, the level of free cash flows varies substantially from year to year. They are even forecasted to be negative in 2017 (when the expansion takes place).

As we noted, free cash flows compute the total cash available to all investors (debt and equity holders). To determine the amount that can be paid out to equity holders, we can adjust the free cash flows to account for all (after-tax) payments to or from debt holders. For example, in 2017 KMS will pay after-tax interest of $199,000 and receive $20 million by issuing new debt as follows:

	2017
Free Cash Flows	−15,015
Less: After-Tax Interest Expense	−199
Plus: Increase in Debt	+20,000
= Free Cash Flows to Equity	= 4,786

Note that the free cash flows that are available to equity holders in 2017, $4.786 million, are exactly the amount of dividends we forecast at the end of Section 18.3. This is no coincidence—we chose in that section to pay out all excess available cash flows as a dividend. This is exactly what the free cash flows to equity tell us—the total amount of excess cash flows that belongs to the equity holders for them to use to pay dividends, repurchase shares, retain in the firm as cash, or retire debt. (See the appendix to this chapter for a forecast of free cash flows to equity and dividends through 2021.)

---

[10]If KMS had some interest income or expenses from working capital, we would *not* include that interest here. We adjust only for interest that is related to the firm's *financing*—that is, interest associated with debt and excess cash (cash not included as part of working capital).

[11]While we are maintaining the assumption that after paying the interest on its debt, KMS will distribute any excess funds to shareholders as dividends, this payout decision has no impact on the amount of free cash flows the firm generates in the first place, and hence has no impact on the value we will compute for KMS.

COMMON MISTAKE

Confusing Total and Incremental Net Working Capital

When calculating free cash flows from earnings, students often make the mistake of subtracting the firm's *total* net working capital each year rather than only the incremental change in net working capital. Remember that only a change in net working capital results in a new cash inflow or outflow for the firm. Subtracting the entire *level* of net working capital will reduce the free cash flows, often even making them negative, and lead the student to understate the NPV of the decision.

KMS Designs' Expansion: Effect on Firm Value

We've accomplished a lot by carefully forecasting the impact of the planned expansion on KMS's net income, capital expenditures, and working capital needs. First, we identified future financing needs, allowing us ample time to plan to secure the necessary funding. Next, in order to construct our pro forma statements, we built an Excel model of the interactions between sales growth, costs, capital investment, working capital needs, and financing choices. This model allows us to study how changes in any of these factors will affect the others and our expansion plans.[12] Remember the lesson from sensitivity and scenario analysis in Chapter 9—these numbers are only forecasts, and as such you need to see how reasonable deviations from the forecast would affect the value of the expansion. Nonetheless, as a starting point, we use these forecasts to provide our best estimate of whether the expansion plan is a good idea—does it increase the value of KMS? There are two ways of doing this: (1) value the whole company with and without the expansion and compare the values or (2) value only the incremental changes to the company caused by the expansion, as we did in Chapter 9's capital budgeting exercise. We will go the first route to provide an example of how to do whole-company valuation. However, you could arrive at the same answer by following the incremental approach.

As we learned in Chapter 16, absent distress costs, the value of a firm with debt is equal to the value of the firm without debt plus the present value of its interest tax shields. Our careful forecast of the financing of KMS's expansion allows us to apply the same approach to valuing the expansion: We compute the present value of the *unlevered* free cash flows of KMS and add to it the present value of the tax shields created by our planned interest payments.[13] However, we have only forecast cash flows out to 2021, so we will need to account for the remaining value of KMS at that point. We do so using the tools developed in Chapter 10 for valuing common stock.

Multiples Approach to Continuation Value. Practitioners generally estimate a firm's continuation value (also called the *terminal value*) at the end of the forecast horizon using a valuation multiple. Explicitly forecasting cash flows is useful in capturing those specific aspects of a company that distinguish the firm from its competitors in the short run. However, because of competition between firms, the long-term expected growth rates, profitability, and risk of firms in the same industry should move toward one another. As a consequence, long-term expectations of multiples are likely to be relatively homogeneous across firms. Thus, a realistic assumption is that a firm's multiple will eventually move toward the industry average. Because distant cash flows are difficult to forecast accurately,

---

[12]You can download a copy of the forecasting model in Excel from the book's Web site and experiment with changes in these factors.

[13]This approach is called the *adjusted present value* because it adjusts the present value of the unlevered free cash flows for the effect of the interest tax shields.

estimating the firm's continuation or terminal value based on a long-term estimate of the valuation multiple for the industry is a common (and, generally, reasonably reliable) approach.

Of the different valuation multiples available, the EBITDA (earnings before interest, taxes, depreciation, and amortization) multiple is most often used in practice. In most settings, the EBITDA multiple is more reliable than sales or earnings multiples because it accounts for the firm's operating efficiency and is not affected by leverage differences between firms. We discussed the use of multiples in valuation in Chapter 10. As in that context, here we estimate the continuation value using an EBITDA multiple as follows:

$$\text{Continuation Enterprise Value at Forecast Horizon}$$
$$= \text{EBITDA at Horizon} \times \text{EBITDA Multiple at Horizon} \qquad (18.7)$$

From the income statement in Table 18.8, KMS's EBITDA in 2021 is forecast to be $34.880 million. Firms in KMS's industry are valued at an average EBITDA multiple of 9. If we assume that the appropriate EBITDA multiple in 2021 is unchanged from the current value of 9, then KMS's continuation value in 2021 is $34.880 \times 9 = \$313.920$ million. This assumption is important—the EBITDA multiple at the horizon will have a large impact on our value calculation. A careful analysis of the prospects for industry growth (which tends to be related to higher multiples) at the horizon is important. Here, we assume that the design and apparel industry is mature and will remain relatively stable, but this assumption can be probed, especially in sensitivity analysis.

KMS Designs' Value with the Expansion. Assume that KMS's financial managers have estimated KMS's unlevered cost of capital to be 10% (specifically, 10% is their pretax WACC; see the details regarding the estimation of the cost of capital in Chapter 13). Now we have all the inputs we need to value KMS with the expansion. Table 18.14 presents the calculation. First, we compute the present value of the forecasted free cash flows of the firm over the next five years. These are the cash flows available to both bondholders and equity holders, so they are free of any effects of leverage. Because they represent cash flows to both debt and equity holders, and because we will account for the benefits of the interest tax shield separately, we discount KMS's free cash flows at the firm's pretax WACC of 10%. Using the free cash flows we forecasted for 2017–2021 in Table 18.13, we get a present value of $4096:

$$PV(FCF) = \frac{-15{,}015}{(1.10)^1} + \frac{3586}{(1.10)^2} + \frac{5320}{(1.10)^3} + \frac{7250}{(1.10)^4} + \frac{9396}{(1.10)^5} = 4096 \quad (18.8)$$

Even though the PV of the cash flows over the next five years is small, the expansion pays off in the long run by providing higher free cash flows from 2021 onward. This growth results in a higher EBITDA in 2021 than would otherwise be possible, and thus a higher continuation value once that EBITDA is multiplied by the continuation multiple of 9. The

TABLE 18.14

Calculation of KMS Firm Value with the Expansion

	Year		2017	2018	2019	2020	2021
1							
2	Free Cash Flow of Firm		−15,015	3,586	5,320	7,250	9,396
3	**PV Free Cash Flow** (at 10%)	4,096					
4	Continuation Value						313,920
5	**PV Continuation Value** (at 10%)	194,920					
6	Net Interest Expense		−306	−1,666	−1,666	−1,666	−1,666
7	Interest Tax Shield		107	583	583	583	583
8	**PV Interest Tax Shield** (at 6.8%)	1,958					
9	**Firm Value (3 + 5 + 8)**	200,974					

$313,920 continuation value in 2021 that we calculated is included in Table 18.14. However, because it is a 2021 value, we need to discount it to the present:

$$\text{PV Continuation Value} = \frac{313,920}{(1.10)^5} = 194,920 \tag{18.9}$$

Finally, because we are financing the expansion with debt, we will have additional interest tax shields. The total net interest expense is included in the table and the interest tax shield in the table is calculated as we did in Chapter 16, by multiplying the interest expense by the tax rate (35% for KMS):

$$\text{Interest Tax Shield} = \text{Net Interest Expense} \times \text{Tax Rate} \tag{18.10}$$

Also as we did in Chapter 16, we calculate the present value of the interest tax shield using the interest rate on debt as the discount rate, *not* using the WACC. Recall that the reason for doing so is that the tax shield is only as risky as the debt that creates it, so that the proper discount rate is the debt's interest rate, here at 6.8%:[14]

$$\text{PV Interest Tax Shield} = \frac{107}{(1.068)^1} + \frac{583}{(1.068)^2} + \frac{583}{(1.068)^3} + \frac{583}{(1.068)^4}$$

$$+ \frac{583}{(1.068)^5} = 1,958 \tag{18.11}$$

The total value of KMS with the expansion is the sum of the present values of the forecasted unlevered free cash flows, the continuation value of the firm, and the interest tax shields. As shown in Table 18.14, the total firm value is $200,974 million.

KMS Designs' Value Without the Expansion. But how do we know if the expansion is a good idea? We can compare KMS's value with the expansion to its value without the expansion. If KMS does not invest in the new equipment, it will be stuck with a maximum capacity of 1100 units. While its sales revenue will grow due to price increases, its main source of growth will be cut off. Table 18.15 shows the sales revenue without the expansion. By 2017, KMS reaches maximum production capacity and can no longer expand. Comparing the sales revenue in the table to the sales revenue with the expansion given in Table 18.8, we see how much higher sales are forecasted to be with the expansion.

TABLE 18.15

Sales Forecast Without Expansion

	Year	2016	2017	2018	2019	2020	2021
1							
2	Production Volume	1,000	1,100	1,100	1,100	1,100	1,100
3	Sales Price	$ 74.89	$ 76.51	$ 78.04	$ 79.60	$ 81.19	$ 82.82
4	Sales Revenue	$74,889	$84,161	$85,844	$87,561	$89,312	$91,099

We can complete the same process for forecasting the free cash flows of the firm without the expansion as we did for the firm with the expansion. In this case, we would find that the 2021 EBITDA would only be $20,042, so that the continuation value would drop to $20,042 \times 9 = $180,378. Also, KMS will not be taking on any additional debt, so the interest expense will remain constant at $306 per year. The final result of the valuation is presented in Table 18.16.

---

[14]We have not ignored the rest of the interest tax shields from the new debt. The value of those shields is subsumed in the continuation value of the firm. When we say that the firm will be worth 9 times EBITDA, we are saying that the total value at that point, including all unused tax shields, will be 9 times EBITDA.

TABLE 18.16

KMS's Value Without
the Expansion

	Year		2017	2018	2019	2020	2021
1							
2	Free Cash Flow of Firm		5,324	8,509	8,727	8,952	9,182
3	**PV Free Cash Flow** (at 10%)	30,244					
4	Continuation Value						180,378
5	**PV Continuation Value** (at 10%)	112,001					
6	Net Interest Expense		−306	−306	−306	−306	−306
7	Interest Tax Shield		107	107	107	107	107
8	**PV Interest Tax Shield** (at 6.8%)	441					
9	**Firm Value (3 + 5 + 8)**	142,686					

While the PV of the free cash flows over the next five years is higher because we don't have to spend $20 million for the new equipment, the lower growth substantially reduces our continuation value and the reduced debt (because we do not need to borrow to fund the equipment) produces a much lower present value of interest tax shields as well. The resulting firm value is almost $60 million lower without the expansion than it is with the expansion. Thus, the expansion is certainly a good idea for KMS.

Optimal Timing and the Option to Delay

We just showed that if the alternative is not to expand at all, KMS should definitely expand in 2017. However, what if it also has the option to simply delay expansion to 2018 or later, rather than not to expand at all? If we repeat the valuation analysis above for expansion in each year from 2017 to 2021, we get the following firm values in 2016:[15]

Expand in . . .	2017	2018	2019	2020	2021
KMS's Firm Value in 2016:	200,974	203,553	204,728	204,604	203,277

KMS's firm value is maximized by delaying the expansion to 2019. The reason is that while delaying expansion means that KMS cannot produce enough units to meet demand, the shortfall is not too great until 2019. The value gained from putting off such a large financial outlay is greater than the value lost from forgone sales.

The timing analysis recalls an important point from Chapter 9: Managers often have real options embedded in capital budgeting decisions. In this case, it is important for KMS's managers to realize that the alternative is not expand or do nothing. Rather, it is expand or delay expansion for another year (or more). As we see here, this option is valuable, allowing KMS's managers to add almost $4 million in additional value to the firm.

**CONCEPT
CHECK**

9. What is the multiples approach to continuation value?

10. How does forecasting help the financial manager decide whether to implement a new business plan?

---

[15]Interested students may perform this analysis using the spreadsheet that accompanies this chapter on the book's Web site.

MyFinanceLab

Here is what you should know after reading this chapter. MyFinanceLab will help you identify what you know, and where to go when you need to practice.

KEY POINTS AND EQUATIONS	KEY TERMS	ONLINE PRACTICE
18.1 Goals of Long-Term Financial Planning Building a financial model to forecast the financial statements and free cash flows of a firm allows the financial manager to: • Identify important linkages. • Analyze the impact of potential business plans. • Plan for future funding needs.		MyFinanceLab Study Plan 18.1
18.2 Forecasting Financial Statements: The Percent of Sales Method • One common approach to forecasting is the percent of sales approach, where you assume that costs, working capital, and total assets will remain a fixed percent of sales as sales grow. • A pro forma income statement projects the firm's earnings under a given set of hypothetical assumptions. • A pro forma balance sheet projects the firm's assets, liabilities, and equity under the same assumptions used to construct the pro forma income statement. • Forecasting the balance sheet with the percent of sales method requires two passes. • The first pass reveals by how much equity and liabilities would fall short of the amount needed to finance the expected growth in assets. • In the second pass, the pro forma balance sheet shows the necessary financing from the planned sources and is in balance.	net new financing, p. 577 percent of sales method, p. 575	MyFinanceLab Study Plan 18.2 Spreadsheet Tables 18.1–18.4
18.3 Forecasting a Planned Expansion • An improvement over the percent of sales method is to forecast the firm's working capital and capital investment, along with planned financing of those investments directly. • Such a financial model will have the correct timing of external financing and capital investment so that we can estimate the firm's future free cash flows.		MyFinanceLab Study Plan 18.3 Spreadsheet Tables 18.5–18.10

18.4 Growth and Firm Value
• Two common concepts are internal growth rate and sustainable growth rate.
• The internal growth rate identifies the maximum rate at which the firm can grow without external financing:
  Internal Growth Rate $= \text{ROA} \times \text{Retention Rate}$ (18.4)
• The sustainable growth rate identifies the maximum rate at which the firm can grow if it wants to keep its D/E ratio constant without any new equity financing:
  Sustainable Growth Rate $= \text{ROE} \times \text{Retention Rate}$ (18.5)
	internal growth rate, p. 586
	plowback ratio, p. 586
	sustainable growth rate, p. 586
		MyFinanceLab
		Study Plan 18.4

- Neither the internal growth rate nor the sustainable growth rate indicates whether planned growth is good or bad. Only an NPV analysis can tell us whether the contemplated growth will increase or decrease the value of the firm.

18.5 Valuing the Expansion

- In addition to forecasting cash flows for a few years, we need to estimate the firm's continuation value at the end of the forecast horizon.
- One method of estimating the continuation value is to use a valuation multiple based on comparable firms.
- Given the forecasted cash flows and an estimate of the cost of capital, the final step is to combine these inputs to estimate the value of the firm based on the business plan. We can compare this to the value of the firm without the new plan to determine whether to implement the plan.

MyFinanceLab
Study Plan 18.5

Interactive
Financial
Statement Model

Spreadsheet
Tables
18.13–18.16

CRITICAL THINKING

1. What is the purpose of long-term forecasting?

2. What are the advantages and disadvantages of the percent of sales method?

3. What is gained by forecasting capital expenditures and external financing specifically?

4. What can the sustainable growth rate tell a financial manager and what can it not tell?

5. How can the financial manager use the long-term forecast to decide on adopting a new business plan?

PROBLEMS

All problems are available in MyFinanceLab. *The* 🖩 *icon indicates problems that are easier to solve using Excel and have data in an Excel format available in* MyFinanceLab.

Forecasting Financial Statements: The Percent of Sales Method

1. Your company has sales of $100,000 this year and cost of goods sold of $72,000. You forecast sales to increase to $110,000 next year. Using the percent of sales method, forecast next year's cost of goods sold.

2. For the next fiscal year, you forecast net income of $50,000 and ending assets of $500,000. Your firm's payout ratio is 10%. Your beginning stockholders' equity is $300,000 and your beginning total liabilities are $120,000. Your non-debt liabilities such as accounts payable are forecasted to increase by $10,000. What is your net new financing needed for next year?

3. Assume your beginning debt in Problem 2 is $100,000. What amount of equity and what amount of debt would you need to issue to cover the net new financing in order to keep your debt-equity ratio constant?

For Problems 4–7, use the following income statement and balance sheet for Jim's Espresso:

Income Statement		Balance Sheet	
Sales	200,000	<u>Assets</u>	
Costs Except Depreciation	(100,000)	Cash and Equivalents	15,000
EBITDA	100,000	Accounts Receivable	2,000
Depreciation	(6,000)	Inventories	4,000
EBIT	94,000	Total Current Assets	21,000
Interest Expense (net)	(400)	Property, Plant, and Equipment	10,000
Pretax Income	93,600	Total Assets	31,000
Income Tax	(32,760)		
Net Income	60,840	<u>Liabilities and Equity</u>	
		Accounts Payable	1,500
		Debt	4,000
		Total Liabilities	5,500
		Stockholders' Equity	25,500
		Total Liabilities and Equity	31,000

 4. Jim's expects sales to grow by 10% next year. Using the percent of sales method, forecast (*see* MyFinanceLab *for the data in Excel format*):
   a. Costs
   b. Depreciation
   c. Net income
   d. Cash
   e. Accounts receivable
   f. Inventory
   g. Property, plant, and equipment

 5. Assume that Jim's pays out 90% of its net income. Use the percent of sales method to forecast (*see* MyFinanceLab *for the data in Excel format*):
   a. Stockholders' equity
   b. Accounts payable

 6. What is the amount of net new financing needed for Jim's (*see* MyFinanceLab *for the data in Excel format*)?

7. If Jim's adjusts its payout policy to 70% of net income, how will the net new financing change?

For Problems 8–11, use the following income statement and balance sheet for Global Corp.:

Figures in $ millions

Net sales	186.7	**Assets**	
Costs Except Depreciation	−175.1	Cash	23.2
EBITDA	11.6	Accounts Receivable	18.5
Depreciation and Amortization	−1.2	Inventories	15.3
EBIT	10.4	Total Current Assets	57
Interest Income (expense)	−7.7		
Pretax Income	2.7	Net Property, Plant, and Equipment	113.1
Taxes	−0.7	Total Assets	170.1
Net Income	2.0		
		Liabilities and Equity	
		Accounts Payable	34.7
		Long-Term Debt	113.2
		Total Liabilities	147.9
		Total Stockholders' Equity	22.2
		Total Liabilities and Equity	170.1

8. Global expects sales to grow by 8% next year. Using the percent of sales method, forecast (*see* MyFinanceLab *for the data in Excel format*):

    a. Costs except depreciation   e. Accounts receivable

    b. Depreciation   f. Inventory

    c. Net income   g. Property, plant, and equipment

    d. Cash   h. Accounts payable

9. Assume that Global pays out 50% of its net income. Use the percent of sales method to forecast stockholders' equity (*see* MyFinanceLab *for the data in Excel format*).

10. What is the amount of net new financing needed for Global (*see* MyFinanceLab *for the data in Excel format*)?

11. If Global decides that it will limit its net new financing to no more than $9 million, how will this affect its payout policy (*see* MyFinanceLab *for the data in Excel format*)?

Forecasting a Planned Expansion

For problems in this section, you should download the KMS spreadsheets available on the book's Web site.

12. Assume that KMS's market share will increase by 0.25% per year rather than the 1% used in the chapter (see Table 18.5) and that its prices remain as in the chapter. What production capacity will KMS require each year? When will an expansion become necessary (that is, when will production volume exceed 1100)?

13. Under the assumption that KMS's market share will increase by 0.25% per year, you determine that the plant will require an expansion in 2018. The expansion will cost $20 million. Assuming that the financing of the expansion will be delayed accordingly, calculate the projected interest payments and the amount of the projected interest tax shields (assuming that KMS still uses a 10-year bond and interest rates remain the same as in the chapter) through 2021.

14. Under the assumption that KMS's market share will increase by 0.25% per year (and the investment and financing will be adjusted as described in Problem 13), you project the following depreciation:

Year	2016	2017	2018	2019	2020	2021
Depreciation	5,492	5,443	7,398	7,459	7,513	7,561

Using this information, project net income through 2021 (that is, reproduce Table 18.8 under the new assumptions).

15. Assuming that KMS's market share will increase by 0.25% per year (implying that the investment, financing, and depreciation will be adjusted as described in Problems 13 and 14), and that the working capital assumptions used in the chapter still hold, calculate KMS's working capital requirements through 2021 (that is, reproduce Table 18.9 under the new assumptions).

Growth and Firm Value

16. Using the information in the following table, calculate this company's:

Net Income	50,000
Beginning Total Assets	400,000
Beginning Stockholders' Equity	250,000
Payout Ratio	0%

a. Internal growth rate.
b. Sustainable growth rate.
c. Sustainable growth rate if it pays out 40% of its net income as a dividend.

17. Did KMS's expansion plan call for it to grow slower or faster than its sustainable growth rate?

18. Your firm has an ROE of 12%, a payout ratio of 25%, $600,000 of stockholders' equity, and $400,000 of debt. If you grow at your sustainable growth rate this year, how much additional debt will you need to issue?

19. IZAX, Co. had the following items on its balance sheet at the beginning of the year:

Assets		Liabilities and Equity	
Cash	50,000	Debt	100,000
PPE	350,000	Equity	300,000

Its net income this year is $20,000 and it pays dividends of $5,000. If its assets grew at its internal growth rate, what is its new D/E ratio?

Valuing the Expansion

20. Forecast KMS's free cash flows (reproduce Table 18.13), assuming KMS's market share will increase by 0.25% per year; investment, financing, and depreciation will be adjusted accordingly; and working capital will be as you projected in Problem 15.

21. Calculate the continuation value of KMS using your reproduction of Table 18.8 from Problem 14, and assuming an EBITDA multiple of 8.5.

22. Assuming a cost of capital of 10%, compute the value of KMS under the 0.25% growth scenario.

<table>
<tr><td>**Chapter 18**
Appendix</td><td>## The Balance Sheet and
Statement of Cash Flows</td></tr>
</table>

The information we have calculated so far can be used to project KMS's balance sheet and statement of cash flows through 2021. While these statements are not critical for our valuation of the expansion, they often prove helpful in providing a more complete picture of how a firm will grow during the forecast period. These statements for KMS are shown in the spreadsheets in Tables 18.17 and 18.18.

TABLE 18.17

Pro Forma Balance Sheet for KMS, 2016–2021

	Year	2016	2017	2018	2019	2020	2021
2	**Balance Sheets ($000s)**						
3	**Assets**						
4	Cash and Cash Equivalents	11,982	14,139	16,520	19,167	22,107	25,367
5	Accounts Receivable	14,229	16,790	19,617	22,761	26,252	30,124
6	Inventories	14,978	17,674	20,649	23,959	27,633	31,709
7	**Total Current Assets**	41,189	48,603	56,786	65,886	75,992	87,201
8	Property, Plant, and Equipment	49,427	66,984	67,486	67,937	68,344	68,709
9	**Total Assets**	90,616	115,587	124,272	133,823	144,335	155,910
10							
11	**Liabilities**						
12	Accounts Payable	11,982	14,139	16,520	19,167	22,107	25,367
13	Debt	4,500	24,500	24,500	24,500	24,500	24,500
14	**Total Liabilities**	16,482	38,639	41,020	43,667	46,607	49,867
15							
16	**Stockholders' Equity**						
17	Starting Stockholders' Equity	69,275	74,134	76,948	83,252	90,156	97,729
18	Net Income	6,940	7,600	8,807	11,141	13,739	16,627
19	Dividends	−2,082	−4,786	−2,503	−4,237	−6,167	−8,313
20	**Stockholders' Equity**	74,134	76,948	83,252	90,156	97,729	106,042
21	**Total Liabilities and Equity**	90,616	115,587	124,272	133,823	144,335	155,910

TABLE 18.18

Pro Forma Statement of Cash Flows for KMS, 2016–2021

	Year	2016	2017	2018	2019	2020	2021
2	**Statement of Cash Flows ($000s)**						
3	**Net Income**		7,600	8,807	11,141	13,739	16,627
4	Depreciation		7,443	7,498	7,549	7,594	7,634
5	**Changes in Working Capital**						
6	Accounts Receivable		−2,561	−2,827	−3,144	−3,491	−3,872
7	Inventory		−2,696	−2,976	−3,309	−3,675	−4,076
8	Accounts Payable		2,157	2,381	2,647	2,940	3,261
9	**Cash from Operating Activities**		11,942	12,884	14,884	17,107	19,574
10	Capital Expenditures		−25,000	−8,000	−8,000	−8,000	−8,000
11	Other Investment		—	—	—	—	—
12	**Cash from Investing Activities**		−25,000	−8,000	−8,000	−8,000	−8,000
13	Net Borrowing		20,000	—	—	—	—
14	Dividends		−4,786	−2,503	−4,237	−6,167	−8,313
15	**Cash from Financing Activities**		15,214	−2,503	−4,237	−6,167	−8,313
16							
17	**Change in Cash (9 + 12 + 15)**		2,157	2,381	2,647	2,940	3,261

The balance sheet (Table 18.17) continues the work we started in Table 18.10. Current assets and liabilities come from the net working capital spreadsheet (Table 18.9). The inventory entry on the balance sheet includes both raw materials and finished goods. Property, plant, and equipment information comes from the forecasted capital expenditure spreadsheet (Table 18.6), and the debt comes from Table 18.7.

KMS's book value of equity will steadily grow as it expands and remains profitable, paying out only a portion of its net income each year. Its debt will jump from $4500 to $24,500 in 2017 when it finances its expansion. KMS's other liabilities—accounts payable—will grow steadily with sales. KMS's book debt-equity ratio will jump from 4500/74,134 = 6% in 2016 to 24,500/76,948 = 32% in 2017, and then will steadily decline to 23% by 2021.

The statement of cash flows in Table 18.18 starts with net income. Cash from operating activities includes depreciation as well as *changes* to working capital items (other than cash) from Table 18.9. Cash from investing activities includes the capital expenditures in Table 18.6. Cash from financing activities includes net borrowing from Table 18.7, and dividends are equal to free cash flows to equity because we assume KMS pays out all excess cash. We can compute FCF to equity from Table 18.13 using the following equation:

$$\text{FCF to Equity} = \text{FCF of the Firm} + \text{Net Borrowing}$$
$$- \text{After-Tax Interest Expense} \qquad (18.12)$$

KMS is not planning to raise any additional equity financing, so there are no capital contributions on the cash flow statement. As a final check on the calculations, note that the change in the minimum cash balance shown on the balance sheet (Table 18.17). For example, in 2017, the change in cash and cash equivalents is 2157, which is the amount by which 2017 cash exceeds 2016 cash on the balance sheet.

19

Working Capital Management

LEARNING OBJECTIVES

- Understand the cash cycle of the firm and why managing working capital is important

- Use trade credit to the firm's advantage

- Make decisions on extending credit and adjusting credit terms

- Manage accounts payable

- Know the costs and benefits of holding additional inventory

- Contrast the different instruments available to a financial manager for investing cash balances

notation

CCC	cash conversion cycle	NPV	net present value
EAR	effective annual rate	PV	present value
g	perpetuity growth rate	r	discount rate

In Chapter 2, we defined a firm's net working capital as its current assets minus its current liabilities. Net working capital is the capital required in the short term to run the business. Thus, working capital management involves short-term asset accounts such as cash, inventory, and accounts receivable, as well as short-term liability accounts such as accounts payable. The level of investment in each of these accounts differs from firm to firm and from industry to industry. It also depends on factors such as the type of business and industry standards. Some firms, for example, require heavy inventory investments because of the nature of their business.

Consider The Kroger Company, a retail grocery chain, and Southwest Airlines, a regional airline. Inventory amounted to over 18% of Kroger's total assets in early 2016 whereas Southwest's investment in inventory was just over 1%. A grocery store requires a large investment in inventory, but an airline's profitability is generated primarily from its investment in plant, property, and equipment—that is, its airplanes.

There are opportunity costs associated with investing in inventories and accounts receivable, and from holding cash. Excess funds invested in these accounts could instead be used to pay down debt or returned to shareholders in the form of a dividend or share repurchase. This chapter focuses on the tools firms use to manage their working capital efficiently and thereby minimize these opportunity costs. We begin by discussing why firms have working capital and how it affects firm value. In a perfect capital market, many of the working capital accounts would be irrelevant. Not surprisingly, the existence of these accounts for real firms can be traced to market frictions. We discuss the costs and benefits of trade credit and evaluate the tradeoffs firms make in managing various working capital accounts. Finally, we discuss the cash balance of a firm and provide an overview of the short-term investments in which a firm may choose to invest its cash.

19.1 Overview of Working Capital

Most projects require the firm to invest in net working capital. The main components of net working capital are cash, inventory, receivables, and payables. Working capital includes the cash that is needed to run the firm on a day-to-day basis. It does not include excess cash, which is cash that is not required to run the business and can be invested at a market rate. As we discussed in Chapter 13, excess cash may be viewed as part of the firm's capital structure, offsetting firm debt. In Chapter 9, we discussed how any increases in net working capital represent an investment that reduces the cash that is available to the firm. The Valuation Principle tells us that the value of the firm is the present value of its free cash flows. Therefore, working capital alters a firm's value by affecting its free cash flows. In this section, we examine the components of net working capital and their effects on the firm's value.

The Cash Cycle

The level of working capital reflects the length of time between when cash goes out of a firm at the beginning of the production process and when it comes back in. Take Intel, for example. Let's trace the path of $1000 worth of inventory and raw materials through Intel's production process.

- First, Intel buys $1000 of raw materials and inventory from its suppliers, purchasing them on credit, which means that the firm does not have to pay cash immediately at the time of purchase.

- About 36 days later, Intel pays for the materials and inventory, so five weeks have passed between when Intel purchased the materials and when the cash outflow occurred.

- After another 55 days, Intel sells the materials (now in the form of finished microprocessors) to a computer manufacturer, but the sale is on credit, meaning that the computer manufacturer does not pay cash immediately. A total of 91 days have passed between when Intel purchased the materials and when it sold them as part of the finished product.

operating cycle The average length of time between when a firm originally receives its inventory and when it receives the cash back from selling its product.

- About 32 days later, the computer manufacturer pays for the microprocessors, producing a cash inflow for Intel.

A total of $36 + 55 + 32 = 123$ days have passed from when Intel originally bought the raw materials until it received the cash from selling the finished product. Thus, Intel's *operating cycle* is 123 days: a firm's **operating cycle** is the average length of time between when the firm originally purchases its inventory and when it receives the cash back from

cash cycle The length of time between when a firm pays cash to purchase its initial inventory and when it receives cash from the sale of the output produced from that inventory.

selling its product. A firm's **cash cycle** is the length of time between when the firm pays cash to purchase its initial inventory and when it receives cash from the sale of the output produced from that inventory. For Intel, the cash cycle is 87 days: the 55 days it holds the material after paying for it plus the 32 days it waits to receive cash after selling the finished product. Some companies actually have a *negative* cash cycle; they are paid for the product before they have to pay for the cost of producing it! This is generally possible only if companies keep very low inventory and have the size to force their suppliers to wait to be paid. Example 19.1 goes through an example of this for Apple. Figure 19.1 illustrates the operating and cash cycle.

cash conversion cycle A measure of the cash cycle calculated as the sum of a firm's inventory days and accounts receivable days, less its accounts payable days.

Some practitioners measure the cash cycle by calculating the *cash conversion cycle*. The **cash conversion cycle (CCC)** is defined as:

$$CCC = \text{Inventory Days} + \text{Accounts Receivable Days} - \text{Accounts Payable Days} \quad (19.1)$$

where

$$\text{Inventory Days} = \frac{\text{Inventory}}{\text{Average Daily Cost of Goods Sold}}$$

$$\text{Accounts Receivable Days} = \frac{\text{Accounts Receivable}}{\text{Average Daily Sales}}$$

$$\text{Accounts Payable Days} = \frac{\text{Accounts Payable}}{\text{Average Daily Cost of Goods Sold}}$$

All these ratios can be computed from the firm's financial statements. We discussed how to compute and use them in Chapter 2. Even though the cash conversion cycle is an important metric on its own, a financial manager needs to keep an eye on each of its components, because they all contain valuable information about how efficiently the firm is managing its working capital. Higher accounts receivable days may signal that the firm is having trouble collecting from its customers, and low accounts payable days might suggest it is not taking full advantage of opportunities to delay payment to suppliers. Finally, high inventory days would focus a manager on why the firm needs to have its inventory on hand so long before it sells the product.

FIGURE 19.1

The Cash Cycle and Operating Cycle for a Firm

The cash cycle is the average time between when a firm pays for its inventory and when it receives cash from the sale of its product. If the firm pays cash for its inventory, this period is identical to the firm's operating cycle. However, most firms buy their inventory on credit, which reduces the amount of time between the cash investment and the receipt of cash from that investment.

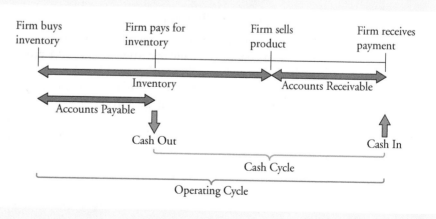

EXAMPLE 19.1

Computing the Cash
Conversion Cycle

MyFinanceLab

PROBLEM

The following information is from Apple's 2015 income statement and balance sheet (numbers are in $ millions). Use it to compute Apple's cash conversion cycle.

Sales	233,715
Cost of Goods Sold	140,089
Accounts Receivable	16,849
Inventory	2,349
Accounts Payable	35,490

SOLUTION

PLAN

The CCC is defined in Eq. 19.1 as Inventory Days + Accounts Receivable Days − Accounts Payable Days. Thus, we need to compute each of the three ratios in the CCC. In order to do that, we need to convert Sales and COGS into their average daily amounts simply by dividing the total given for the year by 365 days in a year.

EXECUTE

Average Daily Sales = Sales/365 Days = 233,715/365 = 640.32

Average Daily COGS = COGS/365 Days = 140,089/365 = 383.81

$$\text{Inventory Days} = \frac{\text{Inventory}}{\text{Average Daily Cost of Goods Sold}} = \frac{2,349}{383.81} = 6.12$$

$$\text{Accounts Receivable Days} = \frac{\text{Accounts Receivable}}{\text{Average Daily Sales}} = \frac{16,849}{640.32} = 26.31$$

$$\text{Accounts Payable Days} = \frac{\text{Accounts Payable}}{\text{Average Daily Cost of Goods Sold}} = \frac{35,490}{383.81} = 92.47$$

Thus, Dell's CCC = 6.12 + 26.31 − 92.47 = −60.04!

EVALUATE

Apple actually has a *negative* cash conversion cycle, meaning that it generally receives cash for its computers and other products *before* it pays its suppliers for the parts in its products. Apple is able to do this because its combination of direct sales to the consumer (it charges your credit card as soon as you order) and sales through retailers keep its receivables low. Due to its size and bargaining power, its suppliers allow it to wait nearly 93 days before paying them!

Working Capital Needs by Industry

The longer a firm's cash cycle, the more working capital it has, and the more cash it needs to carry to conduct its daily operations. Table 19.1 provides data on the working capital needs for selected firms in a variety of industries.

Because of the characteristics of the different industries, working capital levels vary significantly. For example, a large portion of a retail grocery store's customers pay cash when they buy their groceries, so you would expect accounts receivable to be a very small percentage of its sales.[1] For Kroger, accounts receivable represent only four days worth of

---

[1]When you use your credit card to pay for your groceries, it is a cash sale for the store. The credit card company pays the store cash upon confirmation of the transaction, even if you do not pay your credit card bill on time.

TABLE 19.1

Cash Conversion Cycles of Various Companies (2015)

Cash Conversion Cycle (CCC)	Company	Industry	Accounts Receivable Days	Inventory Days	Accounts Payable Days	CCC
	Molson Coors Brewing Company	Brewing	48	37	184	-99
	Pepsico	Beverages	40	40	164	-84
	Verizon Communications	Telecommunications	37	8	117	-72
	Apple	Computer Hardware	26	6	92	-60
	Bristol-Myers Squibb	Pharmaceuticals	72	126	223	-25
	Southwest Airlines	Airlines	9	9	32	-14
	Amazon.com	Internet Retail	19	45	73	-9
	Chipotle Mexican Grill	Restaurants	2	2	10	-6
	The Kroger Co.	Grocery Stores	4	24	23	5
	Walmart Stores	Superstores	4	47	39	12
	Microsoft	Software	62	33	77	18
	Macy's	Department Stores	4	147	133	18
	FedEx	Air Freight	43	5	22	26
	Starbucks	Restaurants	12	30	16	26
	Nordstrom	Department Stores	29	79	62	46
	Nike	Footwear	36	91	41	86
	AGL Resources	Gas Utilities	150	76	132	94
	Brown-Forman	Distillers and Vintners	72	440	90	422
	Lennar	Homebuilding	3	463	23	443
	Tiffany & Co.	Luxury Goods	17	546	66	497

-100 -50 0 50 100 400 450 500

Source: www.capitaliq.com.

sales. Similar results hold for Southwest Airlines, because many of its customers pay in advance for airline tickets with cash or credit cards. Inventory represents a large percentage of sales for firms such as Lennar, which have a long development and sales cycle. Note also the wide variation in the firms' cash conversion cycles. For example, Southwest's cash conversion cycle is negative, reflecting the fact that it receives cash from its customers before having to pay its suppliers.

Firm Value and Working Capital

To understand why working capital management can increase firm value, recall that any funds your company has from investors need to earn an opportunity cost of capital for those investors. Working capital ties up funds that could be deployed elsewhere in the firm to earn a return. For example, imagine $50,000 in raw materials sitting in a factory waiting to be used. That $50,000 needs to earn a return, so any delay in converting that material into a product that can be sold reduces its return. If you could improve your production process so that only $30,000 of raw material was waiting to be used at any one time, you would have freed up $20,000 to be invested elsewhere or returned to the shareholders. Similarly, when you allow your customers to pay within 30 days, you are giving them a 30-day interest-free loan. However, your investors and banks have not given you interest-free funds! If you can reduce the time it takes customers to pay without reducing sales, you can improve the return your investors earn on the business.

Any reduction in working capital requirements generates a positive free cash flow that the firm can distribute immediately to shareholders. For example, if a firm is able to reduce its required net working capital by $50,000, it will be able to distribute this $50,000 as a dividend to its shareholders immediately.

Recall that the Valuation Principle implies that the value of the firm is the present value of its free cash flows. Managing working capital efficiently will increase those free cash flows, allowing a manager to maximize firm value. We now turn our attention to some specific working capital accounts.

EXAMPLE 19.2

The Value of Working
Capital Management

MyFinanceLab

PROBLEM

The projected net income and free cash flows next year for Emerald City Paints are given in the following table in $ thousands:

Net Income	20,000
+ Depreciation	+5,000
− Capital Expenditures	−5,000
− Increase in Working Capital	−1,000
= Free Cash Flow	19,000

Emerald City expects capital expenditures and depreciation to continue to offset each other, and for both net income and increase in working capital to grow at 4% per year. Emerald City's cost of capital is 12%. If Emerald City were able reduce its annual increase in working capital by 20% by managing its working capital more efficiently without adversely affecting any other part of the business, what would be the effect on Emerald City's value?

SOLUTION

PLAN

A 20% decrease in required working capital increases would reduce the starting point from $1,000,000 per year to $800,000 per year. The working capital increases would still grow at 4% per year, but each increase would then be 20% smaller because of the 20% smaller starting point. We can value Emerald City using the formula for a growing perpetuity from Chapter 4 (Eq. 4.7):

$$PV = \frac{Cash\ Flow}{r - g}$$

As shown in the table above, we can determine Emerald City's free cash flow as:

Net Income + Depreciation − Capital Expenditures − Increases in Working Capital.

EXECUTE

Currently, Emerald City's value is:

$$\frac{20,000,000 + 5,000,000 - 5,000,000 - 1,000,000}{.12 - .04} = 237,500,000$$

If they can manage their working capital more efficiently, the value will be:

$$\frac{20,000,000 + 5,000,000 - 5,000,000 - 800,000}{.12 - .04} = 240,000,000$$

EVALUATE

Although the change will not affect Emerald City's earnings (net income), it will increase the free cash flow available to shareholders and increase the value of the firm by $2.5 million.

CONCEPT CHECK

1. What is the difference between a firm's cash cycle and operating cycle?

2. How does working capital impact a firm's value?

19.2 Trade Credit

When a firm allows a customer to pay for goods at some date later than the date of purchase, it creates an account receivable for the firm and an account payable for the customer. Accounts receivable represent the credit sales for which a firm has yet to receive payment. The accounts payable balance represents the amount that a firm owes its suppliers for goods that it has received but for which it has not yet paid. The credit that the firm is extending to its customer is known as **trade credit**—the difference between receivables

trade credit The difference between receivables and payables that is the net amount of a firm's capital consumed as a result of those credit transactions; the credit that a firm extends to its customers.

and payables that is the net amount of a firm's capital consumed as a result of those credit transactions. A firm would, of course, prefer to be paid in cash at the time of purchase. A "cash-only" policy, however, may cause it to lose its customers to competition. Even after a customer decides to pay a bill, there is a delay before the money is credited to the firm because of processing and mailing the payment. In this section, we demonstrate how managers can compare the costs and benefits of trade credit to determine optimal credit policies.

Trade Credit Terms

To see how the terms of trade credit are quoted, let's consider some examples. If a supplier offers its customers terms of "net 30," payment is not due until 30 days from the date of the invoice. Essentially, the supplier is letting the customer use its money for an extra 30 days. (Note that "30" is not a magic number; the invoice could specify "net 40," "net 15," or any other number of days as the payment due date.)

cash discount The percentage discount offered if the buyer pays early.

discount period The number of days a buyer has to take advantage of the cash discount.

credit period The total length of time credit is extended to the buyer.

Sometimes the selling firm will offer the buying firm a discount if payment is made early. The terms "2/10, net 30" mean that the buying firm will receive a 2% discount if it pays for the goods within 10 days; otherwise, the full amount is due in 30 days. The **cash discount** is the percentage discount offered if the buyer pays early, in this case 2%. The **discount period** is the number of days the buyer has to take advantage of the cash discount; here it is 10 days. Finally, the **credit period** is the total length of time credit is extended to the buyer—the total amount of time the buyer has to pay. It is 30 days in our example. Firms offer discounts to encourage customers to pay early so that the selling firm gets cash from the sale sooner. However, the amount of the discount also represents a cost to the selling firm because it does not receive the full selling price for the product. This timeline shows the terms of our 2/10, net 30 example:

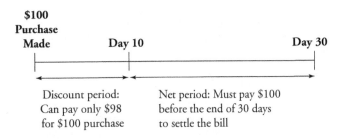

Trade Credit and Market Frictions

In a perfectly competitive market, trade credit is just another form of financing. As we learned in Chapter 16, financing decisions are irrelevant under the assumptions of perfect capital markets. In reality, product markets are rarely perfectly competitive, so firms can maximize their value by using their trade credit options effectively.

Cost of Trade Credit. Trade credit is, in essence, a loan from the selling firm to its customer. The price discount represents an interest rate. Often, firms offer favorable interest rates on trade credit as a price discount to their customers. Therefore, financial managers should evaluate the terms of trade credit to decide whether to use it.

How do we compute the interest rate on trade credit? Suppose a firm sells a product for $100 but offers its customer terms of 2/10, net 30. The customer doesn't have to pay anything for the first 10 days, so it effectively has a zero-interest loan for this period. If the customer takes advantage of the discount and pays within the 10-day discount period, the customer pays only $98 for the product. The cost of the discount to the selling firm is equal to the discount percentage times the selling price. In this case, it is 0.02 × $100, or $2.

Using APR Instead of EAR to Compute the Cost of Trade Credit

Some managers fail to fully recognize the cost of trade credit by using APR (simple interest) rather than EAR to compute the annual cost for comparison with other financing options. Recall from Chapter 5 that whereas the EAR appropriately accounts for the compounding "interest on interest" effect over the year, APR ignores compounding. Thus, in our example below with 2.04% interest over 20 days, the corresponding APR would be $(365/20) \times 2.04\% = 37.23\%$, which is less than the true effective annual cost of this credit: 44.6%.

Rather than pay within 10 days, the customer has the option to use the $98 for an additional 20 days $(30 - 10 = 20)$. The interest rate for the 20-day term of the loan is $2/\$98 = 2.04\%$. To compare this 20-day interest rate with interest rates available from other financing sources, we convert it to an effective annual rate using Eq. 5.1 from Chapter 5, where n is the number of 20-day periods in a year:

$$EAR = (1 + r)^n - 1$$

With a 365-day year, there are 365/20 (18.25) 20-day periods in a year. Thus, this 2.04% rate over 20 days corresponds to an effective annual rate of:

$$EAR = (1.0204)^{365/20} - 1 = 44.6\%$$

Therefore, by not taking the discount, the firm is effectively paying 2.04% to borrow the money for 20 days, which translates to an effective annual rate of 44.6%! If the firm can obtain a bank loan at a lower interest rate, it would be better off borrowing at the lower rate and using the cash proceeds of the loan to take advantage of the discount offered by the supplier.

EXAMPLE 19.3

Estimating the Effective Cost of Trade Credit

MyFinanceLab

PROBLEM

Your firm purchases goods from its supplier on terms of 1/15, net 40. What is the effective annual cost to your firm if it chooses not to take advantage of the trade discount offered?

SOLUTION

PLAN

Using a $100 purchase as an example, 1/15, net 40 means you get a 1% discount if you pay within 15 days, or you can pay the full amount within 40 days. 1% of $100 is a $1 discount, so you can either pay $99 in 15 days, or $100 in 40 days. The difference is 25 days, so you need to compute the interest rate over the 25 days and then compute the EAR associated with that 25-day interest rate.

EXECUTE

$1/\$99 = 0.0101$, or 1.01% interest for 25 days. There are 365/25 = 14.6 25-day periods in a year. Thus, your effective annual rate is $(1.0101)^{14.6} - 1 = 0.158$, or 15.8%.

EVALUATE

If you really need to take the full 40 days to produce the cash to pay, you would be better off finding a bank that would lend you the $99 at a lower rate so you could take advantage of the discount.

Benefits of Trade Credit. For a number of reasons, trade credit can be an attractive source of funds. First, trade credit is simple and convenient to use, and it has lower transaction costs than alternative sources of funds. For example, no paperwork must be completed, as would be the case for a loan from a bank. Second, it is a flexible source of funds and can be used as needed. Finally, it is sometimes the only source of funding available to a firm.

Trade Credit Versus Standard Loans. You might wonder why companies would ever provide trade credit. After all, most companies are not banks, so why are they in the business of making loans? Several reasons explain their willingness to offer trade credit. First, providing financing at below-market rates is an indirect way to lower prices for only certain customers. Consider, for example, an automobile manufacturer. Rather than lowering prices on all cars, the financing division may offer specific credit terms that are attractive to customers with bad credit, but unattractive to customers with good credit. In this way, the car manufacturer is able to discount the price only for those customers with bad credit who otherwise might not be able to afford the car.

Second, because a supplier may have an ongoing business relationship with its customer, it may have more information about the credit quality of the customer than a traditional outside lender such as a bank would have. The supplier may also be able to increase the likelihood of payment by threatening to cut off future supplies if payment is not made. Finally, if the buyer defaults, the supplier may be able to seize the inventory as collateral. This inventory is likely to be more valuable to a company within the industry such as the supplier (which presumably has other customers) than to an outsider.

Managing Float

One factor that contributes to the length of a firm's receivables and payables is the delay between the time a bill is paid and the cash is actually received. This delay, or *processing float*, will impact a firm's working capital requirements.

collection float The amount of time it takes for a firm to be able to use funds after a customer has paid for its goods.

Collection Float. The amount of time it takes for a firm to be able to use funds after a customer has paid for its goods is referred to as **collection float**. Firms can reduce their working capital needs by reducing their collection float. Collection float is determined by three factors, as shown in Figure 19.2:

mail float The time it takes a firm to receive a customer's payment check after the customer has mailed it.

- **Mail float:** The time it takes the firm to receive a payment check after the customer has mailed it.

processing float The time it takes a firm to process a customer's payment check and deposit it in the bank.

- **Processing float:** The time it takes the firm to process a customer's payment check and deposit it in the bank.

availability float The time it takes a bank to give a firm credit for customer payments the firm has deposited in the bank.

- **Availability float:** The time it takes a bank to post the funds from customer payments the firm has deposited in the bank.

FIGURE 19.2

Collection Float

Disbursement Float. The time it takes before payments to suppliers actually result in a cash outflow for the firm is referred to as **disbursement float**. Similar to collection float, it is a function of mail time, processing time, and check-clearing time. Although a firm may try to extend its disbursement float in order to lengthen its payables and reduce its working capital needs, it risks making late payments to suppliers. In such a case, the firm may be charged an additional fee for paying late or may be required to pay cash before delivery (CBD) or cash on delivery (COD) for future purchases. In some cases, the supplier may refuse to do business in the future with the delinquent firm.

disbursement float The time it takes before a firm's payments to its suppliers actually result in a cash outflow for the firm.

Electronic Check Processing. Firms can employ several methods to reduce their collection and disbursement floats. The **Check Clearing for the 21st Century Act (Check 21)**, which became effective on October 28, 2004, eliminated the part of the disbursement float due to the check-clearing process. Under the act, banks can process check information

Check Clearing for the 21st Century Act (Check 21) Eliminates the disbursement float due to the check-clearing process. Banks can process check information electronically and, in most cases, the funds are deducted from a firm's checking account on the same day that the firm's supplier deposits the check in its bank.

electronically and, in most cases, the funds are deducted from a firm's checking account on the same day the firm's supplier deposits the check in its bank. Unfortunately, even though the funds are taken out of the check writer's account almost immediately under Check 21, the check recipient's account is not credited as quickly. As a result, the act does not serve to reduce collection float.

There are, however, several ways that a firm *can* reduce its collection float. For example, the firm may streamline its in-house check-processing procedures. In addition, with electronic collection, funds are automatically transferred from the customer's bank account to the firm's bank account on the payment date, reducing the collection float to zero. The methods a firm employs to reduce its collection float are not without costs, of course. New check-processing systems could be expensive and disruptive, and hiring a collection agency to speed up collections generates costs such as fees to the agency as well as bad will with the firm's customers. Therefore, to decide which method, if any, to employ, the firm must compare the costs and benefits of systems that allow it to use its cash for a longer period.

CONCEPT CHECK

3. What does the term "2/10, net 30" mean?

4. List three factors that determine collection float.

19.3 Receivables Management

So far, we have discussed the costs and benefits of trade credit in general. Next, we look at some issues that arise specifically from the management of a firm's accounts receivable. In particular, we focus on how a firm adopts a policy for offering credit to its customers and how it monitors its accounts receivable on an ongoing basis.

Determining the Credit Policy

Establishing a credit policy involves three steps that we will discuss in turn:

1. Establishing credit standards
2. Establishing credit terms
3. Establishing a collection policy

 The 5 C's of Credit

Lenders have coined the phrase "The 5 C's of Credit" to summarize the qualities they look for before granting credit:

Character: Is the borrower trustworthy, with a history of meeting its debt obligations?

Capacity: Will the borrower have enough cash flow to make its payments?

Capital: Does the borrower have enough capital (net worth) to justify the loan?

Collateral: Does the borrower have any assets that can secure the loan?

Conditions: How are the borrower and the economy performing and how are they expected to perform?

Establishing Credit Standards. Management must first decide on its credit standards. Will it extend credit to anyone who applies for it? Or will it be selective and extend credit only to those customers who have very low credit risk? Unless the firm adopts the former policy, it will need to assess the credit risk of each customer before deciding whether to grant credit. Large firms perform this analysis in-house with their own credit departments. Small firms purchase credit reports from credit rating agencies such as Dun & Bradstreet.

Many firms will consider additional factors when deciding whether to grant credit to a particular customer. For example, in order to win sales a firm may be more likely to grant credit if the customer is expected to be a repeat customer. If the cost of the credit is small relative to the purchase price, it may also adopt a less restrictive policy. Thus, while credit risk is the starting point, the firm's managers may choose to extend credit strategically when dealing with potentially important customers or high-margin sales.

The decision of how much credit risk to assume plays a large role in determining how much money a firm ties up in its receivables. Although a restrictive policy can result in a lower sales volume, the firm will have a smaller investment in receivables. Conversely, a less selective policy will produce higher sales, but the level of receivables will also rise.

Establishing Credit Terms. After a firm decides on its credit standards, it must next establish its credit terms. The firm decides on the length of the period before payment must be made (the "net" period) and chooses whether to offer a discount to encourage early payments. If it offers a discount, it must also determine the discount percentage and the discount period. If the firm is relatively small, it will probably follow the lead of other firms in the industry in establishing these terms.

EXAMPLE 19.4
Evaluating a Change in Credit Policy

MyFinanceLab

PROBLEM

Your company currently sells its product with a 1% discount to customers who pay cash immediately. Otherwise, the full price is due within 30 days. Half of your customers take advantage of the discount. You are considering dropping the discount so that your new terms would just be net 30. If you do that, you expect to lose some customers who were only willing to pay the discounted price, but the rest will simply switch to taking the full 30 days to pay. Altogether, you estimate that you will sell 20 fewer units per month (compared to 500 units currently). Your variable cost per unit is $60 and your price per unit is $100. If your required return is 1% per month, should you switch your policy?

SOLUTION

PLAN

To decide whether to change your policy, compute the NPV of the change. It costs you $30,000 to make the 500 units. You receive payment for half of the units immediately at a price of $99 per unit (1% discount). The other half comes in 30 days at a price of $100 per unit. At that point, you are starting over again with the next set of product. Thus, you can think of your cash flows in any 30-day period as:

	Now	30 days	
Produce first set of 500 units at $60 apiece	−30,000		
Customers pay for 250 units at $99 apiece	+24,750		
Customers pay for 250 units at $100 apiece		+25,000	...
Produce next set of 500 units at $60 apiece		−30,000	...
Customers pay for 250 units at $99 apiece		+24,750	...
Total	−5,250	+25,000 − 5,250	...

Under the new policy, your cash flows would switch to:

	Now	30 days	
Produce first set of 480 units at $60 apiece	−28,800		
Customers pay for 480 units at $100 apiece		+48,000	...
Produce next set of 480 units at $60 apiece		−28,800	...
Total	−28,800	+48,000 − 28,800	...

With these cash flows, we are ready to compute the NPV of the policy change.

(Continued)

EXECUTE

$$NPV_{current} = -5250 + \frac{25{,}000 - 5250}{.01} = 1{,}969{,}750$$

$$NPV_{new} = -28{,}800 + \frac{48{,}000 - 28{,}800}{.01} = 1{,}891{,}200$$

So the NPV of the switch will be $1,969,750 - $1,891,200 = -$78,550.

EVALUATE

You shouldn't make the switch because you will lose too many customers, even though your remaining customers will be paying the full price. The NPV helps us weigh this tradeoff—the present value of the costs outweighs the present value of the benefits, so the decision is not a good one.

Establishing a Collection Policy. The last step in the development of a credit policy is to decide on a collection policy. The content of this policy can range from doing nothing if a customer is paying late (generally not a good choice), to sending a polite letter of inquiry, to charging interest on payments extending beyond a specified period, to threatening legal action at the first late payment.

Monitoring Accounts Receivable

After establishing a credit policy, a firm must monitor its accounts receivable to analyze whether its credit policy is working effectively. Two tools that firms use to monitor the accounts receivable are the *accounts receivable days* (or average collection period) and the *aging schedule*.

Accounts Receivable Days. The accounts receivable days is the average number of days that it takes a firm to collect on its sales. A firm can compare this number to the payment policy specified in its credit terms to judge the effectiveness of its credit policy. If the credit terms specify "net 30" and the accounts receivable days outstanding is 50 days, the firm can conclude that its customers are paying 20 days late, on average.

The firm should also look at the trend in the accounts receivable days over time. If the accounts receivable days ratio of a firm has been approximately 35 days for the past few years and it is 43 days this year, the firm may want to reexamine its credit policy. Of course, if the economy is sluggish, the entire industry may be affected. Under these circumstances, the increase might have little to do with the firm itself.

Accounts receivable days can be calculated from the firm's financial statements. Outside investors commonly use this measure to evaluate a firm's credit management policy. A major weakness of the accounts receivable days is that it is merely one number and conceals much useful information. Seasonal sales patterns may cause the number calculated for the accounts receivable days to change depending on when the calculation takes place. The number can also look reasonable even when a substantial percentage of the firm's customers are paying late.

aging schedule
Categorizes a firm's accounts by the number of days they have been on the books. It can be prepared using either the number of accounts or the dollar amount of the accounts receivable outstanding.

Aging Schedule. An **aging schedule** categorizes a firm's accounts by the number of days they have been on the books. It can be prepared using either the number of accounts or the dollar amount of the accounts receivable outstanding. For example, assume that a firm selling on terms of 2/15, net 30 has $530,000 in accounts receivable that has been on the books for 15 or fewer days in 220 accounts. Another $450,000 has been on the books for 16 to 30 days and is made up of 190 accounts, and $350,000 has been on the books for 31 to 45 days and represents 80 accounts. The firm has $200,000 that has been on the books for 46 to 60 days in 60 accounts. Yet another $70,000 has been on the books for more than 60 days and is made up of 20 accounts. Table 19.2 includes aging schedules based on the number of accounts and dollar amounts outstanding.

In this case, if the firm's average daily sales are $65,000, its accounts receivable days is $1,600,000/$65,000 = 25 days. But on closer examination, using the aging schedules in Table 19.2, we can see that 28% of the firm's credit customers (and 39% by dollar amounts) are paying late.

TABLE 19.2

Aging Schedules

(a) Number of Accounts

Days Outstanding	Number of Accounts	Percentage of Accounts (%)
1–15	220	38.6
16–30	190	33.3
31–45	80	14.0
46–60	60	10.5
60+	20	3.5
	570	100.0

(b) Dollar Amounts Outstanding

Days Outstanding	Amount Outstanding ($)	Percentage Outstanding (%)
1–15	530,000	33.1
16–30	450,000	28.1
31–45	350,000	21.9
46–60	200,000	12.5
60+	70,000	4.4
	1,600,000	100.0

EXAMPLE 19.5

Aging Schedules

MyFinanceLab

PROBLEM

Financial Training Systems (FTS) bills its accounts on terms of 3/10, net 30. The firm's accounts receivable include $100,000 that has been outstanding for 10 or fewer days, $300,000 outstanding for 11 to 30 days, $100,000 outstanding for 31 to 40 days, $20,000 outstanding for 41 to 50 days, $10,000 outstanding for 51 to 60 days, and $2000 outstanding for more than 60 days. Prepare an aging schedule for FTS.

SOLUTION

PLAN

An aging schedule shows the amount and percent of total accounts receivable outstanding for different lengths outstanding. With the available information, we can calculate the aging schedule based on dollar amounts outstanding. (The numbers don't add to exactly 100% because of rounding.)

EXECUTE

Days Outstanding	Amount Outstanding ($)	Percentage Outstanding (%)
1–10	100,000	18.8
11–30	300,000	56.4
31–40	100,000	18.8
41–50	20,000	3.8
51–60	10,000	1.9
60+	2,000	0.4
	532,000	100.0

(Continued)

If the aging schedule gets "bottom-heavy"—that is, if the percentages in the lower half of the schedule representing late-paying firms begin to increase—the firm will likely need to revisit its credit policy. The aging schedule is also sometimes augmented by analysis of the **payments pattern**, which provides information on the percentage of monthly sales that the firm collects in each month after the sale. By examining past data, a firm may observe that 10% of its sales are usually collected in the month of the sale, 40% in the month following the sale, 25% two months after the sale, 20% three months after the sale, and 5% four months after the sale. Management can compare this normal payments pattern to the current payments pattern. Knowledge of the payments pattern is also useful for forecasting the firm's working capital requirements.

payments pattern
Provides information on the percentage of monthly sales that the firm collects in each month after the sale.

CONCEPT CHECK

5. Describe three steps in establishing a credit policy.

6. What is the difference between accounts receivable days and an aging schedule?

19.4 Payables Management

A firm should choose to borrow using accounts payable only if trade credit is the cheapest source of funding. The cost of the trade credit depends on the credit terms. The higher the discount percentage offered, the greater the cost of forgoing the discount. The cost of forgoing the discount is also higher with a shorter loan period. When a company has a choice between trade credit from two different suppliers, it should take the less expensive alternative.

In addition, a firm should always pay on the latest day allowed. For example, if the discount period is 10 days and the firm is taking the discount, payment should be made on day 10, not on day 2. If the discount is not taken and the terms are 2/10, net 30, the full payment should be made on day 30, not on day 16. A firm should strive to keep its money working for it as long as possible without developing a bad relationship with its suppliers or engaging in unethical practices. In this section, we examine two techniques that firms use to monitor their accounts payable: determining the accounts payable days outstanding and stretching accounts payable.

Determining Accounts Payable Days Outstanding

Similar to the situation with its accounts receivable, a firm should monitor its accounts payable to ensure that it is making its payments at an optimal time. One method is to calculate the accounts payable days outstanding and compare it to the credit terms. The accounts payable days outstanding is the accounts payable balance expressed in terms of the number of days of cost of goods sold. If the accounts payable outstanding is 40 days and the terms are 2/10, net 30, the firm can conclude that it generally pays late and may be risking supplier difficulties. Conversely, if the accounts payable days outstanding is 25 days and the firm has not been taking the discount, the firm is paying too early. It could be earning another five days' interest on its money.

EXAMPLE 19.6

Accounts Payable Management

MyFinanceLab

PROBLEM

The Rowd Company has an average accounts payable balance of $250,000. Its average daily cost of goods sold is $14,000, and it receives terms of 2/15, net 40 from its suppliers. Rowd chooses to forgo the discount. Is the firm managing its accounts payable well?

SOLUTION

PLAN

Given Rowd's AP balance and its daily COGS, we can compute the average number of days it takes to pay its vendors by dividing the average balance by the daily costs. Given the terms from its suppliers, Rowd should either be paying on the 15th day (the last possible day to get the discount), or on the 40th day (the last possible day to pay). There is no benefit to paying at any other time.

EXECUTE

Rowd's accounts payable days outstanding is $250,000/$14,000 = 17.9 days. If Rowd made payment three days earlier, it could take advantage of the 2% discount. If, for some reason, it chose to forgo the discount, it should not be paying the full amount until the 40th day.

EVALUATE

The firm is not managing its accounts payable well. The earlier it pays, the sooner the cash leaves Rowd. Thus, the only reason to pay before the 40th day is to receive the discount by paying before the 15th day. Paying on the 18th day not only misses the discount, but costs the firm 22 days (40–18) use of its cash.

Stretching Accounts Payable

stretching the accounts payable When a firm ignores a payment due period and pays later.

Some firms ignore the payment due period and pay the amount owed later, in a practice referred to as **stretching the accounts payable**. Given terms of 2/10, net 30, for example, a firm may choose not to pay the amount owed until 45 days have passed. Doing so reduces the direct cost of trade credit because it lengthens the time that a firm has use of the funds. Although the interest rate per period remains the same—$2/$98 = 2.04%—the firm is now using the $98 for 35 days beyond the discount period, rather than 20 days as provided by the trade credit terms.

EXAMPLE 19.7

Cost of Trade Credit with Stretched Accounts Payable

MyFinanceLab

PROBLEM

What is the effective annual cost of credit terms of 1/15, net 40 if the firm stretches the accounts payable to 60 days?

SOLUTION

PLAN

First, we need to compute the interest rate per period. The 1% discount means that on a $100 purchase, you can either pay $99 in the discount period, or keep the $99 and pay $100 later. Thus, you pay $1 interest on the $99. If you pay on time, then this $1 in interest is over the 25-day period between the 15th day and the 40th day. If you stretch, then this $1 in interest is over the 45-day period between the 15th day and the 60th day.

EXECUTE

The interest rate per period is $1/$99 = 1.01%. If the firm delays payment until the 60th day, it has use of the funds for 45 days beyond the discount period. There are 365/45 = 8.11 45-day periods in one year. Thus, the effective annual cost is $(1.0101)^{8.11} - 1 = 0.0849$, or 8.49%.

EVALUATE

Paying on time corresponds to a 25-day credit period and there are 365/25 = 14.6 25-day periods in a year. Thus, if the firm pays on the 40th day, the effective annual cost is $(1.0101)^{14.6} - 1 = .1580$, or 15.8%. By stretching its payables, the firm substantially reduces its effective cost of credit.

Firms may also make a payment on the 30th day but pay only the discounted price. Some may pay only the discounted price and pay even later than the 30th day. Although all these actions will reduce the effective annual rate associated with the trade credit, the firm may incur costs as a result of these actions. Suppliers may react to a firm whose payments are always late by imposing terms of cash on delivery (COD) or cash before delivery (CBD). The delinquent firm then bears the additional costs associated with these terms and may have to negotiate a bank loan to have the cash available to pay. The supplier may also discontinue business with the delinquent customer, leaving the customer to find another source, which may be more expensive or of lower quality. A poor credit rating might also result, making it difficult for the firm to obtain good terms with any other supplier. Moreover, when a firm explicitly agrees to the terms of the sale, violating these terms constitutes unethical business behavior.

CONCEPT   7. What is the optimal time for a firm to pay its accounts payable?
CHECK   8. What do the terms COD and CBD mean?

19.5   Inventory Management

As we discussed, in a perfect capital markets setting, firms would not need to have accounts payable or receivable. Interest rates on trade credit would be competitive, and firms could use alternative sources of financing. However, unlike trade credit, inventory represents one of the required factors of production. Therefore, even in a perfect markets setting, firms still need inventory.

Inventory management receives extensive coverage in a course on operations management. Nevertheless, it is the firm's financial manager who must arrange for the financing necessary to support the firm's inventory policy and who is responsible for ensuring the firm's overall profitability. Therefore, the role of the inventory manager is to balance the costs and benefits associated with inventory. Because excessive inventory uses cash, efficient management of inventory increases firm value.

Benefits of Holding Inventory

A firm needs its inventory to operate for several reasons. First, inventory helps minimize the risk that the firm will not be able to obtain an input it needs for production. If a firm holds too little inventory, **stock-outs**, the situation when a firm runs out of inventory, may occur and lead to lost sales. Disappointed customers may switch to one of the firm's competitors.

stock-outs The situation that occurs when a firm runs out of inventory.

Second, firms may hold inventory because factors such as seasonality in demand mean that customer purchases do not perfectly match the most efficient production cycle. Consider the case of the Sandpoint Toy Company. As is typical for many toy manufacturers, 80% of Sandpoint's annual sales occur between September and December, in anticipation of the holiday gift season. It is more efficient for Sandpoint to manufacture toys at relatively constant levels throughout the year. If Sandpoint produces its toys at a constant rate, its inventory levels will increase to very high levels by August, in anticipation of the increase in sales beginning in September. In contrast, Sandpoint may consider a seasonal manufacturing strategy, producing more toys between September and December when sales are high. Under this strategy, inventory would not accumulate, freeing up cash flow from working capital and reducing the costs of inventory. However, seasonal manufacturing incurs additional costs, such as increased wear and tear on the manufacturing equipment during peak demand and the need to hire and train seasonal workers. Sandpoint must weigh the costs of the inventory buildup under constant production against the benefits of more efficient production. The optimal choice is likely to involve a compromise between the two extremes, so that Sandpoint will carry some inventory.

Costs of Holding Inventory

As suggested by the Sandpoint Toy example, tying up capital in inventory is costly for a firm. We can classify the direct costs associated with inventory into three categories:

- *Acquisition costs* are the costs of the inventory itself over the period being analyzed (usually one year).
- *Order costs* are the total costs of placing an order over the period being analyzed.
- *Carrying costs* include storage costs, insurance, taxes, spoilage, obsolescence, and the opportunity cost of the funds tied up in the inventory.

Minimizing these total costs involves some tradeoffs. For example, if we assume no quantity discounts are available, the lower the level of inventory a firm carries, the lower its carrying cost, but the higher its annual order costs because it needs to place more orders during the year.

"just-in-time" (JIT) inventory management When a firm acquires inventory precisely when needed so that its inventory balance is always zero, or very close to it.

Some firms seek to reduce their carrying costs as much as possible. With **"just-in-time" (JIT) inventory management**, a firm acquires inventory precisely when needed so that its inventory balance is always zero, or very close to it. This technique requires exceptional coordination with suppliers as well as a predictable demand for the firm's products. In 2007, Boeing established a global production system for its new 787 "Dreamliner." Very little of the new plane is actually produced at its plant in Everett, Washington. Rather, all of its major systems, including the fuselage and wings, are produced elsewhere and are flown to the final assembly plant using a specially modified 747 cargo plane. The pieces arrive very shortly before they are needed in the final assembly of the airplane, so Boeing does not have to face the carrying costs of maintaining a large inventory. However, such a plan has risks, as Boeing initially had substantial troubles with its contracted producers finishing their parts on time. Consequently, it delayed the delivery of the first planes and suffered financial penalties from doing so. By 2010, with the 787 in flight-testing, Boeing remained committed to the new production system, although it had to send thousands of its own engineers out to suppliers to help solve bottleneck problems. In some cases, it even bought its suppliers.

Inventory Management Adds to the Bottom Line at Gap

In 2003, the apparel chain GAP reduced its investment in inventory significantly by reducing its inventory days outstanding by 24%. This change freed up $344 million for other purposes. GAP invested some of this cash in short-term securities—primarily in U.S. government and agency securities and in bank certificates of deposit with maturities between three months and one year. The firm reported an increase of *$1.2 million* in interest income in fiscal year 2003 compared with fiscal year 2002. It attributed the increase in interest income to increases in the average cash balances available for investment.

Source: GAP 2003 annual report.

Even if your company does not practice JIT inventory management, it may be forced to adopt it if a major customer does so. For example, in 1999, Toys "R" Us instituted JIT, which caused one of its suppliers, toy manufacturer Hasbro, to make changes in its production schedule.[2]

CONCEPT CHECK

9. What are the direct costs of holding inventory?

10. Describe "just-in-time" inventory management.

---

[2]Hasbro 1999 annual report.

19.6   Cash Management

In the perfect markets setting, the level of cash is irrelevant. With perfect capital markets, a firm is able to raise new money instantly at a fair rate, so it can never be short of cash. Similarly, the firm can invest excess cash at a fair rate to earn an NPV of zero.

In the real world, of course, markets are not perfect. Liquidity has a cost; for example, holding liquid assets may earn a below-market return, and a firm may face transaction costs if it needs to raise cash quickly. Similarly, recall from Chapter 16 that holding excess cash has a tax disadvantage. In these cases, the optimal strategy for a firm is to hold cash in anticipation of seasonalities in demand for its products and random shocks that affect its business. Risky firms and firms with high-growth opportunities tend to hold a relatively high percentage of assets as cash. Firms with easy access to capital markets (for which the transaction costs of accessing cash are therefore lower) tend to hold less cash.[3] In this section, we examine the firm's motivation for holding cash, tools for managing cash, and the short-term securities in which firms invest.

Motivation for Holding Cash

There are three reasons why a firm holds cash:

- To meet its day-to-day needs
- To compensate for the uncertainty associated with its cash flows
- To satisfy bank requirements

We will now examine each of these motivations for holding cash in detail.

transactions balance
The amount of cash a firm needs to pay its bills.

Transactions Balance. Just like you, a firm must hold enough cash to pay its bills. The amount of cash a firm needs to be able to pay its bills is sometimes referred to as a **transactions balance**. The amount of cash a firm needs to satisfy the transactions balance requirement depends on both the average size of the transactions made by the firm and the firm's cash cycle, discussed earlier in the chapter.

precautionary balance
The amount of cash a firm holds to counter the uncertainty surrounding its future cash needs.

Precautionary Balance. The amount of cash a firm holds to counter the uncertainty surrounding its future cash needs is known as a **precautionary balance**. The size of this balance depends on the degree of uncertainty surrounding a firm's cash flows. The more uncertain future cash flows are, the harder it is for a firm to predict its transactions need, so the larger the precautionary balance must be.

compensating balance
An amount a firm's bank may require the firm to maintain in an account at the bank as compensation for services the bank performs.

Compensating Balance. A firm's bank may require it to hold a **compensating balance** in an account at the bank as compensation for services that the bank performs. Compensating balances are typically deposited in accounts that earn either little or no interest. This arrangement is similar to a bank offering individuals free checking as long as their balances do not fall below a certain level—say, $1000. Essentially, the customer has $1000 cash that she cannot use unless she is willing to pay a service charge. Similarly, the cash that a firm has tied up to meet a compensating balance requirement is unavailable for other uses.

Alternative Investments

In our discussion of collection and disbursement floats, we assumed that the firm will invest any cash in short-term securities. In fact, the firm may choose from a variety of

---

[3]See T. Opler, L. Pinkowitz, R. Stulz, and R. Williamson, "The Determinants and Implications of Corporate Cash Holdings," *Journal of Financial Economics*, 52 (1) (1999): 3–46.

short-term securities that differ somewhat with regard to their default risk and liquidity risk. The greater the risk, the higher the expected return on the investment. The financial manager must decide how much risk she is willing to accept in return for a higher yield. If her firm expects to need the funds within the next 30 days, the manager will probably avoid the less liquid options. Table 19.3 briefly describes the most frequently used short-term investments; these short-term debt securities are collectively referred to as **money market securities**.

money market Market for safe, short-term debt issued by high-quality borrowers, such as governments or high credit quality firms.

TABLE 19.3

Money Market Investment Options

Investment	Description	Maturity	Risk	Liquidity
Treasury Bills	Short-term debt of the U.S. government.	Four weeks, three months (91 days), six months (182 days), or 52 weeks when newly issued.	Default risk free.	Very liquid and marketable.
Certificates of Deposit (CDs)	Short-term debt issued by banks. Minimum denomination of $100,000.	Varying maturities up to one year.	If the issuing bank is insured by the FDIC, any amount up to $250,000 is free of default risk because it is covered by the insurance. Any amount in excess of $250,000 is not insured and is subject to default risk.	Unlike CDs purchased by individuals, these CDs sell on the secondary market, but are less liquid than Treasury bills.
Repurchase Agreements	Essentially a loan arrangement wherein a securities dealer is the "borrower" and the investor is the "lender." The investor buys securities, such as U.S. Treasury bills, from the securities dealer, with an agreement to sell the securities back to the dealer at a later date for a specified higher price.	Very short term, ranging from overnight to approximately three months in duration.	The security serves as collateral for the loan, and therefore the investor is exposed to very little risk. However, the investor needs to consider the creditworthiness of the securities dealer when assessing the risk.	No secondary market for repurchase agreements.
Banker's Acceptances	Drafts written by the borrower and guaranteed by the bank on which the draft is drawn. Typically used in international trade transactions. The borrower is an importer who writes the draft in payment for goods.	Typically one to six months.	Because both the borrower and a bank have guaranteed the draft, there is very little risk.	When the exporter receives the draft, he may hold it until maturity and receive its full value or he may sell the draft at a discount prior to maturity.
Commercial Paper	Short-term, unsecured debt issued by large corporations. The minimum denomination is $25,000, but most commercial paper has a face value of $100,000 or more.	Typically one to six months.	Default risk depends on the creditworthiness of the issuing corporation.	No active secondary market, but issuer may repurchase commercial paper.
Short-Term Tax Exempts	Short-term debt of state and local governments. These instruments pay interest that is exempt from federal taxation, so their pretax yield is lower than that of a similar-risk, fully taxable investment.	Typically one to six months.	Default risk depends on the creditworthiness of the issuing government.	Moderate secondary market.

Hoarding Cash

Corporate liquidity is measured as corporate investments in short-term, marketable securities. In the United States, it rose from $3.9 trillion in 1999 to $9.7 trillion in 2013, for an increase of nearly 150%. Indeed, in 2015 more than 39% of U.S. publicly traded firms were net investors, having more cash and short-term investments than debt outstanding.

Why have companies been accumulating more cash? Factors include a shift away from industries such as manufacturing that spend heavily on plant and equipment, strength in sectors such as financial services that have low capital expenditures and high cash flows, avoidance of repatriation taxes by multinational firms, and a desire by companies to preserve liquidity and maintain financial flexibility. As a result, corporate savings have reached an all-time high.

How are companies investing their cash? A 2007 survey by Treasury Strategies indicated that 20% is invested in money market funds and accounts, 18% is invested in bonds and notes, and

the remainder is invested directly in commercial paper, CDs, repurchase agreements, and other investments.

During the 2008 financial crisis, short-term credit markets froze and many businesses that relied on short-term credit found themselves unable to conduct business, You might expect that businesses that held a lot of cash were in good shape. However, cash-holding firms during the crisis did not know what to do with the cash. Before it became clear that governments were going to bail out large banks, firms had to worry about how secure their cash was. In the event of a bank bankruptcy, the firm risked losing access to its cash in the short term and perhaps ultimately losing the cash altogether. For firms that relied on cash balances to conduct business, the impact of the breakdown in financial markets was potentially as big as for firms that relied on credit.

Source: Authors' calculations from Internal Revenue Service Data and Treasury Strategies 2007 Corporate Liquidity Research Overview.

Thus, a financial manager who wants to invest the firm's funds in the least risky security will choose to invest in Treasury bills. However, if a financial manager wishes to earn a higher return on the firm's short-term investments, she may opt to invest some or all of the firm's excess cash in a riskier alternative, such as commercial paper.

CONCEPT CHECK

11. List three reasons why a firm holds cash.

12. What tradeoff does a firm face when choosing how to invest its cash?

MyFinanceLab

Here is what you should know after reading this chapter. MyFinanceLab will help you identify what you know, and where to go when you need to practice.

KEY POINTS AND EQUATIONS	KEY TERMS	ONLINE PRACTICE
19.1 Overview of Working Capital • Working capital management involves managing a firm's short-term assets and short-term liabilities. • A firm's cash cycle is the length of time between when the firm pays cash to purchase its initial inventory and when it receives cash from the sale of the output produced from that inventory. The operating cycle is the average length of time between when a firm originally purchases its inventory and when it receives the cash back from selling its product.	cash conversion cycle, p. 605 cash cycle, p. 605 operating cycle, p. 604	MyFinanceLab Study Plan 19.1

19.2 Trade Credit

- Trade credit is effectively a loan from the selling firm to its customer. The cost of trade credit depends on the credit terms. The cost of not taking a discount that is offered by a supplier implies an interest rate for the loan.
- Firms provide trade credit to their customers for two reasons: (a) as an indirect way to lower prices and (b) because they may have advantages in making loans to their customers relative to other potential sources of credit.
- A firm should compare the cost of trade credit with the cost of alternative sources of financing in deciding whether to use the trade credit offered.
- Collection float is the amount of time it takes for a firm to be able to use funds after a customer has paid for its goods. Firms can reduce their working capital needs by reducing their collection float.

availability float, p. 611
cash discount, p. 609
Check Clearing for the 21st Century Act (Check 21), p. 611
collection float, p. 611
credit period, p. 609
disbursement float, p. 611
discount period, p. 609
mail float, p. 611
processing float, p. 611
trade credit, p. 609

19.3 Receivables Management

- Establishing a credit policy involves three steps: establishing credit standards, establishing credit terms, and establishing a collection policy.
- The accounts receivables days and aging schedule are two methods used to monitor the effectiveness of a firm's credit policy.

aging schedule, p. 614
payments pattern, p. 616

MyFinanceLab
Study Plan 19.3

19.4 Payables Management

- Firms should monitor accounts payable to ensure that they are making payments at an optimal time.
- Paying late, known as stretching accounts payable, can reduce the direct costs of trade credit, but may result in worse terms from suppliers.

stretching the accounts payable, p. 617

MyFinanceLab
Study Plan 19.4

19.5 Inventory Management

- Because excessive inventory uses cash, efficient inventory management increases the firm's free cash flow and thus increases firm value.
- Firms hold inventory to avoid lost sales due to stock-outs and because of factors such as seasonal demand.
- The costs of inventory include acquisition costs, order costs, and carrying costs.

"just-in-time" (JIT) inventory management, p. 619
stock-outs, p. 618

MyFinanceLab
Study Plan 19.5

19.6 Cash Management

- If a firm's need to hold cash is reduced, the funds can be invested in a number of different short-term securities, including Treasury bills, certificates of deposit, commercial paper, repurchase agreements, banker's acceptances, and short-term tax exempts.

compensating balance, p. 620
precautionary balance, p. 620
transactions balance, p. 620

MyFinanceLab
Study Plan 19.6

CRITICAL THINKING

1. What does a firm's cash cycle tell us?

2. Answer the following:
   a. What is the difference between a firm's cash cycle and its operating cycle?
   b. How will a firm's cash cycle be affected if it increases its inventory, all else being equal?
   c. How will a firm's cash cycle be affected if it begins to take the discounts offered by its suppliers, all else being equal?

3. Does an increase in a firm's cash cycle necessarily mean that the firm is managing its cash poorly?

4. Why is trade credit important?

5. What are the ways that receivables management can affect a firm's value?

6. What are the three steps involved in establishing a credit policy?

7. What factors determine how a firm should manage its payables?

8. What is meant by "stretching the accounts payable"?

9. What are the tradeoffs involved in reducing inventory?

10. What are the different ways you can invest your firm's cash?

11. Which of the following short-term securities would you expect to offer the highest before-tax return: Treasury bills, certificates of deposit, short-term tax exempts, or commercial paper? Why?

PROBLEMS

All problems are available in MyFinanceLab. *The* 📊 *icon indicates problems that are easier to solve using Excel and have data in an Excel format available in* MyFinanceLab. *An asterisk * indicates problems with a higher level of difficulty.*

Overview of Working Capital

1. Homer Boats has accounts payable days of 20, inventory days of 50, and accounts receivable days of 30. What is its operating cycle?

2. FastChips Semiconductors has inventory days of 75, accounts receivable days of 30, and accounts payable days of 90. What is its cash conversion cycle?

3. Westerly Industries has the following financial information. What is its cash conversion cycle?

Sales	100,000
Cost of Goods Sold	80,000
Accounts Receivable	30,000
Inventory	15,000
Accounts Payable	40,000

4. Aberdeen Outboard Motors is contemplating building a new plant. The company anticipates that the plant will require an initial investment of $2 million in net working capital today. The plant will last 10 years, at which point the full investment in net working capital will be recovered. Given an annual discount rate of 6%, what is the net present value of this working capital investment?

5. Your firm currently has net working capital of $100,000 that it expects to grow at a rate of 4% per year forever. You are considering some suggestions that could slow that growth to 3% per year. If your discount rate is 12%, how would these changes impact the value of your firm?

6. The Greek Connection had sales of $32 million in 2015, and a cost of goods sold of $20 million. A simplified balance sheet for the firm appears below:
   a. Calculate The Greek Connection's net working capital in 2015.
   b. Calculate the cash conversion cycle of The Greek Connection in 2015.
   c. The industry average accounts receivable days is 30 days. What would have been the cash conversion cycle for The Greek Connection in 2015 had it matched the industry average for accounts receivable days (*see* MyFinanceLab *for the data in Excel format*)?

The Greek Connection
Balance Sheet as of December 31, 2015
(thousands of dollars)

Assets		Liabilities and Equity	
Cash	$ 2,000	Accounts payable	$ 1,500
Accounts receivable	3,950	Notes payable	1,000
Inventory	1,300	Accruals	1,220
Total current assets	$ 7,250	Total current liabilities	$ 3,720
Net plant, property, and equipment	8,500	Long-term debt	$ 3,000
		Total liabilities	$ 6,720
Total assets	$ 15,750	Common equity	$ 9,030
		Total liabilities and equity	$ 15,750

Trade Credit

7. Assume the credit terms offered to your firm by your suppliers are 3/5, net 30. Calculate the cost of the trade credit if your firm does not take the discount and pays on day 30.

8. Your supplier offers terms of 1/10, net 45. What is the effective annual cost of trade credit if you choose to forgo the discount and pay on day 45?

*9. The Fast Reader Company supplies bulletin board services to numerous hotel chains nationwide. The owner of the firm is investigating the desirability of employing a billing firm to do her billing and collections. Because the billing firm specializes in these services, collection float will be reduced by 20 days. Average daily collections are $1200, and the owner can earn 8% annually (expressed as an APR with monthly compounding) on her investments. If the billing firm charges $250 per month, should the owner employ the billing firm?

*10. The Saban Corporation is trying to decide whether to switch to a bank that will accommodate electronic funds transfers from Saban's customers. Saban's financial manager believes the new system would decrease its collection float by as much as five days. The new bank would require a compensating balance of $30,000, whereas its present bank has no compensating balance requirement. Saban's average daily collections are $10,000, and it can earn 8% on its short-term investments. Should Saban make the switch? (Assume the compensating balance at the new bank will be deposited in a non-interest-earning account.)

Receivables Management

11. The Manana Corporation had sales of $60 million this year. Its accounts receivable balance averaged $2 million. How long, on average, does it take the firm to collect on its sales?

12. The Mighty Power Tool Company has the following accounts on its books:

Customer	Amount Owed ($)	Age (days)
ABC	50,000	35
DEF	35,000	5
GHI	15,000	10
KLM	75,000	22
NOP	42,000	40
QRS	18,000	12
TUV	82,000	53
WXY	36,000	90

The firm extends credit on terms of 1/15, net 30. Develop an aging schedule using 15-day increments through 60 days, and then indicate any accounts that have been outstanding for more than 60 days.

Payables Management

13. Simple Simon's Bakery purchases supplies on terms of 1/10, net 25. If Simple Simon's chooses to take the discount offered, it must obtain a bank loan to meet its short-term financing needs. A local bank has quoted Simple Simon's owner an interest rate of 12% on borrowed funds. Should Simple Simon's enter the loan agreement with the bank and begin taking the discount?

14. Your firm purchases goods from its supplier on terms of 3/15, net 40.
    a. What is the effective annual cost to your firm if it chooses not to take the discount and makes its payment on day 40?
    b. What is the effective annual cost to your firm if it chooses not to take the discount and makes its payment on day 50?

*15. Use the financial statements supplied below and on the next page for International Motor Corporation (IMC) to answer the following questions (*see* MyFinanceLab *for the data in Excel format*):
    a. Calculate the cash conversion cycle for IMC for both 2015 and 2016. What change has occurred, if any? All else being equal, how does this change affect IMC's need for cash?
    b. IMC's suppliers offer terms of net 30. Does it appear that IMC is doing a good job of managing its accounts payable?

International Motor Corporation
Income Statement (in millions)
for the Years Ending December 31

	2015	2016
Sales	$60,000	$75,000
Cost of goods sold	52,000	61,000
Gross profit	$ 8,000	$14,000
Selling, general, and administrative expenses	6,000	8,000
Operating profit	$ 2,000	$ 6,000
Interest expense	1,400	1,300
Earnings before taxes	$ 600	$ 4,700
Taxes	300	2,350
Earnings after taxes	$ 300	$ 2,350

International Motor Corporation
Balance Sheet (in millions) as of December 31

	2015	2016		2015	2016
Assets			**Liabilities**		
Cash	$ 3,080	$ 6,100	Accounts payable	$ 3,600	$ 4,600
Accounts			Notes payable	1,180	1,250
receivable	2,800	6,900	Accruals	5,600	6,211
Inventory	6,200	6,600	Total current		
Total current assets	$12,080	$19,600	liabilities	$10,380	$12,061
Net plant, property,			Long-term debt	$ 6,500	$ 7,000
and equipment	$23,087	$20,098			
			Total liabilities	$16,880	$19,061
Total assets	$35,167	$39,698	**Equity**		
			Common stock	$ 2,735	$ 2,735
			Retained earnings	$15,552	$17,902
			Total equity	$18,287	$20,637
			Total liabilities and equity	$35,167	$39,698

Inventory Management

16. Your company had $10 million in sales last year. Its cost of goods sold was $7 million and its average inventory balance was $1,200,000. What was its average days of inventory?

17. Happy Valley Homecare Suppliers, Inc. (HVHS), had $20 million in sales in 2015. Its cost of goods sold was $8 million, and its average inventory balance was $2 million.
    a. Calculate the average number of days inventory outstanding ratios for HVHS.
    b. The average days of inventory in the industry is 73 days. By how much would HVHS reduce its investment in inventory if it could improve its inventory days to meet the industry average?

DATA CASE [4]

You are the Chief Financial Officer (CFO) of Walmart. This afternoon you played golf with a member of the company's board of directors. Somewhere during the back nine, the board member enthusiastically described a recent article she had read in a leading management journal. This article noted several companies that had improved their stock price performance through effective working capital management, and the board member was intrigued. Even though Walmart was known for working capital management, she wondered if it could do even better. How was Walmart managing its working capital, and how does it compare to Costco, another company well known for working capital management?

Upon returning home, you decide to do a quick preliminary investigation using information freely available on the Internet.

1. Obtain Costco's financial statements for the past four years from http://moneycentral.msn.com.
   a. Enter the stock symbol (COST) in the box and click "Get Quote."
   b. Next click "Income Statement" in the left column.

---

[4]If the data sets on the Web sites indicated for this case become unavailable in the future, the data sets will be posted on the book's Web site.

    c. Select "Annual," and if you are using Internet Explorer, place the cursor in the statement and right-click the mouse. Select "Export to Microsoft Excel" from the menu. If you do not have that option, you can copy and paste the data into Excel.

    d. Go back to the Web page and click "Balance Sheet" at the left of the page; repeat the download procedure for the balance sheets.

    e. Copy and paste the balance sheet so that it is on the same worksheet as the income statement.

2. Following the same steps as you did for Costco, Obtain Walmart's (WMT) financial statements for comparison from http://moneycentral.msn.com.

3. Compute the cash conversion cycle for Walmart and Costco for each of the last four years.

    a. Compute the inventory days using "Cost of Revenue" as cost of goods sold and a 365-day year.

    b. Compute accounts receivable days using a 365-day year.

    c. Compute accounts payable days using a 365-day year.

    d. Compute the cash conversion cycle for each year.

4. How has Walmart's CCC changed over the last few years?

5. Compare Walmart's inventory and receivables turnover ratios for the most recent year to Costco's.

    a. Compute the inventory turnover ratio as cost of revenue/inventory.

    b. Compute the receivable turnover ratio as total revenue/net receivables.

6. Now assume Walmart matches Costco's inventory and receivables turnover ratios without changing its payable days.

    a. How much would Walmart's free-cash flow change relative to its current situation?

    b. What would Walmart's CCC be in this case?

7. What are your impressions regarding Walmart's working capital management based on this preliminary analysis? Discuss any advantages and disadvantages of attempting to match Costco's cash conversion cycle.

21

Option Applications and Corporate Finance

LEARNING OBJECTIVES

- Understand basic option terminology

- Explain the difference between *calls* and *puts*, how they pay off, and the profit from holding each to expiration

- Analyze the factors that affect option prices

- Become familiar with the Black-Scholes option pricing formula

- Describe the relationship that must hold between the prices of similar *calls* and *puts* on the same stock

- Demonstrate how options are applied in corporate finance

notation

NPV	net present value
PV	present value

Since the introduction of publicly traded options on the Chicago Board Options Exchange (CBOE) in 1973, financial options have become one of the most important and actively traded financial assets. Today, options are everywhere. Over 2000 companies in the United States alone have options on their stock— including Google, Amazon.com, and Apple. Many public companies such as Nike pay their executives partly in stock options. The 1997 Nobel Prize in Economics was awarded for an option pricing formula. Huge quantities of commodities such as corn, wheat, oil, soybeans, and gold are traded through options. Companies such as Dell spend millions of dollars each year buying options on foreign currencies. Even the plot of the James Bond film *Casino Royale* featured the villain losing a fortune when his options expired worthless. As the use of options grows, so does the value of understanding them.

In this chapter, we introduce the financial option, a financial contract between two parties. In Chapter 9, we briefly discussed the idea of *real options*, or the value of flexibility when managing projects. Here, we delve further into understanding what options are and what factors affect their value. To start, we provide an overview of the basic types of financial options, introduce important terminology, and describe the payoffs of various option-based strategies. Next, we discuss the factors that affect option prices. Finally, we model the equity and debt of the firm as options to gain insight into the conflicts of interest between equity and debt holders, as well as the pricing of risky debt.

Option Basics

financial option A contract that gives its owner the right (but not the obligation) to purchase or sell an asset at a fixed price at some future date.

call option A financial option that gives its owner the right to buy an asset.

put option A financial option that gives its owner the right to sell an asset.

option writer The seller of an option contract.

derivatives Securities whose cash flows depend solely on the prices of other marketed assets.

warrant A call option written by a company itself on new stock.

exercising (an option) When a holder of an option enforces the agreement and buys or sells a share of stock at the agreed-upon price.

strike (exercise) price The price at which an option holder buys or sells a share of stock when the option is exercised.

American options The most common kind of option, they allow their holders to exercise the option on any date up to and including the expiration date.

expiration date The last date on which an option holder has the right to exercise the option.

European options Options that allow their holders to exercise the option only on the expiration date.

A **financial option** contract gives its owner the right (but not the obligation) to purchase or sell an asset at a fixed price at some future date. There are two distinct kinds of option contracts: *call options* and *put options*. A **call option** gives the owner the right to *buy* the asset; a **put option** gives the owner the right to *sell* the asset. An option is a contract between two parties. For every owner of a financial option, there is also an **option writer**, the seller of an option contract, who is the person who takes the other side of the contract. Options are part of a broader class of securities called **derivatives** because they derive their value solely from the price of another asset.

The most common option contracts are options on shares of stock. A stock option gives the holder the option to buy or sell a share of stock on or before a given date for a given price. For example, a call option on 3M Corporation stock might give the holder the right to purchase a share of 3M for $180 per share at any time up to, for example, January 18, 2019. Similarly, a put option on 3M stock might give the holder the right to sell a share of 3M stock for $175 per share at any time up to, say, February 15, 2019.

When a company writes a call option on *new* stock in the company, it is called a **warrant**. A regular call option is written by a third party on existing stock. When a holder of a warrant exercises it and thereby purchases stock, the company delivers this stock by issuing new stock. In all other respects, a warrant is identical to a call option.

Option Contracts

Practitioners use specific words to describe the details of option contracts. When a holder of an option enforces the agreement and buys or sells a share of stock at the agreed-upon price, he is **exercising** the option. The price at which the option holder buys or sells the share of stock when the option is exercised is called the **strike price** or **exercise price**.

There are two kinds of options. **American options**, the most common kind, allow their holders to exercise the option on any date up to and including a final date called the **expiration date**. **European options** allow their holders to exercise the option *only* on the expiration date—holders cannot exercise before the expiration date. The names *American* and *European* have nothing to do with the location where the options are traded: Both types are traded worldwide. For options on equity (stock), the expiration date is the Saturday following the third Friday of the expiration month. However, trading of the option stops on that Friday.

As with other financial assets, options can be bought and sold. Standard stock options are traded on organized exchanges, while more specialized options are sold through dealers. The oldest and largest options exchange is the Chicago Board Options Exchange (CBOE). By convention, all traded options expire on the Saturday following the third Friday of the month. The market price of the option is also called the *option premium*.

The *option buyer*, also called the *option holder*, holds the right to exercise the option and has a *long* position in the contract. The *option seller*, also called the *option writer*, sells (or writes) the option and has a *short* position in the contract. Because the long side has the option to exercise, the short side has an *obligation* to fulfill the contract. For example, suppose you own a call option on Hewlett-Packard stock with an exercise price of $25. Hewlett-Packard stock is currently trading for $40, so you decide to exercise the option. The person holding the short position in the contract is obligated to sell you a share of Hewlett-Packard stock for $25. Your $15 gain—the difference between the price you pay for the share of stock and the price at which you can sell the share in the market—is the short position's loss.

Investors exercise options only when they stand to gain something. Consequently, whenever an option is exercised, the person holding the short position funds the gain. That is, the obligation will be costly. Why, then, do people write options? The answer is that when you sell an option you get paid for it—options always have positive prices. This up-front payment compensates the seller for the risk of loss in the event that the option holder chooses to exercise the option. If all this new terminology is confusing, rest assured that you will become comfortable with it as you proceed through the chapter. We provide a summary of the new terms in Table 21.1.

Stock Option Quotations

Table 21.2 shows near-term options on Amazon.com taken from the CBOE Web site (www.cboe.com) on July 18, 2016. Call options are listed on the left and put options on the right. Each line corresponds to a particular option. The first two digits in the option name refer to the year of expiration. The option name also includes the month of expiration and the strike or exercise price. Looking at Table 21.2, the first line of the left column is a call option with an exercise price of $715 that expires on the Saturday following the third Friday of August 2016 (Saturday, August 20, 2016). The columns to the right of the name display market data for the option. The first of these columns shows the last sale price, followed by the net change from the previous day's last reported sale price, the current bid and ask

open interest The total number of contracts of a particular option that have been written and not yet closed.

prices, and the daily volume. The final column is the **open interest**, the total number of contracts of that particular option that have been written and not yet closed.

The top line of the option quote displays information about the stock itself. In this case, Amazon's stock last traded at a price of $736.07 per share, which is $0.63 less than where it closed the previous day (red indicates a decline).

at-the-money Describes options whose exercise prices are equal to the current stock price.

When the exercise price of an option is equal to the current price of the stock, the option is said to be **at-the-money**. Notice that much of the trading occurs in options that are closest to being at-the-money—that is, calls and puts with exercise prices of $735. Note how the August 735 calls have high volume. They last traded for $34.04, which is above the

TABLE 21.1

The Language of Options

Call option	Option to <u>buy</u> the stock at a prespecified price
Put option	Option to <u>sell</u> the stock at a prespecified price
Strike (exercise) price	The prespecified price in the option contract
Write an option	Sell an option
Exercise (an option)	Enforce your right to buy or sell the stock as specified in the option contract
Short/Long position	The writer (seller) has a short position and the buyer has a long position in the option
American option	You can exercise the option any time on or before the expiration date
European option	You can exercise the option only on the expiration date
Warrant	A call option written by the firm whereby new stock will be issued if the warrant is exercised

TABLE 21.2

Option Quotes for Amazon.com Stock

The description of each traded option can be read as: year and month of expiration, followed by the strike price. For example, the first call listed expires in August 2016 and has an exercise (strike) price of 715.00.

AMZN (AMAZON.COM INC)   736.07   0.63
Jul 18 2016 @ 17:47 ET

Calls	Last Sale	Net	Bid	Ask	Vol	Open Int	Puts	Last Sale	Net	Bid	Ask	Vol	Open Int
16 Aug 715.00	44.20	0.09	43.55	44.35	44	1253	16 Aug 715.00	22.10	−1.47	22.05	22.75	97	590
16 Aug 720.00	41.79	0.52	40.55	41.35	135	806	16 Aug 720.00	24.00	−1.87	24.05	24.70	158	610
16 Aug 725.00	38.79	0.74	37.60	38.45	149	602	16 Aug 725.00	25.60	−2.09	26.15	26.80	37	624
16 Aug 730.00	36.07	0.47	34.95	35.65	168	1496	16 Aug 730.00	27.81	−2.24	28.40	29.15	49	714
16 Aug 735.00	34.04	1.26	32.20	33.00	156	656	16 Aug 735.00	30.31	−2.04	30.70	31.40	28	318
16 Aug 740.00	30.36	0.16	29.70	30.40	185	669	16 Aug 740.00	33.10	−1.12	33.10	33.65	65	657
16 Aug 745.00	28.65	0.71	27.30	27.95	51	602	16 Aug 745.00	35.70	−1.65	35.70	36.50	19	338
16 Aug 750.00	25.70	0.10	24.80	25.60	378	1671	16 Aug 750.00	38.60	−1.50	38.35	39.10	25	615
16 Aug 755.00	24.20	0.75	22.90	23.35	57	682	16 Aug 755.00	41.00	−1.41	41.10	41.90	8	305

Source: Chicago Board Options Exchange at www.cboe.com.

current bid price ($32.20) and the ask price ($33.00). This indicates that the trade likely did not occur recently because the last traded price is not a current market price.

Stock option contracts are always written on 100 shares of stock. If, for instance, you decided to purchase one August 715 call contract, you would be purchasing an option to buy 100 shares at $715 per share. Option prices are quoted on a per-share basis, so the ask price of $44.35 implies that you would pay $100 \times 44.35 = \$4,435$ for the contract. Similarly, if you decide to buy an August 715 put contract, you would pay $100 \times 22.75 = \$2,275$ for the option to sell 100 shares of Amazon's stock for $715 per share.

Note from Table 21.2 that for the August 2016 expiration date, call options with lower strike prices have higher market prices—the right to buy the stock at a lower price is more valuable than the right to buy it for a higher price. Conversely, because the put option gives the holder the right to sell the stock at the strike price, puts with higher strikes are more valuable (for the same expiration date). On the other hand (not shown in the table), holding fixed the strike price, both calls and puts are more expensive for a longer time to expiration. Because these options are American-style options that can be exercised at any time, having the right to buy or sell for a longer period is valuable.

in-the-money Describes an option whose value if immediately exercised would be positive.

out-of-the-money Describes an option that if exercised immediately results in a loss of money.

deep in-the-money Describes options that are in-the-money and for which the strike price and the stock price are very far apart.

deep out-of-the-money Describes options that are out-of-the-money and for which the strike price and the stock price are very far apart.

If the payoff from exercising an option immediately is positive, the option is said to be **in-the-money**. Call options with strike prices below the current stock price are in-the-money, as are put options with strike prices above the current stock price. At the time of the quotes in Table 21.2, Amazon's stock price was $736.07, so any call option with a strike price below $736.07 would be in-the-money, such as the August 715 through 735 calls, and any put option with a strike price above $736.07 would be in the money, such as the August 740 through 755 puts. Conversely, if the payoff from exercising the option immediately is negative, the option is **out-of-the-money**. Call options with strike prices above the current stock price are out-of-the-money, as are put options with strike prices below the current stock price. In Table 21.2, the August 740 through August 755 calls are out-of-the money, as are the August 715 through 735 puts. Of course, a holder would not exercise an out-of-the-money option. Options where the strike price and the stock price are very far apart are referred to as **deep in-the-money** or **deep out-of-the-money**.

EXAMPLE 21.1
Purchasing Options

MyFinanceLab

PROBLEM

It is July 18, 2016, and you have decided to purchase 10 August call contracts on Amazon's stock with an exercise price of $740. Because you are buying, you must pay the ask price. How much money will this purchase cost you? Is this option in-the-money or out-of-the-money?

SOLUTION

PLAN

From Table 21.2, the ask price of this option is $30.40. Remember that the price quoted is per share and that each contract is for 100 shares.

EXECUTE

You are purchasing 10 contracts and each contract is on 100 shares, so the transaction will cost $30.40 \times 10 \times 100 = \$30,400$ (ignoring any commission fees). Because this is a call option and the exercise price is above the current stock price ($736.07), the option is currently out-of-the-money.

EVALUATE

Even though the option is currently out-of-the-money, it still has value. During the time left to expiration, the stock could rise above the exercise (strike) price of $740.

Options on Other Financial Securities

hedging To reduce risk by holding contracts or securities whose payoffs are negatively correlated with some risk exposure.

speculate When investors use securities to place a bet on the direction in which they believe the market is likely to move.

Although the most commonly traded options are written on stocks, options on other financial assets do exist. Perhaps the most well known are options on stock indexes such as the S&P 100 index, the S&P 500 index, the Dow Jones Industrial Average index, and the NYSE index. These popular options allow investors to protect the value of their investments from adverse market changes. As we will see shortly, a stock index put option can be used to offset the losses on an investor's portfolio in a market downturn. Using an option to reduce risk by holding contracts or securities whose payoffs are negatively correlated with some risk exposure is called **hedging**. Options also allow investors to **speculate**, or place a bet on the direction in which they believe the market is likely to move. By purchasing a call, for example, investors can bet on a market rise with a much smaller investment than they could by investing in the market index itself.

Options Are for More Than Just Stocks

Although the examples in this chapter are mainly about options on stocks, there are options on a wide variety of other assets. For example, options are also traded on Treasury securities. These options allow investors to bet on or hedge interest rate risk. There are also options on currencies (we discuss these in more detail in Chapter 23), gold, platinum, and other commodities such as copper or oil. There are also many options on agricultural products such as wheat, soybeans, livestock, cotton, orange juice, and sugar. These options allow both farmers and large agribusinesses to hedge their risks from fluctuations in production and prices.

CONCEPT
CHECK

1. Does the holder of an option have to exercise it?
2. What is the difference between an American option and a European option?

21.2   Option Payoffs at Expiration

With our new understanding of the basics of puts and calls, we are now prepared to examine their values. From the Valuation Principle, the value of any security is determined by the future cash flows an investor receives from owning it. Therefore, before we can assess what an option is worth, we must determine an option's payoff at the time of expiration.

The Long Position in an Option Contract

Assume you own an option with a strike price of $20. If, on the expiration date, the stock price is greater than the strike price, say $30, you can make money by exercising the call (by paying $20, the strike price for the stock) and immediately selling the stock in the open market for $30. The $10 difference is what the option is worth. Consequently, when the stock price on the expiration date exceeds the strike price, the value of the call is the difference between the stock price and the strike price. When the stock price is less than the strike price at expiration, the holder will not exercise the call, so the option is worth nothing. These payoffs are plotted in Figure 21.1.

Thus, the value of the call at expiration is:

Call Value at Expiration

Call Value = Stock Price − Strike Price, if Stock Price > Strike Price

$$= 0, \qquad \text{if Stock Price} \leq \text{Strike Price} \qquad (21.1)$$

The holder of a put option will exercise the option if the stock price is below the strike price. Because the holder receives the strike price when the stock is worth less, the holder's gain is equal to Strike Price − Stock Price. Thus, the value of a put at expiration is:

Put Price at Expiration

Put Value = Strike Price − Stock Price, if Stock Price < Strike Price

$$= 0, \qquad \text{if Stock Price} \geq \text{Strike Price} \qquad (21.2)$$

FIGURE 21.1

Payoff of a Call Option with a Strike Price of $20 at Expiration

If the stock price is greater than the strike price ($20), the call will be exercised. The holder's payoff is the difference between the stock price and the strike price. If the stock price is less than the strike price, the call will not be exercised, and so has no value.

EXAMPLE 21.2

Payoff of a Put Option
at Maturity

MyFinanceLab

PROBLEM

You own a put option on Oracle stock with an exercise price of $20 that expires today. Plot the value of this option as a function of the stock price.

SOLUTION

PLAN

From Eq. 21.2, and the fact that the strike price is $20, we see that the value of the put option is:

Put Value = 20 − Stock Price, if Stock Price < 20; = 0, if Stock Price ≥ 20

EXECUTE

Plotting this function gives:

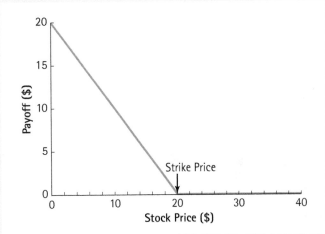

EVALUATE

Because the put option allows you to force the put writer to buy the stock for $20, regardless of the current market price, we can see that the put option payoff increases as Oracle's stock price decreases. For example, if Oracle's price were $10, you could buy a share of Oracle in the market for $10 and then sell it to the put writer for $20, making a profit of $10.

The Short Position in an Option Contract

An investor holding a short position in an option has an obligation: This investor takes the opposite side of the contract to the investor who is long. Thus, the short position's cash flows are the negative of the long position's cash flows. Because an investor who has a long position in an option can only receive money at expiration—that is, the investor will not exercise an option that is out-of-the-money—a short investor can only pay money.

To demonstrate, assume you have a short position in a call option with an exercise price of $20. If the stock price is greater than the strike price of a call—for example, $25—the holder will exercise the option. You then have the obligation to sell the stock for the strike price of $20. Because you must purchase the stock at the market price of $25, you lose the difference between the two prices, or $5. However, if the stock price is less than the strike price at the expiration date, the holder will not exercise the option, so in this case you lose nothing; you have no obligation. These payoffs are plotted in Figure 21.2.

FIGURE 21.2

Short Position in a
Call Option at
Expiration

If the stock price is greater than the strike price, the call will be exercised. A person on the short side of a call will lose the difference between the stock price and the strike price. If the stock price is less than the strike price, the call will not be exercised, and the seller will have no obligation.

EXAMPLE 21.3

Payoff of a
Short Position in
a Put Option

MyFinanceLab

PROBLEM

You are short a put option on Oracle stock with an exercise price of $20 that expires today. Plot the value of this option as a function of the stock price.

SOLUTION

PLAN

Again, the strike price is $20 and in this case your cash flows will be opposite of those from Eq. 21.2, as depicted in the previous example. Thus, your cash flows will be

$$-(20 - \text{Stock Price}) = -20 + \text{Stock Price, if Stock Price} < 20$$
$$= 0, \text{ if Stock Price} \geq 20$$

EXECUTE

The graph plots
your cash flows:

EVALUATE

If the current stock price is $30, the put will not be exercised and you will owe nothing. If the current stock price is $15, the put will be exercised and you will lose $5. Comparing the graph here and in Example 21.2, we see that the payoffs are mirror images of each other.

Notice that because the stock price cannot fall below zero, the downside for a short position in a put option is limited to the strike price of the option. A short position in a call, however, has no limit on the downside (see Figure 21.2).

Profits for Holding an Option to Expiration

Although payouts on a long position in an option contract are never negative, the *profit* from purchasing an option and holding it to expiration could be negative. That is, the payout at expiration might be less than the initial cost of the option.

To illustrate, let's consider the potential profits from purchasing the "16 August 735" call option on Amazon's stock quoted in Table 21.2. The option costs $33.00 \times 100 = \$3{,}300$ and expires on Saturday, August 20, 2016 (33 days). Assume you choose to finance the purchase by borrowing $3,300 at an interest rate of 3% per year. At the end of 33 days, you will need $3,308.83 to pay off the loan $(3{,}300 \times 1.03^{33/365} = 3{,}308.83)$. The profit is the call payoff minus the $3,308.83 owed on the loan, shown as the brick-colored curve in Figure 21.3. Once the cost of the position is taken into account, you make a positive profit only if the stock price exceeds $768.09. For example, if the price of the stock is $768.10, then you can exercise your option to buy at $735, sell at $768.10, gaining $33.10 per share. With 100 shares, you have a total gain of $3,310, which will be enough to pay off your loan. As we can see from Table 21.2, the further in-the-money the option is, the higher its initial price and thus the larger your potential loss. An out-of-the-money option has a smaller

FIGURE 21.3

Profit from Holding a Call Option to Expiration

The curves show the profit per share from purchasing a few of the August call options in Table 21.2 on July 18, 2016, paying for this purchase by borrowing at 3%, and holding the position until the expiration date. Note that all of the payoff diagrams are shifted down by the amount of the option's premium. Thus, even if the payoff is positive, if it is not enough to offset the premium you paid to acquire the option, your profit will be negative.

initial cost and hence a smaller potential loss. The probability of a gain, however, is also smaller because the point where profits become positive is higher.

Because a short position in an option is the other side of a long position, the profits from a short position in an option are the negative of the profits of a long position. For example, a short position in an out-of-the-money call such as the "16 August 740" Amazon call in Figure 21.3 produces a small positive profit if Amazon's stock is below $770.49, but leads to losses if the stock price is above $770.49.

EXAMPLE 21.4

Profit on Holding a Position in a Put Option Until Expiration

MyFinanceLab

PROBLEM

Assume you decided to purchase the August 725 through 740 put options quoted in Table 21.2 on July 18, 2016, and you financed each position by borrowing at 3% for 33 days. Plot the profit of each position as a function of the stock price on expiration.

SOLUTION

PLAN

Suppose P is the price of each put option on August 21. Then your cash flows on the expiration date will be:

$$(\text{Strike Price} - \text{Stock Price}) - P \times 1.03^{33/365}, \text{ if Stock Price} < \text{Strike Price}$$

$$\text{or } 0 - P \times 1.03^{33/365}, \text{ if Stock Price} \geq \text{Strike Price}$$

EXECUTE

The graph plots your profits:

EVALUATE

The graph illustrates the same tradeoff between the maximum loss and the potential for profit as for the call options in Figure 21.3. The greatest profit potential comes from the most expensive option, so if that option expires worthless, you have lost the greatest amount.

Returns for Holding an Option to Expiration

We can also compare options based on their potential returns. Figure 21.4 shows the return from purchasing one of the August 2016 options in Table 21.2 on July 18, 2016, and holding it until the expiration date. Let's begin by focusing on call options, shown in Panel (a). In all cases, the maximum loss is 100%—the option may expire worthless. Notice how the curves change as a function of the strike price—the potential returns for out-of-the-money call options are more extreme than those for in-the-money calls. That is, an out-of-the money call option is more likely to have a −100% return. If the stock goes up sufficiently, however, it will also have a much higher return than an in-the-money call option. Similarly, all call options have more extreme returns than the stock itself (given Amazon's initial price of $736.07, the range of stock prices shown in the plot represent returns from about −10% to +10%). Consequently, the risk of a call option is amplified relative to the risk of the stock. The amplification is greater for deeper out-of-the-money calls. Thus, if a stock had a positive beta, call options written on the stock will have even higher betas and expected returns than the stock itself.

Now consider the returns for put options. Look carefully at Panel (b) in Figure 21.4. The put position has a higher return in states with *low* stock prices; that is, if the stock has a positive beta, the put has a negative beta. Hence, put options on positive beta stocks have lower expected returns than the underlying stocks. The deeper out-of-the-money the put option is, the more negative its beta, and the lower its expected return. As a result, put options are generally not held as an investment, but rather as insurance to hedge other risk in a portfolio. We explore the idea of using options for insurance further in Section 21.5.

At this point, we have discussed the cost (premium) of buying an option, the payoffs at expiration, and the profits. It is a lot to keep track of, but it is usually helpful to remember

FIGURE 21.4

Option Returns from Purchasing an Option and Holding It to Expiration

Panel (a) shows the return on the expiration date from purchasing one of the August call options in Table 21.2 on July 18, 2016, and holding the position until the expiration date. Panel (b) shows the same return for the September put options in the table. Notice how the returns are more sensitive to a change in the stock price the further out-of-the-money the option is. For example, in Panel (a), the slope of the return line after the strike price is reached is steeper for options that are further out-of-the-money. For the August 740 call, a small change in the stock price can lead to a large change in the return. A similar effect is seen for puts in Panel (b).

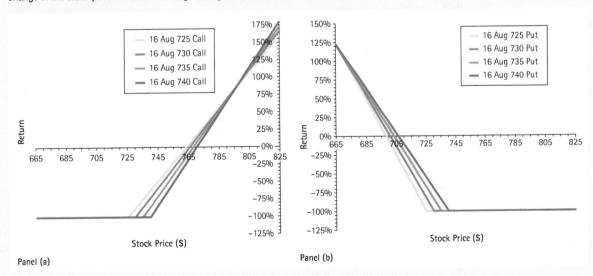

that there are only three things being exchanged: (1) the option premium, (2) the strike price, and (3) the share of stock. Furthermore, because an option is a contract between two parties, the losses of one party are the gains of the other. We summarize these relationships in Table 21.3 for the "16 August 735" calls and puts on Amazon.com stock from Table 21.2. When reading the table, keep in mind that if you own the option and exercising it would create a negative payoff, you will choose not to exercise, so the payoff will be zero (see Eqs. 21.1 and 21.2).

TABLE 21.3

Payoffs, Profits, and Returns to Buying or Writing Options in Table 21.2

	At Purchase	At Expiration If Stock Price = 695		At Expiration If Stock Price = 775	
		Payoff	**Profit**	**Payoff**	**Profit**
Buy a 16 Aug 735 Call	Pay 33.00	0	−33.00 −100% return	775 − 735 = **40**	40 − 33 = **7** 7/33 = 21% return
Write a 16 Aug 735 Call	Receive 33.00	0	**33.00**	735 − 775 = **−40**	33.40 = **−7**
Buy a 16 Aug 735 Put	Pay 31.40	735 − 695 = **40**	40 − 31.40 = **8.60** 8.60/31.40 = 27% return	0	**−31.40** −100% return
Write a 16 Aug 735 Put	Receive 31.40	695 − 735 = **−40**	31.40 − 40 = **−8.60**	0	**31.40**

Contracts are for 100 shares. Payoffs shown are per share.

CONCEPT
CHECK

3. How are the profits from buying an option different from the payoff to the option at expiration?

4. How are the payoffs to buying a call option related to the payoffs from writing a call option?

21.3   Factors Affecting Option Prices

When we discussed Table 21.2, we noted some relations between the option prices and different characteristics of the options. In this section, we identify and explain all the factors that affect the price of an option.

Strike Price and Stock Price

As we noted earlier for the Amazon.com option quotes in Table 21.2, the value of an otherwise identical call option is higher if the strike price the holder must pay to buy the stock is lower. Because a put is the right to sell the stock, puts with a lower strike price are less valuable.

For a given strike price, the value of a call option is higher if the current price of the stock is higher, as there is a greater likelihood the option will end up in-the-money. Conversely, put options increase in value as the stock price falls.

Option Prices and the Exercise Date

For American options, the longer the time to the exercise date, the more valuable the option. To see why, let's consider two options: an option with one year until the exercise date and an option with six months until the exercise date. The holder of the one-year option can turn her option into a six-month option by simply exercising it early. That is, the one-year option has all the same rights and privileges as the six-month option, so by the Valuation Principle, it cannot be worth less than the six-month option. That is, *an American option with a later exercise date cannot be worth less than an otherwise identical American option with an earlier exercise date*. Usually the right to delay exercising the option is worth something, so the option with the later exercise date will be more valuable.

What about European options? The same argument will not work for European options, because a one-year European option cannot be exercised early at six months. As a consequence, a European option with a later exercise date may potentially trade for less than an otherwise identical option with an earlier exercise date. For example, think about a European call on a stock that pays a liquidating dividend in six months (a *liquidating dividend* is paid when a corporation chooses to go out of business, sells off all of its assets, and pays out the proceeds as a dividend). A one-year European call option on this stock would be worthless, but a six-month call would have value.

Option Prices and the Risk-Free Rate

The value of a call option is increasing in the risk-free rate, but the value of a put option is decreasing in the risk-free rate. The intuition is that a higher discount rate reduces the present value of the strike price: Because you must pay the strike price to exercise a call option, reducing the present value of your payment increases the value of the option. However, because you *receive* the strike price when you exercise a put, reducing the present value decreases the value of the put option. We note, however, that given normal swings in the risk-free rate, they would be unlikely to change enough over the life of an option to have a substantial impact on the price of the option—that is, option values are not particularly sensitive to changes in the risk-free rate.

Option Prices and Volatility

An important criterion that determines the price of an option is the volatility of the underlying stock. In fact, *the value of an option generally increases with the volatility of the stock*.[1] The intuition for this result is that an increase in volatility increases the likelihood of very high and very low returns for the stock. The holder of a call option benefits from a higher payoff when the stock goes up and the option is in-the-money, but earns the same (zero) payoff no matter how far the stock drops once the option is out-of-the-money. *Because of this asymmetry of the option's payoff, an option holder generally gains from an increase in volatility*. Consider the following example.

<table>
<tr><td>

EXAMPLE 21.5

Option Value and
Volatility

MyFinanceLab

</td><td>

PROBLEM

Two European call options with a strike price of $50 are written on two different stocks. Suppose that tomorrow, the *low-volatility* stock will have a price of $50 for certain. The *high-volatility* stock will be worth either $60 or $40, with each price having equal probability. If the exercise date of both options is tomorrow, which option will be worth more today?

SOLUTION

PLAN

The value of the options will depend on the value of the stocks at expiration. The value of the options at expiration will be the stock price tomorrow minus $50 if the stock price is greater than $50, and $0 otherwise.

(Continued)

</td></tr>
</table>

---

[1]This relation between the stock's volatility and the value of an option holds for realistic distributions of stock prices assumed by practitioners, in which an increase in volatility implies a more "spread out" distribution for the entire range of future stock prices. That said, it need not hold, for example, if the volatility of the stock increases in some ranges but falls in others.

EXECUTE

The low-volatility stock will be worth $50 for certain, so its option will be worth $0 for certain. The high-volatility stock will be worth either $40 or $60, so its option will pay off either $0 or $60 − $50 = $10. Because options have no chance of a negative payoff, the one that has a 50% chance of a positive payoff has to be worth more than the option on the low-volatility stock (with no chance of a positive payoff).

EVALUATE

Because volatility increases the chance that an option will pay off, the options have very different values even though the expected value of *both* stocks tomorrow is $50—the low-volatility stock will be worth this amount for sure, and the high-volatility stock also has an expected value of $40 $\left(\frac{1}{2}\right)$ + $60 $\left(\frac{1}{2}\right)$ = $50.

Example 21.5 confirms our intuition that the value of a call option is increasing in the volatility of the underlying stock. The same holds for puts. Recall that adding a put option to a portfolio is akin to buying insurance against a decline in value. Insurance is more valuable when there is higher volatility—hence, put options on more volatile stocks are also worth more. Table 21.4 summarizes the factors that affect option values and how an increase in each factor affects those values.

TABLE 21.4

How an Increase in Each Factor Affects Option Values

	American		European	
	Call	**Put**	**Call**	**Put**
Stock Price	Increases Value	Decreases Value	Increases Value	Decreases Value
Strike Price	Decreases Value	Increases Value	Decreases Value	Increases Value
Time to Expiration	Increases Value	Increases Value	Uncertain	Uncertain
Risk-Free Rate	Increases Value	Decreases Value	Increases Value	Decreases Value
Volatility of Stock Price[2]	Increases Value	Increases Value	Increases Value	Increases Value

CONCEPT CHECK

5. Can a European option with a later exercise date be worth less than an identical European option with an earlier exercise date?

6. Why are options more valuable when there is increased uncertainty about the value of the stock?

21.4 The Black-Scholes Option Pricing Formula

In Nobel Prize-winning research, Professors Fischer Black and Myron Scholes derived a formula for the price of a European-style call option for a non-dividend-paying stock. The formula now serves as the basis of pricing for options contracts traded worldwide. Their formula is:

Black-Scholes Price of a Call Option on a Non-Dividend-Paying Stock

$$\text{Call Price} = \text{Stock Price} \times N(d_1) - PV(\text{Strike Price}) \times N(d_2) \qquad (21.3)$$

The present value is calculated using the risk-free rate and $N(d_1)$ and $N(d_2)$ are probabilities. The expressions for d_1 and d_2 are complicated and explaining them is better left to your later finance courses.[3] However, we note here that they contain only the stock price,

---

[2]See footnote 1 on page 673.

[3]For the curious student, they are:

$$d_1 = \frac{\ln\left[\text{Stock Price}/PV(\text{Strike Price})\right]}{\sigma\sqrt{T}} + \frac{\sigma\sqrt{T}}{2} \text{ and } d_2 = d_1 - \sigma\sqrt{T},$$

where σ is the annual standard deviation of the stock return and T is the time to expiration of the option (in years). We also note that $N(\cdot)$ in Eq. 21.3 refers to the cumulative normal distribution function.

strike price, risk-free rate, time to expiration of the option, and volatility of the stock. Thus, Black and Scholes confirmed our discussion from the last section that these five factors are the only ones relevant to the value of an option. What is just as notable is what is *not* relevant: We do not need to know the expected return of the stock. You might wonder how it is possible to compute the value of a security such as an option that appears to depend critically on the future stock price without knowing the expected return of the stock. In fact, the expected return of the stock is already incorporated into the current stock price, and the value of the option today depends on the stock price today.

Fortunately, you do not need to understand the Black-Scholes formula to use it. There are many online option pricing calculators and even add-ins for Excel based on the formula. In Figure 21.5, we show one such calculator from the Options Industry Council.

So far, we have discussed the factors affecting the prices of individual calls and puts. You may have noticed in Figure 21.5 that the prices of both the put and call for the stock are displayed. In fact, those prices cannot move independently of each other. In the next section, we will demonstrate a powerful relation that links the price of a put to the price of a call on the same stock.

FIGURE 21.5

Online Option Pricing Calculator

This option pricing calculator is based on the Black-Scholes option pricing formula. Here, we selected "Black-Scholes (European)" in the "Model/Exercise" box and then entered a stock price of $46, a strike price of $45, expiration in September 2016, a risk-free interest rate of 1%, annual volatility (standard deviation) of the stock return of 25%, and no dividends. The right side of the screen shows that the call value is $2.42 (and the put value is $1.35). The other outputs on the right side of the screen are called "the Greeks" because they are mostly Greek letters (vega is not a real Greek letter). Interested students can go to the Web site and click the question mark next to each Greek letter to learn its meaning. Note that the option values will vary depending on how close you are to the expiration date, so you should not expect to get the same values shown when you try the calculator.

Source: http://www.optionseducation.org. Courtesy of The Options Industry Council. Used with permission.

CONCEPT CHECK

7. What factors are used in the Black-Scholes formula to price a call option?

8. How can the Black-Scholes formula not include the expected return on the stock?

Put-Call Parity

As we have seen, the payoffs to both puts and calls depend on the price of the underlying stock. The expected payoffs determine the prices of the options, so the prices of puts and calls depend partly on the price of the underlying stock. Because the prices of both a put and a call on a given stock are influenced by the price of that same stock, their prices are related. In this section, we develop that relation by showing that both puts and calls can be packaged in different ways to achieve the same objective—to provide insurance against a drop in the price of a stock. Then we use the Valuation Principle's Law of One Price to show that if the two packages provide exactly the same payoffs, they must have the same price.

Portfolio Insurance

Let's see how we can use combinations of options to insure a stock against a loss. Assume you currently own a stock worth $80 and you would like to insure the stock against the possibility of a price decline. To do so, you could simply sell the stock, but you would also give up the possibility of making money if the stock price increases. How can you insure against a loss without relinquishing the upside? You can purchase a put option while still holding the stock, sometimes known as a **protective put**.

protective put
Purchasing a put option on a stock you already own.

For example, suppose you want to insure against the possibility that the stock price will drop below $75. You decide to purchase a European put option with a strike price of $75. The yellow line in Figure 21.6, Panel (a), shows the value of the combined position on the expiration date of the option. If the stock price is above $75 at expiration, you keep the stock. If it is below $75, you exercise your put and sell it for $75. Thus, you get the upside, but are insured against a drop in the price of the stock.

You can use the same strategy to insure against a loss on an entire portfolio of stocks by using put options on the portfolio as a whole rather than just a single stock.

FIGURE 21.6

Portfolio Insurance

The plots show two different ways with identical payoffs for insuring against the possibility of a stock's price falling below $75. The yellow line in Panel (a) indicates the value on the expiration date of a position that consists of buying one share of the stock and one European put option with a strike of $75 (the blue dashed line is the payoff of the stock itself). The yellow line in Panel (b) shows the value on the expiration date of a position that consists of buying a zero-coupon risk-free bond with a face value of $75 and a European call option on the stock with a strike price of $75 (the green dashed line is the bond payoff).

Panel (a)   Panel (b)

portfolio insurance A protective put written on a portfolio rather than a single stock.

Consequently, holding stocks and put options in this combination is known as **portfolio insurance**.

Put-Call Parity: Non-Dividend-Paying Stock. You can also achieve portfolio insurance by purchasing a bond and a call option. Let's return to the insurance we purchased on the $80 stock. Assume that the stock does not pay dividends, so there are no cash flows before the expiration of the option. Thus, instead of holding a share of stock and a put, you could get the same payoff by purchasing a risk-free zero-coupon bond with a face value of $75 and a European call option with a strike price of $75. In this case, if the stock price is below $75, you receive the payoff from the bond. If the stock price is above $75, you can exercise the call and use the payoff from the bond to buy the stock for the strike price of $75. The yellow line in Figure 21.6, Panel (b), shows the value of the combined position on the expiration date of the option; it achieves exactly the same payoffs as owning the stock itself and a put option.

Consider the two different ways to construct portfolio insurance illustrated in Figure 21.6: (1) Purchase the stock and a put or (2) purchase a bond and a call. Because both positions provide exactly the same payoff, the Valuation Principle and, in particular, the Law of One Price, requires that they must have the same price:

$$\text{Stock Price} + \text{Put Price} = PV(\text{Strike Price}) + \text{Call Price}$$

The left side of this equation is the cost of buying the stock and a put; the right side is the cost of buying a zero-coupon bond with face value equal to the strike price of the put and a call option (with the same strike price as the put). Recall that the price of a zero-coupon bond is the present value of its face value, which we have denoted by PV(Strike Price). Rearranging terms gives an expression for the price of a European call option for a non-dividend-paying stock:

put-call parity (for non-dividend paying stocks) The relationship that gives the price of a call option in terms of the price of a put option plus the price of the underlying stock minus the present value of the strike price.

$$\text{Call Price} = \text{Put Price} + \text{Stock Price} - PV(\text{Strike Price}) \qquad (21.4)$$

This relationship between the value of the stock, the bond, and the call and put options is known as **put-call parity**. It says that the price of a European call equals the price of the stock plus an otherwise identical put minus the price of a bond with a face value equal to the strike price that matures on the exercise date of the option. In other words, you can think of a call as a combination of a levered position in the stock, Stock Price $- PV$(Strike Price), plus insurance against a drop in the stock price, the put.

EXAMPLE 21.6
Using Put-Call Parity

MyFinanceLab

PROBLEM

You are an options dealer who deals in non-publicly traded options. One of your clients wants to purchase a one-year European call option on HAL Computer Systems stock with a strike price of $20. Another dealer is willing to write a one-year European put option on HAL stock with a strike price of $20, and sell you the put option for a price of $2.50 per share. If HAL pays no dividends and is currently trading for $18 per share, and if the risk-free interest rate is 6%, what is the lowest price you can charge for the call option and still guarantee yourself a profit?

SOLUTION

PLAN

We can use put-call parity to determine the price of the option:

$$\text{Call Price} = \text{Put Price} + \text{Stock Price} - PV(\text{Strike Price}).$$

In order to price a one-year European call with a strike price of $20, we need to know the price of a one-year European put with the same strike price, the current stock price, and the risk-free interest rate. We have all of that information, so we're ready.

(Continued)

EXECUTE

$$\text{Call Price} = \text{Put Price} + \text{Stock Price} - PV(\text{Strike Price})$$
$$= \$2.50 + \$18 - \$20/1.06 = \$1.632.$$

EVALUATE

Put-call parity means that we can replicate the payoff of the one-year call option with a strike price of $20 by holding the following portfolio: Buy the one-year put option with a strike price of $20 from the dealer, buy the stock, and sell a one-year, risk-free zero-coupon bond with a face value of $20. With this combination, we have the following final payoff, depending on the final price of HAL stock in one year, S_1:

		Payoff	
		Final HAL Stock Price	
		$S_1 < \$20$	$S_1 \geq \$20$
	Buy Put Option	$20 - S_1$	0
+	Buy Stock	S_1	S_1
+	Sell Bond	-20	-20
=	Portfolio	0	$S_1 - 20$
+	Sell Call Option	0	$-(S_1 - 20)$
=	Total Payoff	0	0

Note that the final payoff of the portfolio of the three securities matches the payoff of a call option. Therefore, we can sell the call option to our client and have future payoff of zero no matter what happens. Doing so is worthwhile as long as we can sell the call option for more than the cost of the portfolio, which we found to be $1.632.

Put-Call Parity: Dividend-Paying Stock. What happens if the stock pays a dividend? In that case, the two different ways to construct portfolio insurance do not have the same payout because the stock will pay a dividend while the zero-coupon bond will not. Thus, the two strategies will cost the same to implement only if we add the present value of future dividends to the combination of the bond and the call:

$$\text{Stock Price} + \text{Put Price} = PV(\text{Strike Price}) + PV(\text{Dividends}) + \text{Call Price}$$

The left side of this equation is the value of the stock and a put; the right side is the value of a zero-coupon bond, a call option, and the future dividends paid by the stock during the life of the options. Rearranging terms gives the general put-call parity formula:

Put-Call Parity

$$\text{Call Price} = \text{Put Price} + \text{Stock Price} - PV(\text{Strike Price}) - PV(\text{Dividends}) \quad (21.5)$$

In this case, the call is equivalent to having a levered position in the stock without dividends plus insurance against a fall in the stock price.

CONCEPT CHECK

9. Explain put-call parity.

10. If a put option trades at a higher price from the value indicated by the put-call parity equation, what action should you take?

Options and Corporate Finance

We briefly explored real options in capital budgeting in Chapter 9. There, we stressed the value of the flexibility provided by a real option—the option to delay, change, or abandon a project. These are options because, like the ones discussed in this chapter, you would only exercise a real option if doing so would make you better off.

We also noted in Chapter 15 that the ability to retire (or call) a bond early is a valuable option for a firm, and that the ability to convert the bond into shares of stock is an option for the bondholders. We can now say more formally that when a firm issues a callable bond, it is selling a bond that has a call option on it with a strike price equal to the call price. Because the buyers of the bond are granting a valuable call option to the firm, they will pay less for a callable bond than they would for an equivalent non-callable bond. Similarly, when a firm issues a convertible bond, it is essentially issuing a package of a straight bond and warrants on its stock. Those warrants are valuable options, so buyers of convertible bonds will pay more than they would for similar non-convertible bonds.

Options are plentiful in corporate finance. In Chapter 14, we described another one—the "greenshoe option," which gives the underwriter the option to sell additional shares in an oversubscribed equity offering. Many start-up and high-tech firms compensate their employees by granting them options on the firm's stock, and it is common for the majority of a CEO's compensation to come in this form.

One other very important corporate finance application of options is interpreting the capital structure of the firm as options on the firm's assets. Specifically, a share of stock can be thought of as a call option on the assets of the firm with a strike price equal to the value of debt outstanding.[4] To illustrate, consider a single-period world in which at the end of the period the firm is liquidated. If the firm's value does not exceed the value of debt outstanding at the end of the period, the firm must declare bankruptcy and the equity holders receive nothing. Conversely, if the value exceeds the value of debt outstanding, the equity holders get whatever is left once the debt has been repaid. Figure 21.7 illustrates this payoff. Note how the payoff to equity looks exactly the same as the payoff of a call option.

Viewed this way, a share of equity is a call option on the firm's assets. In fact, debt holders can be thought of as owning the firm, but they have *written* to equity holders a call option on the firm's assets with a strike price equal to the required debt payment. Recall that the price of an option increases with the volatility level of the underlying security. That means equity holders benefit from high-volatility investments. Because the price of equity is increasing with the volatility of the firm's assets, equity holders benefit from a zero-NPV project that increases the volatility of the firm's assets. However, debt holders, as lenders to the firm, do not benefit from an increase in the risk of the firm's assets. Thus, the project increases the value of equity, but decreases the value of the debt claims. In fact, because the project is zero-NPV, taking it on does not change the value of the firm as a whole. The value of the debt claims decreases by exactly the amount the value of the equity increases. This effect creates a conflict of interest between equity holders and debt holders. Options pricing theory helps us understand why this conflict of interest arises.

---

[4]This insight has been known at least since Black and Scholes wrote their pathbreaking option valuation paper. See F. Black and M. Scholes, "The Pricing of Options and Corporate Liabilities," *Journal of Political Economy*, 81 (3) (1973): 637–654.

FIGURE 21.7

Equity as a Call Option

If the value of the firm's assets exceeds the required debt payment, the equity holders receive the value that remains after the debt is repaid. Otherwise, the firm is bankrupt and its equity is worthless. Thus, the payoff to equity is equivalent to a call option on the firm's assets with a strike price equal to the required debt payment.

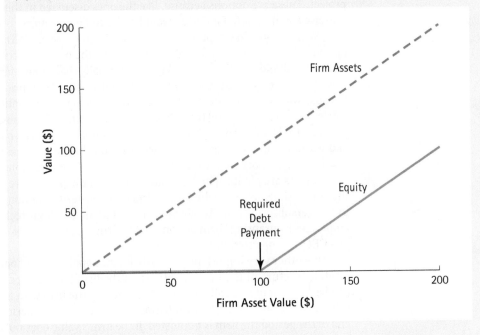

The option price is more sensitive to changes in volatility for at-the-money options than it is for in-the-money options. In the context of corporate finance, equity is at-the-money when a firm is close to bankruptcy. In this case, the loss in equity value that results from taking on a negative-NPV investment might be outweighed by the gain in equity value from the increase in volatility. Hence, equity holders have an incentive to take on negative-NPV, high-volatility investments. As we saw in Chapter 16, this excessive risk-taking problem is of concern to debt holders, who bear its cost.

CONCEPT CHECK

11. Explain how equity can be viewed as a call option on the firm.

12. Under what circumstances would equity holders have a possible incentive to take on negative-NPV investments?

MyFinanceLab

Here is what you should know after reading this chapter. MyFinanceLab will help you identify what you know, and where to go when you need to practice.

KEY POINTS AND EQUATIONS	KEY TERMS	ONLINE PRACTICE

21.1 Option Basics

- An option that gives the holder the right (but not the obligation) to purchase an asset at some future date is known as a call option.
- An option that gives the holder the right to sell an asset at some future date is known as a put option.
- When a holder of an option enforces the agreement and buys or sells the share of stock at the agreed price, the holder is exercising the option.
- The price at which the holder agrees to buy or sell the share of stock when the option is exercised is known as the strike price or exercise price.
- The last date on which the holder has the right to exercise the option is known as the expiration date.
- An American option can be exercised on any date up to, and including, the exercise date. A European option can be exercised only on the expiration date.
- If you would make money by exercising an option immediately, the option is in-the-money. Conversely, if you would lose money by exercising an option immediately, the option is out-of-the-money.

American options, p. 662
at-the-money, p. 663
call option, p. 662
deep in-the-money, p. 664
deep out-of-the-money, p. 664
derivatives, p. 662
European options, p. 662
exercising (an option), p. 662
expiration date, p. 662
financial option, p. 662
hedging, p. 665
in-the-money, p. 664
open interest, p. 663
option writer, p. 662
out-of-the-money, p. 664
put option, p. 662
speculate, p. 665
strike (exercise) price, p. 662
warrant, p. 662

MyFinanceLab
Study Plan 21.1

21.2 Option Payoffs at Expiration

- The value of a call option at expiration
  = Stock Price − Strike Price,
  if Stock Price > Strike Price;
  = 0, if Stock Price ≤ Strike Price   (21.1)

- The value of a put option at expiration
  = Strike Price − Stock Price,
  if Stock Price < Strike Price;
  = 0, if Stock Price ≥ Strike Price   (21.2)

- An investor holding a short position in an option has an obligation; he or she takes the opposite side of the contract to the investor who holds the long position.

MyFinanceLab
Study Plan 21.2

21.3 Factors Affecting Option Prices

- Call options with lower strike prices are more valuable than otherwise identical calls with higher strike prices. Conversely, put options are more valuable with higher strike prices.
- Call options increase in value, and put options decrease in value, when the stock price rises.
- The value of an option generally increases with the volatility of the stock.

MyFinanceLab
Study Plan 21.3

21.4 The Black-Scholes Option Pricing Formula • The Black-Scholes option pricing formula shows that the price of an option on a non-dividend-paying stock is a function of only the current stock price, the strike price, the time to expiration, the volatility of the stock, and the risk-free rate.		MyFinanceLab Study Plan 21.4

21.5 Put-Call Parity
• Put-call parity relates the value of the European call to the value of the European put and the stock:
  Call Price = Put Price + Stock Price −
  $PV(\text{Strike Price}) - PV(\text{Dividends})$ (21.5)
	portfolio insurance,
	   p. 677
	protective put, p. 676
	put-call parity, p. 677
		MyFinanceLab
		Study Plan 21.5

21.6 Options and Corporate Finance • Equity can be viewed as a call option on the firm. • The debt holders can be viewed as owning the firm *and* having sold a call option with a strike price equal to the required debt payment.		MyFinanceLab Study Plan 21.6

CRITICAL THINKING

1. Explain the meanings of the following financial terms:
   a. Option
   b. Expiration date
   c. Strike price
   d. Call
   e. Put

2. What is the difference between a European option and an American option?

3. Explain the difference between a long position in a put and a short position in a call.

4. What position has more downside exposure: a short position in a call or a short position in a put? That is, in the worst case, in which of these two positions would your losses be greater?

5. If you own a call option at expiration and the stock price equals the strike price, is your *profit* zero?

6. Is an increase in a stock's volatility good for the holder of a call option? Is it good for the holder of a put option?

7. Why are the prices of puts and calls on the same stock related?

8. Explain why an option can be thought of as an insurance contract.

9. Explain why equity can be viewed as a call option on a firm.

PROBLEMS

All problems are available in MyFinanceLab. *An asterisk * indicates problems with a higher level of difficulty.*

Option Basics

1. See the option quote on IBM from the CBOE Web site on the next page.
   a. Which option contract had the most trades today?
   b. Which option contract is being held the most overall?

c. Suppose you purchase one option with symbol IBM1616I155-E. How much will you need to pay your broker for the option (ignoring commissions)?

d. Suppose you sell one option with symbol IBM1619H165-E. How much will you receive for the option (ignoring commissions)?

e. The calls with which strike prices are currently in-the-money? Which puts are in-the-money?

IBM (INTL BUSINESS MACHINES)   161.36   1.78

Jul 20 2016 @ 17:21 ET   Bid 161.11   Ask 161.3 Size 3 × 1   Vol 4372921

Calls	Last Sale	Net	Bid	Ask	Vol	Open Int	Puts	Last Sale	Net	Bid	Ask	Vol	Open Int
16 Aug 155.00 (IBM1619H155-E)	6.45	0.75	6.95	7.25	9	7640	16 Aug 155.00 (IBM1619T155-E)	1.18	−0.75	1.17	1.25	61	4505
16 Aug 160.00 (IBM1619H160-E)	3.3	0.85	3.15	3.3	101	12811	16 Aug 160.00 (IBM1619T160-E)	2.76	−1.24	2.71	2.84	61	2114
16 Aug 165.00 (IBM1619H165-E)	1.05	0.3	0.96	1.06	178	27064	16 Aug 165.00 (IBM1619T165-E)	7.1	−0.4	5.7	5.9	1	332
16 Aug 170.00 (IBM1619H170-E)	0.21	−0.01	0.21	0.27	20	6086	16 Aug 170.00 (IBM1619T170-E)	12.25	0	9.95	10.3	0	393
16 Sep 155.00 (IBM1616I155-E)	7.77	1.58	7.5	7.7	2	122	16 Sep 155.00 (IBM1616U155-E)	2.34	−0.59	2.13	2.22	3	251
16 Sep 160.00 (IBM1616I160-E)	4.05	0.76	4	4.2	6	380	16 Sep 160.00 (IBM1616U160-E)	4	−1.09	3.8	4	1	476
16 Sep 165.00 (IBM1616I165-E)	1.87	0.47	1.76	1.88	161	297	16 Sep 165.00 (IBM1616U165-E)	6.65	−2.1	6.55	6.75	1	27
16 Sep 170.00 (IBM1616I170-E)	0.65	0.07	0.63	0.71	2	498	16 Sep 170.00 (IBM1616U170-E)	12.35	0	10.4	10.7	0	47

Source: Chicago Board Options Exchange at www.cboe.com.

Option Payoffs at Expiration

2. You own a call option on Intuit stock with a strike price of $40. The option will expire in exactly three months.
   a. If the stock is trading at $55 in three months, what will be the payoff of the call?
   b. If the stock is trading at $35 in three months, what will be the payoff of the call?
   c. Draw a payoff diagram showing the value of the call at expiration as a function of the stock price at expiration.

3. Assume that you have shorted the call option in Problem 2.
   a. If the stock is trading at $55 in three months, what will you owe?
   b. If the stock is trading at $35 in three months, what will you owe?
   c. Draw a payoff diagram showing the amount you owe at expiration as a function of the stock price at expiration.

4. You own a put option on Ford stock with a strike price of $10. The option will expire in exactly six months.
   a. If the stock is trading at $8 in six months, what will be the payoff of the put?
   b. If the stock is trading at $23 in six months, what will be the payoff of the put?
   c. Draw a payoff diagram showing the value of the put at expiration as a function of the stock price at expiration.

5. Assume that you have shorted the put option in Problem 4.
   a. If the stock is trading at $8 in three months, what will you owe?
   b. If the stock is trading at $23 in three months, what will you owe?
   c. Draw a payoff diagram showing the amount you owe at expiration as a function of the stock price at expiration.

6. You are long both a call and a put on the same share of stock with the same exercise date. The exercise price of the call is $40 and the exercise price of the put is $45. Plot the value of this combination as a function of the stock price on the exercise date.

7. You are long two calls on the same share of stock with the same exercise date. The exercise price of the first call is $40 and the exercise price of the second call is $60. In addition, you are short two otherwise identical calls, both with an exercise price

of $50. Plot the value of this combination as a function of the stock price on the exercise date.

*8. A *forward contract* is a contract to purchase an asset at a fixed price on a particular date in the future. Both parties are obligated to fulfill the contract. Explain how to construct a forward contract on a share of stock from a position in options.

9. You own a share of Costco stock. You are worried that its price will fall and would like to insure yourself against this possibility. How can you purchase insurance against a fall in the price of the stock?

Factors Affecting Option Prices

10. What is the maximum value that a call option and a put option can have?

11. Why is an American option with a longer time to expiration generally worth more than an otherwise identical option with a shorter time to expiration?

Put-Call Parity

12. Dynamic Energy Systems stock is currently trading for $33 per share. The stock pays no dividends. A one-year European put option on Dynamic with a strike price of $35 is currently trading for $2.10. If the risk-free interest rate is 10% per year, what is the price of a one-year European call option on Dynamic with a strike price of $35?

13. You happen to be checking the newspaper and notice an arbitrage opportunity. The current stock price of Intrawest is $20 per share and the one-year risk-free interest rate is 8%. A one-year put on Intrawest with a strike price of $18 sells for $3.33, while the identical call sells for $7. Explain what you must do to exploit this arbitrage opportunity.

Options and Corporate Finance

*14. Express the position of an equity holder in terms of put options.

15. Express the position of a debt holder in terms of put options.

DATA CASE

Your uncle owns 10,000 shares of Walmart stock. He is concerned about the short-term outlook for Walmart's stock due to an impending "major announcement." This announcement has received much attention in the press so he expects the stock price will change significantly in the next month, but is unsure whether it will be a profit or a loss. He hopes the price will increase, but he also doesn't want to suffer if the price were to fall in the short term.

His broker recommended he buy a "protective put" on the stock, but your uncle has never traded options before and is not much of a risk taker. He wants you to devise a plan for him to capitalize if the announcement is positive but still be protected if the news causes the price to drop. You realize that a protective put will protect him from the downside risk, but you think a strategy of purchasing a call and a put with the same exercise price (known as a "straddle") may offer similar downside protection, while increasing the upside potential. You decide to show him both strategies and the resulting profits and returns he could face from each.

1. Download option quotes on options that expire in approximately one month on Walmart from the Chicago Board Options Exchange (www.cboe.com) into an Excel spreadsheet. If you choose to download "near-term at-the-money" options you will get a range of options expiring in about a month. You can only get active quotes while the exchange is open; bid or ask prices are not available when it is closed.

2. Determine your uncle's profit and return using the protective put.
   a. Identify the expiring put with an exercise price closest to, but not below, the current stock price. Determine the investment required to protect all 10,000 shares.
   b. Determine the put price at expiration for each stock price at $5 increments within a range of $20 above and below Walmart's current price using Eq. 21.2.
   c. Compute the profit (or loss) on the put for each stock price used in (b).
   d. Compute the profit on the stock from the current price for each stock price used in (b).
   e. Compute his overall profit (or loss) of the protective put; that is, combining the put and his stock for each price used in (c) and (d).
   f. Compute the overall return of the protective put.

3. Determine your uncle's profit and return using the straddle.
   a. Compute the investment your uncle would have to make to purchase the call and put with the same exercise price and expiration as the put option in Question 2, to cover all 10,000 of his shares.
   b. Determine the value at expiration of the call and the put options at each $5 increment of stock prices within a range of $20 above and below Walmart's current price using Eqs. 21.1 and 21.2.
   c. Determine the profit (or loss) on the options at each stock price used in (b).
   d. Determine the profit (or loss) on the stock from the current price for each stock price used in (b).
   e. Compute his overall profit (or loss) of the stock plus the straddle; that is, combining the position in both options and his stock for each price used in (c) and (d).
   f. Compute the overall return of this position.

4. Was the broker correct that the protective put would prevent your uncle from losing if the announcement caused a large decrease in the stock value? What is your uncle's maximum possible loss using the protective put?

5. What is the maximum possible loss your uncle could experience using the straddle?

6. Which strategy, the protective put or the straddle, provides the maximum upside potential for your uncle? Why does this occur?

Index